READINGS
ON READING
INSTRUCTION

Third Edition

READINGS ON READING INSTRUCTION

Edited by

ALBERT J. HARRIS
and
EDWARD R. SIPAY

LONGMAN INC.
NEW YORK AND LONDON

Readings on Reading Instruction

Longman Inc., 95 Church Street, White Plains, N.Y. 10601
Associated companies, branches, and representatives
throughout the world.

Developmental Editor: Nicole Benevento
Editorial and Design Supervisor: Joan Matthews
Production Supervisor: Ferne Y. Kawahara
Manufacturing Supervisor: Marion Hess

Library of Congress Cataloging in Publication Data

Main entry under title:

Readings on reading instruction.

   Includes index.
   1. Reading (Elementary)—Addresses, essays, lectures.
I. Harris, Albert Josiah. II. Sipay, Edward R.
LB1573.R294   1983   372.41'1   82-24975
ISBN 0-582-28311-6

Manufactured in the United States of America
Printing: 9 8 7 6 5 4 3 2   Year: 92 91 90 89 88 87 86 85

Contents

PREFACE   *ix*
CONTRIBUTORS *xi*

I. An Overview of Reading Instruction   1
  1. Reading Instruction and Research: In Historical Perspective,   1
     H. Alan Robinson
  2. Reading Instruction Today, *Joanna Williams*   12
  3. The Status of Reading Achievement: Is There a Halo around the   20
     Past?, *Leo Fay*
  4. How Well Does the Average American Read? Some Facts,   25
     Figures and Opinions, *Mary K. Monteith*

II. Contrasting Views about Reading Instruction   30
  5. The Nature of the Reading Process, *John B. Carroll*   30
  6. Subskill and Holistic Approaches to Reading Instruction, *Phyllis* 34
     Weaver and Fredi Shonhoff
  7. Controversial Issues in Beginning Reading Instruction: Meaning   37
     versus Subskill Emphasis, *S. Jay Samuels and Sumner W.*
     Schachter
  8. Reading: A Psycholinguistic Guessing Game, *Kenneth S.*   45
     Goodman
  9. The Contributions of the Psycholinguists to the Teaching of   53
     Reading: Part I—An Appreciation and a Critique, *Denis H. Stott*

III. Language and Reading   59
  10. Language Development: The Elementary School Years, *Richard*   59
      E. Hodges
  11. On Developmental Relations between Language—Learning and   65
      Reading, *Sara W. Lundsteen*
  12. Research Update: Listening Comprehension, *P. David Pearson and*   74
      Linda Fielding
  13. Integrating Reading and Writing Instruction, *Fran Lehr*   85

IV. **Reading Readiness and Prereading Development**   89
  14. Effects of Early Intervention Programs, *Doris Roettger*   89
  15. Facts About Pre-First Grade Reading, *Dolores Durkin*   95
  16. When Should We Begin to Teach Reading?, *Walter H. MacGinitie*   103
  17. Readiness for Reading: A Practical Approach, *John Pikulski*   107
  18. New Thoughts about Reading Readiness, *Gloria M. McDonell and E. Bess Osburn*   112

V. **Beginning Reading Instruction**   116
  19. Beginning Reading in North America, *Lloyd O. Ollila and Joanne R. Nurss*   116
  20. Features of the Basal Series of the 1980s, *Robert C. Aukerman*   122
  21. Beginning Reading: Theory and Practice, *Marilyn Jager Adams, Richard C. Anderson, and Dolores Durkin*   126
  22. The Teacher's Role, *Frank Smith*   132
  23. The Effectiveness of Code- and Meaning-Emphasis Beginning Reading Programs, *Robert Dykstra*   136
  24. Linguistically Speaking, Why Language Experience?, *Maryanne Hall*   142

VI. **Measuring Reading Outcomes and Determining Needs**   146
  25. Areas of Concern in Evaluation, *Albert J. Harris*   146
  26. Informal Inventories, *Emmett Albert Betts*   153
  27. Using an Informal Reading Inventory to Affect Instruction, *Robert A. McCracken*   156
  28. If Not Grade Equivalent Scores—Then What?, *Jeanne M. Plas*   160
  29. Learning about Psycholinguistic Processes by Analyzing Oral Reading, *Kenneth S. Goodman and Yetta M. Goodman*   165
  30. Is Miscue Analysis Practical for Teachers, *Joyce Hood*   170

VII. **Adapting Reading Instruction to Individual Differences**   177
  31. Personalize Your Group Teaching, *Gary R. McKenzie*   177
  32. Individualizing Reading Assignments, *Richard A. Earle and Peter L. Sanders*   180
  33. Pupil Partners, *Nancy G. Whisler*   184
  34. Peer Tutoring in the Regular Classroom, *Stewart Ehly and Stephen C. Larsen*   187
  35. Six Steps to the Individualized Reading Program (IRP), *Lyman C. Hunt, Jr.*   189
  36. The Effective Teacher of Reading, Revisited, *Albert J. Harris*   195

VIII. **Word Recognition and Decoding**   202
  37. A Compare/Contrast Theory of Mediated Word Identification, *Patricia M. Cunningham*   202
  38. Automatic Decoding and Reading Comprehension, *S. Jay Samuels*   207

39. Designing Instruction in Reading: Initial Reading, *Lauren B. Resnick and Isabel L. Beck* — 210
40. Teaching Basic Function Words, *Hayden B. Jolly, Jr.* — 215
41. Using Children's Reading Miscues for New Teaching Strategies, *Yetta M. Goodman* — 216
42. There Is a Need for Word Attack Generalizations, *Judi Lesiak* — 223

IX. Development of Reading Vocabulary — 226
43. The Need for a Planned Vocabulary Program, *Edgar Dale and Joseph O'Rourke* — 226
44. Reading to Learn about the Nature of Language, *A. Barbara Pilon* — 231
45. Figurative Language: Deceitful Mirage or Oasis for Reading?, *Thomas N. Turner* — 236
46. Ten Creative Ways to Build Vocabulary Skills, *Nicholas P. Criscuolo* — 240
47. Stimulate Reading . . . with a Dictionary, *Edith F. Miller* — 242
48. Vocabulary Development in the Classroom, *Lee C. Deighton* — 245

X. Improvement of Reading Comprehension — 248
49. What Is the Value of the New Interest in Reading Comprehension?, *Dolores Durkin* — 249
50. Instructional Implications of a Conceptual Theory of Reading Comprehension, *Michael Strange* — 267
51. Asking Questions about Stories, *P. David Pearson* — 274
52. Improving Classroom Comprehension, *Robert B. Ruddell* — 283
53. Developing Sentence Comprehension in Reading, *John G. Barnitz* — 286
54. Clozing the Reading Gap, *V. Patricia Gunn and John Elkins* — 293
55. Ten Ways to Sort Out Reading Comprehension Problems, *Dixie Lee Spiegel* — 298
56. The Perils of Reading, *Edwin J. Swineford* — 302

XI. Reading for Content — 308
57. Questioning Is Not the Answer, *Harold L. Herber and Joan B. Nelson* — 309
58. The Study Guide—Types, Purpose and Value, *Daniel J. Tutolo* — 313
59. Learning to Learn: On Training Students to Learn from Texts, *Ann L. Brown, Joseph C. Campione, and Jeanne D. Day* — 317
60. Strategies for Enhancing Readiness and Recall in Content Areas: The Encoding Specificity Principle, *John E. Readance and David Moore* — 326
61. Notetaking: Theory and Research, *John P. Rickards* — 331
62. Graphical Literacy, *Edward Fry* — 337

XII. Recreational Reading   344

63. Assessing Reading Interests of Elementary and Middle School Students, *Ken L. Dulin*   344

64. The Effects of TV on Reading, *Lilya Wagner*   358

65. Approaches to the Use of Literature in the Reading Program, *Helen Huus*   363

66. Humor and the Reading Program, *Lance M. Gentile and Merna M. McMillan*   369

67. Dr. Criscuolo's 30 Miracle Motivators for Reluctant Readers, *Nicholas P. Criscuolo*   374

68. Children's Responses to Literature: What Happens in the Classroom, *Janet Hickman*   377

XIII. Some Special Issues Concerning Reading Instruction   383

69. The Missing Ingredient: Fluent Oral Reading, *Betty Anderson*   383

70. Reading in Silence—A Chance to Read, *Martha Efta*   387

71. Six Alternatives to the Directed Reading Activity, *Dixie Lee Spiegel*   391

72. Techniques for Increasing Reading Rate, *James I. Brown*   397

73. Developing Flexible Reading Habits, *Sumner W. Schachter*   402

74. The Teacher's Dilemma: How to Gauge the Suitability of Reading Materials, *Jonathan Anderson and Jim Coates*   405

75. Parents as Partners in Reading Development, *Norma Noonan*   410

76. Computer Literacy, Part II: Classroom Applications, *Holly O'Donnell*   413

XIV. Teaching Reading to Children with Special Needs   416

77. The Diagnosis of Reading Disabilities, *Albert J. Harris*   416

78. Corrective Reading in the Classroom, *Marianne Frostig*   420

79. What Is New in Remedial Reading?, *Albert J. Harris*   427

80. The Reading Program and Its Potential Obstacles for Minority Children, *Susan W. Masland*   432

81. Dialects and Reading, *Pose Lamb*   436

82. Beginning English Reading for ESL Students, *Phillip C. Gonzales*   443

83. Teaching Reading to the Gifted, *Robert L. Trezise*   452

INDEX   *457*

Preface

The dozen years since the completion of the Second Edition of this book have witnessed a continuing increase in the amount of research and writing about the teaching of reading. For example, the number of abstracts in the *Annual Summary of Investigations Relating to Reading* grew from 307 in 1970–71 to 1,165 in 1979–80.

Our task in reviewing this outpouring of publications has been to select contributions that have meaning and value for the reading teacher and teacher-to-be. We looked for the following qualities: representation of current and forward-looking points of view; contributions that have made an impact on both theory and practice; emphasis on applications of theory rather than theory for its own sake; relevance to the problems of today's teachers of reading; clarity and readability of style; and brevity. On controversial issues we tried to find papers that explain the contrasting viewpoints clearly and to make sure that opposing views are well presented.

Most of the 83 selections are quite recent. Only ten were published before 1970, and most of those have been retained from the Second Edition. Six were published between 1970 and 1974; forty-five, between 1975 and 1979; and twenty-one in 1980–82. The most recent is dated September, 1982.

We expect that this book's major use will be as supplementary reading in courses on reading instruction in the elementary school. Its usefulness in off-campus courses is obvious. The library of a college or university is likely to have only one copy of the journal or other publication in which one of the selections originally appeared. If such an article is assigned as required reading, in order to have group discussion about it, the one copy is likely to disappear. Inclusion of the article in a book of readings makes it possible for all students in a course to read the same article. Excessive reliance on a single textbook is less likely, and the students can become acquainted with samples of the writing of many leaders in the field of reading.

The chapter organisation of this Third Edition is quite similar to that of the preceding editions. Chapter 1 provides a brief history of reading instruction and reviews evidence on the complaint that reading achievement has been deteriorating. Both sides of the argument concerning the merits of subskill and holistic approaches in reading instruction are presented in Chapter 2. Chapter 3, a new chapter, explores the relations of reading to listening, speaking, and writing. Early reading instruction and recent changes in the concept of reading readiness are considered in Chapter 4, and an overview of current trends in beginning reading instruction takes up Chapter 5. Chapter 6 covers informal and standardized ways of measuring attainment in reading. Chapter 7 considers grouping, individualized instruction, the use of peers as tutors, and the characteristics that make for effective reading instruction. Viewpoints on the teaching of word recognition and decoding are explored in Chapter 8, and Chapter 9 deals with the development of word meanings. The length of Chapter 10 (the longest in the book) reflects the recent great increase in concern about reading for meaning; the papers in this chapter range from sentence meaning to critical reading. Chapter 11 provides ideas about the development of skills that are generally useful in studying. Chapter 12 begins with ways of exploring reading interests and describes many ideas on how to enhance enjoyment of reading. The eight articles in Chapter 13 did not fit into the preceding chapters, but present ideas that are too good to leave out. Finally, Chapter 14 deals with the special learning problems of disabled readers, children with linguistic and social disadvantages, and the often-neglected gifted child.

We have preferred to let authors speak for themselves. Some of the papers have been shortened by deleting sentences or paragraphs, but we have not changed the authors' words. Deletions that have been made are indicated by a short series of dots: . . . . Aside from deletions, all selections are presented exactly as originally published. No changes have been made in figures or tables, and these keep their original numbering.

We are, of course, greatly indebted to the many authors and publishers who have agreed to allow their copyrighted selections to be republished in this volume. A full acknowledgement will be found as a footnote to the title of each selection.

Albert J. Harris
Edward R. Sipay

Contributors

Marilyn Jager Adams, Center for the Study of Reading, University of Illinois, Champaign, IL.

Betty Anderson, Professor of Education, University of Central Florida, Orlando, FL.

Jonathan Anderson, Flanders University of South Australia, Bedford Park, South Australia, Australia.

Richard C. Anderson, Professor and Director, Center for the Study of Reading, University of Illinois, Champaign, IL.

Robert C. Aukerman, Professor Emeritus, University of Rhode Island, Kingston, RI.

John G. Barnitz, Associate Professor of Education, University of New Orleans, New Orleans, LA.

Isabel L. Beck, Senior Scientist, Learning Research and Development Center, and Professor of Education, University of Pittsburgh, Pittsburgh, PA.

Emmett A. Betts, Professor Emeritus, University of Miami, Miami, FL.

Anne L. Brown, Professor of Psychology and Educational Psychology, Center for the Study of Reading, University of Illinois, Champaign, IL.

James I. Brown, Professor Emeritus, Department of Rhetoric, University of Minnesota, St. Paul, MN.

James C. Campione, Professor of Psychology, Center for the Study of Reading, University of Illinois, Champaign, IL.

John B. Carroll, W. R. Kenan, Jr., Professor of Psychology, Emeritus, University of North Carolina, Chapel Hill, NC.

Jim Coates, Copland College, Canberra, Australia.

Nickolas P. Criscuolo, Supervisor of Reading, New Haven Public Schools, New Haven, CT.

Patricia M. Cunningham, Associate Professor, Wake Forest University, Winston Salem, NC.

Edgar Dale, Professor Emeritus, The Ohio State University, Columbus, OH.

Jeanne D. Day, Assistant Professor, Department of Psychology, University of Notre Dame, Notre Dame, IN.

Lee. C. Deighton, Formerly President, The MacMillan Publishing Company, New York, NY.

Dolores Durkin, Professor of Education, University of Illinois, Champaign, IL.

Robert Dykstra, Professor of Education, University of Minnesota, Minneapolis, MN.

Richard A. Earle, Professor of Education and Associate Director, Reading Centre, McGill University, Montreal, Quebec, Canada.

Martha Efta, Teacher of EMR Children, Dover Elementary Schools, Westlake, OH.

Stewart Ehly, Associate Professor, University of Iowa, Ames, IA.

John Elkins, Schonell Educational Research Centre, University of Queensland, St. Lucia, Australia.

Leo Fay, Professor of Education, Indiana University, Bloomington, IN.

Linda Fielding, Doctoral Student, University of Illinois, Champaign, IL.

Marianne Frostig, Formerly Executive Director, Marianne Frostig Center of Educational Therapy, Los Angeles, CA.

Edward Fry, Professor of Education and Director of the Reading Clinic, Rutgers University, New Brunswick, NJ.

Lance M. Gentile, Professor of Education and Director of the Pupil Appraisal Center, North Texas State University, Denton, TX.

Phillip C. Gonzales, Associate Professor and Director of the Bilingual Education Service Center for Alaska and the Northwest, University of Washington, Seattle, WA.

Kenneth S. Goodman, Professor and Co-Director of the Program in Language and Literacy, University of Arizona, Tuscon, AZ.

Yetta M. Goodman, Professor and Co-Director of the Program in Language and Literacy, University of Arizona, Tuscon, AZ.

V. Patricia Gunn, Schonell Educational Research Centre, University of Queensland, St. Lucia, Australia.

MaryAnne Hall, Professor of Education, Georgia State University, Atlanta, GA.

Albert J. Harris, Professor Emeritus, City University of New York, New York, NY.

Harold L. Herber, Professor of Education, Syracuse University, Syracuse, NY.

Janet Heckman, Lecturer, The Ohio State University, Columbus, OH.

Richard E. Hodges, Professor and Director, School of Education, University of Puget Sound, Tacoma, WA.

Joyce Hood, Director of the Children's Reading Clinic, University of Iowa, Iowa City, IA.

Lyman C. Hunt, Jr., Director, Reading Center, University of Vermont, Burlington, VT.

Helen Huus, Professor Emeritus, University of Missouri, Kansas City, MO.

Hayden B. Jolly, Jr., Director, The Learning Services, Clarksville, TN.

Pose Lamb, Professor of Education, Purdue University, West Lafayette, IN.

Stephen C. Larsen, Professor and Area Coordinator, Learning Disabilities Program, University of Texas, Austin, TX.

Fran Lehr, Senior Research Associate, ERIC/RCS, Urbana, IL.

Judi Lesiak, Professor of Psychology, Central Michigan University, Mt. Pleasant, MI.

Sara W. Lundsteen, Professor of Education, North Texas State University, Denton, TX.

Walter H. MacGinitie, Lansdowne Scholar and Professor of Education, University of Victoria, British Columbia, Canada.

Susan W. Masland, Associate Dean, School of Education, University of Wisconsin, Milwaukee, WI.

Robert A. McCracken, Professor of Education, Western Washington University, Bellingham, WA.

Gloria M. McDonell, Coordinator, Compensatory Education, Department of Instruction Fairfax County Public Schools, Springfield, VA.

Gary R. McKenzie, Associate Professor of Curriculum and Instruction, University of Texas, Austin, TX.

Merna M. McMillan, Deputy Director, Health Care Services/Mental Health, Santa Barbara, CA.

Edith F. Miller, English Teacher, Grades 5 and 6, Glen Ridge Middle School, Glen Ridge, NJ.

Mary K. Monteith, Research Associate, ERIC/RCS, Urbana, IL.

David Moore, Assistant Professor, University of Northern Iowa, Cedar Falls, IA.

Joan B. Nelson-Herber, Professor of Education, State University of New York, Binghamton, NY.

Norma Noonan, New South Wales Department of Education, Lismore, New South Wales, Australia.

Joanne R. Nurss, Professor of Early Childhood Education, Georgia State University, Atlanta, GA.

Holly O'Donnell, Research Associate, ERIC/RCS, Urbana, IL.

Lloyd O. Ollila, Professor, University of Victoria, Victoria, British Columbia, Canada.

Joseph O'Rourke, Senior Research Associate, The Ohio State University, Columbus, OH.

E. Bess Osburn, Coordinator of Reading and Special Education, Sam Houston University, Huntsville, TX.

P. David Pearson, Professor of Education, School of Education and Center for the Study of Reading, University of Illinois, Champaign, IL.

John Pikulski, Professor of Education, University of Delaware, Newark, DE.

A. Barbara Pilon, Professor of Education, Worcester State College, Worcester, MA.

Jeanne M. Plas, Associate Professor, Psychology Faculty, George Peabody College, Nashville, IN.

John E. Readence, Associate Professor, Reading Department, University of Georgia, Athens, GA.

Lauren B. Resnick, Professor of Psychology and Co-Director, Learning Research and Development Center, University of Pittsburgh, Pittsburgh, PA.

John P. Rickards, Professor and Chairperson, Department of Educational Psychology, University of Connecticut, Storrs, CT.

Doris Roettger, Heartland Education Agency, Ankeny, IA.

Robert B. Ruddell, Professor and Director of the Reading and Language Development Program, University of California, Berkley, CA.

S. Jay Samuels, Professor of Educational Psychology and Curriculum and Instruction, University of Minnesota, Minneapolis, MN.

Peter L. Sanders, Professor of Education, Wayne State University, Detroit, MI.

Sumner W. Schachter, Elementary Coordinator, Roaring Fork School District, Glenwood Springs, CO.

Frank Smith, Lansdowne Professor of Language in Education, University of Victoria, Victoria, British Columbia, Canada.

Dixie Lee Spiegal, Associate Professor of Curriculum and Instruction, University of North Carolina, Chapel Hill, NC.

Denis M. Stott, Professor Emeritus, Department of Psychology, University of Guelph, Ontario, Canada.

Michael Strange, President, E. P. R., Austin, TX.

Edwin J. Swineford, Professor Emeritus, California State College, Fresno, CA.

Robert L. Trezise, Supervisor, Teacher Preparation and Certification, Michigan Department of Education, Lansing, MI.

Thomas N. Turner, Professor of Education, University of Tennessee, Knoxville, TN.

Daniel J. Tutolo, Professor of Education, Department of Curriculum and Instruction, Bowling Green State University, Bowling Green, OH.

Lilya Wagner, Associate Professor, Division of Humanities and Director of the Writing Program, Union College, Lincoln, NE.

Phyllis Weaver, Goldman, Sachs and Co., New York, NY; Formerly Associate Professor, Harvard University, Cambridge, MA.

Joanne P. Williams, Professor of Psychology and Education, Teachers College, Columbia University, New York, NY.

CHAPTER I

An Overview of Reading Instruction

The selections in this chapter provide a historical perspective on trends in reading instruction. H. Alan Robinson summarizes the changing emphasis in reading instruction that took place from the Colonial Period of our country through 1976. Williams describes relatively recent trends in reading theory and instruction.

There have been many complaints in the media, and in books such as Copperman's *The Literary Hoax*, to the effect that students today are less competent readers than in the "good old days." Fay carefully reviews the research on reading then and now, and comments on some of the social factors that affect the reading performance of children. Monteith summarizes evidence about trends in adult literacy, and describes the relationship between the difficulty of reading materials and adult reading ability.

1. Reading Instruction and Research: In Historical Perspective

H. Alan Robinson

In preparing the chapter, I utilized a number of primary and secondary sources—all of value. But, I leaned most heavily on Smith's intensive and extensive review, *American Reading Instruction*, published by the International Reading Association in 1965. In fact, this chapter is organized essentially in line with the time periods Smith used as her framework for looking at reading instruction from a historical perspective. For minutely detailed descriptions of methods and materials up to 1965, I recommend reading Smith's engaging and largely objective document on reading instruction in the United States.

Before Independence

The first instructional materials used in reading (by English-speaking colonists)

From H. Alan Robinson, Reading instruction and research: In historical perspective. In H. A. Robinson (Ed.), *Reading and writing instruction in the United States: Historical trends*. Newark, Del.: International Reading Association, 1977. Pp. 44–58. Reprinted with permission of H. Alan Robinson and the International Reading Association.

were imported from Great Britain. The materials emphasized religious content, and, almost always, at one point or another in the instructional sequence, the Psalter (a book of psalms used primarily for devotional purposes) and the Bible were in evidence.

For the very beginning stages of instruction, the hornbook, also imported from Great Britain, was frequently used. The hornbook was usually about three inches by four inches of paper fastened on a thin paddle-shaped piece of wood, iron, pewter, or even ivory or silver. At first the hornbook only contained the alphabet, but the content was soon expanded to include syllables and some basic religious selections. Smith (1965, p. 6) conjectured that a hornbook made of gingerbread, a favorite of the time, "was perhaps the first attempt to motivate reading instruction."

The ABC book was sometimes used following the completion of the hornbook, but most often the first book was called a primer, not because it was a *first* book, but because it was primary "in containing the 'minimum essentials' deemed necessary for one's spiritual existence" (Smith, p. 8). *The New England Psalter, The Protestant Tutor,* and *The New England Primer* were among the most popular texts of the day. Spellers were introduced, and they added the dimension of spelling instruction but also included instruction in reading, religion, and morals. Strong's *England's Perfect School-Master* was one of the first spellers on the market—1710.

Usually the books were very small, often about two and a half inches by four and a half inches in size. Most of the instructional materials proceeded from simple to complex in respect to number of letters and syllables. No provision was made for repetition or distribution of the words being introduced. The rate of introduction of new words per page ranged from twenty to one hundred.

During this time period, no professional books, manuals, or courses of study existed to provide conceptual bases for the teaching of reading. Methods were imported (for English-speaking colonists) from Great Britain. The following sequence, apparently growing from a simplistic notion that instruction proceeds from small to large units, seemed to be the customary methodology.

1. Learn the alphabet by rote, forward and backward.
2. Point out the individual letters, in the alphabet and as they appear in words. (There appears to have been some use of squares of ivory with pictures and letters on them.)
3. After mastering all the letters, proceed to the syllabarium (organized groups of consonant-vowel clusters) and learn them by rote: *ba, be, bi, bo, bu,* and so on.
4. Then, using the ability to name the letters, spell out lists of short words—using this [magical] means of pronouncing the words.
5. Proceed to memorization of sentences and selections.
6. In some cases, answer general questions about selections.

In all cases, content was considered more important than any methodology directed toward developing independent readers. Oral reading was promoted as *the* reading procedure for social and religious needs. *The* reader in the family read to other family members from what was probably the one piece of reading material in the home—the Bible.

1776 to 1840

Not surprisingly, the emphasis in the content of instructional reading materials from 1776 to 1840 was nationalistic, with a good deal of the moralistic included. (There was overlap, of course, for many of the materials used prior to independence were still in service.) Led by Noah Webster with his blue-back spellers in a variety of editions, authors aimed to purify the language in the U.S., to develop loyalty to the new country, to inculcate high ideals of virtue and moral behavior, and to develop elocutionary ability. Hence, exercises focused on the *right* pronunciation, on patriotic and historical selections, proverbs, moral stories, fables, and so forth, as well as on expressive oral reading. Expository literature dominated the scene, however. Numerous new authors produced popular primers, readers, and spellers. Also the first set of readers was born.

The "spelling" method of teaching reading was still prevalent, but, with Webster and others attempting to unify the language, a type of phonics was developed. Sounds were taught, letter by letter and syllable by syllable, to stress articulation and pronunciation, as well as to "correct" dialects. Worcester, Gallaudet, and Taylor, in the period between 1820 and 1835, advocated a word method which sustained some popularity. Gallaudet introduced the word-to-letter method, in which a word was shown under the picture of a particular object—the beginnings of developing a sight vocabulary; however, at that time, pupils learned each of the letters in the word.

Nevertheless, whatever method was used to try to learn words, the overriding emphasis appeared to be on elocution. The teacher would read a sentence, and the pupils would keep pronouncing it until they said it "properly." This approach necessitated learning much information about commas, colons, and other punctuation and about the rules of reading aloud.

During the latter part of this time period, Keagy, a physician, introduced *The Pestalozzian Primer*, with emphasis on meaning and thinking. Interpreting Pestalozzi, Keagy spoke out against saying words "without having the corresponding ideas awakened in their [the youngsters'] minds" (Mathews 1966, p. 65). He suggested that children be helped to build up

much useful knowledge prior to reading and that they then start reading whole words at sight. He felt that word analysis should follow fluent reading of stories. Keagy appears to have been a minority forerunner of the greater emphasis on thinking during reading which emerged as one definite trend in the next time period.

1840 to 1880

This time period was characterized, according to Smith, by a search for more effective methods of teaching reading, since the national emphasis appeared to focus on promoting intelligent citizenship—not an unexpected trend for a developing nation. The content of readers was turning from patriotic and moral selections (at a slow but steady pace) to emphasis on reading for information, reading to find out about real events, and reading to learn more about nature. Some literary selections were included mainly for elocutionary purposes. Often the content seemed dull, particularly in the beginning books of the extremely popular McGuffey readers. In these beginning books, sentences were emphasized, rather than longer selections; the sentences were usually quite meaningless and uninteresting, as they were "subservient to the phonetic elements which McGuffey selected for drill purposes" (Smith, p. 106). One set of readers, by Willson, featured only scientific content.

During this period, though, another way of approaching reading instruction began to bloom. Although Keagy's *The Pestalozzian Primer*, introduced during the preceding time period (1776 to 1840), had some influence and popularity, it remained for Horace Mann to really guide Pestalozzian principles and methods into American reading instruction. Mann provided the developing discipline of reading instruction with its first conceptual framework. He denounced most existing methods as refusing children a chance to think;

he said that they were so imitative that "a parrot or even an idiot could do the same thing" (Smith, p. 78). The Pestalozzian movement, which stressed use of all senses and immediate application to meaningful situations, resulted in the use of word methods, pictures, and materials dealing with objects and experiences familiar to children.

Word methods appeared to grow out of the application of Pestalozzian principles, but also out of the independent thinking of individuals who rebelled against what they considered to be boring methodology that interfered with learning. Bumstead, who based his *My Little Primer* specifically on a word method, stated that "children are delighted with ideas; and in school exercises . . . they are disgusted with their absence." He also indicated that the words in his readers were chosen regardless of length and "the popular opinion that a word is *easy* because it is *short*." He said a word "is easy or difficult, chiefly, as it expresses an idea easy or difficult of comprehension" (Smith, p. 88).

Word methods, however, did not concentrate on context. Pupils were first confronted with lists of words and then went on to the approaches still used most frequently—the "alphabet-phonetic" methods. The syllabarium method disappeared, but "heightened attention to the principle of 'proceeding from the simple to the complex' was generally and painstakingly applied" (Smith, p. 86). Spelling and reading instruction were closely tied together essentially through concentration on phonetics, or phonics.

At the same time, emphasis was still placed on expressive oral reading and elocutionary ability, in company with many of the overlapping aims of the earlier periods. Nevertheless, the introduction of some stress on meaning was prevalent both in the discussions of individual words and when pupils read passages. "Some attention was now called to meanings in the upper grades through questions on the content and definitions of words, both of which were specified in the book" (Smith, p. 86).

Because of the development of graded schools during this time period (a Pestalozzian influence), graded reading series were introduced, edited by such contemporary educators as McGuffey, Tower, Hillard, and Bumstead. (The McGuffey readers remained the most popular, even into the next era.) The books themselves were longer and narrower than those of the past. Fewer words were introduced in the primers than before, and they were repeated often during the series. Some of the series included instructions to the teacher at the beginning of individual volumes. No teacher's manuals and few professional books were yet introduced. A few meager courses of study existed in some school systems.

1880 to 1910

Smith named this the period of "reading as a cultural asset," for there was a distinctive trend for a stabilizing nation to turn toward the cultivation of taste in literature. Herbart's doctrines centering on reading to discover the truth and on enjoying characters and plots were becoming popular in the United States. Charles W. Elliot, then president of Harvard, advocated the abolishment of basal readers and suggested substituting original literary works in their place.

A few professional books and articles were published during this time period. The most noteworthy book was written by Huey (1908); it is considered the first scientific contribution to reading instruction. This volume was reprinted quite recently (1968), not just for its historical value but because many of the ideas and problems discussed by Huey are even more pertinent today than they were earlier. Full-fledged courses of study also emerged on the educational scene, and many contained pages devoted to reading instruction. A few separate courses of study were focused on reading.

Although basal readers still flourished, supplemental materials were introduced to balance the reading diet. Smith (p. 125) quoted from a contemporary article which clarified the trend.

> Now it is very evident that the advantages which the readers have as exercises in elocution and drill-books prevent them in most cases from inspiring any love of good reading and from giving the power of sustained interest. It is to promote these two objects that supplemental reading has been introduced into many of our schools. Books and magazines are brought forward to do what the reading books from their nature cannot do.

A number of methods were in use during this period, although the alphabet method seems to have died. Phonics, or phonetics, was in wide use, although there were loud voices raised against an overdose of phonics, since there appeared to be many poor readers in the upper grades who had been raised on strong phonics programs. Nevertheless, major emphasis on sound/symbol relationships flourished as *the* approach to learning how to read. Pollard's synthetic method of 1889, with its intense stress on phonics, was popular; on the other hand, Pollard did give careful consideration to children's interests and attempted to make readings and exercises interesting.

At this time, two short-lived, contrived alphabetic-phonetic systems were introduced. The "scientific alphabet," used in the first reader of the Standard Reading Series published in 1902, "reduced the number of characters needed in representing the sounds in the English language by respelling words and by omitting silent letters. Some diacritical markings also appeared in this alphabet" (Smith, p. 127). In the "Shearer system" published

in 1894, "a letter's sound where it might be equivocal is represented by a mark which constantly stands for that sound, and for that sound only, irrespective of what the letter may be. Comparatively few marks are needed and the constant value of the marks is supposed to give an easy guide to pronunciation. The silent letters are indicated by a dot" (Smith, p. 128).

Several basal readers introduced the word method during this period. Phonics was used after a stock of sight words had been developed. Outgrowths of the word method, sentence and story methods focused on familiarization or memorization of the larger language units before working on specific word-attack techniques, essentially phonics.

The instructional materials themselves, both basal and supplementary, were more attractive than in past periods. Cloth covers replaced cardboard covers, type became clearer and larger, volumes were closer in size to present-day books, and colored pictures, although sparse, were introduced.

Concern for children who were having problems learning to read and the ever-broadening significance of reading in daily life in the United States apparently were major factors in the burgeoning of research during this chronological period. Although most of the studies were laboratory-type studies and had little impact on the classroom, these initial investigators called attention to, and began to contribute insights into, such factors as "rate in reading, distinctions between silent and oral reading, and individual differences in reading" (Smith, p. 155).

1910 to 1925

This period in reading history was called the "scientific movement" by Smith, for it marked the advent of instruments of measurement. The Gray Standardized Oral Reading Paragraphs, published in

1915, were soon followed by a number of other reading tests, mainly tests of silent reading. In addition, much more emphasis than ever before was placed on reading research.

A true innovation, unaffected by the overlap principle, emerged—emphasis on silent reading. The rather rapid change from stress on oral reading to the vigorous teaching of silent reading was probably related to several factors. There were increasing demands placed on reading for meaning, instead of on oral exercise, in order to meet the varied needs of society. There were loud cries for improving reading instruction, for it had been found during the war years "that thousands of our soldiers could not read well enough to follow printed instructions used in connection with military life" (Smith, p. 158). Research reports began to show the superiority of silent reading over oral reading for both fluency and comprehension. Contemporary writers urged that schools place emphasis on the teaching of silent reading. Finally, the birth of standardized silent reading tests called for appropriate shifts in teaching methodology.

Although the number of professional texts was small, there were numerous professional articles; both texts and articles focused largely on silent reading. The most popular professional text continued to be Huey's *The Psychology and Pedagogy of Reading*, revised in 1912 and again in 1915. Many courses of study appeared as part of an English or overall curriculum guide. A few cities published separate reading guides. There was a proliferation of manuals, both revisions of old ones and some brand new, accompanying basal programs. The manuals were particularly directed toward the teaching of silent reading. There was usually at least one paper-covered manual for each grade.

The basal readers themselves centered on factual, informative material. According to the authors of a widely used basal series of the time,

to feed the child on an exclusive literary diet that is entirely divorced from the actual situations in the world in which he lives, will defeat one of the fundamental purposes of teaching reading. A certain amount of fanciful material may be legitimate. But at the present time the supply of "Little Red Hen" and "Gingerbread Boy" type of material, largely used in the schools, needs to be supplemented by a suitable proportion of factual material, in order that the child's thinking may be more directly related to the actual experiences which he daily encounters. (Smith, p. 173)

There was an abundance of supplemental materials of all kinds. Since emphasis was placed on silent reading, numerous aids were directed toward helping teachers cope with "seatwork" problems. Flash cards and other devices which could be used independently were prevalent. Pupils were asked to answer objective-type questions—often in written form—about selections in both supplemental and basal programs.

Methods were aimed at improvement of comprehension. Lessons often began at the sentence level, through directions for reading presented orally or on the chalkboard. Children then read silently to find specific answers to questions or to interpret a passage. Some emphasis was placed on speed of reading. Phonics, or phonetics, was still taught in the primary grades as a separate group of lessons. Experience charts were used, to a limited extent, in limited fashion.

During the preceding period, from 1880 to 1910, it had been discovered that many intermediate children were unable to read well. During this period (1910 to 1925) discovery continued, and the first vague beginnings of special help for poor readers became visible. Also, there seemed to be more general concern than ever before for attending to individual differences.

1925 to 1935

Although this period was a brief one in the history of United States reading instruction, it was aptly named by Smith the period of "intensive research and application." Two differing philosophies of reading instruction emerged from the roots developed in earlier periods: (1) There is a sequence of skills to be learned by all children, and these can be plotted out in a basic program by authoritative adults. (2) The reading needs of children can best be met through their reasoning processes as they carry out their own purposes and solve their own problems (the activity movement).

Reading researchers were remarkably prolific during this time period, and the quality of the research was constantly improving. Although researchers focused on many aspects of reading, reading interests, reading disability, and readiness for beginning reading were the topics most frequently studied. Although there was continued interest during the early part of this period in studying silent reading, few researchers seem to have remained interested by the close of the period.

Most reading programs attempted to adhere to an influential set of objectives published in *The Twenty-Fourth Yearbook of the National Society for the Study of Education*, Part 1 (1925). These objectives focused on enabling the reader:

To participate intelligently in the thought life of the world and appreciatively in its recreational activities (p. 9)

To develop strong motives for, and permanent interests in reading that will inspire the present and future life of the reader and provide for the wholesome use of leisure time (p. 11)

To develop the attitudes, habits, and skills that are essential in the various types of reading activities in which children and adults should engage (p. 12)

Many of the professional books and courses of study published during this short time period were devoted to reading. Some courses of study dealt with specific aspects of reading—remedial reading, reading factual material, audience reading, recreational reading, vocabulary development; two were devoted to the reading of mathematics. Manuals accompanying basal readers became much like professional books, were less dogmatic than in the past, contained more optional activities, and suggested many supplementary activities.

Varied instructional materials were used in both "sequence-of-skills" and "activity" programs. Abundant and beautiful supplemental materials were available. Most of the stories in supplemental materials were realistic; few folk tales and fanciful tales were published. Some sets of supplemental materials emerged.

Readers, of course, were the foundation of the sequence-of-skills programs. The preprimer was introduced as readiness for the primer. The books were much more attractive and colorful than in the past. Care was exercised to introduce only words used most frequently according to vocabulary lists; some attention was also paid to reducing the number of words in the early books. Words were repeated often so learners might remember them. Sets of readers were available mainly through the intermediate grades, although one set went to grade seven and another to grade eight. William S. Gray and Arthur I. Gates were prominent developers of basal series.

Reading instruction was generally conducted throughout the school day and not just during a reading period. In most programs, the basal was used daily as the main feature of the reading program. A correlation approach was also in use—if reading a unit on Japan in a basal, pupils would also study Japan in geography, work arithmetic problems about Japan, and so on. Some educators appeared to be reaching toward an integration approach (reading not taught as a separate subject but used as a tool in all subjects), but the result was most often correlation.

Specific methods were varied. All manuals dealt with phonics in some way. Gates developed his "intrinsic" method: word-recognition techniques (including context clues) were to be part of, and not apart from, silent reading exercises. In some programs, phonics was taught only to those who needed it. In other cases, phonics was delayed until children were able to note similarities and differences in words. In sequence-of-skills programs, developmental lessons were planned dealing with specific skills. Exercises provided for both work-type and recreational reading.

Much attention was given to the concept of individual needs. In sequence-of-skills programs, the three-group method was most often employed as a means of providing for individual needs. In the activity movement, the program was organized around the needs and activities of children, through a variety of themes. Some of the activity programs dispensed with basal readers.

Diagnosis and remediation was a chief topic of study during this period. Most manuals of basal series discussed techniques for helping disabled readers. The Fernald technique, introduced in the preceding period, was beginning to be used, particularly by some clinical psychologists. Psychological and educational clinics came into being with primary concentration on diagnosis rather than remediation.

This time period saw the birth of the term "reading readiness," nurtured by Rousseau, Pestalozzi, Froebel, and Herbart, and now crystallized by Dewey. The readiness period for reading was both discussed and recommended in *The Twenty-Fourth Yearbook of the National Society for the Study of Education*, Part 1 (1925). Also, the results of a doctoral study by Reed (1927) demonstrated "that one in every six children failed at the end of the first semester in first grade, and that one in every eight failed at the end of the second semester in first grade" (Smith, p. 261). Reed's results appeared to strengthen the growing awareness of a need for focusing attention on reading readiness.

1935 to 1950

During this fifteen-year span, appropriately named "the period of international conflict" by Smith, emphasis was placed on systematic reading instruction and on reading in contemporary life. A host of materials was published that centered on high school, college, and adult reading as outgrowths of the realization (first arrived at during World War I) that young people entering the armed forces could not read well enough to cope with their duties. Developmental reading programs were instituted in high schools and colleges, with emphasis on reading in content areas.

A number of important professional books were published, and their far-reaching influence may be felt even today: Gates, *The Improvement of Reading*; Betts, *Foundations of Reading Instruction*; Monroe, *Children Who Cannot Read*; Fernald, *Remedial Techniques in Basic School Subjects*; and Helen M. Robinson, *Why Pupils Fail in Reading*. Some of the professional texts were general in nature, but a number concentrated on specific aspects. In fact, the first volumes on secondary school reading were published at this time. Manuals accompanying basals, as well as supplementary materials, were very thorough in nature.

The few new series introduced during this period had reading-readiness books preceding preprimers. There were generally two books per grade, from second grade on. A continued reduction in the total number of words introduced and in the number of words per page was evident. Repetitions of words were better controlled. The stories were predominantly realistic and informative, with a scattering of the fanciful. There tended to be more interrelationship with the other language arts and, in one series, overall emphasis on social studies and science. Reading readiness began to be recognized as an important concept at all levels of instruction.

Long, carefully organized skill charts accompanied basals, and word recognition was broken down into phonics, structural analysis, and context clues. Phonics instruction in grade one was generally limited. Work-type reading was now called work study or study skills and generally was broken down into information locating, evaluation, organization, and retention. Comprehension was segmented in a variety of ways but most often in these general categories: simple comprehension, higher mental processes, and critical thinking or critical reading. Some attention was given speed of reading and skimming.

Attention to individual needs remained a viable concept. Grouping was the main approach to caring for individual needs, and the objective of flexibility was more discussed than achieved.

A great deal of emphasis was placed on remediation, and reading clinics developed at a rapid pace. A number of instruments were invented or adapted for use in diagnosis and instruction: telebinocular, ophthalmograph, metronoscope, tachistoscopes, Harvard Films, and others.

1950 to 1965

Smith called the period from 1950 to 1965 a time of "expanding knowledge and technological revolution." During these fifteen years, many professional books were published. New and revised basals with extensive manuals spanned the elementary grades, sometimes covering grades seven and eight. Stories were mostly realistic. The average number of words introduced in basals was still decreasing. Repetitions of vocabulary words usually were carefully controlled. The civil rights movement raised the moral and economic consciousness of authors and publishers; multicultural readers and supplementary materials were produced. At first the materials were quick responses to a need—change the pictures, alter some stereotypes. By the end of this time period, these materials had improved in quality and in response to at least some of the needs of some of the learners.

At the same time, multiple texts were being introduced into classes, in order to care for individual needs. Individualized reading programs and individualized instruction, visible throughout our history, now emerged with a sound conceptual base partly due to Olson's ideas of "seeking, self-selection, and pacing." The concept of individualized reading was used in collaboration with basal instruction by some teachers, but, in a large number of situations, individualized reading programs replaced basal programs. Programmed reading, with or without hardware, was introduced as part of the concept of individualized instruction; unfortunately, most of the programs concentrated on "pacing" rather than on overall individualization.

Reading-readiness programs were evident, but criticism, particularly of the instructional materials and activities, was growing. Questions were asked, not necessarily about the concept, but rather about the procedures used to develop this readiness. During this time, in some situations, a child could be held back to complete the parts of the structured readiness program, even though he or she was ready, or even able, to read.

Linguists became interested in reading instruction, and "linguistic" readers came into being. Materials were usually based on the gradual introduction of word or spelling patterns, although some attention was focused on sentence patterns. Pitman's initial teaching alphabet (i.t.a.) found its way to this country in a set of materials prepared by Mazurkiewicz and Tanyzer in 1963 and 1964. Other augmented alphabets were tried, but none became as popular as i.t.a.

Essentially, however, instruction incorporated all of the reading skills discovered or developed over the years. All types of word-recognition clues were taught, and phonics, contrary to some notions, never left the basal programs. However, several critics claimed that phonics needed more emphasis (a recurring theme) and, as usual, publishers responded with renewed vigor. Austin and Morrison (1963), in their extensive study of elementary reading, observed that phonics was taught across the nation, often, in their view, at the expense of other learning.

Much stress appeared to be placed on the higher-level reading skills, such as critical reading, although Austin and Morrison found that such skills were discussed by educators more often than they were actually taught. Vocabulary and study-skills instruction seemed universal.

From 1960 on, there was a decided expansion of developmental reading programs in high schools, and many programs, most often of a corrective nature, were organized in colleges. Adult reading programs, for those functionally illiterate, as well as for those who could read well but who wanted to read better, became popular and were offered in adult education centers, as well as in libraries and in business settings. Clinics, private and public, developed at a fast pace to care for the needs of retarded readers in a society where high-level literacy seemed essential.

Research was prolific and improved in design. An increasing number of investigators became interested in the sociology of reading, although studies concentrating on psychological factors in reading also continued to be prominent. Doctoral dissertations were plentiful, and some of those student researchers may be credited

with a movement toward looking intensively at the reading processes rather than stressing, as did so many researchers, evaluation of the products of reading or reading instruction (in essence, the test results).

1965 to 1976

The time period from 1965 to 1976 is too close to the time of publication of this volume to allow us to stand back and look at the decade very objectively or, indeed, to give it a name. At this time, in the view of this writer, the decade in some ways seems to have been almost two separate periods, educationally speaking—the first half, one of hope and abundance; the second half, one of uncertainty and poverty. Certainly the total decade was characterized by overlapping methodologies resulting, as usual, in dichotomous suggestions, procedures, and instructional materials. Reading instruction encompassed emphases on phonics, context clues, content areas, rates of reading, study skills, reasoning, critical reading, and so on. Almost all of the approaches (in modern dress) utilized in the United States since 1840 were visible during this decade. The cry for more phonics issued loud and clear once again as *the* way of solving "the reading problem." And this in spite of a large-scale national study, described by Bond and Dykstra (1967), in which a major conclusion appeared to be that the teacher and the elements in the learning situation were more important than was any single method.

Particularly during the first half of the decade, when funds were available from many sources, authors and publishers answered the demands for many methods and for a multitude of materials. Books, workbooks, instruments, and computers abounded, offering schools a wide choice for their particular needs. Emphasis was placed on helping minority groups, and funds were available for additional personnel in the school system. The demand for reading teachers and the number in training were at all-time highs. The concept of accountability entered the educational arena. For a short time, schools bought programs on trial (payment dependent upon student achievement), and teachers often were judged on the ability of their students to achieve high scores.

During the latter part of the decade, inflation and recession succeeded in restricting budgets, and schools became more selective about their purchases. In addition, publishers had to evaluate the projects they planned to publish or revise. The educational scene reflected a new phenomenon: aside from the influence of lowered budgets, school populations—mainly in suburban areas—diminished as a result of "no growth" and the lowered national birthrate. A number of schools were closed, and thousands of teachers were excised. Although the national concern for eliminating illiteracy by 1980 received priority, numerous factors—even with the valiant efforts of the Right to Read Program—made it sound like "the impossible dream."

During the 1965–1976 period, particularly during the last five years, growing emphasis was placed on communication skills (including reading) that would help learners cope with the tasks confronting them in their everyday lives. Adult education programs began to focus on consumer education, health, job-finding skills, and ecology. In this amazingly complex and ever-changing society, it seems likely that coping skills will receive much more attention in the next decade, for younger learners as well as for adults.

In the opinion of this writer the most significant "innovation" during this decade, and slightly before, was the contribution to reading instruction made by linguistics, psycholinguistics, and sociolinguistics. There is still much to be learned, but I see promising signs of improved reading instruction as a result of increasing knowledge. Strickland (1962) should be thanked for pressuring the profession into looking at written language as it is processed by readers, in terms of syntax rather than just in terms of word difficulty and sentence length. Her study was followed rapidly by other researchers (including Loban 1963–1967; Ruddell 1963; Hunt 1965; O'Donnell, Griffin, and Norris 1967; Goodman 1964–1973; Peltz 1973–1974) who made us realize how much we need to know about learners and their languages if we are to try to facilitate reading achievement. Young (1973), in a doctoral dissertation, critically reviewed and summarized studies concerned with the relationship of reading and linguistics.

Conclusion

Enlightened attitudes toward language usage and dialects, in my opinion, have been, and will continue to be, strong influences for improvement in reading instruction. The promising trend and the hope for the future was summed up well by Gunderson (1971):

> A teacher who has an understanding of language and its structure, and who possesses the requisite skills to understand and to capitalize on a child's particular strengths should be able to provide the proper opportunity for children to learn to read.

References

Austin, Mary C., and Morrison, Coleman. *The First R.* New York: Macmillan Co., 1963.

Bond, Guy L., and Dykstra, Robert. "The Cooperative Research Program in First-Grade Reading Instruction." *Reading Research Quarterly* 2 (summer 1967):1–142. [ED 014 417]

Goodman, Kenneth S. "A Linguistic Study of Cues and Miscues in Reading," 1964. [ED 015 087]

———. "Study of Children's Behavior While Reading Orally." 1964. [ED 021 698]

———. *Theoretically Based Studies of Patterns of Miscues in Oral Reading Performance*. Washington: Bureau of Research, Office of Education, April 1973. [ED 079 708]

Gunderson, Doris V. "Reading: The Past Revisited." November 1971. [ED 085 680]

Huey, Edmund B. *The Psychology and Pedagogy of Reading*. 1908. Reprint. Cambridge, Massachusetts: MIT Press, 1968.

Hunt, Kellogg W. *Grammatical Structures Written at Three Grade Levels*. Research Report, no. 3. Champaign, Illinois: National Council of Teachers of English, 1965. [ED 113 735]

Loban, Walter. *The Language of Elementary School Children*. Research Report, no. 1. Champaign, Illinois: National Council of Teachers of English, 1963. [ED 001 875]

———. "Language Ability: Grades Seven, Eight, and Nine." Cooperative Research Project, no. 1131. Berkeley, California: University of California, 1964. [ED 001 275]

———. "Language Ability: Grades Ten, Eleven, and Twelve." Berkeley, California: University of California, 1967. [ED 014 477]

Mathews, Mitford M. *Teaching to Read: Historically Considered*. Chicago: University of Chicago Press, 1966. [ED 117 649]

O'Donnell, Roy C.; Griffin, W. J.; and Norris, R. C. *Syntax of Kindergarten and Elementary School Children: A Transformational Analysis*. Research Report, no. 8. Champaign, Illinois: National Council of Teachers of English, 1967. [ED 070 093]

Olson, Willard. "Seeking, Self-Selection and Pacing in the Use of Books by Children." *The Packet* (spring 1962):3–10.

Peltz, Fillmore K. "The Effect upon Comprehension of Repatterning Materials Based on Students' Writing Patterns." *Reading Research Quarterly* 9 (1973–1974):603–21. [ED 086 990]

Reed, Mary M. "An Investigation of the Practice for the Admission of Children and the Promotion of Children from First Grade." Doctoral dissertation, Teachers College, Columbia University, 1927.

Ruddell, Robert B. "An Investigation of the Effect of the Similarity of Oral and Written Patterns of Language Structure on Reading Comprehension." Doctoral dissertation, Indiana University, 1963.

Smith, Nila Banton. *American Reading Instruction*, rev. ed. Newark, Delaware: International Reading Association, 1965.

Strickland, Ruth G. "The Language of Elementary School Children: Its Relationship to the Language of Reading Textbooks and the Quality of Reading of Selected Children." *Bulletin of the School of Education, Indiana University* 38 (July 1962). [ED 002 970]

Twenty-Fourth Yearbook of the National Society of the Study of Education. Part 1. Bloomington, Illinois: Public School Publishing Co., 1925.

Young, Sherrye L. S. "The Relationship of Reading and Linguistics: A Critical Essay and Annotated Bibliography." Doctoral dissertation, Ohio University, 1973.

2. Reading Instruction Today

Joanna Williams

People will always bewail the low level of reading ability of the current school population. Such complaints are to be expected, given the central importance of literacy in our society. Indeed, a lack of concern on the part of parents and educators would indicate a serious lack of interest in the foundations of education. These comments are not meant to imply that there is no cause for concern about the quality of today's instruction in reading; there is plenty of room for improvement.

From Joanna Williams, Reading instruction today. *American Psychologist*, October 1979, 34, 917–922. Copyright 1979 by the American Psychological Association. Reprinted by permission of the publisher and author.

But we may sound an optimistic note: The high priority given to literacy means that there is a great deal of motivation for both theoretical and applied work in this area.

This essay describes current achievements in the areas of reading theory and reading instruction. How well are we doing? Have we learned anything from previous generations of theorists and educationists? Are tomorrow's students likely to demonstrate skills superior to those of today's students?

A generation ago, most children were taught to read by one or another version of the "whole-word," or "look-say," method. This approach, which was developed as a reaction to the previously popular drill-heavy and tedious phonics approach, stressed the communication aspect of reading. From the very beginning of instruction, the emphasis was on reading as a meaningful and satisfying activity.

The single whole word was the focus of instruction, for it was the smallest unit of written language that was meaningful. Words selected for teaching were those in the child's oral vocabulary and ones that could be combined easily in sentences and stories.

There was, of course, research evidence to justify the approach. Experiments were cited which demonstrated that a familiar word *is* read as a whole. It was, for example, possible to read a short word, tachistoscopically presented, in the same amount of time as sufficed for the recognition of a single letter. It was also possible to identify a combination of letters that made a word (such as CAT) after a very brief exposure that was too short to allow identification of the same letters in a sequence that did not make a word (such as TCA). But this empirical evidence was certainly not the main reason why the whole-word method became so well established. The fact that Gestalt principles were so highly endorsed at the time this method was promoted in the 1920s, 1930s,

and 1940s probably had much more to do with its success. Gestalt psychology emphasized the importance of a meaningful whole, and a word was a meaningful whole. Moreover, children are better able to handle the familiar and the concrete—and words are both familiar and concrete. Perhaps just as potent an influence was the then prevalent philosophy of education that stressed personal adjustment and the "whole child"; that is, it was harmful to push children to achieve too much too soon. This idea often led to great concern about readiness for learning and then to the postponement of reading instruction until it was clear that the child was "ready."

By the 1950s, however, there was a great deal of concern about the many children who were not reading well. In 1955, Rudolf Flesch published *Why Johnny Can't Read*, a strong indictment of the whole-word method and a call for a return to old-style phonics instruction. The book became a best-seller. New methods, based on proposals by linguists such as Bloomfield and Fries, began to make headway. These new linguistics methods looked suspiciously like the earlier, repudiated phonics instruction, but they were considerably more systematic in presentation, and of course they had the endorsement of current, well-respected scholars.

Discussion became intense. Should there be a change in the way reading was taught? If so, should there be a return to phonics—which had already been found wanting—or was there something else that might be tried? Over the years, novel approaches to instruction were introduced, such as O. K. Moore's talking typewriter and Pitman's initial teaching alphabet. Research findings were reinterpreted; people began to point out, for example, that the tachistoscopic recognition experiments had used adult subjects and that perhaps literate adults were different from 5-year-old nonreaders. But no new ideas appeared that could deflect the thinking in the field away from its perennial question: If the purpose of reading is communication, shouldn't meaning be stressed? And yet English is, after all, based on the alphabetic principle, so shouldn't instruction focus on the correspondences between letters and sounds (as phonics did)? You may recognize this as what Jeanne Chall called, in her landmark book of 1967, "the Great Debate."

On the basis of a careful study of the findings (which included hundreds of studies), Chall pointed out that the debate was not really between teaching or not teaching the alphabetic code; it concerned at what point in the course of instruction, and with what emphasis, the code should be taught. She concluded that early emphasis on decoding involving translating the written code into speech, in terms of the correspondences between letters and sounds, led to higher achievement in word recognition and in spelling. Not even in terms of interest or involvement in reading was a whole-word (meaning-emphasis) approach superior. Chall observed that all children tended to do better with a code approach but that those of low intelligence or of low socioeconomic level were especially likely to achieve more when a code approach was used.

There were other major undertakings in the 1960s besides Chall's study. First, in the First Grade Studies, funded by the U.S. Office of Education (Bond & Dykstra, 1967), 27 independent investigators from all over the United States compared the effects of different instructional methods in the 1st-grade classrooms; about half of them continued their study through the 3rd grade. The report of the findings was disappointing, however; no one method or approach led to better achievement than any other.

Second, Project Literacy was organized to stimulate basic research on reading (Gibson & Levin, 1975). The tremendous growth of the field over the last 15 years is due in large part to Project Literacy, especially to the contributions of Eleanor Gibson. Much of the early work centered on perceptual learning (probably because of Gibson's influence) and also on the nature of the correspondence between written and spoken language. In doing this, perhaps this basic work tended, indirectly, of course, to endorse decoding instruction.

A notable contribution to instructional psychology, task analysis, became popular at about the same time. Robert Gagné (1970) proposed the technique of breaking down a complex task into its component skills and then determining the sequence in which the components should be taught for the most effective and efficient mastery of the complex task.

In the 1970s we have seen a continuation of intense interest in research on reading, both basic and applied, as well as the development of a large number of instructional programs. Most of these curricula seem to subscribe to the notions that the ability to decode is of fundamental importance and that the reading task can be analyzed into component skills, to be taught in sequence. This has come to be known as the "skills approach."

There is still a school of thought which believes that instruction in how to break the code should not be emphasized for beginning readers. It is hard to describe this approach because, unlike the leaders of the old whole-word approach, its proponents do not have a specific proposal about what to do instead of teaching the code. Frank Smith (1975) is probably the best representative of this point of view. According to Smith, getting meaning from the printed page is the main task of the reader; he or she does not need to decode written language into spoken language at all. Researchers should go to the field of language comprehension for ideas of how reading should be defined and how it should be taught.

It seems to be assumed that the processes that occur in the mature, proficient reader are the very ones that should be taught to the beginning reader, and the argument is made that instruction in decoding, or the skills approach, may actually impede the child in his or her attempt to get the meaning of the text. Smith acknowledges that his theories do not "offer prescriptions for methodology. They are not directly translatable into practice. Instead, they aim to inform teachers, to assist them in making their own diagnoses and decisions" (p. 75). In practice, then, this approach usually comes down to instruction that offers the child a great deal of language activity, interesting reading material, and an emphasis on comprehension from the very beginning. Language-experience methods, in which the child dictates a story to be read, can fall within this classification, as can instruction that simply involves reading to the child, sometimes with many repetitions of the same text. Such methods are, in fact, considerably less structured than those of traditional look-say basal readers.

These, then, are the major events and ideas that have led up to today's thinking: dissatisfaction with the results of reading instruction; Chall's conclusion that early instruction in decoding would lead to better achievement; concern that method comparisons in actual school settings might never, by their very nature, give us answers; and most recently, large-scale investment in the development of instructional programs.

After 15 years of intense activity, the Great Debate continues. As John Carroll (1978) noted, the debate has shifted slightly from a focus on teaching practices to a focus on reading process. But in terms of its implications for instruction, the debate has not changed much.

Have we made any progress in resolving the matter? Today, educational researchers are considerably less sanguine about how directly basic research can address educational questions. Current research in word recognition, for exam-

ple, is contributing substantially to the field of cognitive psychology, but for the most part the findings are too detailed and specific to yield implications for instruction. And the early applied research, which often consisted of small-scale studies that translated educational assumptions and practices into laboratory analogues, has clearly run its course. We now seem to be at the point—again— where we look for answers in the evaluation of large-scale instructional programs in actual school settings.

I want to describe a couple of recent studies that do seem to me to indicate some progress—if we choose to acknowledge it. First, John Guthrie and his colleagues (Guthrie, Martuza, & Seifert, 1979) reanalyzed the results of the First Grade Studies I mentioned above. They looked specifically at the Word Reading subtest of the Stanford Achievement Test and found that children learned word recognition more readily in those programs that were skills oriented, such as linguistics methods or methods combining phonics and linguistics, than in basal reading programs. In addition, programs that combined a phonics program with a basal method were superior to the traditional basal approaches. However, on another subtest of the SAT, Paragraph Meaning, a measure of reading comprehension, they did not find differences between skills-oriented and basal methods. These investigators concluded that, at least in the 1st grade, an emphasis on decoding seemed beneficial.

Second, analyses of Follow Through, an enormous planned-variation experiment in which different models for educating disadvantaged children were tested, have begun to appear. In an initial major data analysis, Abt Associates (Stebbins, St. Pierre, Proper, Anderson, & Cerva, 1977) compared 13 of the models, looking at children who had been enrolled in Follow-Through models for a four-year period. They reported, first of all, that the effectiveness of a teaching approach varied greatly from one school to the next, and overall, there were not substantive differences between the Follow-Through and the comparison non-Follow-Through groups. The instructional models were categorized into three groups: those in which the instruction focused on Basic Skills—that is, vocabulary, arithmetic computation, spelling, and language; those that were cognitive-conceptual in orientation; and those that were affective-cognitive, or in other words, child centered. It was found that on the Metropolitan Achievement Test, the Basic Skills models led to better performance than did the other two models. Within the Basic Skills models, it was the Direct Instructional Model of the University of Oregon (known as DISTAR) that seemed to show up best. This program is highly structured and has a strong emphasis on decoding. The superiority of this program was clearest at the 1st- and 2nd-grade levels and no longer appeared at the 4th-grade level. (Other studies in which an effect of instruction is seen in the early grades also show no effect at Grades 3, 4, and beyond; this is typically attributed to the fact that reading tests change their focus at about the 4th-grade level, shifting from assessment of word recognition, that is, those skills that are specifically and sometimes directly taught in programs that emphasize decoding, to assessment of comprehension.) It should be noted that, as expected, the Abt report has become highly controversial, and strong critiques of both methodology and conclusions have appeared. House, Glass, McLean, and Walker, for example, in the May 1978 *Harvard Educational Review*, objected strongly to the conclusion that there are any differences at all among the instructional models. These investigators, funded by the Ford Foundation, emphasized the fact that the effectiveness of every one of the teaching approaches varied widely among school districts, and they argued that this is the finding that should serve as a basis for educational policy; that is, we should "honor local individuality."

Lauren Resnick (Note 1) reviewed these studies and others, some of which have not demonstrated the superiority of any method, including another reanalysis by Guthrie, this time of the Educational Testing Service evaluation of compensatory reading programs across the country, and the work of Berliner, Rosenshine, and others on the California Teacher Study. Several of these studies indicated that more time spent in instruction and more direct instruction lead to greater achievement in reading (as well as in other school subjects), especially for low-socioeconomic-level children. Resnick pointed out that it is the proponents of an approach that emphasizes decoding who tend also to recommend direct instruction; that it is likely that when more instructional time is spent on reading in the classroom, the teacher is doing direct teaching; and that that direct teaching is of decoding. Resnick also raised the important question of whether the effects are due to teaching decoding specifically or to direct teaching per se; we cannot tell, because these two variables are usually confounded.

The evidence, then, is far from clear. Overall, the bits and pieces suggest that sometimes skills-oriented approaches lead to significantly greater achievement on reading tests and sometimes they don't. The effects, when they occur, show up at the 1st and perhaps the 2nd grade and wash out at later grades. The outcome measures that demonstrate the effects are limited to word-recognition skills. The effects are more likely to be seen when children of low socioeconomic level are studied. And the effects, when they occur, are never very large.

These findings suffer from the many thorny problems inherent in the evaluation of large-scale educational programs in natural settings. But they are certainly similar to those of smaller scale and/or more basic studies. To give just a single example, the old studies done within the framework of programmed instruction found that sometimes material incorporating "good principles," like sequenced presentation, led to higher achievement than did material that did not follow the principles, and sometimes it didn't. But poorly organized material never proved superior. And it was low-aptitude pupils whose scores suffered particularly from the lack of a well-structured program.

Such studies obviously have less ecological validity than do actual program comparisons. But they should make us more willing to accept the notion that even if we find no differences in large-scale comparisons of total instruction programs, with the myriad pragmatic difficulties involved in implementing the design, managing the treatment, handling attrition, choosing criterion measures, and so forth, ad infinitum, the variables might actually be important after all.

It seems to me that at this point, in order to argue against using a code approach, one is forced to claim that (a) there are positive gains from programs that emphasize meaning but we cannot assess them, and (b) those outcomes are more important than the outcomes we can measure. There are those who say just that. I don't believe it, myself. It seems to me that the evidence suggests that you might as well provide the child with a good decoding program; such instruction teaches basic skills more effectively. As far as comprehension is concerned, it hasn't been demonstrated that instruction in decoding helps, but it certainly doesn't seem to hurt.

Why is it that there is so much resistance to the idea of teaching decoding skills? We hear that it is the publishers' fault, that they have million-dollar investments to protect, so they resist strongly any fundamental change in approach. To some extent this is plausible, especially in light of today's extraordinarily high publishing costs. Yet most widely used basal reading series now incorporate some emphasis on decoding in their approach. Helen Popp (1975) recently surveyed the current materials on the market, and in addition to finding that most current instructional programs today offer a balance between decoding and comprehension instruction, she noted other trends: increased emphasis on literature, writing, and communication skills; more audio and visual aids; greater diversity of ethnic groups and socioeconomic levels portrayed in basal readers; more attempts to individualize instruction; and more emphasis on criterion-referenced testing. These recent developments in instructional materials clearly reflect the eagerness with which innovations are sought and used.

Why, then, is there such resistance to change? I do not believe that we can attribute it to the dearth of empirical evidence. Today, as in the past, data do not carry a great deal of weight in determining educational practice. I mentioned theory and general social philosophy as having previously contributed greatly to decisions about method. We can see similar forces operating today, and most of them support programs that emphasize meaning.

First of all, let us consider theory. The exciting new areas in psychology for the last decade or more have been language and cognitive processing. These areas speak much more to issues of comprehension than they do to decoding. Indeed, the term *language approach* is coming to be used for what has usually been referred to as *meaning emphasis*.

On the other hand, *decoding* smacks of rote learning, drill, and practice, all unappealing concepts these days. The recent major improvements in the teaching of decoding are, in my opinion, largely due to the use of task analysis as a model. Though task analysis has been accepted by cognitive psychologists, and indeed it makes sense to consider it under this rubric, it had at its inception many proponents who were committed to the old stimulus-response, behaviorist point of view. It is one of the strengths of task analysis, incidentally, to have straddled successfully the behaviorist and cognitive paradigms. But it leaves the resulting decoding instruction too much associated with the old, out-of-favor psychology.

Second, the approach that emphasizes meaning seems more "professional." One of the genuine contributions of educational psychology over the years, accomplished very often through college courses in teacher preparation, is the emphasis on the teacher as a hypothesis tester and decision maker. With an understanding of general principles, we say, and an ability to make careful observations in one's own classroom, the good teacher can try out techniques and see what works. He or she can assess the effectiveness of new materials. The good teacher is in charge.

I agree that these kinds of skills and attitudes on the part of the teacher are absolutely essential and of the highest priority. But at times this approach may well boomerang, because when there is something specific that really should be done, it sometimes does not claim any more importance in the teacher's decision making than anything else. And training in decoding is often considered boring and uncreative. Moreover, it is hard work. It is no surprise to find that successful programs of direct instruction often have backup teachers to share the load. Teachers are only human; it is not unreasonable to consider that, without strong inducement on the grounds that it is really very important to give direct instruction in decoding, a decision will often be made in favor of a less effortful and more enjoyable procedure. Please note that I am talking about the enjoyment of the teacher: Good direct teaching, however repetitious and drill oriented, can be highly stimulating and fun for the children—but of course this is exactly what takes an enormous amount out of the teacher!

Last but not least, there is the matter of social philosophy. Today's schools have taken over many tasks that used to be the responsibility of other institutions in the society. At the same time, as Resnick and Resnick (1977) pointed out, the United States has taken on an educational task that is really quite new: We are now committed to educating all children to a high level of literacy. Our aspirations on this score today are far different from what they were in earlier times. But we have other social-educational goals as well. Old ideas about education for the elite are not acceptable now; we want children from all walks of life to learn together in order that they may learn to live together. Thus, today as before, other goals take priority over the goal of producing the highest possible achievement scores in basic skills. Perhaps this should always be true in a democracy.

Comprehension of meaning from a written text—often expressed these days in terms of processing the information in a text—is, of course, the ultimate goal of reading. The state of the art in both theoretical work and instructional development in comprehension is not well advanced.

Theoretical work in psychology, linguistics, and artificial intelligence is moving forward very rapidly right now. The concentration in the 1960s on transformational grammar did not lead to much progress in the way of new teaching practices or even teaching goals, although there were many attempts to use it. (Some people even went so far as to teach transformational grammar to junior high school students in the hope of improving their reading.) The recent emphasis on semantics and the new advances in theory, especially the development of discourse analysis, are much more promising.

For those of you who are skeptical that we shall actually be able to modify children's comprehension by any kind of direct instruction, let me say, first, it is worth a try; and second, even if that aspiration turns out to be too grand, there will no doubt be other valuable outcomes. We shall, I am sure, learn a great deal about ways of writing expository texts to ensure maximally effective processing. It may be that presentation formats will undergo revolutionary changes as a result of this work.

Let us look ahead to the next decade. As research on comprehension proceeds, new ideas for teaching procedures and new techniques will be identified and tried. Some will work and will be incorporated quickly into classroom activities. Some, for all sorts of reasons, good and bad, will not catch on. It is likely that in a few years, large-scale instructional programs for the middle years (Grades 4–6) will be developed, similar to those available now for the beginning stages of reading. It is to be hoped—but not expected—that these will prove to be clearly effective, efficient, and noncontroversial.

Reference Note

1. Resnick, L. *Theory and practice in beginning reading instruction.* Paper presented at the meeting of the National Academy of Education, New York, October 1977.

References

Bond, G., & Dykstra, R. The cooperative research program in first-grade reading. *Reading Research Quarterly*, 1967, 2, 5–142.

Carroll, J. B. Psycholinguistics and the study and teaching of reading. In S. Pflaum-Connor (Ed.), *Aspects of reading education.* Berkeley, Calif.: McCutchan, 1978.

Chall, J. S. *Learning to read: The great debate.* New York: McGraw-Hill, 1967.

Flesch, R. *Why Johnny can't read and what you can do about it.* New York: Harper, 1955.

Gagné, R. M. *The conditions of learning* (2nd ed.). New York: Holt, Rinehart & Winston, 1970.

Gibson, E. J., & Levin, H. *Psychology of reading.* Cambridge, Mass.: MIT Press, 1975.

Guthrie, J. T., Martuza, V., & Seifert, M. Impacts of instructional time in reading. In L. B. Resnick & P. A. Weaver (Eds.), *Theory and practice of early reading.* Vol. 3. Hillsdale, N. J.: Erlbaum, 1979.

House, E. R., Glass, G. V, McLean, L. D., & Walker, D. F. No simple answer: Critique of the Follow Through evaluation. *Harvard Educational Review*, 1978, 48, 128–160.

Popp, H. Current practices in the teaching of beginning reading. In J. B. Carroll & J. S. Chall (Eds.), *Toward a literate society.* New York: McGraw-Hill, 1975.

Resnick, D. P., & Resnick, L. B. The nature of literacy: An historical exploration. *Harvard Educational Review*, 1977, 47, 370–385.

Smith, F. *Comprehension and learning.* New York: Holt, Rinehart & Winston, 1975.

Stebbins, L. B., St. Pierre, R. G., Proper, E. C., Anderson, R. B., & Cerva, T. R. *Education as experimentation: A planned variation model: Vol. IV–A. An evaluation of Follow Through.* Cambridge, Mass.: Abt Associates, 1977.

3. The Status of Reading Achievement: Is There a Halo around the Past?

Leo Fay

When I first considered this topic, I had a clear idea of what the presentation would be. In fact, I gathered a vast amount of data concerning the status of reading achievement in the United States and, with Roger Farr, systematically tested 10,000 sixth graders and 10,000 tenth graders in Indiana using the same tests given to comparable groups in 1944. It all seemed so straightforward, but then some unusual things happened that changed the nature of this presentation in some significant ways.

I received and accepted an invitation to serve as a consultant to the Institute of Education and Research at the University of Punjab in Lahore, Pakistan. The institute faculty is divided into two parts—a teaching faculty offering the master's and Ph.D. degrees to prepare a cadre of educational leaders and a research faculty engaged in attempting to develop a research and development base for education in the country. Pakistan is both an old civilization with a history extending beyond 2500 B.C., and a new country having been formed by the partition of the Indian subcontinent in 1947 into two independent countries—India and Pakistan. The development needs of the country are tremendous—almost overwhelming—in agriculture, commerce, health, and education. Unesco, the U.S. Agency for International Development, and the Institute are all working to strengthen the educational base upon which all other development depends. Recently the World Bank provided Pakistan with a 50 million dollar loan to develop a better base of literacy in

the country. Think what it must be like to try to develop anything if your labor pool is over 85 percent illiterate.

Later, I received an invitation from Unesco to serve as a consultant to the Ministry of Education in Saudi Arabia to establish a system to evaluate their five year plan for educational development. I could not accept this invitation but did stop by Unesco in Paris to meet the head of the Arab section and several others concerned with educational development in the Arab nations. When I walked into the office of the head of the Arab section, he asked me what I thought a certain sign in his office meant. It was a strange question because the sign was in Arabic, but he went on to say, "Those are the first words of the Koran. They say, 'Read what God has revealed to you.' Our holy book tells us to read and yet we are the most illiterate people on earth."

The Importance of Education for Everyone

The following conversation made a deep impact on me. I saw how blessed we are and have been as a people. How wise our early leaders had been in emphasizing the importance of education for everyone. To read is to possess a power for transcending whatever physical power humans can muster. And we, my friends, have been blessed with this power in ever increasing measure throughout our history. We have enjoyed the presence in our past of the halo referred to in the title of the paper; it is here in our present; and it will continue into our future.

From Leo Fay, The status of reading achievement: Is there a halo around the past? In Constance McCullough (Ed.), *Inchworm, inchworm: Persistent problems in reading education.* Newark, Del.: International Reading Association, 1980. Pp. 13–21. Reprinted with permission of Leo Fay and the International Reading Association.

The development of literacy in our country is interesting to trace. At the time of the first census in 1790, the estimate was that 15 percent of the people were literate in that they could read and write their own names. It was not until after World War I that half the people were literate, defined in terms of having attended four years of school. As late as 1943, 750,000 men had been rejected for military service because of illiteracy. Most of these young men were from remote rural areas and were predictors of the postwar problems that urban areas experienced with the mass movement of people out of rural areas to the large cities. By 1960, 75 percent of the children who were in fifth grade went on to complete high school; today, over 50 percent of our youth go on to postsecondary education and by some definitions we are 90+ percent literate. This is a truly phenomenal accomplishment. But too often we simply do not appreciate the significance of the contribution that schooling of *all* of our youth has made to the well being and power of this nation.

In his "A Letter to the President-Elect" (*Change* magazine, December 1976), Wilbur Cohen reminded Mr. Carter that "Education has been a critical key to our national development and the quality of our life." Edward Denison (in a Brookings Institution report) found that the biggest single stimulus of our economic growth during 1962–1969 was increase of knowledge. Another major source was the increased education of our labor force. Fourteen percent of our economic growth during this period came from increased education per worker and 41 percent from advances in knowledge.

"According to Denison, educational background decisively conditions the type of work individuals can perform as well as their proficiency." Cohen then comments about the upward shift in the educational background of the labor force from 1929 to 1969 and concludes his letter with the observation that "Nothing is more important [than education of the people] for the fulfillment of the nation's goals." The truth is schools and teachers have served the nation well.

Achieving Our Literacy Potential

Having said this, let us look at the present state of reading achievement and try to determine where we are now. As we do this, I would also like to comment about some potential dangers on the horizons that we can and must avoid if our literacy potential is to be achieved.

It is a difficult if not impossible task to pick a particular moment in time to understand the status of any social phenomenon. This is certainly true of school achievement data. Usually it is more useful, in attempting to make judgments about the present, to look at trend lines over some span of time. Fortunately, various researchers have done this. In their study, "Reading: Then and Now," Farr and Tuinman and Rawls reported a compilation of studies which over the span of time from about 1920 through the middle sixties showed a continuing improvement in reading achievement. More recently, in their report, "The Decline in Reading Achievement: Need We Worry?" Harnischfeger and Wiley presented additional data that supported the same findings.

But then something seemed to happen, at least as far as test scores were concerned, from the middle grades through college levels. From about 1967, reading test scores for people beyond the age of nine started to drift down. This drift continued into the 70s, and at best is only now beginning to level off. The magnitude of this drop is such that one can say that while today's students perform better than their parents did at comparable ages, they are not doing as well, at least on standard tests, as their older siblings.

The evidence for this conclusion is found in two sets of data. The first, from the Iowa statewide testing program, shows the following drops in grade scores over the decade from 1965–1975:

	Grade 5	Grade 6	Grade 7	Grade 8
Reading	1.9 mo.	2.5 mo.	5.2 mo.	5.5 mo.
Vocabulary	.5 mo.	1.4 mo.	3.9 mo.	4.3 mo.
Math Concepts	3.1 mo.	4.8 mo.	6.5 mo.	7.0 mo.
Math Problem Solving	3.2 mo.	5.0 mo.	7.4 mo.	7.3 mo.

The second set of data is derived from a comparison of 1945 with 1976 reading achievement for a systematic, statewide sampling of sixth and tenth grade children. (Farr, Fay, Negley, *Then and Now: Reading Achievement in Indiana, 1944–1945 and 1976* [1978].) Because 1976 sixth grade students were ten months younger than their 1945 counterparts and 1976 tenth graders were fourteen months younger than the 1945 students, comparisons were adjusted by age. These comparisons resulted in a superiority of ten percentile points for the 1976 tenth grade students. The marked reduction in dropout rates over this period suggests that the difference was, in fact, substantially larger at the tenth grade level.

It should also be noted that the National literacy assessment data for seventeen year olds showed an increase of 2 percent over the period of 1971–1974. The NAEP data reported for nine year olds also showed an increase. The Iowa and NAEP data are based upon very different kinds of instruments and as a consequence are not directly comparable. The Iowa tests show a lower mean performance over the span of time whereas the NAEP shows an increase in the percentage of a given group that can perform successfully on the instruments. One interpretation is that NAEP data show that the percentage of functional literates has increased while the Iowa data show that the average performance of students has decreased.

Data from the city of Minneapolis and the state of Minnesota show patterns comparable to the above. Standardized tests show an improvement in the early elementary grades with some drop after the fourth grade, and National Assessment data show a high and increasing level of functional literacy within the state. Data from other communities indicate that this is a general pattern across the country, although actual levels of performance may differ.

In essence, then, on the long term, achievement has gone up. On the short term, achievement has appeared to have dropped. At this time there is no research to justify a stronger term than *appears* in this context. While there is no hard evidence, however, there is much speculation as to whether the observed change is real and, if it is real, what the reasons for the change might be.

At first glance, it would appear that there has been a real change. After all, the same instruments were used and the difference without question is there. This conclusion, however, assumes that conditions have remained constant enough for the instruments to remain valid. You could also speculate that the nature of literacy itself has broadened over the past decade to the extent that it can no longer be assessed by reading tests that are based upon models of forty or more years ago. The recent activities of the Association for Visual Literacy and the most recent definitions of literacy appearing in IRA publications would suggest this might be a distinct possibility. Badly needed are studies to determine the dimensions of reading and literacy in our society at this time.

The research is yet to be done. Perhaps it can be structured by speculation as to possible causes relating to the apparent drop in achievement in reading as well as the other school subjects. Strong opinions exist in regard to this matter. In the eighth annual Gallup Poll on Education (*Phi Delta Kappan*, October 1976), it is reported that 59 percent of the population believes that the quality of education today is declining as evidenced by the decline in national test scores. Furthermore, the poll revealed that the public places the greatest blame for declining scores on parents, on society, on children's lack of motivation, and too much viewing of television. Others blame the schools. The Hudson Institute Report by Frank Armbruster and others (*Wall Street Journal*, July 23, 1976) concluded that schools are deteriorating everywhere and that teachers and administrators are the ones primarily responsible. In both cases, the assumption is accepted that school achievement was indeed better in the past. School people have had to live with that contention probably for as long as schools have existed. Will Rogers used to comment that, "The schools ain't as good as they used to be—and they probably never were." In an address on April 21, 1932, Arthur Gates observed that teachers and schools were not responsible for the Great Depression.

Today's Schools

Schools do not exist in a void. They are a basic institution and in many ways reflect the society they serve. The period from the mid-sixties to the mid-seventies was not the most tranquil decade in our history. It was a time of conflict and of loud and serious questioning of our basic institutions. The home, church, state, and schools have all felt the negative impact of this period. Interestingly, this period was marked by a significant drop in the productivity of the American worker as measured by output per hour of work. Could this phenomenon bear any relationship to the apparent drop in school achievement? Is it reasonable to expect the school to run counter to a major opposite force in the society?

Look again at the American family. The children in school during this period were the later children of the relatively large postwar families. For some reason, later children tend toward lower achievement in school than their older siblings. This is the period when large numbers of women joined the labor force and family patterns started to change. Drug and alcohol abuse had a devastating effect on middle class America with the eight to fourteen year olds becoming the fastest growing group of drug users. Last year there were 300,000 births to unwed mothers ages fifteen and less. While not exactly a new phenomenon, the rate of increase is up more than 300 percent over a decade ago. In the report, "Greening of the High School—A Look at the Clients," the conclusion is documented that today's youth is far different from his parents and grandparents.

The school became the battleground for desegregation and racial balance which is but another societal problem cast upon the school. Yet, in spite of these changes in society, critics maintain that teachers and administrators are primarily responsible for the deterioration of school achievement. That is like saying that doctors and hospital staffs are responsible for the frightening trends in the increased incidence of cancer.

During this period, the value of schooling has been questioned in the various media. The lower economic payoff of education has been so publicized that there is a growing drop in enrollment in higher education among middle class families. Related is a change in values concerning work with a consequent drop in purpose for education. In a 1973 Gallup Poll, over one-third of the eighteen to twenty year olds did not consider education as important as success. Older populations had a much higher percentage of positive response, thus reflecting a major change in attitude between the two groups.

Patterns have shifted in school as well. Retention rates have increased during this period but unfortunately, attendance has dropped significantly. A group of Illinois teachers reported to me that when students were in school they attended fewer classes. A typical pattern was a work study assignment, study halls, and only two academic classes a day. Courses in English, foreign languages, and general mathematics all show drops in enrollment. The anti-schooling, anti-intellectual attitudes commonly held in our society apparently are having their impact.

One could hardly comment about school achievement without commenting about television. TV appears to be a positive force for the young learner up to ages eight and nine. After that age, TV begins to detract from reading and home study. Furthermore, TV watching may result in changes in thinking patterns that may affect school performance and performance on tests. This is another area for further research.

If you reflect upon these factors that may impinge upon school achievement, you realize that we must know much more before we can interpret what the nature of reading achievement really is. However, in spite of all the problems, the school has remained a viable institution. It continues to serve large numbers of people well. The Minnesota assessment revealed that the vast majority of students reacted very positively to their schooling and, furthermore, that this attitude is a positive force for higher achievement—more important than amount of money spent or various types of school interventions. Judging from past performance, the schools will be a major factor in building a better future for our nation.

New Developments to Be Considered

There are two major current developments, however, that need to be dealt with cautiously. One is the back to basics movement and the second is the trend toward forcing equal expenditures for the education of all children. On the surface, both developments appear attractive. Both, however, can result in mediocrity. The March 1977 issue of the *Phi Delta Kappan* features a series of articles discussing the back to basics movement and its meaning. This issue merits careful review. ''Back to'' suggests to the practices of some golden period, and ''basics'' needs definition as well. As Farr and his colleagues suggest, there was no golden period of American schooling. Rather, the schools have generally successfully adjusted to changing conditions and will most likely continue to do so. Basics or fundamentals as the terms are generally used mean a restriction of the curriculum to the teaching of skills that can be easily measured. This is a sure route to mediocre performance as has been demonstrated over and over again in American education. Superior performance is not achieved this way. Basics can be defined differently to mean the development of high levels of performance in the skills of communicating, of problem solving, and of creative behavior. A broad and demanding curriculum is essential if students are to come anywhere close to achieving their potential. I can agree that education should be concerned with the basics, but I further believe that professional teachers should be deeply involved with the definition of what this means in school practice.

The second condition currently being legislated in many places, that of necessity will lead schools to mediocrity, is the move to force the same level of expenditure on all schools within a state. No more, no less. Even if a district wanted to add to the support of its schools, it is not permitted to do so. Where are the centers of excellence to come from that test out the adaptations to changing conditions or that attempt to find the better way to provide schooling? American education sorely needs to encourage centers of excellence and this of necessity involves differential funding.

In conclusion, American schools have long merited a halo for their contribution to the strength of the nation. That halo is still merited, for the school continues to perform well in spite of the massive changes and problems that have characterized our recent history. In regard to reading achievement, the picture is any-thing but bleak. Basic functional literacy has increased particularly among our younger people. This is not to deny that a literacy problem exists. The recent IRA publication, *Adult Literacy Education in the United States*, by Wanda Cook, documents the problem thoroughly. However, as we study the ways to help our students become increasingly effective, let's do so with the confidence and pride that come from a solid record of accomplishment.

4. How Well Does the Average American Read? Some Facts, Figures, and Opinions

Mary K. Monteith

What's the average reading level in the United States? How well does the average American read? Several times a year one of the research specialists at the ERIC Clearinghouse on Reading and Communication Skills picks up the phone and is asked similar questions. This article is a compilation of many partial answers collected from the most recent studies, facts, figures, and opinions related to reading. The information should prove useful to reading teachers and other educators who are frequently held responsible for the answers to these questions or who may be asked to speak formally or informally on this topic. For more detailed discussions of each question, the original sources should be consulted.

What's the Average Reading Level in the U.S.?

How well does the average American read? The question is so basic it's hard to believe no one answer exists. The problem lies with the fact that most of the standardized reading tests taken by students in our high schools are norm-referenced. The score is a comparison or rank score, not a criterion-referenced score based upon the difficulty of what is read. A score of grade level 12 for a twelfth grader means that the student reads as well as an average twelfth grader, but it doesn't indicate the difficulty of the material read, according to a readability level, or the type of material. We have found no studies that analyze both the readability of the passages and the questions of a norm-referenced test and that compare them to norm rankings.

We do know that the mean educational attainment is now near the twelfth grade level. Several sources support this fact. A 1971 Harris survey [ED 068 813] shows that people in the age groups 16 to 49 attain an average of 11.5 to 12.5 years of schooling. An Educational Testing Service study conducted by Richard Murphy [ED 109 650] indicates that people between 16 and 60 have an average educational

From Mary K. Monteith. How well does the average American read? Some facts, figures, and opinions. *Journal of Reading*, February 1980, *20*, 460–464. Reprinted with permission of Mary K. Monteith and the International Reading Association.

attainment of 11.2 to 12.59, and a 1974 U.S, Bureau of the Census report had found the mean educational level is 12.3 for persons 25 years old and over.

In a comprehensive study of the research on literacy in the U.S., Fisher [ED 151 760] cites a 1971 study by Corder which indicates that half of the total U.S. population entering the twelfth grade will score at grade level 12 and above, and about 87% will score above grade level 8. Using these figures, Fisher estimates that there are about 45 million persons (37% of the adult population) scoring below an equivalent of 8.0 on standardized tests. Therefore we can predict that a certain percentage of Americans will score below or above an eighth- or twelfth-grade equivalent level, but we need to look at some of the other questions in this article to form a more adequate concept of how well Americans read.

How Well Does the Average American Need to Read?

Many studies have applied a variety of readability formulas to materials commonly read by adults. Several of these reports are cited here with the cautionary note that readability formulas are still imperfect measures of what is to be read and do not measure how well something is actually read.

A report in the *Illinois Reading Council Journal* (Wheat, Lindberg and Nauman 1977) suggests that newspapers are written at a considerably more difficult reading level than the sixth-grade level the authors had found was assumed by many other writers. The researchers found the mean readability level of wire service articles in metropolitan newspapers to be eleventh grade, nonwire articles ninth to tenth grade, and an average readability level to be tenth grade.

Payne [ED 163 419] analyzed the materials required for entry-level job performance for Washington, D.C. Fire Department workers and found most of the materials were written at a junior college level. Duffy and Nugent [ED 154 363] indicate that manuals for recruits training in the Navy are written at eleventh-and twelfth-grade levels while the median score of over 30,000 recruits on the Gates-MacGinitie Reading Text was 10.7.

Studies by Sticht and Vineberg in Fisher [ED 151 760] indicate that reading grade level scores of 7, 8, and 9 were attained by men performing at a satisfactory level of job proficiency in the military occupational specialties of cook, repairman, and supply clerk, respectively. However, the readability levels of materials written for these jobs are at 9.0 for cook, 14.5 for repairman, and 16.0 for supply clerk. This may indicate an incompatibility between reading test scores and readability formula levels, or it may indicate the many other factors besides reading performance necessary to many jobs.

An interesting study by Schulze [ED 120 682] analyzed the readability of best-sellers from a fifty-year period. The Fry Readability Formula was applied to each of sixty adult fiction best-sellers, representing the top ten best-sellers, beginning in 1923 and proceeding every ten years up to 1973. The mean readability score for 1923 was 7.3, with a range of 6 to 9, in 1974 the mean score was 7.4, with a range from 6 to 10 with similar scores in the decades between.

In *Reporting on Reading: Right to Read* (August 1978) Roger Farr noted that a ninth-grade reading level is required in order to answer the questions on the SAT.

Zingman [ED 142 933] analyzed mass political literature which appeared in newspapers and magazines during convention and election periods of the 1976 presidential election campaign. She concludes that the readability level ranges from the tenth to eleventh grades in magazines, to college level in newspapers. She suggests that election materials available from newspapers and magazines may be too difficult to serve the purpose of informing the public.

Fifty commonly used forms were compared with respect to length, readability, t-unit density, and word-length variables by Abbass [ED 146 623]. The forms were also compared against two word-frequency lists. Results showed that many of the words appearing often on forms do not appear on the high-frequency word list, that the readability of the forms ranges from the eighth-grade level to above the sixteenth-grade level, and that language of forms combines difficult semantics with overly simplistic syntax.

What Can the Average American Read?

Studies of what the American public can read are relatively recent and focus on functional literacy, the skills necessary for functioning in everyday life. The NAEP Assessment of Functional Literacy (Gadway and Wilson [ED 112 350], assessed the performance of 17-year-old students in 1971, 1974, and 1975. Students performed highest on exercises containing drawings, pictures, signs, and labels; second highest on charts, maps, and graphs. Most of the students performed next highest on reading passages, fourth highest on forms, and least well on reference materials. Over 90% of the students could read a help wanted ad and describe the product appeal of a coupon. Given a replica of a report card, only 68% were able to identify the subject in which improvement was shown. On three exercises performance was consistently low in all three assessment years. Given a replica of an automobile insurance policy statement, about 18% were able to identify the correct amount of coverage for bodily injury liabilities. Given a facsimile of a book club membership application only approximately 43% recognized that no money was required to be sent in with the application. Given a replica of a traffic ticket only 41 to 49% could identify the correct date for paying the fine.

The Survival Literacy Study conducted by Harris [ED 068 813] in 1970 asked adults to answer items on five different application forms. Three percent answered more than 10% of an application for public assistance incorrectly, or not at all; 7% answered more than 10% of an identification form similar to a social security information form, incorrectly or not at all; 8% answered more than 10% of an application for a driver's license, incorrectly or not at all; 11% had the same difficulty with completing a form for an application for a personal bank loan; and 34% had the same difficulty completing an application for Medicaid. In his study of the reports on literacy, Fisher [ED 151 760] points out that many of these questions test not only reading ability but recall of personal, economic and legal facts. He adjusts the survey calculations by excluding the figures from the Medicaid application which asks whether one's life insurance is 20 payment life, 20 year endowment, or another kind.

As part of the Adult Functional Reading Study (Murphy [ED 109 650]), a national reading performance survey consisting of 180 reading tasks was constructed and portions were administered to 7,866 adults. Items were intended to correspond to the ordinary reading tasks identified in the survey of reading habits. Examples of the reading tasks included answering questions concerning a TV schedule, a legal form, a group insurance plan, a train schedule, and election ballot instructions. The number of persons (and percentages) answering each of the 170 items correctly, incorrectly, or not at all is given for each item.

What Does the Average American Read?

As part of the Adult Functional Reading Study, Sharon [EJ 092 583] in 1973 indicated that 5,000 randomly selected persons were surveyed about their reading habits. The most common reading activity in the U.S. was reported to be newspaper reading, with more than seven out of ten readers reporting that they read or looked at a newspaper for an average of 35 minutes. The next most common reading activity was that occurring while traveling. Seven out of ten respondents reported reading while traveling; however, only three minutes a day were spent in such activity. Respondents indicated that they spent 61 minutes a day reading at work and 47 minutes reading books. The most commonly read book was the Bible, which 5% of all adults read for an average of 29 minutes per day. General fiction was read by 5% of the respondents; newspapers, by 73%; magazines, by 39%; books, by 33%; and mail, by 54%.

A large-scale research report in 1978 done for the Book Industry Study Group (Yankelovich, Skelly and White, Inc.) surveyed over 1,500 persons and found that 94% of the American public age 16 or older read magazines and newspapers, 33% read at least a book a month, and 55% had read at least one book in the past six months. While 39% never read a book, they do read newspapers and magazines, and many do buy books for others. Of the 6% who read nothing, 28% say they don't like to read. The most popular fiction categories were action and adventure stories, followed by historical fiction and historical romance. The top nonfiction categories were biography and autobiography, followed by cooking, home economics, and history.

A Gallup poll (1978) conducted for the American Library Association similarly found that many Americans are book readers and that fiction is still the most widely read genre.

How Well Does the Average American Read?

Poorly, according to Paul Copperman, author of *The Literacy Hoax*, who reiterates his conclusion in "The Achievement Decline of the 1970s" [*Phi Delta Kappan* (June 1977)].

Worse, when comparing the scores of college bound students on the SAT and other college admissions tests. Verbal scores on the SAT dropped 49 points between 1963 and 1977 (*On Further Examination*, College Board Publications).

The same or better, when referring to Roger Farr's historical analyses of reading achievement scores over several decades (*Reading Achievement in the United States: Then and Now* [ED 109 595] and *Then and Now: Reading Achievement in Indiana* (1944–45 and 1976) [ED 158 262]).

Better, when looking at scores over several years from the National Assessment of Educational Progress (Gadway and Wilson [ED 112 350]).

OK, according to Donald Fisher in *Functional Literacy and the Schools* [ED 151 760]. He has reexamined many of the literacy studies mentioned in this article, concluding that there is no reason to believe that high school graduates who perform poorly on a measure of functional literacy are held back in life. He has found that a population which might be considered functionally illiterate is those students who are held back one or more years and who frequently drop out before they graduate.

Fine, according to John Bormuth, in "Trends, Level, and Value of Literacy in the U.S." (*Slate Newsletter*, August 1979). He notes that the percentage of students dropping out of school has dropped in the last decade from 8 to 2%. Since 1947 the percentage of youth enrolled in college has risen from 13 to 30, and the percentage of workers employed in white collar jobs has risen from 36 to 50. Bormuth provides evidence of high expenditures on our nation's literacy-related activities and insists that the nation's rate of literacy is very high and is rising rapidly.

References

Abbass, Mazin. The Language of Fifty Commonly Used Forms. Doctoral dissertation,

Southern Illinois University, Carbondale, Ill., 1976. 520 pp. [ED 146 623] Not available from EDRS. Available from University Microfilms, P.O. Box 1764, Ann Arbor, Michigan 48106, U.S.A.

American Library Association. *Gallup Poll: Reading and Library Usage: A Study of Habits and Perceptions.* Chicago, Ill.: American Library Association, 1978.

Bormuth, John R. "Trends, Level, and Value of Literacy in the U.S." *Slate Newsletter*, vol. 4, no. 4 (August 1979).

Copperman, Paul. "The Achievement Declines of the 1970s." *Phi Delta Kappan*, vol. 60, no. 10 (June 1979), pp. 736–39.

Duffy, Thomas M. and William A. Nugent. *Reading Skill Levels in the Navy.* San Diego, Calif.: Navy Personnel Research and Development Center, 1978, 39 pp. [ED 154 363]

Farr, Roger. "Competency Testing and Reading Performance." *Reporting on Reading: Right to Read*, vol. 4, no. 5 (August 1978), pp. 2–6.

Farr, Roger and others. *Reading Achievement in the United States: Then and Now.* Princeton, N.J.: Educational Testing Service and Bloomington, Ind.: Institute for Child Study and Reading Program Center, Indiana University, 1974. 174 pp. [ED 109 595]

Farr, Roger and others. *Then and Now: Reading Achievement in Indiana (1944–45 and 1976).* Bloomington. Ind.: Indiana University, 1978. 146 pp. [ED 158 262]

Fisher, Donald L. *Functional Literacy and the Schools.* Washington, D.C.: National Institute of Education (DHEW), 1978. 77 pp. [ED 151 760]

Gadway, Charles and H. A. Wilson. *Functional Literacy: Basic Reading Performance. An Assessment of In-School 17-Year-Olds in 1974.* Technical Summary. Denver, Colo.: Education Commission of the States, National Assessment of Educational Progress, 1975, 32 pp. [ED 112 350]

Harris (Louis) and Associates, Inc. *Survival Literacy Study.* Washington, D.C.: National Reading Council, 1970. 38 pp. [ED 068 813]

Murphy, Richard T. *Adult Functional Reading Study: Project 1: Targeted Research and Development Reading Program Objective, Sub-parts 1, 2, and 3.* Final Report with Appendixes A, B, C. Princeton, N.J.: Educational Testing Service, 1973. 438 pp. [ED 109 650]

On Further Examination. Princeton, N.J.: College Board Publications, 1977.

Payne, Sandra S. *Reading Ease Level of D.C. Fire Department Written Materials for Entry-Level Job Performance.* Washington, D.C.: Civil Service Commission, Bureau of Policies and Standards, 1976. [ED 163 419]

Sharon, Amiel. "What Do Adults Read?" *Reading Research Quarterly*, vol. 9, no. 2 (1973–74), pp. 148–69. [EJ 092 583]

Schulze, Lydia D. Best Sellers Evaluated for Readability and Portrayal of Female Characters. Unpublished master's thesis, Rutgers University, New Brunswick, New Jersey, 1976. 105 pp. [ED 120 682]

Wheat, Thomas E., Martha Morrow Lindberg and Mary Jean Nauman. "An Exploratory Investigation of Newspaper Readability." *Illinois Reading Council Journal*, vol. 5 (March 1977), pp. 4–7.

Yankelovich, Skelly and White, Inc. *The 1978 Consumer Research Study on Reading and Book Purchasing.* BISG Report No. 6. Book Industry Study Group, Inc., 1978.

Zingman, Doris E. *Readability and Mass Political Literature: The 1976 Presidential Election Campaign.* Master's thesis, Rutgers The State University of New Jersey, 1977. 72 pp. [ED 142 933]

CHAPTER II

Contrasting Views about Reading Instruction

Carroll singles out eight components of reading skill that he regards as essential, and proposes that there is agreement about what these skills are among theorists with a variety of viewpoints, while they disagree about the relative emphasis to be given to each and the sequence in which the skills should be taught. Weaver and Shonhoff provide an objective explanation of the controversy between those who stress reading subskills and those who advocate a holistic view of reading instruction.

The next two readings in this chapter express the contrasting points of view. Samuels and Schachter argue persuasively for an emphasis on subskills. Goodman's description of reading as a psycholinguistic guessing game is the most widely cited statement of the holistic emphasis. In the final article, Stott questions the viewpoint of some psycholinguists as to how reading should be taught.

5. The Nature of the Reading Process

John B. Carroll

The *essential* skill in reading is getting meaning from a printed or written message. In many ways this is similar to getting meaning from a *spoken* message, but there are differences, because the cues are different. Spoken messages contain cues that are not evident in printed messages, and conversely. In either case, understanding language is itself a tremendous feat, when one thinks about it. When you get the meaning of a verbal message, you have not only recognized the words themselves; you have interpreted the words in their particular grammatical functions, and you have somehow apprehended the general grammatical patterning of each sentence. You have unconsciously recognized what words or phrases constitute the subjects and predicates of the sentence, what words or phrases modify those subjects or predicates, and so on. In addition, you have given a "semantic" interpretation of the sentence, assigning meanings to the key words in the sentence. For example,

From John B. Carroll, The nature of the reading process. In Harry Singer and Robert B. Ruddell (Eds.), *Theoretical models and processes in reading* (2nd ed). Newark, Del.: International Reading Association, 1976. Pp. 11–16. Reprinted with permission of John B. Carroll and the International Reading Association.

in reading the sentence "He understood that he was coming tonight" you would know to whom each "he" refers, and you would interpret the word *understood* as meaning "had been caused to believe" rather than "comprehended." Somehow you put all these things together in order to understand the "plain sense" of what the message says.

Even beyond getting the simple meaning of the material you are reading, you are probably reacting to it in numerous ways. You may be trying to evaluate it for its truth, validity, significance, or importance. You may be checking it against your own experience or knowledge. You may find that it is reminding you of previous thoughts or experiences, or you may be starting to think about its implications for your future actions. You may be making inferences or drawing conclusions from what you read that go far beyond what is explicitly stated in the text. In doing any or all of these things, you are "reasoning" or "thinking." Nobody can tell you exactly what to think; much of your thinking will be dependent upon your particular background and experience. At the same time, some thinking is logical and justified by the facts and ideas one reads, while other kinds of thinking are illogical and not adequately justified by the facts and ideas one reads. One aspect of a mature reader's skill consists in his being able to think about what he reads in a logical and well-informed way. This aspect of reading skill sometimes takes years to attain.

We have described the process of reading in the skilled reader—a process that is obviously very complex. How is this process learned or attained?

As in the case of any skill, reading skill is not learned all at once. It takes a considerable amount of time. Furthermore, the process of learning to read is *not* simply a slow motion imitation of the mature reading process. It has numerous components, and each component has to be learned and practiced.

There are probably a great many ways to attain reading skill, depending upon the order in which the various components are learned and mastered. It may be the case that some ways are always better than others. On the other hand, children differ in their aptitudes, talents, and inclinations so much that it may also be the case that a particular way of learning is better for one child while another way is better for another child. It all depends upon which components of reading skill a given child finds easier to learn at a given stage of his development. In referring to different orders in which component skills would be learned, we do not mean to imply a lock-step procedure in which the child first learns and masters one skill, then goes on to learn and master another skill, and so on. Actually, a child can be learning a number of skills simultaneously, but will reach mastery of them at different periods in his development. From the standpoint of the teacher, this means that different skills may need to be emphasized at different periods, depending upon the characteristics of the individual child. This is particularly true in the case of the child who is having difficulty in learning to read.

Let us try to specify the components of reading skill. Some of these components come out of our analysis of the mature reading process; others out of a further analysis of *those* components.

1. *The child must know the language that he is going to learn to read.* Normally, this means that the child can speak and understand the language at least to a certain level of skill before he starts to learn to read, because the purpose of reading is to help him get messages from print that are similar to the messages he can already understand if they are spoken. But language learning is a lifelong process, and normally there are many aspects of language that the individual learns solely or mainly through reading. And speaking and understanding the language is not an absolute prerequisite for beginning to

learn to read; there are cases on record of children who learn to read before they can speak, and of course many deaf children learn the language only through learning to read. Foreign-born children sometimes learn English mainly through reading. Children who, before they begin to read, do not know the language, or who only understand but do not speak, will very likely require a mode of instruction specially adapted to them.

2. *The child must learn to dissect spoken words into component sounds.* In order to be able to use the alphabetic principle by which English words are spelled, he must be able to recognize the separate sounds composing a word and the temporal order in which they are spoken—the consonants and vowels that compose spoken words. This does not mean that he must acquire a precise knowledge of phonetics, but it does mean that he must recognize those aspects of speech sound that are likely to be represented in spelling. For example, in hearing the word *straight*, the child must be able to decompose the sounds into the sequence /s, t, r, ey, t/.

3. *The child must learn to recognize and discriminate the letters of the alphabet in their various forms (capitals, lower case letters, printed, and cursive).* (He should also know the names and alphabetic ordering of the letters.) This skill is required if the child is to make progress in finding correspondences between letters and sounds.

4. *The child must learn the left-to-right principle by which words are spelled and put in order in continuous text.* This is, as we have noted, a very general principle, although there are certain aspects of letter-sound correspondences that violate the principle—e.g., the reverse order of *wh* in representing the sound cluster /hw/.

5. *The child must learn that there are patterns of highly probable correspondence between letters and sounds, and he must learn those patterns of correspondence that will help him recognize words that he already knows in his spoken language or that will help him determine* *the pronunciation of unfamiliar words.* There are few if any letters in English orthography that always have the same sound values; nevertheless, spellings tend to give good clues to the pronunciation of words. Often a letter will have highly predictable sound values if it is considered in conjunction with surrounding letters. Partly through direct instruction and partly through a little-understood process of inference, the normal child can fairly readily acquire the ability to respond to these complex patterns of letter-sound correspondences.

6. *The child must learn to recognize printed words from whatever cues he can use— their total configuration, the letters composing them, the sounds represented by those letters, and/or the meanings suggested by the context.* By "recognition" we mean not only becoming aware that he has seen the word before, but also knowing the pronunciation of the word. This skill is one of the most essential in the reading process, because it yields for the reader the equivalent of a speech signal.

7. *The child must learn that printed words are signals for spoken words and that they have meanings analogous to those of spoken words. While decoding a printed message into its spoken equivalent, the child must be able to apprehend the meaning of the total message in the same way that he would apprehend the meaning of the corresponding spoken message.* As in the case of adult reading, the spoken equivalent may be apprehended solely internally, although it is usual, in early reading efforts, to expect the child to be able to read aloud, at first with much hesitation, but later with fluency and expression.

8. *The child must learn to reason and think about what he reads, within the limits of his talent and experience.*

It will be noticed that each of these eight components of learning to read is somehow involved in the adult reading process—knowing the language, dissecting spoken words into component sounds, and so forth. Adult reading is skilled only because all the eight components are so highly practiced that they merge together, as it were, into one unified performance. The well-coordinated, swift eye movements of the adult reader are a result, not a cause, of good reading; the child does not have to be *taught* eye movements and therefore we have not listed eye-coordination as a component skill. Rather, skilled eye movements represent the highest form of the skill we have listed as 4—the learning of the left-to-right principle. The instantaneous word recognition ability of the mature reader is the highest form of the skill we have listed as 6—recognition of printed words from whatever cues are available, and usually this skill in turn depends upon the mastery of some of the other skills, in particular 5—learning patterns of correspondence between letters and sounds. The ability of the adult reader to apprehend meaning quickly is an advanced form of skill 7, and his ability to think about what he reads is an advanced form of skill 8.

The "great debate" about how reading should be taught is really a debate about the *order* in which the child should be started on the road toward learning each of the skills. Few will question that mature reading involves all eight skills; the only question is which skills should be introduced and mastered first. Many points of view are possible. On the one hand there are those who believe that the skills should be *introduced* in approximately the order in which they have been listed; this is the view of those who believe that there should be an early emphasis on the decoding of print into sound via letter-sound relations. On the other hand, there are those who believe that the skills should be introduced approximately in the following order:

1. The child should learn the language he is going to read.
6. The child should learn to recognize printed words from whatever cues he can use, but initially only from total configurations.
7. The child should learn that printed words are signals for spoken words, and that meanings can be apprehended from these printed words.
8. The child must learn to reason and think about what he reads.
4. The child should learn the left-to-right principle, but initially only as it applies to complete words in continuous text.
3. The child should learn to recognize and discriminate the letters of the alphabet.
2. The child should learn to dissect spoken words into component sounds.
5. The child should learn patterns of correspondence between letters and sounds, to help him in the advanced phases of skill 6.

This latter view is held by those who argue that there should be an early emphasis on getting the meaning from print, and that the child should advance as quickly as possible toward the word-recognition and meaning-apprehension capacities of the mature reader. Skills 2, 3, and 5 are introduced only after the child has achieved considerable progress towards mastery of skills 4, 6, 7, and 8.

These are the two main views about the process of teaching reading. If each one is taken quite strictly and seriously, there can be very clear differences in the kinds of instructional materials and procedures that are used. It is beyond our scope to discuss whether the two methods differ in effectiveness. We would emphasize, rather, that methods may differ in effectiveness from child to child. Furthermore, it is possible to construct other reasonable orders in which the various components of reading skill can be introduced to the child. There is currently a tendency to interlace the approaches distinguished above in such a way that the child can attain rapid sight recognition of words at the same time that he is learning letter-sound correspondences that will help him "attack" words that he does not already know.

For the child who is having difficulty in learning to read, it may be necessary to determine exactly which skills are causing most difficulty. The dyslexic child may be hung up on the acquisition of just one or two skills. For example, he may be having particular trouble with skill 3—the recognition and discrimination of the letters of the alphabet, or with skill 2—the dissection of spoken words into component sounds. On determining what skills pose obstacles for a particular child, it is usually necessary to give special attention to those skills while capitalizing on those skills which are easier for the child to master.

6. Subskill and Holistic Approaches to Reading Instruction

Phyllis Weaver and Fredi Shonhoff

Question

Our school district is conducting a review on the objectives established to guide reading instruction in the elementary grades (one through six). The language arts curriculum committee has identified a large number of separate subskills that they claim should be taught in the six grades. I am a new teacher, and I don't want to make waves, but I can't imagine that anyone, let alone a child, could do so many different things during something that takes place as fast as reading. Is reading really just a lot of separate skills that are performed rapidly, or is it more like a single process that cannot be separated into component skills?

Discussion

Some researchers believe that reading is a single process, that it is *holistic* in nature. This term implies that reading is much more than decoding plus comprehension and that it should not be subdivided, even for teaching purposes. Other researchers believe that reading is comprised of different components, or subskills. Reading, and understanding what is read, are seen as the integration of a number of separate skills that are interrelated.

In this debate among theorists and researchers, we can identify three major positions: all reading (beginning or skilled) is holistic in nature; all reading consists of separate but integrated subskills; and skilled reading is holistic, but early reading consists of subskills. Some discussion of these positions should provide a framework for answering this teacher's question.

All reading is holistic

Those who contend that reading is holistic in nature view skilled reading as a high speed process wherein the reader does not have to recognize every letter or word but can construct the meaning of the text by making predictions regarding the message

From Phyllis Weaver with Fredi Shonhoff, Subskill and holistic approaches to reading instruction. In Phyllis Weaver with Fredi Shonhoff. *Research within reach: A research-based response to concerns of reading educators.* St. Louis: CEMREL, Inc., 1978. Pp. 3–8. Reprinted by permission of Research Development Interpretation Service, CEMREL, Inc., St Louis, MO.

and then sampling only as much of the printed material as is necessary to confirm or reject those predictions and make new ones. This ability to derive meaning from minimal textual cues theoretically comes from a well-developed awareness of the spelling patterns and syntactic rules of our language.

Beginning readers have only begun to develop this awareness of oral and written language patterns. Therefore, they are less efficient than skilled readers at deriving meaning from sampling the text and need to be exposed, even immersed, in an environment that is rich in language. What ought to be remembered about the holistic view of reading is the notion that reading at any level is not conceived as a combination of separable subskills but is instead viewed as a process whose focus is the communication of meaning.

All reading consists of subskills

Individuals who hold this position argue that although skilled reading may appear to be a single process, it is not. In skilled reading, the separate subskills have become so well integrated that readers don't have to pay any attention to them—they all seem to operate automatically. For example, although the process of walking can be divided into a number of specific acts, once we have learned to walk the individual acts are performed so smoothly that they do not seem separable. Similarly, everything happens so fast and smoothly in reading that skilled readers probably couldn't be aware of the various subskills they are using without interrupting the reading process. Despite this, supporters of the subskill position contend that the many subprocesses are all in operation even if they are not apparent.

Unlike skilled readers, beginning readers haven't learned all the subskills, and the ones they know aren't used together very smoothly. For example, they often concentrate on pronouncing individual words (even parts of words), and they can only recognize a limited number of them. Beginners often read in a slow, choppy manner; sometimes it sounds as if they are reading a list. It is common for beginners to come to the end of a sentence or passage and seem not to understand or remember what they just finished reading. This is because they have to pay attention to the separate parts of reading—word recognition takes so much attention that comprehension suffers.

The subskills position on teaching reading is obvious: reading can be analyzed into a number of separate skills that can be taught and integrated, with the result being reading. Most individuals who support this view believe that teaching the subskills is not enough; you must provide plenty of practice using easy materials so that the subskills will not need conscious attention and will become integrated into what looks more and more like skilled reading.

Reading is a combination of the holistic and subskills positions

A third view on the nature of reading combines the other two. Supporters of this position make a distinction between beginning readers and skilled readers, that is, they think that the nature of the reading process actually changes as skill develops. In the early stages reading is accomplished by attending to identifiable component skills or parts; by the time the skilled level is reached, reading has become a meaning-oriented process and is no longer divisible into subskills. The component parts are no longer relevant or existent when the nature of fluent reading is analyzed.

What actually is the nature of reading? Which of the above descriptions is accurate? The research findings currently available do not provide conclusive information, and it may take a long time for these issues to be resolved and supported by the results of research. Reading educators do not have time to wait. Whatever view of reading is accurate, an equally pertinent question for educators as we see it is, How should reading be viewed so that its acquisition and development are facilitated? We think it is helpful to make the distinction between the reading process and effective teaching of reading. An example from teaching sports might help make this point.

In learning to play tennis, a very complex activity, students are taught components of the skill. They learn footwork, how to grip the racket, how to hit backhand and forehand shots, how to serve, and so on. And most of these components are broken down further into even smaller steps for teaching purposes. Although the instructor may often demonstrate the whole skill, mere demonstration is never the only means of teaching. The students practice the components and play the game at all stages. This kind of tennis instruction is similar to the sort of reading instruction that we are proposing.

Although some research suggests that *skilled* reading is a single, holistic process, there is no research to suggest that children can learn to read and develop reading skill if they are taught using a method that treats reading as if it were a single process. Therefore, for instructional purposes, it is probably best to think of reading as a set of interrelated subskills. The separate skills should be taught, practiced, and integrated with other skills being taught and with those that have already been learned. The important thing to remember is that although reading may be taught subskill by subskill, students should always have ample opportunity to practice the whole activity.

Summary

We do not know whether skilled reading is a holistic process or a set of interrelated subprocesses; researchers have not yet resolved this problem. In this case, we do not think reading educators can wait for resolution. Based on our analysis of reading theory and reading research, we recommend for teaching purposes that reading be viewed as a set of subskills that can be taught and integrated. We feel that development of subskills is important for learning to read and will prove useful to skilled readers when they encounter difficulty in a text.

Suggested Reading

Athey, I. *Essential skills and skill hierarchies in reading.* Washington, DC: National Institute of Education, 1975.

Calfee, R. C., & Drum, P. A. How the researcher can help the reading teacher with classroom assessment. In L. B. Resnick & P. A. Weaver (Eds.), *Theory and practice of early reading.* Vol. 2. Hillsdale, NJ: Erlbaum, 1979.

Goodman, K. Reading: A psycholinguistic guessing game. In H. Singer & R. Ruddell (Eds.), *Theoretical models and processes of reading.* Newark, DE: International Reading Association, 1976.

Guthrie, J. Models of reading and reading disability. *Journal of Educational Psychology,* 1973, 65(1), 9–18.

Perfetti, C., & Lesgold, A. Coding and comprehension in skilled reading and implications for reading instruction. In L. B. Resnick & P. A. Weaver (Eds.), *Theory and practice of early reading.* Vol. 1. Hillsdale, NJ: Erlbaum, 1979.

Samuels, S. J. Hierarchical subskills in the reading acquisition process. In J. Guthrie (Ed.), *Aspects of reading acquisition.* Baltimore, MD: Johns Hopkins University Press, 1976.

Smith, F. *Understanding reading.* New York: Holt, Rinehart & Winston, 1971.

Williams, J. Learning to read: A review of theories and models. *Reading Research Quarterly,* 1972–73, 8(2), 121–146.

7. Controversial Issues in Beginning Reading Instruction: Meaning versus Subskill Emphasis

S. Jay Samuels and Sumner W. Schachter

Two Views of Instruction

The labels "holistic" and "subskill" are universal and are used to describe whole-to-part and part-to-whole conceptualizations of developmental aspects of reading. Researchers who favor either view would tend to agree that proficient reading represents a highly complex process in which subordinate units are integrated in the formation of higher-order skills. While researchers may share somewhat similar viewpoints concerning proficient reading, however, they differ in significant ways regarding the best way to instruct beginning readers.

The holistic view

The most significant characteristic of the holistic view is that from the outset beginning instruction tends to focus on deriving meaning from the printed page. In this sense, reading and speaking are basically the same process of meaningful communication. From the start the child becomes aware that printed symbols represent meaning and are not a concatenation of meaningless sounds. The unit of instruction, therefore, becomes the word, phrase, sentence, or some unit that carries meaning.

According to Kenneth Goodman, reading can be considered a natural language process that has the potential for being learned with the same ease and speed at which speech is learned.[1] One of the reasons why speech is acquired with

some degree of ease is that it fulfills the human needs of communication and of acquiring information. If the environment of reading instruction could be engineered to meet these basic communication needs, reading should also be acquired with relative ease. Regarding the sequencing of instruction, Goodman claims that "Sequencing of skill instruction in reading has often been strongly advocated by publishers and curriculum workers. But the reading process requires that a multitude of skills be used simultaneously. As we have indicated, many of these skills are already employed by the learner in listening. Any sequence will necessarily be arbitrary."[2]

Those who favor the holistic approach believe that the a priori assumption that children should be taught subskills is incorrect and may, in fact, be detrimental to the acquisition of fluent reading. It is believed that children learn to speak and listen without formal instruction and that reading—as a natural outgrowth of listening—could, under certain conditions, be learned with equal ease and proficiency. Kenneth and Yetta Goodman state: "We take as our principal premise in designing initial reading instruction that our goal is to create conditions which help all students to learn as naturally as some do."[3] And, with regard to sequencing of instruction, they write: "Our research has convinced us that the skills displayed by the proficient reader derive from the meaningful use of written language and that sequential instruction in these skills is as pointless and fruitless as instruction in the skills of a proficient listener would be to teach infants to comprehend speech."[4]

It should be pointed out that advocates of the holistic approach would teach subskills under certain conditions. These conditions would arise when the reader fails to get meaning because a particular skill is lacking. Then the instructor would teach the appropriate skill.

The subskill view

Advocates of the subskill approach look upon proficient reading as the acquisition of a developmental skill. This means that the acquisition of highly complex skills such as reading may be viewed on a continuum that represents beginning, intermediate, and fluent levels of skill. Thus, beginning and fluent reading are viewed as quite different processes. For example, since so much of the beginning reader's attention is taken up with decoding printed symbols, meaning is not easily assessed. On the other hand, the skilled reader is able to decode printed symbols automatically, and, consequently, the limited attention capacity may be used for processing meaning.

One of the major premises of the subskill approach is that reading is not a natural language process and that learning to read requires specific instruction. Another assumption is that reading, as a complex skill, is comprised of subordinate units that must be mastered and integrated to form higher-order skills. Consequently, to accomplish this developmental task, a variety of subskills thought to be essential are taught routinely to students. The order of progression in these skills is from prerequisite smaller units to larger units.

Reading and Speech Acquisition Compared

Since some advocates of the holistic approach to reading emphasize the similarities between speech and reading, whereas advocates of the subskill approach look upon reading and speech acquisition as being quite different, it would be appropriate at this point to examine these counterclaims.

The development of the communication skills of speech and listening takes place over a relatively long period of time. Although they may be acquired in a naturalistic manner without formal instruction, these skills are not developed without considerable time, effort, and practice. Charles Fries has pointed out that the child has developed, and practiced, language skills for over ten thousand hours before formal reading instruction begins.[5]

Interesting comparisons can be made between the acquisition of speech and learning to read. Learning to speak is generally accomplished with little difficulty[6] whereas learning to read requires considerably more effort. According to Arthur and Carolyn Staats, although the acquisition of speech is gradual, beginning at infancy and extending for a considerable period of time, the introduction to reading is much more abrupt and less gradual.[7] Also, there are strong sources of reinforcement involved with the acquisition of speech, while in the typical classroom sources of reinforcement for reading appear to be much less forceful. The strong reinforcers involved in acquiring speech seem to be applied almost immediately following appropriate speech behaviors, but in learning to read the much weaker reinforcers are often delayed or may be nonexistent. The Staatses feel that perhaps the most important difference between acquiring speech and learning to read is that in the latter process intensive periods of concentration are required that may easily take on aversive characteristics.

To summarize the differences between speech and reading, it is indeed accurate to say that for nearly all people the acquisition of a first language appears to be easily mastered, but many people achieve literacy only with difficulty, if at all. Reading is not a behavior common to all humans, and its acquisition frequently requires the expenditure of considerable time and effort.

Role of Subskills in Learning

Critics of the subskill approach have claimed that sequential subskill instruction probably represents improper reading pedagogy. What justification is there, then, for any method of reading instruction that attempts a part-to-whole instructional sequence?

The research of William Bryan and Noble Harter in 1897 on learning Morse code has contributed knowledge regarding requirements for learning a complex task. They noted that in developing skill in Morse code there were plateaus in the learning curves during which practice did not lead to further improvement. Their interpretation of this finding was that in learning Morse code numerous lower-order skills had to be learned and integrated. These plateaus, they thought, indicated temporary periods devoted to learning the component skills or to organizing component skills into higher-order skills. Thus, before one became skilled in Morse code the subordinate skills had to be mastered and integrated.[8]

John Guthrie has provided additional support for the view that complex skill development requires the learning and integration of subordinate skills. He examined the intercorrelations among reading subskills for good and poor readers. With the good readers the intercorrelations among the skills were highly significant, suggesting that these readers had integrated the skills into higher-order units. With the poor readers, the intercorrelations were low, suggesting that these readers were still at the level of separate skills. Guthrie concluded that one source of disability among poor readers was the lack of subskill mastery and the lack of integration of these skills into higher-order units.[9]

Ernest Hilgard and Donald Marquis have written that most learning is complex and requires the simultaneous learning of several components.[10] A question remains about simple learning, such as associational learning: is the formation of simple associations influenced by subsystems?

Associational learning was traditionally believed to be a simple, single-stage process, but as psychologists continued to investigate its nature, they discovered that stimulus-response learning was anything but a simple, single-stage process. Research in associational learning over the past twenty-five years has revealed that there are stimulus-learning stages, response-learning stages, and associational stages. And these stages are influenced by other factors such as overt attention, perceptual learning, memory, and mediational strategies.

Thus, even the so-called simple learning tasks have their complex aspects, and fractionating a simple associational task into subskills can facilitate the learning process. For example, in an associational task such as learning the name of a letter, it appears that breaking the task into subskills facilitates learning. In S. Jay Samuels's experiment, an experimental group received visual discrimination training on noting distinctive features of letters. Following perceptual training, they learned the letter names. A control group was taught using a holistic approach; this group did not get perceptual pretraining. They were shown the letters and were told to learn their names. The experimental group that received subskill training learned in significantly fewer trials, and the savings were sufficient to make a practical difference as well.[11]

In what is now considered to be a classical study on instruction, Robert Gagné took a terminal behavior in mathematics, fractionated it into subskills that were ranked from lower-order to higher-order, and developed tests for each level. Following instruction on the mathematics skill, he tested the students and found that those who failed a lower-order task were unable to pass a test at the higher level. He then taught the unit again requiring the students to master each of the subordinate skills. All the students were able to complete the terminal task after having mastered the subordinate tasks.[12]

There is evidence that perceptual learning also seems to follow a pattern from smaller to larger units. At one time, Gestalt psychology formed the basis for the belief that when a beginning reader encountered a word, the perceptual unit was the whole word. Contrary to this belief, however, research has indicated that children tend to select a single letter rather than the whole word as the cue for word recognition.[13] In fact, it is usually not until the tenth grade that a single eye fixation suffices to take in the whole word at once.[14]

One can find examples from perception and reading to illustrate the principle that smaller units are mastered prior to larger units. The model of perceptual learning developed by David LaBerge and S. Jay Samuels is hierarchical and suggests that the sequence of learning is from distinctive features, to letters, to letter clusters, and to words.[15] In the process of learning to recognize a letter, the student must first identify the features that comprise it. For the lower-case letters *b*, *d*, *p*, and *q*, the features are a vertical line and a circle in a particular relationship to each other; that is, the circle may be high or low and to the left or right side of the vertical line. Having identified the parts and after an extended series of exposure to the letters, the learner sees it as a unit; that is, the parts are perceptually unitized. We have recently gathered evidence at our laboratory that skilled readers appear to have perceptually unitized—or chunked— digraphs such as *th*, *ch*, and *sh*. These are not processed as *t* + *h*, *c* + *h*, or *s* + *h*, but as a single unit. Evidence gathered elsewhere indicates that units longer than the letter, such as affixes *ed* and *ing*, can

become perceptually unitized.[16] These findings from different laboratories suggest that perceptual learning seems to follow a pattern from smaller to larger units.

Additional evidence illustrates the point that subskill mastery may be essential for achieving reading fluency. Donald Shankweiler and Isabelle Liberman investigated whether the main source of difficulty in beginning reading is at the word level or at the level of reading connected text. In other words, how well could one predict a child's fluency in oral reading of paragraph material from his performance on selected words presented in tests? The average correlation was .70 between reading individual words on a list and reading connected discourse.[17] Thus, roughly 50 percent of the variability in oral reading of connected words is associated with how well one can read these words in isolation. The authors concluded: "These correlations suggest that the child may encounter his major difficulty at the level of the word—his reading of connected text tends to be only as good or poor as his reading of individual words."[18]

Still other investigators have discovered the importance of reading subskills. Harry Silberman reported on an experimental program used to teach beginning reading. He found that the brighter children acquired the necessary reading skill he wanted them to learn, but that the less bright seemed unable to transfer their knowledge to words not specifically taught. Classroom teachers brought in to evaluate the program discovered that a necessary subskill had been omitted. Only after that subskill had been included in the program were all the children able to master the transfer to untaught words. It is interesting to note that, even with an important subskill missing, the brighter children were able to surmount this obstacle.[19] Silberman's study suggests, therefore, that brighter children may be able to overcome an inadequate program, but the less bright have great difficulty.

Pragmatic Concerns

One may raise the question as to the existence of exemplary reading programs and their characteristics. Information on successful programs was provided by the American Institutes for Research (AIR),[20] George Weber,[21] the New York State Office of Education,[22] and the CRAFT Project.[23]

The above reports, which identified outstanding reading programs, shared a common assumption: that a good reading program is more than a method; it is a system with individual elements to which there is an order and with interdependent components contributing to the whole of the system. These components, which were examined for overlap among successful programs, included needs, objectives, staffing, costs and budget, management, facilities, participants' characteristics, and procedures for evaluation. It is important to keep these components in mind as the programs are discussed and to realize that each program does not excel in all the various components.

Seven programs selected by the AIR had as their primary concern the initial teaching of reading in elementary school settings. Although representing different geographical areas and school populations, the programs appeared to share several common elements. Eight components appeared to account for the common success of a number of programs: academic objectives that were clearly stated, that were broken into smaller units, and that gave evidence of careful planning; teacher training in the methods of the program; small group or individualized instruction; highly structured teaching directly relevant to the objectives; high intensity of treatment; active parental involvement; utilization of additional reading personnel; and some sort of continuous assessment, providing both feedback and diagnostic information.[24]

Weber studied successful reading achievement in four inner-city ghetto schools. Although he acknowledged that nonschool factors can contribute to success or failure in beginning reading, he argued that a great difference in reading achievement can result from the school's effectiveness in teaching beginning reading. Weber found that forceful leadership, a pleasant and happy atmosphere, a strong emphasis on reading, additional reading personnel, use of a phonics subskill approach, individualization, and careful evaluation of pupils' progress contributed to successful reading programs. He believed that the attitude and approaches of the faculty, combined with a purposeful and pleasurable learning environment and a well-structured reading program, were responsible for improved reading achievement in these four inner-city ghetto schools.[25]

The New York State Office of Education Performance Review identified at least four factors under the control of the schools that contributed to a successful reading program. They were effective use of reading time, much positive reinforcement, extensive evaluations of pupils, and high expectations.[26]

Investigations of the CRAFT Project indicated that efficient use of time in reading instruction may be a relevant factor in successful programs. Thus, when a considerable amount of time was spent on activities that required little or no reading, the effect on reading achievement tended to be unfavorable; the amount of time spent in actual reading activities was positively correlated with achievement for all methods.[27] This study suggests that neither the method used nor the amount of time allocated on the class schedule was related to achievement, but the time spent in actual reading activities was related to achievement.

From the studies investigated in this chapter, we must now attempt to distill the characteristics that appear to contribute to success in reading programs. Perhaps, at the risk of overgeneralizing, one may draw some tentative conclusions. At the organizational level, the evidence points to a district that has strong administrative leadership, cooperation, and involvement of staff in planning a coordinated reading program. An expectation of success permeates the educational enterprise. Further, the successful district is one in which fiscal resources are predominantly invested in personnel rather than facilities: pupil-teacher ratios are acceptable; aides assist in individualized instruction; and there is often a reading specialist or program coordinator.

At the instructional level, the variables may not be as neatly defined as one might wish, and it is clear that no one method of reading instruction is consistently superior. Certain characteristics of instruction are important, however: the successful programs break the reading task into subskills or units that are specifically sequenced; and the student moves through these units at an individual pace and must attain mastery of each before going on to the next. The continuous feedback resulting from such a system reinforces the student and provides a diagnostic aid for the instructor.

Practical Implications for Reading Instruction

The current debate concerning the holistic versus the subskill approach may be somewhat overdrawn and may have established a false dichotomy, especially if one realizes that many teachers are eclectic in their approach to reading instruction. Furthermore, despite the claims of some teachers regarding their adherence to a particular approach to reading, there may be a significant gap between what they say and what they do.

Our problem may be reduced to one of focus, emphasis, and sequence. Regardless of which size unit one uses for beginning reading, one must also include units at the other end of the scale.

As Richard Venezky points out: "almost all methods for teaching reading include letter-sound learning somewhere in the teaching sequence, although the amount and exact placement of this training account for the central disagreement between methods."[28] This view was expressed in an article by Harry Singer, S. Jay Samuels, and Jean Spiroff, who state: "While this study has demonstrated that for the purpose of teaching children to identify a word it is best to present that word in isolation . . . the child [also] needs to get ample practice reading meaningful and interesting material in context so that he will develop strategies for using semantic and syntactic constraints in passages as aids in word identification."[29]

A major point made by critics of the subskill approach is that fractionating the reading process interferes with the essential characteristic of reading, which is comprehension. This point is well taken. Many teachers who use the subskill approach have lost sight of the fact that the approach is simply a means to an end. In many classrooms there has been a displacement of goals, and the means have become ends. In the subskill approach, care must be taken to prevent the subskills from becoming the focal point of instruction. Once again, perhaps, the point should be made that it is important for the child to get ample practice reading meaningful and interesting material in context.

We agree with the critics of the subskill approach that too much emphasis can be placed on these subordinate skills. The critics probably are in error, however, in failing to recognize the importance of subskills in the developmental sequence of skill attainment. Just because fluent readers are able to determine the meaning on a printed page is no reason to believe that beginning readers can do the same or that we can transfer the sophisticated strategies of the fluent reader to the beginning reader. Downing shares this view: "It seems quite unlikely that the learning-to-read process is directly derivable from the behavior observed in a fluent reader as is assumed in the theories of Smith and Goodman."[30]

Both the advocates of holistic and subskill approaches recognize that reading is comprised of subordinate skills. There is a problem, however, concerning who determines which subskills should be taught and when they should be introduced. According to one school of thought, when the student encounters a problem, the teacher should analyze the nature of the difficulty and remedy it. This approach places the teacher in the role of a troubleshooter. Thus, the particular subskills that are taught are determined by the student, that is, by an analysis of the student's weaknesses, and the skills are introduced after the problem is uncovered. According to the other school of thought, certain subskills must be mastered in the reading acquisition process, and these skills can be taught routinely before the student shows signs of having a problem. Thus, with this approach, it is the teacher or curriculum expert who determines a priori which skills are to be taught and when.

Many critics of the subskill approach suggest that meaningful reading material should be given to a child and that subskills should be taught when the student asks for help or shows evidence of needing particular skills. The shortcomings of this approach become obvious when one realizes the logistical and managerial problems facing the teacher with a large number of students. With regard to this last point, it is important to realize that many students do not know what kind of help to request, and a good number of teachers are not sufficiently trained to pinpoint the cause of the student's difficulty. Even when the teacher is able to diagnose accurately the cause of the problem, the managerial problems of providing individual help are so large as to make the system difficult to operate, if not unworkable. It would seem more manageable to assume on a priori grounds that beginning readers require

certain subskills, which would be taught routinely to students. For those students who fail to master these skills, additional time could be allocated, and different methods could be tried.

We made the point earlier in this chapter that the adverse relationship between holistic and subskill approaches may not exist. Both approaches recognize there are subskills. Subskill approaches start with smaller units and move to larger and more complex units. The holistic approach, on the other hand, begins with the larger unit and moves to smaller units. Thus, one of the important factors differentiating the two approaches is that of sequencing. In considering this factor, we must think about which tasks and which unit size one would use to start instruction and how one would program the sequence of skills to be taught as the student progresses in skill. Another similarity between the two approaches is that both recognize the importance of diagnosis of difficulty in reading and the need to remedy the problem. The subskill approach, however, attempts to reduce the number of students who will experience difficulties in reading by teaching the prerequisite skills before a problem appears.

In summary, we must keep in mind that reading is a developmental skill, and, while the goal of reading is to acquire meaning, there are certain prerequisites. One important prerequisite is the development of decoding skills. These skills must be brought beyond the level of mere accuracy to the level of automaticity. When these skills become automatic, the student is able to decode the printed symbols without the aid of attention, thereby freeing attention for the all-important task of processing meaning.

Notes

1. Kenneth A. Goodman, "Acquiring Literacy Is Natural: Who Killed Cock Robin," paper presented at Sixth World Reading Congress, Singapore, August 1976.
2. Kenneth A. Goodman, "Behind the Eye:

What Happens in Reading," in *Theoretical Models and Processes in Reading*, ed. Harry Singer and Robert Ruddell, 2d ed. (Newark, Del.: International Reading Association, 1976), 494.

3. Kenneth A. Goodman and Yetta Goodman, "Learning to Read Is Natural," paper presented at Conference on Theory and Practice of Beginning Reading Instruction, Pittsburgh, April 1976, 21.

4. *Ibid.*

5. Charles C. Fries, *Linguistics and Reading* (New York: Holt, Rinehart, and Winston, 1963).

6. William N. Dember and James Jenkins, *General Psychology: Modeling Behavior and Experience* (Englewood Cliffs, N.J.: Prentice-Hall, 1970).

7. Arthur W. Staats and Carolyn K. Staats, *Complex Human Behavior* (New York: Holt, Rinehart, and Winston, 1963).

8. William L. Bryan and Noble Harter, "Studies in the Physiology and Psychology of the Telegraphic Language," *Psychological Review* 4 (January 1897): 27–53.

9. John T. Guthrie, "Models of Reading and Reading Disability," *Journal of Educational Psychology* 65 (August 1973): 9–18.

10. Ernest R. Hilgard and Donald G. Marquis, *Conditioning and Learning*, 2d ed. (New York: Appleton-Century-Crofts, 1961).

11. S. Jay Samuels, "Effect of Distinctive Feature Training on Paired Associate Learning," *Journal of Educational Psychology* 64 (April 1973): 164–170.

12. Robert M. Gagné, "The Acquisition of Knowledge," *Psychological Review* 69 (No. 4, 1962): 355–365.

13. Gabrielle Marchbanks and Harry Levin, "Cues by Which Children Recognize Words," *Journal of Educational Psychology* 56 (April 1965): 57–62; S. Jay Samuels and Wendell F. Jeffrey, "Discriminability of Words, and Letter Cues Used in Learning to Read," *ibid.*, 57 (December 1966): 337–340.

14. Stan E. Taylor, Helen Frackenpohl, and J. L. Pettee, *Grade Level Norms for the Components of the Fundamental Reading Skill* (Huntington, N.Y.: Educational Developmental Laboratories, Inc., 1960).

15. David LaBerge and S. Jay Samuels, "Toward a Theory of Automatic Information Processing in Reading," *Cognitive Psychology* 6 (April 1974): 293–323.

16. Eleanor J. Gibson and Lynne Guinet, "The Perception of Inflections in Brief Visual Presentations of Words," *Journal of Verbal Learning and Verbal Behavior* 10 (April 1971): 182–189.

17. Donald Shankweiler and Isabelle Y. Liberman, "Misreading: A Search for Causes." in *Language by Ear and by Eye*, ed. J. F. Kavanagh and Ignatius G. Mattingly (Cambridge, Mass.: M.I.T. Press, 1972), 293–317.

18. *Ibid.*, 298.

19. Harry F. Silberman, *Exploratory Research in a Beginning Reading Program* (Santa Monica, Calif.: System Development Corp., 1964), 430–432.

20. John E. Bowers *et al.*, *Final Report Identifying, Validating, and Multi-Media Packaging of Effective Reading Programs* (Palo Alto, Calif.: American Institutes for Research, 1974).

21. George Weber, *Inner-City Children Can Be Taught to Read: Four Successful Schools* (Washington, D.C.: Council for Basic Education, 1971).

22. New York State Office of Education, *School Factors Influencing Reading Achievement: A Performance Review* (Albany: New York State Office of Education, 1974).

23. Albert J. Harris and Blanche L. Serwer, "The CRAFT Project: Instructional Time in Reading Research," *Reading Research Quarterly* 2 (Fall 1966): 27–56.

24. Bowers *et al.*, *Final Report*.

25. Weber, *Inner-City Children Can Be Taught to Read*. [Note incomplete in original.]

26. New York State Office of Education, *School Factors Influencing Reading Achievement*.

27. Harris and Serwer, "The CRAFT Project."

28. Richard Venezky, *Language and Cognition in Reading*, Technical Report No. 188, University of Wisconsin-Madison (Washington, D.C.: U.S. Office of Education, 1972), 19.

29. Harry Singer, S. Jay Samuels, and Jean Spiroff, "Effects of Pictures and Contextual Conditions on Learning to Read," *Reading Research Quarterly* 9 (No. 4, 1974): 566.

30. John Downing, "The Child's Understanding of the Function and Processes of Communication," unpublished paper, University of Victoria, Canada, 1977, 33.

8. Reading: A Psycholinguistic Guessing Game

Kenneth S. Goodman

As scientific understanding develops in any field of study, pre-existing, naive, common sense notions must give way. Such outmoded beliefs clutter the literature dealing with the process of reading. They interfere with the application of modern scientific concepts of language and thought to research in reading. They confuse the attempts at application of such concepts to solution of problems involved in the teaching and learning of reading. The very fact that such naive beliefs are based on common sense explains their persistent and recurrent nature. To the casual and unsophisticated observer they appear to explain, even predict, a set of phenomena in reading. This paper will deal with one such key misconception and offer a more viable scientific alternative.

Simply stated, the common sense notion I seek here to refute is this:

"Reading is a precise process. It involves exact, detailed, sequential perception and identification of letters, words, spelling patterns and larger language units."

In phonic-centered approaches to reading, the preoccupation is with precise letter identification. In word-centered approaches, the focus is on word identification. Known words are sight words, precisely named in any setting.

This is not to say that those who have worked diligently in the field of reading are not aware that reading is more than precise, sequential identification. But, the common sense notion, though not adequate, continues to permeate thinking about reading.

Spache presents a word version of this common sense view: "Thus, in its simplest form, reading may be considered a series of word perceptions."[1]

The teacher's manual of the Lippincott *Basic Reading* incorporates a letter by letter variant in the justification of its reading approach: "In short, following this program the child learns from the beginning to see words exactly as the most skillful readers see them . . . as whole images of complete words with all their letters."[2]

In place of this misconception, I offer this: "Reading is a selective process. It involves partial use of available minimal language cues selected from perceptual input on the basis of the reader's expectation. As this partial information is processed, tentative decisions are made to be confirmed, rejected or refined as reading progresses."

More simply stated, reading is a psycholinguistic guessing game. It involves an interaction between thought and language. Efficient reading does not result from precise perception and identification of all elements, but from skill in selecting the fewest, most productive cues necessary to produce guesses which are right the first time. The ability to anticipate that which has not been seen, of course, is vital in reading, just as the ability to anticipate what has not yet been heard is vital in listening.

Consider this actual sample of a relatively proficient child reading orally. The reader is a fourth-grade child reading the opening paragraphs of a story from a sixth-grade basal reader.

From Kenneth S. Goodman, Reading: A psycholinguistic guessing game. *Journal of the Reading Specialist*, May 1967, *6*, 126–135. Reprinted by permission of the author and the College Reading Association.

"If it bothers you to think of it as baby sitting," my father said, "then don't think of it as baby sitting. Think of it as homework. Part of your education. You just happen to do your studying in the room where the baby brother is sleeping, that's all." He helped my mother with her coat, and then they were gone.

hoped © a

So education it was! I ~~opened~~)the dic-

tionary and picked out a word that

    s   PH———   He
sounded good. "Phil/oso/phi/cal!" ✗

                             what it means
yelled. Might as well study ~~word meanings~~

   1. Phizo   2. Phiso/soophical
~~first.~~ "~~Philosophical~~: showing calmness

           his   1. fort
and courage in ~~the~~ face of ill fortune."

2. future   3. futshion
I mean I really yelled it. I guess a fellow

has to work off steam once in a while.[3]

He has not seen the story before. It is, by intention, slightly difficult for him. The insights into his reading process come primarily from his errors, which I choose to call miscues in order to avoid value implications. His expected responses mask the process of their attainment, but his unexpected responses have been achieved through the same process, albeit less successfully applied. The ways that they deviate from the expected reveal this process.

In the common sense view that I am rejecting, all deviations must be treated as errors. Furthermore, it must be assumed in this view that an error either indicates that the reader does not know something or that he has been "careless" in the application of his knowledge.

For example, his substitution of *the* for *your* in the first paragraph of the sample must mean that he was careless, since he has already read *your* and *the* correctly in the very same sentence. The implication is that we must teach him to be more careful, that is to be more precise in identifying each word or letter.

But now let's take the view that I have suggested. What sort of information could have led to tentatively deciding on *the* in this situation and not rejecting or refining this decision? There obviously is no graphic relationship between *your* and *the*. It may be of course, that he picked up *the* in the periphery of his visual field. But, there is an important non-graphic relationship between *the* and *your*. They both have the same grammatical function: They are, in my terminology, noun markers. Either the reader anticipated a noun marker and supplied one paying no attention to graphic information or he used *your* as a grammatical signal ignoring its graphic shape. Since the tentative choice *the* disturbs neither the meaning nor the grammar of the passage, there is no reason to reject and correct it. This explanation appears to be confirmed by two similar miscues in the next paragraph. *A* and *his* are both substituted for *the*. Neither is corrected. Though the substitution of *his* changes the meaning, the peculiar idiom used in this dictionary definition, "in the face of ill fortune," apparently has little meaning to this reader anyway.

The conclusion this time is that he is using noun markers for grammatical, as well as graphic, information in reaching his tentative conclusions. All together in reading this ten-page story, he made twenty noun marker substitutions, six omissions, and two insertions. He corrected four of his substitutions and one omission. Similar miscues involved other function words (auxiliary verbs and prepositions, for example). These miscues appear to have little effect on the meaning of what he is reading. In spite of their frequency, their elimination would not substantially improve the child's reading. Insistence on more precise identification of each word might cause this reader to stop seeking grammatical information and use only graphic information.

The substitution of *hoped* for *opened* could again be regarded as careless or imprecise identification of letters. But, if we dig beyond this commonsense explanation, we find (a) both are verbs and (b) the words have *key* graphic similarities. Further, there may be evidence of the reader's bilingual French-Canadian background here, as there is in subsequent miscues (*harms* for *arms, shuckled* for *chuckled, shoose* for *choose, shair* for *chair*). The correction of this miscue may involve an immediate rejection of the tentative choice made on the basis of a review of the graphic stimulus, or it may result from recognizing that it cannot lead to the rest of the sentence, "I hoped a dictionary . . ." does not make sense. (It isn't decodable.) In any case, the reader has demonstrated the process by which he constantly tests his guesses, or tentative choices, if you prefer.

Sound*s* is substituted for sound*ed*, but the two differ in ending only. Common sense might lead to the conclusion that the child does not pay attention to word endings, slurs the ends or is otherwise careless. But, there is no consistent similar occurrence in other word endings. Actually, the child has substituted one inflectional ending for another. In doing so he has revealed (a) his ability to separate base and inflectional suffix, and (b) his use of inflectional endings as grammatical signals or markers. Again he has not corrected a miscue that is both grammatically and semantically acceptable.

He for *I* is a pronoun-for-pronoun substitution that results in a meaning change, though the antecedent is a bit vague, and the inconsistency of meaning is not easily apparent.

When we examine what the reader did with the sentence *"Might as well study word meanings first,"* we see how poorly the model of precise sequential identification fits the reading process. Essentially this reader has decoded graphic input for meaning and then encoded meaning in oral output with transformed grammar and changed vocabulary, but with the basic meaning retained. Perhaps as he encoded his output, he was already working at the list word which followed, but the tentative choice was good enough and was not corrected.

There are two examples, in this sample, of the reader working at unknown words. He reveals a fair picture of his strategies and abilities in these miscues, though in neither is he successful. In his several attempts at *philosophical*, his first attempt comes closest. Incidentally, he reveals here that he can use a phonic letter-sound strategy when he wants to. In subsequent attempts he moves away from this sounding out, trying other possibilities, as if trying to find something which at least will sound familiar. Interestingly, here he has a definition of sorts, but no context to work with. *Philosophical* occurs as a list word a number of times in the story. In subsequent attempts, the child tried *physica, physicacol, physical, philosovigul, phizzlesovigul, phizzo sorigul, philazophgul*. He appears to move in concentric circles around the phonic information he has, trying deviations and variations. His three unsuccessful attempts at *fortune* illustrate this same process. Both words are apparently unknown to the reader. He can never really identify a word he has not heard. In such cases, unless the context or contexts sufficiently delimit the word's meaning, the reader is not able to get meaning from the words. In some instances, of course, the reader may form a fairly accurate definition of the word, even if he never recognizes it (that is matches it with a known oral equivalent) or pronounces it correctly. This reader achieved that with the word *typical* which occurred many times in the story. Throughout his reading he said *topical*. When he finished reading a check of his comprehension indicated that he knew quite well the meaning of the word. This phenomenon is familiar to any adult reader. Each of us has many well-defined words in our reading vocabulary which we either mispronounce or do not use orally.

I've used the example of this youngster's oral reading not because what he's done is typical of all readers or even of readers his age, but because his miscues suggest how he carries out the psycholinguistic guessing game in reading. The miscues of other readers show similarities and differences, but all point to a selective, tentative, anticipatory process quite unlike the process of precise, sequential identification commonly assumed.

Let's take a closer look now at the components the reader manipulates in this psycholinguistic guessing game.

At any point in time, of course, the reader has available to him and brings to his reading the sum total of his experience and his language and thought development. This self-evident fact needs to be stated because what appears to be intuitive in any guessing is actually the result of knowledge so well learned that the process of its application requires little conscious effort. Most language use has reached this automatic, intuitive level. Most of us are quite unable to describe the use we make of grammar in encoding and decoding speech, yet all language users demonstrate a high degree of skill and mastery over the syntax of language even in our humblest and most informal uses of speech.

Chomsky has suggested this model [shown below] of sentence production by speakers of a language.[4]

Thus, in Chomsky's view, encoding of speech reaches a more or less precise level and the signal which results is fully formed. But in decoding, a sampling process aims at approximating the message and any matching or coded signal which results is a kind of by-product.

In oral reading, the reader must perform two tasks at the same time. He must produce an oral language equivalent of the graphic input which is the *signal* in reading, and he must also reconstruct the

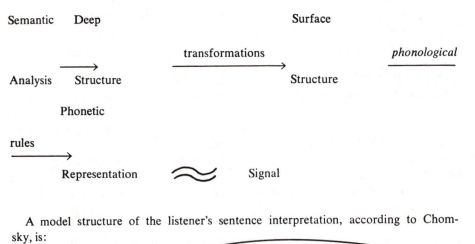

A model structure of the listener's sentence interpretation, according to Chomsky, is:

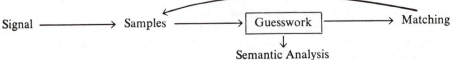

meaning of what he is reading. The matching in Chomsky's interpretation model is largely what I prefer to call a recoding operation. The reader recodes the coded graphic input as phonological or oral output. Meaning is not normally involved to any extent. This recoding can even be learned by someone who doesn't speak the language at all, for example, the bar-mitzvah boy may learn to recode Hebrew script as chanted oral Hebrew with no ability to understand what he is chanting; but when the reader engages in semantic analysis to reconstruct the meaning of the writer, only then is he decoding.

In oral reading there are three logical possible arrangements of these two operations. The reader may recode graphic input as oral language and then decode it. He may recode and decode simultaneously. Or, he may decode first and then encode the meaning as oral output.

On the basis of my research to date, it appears that readers who have achieved some degree of proficiency decode directly from the graphic stimulus in a process similar to Chomsky's sampling model and then encode from the deep structure, as illustrated in Chomsky's model of sentence production. Their oral output is not directly related to the graphic stimulus and may involve transformation in vocabulary and syntax, even if meaning is retained. If their comprehension is inaccurate, they will encode this changed or incomplete meaning as oral output.

The common misconception is that graphic input is precisely and sequentially recoded as phonological input and then decoded bit by bit. Meaning is cumulative, built up a piece at a time, in this view. This view appears to be supported by studies of visual perception that indicate that only a very narrow span of print on either side of the point of fixation is in sharp focus at any time. We might dub this the "end of the nose" view, since it assumes that input in reading is that which lies in sharp focus in a straight line from the end of the nose.

Speed and efficiency are assumed to come from widening the span taken in on either side of the nose, moving the nose more rapidly or avoiding backward movements of the eyes and nose, which of course must cut down on efficiency.

This view cannot possibly explain the speed with which the average adult reads, or a myriad of other constantly occurring phenomena in reading. How can it explain, for example, a highly proficient adult reader reading and rereading a paper he's written and always missing the same misprints? Or how can it explain our fourth-grader seeing "study word meanings first" and saying "study what it means"?

No, the "end of the nose" view of reading will not work. The reader is not confined to information he receives from a half inch of print in clear focus. Studies, in fact, indicate that children with severe visual handicaps are able to learn to read as well as normal children. Readers utilize not one, but three kinds of information simultaneously. Certainly without graphic input there would be no reading. But the reader uses syntactic and semantic information as well. He predicts and anticipates on the basis of this information, sampling from the print just enough to confirm his guess of what's coming, to cue more semantic and syntactic information. Redundancy and sequential constraints in language, which the reader reacts to, make this prediction possible. Even the blurred and shadowy images he picks up in the peripheral area of his visual field may help to trigger or confirm guesses.

Skill in reading involves not greater precision, but more accurate first guesses based on better sampling techniques, greater control over language structure, broadened experiences and increased conceptual development. As the child develops reading skill and speed, he uses increasingly fewer graphic cues. Silent reading can then become a more rapid and efficient process than oral reading, for two reasons: (1) the reader's attention is not divided between decoding and recoding or encoding as oral output, and (2) his speed is not restricted to the speed of speech production. Reading becomes a more efficient and rapid process than listening, in fact, since listening is normally limited to the speed of the speaker.

Recent studies with speeded-up electronic recordings where distortion of pitch is avoided have demonstrated that listening can be made more rapid without impairing comprehension too.

Though the beginning reader obviously needs more graphic information in decoding and, therefore, needs to be more precise than skilled readers, evidence from a study of first graders by Yetta Goodman[5] indicates that they begin to sample and draw on syntactic and semantic information almost from the beginning, if they are reading material which is fully formed language.

Here are excerpts from two primer stories as they were read by a first-grade child at the same session. Ostensibly (and by intent of the authors) the first, from a second preprimer, should be much easier than the second, from a third preprimer. Yet she encountered problems to the point of total confusion with the first and was able to handle exactly the same elements in the second.

Note, for example, the confusion of *come* and *here* in "Ride In." This represents a habitual association in evidence in early reading of this child. Both *come* and *here* as graphic shapes are likely to be identified as *come* or *here*. In "Stop and Go," the difficulty does not occur when the words are sequential. She also substitutes *can* for *and* in the first story, but encounters no problem with either later. *Stop* stops her completely in "Ride In," a difficulty that she doesn't seem to know she has when she reads "Stop and Go" a few minutes later. Similarly, she calls (ride) run in the first story, but gets it right in the latter one.

RIDE IN

Run
~~Ride~~ in, Sue.
Run
~~Ride~~ in here.
Come   here
~~Here I come~~, Jimmy.
Can Come
~~And here I~~ (stop).[6]

STOP AND GO

Jimmy said, "Come here, Sue,
    too
Look at my ~~toy~~ (train.)

See it go.
       toy
Look at my lit/tle ~~train~~ go."
         toy
  Sue said, Stop the ~~train~~.
  Come
Stop it ~~here~~, Jimmy."
              toy
  Jimmy said, "I can stop the ~~train~~.
  toy
See the ~~train~~ stop."
           too.
  Sue said, "Look at my ~~toy~~.
      toy.
It is in the ~~train~~.
       too
See my little red ~~toy~~, Jimmy.
        toy
It can ride in the ~~train~~."
           toy
  Jimmy said, "See the ~~train~~ go.
Look at it go."
  Suzie   too
  ~~Sue~~ said, "Look at my little red ~~toy~~.
      toy
See it go for a ~~train~~ ride."
  Suzie   too
  ~~Sue~~ said, "My little red ~~toy~~!
  said too
© Jimmy, my ~~toy~~ is not here.
        toy
It is not in the ~~train~~.
     toy
Stop the ~~train~~, Jimmy.
       too
Stop it and look for my ~~toy~~."[7]

Though there are miscues in the second story, there is a very important difference. In the first story she seems to be playing a game of name the word. She is recoding graphic shapes as phonological ones. Each word is apparently a separate problem. But in "Stop and Go" what she says, including her miscues, in almost all instances makes sense and is grammatically acceptable. Notice that as *Sue* becomes better known she becomes *Suzie* to our now confident reader.

A semantic association exists between *train* and *toy*. Though the child makes the same substitution many times, nothing causes her to reject her guess. It works well each time. Having called (train) *toy*, she calls (toy) *too* (actually it's an airplane in the pictures), not once, but consistently throughout the story. That doesn't seem to make sense. That's what the researcher thought too, until the child spoke of a "little red *too*" later in retelling the story. "What's a 'little red too,'" asked the researcher. "An airplane," she replied calmly. So a train is *toy* and a plane is a *too*. Why not? But, notice that when *toy* occurred preceding *train*, she could attempt nothing for *train*. There appears to be a problem for many first graders when nouns are used as adjectives.

Common sense says go back and drill her on *come, here, can, stop, ride, and*; don't let her go to the next book which she is obviously not ready to read.

But the more advanced story, with its stronger syntax, more fully formed language and increased load of meaning makes it possible for the child to use her graphic cues more effectively and supplement them with semantic and syntactic information. Teaching for more precise perception with lists and phonics charts may actually impede this child's reading development. Please notice, before we leave the passage, the effect of immediate experience on anticipation. Every one of the paragraphs in the sample starts with "Jimmy said" or "Sue said." When the reader comes to a line starting *Jimmy*, she assumes that it will be followed by *said* and it is not until her expectation is contradicted by subsequent input that she regresses and corrects her miscue.

Since they must learn to play the psycholinguistic guessing game as they develop reading ability, effective methods and materials, used by teachers who understand the rules of the game, must help them to select the most productive cues, to use their knowledge of language structure, to draw on their experiences and concepts. They must be helped to discriminate between more and less useful available information. Fortunately, this parallels the processes they have usd in developing the ability to comprehend spoken language. George Miller has suggested ". . . psycholinguists should try to formulate performance models that will incorporate, . . . hypothetical information storage and information processing components that can simulate the actual behavior of language users."[8]

I'd like to present now my model of this psycholinguistic guessing game we call reading English. Please understand that the steps do not necessarily take place in the sequential or stretched out form they are shown here.

1. The reader scans along a line of print from left to right and down the page, line by line.
2. He fixes at a point to permit eye focus. Some print will be central and in focus, some will be peripheral; perhaps his perceptual field is a flattened circle.
3. Now begins the selection process. He picks up graphic cues, guided by constraints set up through prior choices, his language knowledge, his cognitive styles and strategies he has learned.
4. He forms a perceptual image using these cues and his anticipated cues.

This image then is partly what he sees and partly what he expected to see.

5. Now he searches his memory for related syntactic, semantic and phonological cues. This may lead to selection of more graphic cues and to reforming the perceptual image.

6. At this point, he makes a guess or tentative choice consistent with graphic cues. Semantic analysis leads to partial decoding as far as possible. This meaning is stored in short-term memory as he proceeds.

7. If no guess is possible, he checks the recalled perceptual input and tries again. If a guess is still not possible, he takes another look at the text to gather more graphic cues.

8. If he can make a decodable choice, he tests it for semantic and grammatical acceptability in the context developed by prior choices and decoding.

9. If the tentative choice is not acceptable semantically or syntactically, then he regresses, scanning from right to left along the line and up the page to locate a point of semantic or syntactic inconsistency. When such a point is found, he starts over at that point. If no inconsistency can be identified, he reads on seeking some cue which will make it possible to reconcile the anomalous situation.

10. If the choice is acceptable, decoding is extended, meaning is assimilated with prior meaning and prior meaning is accommodated, if necessary. Expectations are formed about input and meaning that lies ahead.

11. Then the cycle continues.

Throughout the process there is constant use of long and short term memory.

I offer no apologies for the complexity of this model. Its faults lie, not in its complexity, but in the fact that it is not yet complex enough to fully account for the complex phenomena in the actual behavior of readers. But such is man's destiny in his quest for knowledge. Simplistic folklore must give way to complexity as we come to know.

Notes

1. George Spache, *Reading in the Elementary School* (Boston: Allyn and Bacon, Inc., 1964), p. 12.
2. Glenn McCracken and Charles C. Walcutt, *Basic Reading*, Teacher's Edition for the Pre-Primer and Primer (Philadelphia: J. B. Lippincott Co., 1963), p. vii.
3. William D. Hayes, "My Brother Is a Genius," in Emmett A. Betts and Carolyn M. Welch (eds.), *Adventures Now and Then*, Book 6, Betts Basic Readers, Third Edition (New York: American Book Co., 1963), p. 246.
4. Noam Chomsky, lecture at Project Literacy, Cornell University, June 18, 1965.
5. Yetta M. Goodman, College of Education, Wayne State University, Doctoral Study of Development of Reading in First Grade Children. See Reading 41 in this book.
6. Emmett A. Betts and Carolyn M. Welch, "Ride In," *Time to Play*, Second Pre-Primer, Betts Basic Readers, 3rd Edition, Language Arts Series (New York: American Book Co., 1963).
7. Emmett A. Betts and Carolyn M. Welch, "Stop and Go," *All in a Day*, Third Pre-Primer, Betts Basic Readers (New York: American Book Co., 1963).
8. George A. Miller, "Some Preliminaries to Psycholinguistics," *American Psychologist*, 20 (1965), 18.

9. The Contribution of the Psycholinguists to the Teaching of Reading

Part I—An Appreciation and a Critique[1]

Denis H. Stott

Our Common Ground

On our fundamentals there is little to fight about. Theoretically Frank Smith and Ken Goodman are on the side of the angels. At least we are on the same side in deploring contemporary practices in the teaching of reading. Everything they say about explaining rules and expecting children to apply them I endorse. When I peep into an empty classroom and see the blackboard strewn with abstruse grammatical terms of the meaning of which I am uncertain, but of the irrelevance of which I am sure, I wonder that generation after generation of teachers can persist in such ineffectiveness.

It is the same with the teaching of phonics. To drill beginning readers in the "sounds of the letters" and then expect them to blend these pseudophonemes into words is not only linguistically artificial— the variations of the flow of breath in speech bear little resemblance to these isolated "sounds"—it imposes the same strain on the intellect as the application of grammatical rules. The learner is expected to bear in mind too many considerations at the same moment. Smith calls this an overloading of the short-term memory; the problem is one of trying to remember to do a dozen things in one fraction of a second.

Smith rightly sees learning as a form of behavior. Children learn by testing hypotheses—deciding which is the most likely answer and seeing if they are right. If the hypothesis is wrong, the learner can examine the problem more closely, get further clues, and make a more accurate hypothesis, until he gets the right answer. A child learns in dealing with his own experiences. To quote Smith and Goodman, "learning is rarely the result of a passive exposure to 'instruction' but rather the result of an active search for specific kinds of information, which is another reason why rules can be learned but not taught" (Smith and Goodman, 1973, p. 179).

I am also at one with Smith when he writes that, "what matters for progress in reading is a child's own capacity to derive sense and pleasure" from the activity of reading (Smith, 1978, p. 194). Elsewhere I have argued that, if learning is made disagreeable, it will either be avoided or the minimum performed to meet the teacher's demands (Stott, 1978a). My particular bugbear is the all-too-popular comprehension exercise, which might have been designed by some obscurantist reactionary intent on destroying interest in reading in order to keep the masses ignorant. Smith (1973) points out that these comprehension exercises are a perversion of the true purpose of reading, which is understanding what the passage or book is about, not a game of recalling details (p. 191).

From Denis H. Stott, The contribution of the psycholinguists to the teaching of reading: Part I—An appreciation and a critique. *Reading—Canada—Lecture*, January 1981, *1*, 11–18. Reprinted by permission of the author and the publisher.

The Psycholinguists' Armchair (or Platform?) Counsel

Where then, with this consensus on the basics of learning, do I part company with these psycholinguists? It is, first, that they commit a major error of scientific method. From their insights into the nature of the reading process (many of which are good) they deduce certain principles for the teaching of reading. These general precepts are in the nature of hypotheses; but they fail to test them by seeing how they apply to the realities of the classroom. They are like drivers who decide to set the steering wheel in a certain position and drive on without taking account of the course of the road ahead. It is beyond the ingenuity of the human brain to work out a course of action so accurately that no later adaptations are needed. In our Centre for Educational Disabilities at the University of Guelph we would confidently design some new technique for overcoming children's faulty ways of learning, only repeatedly to find that things did not work out as we anticipated. The theoretician can help the practitioner by giving him insights into the nature of the problems he faces, but he would be rash to prescribe a course of action without first testing it stage by stage. This Smith and Goodman have not done; consequently they do not learn from their "miscues." They have become platform philosophers, substituting catchy phrases for experiment.

Despite his disclaimers, Smith (1978) does prescribe a method of teaching reading (p. iii). Goodman (1979) goes even further: he advises the teacher to "interfere with the learning as little as possible and facilitate the learning that is taking place." In the address to teachers in which he made this pronouncement he went on to say that he did "not see any place for a sequence of skills because we are convinced reading has to be wholistic." The teacher has simply to "interact" with the children. Interacting evidently doesn't involve teaching, which is old-fashioned and to be avoided. "We assumed that they [children] had to be taught to read and write." All the teacher has to do now, according to Goodman, is to see that there is a lot of reading going on and to create an environment in which kids are willing to take risks, i.e., not be afraid of guessing wrong.

The answer to the problem of how children can be expected to read before they have learned to do so is, in Smith's (1978) view, "very simple. At the beginning—and at any other time when it is necessary—the reading has to be done for the children. . . . everything will have to be read to them. . . ." (p. 180). He even suggests the use of recordings. This is a direct contradiction of his own theory of learning, to which I gave endorsement above. It requires that the child be given the opportunity to form hypotheses and to see which are right and which are wrong. He has to have what Smith (1973) calls "non-examples" (p. 187). He instances the case of a child learning to read the word *John*, arguing that "until the child comes across another word that is not *John*, there can be no learning . . ." (Smith, 1978, p. 129). But when a passage is simply read to a child he cannot make his own attempts to read words, and, in doing so, make mistakes; hence he has no "non-examples" which enable him to identify the distinctive features of words. He occupies the passive role of a listener, which Smith rightly points out is a poor situation for learning.

The Psycholinguistic Prescription Might Work—with the Ideal Scholar

Despite its title, "Reading—and Learning to Read," the final chapter of Smith's (1978) book has little to add about the actual teaching of reading. "Where children have difficulty in reading, teachers must see that they are helped." This consists chiefly in "developing the confidence of children to read by themselves, in their own way, taking the risk of making mistakes and being willing to ignore the completely incomprehensible" (p. 187). The teacher's role is essentially a passive one, relying on the child's initiative and desire to learn, and being there as a resource.

This reliance upon the child's own motivation and learning skills betrays Smith's lack of acquaintance with the realities of teaching. He has a stereotypic image of the child as an ideal student. "Learning," he tells us, "is a continuous and natural process, as natural as breathing" (Smith, 1978, p. 96). "Children are motivated to learn whenever there is something they do not understand, provided they feel there is a chance that they can learn" (p. 97). This certainly applies to the natural learning of the young child who is gifted with a desire to explore and master his environment; but not all children, even of this sort, have a natural desire to direct their learning towards reading. Evidently Smith has never had to deal with the not uncommon careless reader who will blithely read on, ignoring small words which hold the key to the sense and satisfying himself with guesses which make nonsense—or the nervous child, equally common, who refuses to make guesses but goes into a state of non-responding anxiety. Smith seems unaware of the fact that some children may have come from social backgrounds where little importance is attached to literacy and where reading is not regarded as one of the pleasures of life.

The extent of Smith's unrealism is illustrated from the results of the survey of 2013 five and six year old children in English schools by Green and Francis (1979). The Preliminary Screening of the Guide to the Child's Learning Skills (Stott, 1978a, 1978b) completed by their teachers showed that only some 48 percent had uniformly good learning styles in the sense of being able to attend to the teachers and to concentrate on a learning task, having the confidence to tackle a task on

their own yet being willing to seek the teacher's help when necessary, being prepared to think out a problem and being generally alert and well motivated. Smith's assertion that "children find out soon enough the mistakes that make a difference" (Smith, 1978, p. 187) could apply, at best, only to this 48 percent of naturally good listeners. Only they, at best, would learn from their "miscues."

A similar lack of realism pervades Goodman's (1979) utterances. Among the "wholistic things the teacher can do" is to have books with accompanying tapes. "The children then follow along as they hear the story read." Or "the teacher reads, the kid follows. The kid reads and the teacher fades out." Just as simple as that! What a teacher's dream to have a room-full of such budding scholars! Goodman evidently doesn't know the variety of non-reading games a child can play with tapes or how few children have the requisite habits of close attention and enduring concentration. We cannot just take good learning skills or the motivation to read for granted.

In sum, this laissez-faire philosophy of Smith and Goodman, relying on the child to teach himself, favors those who have been reared in an education-conscious environment where they are faced with the challenge of learning to read. It heaps further disadvantages upon those who are deprived of such social incentives or don't have the kind of temperament that takes easily to learning. When Smith absolves the teacher from making any effort to teach children to read ("Learning to read is a problem for the child to solve"— Smith, 1973, p. 195) he is promulgating a socially retrograde doctrine.

Little Help for the Primary Teacher

It becomes apparent that the psycholinguists, as represented by Smith and Goodman, have little to offer the teacher with a class of beginning readers. Their counsel applies only to children who already have a sufficient mastery of reading to get along with only occasional help. They are, of course, quite right in insisting that what these children need is the opportunity to read without being forced to stop and identify every word or being interrupted and bored by comprehension exercises. Their advice, at this stage of reading, that children should be allowed to pass over or to make guesses at unknown words is sound. But inferring the meaning of a word from its context only works when the important words in the sentence can be read. This is well illustrated by Goodman's (1968) nonsense-story, "A marlup was poving his kump," (p. 23). It is quite impossible, without using the deciphering skills of a counter-intelligence expert, even to get any hypotheses as to what the text is about. To expect a child to solve such puzzles leads only to frustration and discouragement. Moreover guessing, for many children, can become a bad habit. They guess in the literal sense of the word—"to form an opinion or estimate without means of knowledge; to judge at random" (Webster, 1975).

The Value of Phonics in Learning to Read

A second reason why Smith and Goodman have so little to offer the primary teacher lies in their misconceptions about the teaching of phonics.

Goodman goes some way toward recognizing the value of the phonic cues. He sees these as being *re-coded* into sound-sequences at the early stages of reading, which are then *decoded* into meaning. He recognizes also that the beginning reader will use a mixture of single-letter, letter-pattern and whole-word strategies (Goodman, 1968, pp. 17–18). He is rightly worried about children being taught to use exclusively the single-letter approach; but he overgeneralizes this into a general dislike of "direct instruction" in phonics. He warns that "excessive stress . . . on phon-

ics or word attack skills will tend to make recoding an end in itself, and may actually distract the child from the real end: decoding written language for meaning" (p. 21). This warning would be valid only if the teaching of phonics is conceived of as the conscious building up of words from the "sounds of the letters." It is evident that Goodman has this narrow conception, and contrasts it to "self-induction" of the phonic cues. It does not occur to him that this process of self-induction (which, as I show below, is the basis of my own approach) can be immensely facilitated by careful sequencing of the child's phonic experiences. This is not an alternative to the teaching of phonics; as I argue in the second part of this article, it is the only valid way of doing so. It demands the sophisticated professional technique—technology if you will—that Smith dismisses as "trickery." Goodman is opposed to an organized, stage-by-stage nurturing of phonic skills. His "wholistic" approach leaves the child without guidance in reaching understanding of the phonic principle and in the mastery of the letter-sound correspondences. By his undiscriminating rejection of phonics teaching he wholistically empties out the baby with the bathwater.

Smith likewise assumes that phonics can be taught only by the memorizing of rules and the sounding out of individual letters (Smith, 1978, pp. 149, 179). He uses two further arguments in his crusade against phonics.

The first of these is what he terms the unpredictability of the letter-sound correspondences (Smith, 1973, p. 184), claiming that even the 166 rules of such which have been identified still do not even cover the words children might be expected to meet in their early reading (Smith, 1978, p. 141). On this issue Goodman (1969) disagrees with him. He points out that what appear as phonic irregularities are different systems by which letters relate to sounds (p. 26). Drawing on the work of Venezky, he—rightly in my view—argues that these minor-pattern regularities are "so firmly based in the operation of the language . . . that they cause no particular problem in reading" (Goodman, 1973, p. 164).

Smith's second objection to phonics teaching is that the attempt to teach its rules overloads the child's memory. Hence he dismisses the learning of phonic skills as an aid to reading (Smith, 1973, p. 147). These, for him, are something children pick up incidentally as a *result* of learning to read—for what purpose he does not say. Smith can envisage no means by which children might master the basic phonic concepts as an aid to reading, and can even begin to do so in advance of reading through pre-reading activities.

The acquisition of phonic concepts does not in effect require the conscious learning of innumerable complex rules. When the manager of a disco puts up a notice about his *Saturday nite attraction* or a garage owner announces *lube* as one of the services he offers, it is highly unlikely that they have remembered, or have even been aware of, a rule about a vowel being "long" when it precedes a "silent *e*." They go by the analogy of *white, kite, rule,* etc. Unconsciously they have induced a "minor-pattern regularity."

If the child is to be denied the help of the phonic cues, what then? Smith recommends that the beginning reader be given an extensive vocabulary of "sight words" (Smith, 1978, p. 149); but what he says about overloading children's memories condemns this look-and-say method of teaching reading. There are not enough differences in the shapes of words to distinguish them; and to have to learn up to 50,000 letter-sequences (Smith's own estimate of the ordinary person's vocabulary) without any insight into the phonic values of the letters would be like learning a similar quantity of telephone numbers. He swallows an elephant while straining at a gnat.

Smith himself produces the strongest argument for equipping the beginning reader with the phonic cues. He admits

(Smith, 1978, p. 147) that "phonic generalizations can work if all they are required to do is to reduce alternatives" when a child is trying to figure out a word. The extent of his blind spot for phonics can be gauged by his failure to realize that this grudging admission gives away his whole case. If the child takes his cue from the sound-value of only the initial letter of a word, he increases by some 28 times his chance of reading it correctly (there being 25 initial letters and three letter-pairs—*ch, sh, th*—which make 28 different phonemes). It is true that the vowels among them will tend to vary, but few words begin with vowels, and their variations are mostly "long" forms, which follow the minor-regularity rules. How much a knowledge of the sound-values of only initial letters can reduce uncertainty is demonstrated by the well-known game "I spy with my little eye." If a player is asked to spot something beginning with *p* his choice is narrowed down to only a few objects (plant, picture, piano). On the other hand, if the player had to guess without the letter-sound cue he might have to name scores of objects before getting the right answer. (Incidentally the above game is an excellent way of introducing phonics because the initial sounds are heard by the child as parts of words.)

Those, like Smith, who make so much of the irregularities of English spelling, overlook the fact that the consonants are nearly always regular, and that their variants—except for the voiced and unvoiced forms of *s* and *th*—form easily memorized conventions (*ph, wh, wr, kn, ch, sh,* the soft *c* and *g*). Moreover one can decode a passage of reading fairly accurately solely from the consonants, as this passage taken from a story shows:

-t w-s s-mm-r. Th-s-n w-s
h-t. Th- gr-ssh-pp-r s-t -n th-
l-ng gr-ss -nd s-ng -nd s-ng.
H- w-s v-ry h-ppy.

It is not suggested of course that children should be encouraged to rely entirely on the consonants. The regular "short" vowels, learned in the first place as initial letters, are equally useful and prepare the way for decoding by the first two or three letters of a word. The phonic conventions ("minor-pattern regularities") can be phased in without making the early reading stilted. In the above passage the only such used are those in *was, the, er* and the terminal *y*.

We forget, also, that, from our own schooling and training, we have become conditioned to the idea of "rules," and are apt to get worried about their exceptions. But the child's world, from which he draws his concepts about the nature of things, is full of exceptions. The weather, other people's behavior, what is expected to eat, and so on, are to some degree unpredictable. What matters in the formation of the expectations that become our concepts is that they should have sufficient regularity to serve us as a guide to action. The same applies to the phonic correspondences. They are many times better than just having to guess from the context, which is in any case often impossible.

Notes

1. Dr. Goodman's response to this two-part series appears in *Reading-Canada-Lecture*, April 1981, *1*, 118–120.

References

Goodman, K. S. (1968), Words and morphemes in reading. In Goodman, K. S., and Fleming, J. T. (eds.), *Psycholinguistics and the teaching of reading*. Newark, Delaware: IRA.

Goodman, K. S. (1969), The psycholinguistic nature of the reading process. In Goodman, K. S. (ed.), *The psycholinguistic nature of the reading process*. Detroit, Michigan: Wayne State University Press.

Goodman, K. S. (1973), Analysis of oral miscues. In Smith, F. (ed.), *Psycholinguistics and reading*. New York, N.Y.: Holt, Rinehart and Winston.

Goodman, K. S. (1979), Address to conference "Reading—No One Way," Faculty of Education, Queen's University, Kingston, Ontario.

Green, L. F., and Francis, J. (1970), personal communication.

Smith, F. (1978), *Understanding reading*. New York, N.Y.: Holt, Rinehart and Winston.

Smith, F. (1973), Twelve easy ways to make learning to read difficult. In Smith, F. (ed.), *Psycholinguistics and reading*. New York, N.Y.: Holt, Rinehart and Winston.

Stott, D. H. (1978a), Harnessing children's play to the business of learning. *Oxford Review of Education*, 4, 65–76.

Stott, D. H. (1978b), *The hard-to-teach child*. Baltimore, Maryland: University Park Press.

Webster's New 20th Century Dictionary, unabridged 2nd ed. (1975). New York, N.Y.: Collins.

CHAPTER III

Language and Reading

In recent years, there has been a marked increase in emphasis on the interrelatedness of the four main aspects of language: listening, speaking, reading, and writing.

Hodges provides a comprehensive survey of what is known about language development during the elementary school years. Lundsteen compares the process of learning to read with that of learning oral language. Pearson and Fielding summarize the research on listening comprehension, and present five recommendations concerning instructional practices. In the final article, Lehr presents some recent evidence about ways to integrate reading with instruction in writing.

10. Language Development: The Elementary School Years

Richard E. Hodges

Oral and Written Language Trends

Phonological development.—Most children by school entrance age have control of the phonemic stock of their dialect, although misarticulations do continue to occur. Templin analyzed the articulations of spontaneously produced and repeated words of 480 boys and girls, ages three to eight, and found that three-year-olds have about 50 percent of the articulatory accuracy of eight-year-olds, whille eight-year-olds achieved about 95 percent accuracy on the articulation measures Templin employed (24).

The age at which individual children acquire general mastery of speech-sound articulation can vary considerably—an observation that tends to be obscured in normative studies. Templin's recent longitudinal investigation of the articulatory development of 436 boys and girls who were followed from prekindergarten through the fourth grade substantiates her earlier finding. Her longitudinal data, however, show that some children display

From Richard E. Hodges, Language development: The elementary school years. In A. H. Marquardt (Ed.), *Linguistics in school programs.* Sixty-ninth yearbook of the National Society for the Study of Education, Part II. Chicago: University of Chicago Press, 1970. Pp. 215–218. Reprinted by permission of the author, the National Society for the Study of Education and the University of Chicago Press. Copyright 1970 by the National Society for the Study of Education.

functional articulatory control as early as age four and one-half, while some ten-year-olds still manifest certain misarticulations (25).

Wepman and Morency report somewhat similar relationships between misarticulation and age (26). Employing the concept of "age-appropriate misarticulation" in studying articulatory development, they call attention to a need to distinguish between developmental and pathological factors when observing the misarticulations of young children. From data obtained in a longitudinal study of 177 children followed from first through third grades, they unequivocally state that children who enter school with age-appropriate misarticulations are not hampered in general school learning—at least in the early grades. They reiterate the point that speech accuracy develops at its own rate, but in an expected order, for each individual. However, they also noted, as have others, that while developmentally caused misarticulations appear not to have significant effects upon school achievement, the ability to discriminate among speech sounds may (26, 5, 20)—a distinction of significance for spelling and reading instruction.

Morphological development.—The child's control of morphology proceeds, as do other language features, along a course of mastering the highly predictable and productive features toward the mastering of uncommon forms of limited distribution—for example, derivational suffixes and irregular inflections. The morphological "errors" of the beginning elementary school child quite clearly demonstrate his preference for the most generalizable patterns (2). His errors are in large part errors of analogy. On the other hand, the young child's inability to correctly employ uncommon forms in his own speech does not preclude his ability to comprehend them when used in the speech of others (15).

The elementary school years thus mark a time when the child gains mastery over most of the remaining morphological features, provided that adequate spoken language is available from which those features may be derived.

Syntactic development.—Although the groundwork has been laid in early childhood for the full development of native language skills, that achievement requires the whole period of childhood and adolescence (4:69). Recognition of this fact underlies in part the growing interest in describing and analyzing the language of the elementary school child.

Contemporary studies of child grammar have usually attempted to classify children's syntactic constructions with reference to adult language norms, with the system of classification being determined by the grammar model the researcher chooses to employ.

Strickland's cross-sectional study (23) involved the analysis of 25 spontaneously produced phonological units obtained in an interview setting for each of 575 randomly selected children taken in approximately equal numbers from each of grades one through six. She found that the most commonly used pattern at all grade levels was the "1|2|4" pattern, consisting of subject, verb, and outer complement or direct object. Strickland further observed that ten sentence patterns used by older children did not appear at all in the speech of first-graders, although there was considerable overlap among the 25 predominant sentence patterns found at each grade level. Children at all grade levels were seen to employ adverbial expressions—the movables—but the incidence of such expressions increased with advance in grade as well as did increased flexibility in how they were placed within a slot.

Strickland also compared the speech of a subsample of 15 first-graders and 15 fifth-graders in an attempt to provide a detailed analysis of growth of syntactic complexity. Although the small number of phonological units (750) that were analyzed limits her findings, progression toward mature speech is clearly identifiable. Fifth-graders consistently made greater use of "fillers" than did first-graders; indeed, the heavy use of long compound subject-predicate forms was found significantly to differentiate the speech of older children from that of the younger subjects.

Loban (13) undertook a longitudinal study of the language development of 338 subjects from kindergarten through the first twelve years of school. His first report encompassed his analysis of the syntactic growth of children through the sixth grade. Language samples were obtained yearly by having individual subjects discuss a series of six still pictures shown to them. The communication units that were obtained were then given a two-level analysis in order to determine each subject's effectiveness in and control of language— (*a*) the Level I analysis providing evidence of an ability to use and vary English structural patterns, and (*b*) the Level II analysis indicating the dexterity with which children vary elements within these patterns. In addition to his analysis of the complete sample of 338 children, Loban also undertook an intensive comparative study of the language production of 30 children designated as exceptionally high, and 24 children designated as exceptionally low, in language ability.

As might be expected, all children at each succeeding year were found to say more, both in terms of number of communication units and the number of words within these units; but noticeable contrasts were identified between the high-ability and low-ability children. Although there were only negligible differences between groups at the first level of analysis (excepting noticeable differences in the use of linking verbs and partials), the dexterity with which elements within basic patterns were manipulated strikingly differentiated the high-ability group from the low-ability group. Moreover, Loban found that the frequency of use and the complexity of

subordination varied according to general language proficiency as well as to socioeconomic status and chronological age. In addition, Loban provided evidence to question the commonly held view of the general linguistic superiority of girls (14:577). His findings indicated that boys in the low-ability group were least proficient, but the boys in the high-ability group excelled girls on the measures used.

Strickland and Loban were generally concerned with analyses of the oral language of children, although Loban did obtain samples of child writing from the third grade on for purposes of relating writing ability (rated on a five-point scale ranging from "superior" to "primitive") to achievement in reading, oral language, and other aspects of language. Other researchers, however, have looked expressly at contrasts between oral and written language development, as well as specifically at language development in the written mode. Riling's investigation of the oral and written language of fourth- and sixth-grade children represents one such study that employs the two-level structural analysis initiated by Strickland and Loban (19).

Riling's findings further substantiate the developmental characteristics of child language, her sixth-grade subjects speaking with greater clarity than fourth-graders and writing longer, more complex sentences with greater variation than their younger counterparts. Of particular interest was Riling's observation that, even in fourth grade, some structural patterns which appeared in writing seldom appeared in speech, leading her to speculate that such differences result from the child's growing awareness of distinctions between oral and written communication.

As had Loban, Riling also observed in the high-ability group the general linguistic superiority of boys as compared to girls, while boys in the low-ability group were indeed "at the bottom of the heap" (19:87). She also noted differences in written language among her subjects when differentiated in terms of rural and urban origins— the former writing less, and doing so in shorter and more repetitious syntactic patterns.

Hunt's study of the grammatical structures used in writing by older children focused expressly on the written mode (9). However, unlike Riling, Strickland, and Loban (13:62), Hunt applied transformational grammar techniques to distinguish levels of linguistic maturity. The particular consequence of Hunt's study lies in its baseline data concerning the grammar of young writers—fourth-graders—compared with older writers and in his observations of the development of skills of individuals to consolidate sentences, reduce redundancies, and to communicate through the written medium with increasing succinctness.

Hunt provided information about the written language abilities of older elementary children. O'Donnell, Griffin, and Norris applied Hunt's "T-unit" (a single independent predication together with any subordinate clauses which may be grammatically related to it) in the study of both the oral and written syntax of 180 children in kindergarten and in Grades I, II, III, V, and VII (17). The investigators did not concern themselves with the full range of possible grammatical structures and functions but selected for study main-clause patterns and those structures dependent on sentence-combining transformations.

As had Hunt, they also observed that the length of the T-unit increased grade by grade. But they also found that, though third-graders used longer T-units in speech than in writing, the reverse situation was true for the fifth-graders, suggesting that older children learn to control written expression with greater care than oral language, an observation not unlike that of Riling (19). However, the greatest advances in oral language development were found in the earliest grades (kindergarten through first grade) and the later grades (sixth and seventh), a finding which led the investigators to speculate about the effectiveness of language instruction during the middle elementary school years (17).

The development of grammatical control during the early school years is further clarified by Slobin's study of the extent to which and the manner in which children and adults comprehend negative and passive forms of basic sentences (22). Kindergarten, second-, fourth-, and sixth-grade children and a group of adults were presented with pictures and spoken sentences. For each picture-sentence pair, the subjects had to determine whether the sentence was true or false in reference to the picture. Four grammatical types of sentences were used which included (in presumed order of difficulty) kernel, negative, passive and passive negative. Response times and errors were tabulated.

Contrary to prediction, the syntactically more complex passive sentences were simpler to evaluate than were the negative sentences. Moreover, this was true for both adults and children, although both response times and errors diminished with age, with a rapid change in response time between the ages of six to ten and a slowing down between ages ten and twelve. It could be inferred that grammatical control continues to improve fairly rapidly in the early school years, slowing down as mature levels of control are reached. Slobin's study demonstrates how, during the elementary school years, the child is involved in increasing skill in the manipulation of more complex and subtle features of the grammatical system.

The foregoing studies illustrate the increased efforts to describe child language in more precise and definitive ways. There can be little question but that language skills continue to develop throughout much of one's lifetime and that the elementary school years are important in the individual's growth toward linguistic maturity.

Whether or not the maturation process can be enhanced through explicit and systematic instruction in such linguistic devices as sentence combining transformations (9) has yet to be investigated substantively at the elementary school level. In one of the few such studies reported, Miller and Ney concluded that oral practice in sentence-combining did produce greater fluency and facility of writing among their fourth-grade subjects (16).

Language variations.—Studies of child language have, for the most part, assumed a model grammar, Standard English. That spoken language varies widely with reference to that model is noticeable by even the most casual language observer.

When language variations, either structural or functional, impede communication, there are likely to be adverse consequences for formal education since oral and written language are primary media of instruction (10). Conflicts between the child's linguistic system and the language of instruction not only can interfere with learning but, unfortunately, can also have social consequences. On both instructional and social grounds, language variations can be a major school problem (1, 21). The increasing literature concerning the language of the "disadvantaged child" is a visible commentary on the relevance of this problem (18, 6). In the main, examinations of language variations have been approached in terms of (*a*) the possible interrelationships between language and cognitive functioning and (*b*) their possible effects on spoken and written communication.

One theoretical position of current interest is that of Bernstein, who posits a relationship between social class speech systems, or codes, and orientations to abstract formulation (3).[1] According to Bernstein, these codes can be described as *restricted* and *elaborated*, the former being characterized by its relatively simple syntax, redundancy, and high predictability, the latter being characterized by its complex syntax and low predictability. Because of the greater number of syntactic options that are possible, an elaborated code permits a greater range of possibilities in organizing experience.

Bernstein stipulates that neither code is necessarily better than the other in terms of its own possibilities. But the larger society may place different values on the kinds of experiences which the different codes may elicit, maintain, and reinforce. Further, although the middle-class person can and does use codes, the individual from the lower class can be expected to be limited to a restricted code. And, because the language of instruction is typically that of the middle class—an elaborated code—it is crucial that the lower-class child be helped to possess, or at least be oriented toward, the elaborated code (3:164–65).

The attractiveness of Bernstein's approach as a means of accounting for differential learning behaviors among lower- and middle-class children establishes a potential for stereotyping the language capabilities of the lower-class child. It is, of course, apparent to the careful observer of child language that children do not fit so neatly into theoretical categories. Nonetheless, the possible consequences of such attempts for elementary school instruction are not to be lightly dismissed. It seems fair to note that to the extent to which language ability is a prerequisite to school learning, disparities with the model of the language used in the classroom can affect learning.

Other effects of language variation on school learning have been reported by numerous investigators. Deutsch and his associates evaluated elements of expressive and receptive speech of Negro and white first- and fifth-grade children representative of three socioeconomic levels.

The language measure included (*a*) total verbal output, (*b*) number of different words, (*c*) the number of nouns, verbs, adjectives, and adverbs, and (*d*) mean sentence length. Factor analysis revealed that language performance and intelligence test scores as measured by the nonverbal form of the *Lorge-Thorndike Intelligence Test* were significantly related, and that although intelligence test scores of advantaged children increased over time, fifth-grade disadvantaged children did relatively poorer on the tests than did their first-grade counterparts. The adverse effects of social disadvantage thus appear to become more pronounced with age, a "cumulative deficit," and are particularly noticeable in language measures among social classes (7, 8).[2]

The relationship of language variations to instruction can be particularly important in the area of reading, where the language of instruction is most formalized. Labov suggests that phonological variations can have both grammatical and motivational consequences, the former in respect to such factors as "*r*-lessness" (*caught* for *court*), "*l*-lessness" (*toe* for *toll*), and simplification of consonant clusters (*pass* for *past* and *passed*), the latter in respect to the hypercorrective teacher (10). Labov also calls attention to the influence of the informal vernacular of peers on the language behavior of the elementary school child (11).

Notes

1. For a comprehensive critique of Bernstein's view, see Lawton (12).
2. For a recent summary, see Whiteman and Deutsch (27).

Bibliography

1. Bailey, Beryl L. "Some Aspects of the Impact of Linguistics on Language Teaching in Disadvantaged Communities," *Elementary English*, XLV (May, 1968), 570–78, 626.
2. Berko, Jean. "The Child's Learning of English Morphology," *Word*, XIV (1958), 150–77.
3. Bernstein, Basil. "A Socio-Linguistic Approach to Social Learning." In *Penguin Survey of the Social Sciences*, 1965, pp. 144–68. Edited by Julius Gould. Baltimore, Maryland: Penguin Books, 1965.
4. Carroll, John B. *Language and Thought*. Englewood Cliffs, N.J.: Prentice-Hall, 1964.
5. Cavoures, Dorothy G. "Phoneme Identification in Primary Reading and Spelling." Doctor's dissertation, Boston University School of Education, 1964.
6. Cazden, Courtney B. "Subcultural Differences in Child Language: An Inter-Disciplinary Review," *Merrill-Palmer Quarterly*, XII (July, 1966), 185–219.
7. Deutsch, Martin *et al. Communication of Information in the Elementary School Classroom*. Cooperative Research Project No. 908, 1964.
8. Deutsch, Martin. "The Role of Social Class in Language Development and Cognition," *American Journal of Orthopsychiatry*, XXXV (January, 1965), 78–88.
9. Hunt, Kellogg W. *Grammatical Structures Written at Three Grade Levels*. NCTE Research Report No. 3. Champaign, Ill.: National Council of Teachers of English, 1965.
10. Labov, William. "Some Sources of Reading Problems for Negro Speakers of Nonstandard English." In *New Directions in Elementary English*. Edited by Alexander Frazier. Champaign, Ill.: National Council of Teachers of English, 1967.
11. ———. "Stages in the Acquisition of Standard English." In *Social Dialects and Language Learning*, pp. 77–103. Edited by Roger Shuy. Champaign, Ill.: National Council of Teachers of English, 1965.
12. Lawton, Denis. *Social Class. Language, and Education*. London: Routledge & Kegan Paul, 1968.
13. Loban, Walter D. *The Language of Elementary School Children*. NCTE Research Report No. 1. Champaign, Ill.: National Council of Teachers of English, 1963.
14. McCarthy, Dorothea. "Language Development in Children." Chapter ix in *Manual of Child Psychology*. 2d. ed., Edited by Leonard R. Carmichael. New York: John Wiley & Sons, 1954.
15. Menyuk, Paula. "Children's Learning and

Reproduction of Grammatical and Non-grammatical Phonological Sequences," *Child Development*, XXXIX (September, 1968), 849–59.

16. Miller, Barbara D. and Ney, James W. "The Effect of Systematic Oral Exercises on the Writing of Fourth-Grade Students," *Research in the Teaching of English*, II (Spring, 1968), 44–61.

17. O'Donnell, Roy C.; Griffin, William J.; and Norris, Raymond C. *Syntax of Kindergarten and Elementary School Children: A Transformational Analysis*. NCTE Research Report No. 8. Champaign, Ill.: National Council of Teachers of English, 1967.

18. Raph, J. B. "Language Development in Socially Disadvantaged Children," *Review of Educational Research*, XXXV (1965). 389–400.

19. Riling, Mildred E. *Oral and Written Language of Children in Grades 4 and 6 Compared with the Language of Their Textbooks*. Cooperative Research Project No. 2410. Washington, D.C.: U.S. Department of Health, Education and Welfare, Office of Education, 1965.

20. Sandy, Don G. "Auditory Discrimination and Articulatory Proficiency of Kindergarten Children." Doctor's dissertation, Boston University School of Education, 1965.

21. Shuy, Roger W. "Detroit Speech: Careless, Awkward, and Inconsistent, or Systematic, Graceful, and Regular?" *Elementary English*, XLV (May, 1968), 565–69.

22. Slobin, Dan I. "Grammatical Transforma-tions and Sentence Comprehension in Childhood and Adulthood," *Journal of Verbal Learning and Verbal Behavior*, V (1966), 219–27.

23. Strickland, Ruth G. *The Language of Elementary School Children: Its Relationship to the Language of Reading Textbooks and the Quality of Reading of Selected Children*. Bulletin of the School of Education, Indiana University, Vol. 38. Bloomington, Ind., 1962.

24. Templin, Mildred C. *Certain Language Skills in Children: Their Development and Interrelationships*. Minneapolis: University of Minnesota Press, 1957.

25. ———. *Longitudinal Study Through the Fourth Grade of Language Skills of Children with Varying Speech Sound Articulation in Kindergarten*. USOE Project H2220. Minneapolis: Institute of Child Development, University of Minnesota, January, 1968.

26. Wepman, Joseph M. and Morency, Anne S. *School Achievement as Related to Developmental Speech Inaccuracy*. Unpublished report, Cooperative Research Project No. 2225, Office of Education, U.S. Department of Health, Education, and Welfare, July, 1967. University of Chicago.

27. Whiteman, Martin and Deutsch, Martin. "Social Disadvantage as Related to Intellectual and Language Development." *Social Class, Race, and Psychological Development*, pp. 86–114. Edited by Martin Deutsch, Irwin Katz, and Arthur R. Jensen. New York: Holt, Rinehart & Winston, 1968.

11. On Developmental Relations between Language-Learning and Reading

Sara W. Lundsteen

It helps to know where we are going, what we are doing and why. When we have this knowledge, much that we do in the classroom falls into place in a meaningful and long lasting way. Each of us needs to work out a rationale for our reading program. If we understand cognitive, affective, and linguistic aspects of our learners' development; if we understand differences (and similarities) between learning a native lan-

Adapted from Sara W. Lundsteen, On developmental relations between language learning and reading. *Elementary School Journal*, January 1977, 77, 193–203. Reprinted by permission of the University of Chicago Press. Copyright 1977 by the University of Chicago Press.

guage and learning to read, we make learning easier and more long lasting for children. I have found it so.

In my work I have found it useful to examine nine elements of language-learning and reading. They are suddenness of onset, anxiety, blame laid on the child for failure, appeal of rewards, surface features of oral and written language, social interaction, correction of "errors," grasp of language concepts, and amount of control and breaking apart of language. We can use these elements as a framework for exploring differences and similarities between native language-learning and learning to read.

What Are the Differences between Learning a Native Language and Learning to Read?

1. Suddenness of onset. Language acquisition has no conscious beginning: typically reading instruction is introduced abruptly. Sometimes the introduction is traumatic. Children ease into using their native language over many years. But in most reading systems the demand for production in reading is abrupt.

When the children come to us for reading, we forget how much they already know and do not know. We forget the saying: "Reading begins at birth." We forget that reading means relating new concepts to what one already knows—and making sense of it. We forget that reading is asking predictive questions—"Is that a new idea coming along? Does this category go with that one?"—a whole jigsaw of thoughts in meaningful relationship. Reading seems so simple to most adults—so difficult to most beginners.

When we use or build background for reading in natural ways (as in oral language-learning), we reduce the "suddenness" of the onset of reading, making it easier (1–7). Again, "Reading begins at birth."

2. Anxiety. Parents and their children generally show little anxiety while the child is learning to talk. But anxiety for learning to read may be great. Anxiety is related to the child's expectancy of success or failure. If children expect to fail, their interest in tasks is likely to decrease and they may finally withdraw. Motivation and persistence in reading tasks hang delicately in the balance between hope and fear (8). A certain amount of freedom from anxiety enables a child to take risks, make predictions, and take leaps toward meaning.

One ingredient related to anxiety in the classroom is mutual respect between teacher and pupil. When there is mutual respect, pupils and teachers think to themselves, "You are not a threat to me, and I am not a threat to you." In such an atmosphere children believe that what they want to say, they will be able to say. What they want to read, they will be able to read. Sometimes educators forget the crucial idea that "nothing succeeds like success." Even small successes help dispel anxiety. ("You really understand what that sentence means, don't you!")

Reading comprehension is impossible for children if they are uptight. To be right much of the time while reading one needs to be able to risk being wrong some of the time. A relaxed frame of mind enables children to try out the probabilities of their language and to use their experience to make sense of print. Helping children to relax makes learning to read easier.

3. Blame laid on the child for failure. Some children are blamed for failing to learn to read but are usually given understanding and help when they fail to learn to speak. Children who are slow in learning to read are sometimes labeled lazy, inattentive, ornery, hyperactive. It may not occur to us that the child is having difficulty reading because we are demanding a conceptual level that the child simply has not yet attained. Or the difficulty may grow out of any of a host of other factors over which the child has little or no control. Reading is easier for children if they are given the same support in mastering print that they were given earlier in mastering oral language.

4. *Appeal of rewards.* Consider another comparison. Rewards for learning to speak are obvious: internal benefits from learning to read may appear too distant and abstract to a child. Usually children are motivated to learn if the content of what they are asked to read encourages and supports their natural ways of thinking.

This kind of motivation is at work when teachers have children read their own dictated stories of their experiences (9–11). At times teachers stimulate children's compositions by using patterns from appealing, high-quality literature for children (12: 95, 399–401). The use of the child's experience for reading material makes sense because it takes into account the common developmental course in growth of language and thought. This method reduces a child's overdependence on print and gives great personal satisfaction.

5. *Surface features of oral and written language*. Printed material, however, is not simply "talk written down." Oral language and reading materials differ in conciseness, in abstractness, and in the special skills of visual discrimination required by reading.

We might say that oral language is to reading as walking is to swimming. Whatever the differences, oral language and thought support reading proficiency, serving as background. If the child's oral language/thought differs from the printed message, the effect is inhibiting. Teachers who are aware of these contrasts in conciseness, abstractness, and redundancy can help make reading easier for children.

6. *Social interaction.* Consider social interaction. Language development is supported by social interaction: Reading instruction often leaves little room for dialoguing as a natural accompaniment to the child's learning.

Consider some positive examples of social interaction. There is interaction when pairs of children dictate, write, and read, and when children use group procedures with literature (12: 198, 201, 204, 212, 220; 13). The activity called "Three in a Tub" encourages social feeling while learning. For this activity one teacher painted an old bathtub orange, tossed in some cushions, and declared it a reading center. Users had to abide by three rules: only three in the tub; keep reading; no splashing.

7. *Correction of "errors."* The next comparison between language acquisition and beginning reading deals with the instructor's correction of errors (or miscues) during learning. Correcting, controlling, and forcing the child to imitate and repeat apparently have not helped much in promoting early language development (14), but similar techniques seem to be typical in reading instruction. A teacher in a reading circle may say to a child, "No, the book says 'toward,' not 'to.' Read it again." Some errors a child makes stem from the rules or generalizations about language that he or she is exploring at a particular time. ("Yesterday I cutted my finger.") Errors of this kind do not mean that the child lacks basic, developing competence.

When errors do not hinder comprehension, the miscues in reading deserve the same attention they usually get in conversational speech—no attention at all. Some teachers tend to jump on minor problems (or "non-problem problems"), failing to see the child's overall comprehension of the printed message. Fluent reading requires a willingness to risk mistakes or miscues.

Children who are linguistically different translate written language into their own dialect as they read. Minority children may read "be goin' disaway" for "going this way." Their translation shows a high level of comprehension. Some teachers do not recognize this achievement. The psychological laws of immediate, corrective feedback about rightness and wrongness, apparently so useful in shaping animal learning, are rarely if ever justifiable in language instruction.

We cannot identify and correct everything that children do wrong while reading. Proficient readers, who are rarely tested individually, sometimes have problems that are similar to those of poor readers. Correction of trivial errors has been overdone. Why not put learners' language achievements, not their deficits, in the spotlight for observation and teaching?

8. Grasp of language concepts. Most children have a fairly broad and deep understanding of what speaking and listening are used for (though they can't tell you abstractly). But many children may not understand what reading is and what they are supposed to be doing (16). They may have no idea, only partial ideas, or misconceptions about terms used in reading instruction. They may not have adequate concepts for terms such as *word, beginning sound, blend, phrase,* or *sentence.*

The teacher may assume that children know abstract concepts such as *word* and *sound.* The teacher is operating on Piaget's highest intellectual level of formal operations; the child is on the pre-operational level. And communication between them may be like "trains passing in the night" (15).

Confusion About Reading

For young beginners, reading is usually a mysterious activity. They have only vague notions as to how their parents read. Children do not seem to know that their parents look at printed symbols. Some children, confused perhaps by a fragmented approach, deny that books at school have stories in them (16). Some children may have difficulty in understanding the informative and delight-producing purposes of the written form of language. The relevance of literature to life becomes clouded by school ritual.

Children need to share ideas of what reading is all about with someone who knows the communicative purpose of literature and exposition. Children need to share with someone who can make it plain that those scratches on paper are telling them something meaningful. They need a loving triangle of Adult, Book, and Child. (Some have called this the "lap method" of reading instruction.)

Confusion About the Terminology of Reading Instruction

Let me give some further examples to show that beyond the confusion about the main purposes of reading, children have misconceptions about its parts. They call numbers letters and letters numbers. They say that *Balfore Street* begins with 3; *L* is called 7. Some children have not categorized words in the adult sense. They may think that the term *word* includes nonhuman sounds (the sound of a bell); any single, short-vowel sound (/ă/,/ĕ/,/ĭ/); phrases (*ham and eggs*); and sentences (*She's a funny girl*). Children may misconstrue *word* to include one, or a combination of, these examples (16).

In the beginning year of one study, few children grasped the fact that spaces act as boundaries between words. Or children used irrelevant attributes, such as length of the word. (For example, they said that *a, an,* and *the* are not words.) One child said, "*In* is not a word, because inside it has only two *words.*" (The child meant *letters,* not *words.*) Another child said that the word *have* is difficult because it has really only three words, not four. He meant *phonemes* not *words* (16).

Oral language a child hears is not segmented into words (for example, *Pleasitdown*; *hamandeggs*). Portions of continuous discourse contain little or no spaces of time between many spoken words. Thus, it is not surprising that children fail to understand the concept *word*.

Duration of Confusion

How long do such confusions continue? Vernon (17) suggests that these confusions are characteristic of reading disability at any age. Study has shown that confusions extend at least nine months into the first year of reading instruction. During this time children make little progress from month to month (16).

Developing Teaching Strengths

What can the teacher do to avoid adding to children's cognitive confusion and to develop clarity? Vygotsky (18) told us long ago that the teacher who simply states a concept does a child little or no good. The ritual of first learning letter names (prevalent in many beginning reading programs) does little to reduce cognitive confusion and teach reading comprehension (19).

Piaget and other developmental psychologists (8) have shown that the appropriate time to teach a child a verbal label is after the child has experienced the concept that is being labeled. To give the label and then the experience is like saying to a child, "This is a shell; this is a wave," and then taking the child to the beach. Isolated drill on letter names and sounds gives a child a wrong initial concept of what reading is all about. A teacher's instructions may throw many concepts at children and place a big load on their memory. The teacher who says to a very young child, "Put a circle around the first letter of the first word of the sentence" is not giving him a simple task.

But teachers can use better methods. They can shape the curriculum to the natural order of intellectual development in young children. They can use the child's own modes of thinking as the starting point for decisions about teaching method and curriculum in reading.

9. Amount of control and breaking apart of language. A final comparison: language acquisition goes on informally, unconsciously, nourished by a wide range of happenings, but reading instruction may not. Usually reading instruction is deliberately formal. The teacher uses techniques that require children to take apart and put together. Sometimes reading instruction has a big, heavy dose of phonics (drill on complex and sometimes merely supposed sound-letter correspondences). To develop this comparison, I will explore aspects of control, fragmentation, integration, and long-term and short-term goals.

Attempts to Control

Designers of most reading systems deliberately select the reading environment. The purpose is to encourage children to construct generalizations and to avoid exceptions to the generalizations. Accordingly, designers may introduce concepts that contain few bits of information. Later more complex concepts are introduced. Designers may introduce two-syllable words before three- and four-syllable words. Designers may avoid irrelevant information, for example, pictures. Designers may arrange for the teaching of similar concepts in sequence. For example, words with *c*, *o*, and *e* may be taught together because the shapes of these letters are similar and require fine discrimination. Or designers may keep these letters separate to avoid possible confusion and negative transfer. Designers may employ a great number of words that show a consistent use of some one vowel sound just introduced (for example, "Jim Reed sowed beet seeds").

Some of this concern with consistency of generalizations that are introduced to the learner may grow out of the thinking that children who are at Piaget's preoperational stage of intellectual growth can attend to only one dimension at a time. Children who are given a collection of white beads and dark beads cannot attend to white beads and dark beads at the same time. Children lack duality in thought. They cannot see that there are more beads altogether than there are of either color. They cannot use simultaneous reasoning about class and subgroups. Along this line, children may have trouble discriminating between letters and at the same time dealing with their sound (6). In this early stage of intellectual growth the child is also having trouble in using rules and in applying them correctly to specific instances. This difficulty applies to the use of phonics rules, such as when there are two vowels together in a word you sound the first one—as in *rain* or *pain*.

Harm from Overcontrol and Fragmentation

Designers of beginning reading programs can overdo the selection and control of material. In their urge to be consistent and help children avoid too many wild guesses, they go to extremes. How much fragmentation of the process can children profit from without harm to their awareness of related, interacting parts? (20) Overcontrol may, and usually does, sacrifice meaning, interest, and familiarity of language.

Phonics—"A Little Dab Will Do You"

When it comes to phonics in reading instruction, the motto "Just a little dab will do you" seems appropriate. All the terminology in some reading series about long- and short-vowel sounds acts to stand

between children and reading, creating a longer, more tortuous path for them. Teachers do not need linguists who are phoneticians to tell them that in normal rapid discourse there is often little difference between supposedly long-vowel sounds and short-vowel sounds. A teacher knows that instructional reading material (along with its rationale) is out-of-date if it has language such as, "What does the letter say?" Letters do not say anything, no matter how close children put their ears to the page. Phonics works when you already know the word—or at least how likely it is that the word will occur in a given context. Does training of young children that breaks reading tasks down into tiny fragments in the attempt to accelerate skill mastery prove economical or valuable in the long run? This issue is the subject of much argument (1, 2, 21, 22, 23).

Let's examine the argument in the light of long-term consequences because they need to be our prime concern if our rationale is to be child-centered.

Need for Concern with Long-Range Consequences

Some early childhood programs recognize the need to select activity that contributes most to the child's total development. People holding this point of view believe that it is a mistake to attempt to ready the child intensively for learning in specific subject areas stressed in later schooling.

Short-Term Approaches

What are the sources of short-term views? One short-range view comes from the behaviorist school of thought (24). In this view, events outside of children shape their learning. The child, likened to a camera, has a mind filled with blank film, some behaviorists would say. This film takes separate pictures and stores them in memory. There the world imprints itself in the child's mind.

In accordance with this short-range view some programs teach behavior merely for its own sake or as a cultural "must." An example is the extended ritual of mouthing sounds and letter names in beginning reading. This behavior, taught with a short-term view, may attempt to imitate development in reading behavior, but does not actually stimulate it.

Such short-term, imitative behavior lacks the mental process of prediction, connectedness, transfer, and genuine developmental change in reading behavior. Under short-term methods, the child may quickly forget reading knowledge and processes from one day to the next (25, 26).

Short-term methods stop at the decoding of sounds, at the word as the unit of language, and at simple, recall-type questions. That sort of reading is a long way from the fundamental thinking processes of fitting wholes into the extended jigsaw puzzle of related ideas—a long way from reality. Sometimes we box ourselves in with short-term objectives and never get to long-term objectives and goals. We need to ask ourselves, "Does that material sound like language?"

Long-Term Approaches

In contrast, the developmental view emphasizes children's own long-term action. Children construct their own learning gradually. From the inside out children slowly build and modify their knowledge. This gradual change is durable, permanent. Let me use an example from Piaget's work to show what I mean.

Piaget has used a number of tasks with children to examine the depth and the durability of their understanding of a logical process called *conservation*. The idea of conservation is to counterbalance effects of how things look to one in the present by how they looked to one in the past. Aspects such as quality, length, or number are constant in the face of certain transfor-

mations. One task includes the pouring of water from a tall, thin container into a short, flat, one—holding the same volume. When confronted with this demonstration of conservation of liquid, children behave differently at various stages of mental growth.

Children start with a preoperational misconception or bewilderment when confronted with the fact that one container does not hold more than the other. They can repeat and repeat and repeat and still not understand. You can try giving them logical language such as "It's long but narrow or skinnier," and the child will still think "I just don't understand. Where did all that water come from?"

After many experiences and the making of connections between two factors at the same time children finally move to the decisive, matter-of-fact explanation of conservation of liquid. This ability to hold more than one variable in mind at the same time is crucial to reading comprehension. Children in this later stage of thinking even make incredulous responses to adults who are asking stupid questions ("questions that everyone knows answers for") about conservation. Gradually children achieve a dramatic consistent change in their world view—with genuine, long-lasting learning.

People holding to the long-term view of instruction seek this same kind of genuine, long-lasting quality of notions about the processes and concepts of reading (25, 26). The long-term view is a realization that individuals learn "inside-out." Children need to be ready inside before they can achieve honest, long-lasting, and widely applicable learning.

The long-term, developmental view holds that the child's mind is not like a camera, or any other mechanical contrivance. Children's minds are more like those of creative artists. These child artists use their own impulses and inner visions (in combination with materials from the outer world) in active, self-directed creation.

These creations in a child's reading grow to be wholes of interrelating, interacting thoughts about reading processes, strategies, and author's patterns.

The Relatedness of Human Behavior and Long-Term Goals

Another contrast between beginning reading and natural language-learning lies in the whole area of the relatedness of human behavior. This area is important to a rationale for unified reading instruction. This contrast relates to both the "short-term–long-term argument" and the controversy about the breaking apart of language. The behaviorist view tends to separate educational goals into separate boxes or categories. Examples of divisions are reading, written composition, spelling, grammar, usage—various compartmentalized knowledges. These divisions are still further separated from other more affective areas, such as values and social expertise.

The developmental view stresses the relatedness and the interaction among these learnings. Development—emotional, social, and moral—occurs as an inseparable whole. Thus this long-term view holds that education contributes not only to children's cognitive development but also to their social, moral, and aesthetic development. In this view, reading is to be integrated into a large context of varied experiences in art, music, drama, literature, social science, science. Reading is not to be narrowed and isolated, not to be separated from its contexts.

How can teachers bring about this integration? In this developmental view, a reading program might center on broad problems or themes. Content might be organized around themes or topics, for example, how to get along with others or animal problems and adventures. Authors' treatment of these themes can be compared and contrasted.

In summary, we can see a long-term view of integrated development versus a short-term view that relies on imitative behavior. The short-term view seems to say, "Here is a child who is reading, a miniature adult. We ought to make this child more precocious." When it comes to evaluation, short-term methods of reading instruction might appear to produce dramatic progress on specific reading tests, because of the narrow focus of attention. But such "tunnel vision" methods may produce few or no outcomes of any permanence. Such methods will produce little transfer or actual use in life. Developmental, integrative, varied programs that build on children's language and literature make reading instruction more complex for the teacher; but in the long run they make it easier and more rewarding for children.

Conclusions from Comparing Acquisition of Language and Reading

I have recommended careful examination of rationales for reading programs. I have urged reading that has meaning, reading that matters to children. The rationale I am trying to develop would make learning to read easier and more natural for children.

Sometimes reading instruction seems to be unrelated to beliefs about language acquisition. While oral language-learning comes about informally, unconsciously, from a wide range of inviting stimuli, reading instruction typically is formal, programmed, and contains unwelcome, inappropriate, and abstract learning about language. I have given examples of ritualized instruction, such as beginning with letter names, memorizing many phonics generalizations (19, 28, 29, 30).

There are many methods and materials for teaching reading. Some make learning easier, more humane, and more joyous. Ideally speaking, all teachers want the best for their children. One way to get the best is to carefully think through our programs—understanding what we are doing, where we are going and why. I have urged the use of programs that focus on long-term growth, based on knowledge of the development of language and thought, and creative problem-solving (27, 31, 32).

Each child probably has an optimal rate of learning to read and an optimal reading environment—with apparent rewards, appropriate level of abstractness, social interaction, and not too much anxiety. It is doubtful that designers of beginning reading programs can make one product with optimal control of material for most children. But any program can be more natural, more enjoyable, and use more long-term goals—

1. if children's cognitive and motor skills are brought together gradually during the learning of reading
2. if oral language background is recognized as an important link to reading and to writing
3. if language is treated as a complete whole, introduced warmly, enticingly, through children's own dictated stories and literature from gifted artists
4. if more of us treat reading as creative problem-solving and try to understand and attend to some of its developmental attributes
5. if more of us read to one another for joy and talk about reading more in class and out.

Given these developmental conditions, would we not have better listeners, better speakers, better writers—and better readers?

References

1. F. Smith. *Understanding Reading*. New York, New York: Holt, Rinehart and Winston, 1971.
2. F. Smith. *Psycholinguistics and Reading*. New York, New York: Holt, Rinehart and Winston, 1973.
3. F. Smith. *Comprehension and Learning*. New York, New York: Holt, Rinehart and Winston, 1975.
4. E. Gibson and H. Levin. *The Psychology of Reading*. Cambridge, Massachusetts: M.I.T. Press, 1975.
5. R. Wardhaugh. "Theories of Language Acquisition in Relation to Beginning Reading Instruction," *Reading Research Quarterly*, 7 (Fall, 1971), 168–94.
6. S. F. Wanat. "Language Acquisition: Basic Issues," *The Reading Teacher*, 25 (November, 1971), 142–48.
7. J. B. Carroll. "Some Neglected Relationships in Reading and Language Learning," *Elementary English, 43* (October, 1966), 577–82.
8. J. Kagan. "A Developmental Approach to Conceptual Growth," in *Analyses of Concept Learning*. Edited by H. J. Klausmeier and C. W. Harris. New York, New York: Academic Press, 1966.
9. R. V. Allen. *Learning Experience in Reading*. Chicago, Illinois: Encyclopaedia Britannica Education Corporation, 1975.
10. M. Hall. *Teaching Reading as a Language Experience*. Columbus, Ohio: Charles E. Merrill Publishing Company, 1976 (revised edition).
11. M. Hall. *The Language Experience Approach for the Culturally Disadvantaged*. Newark, Delaware: ERIC/CRIER and the International Reading Association, 1972.
12. S. W. Lundsteen. *Children Learn To Communicate: Language Arts through Creative Problem-Solving*. Englewood Cliffs, New Jersey: Prentice-Hall, Inc., 1976.
13. Sir A. Clegg. *Revolution in the British Primary Schools*. Arlington, Virginia: National Association of Elementary School Principals, 1971.
14. R. Brown, C. Cazden, and U. Bellugi. "The Child's Grammar from I to III," in *Minnesota Symposium on Child Psychology*, vol. 2, pp. 28–73. Edited by J. P. Hill, Minneapolis, Minnesota: University of Minnesota Press, 1969.
15. R. Shuy. "What Teachers Should Know about the Language of Children." Paper presented at the Fifth Annual National Conference on the Language Arts in the Elementary School, Chicago, Illinois, April 7, 1973.
16. J. Downing. "The Development of Linguistic Concepts in Children's Thinking,"

Research in the Teaching of English, 4 (Spring, 1970), 5–19.

17. M. D. Vernon. *Backwardness in Reading*. London, England: Cambridge University Press, 1957.

18. L. Vygotsky. *Thought and Language*. Cambridge, Massachusetts: M.I.T. Press, 1962.

19. S. J. Samuels. "Letter-Name Versus Letter-Sound Knowledge in Learning To Read," *The Reading Teacher*, 24 (April, 1971), 604–08, 662.

20. C. McCullough, "A Mess of Pottage," *The Reading Teacher*, 26 (March, 1973), 550–52.

21. R. Strang. "Is It Debate or Is It Confusion?" *The Reading Teacher*, 21 (March, 1968), 575–77.

22. K. S. Goodman. "Decoding—from Code to What?" *Journal of Reading*, 14 (April, 1971), 455–62, 498.

23. Y. Goodman. "Using Children's Miscues for Teaching Reading Strategies," *The Reading Teacher*, 23 (February, 1970), 455–59.

24. A. W. Staats and C. K. Staats. *Language, Learning, and Cognition*. New York, New York: Holt, Rinehart and Winston, 1968.

25. F. J. Di Vesta. "Cognitive Structure, Symbolic Processes and Education." Invited paper presented at the American Educational Research Association annual convention, New Orleans, February, 1973.

26. L. Kohlberg and R. Mayer. "Development as the Aim of Education," *Harvard Educational Review*, 42 (November, 1972), 449–96.

27. W. MacGinitie. "Difficulty with Logical Operations," *The Reading Teacher*, 29, (January, 1976), 371–75.

28. T. Clymer. "The Utility of Phonic Generalizations in the Primary Grades," *The Reading Teacher*, 16 (January, 1963), 252–58.

29. W. D. Page (editor). *Help for the Reading Teacher: New Directions in Research*. Urbana, Illinois: National Conference on Research in English (NCRE)/NCTE/ERIC, 1975.

30. P. Lamb. "How Important Is Instruction in Phonics?" *The Reading Teacher*, 29 (October, 1975), 15–19.

31. S. W. Lundsteen and N. Bernstein-Tarrow. *Guiding Young Children's Learning: A Comprehensive Approach to ECE*. New York, New York: McGraw-Hill (in preparation).

32. W. MacGinitie. *Children's Metalinguistic Concepts and Reading* (ED 078 391). Bethesda, Maryland: ERIC Clearinghouse on Reading and Communication Skills (P. O. Drawer O), (n. d.).

12. Research Update: Listening Comprehension

P. David Pearson and Linda Fielding

Like the television advertisement, we find it ironic that language researchers spend so little time studying a phenomenon that people engage in so many of their waking hours. In surveying a broad range of literature about listening comprehension we concluded the following:

1. The zest for research about how to help students become more effective listeners so characteristic of the fifties and sixties seems to have been quelled in the seventies and early eighties, perhaps because the twin poles of literacy, reading and writing, have dominated our energies.

2. In many instances, when listening comprehension is discussed, it is discussed in relationship to reading comprehension, usually to answer the question, How and when do people become as effective at comprehending the written word as they are at comprehending the spoken word?

3. While listening comprehension is frequently used as an *outcome* measure in

From P. David Pearson and Linda Fielding, Research update: Listening comprehension. *Language Arts*, September 1982, *59*, 617–619. Reprinted by permission of the authors and the National Council of Teachers of English.

psycholinguistic and cognitively-oriented research studies, listening as a phenomenon is incidental to those efforts; instead it is often only a convenient vehicle for evaluating the effects of manipulations in factors like text structure (e.g., story grammar research à la Stein and Glenn 1977; or text analysis à la Meyer 1975), imagery training (e.g., Pressley 1977), sentence combining (e.g., Straw and Schreiner 1982), or mnemonic devices (e.g., Levin, Pressley, McCormick, Miller and Shriberg 1979). This fact about much recent research puts us in an interesting situation: We know, by implication, a lot about what affects listening comprehension, but we do not know much about listening comprehension as a process.

Given this background, we set out to answer four questions about listening comprehension. These questions comprise both the intent and the extent of our review:

1. What is involved in listening comprehension?
2. Can listening comprehension be taught?
3. How does listening comprehension relate to reading comprehension?
4. What affects listening comprehension?

After trying to answer each of these four questions, we will attempt to answer the all-important "so what" question—What does all this mean for the language arts educator who is trying to design curriculum and deliver instruction?

What Is Involved in Listening Comprehension?

It is true, by definition, that you cannot understand auditory messages in a language unless you have some command over key components of that language, namely phonology (sound structure), syntax (sentence structure), semantics (word meanings and the relationships among meanings), and text structure (conven-

tions about how events and assertions in narratives and expositions are typically structured).

At the phonological level, a listener has to be able to distinguish the significant sound "bundles," or phonemes, of the language. For instance, a speaker of English knows that /bat/ differs from /vat/ but a speaker of Spanish along the Rio Grande does not "know" that same distinction. But there are other phonemic requirements essential to competence. The listener has to be sensitive to intonation patterns (rising and falling pitch) that offer cues as to whether the statement is a declaration, question or command, as distinct in examples 1)–3).

1) You are going to buy that new hat.
2) You are going to buy that new hat?
3) You are going to buy that new hat!

The listener also has to be sensitive to variations in stress (loudness) patterns across words because stress patterns tell us what aspect of a sentence to focus upon, as illustrated in 4) and 5).

4) YOU are going to buy that hat?
5) You are going to BUY that new hat?

Notice that in 4) the focus is on *who* is doing the buying (you not someone else), whereas in 5) it is on the action (BUYing as opposed to stealing, we suppose). Finally listeners must be sensitive to the subtle cues that allow them to determine where one word stops and another begins—juncture, we call it—so that they can disambiguate potentially ambiguous strings like 6) and 7):

6) ice cream versus I scream
7) my skis versus mice keys

At the syntactic level, listeners must be able to recognize paraphrase, as in 8) and 9); disambiguate—recognize the two interpretations of—sentences like 10); and recognize cues regarding form class (inflections like -ed or -ing for verbs, -er and -est for adjectives, etc., as well as sentence position cues like subject, verb, and object slots).

    8) John thanked Susan.
    9) Susan was thanked by John.
    10) Mrs. Wilson was cooking.

At the semantic level, the listener needs to know what words mean (a dog is an animal that barks, has a sloppy tongue, and fetches newspapers) and how words relate to one another (dogs are members of the *class* called canines, collies are *examples* of dogs, dogs have *attributes* of barking, sloppy tongues and loyalty, cats and dogs are both pets).

At the text structure level, listeners have to know how things like stories are typically organized in their culture (in Western society characters have problems, goals and conflicts that elicit actions designed to *resolve* problems, overcome the conflicts and achieve the goals).

When listeners can orchestrate all these kinds of knowledge and apply them to achieve a satisfactory interpretation of a text (an interpretation that makes listeners feel like they have experienced "the click of comprehension," i.e., it makes sense to them) we can say that they have experienced listening comprehension.

This primarily linguistic analysis of what must be involved in listening comprehension is not without psycholinguistic support. Various researchers have found that the lack of facility in any one of these components leads to either reduced comprehension or increased processing time. This is true for phonological knowledge (e.g., Melmed 1970), syntactic knowledge (e.g., Gough 1965; Slobin 1966), semantic knowledge (Collins and Quillian 1969; Bransford and Johnson 1972), and text structure knowledge (e.g., Stein and Glenn 1977; Rumelhart 1975). The key to listening comprehension is, of course, the ability to orchestrate all these components simultaneously.

Can Listening Comprehension Be Taught?

By the 1960s researchers had amassed considerable proof that elementary children can improve in listening comprehension through training; research in the seventies added to the evidence. The more difficult questions of what methods work best and what enhances listening comprehension are still being pursued, but there do seem to be some promising directions in the research.

Researchers such as Pratt (1953), Canfield (1961), Trivette (1961), Lundsteen (1963), DeSousa and Cowles (1967), Thorn (1968), the Thompson (Colorado) School District (1970), Kranyik (1972), Morrow (1972), Lemons (1974) and others noted by Early (1960) and Duker (1969) in their respective reviews on listening found that elementary children who received direct training in listening could indeed improve in listening comprehension. The training methods and tests used in these studies generally focused on skills commonly taught in reading comprehension, such as getting the main idea, sequencing, summarizing and remembering facts. The key, though, is that instruction occurred in a listening, *not* in a reading, mode, and that the children were aware that they were receiving listening instruction.

Several experimenters of the seventies tried more specific approaches, with mixed results. On the positive side, Klein and Schwartz (1977) found that second and third grade students trained in either auditory sequential memory *or* sustained attention to a task made significant gains in auditory sequential memory (as measured by following directions to complete a task) over a cognitive enrichment group and a no-treatment control group. Wiedner (1976) noted gains in fourth grade students' listening comprehension scores when the teacher read literature to them for ten minutes every day. On a more negative note, Luderer (1976) found no significant differences between fifth and sixth grade students who received prefatory statements (sort of like advance organizers) before listening to a story and those who did not. Gambrell, Koskinen and Cole (1980) found no effects for induced mental imagery on recall after listening to (or reading) a passage. Fleming (1974) found that auditory high-lighting of the main points of a passage (via voice changes or pauses before main points) had no effect on the listening comprehension of fifth and sixth grade underachievers in reading who learned best through an auditory mode.

A promising approach to assisting listening comprehension seems to lie in combining listening with oral responses from the listeners. Keislar and Stern (1969) found, in a series of studies, that kindergarten children, particularly lower class children, profited from speaking relevant words out loud in programmed instruction designed to teach listening comprehension of information dealing with conceptual rules and subject content (e.g., class inclusion, nature study), but that when more complex thought processes were involved and the spoken responses constituted only part of what was to be assimilated, the training procedure did not help. Glynn and Hartzell (1978) found that second grade students who listened to a speech and then reported on it orally had better recall than a group who listened to the speech and then listened to one of the oral reports of the speech. The researchers suggested that the organizational processes necessary to tell about what was listened to aided the recall. Allison (1971) found that fifth grade students who had listening lessons and then discussed the lessons in small groups with their peers achieved higher listening scores than other groups (those who received no listening instruction, or those who received listening instruction with no reinforcement, with multiple choice tests, or with large group teacher-led discussions). Apparently active

involvement following listening seems to help more than do more passive activities.

A series of studies by Patterson and others (Cosgrove and Patterson 1977*ab*; Massad and Patterson 1978; Patterson, Massad and Cosgrove 1978) focused on referential communication skills in kindergarten and first grade children. They found that listeners performed better in choosing an object being described by a speaker they could not see (a screen separated listener and speaker) when they were given a plan for effective listening which involved asking relevant questions of the speakers as they listened. They speculated that an important listening skill is knowing when and how to request additional information.

Two other studies that deal with improving listening through other areas of the language arts deserve mention. A recent study by Straw and Schreiner (in press) showed that fourth grade students trained in a sentence combining (synthetic) approach to writing performed significantly better on a listening comprehension test (and on one of two reading comprehension tests) than those trained in a sentence reduction or a textbook approach (both analytic) to writing. Kennedy and Weener (1973) found that third grade students below average in reading who received either visual or auditory cloze training improved significantly in listening comprehension.

In summary, the following conclusions about teaching listening comprehension seem warranted. First, listening training in the same skills typically taught in reading comprehension curricula tends to improve listening comprehension. Second, listening comprehension is enhanced by various kinds of active verbal responses on the part of students during and after listening. Third, listening to literature tends to improve listening comprehension. Fourth, certain types of instruction primarily directed toward other areas of the language arts (e.g., writing or reading comprehension) may improve listening comprehension as well. Finally, the direct teaching of listening strategies appears to help children to become more conscious of their listening habits than do more incidental approaches.

Listening Comprehension and Reading Comprehension

We have just presented evidence that listening comprehension (at least the kind required in schools) can be improved through fairly direct instructional strategies that focus on listening strategies that are comparable to those typical of reading comprehension instruction. Yet listening comprehension, thought of as the mundane activity that allows us to communicate with all sorts of people as we march through our daily routines of life, is something that develops quite naturally for most children without any direct attempt on anyone's part to "teach" children how to comprehend.

By contrast, we go to great ends to "teach" children how to comprehend the written word, or, at least, as Durkin (1978–79, 1981) points out, we provide children with innumerable opportunities to practice and learn how to perform various comprehension skills. Part of our zeal for providing so many opportunities for children to practice reading comprehension must stem from our concern that so many children do so poorly on reading comprehension tests (as evidenced by NAEP reports, e.g., 1981). And remember many of these "poor" reading comprehenders must be children who manage to get along quite well in their daily lives, implying, of course, that there must be at least some mismatch between their ability to comprehend the written word versus the spoken word. So it seems useful, in this review, to examine the relative courses of development of listening and reading comprehension. There are two lines of research that are relevant to this comparison. The

first, intensively reviewed by Sticht, Beck, Hauke, Kleiman, and James (1974), focuses upon investigations of the relative advantage accruing to either mode at different age levels. The second involves a linguistic comparison of the tasks that readers versus listeners must engage in in order to make sense of their respective graphic or auditory data displays.

Sticht, et al. reviewed some thirty-one studies that compared reading versus listening comprehension at various grade levels. What they found was that in the elementary grades (one–six), almost all of the comparisons favor the listening comprehension mode. As one moves from grade seven through grade twelve, the proportion of studies showing an advantage to reading comprehension increases, as does the proportion of studies showing no difference between the two modes. These findings are displayed dramatically in Figure 1 (derived from Sticht, et al. 1974, p. 82). Sticht, et al., interpret these data as supporting a definition of "mature" reading as a state in which individuals can read as well as they can listen. They suggest that the extra advantage demonstrated beyond grade eight for reading over listening stems from the fact that the data display for reading is stable and can be reexamined whereas the data display for listening is transitory and not (normally) subject to re-examination. One is tempted, when examining these data, to infer that when decoding skills become automatic, a person can read as well as he or she can listen. However, the data do not allow such an inference since individual measures of decoding competence were not correlated with relative advantages to reading or listening in the studies reviewed by Sticht and his colleagues. Nonetheless, the orderliness of the data reviewed in these analyses does suggest that, in general, reading skills develop at a more accelerated rate than do listening skills up until the point where the two modes of processing become essentially equivalent.

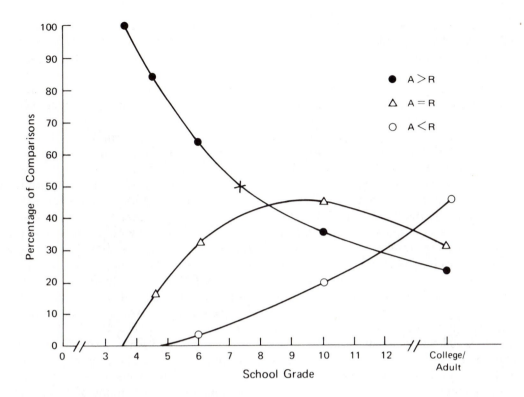

Figure 1. Comparison of Auding and Reading Performance at Five Schooling Levels

Sticht, et al. also reviewed a smaller number of studies that evaluated the transfer of instructional training programs in one modality (mostly listening) to the other modality. Their conclusions are both encouraging and provocative because they suggest that *if* students already had relatively equivalent reading and listening comprehension profiles and *if* the training proved to be effective in the mode in which it was delivered, then it was very likely to transfer to the other mode. They also noted that the intermodal transfer was relatively task-specific; that is, if auditory mode training aided drawing inferences in the auditory mode, then it transferred to drawing inferences in the reading mode but did not transfer, say, to determining sequence in either mode. Sticht, et al. interpret these data as support for a model of languaging which suggests that once lower level reading skills are mastered,

both reading and listening are controlled by the *same* set of cognitive processes (hence the intermodal transfer).

A somewhat different but related perspective comparing listening and reading comprehension is provided by Schreiber (1980), who asks the questions, "What is it that the reader has to learn that happens automatically for the listener?" One might expect Schreiber to answer, "Well, of course, how to recode letters (graphemes) as sounds (phonemes)." While Schreiber does not deny that possibility, he chooses to emphasize other aspects of the auditory message that are not well transmitted in the visual code, namely those aspects of the auditory message that we earlier referred to as stress and pitch, or what many linguistic scholars refer to as "prosodic" features of the auditory message. As we suggested, both of these prosodic features are crucial to comprehension.

Pitch, expressed as intonation patterns, tells us what the speaker wants us to do with his or her message: carry out a command, answer a question, or recognize a fact about the speaker's world. Stress, relative loudness of some words over others, tells us which words (and hence, concepts) the speaker wants us to regard as most important and deserving of our focus.

Neither of these features is well communicated in written language. Punctuation is just not as salient to us as are intonation patterns (besides it comes *after* the sentence), and italics, underlining and quotes are only rarely used to indicate stress. Basically, a reader has to use prior knowledge of the topic of the written text and/or knowledge of sentence structure to *infer* the appropriate prosodic patterns for sentences in a written text. And when a reader is able to make these appropriate inferences, we say that he or she reads with *fluency* or has *good expression* when reading orally.

After discussing these linguistic requirements that are provided for listeners but must be inferred by readers, Schreiber goes on to explain why such seemingly simple-minded instructional strategies like reading along orally with a teacher's model (variously called the impress-method, echo-reading or the oath-of-office approach) or the method of repeated readings (e.g., Samuels 1979; C. Chomsky 1978) seem to result in improved comprehension. They work, according to Schreiber, because they help children determine either what the appropriate prosodic pattern is for a given text and/or because, with lots of practice, they may help children transfer the assignment of appropriate prosody to novel passages. It is precisely because they can assign prosody that they "understand" the passage.

We find Schreiber's analysis fascinating because it suggests that there is something both more subtle and more fundamental than recoding symbols into sounds that readers must learn in order to meet Sticht, et al.'s definition of a mature reader (i.e., one who can read as well as he or she can listen). Schreiber's analysis suggests that what readers must learn to do is to encode "rhythms and melodies" into texts where there is precious little direct evidence concerning what those rhythms and melodies ought to be. Further he implies, when he cites the serendipitous benefits of the overlearning inherent in repeated readings or read-along techniques, that the most efficient route to helping students learn how to do this encoding is to help them learn to rely on their well developed *listening* capabilities to pull their less well developed *reading* capabilities along. This is a case where the reciprocity between language functions is clearly implicated.

The upshot of both these lines of analysis (Sticht, et al. and Schreiber) is that language in all its facets is an integrated phenomenon. Effects in one of its sub-systems will show up in other sub-systems. There appears to be a language comprehension system, of which reading and listening are but complementary facets.

What Affects Listening Comprehension

The decade of the seventies witnessed an explosion of research about the cognitive processes involved in language processes generally and reading comprehension particularly. Beginning with the groundwork of psycholinguists (e.g., Miller 1962; Gough 1965; Slobin 1966), a new branch of psychology, called cognitive psychology, emerged and staked its claim to a study of how the mind encodes, stores, and retrieves (primarily) linguistic information. The pioneering work of people like Sachs (1967) and Bransford and Franks (1971) called into question the behavioristic traditions of an earlier era by rejecting *passive* views of the human information processor as an empty receptacle waiting to be filled by experience in favor of a more *active* processor who guides the search for information from the environment to verify, refine or reconstruct ongoing and ever-changing views about how the linguistic world ought to be organized. In the field of language arts, this more active view is reflected in the work of people like Rosenblatt (1939) in literature and Smith (1971, 1978), Pearson and Johnson (1978) and the Goodmans (K. Goodman 1965; Goodman and Goodman 1979) in reading; more recently, such views have found their way into written composition (e.g., Graves 1978; Flower and Hayes 1981). Ironically, little has been written about listening from this more active cognitive perspective, even though much of the cognitive research supporting this view has been done using listening as the mode through which information has been transmitted to subjects.

For example, much of the work on the development of schemata for stories in children (e.g., the work of Stein and Glenn 1977; Mandler 1978, among others) has been done by having children listen to rather than read stories. Some of the work of Meyer on the influence of text structures in expository prose (e.g., Meyer 1975) has also used listening rather than reading as a mode of input. The intriguing work of Levin and his colleagues (e.g., Levin and Pressley 1981) on the role of pictures and mental imagery training is similarly cast in a predominantly listening rather than reading mode. In fact one of the reasons that cognitive researchers have children listen to rather than read the stories and texts used in their studies is that they do not want differences among students in decoding ability to interfere with their comprehension of these stories and texts. What all this means is that while reading comprehension has been the primary beneficiary of these new cognitive views, we probably have a more substantial basis for applying them to listening comprehen-

sion. It is likely that the reason that people haven't talked much about a revolution in the listening comprehension curriculum (while such rumors of revolution are alive and well in reading and writing) is simply that there really are not very many listening comprehension curricula around.

Nonetheless all the recent talk about active readers who construct a model of meaning for a text (e.g., Collins, Brown and Larkin 1980), all the work on schema theory (e.g., Anderson, Reynolds, Schallert and Goetz 1978) and its application to reading practice (e.g., Pearson and Spiro 1980) should be regarded, if anything, as even more applicable to listening than it is to reading comprehension.

So What?

We begin our implications for practice section with a disclaimer. As researchers, we are tempted to overinterpret and overimply; when we find something that works, we often overstate our case for what it means for practice in our quest not to be perceived as irrelevant. Our disclaimer is this: Just because we can demonstrate that a certain variable (say, a schema for stories) influences comprehension does not mean that teachers should immediately go out and start teaching it (for example, teach kids a schema for stories). It is one thing to be able to demonstrate that students with a better story schema understand stories better than those with a weaker story schema; it is quite another to demonstrate that providing those who are weak with a stronger story schema now comprehend better. And that critical test of determining whether or not instruction helps ought to be a prerequisite to any firm recommendations we make to practitioners. Practitioners, by the way, should require such evidence before they change what they presently do.

Hence we divide our recommendations into two categories; those we feel pretty sure about (because the evidence is in) and those we feel need further testing but are nonetheless worthy of your careful consideration.

The Pretty Sure Recommendations:

1. At almost any age level, students will benefit from direct attempts to improve their ability to perform specific comprehension tasks (e.g., main idea, inference, sequence) in the listening mode. Don't, however, expect much in the way of transfer from one skill to another.

2. After students have become mature readers, then what benefits reading will likely benefit listening comprehension and vice-versa. Prior to that stage, cross-modal transfer is possible but less likely. There is not much reason to believe that there is much transfer between skills even at this more mature level.

The You Ought to Consider Carefully Recommendations:

3. We do not understand why there is so little attention paid to listening comprehension as a matter for a school curriculum when students spend so much time listening. We would like to see more emphasis given to listening comprehension as an entity in its own right. We do not think that what is done ought to be very different from good reading comprehension instruction (see Pearson and Johnson 1978; Goodman and Burke 1979; Pearson 1982 for examples); but we do think it ought to be done more often as a listening activity. Furthermore, if teachers did this, they would be able to work in more advanced content and skills at an earlier age than they can with reading.

4. Helping students learn to read fluently (or with expression) has gotten some pretty bad raps in recent years because

people do not like oral reading. Yet, Schreiber's argument is intriguing, and we'd like to see children get the opportunity to practice reading orally more often so that they can learn how to assign those all important prosodic features to text. In order to do this properly, teachers are going to have to deemphasize accuracy in favor of features like rhythm and melody. So it may not be the kind of oral reading practice we are used to.

5. If we take constructive models of language comprehension seriously, then we have to provide children with many opportunities to "negotiate" a model of meaning for a text with the author of that text. Such practice can proceed just as well in a listening as it can in a reading mode. We can see situations in which teachers work through a story or a text with a group of children. Along the way, the students could *summarize* what it is about so far, discuss things that are *not clear* to them (i.e., monitor for making sense), *predict* what might come next and then continue repeating that cycle. Note that such activities involve verbal response and interaction, which seem to enhance listening comprehension.

There are probably other speculations we could make. But we stop here for fear that we have run out of bridges to help us cross the chasm that sometimes separates research and practice. We end with one conviction: For too long we have neglected listening as a part of our language arts curriculum. Listening is too important a language function to leave to the whims of circumstance; we ought to grant it its rightful place as we plan, implement, and teach the total language arts curriculum.

References

Allison, T. L. "A Comparison of Reinforcement Activities for Listening Comprehension

Skills." Unpublished doctoral dissertation, Syracuse University, 1971. (ED 074 470)

Anderson, R. C.; Reynolds, R. E.; Schallert, D. L.; and Goetz, E. T. "Frameworks for Comprehending Discourse." *American Educational Research Journal* 14 (1977): 367–382.

Bransford, J. and Franks, J. "The Abstraction of Linguistic Ideas." *Cognitive Psychology* 2 (1971): 331–350.

Bransford, J. D. and Johnson, M. K. "Contextual Prerequisites for Understanding: Some Investigations of Comprehension and Recall." *Journal of Verbal Learning and Verbal Behavior* 11 (1972): 717–726.

Canfield, G. R. "How Useful Are Lessons on Listening?" *Elementary School Journal* 62 (1962): 146–151.

Chomsky, C. "When You Still Can't Read in Third Grade: After Decoding, What?" In *What Research Has to Say about Reading Instruction*, edited by S. J. Samuels. Newark, DE: International Reading Association, 1978.

Collins, A. M. and Quillian, M. R. "Retrieval Time from Semantic Memory." *Journal of Verbal Learning and Verbal Behavior* 8 (1969): 240–247.

Cosgrove, J. M. and Patterson, C. J. "Plans and the Development of Referential Communication Skills in Young Listeners." Paper presented at the Annual Meeting of the Society for Research in Child Development, New Orleans, Louisiana, March 1977*a*. (ED 160 196)

Cosgrove, J. M. and Patterson, C. J. "Training Referential Communication Skills: The Relative Effects of Plans and Modeling." Paper presented at the annual meeting of the Eastern Psychological Association, Boston, Massachusetts, April 1977*b*. (ED 146 529)

DeSousa, A. M. and Cowles, M. "An Experimental Study to Determine the Efficacy of Specific Training in Listening." Paper presented at the American Educational Research Convention, February 1967. (ED 016 656)

Duker, S. "Listening." In *Encyclopedia of Educational Research*, 4th ed., edited by R. L. Ebel. London: Collier-Macmillan Ltd., 1969.

Durkin, D. "What Classroom Observations Reveal about Reading Comprehension Instruction." *Reading Research Quarterly* 14 (1978–79): 481–533.

Durkin, D. "Reading Comprehension Instruction in Five Basal Reading Series." *Reading Research Quarterly* 16 (1981): 515–544.

Early, M. J. "Communication Arts." In *Encyclopedia of Educational Research*, 3rd ed., edited by C. W. Harris. New York: Macmillan Co., 1960.

Fleming, J. W. *Auditory Highlighting as a Strategy for Improving Listening Comprehension.* Auditory Learning Monograph Series No. 2, Consortium on Auditory Learning Materials for the Handicapped, East Lansing, Michigan, July 1974. (ED 102 750)

Flower, L. and Hayes, J. R. "The Pregnant Pause: An Inquiry into the Nature of Planning." *Research in the Teaching of English* 15 (1981): 229–243.

Gambrell, L.; Koskinen, P.; and Cole, J. N. "The Effects of Induced Mental Imagery upon Comprehension: A Comparison of Written Versus Oral Presentation." Paper presented at the annual meeting of the National Reading Conference, San Diego, California, December 1980. (ED 198 503)

Glynn, S. M. and Hartzell, L. D. "Children's Retention of Topical and Factual Information Following Oral Report Activities." Paper presented at the annual convention of the Southeastern Psychological Association, Atlanta, Georgia, March 1978. (ED 158 207)

Goodman, K. "A Linguistic Study of Cues and Miscues in Reading." *Elementary English* 42 (1965): 639–643.

Goodman, K. S. and Goodman, Y. M. "Learning to Read Is Natural." In *Theory and Practice of Early Reading*, Vol. 1, edited by L. B. Resnick and P. A. Weaver. Hillsdale, NJ: Erlbaum, 1979.

Goodman, Y. M. and Burke, C. L. *Reading Strategies: Focus on Comprehension.* New York: Holt, Rinehart, & Winston, 1980.

Gough, P. B. "Grammatical Transformations and Speed of Understanding." *Journal of Verbal Learning and Verbal Behavior* 4 (1965): 107–111.

Graves, D. H. "We Won't Let Them Write." *Language Arts* 55 (1978): 635–640.

Keislar, E. R. and Stern, C. *The Value of Spoken Response in Teaching Listening Skills to Young*

Children through Programmed Instruction. Final report. Los Angeles: University of California, January 1969. (ED 027 973)

Kennedy, D. K. and Weener, P. "Visual and Auditory Training with the Cloze Procedure to Improve Reading and Listening Comprehension." *Reading Research Quarterly* 8 (1973): 524–541.

Klein, P. S. and Schwartz, A. A. "Effects of Training Auditory Sequential Memory and Attention on Reading." Unpublished study prepared at Adelphi University, 1977. (ED 159 654)

Kranyik, M. A. "The Construction and Evaluation of Two Methods of Listening Skills Instruction and Their Effects on Listening Comprehension of Children in Grade One." Unpublished doctoral dissertation, Boston University, 1972. (ED 074 486)

Lemons, R. L. "The Effects of Passive Listening upon Reading and Listening Skills of a Group of Black Fourth Graders." Unpublished doctoral dissertation, Syracuse University, 1974. (ED 110 948)

Levin, J. R. and Pressley, M. "Improving Children's Prose Comprehension: Selected Strategies That Seem to Suceed." In *Children's Prose Comprehension: Research and Practice*, edited by C. Santa and B. Hayes. Newark, DE: International Reading Association, 1981.

Levin, J. R.; Pressley, M.; McCormick, C. B.; Miller, G. E.; and Shriberg, L. K. "Assessing the Classroom Potential of the Keyword Method." *Journal of Educational Psychology* 71 (1979): 583–594.

Luderer, E. "The Effects of Prefatory Statements on the Listening Comprehension of Fourth and Fifth Graders." Unpublished master's thesis, Rutgers, The State University of New Jersey, 1976. (ED 127 561)

Lundsteen, S. "Teaching Abilities in Critical Listening in the Fifth and Sixth Grades." Unpublished doctoral dissertation, University of California, Berkeley, 1963.

Mandler, J. M. "A Code in the Node: The Use of a Story Schema in Retrieval." *Discourse Processes* 1 (1978): 14–35.

Massad, C. M. and Patterson, C. J. "Communication among Children: The Role of the Listener." Paper presented at the Biennial Southeastern Conference on Human Development, Atlanta, Georgia, April 1978. (ED 160 196)

Melmed, P. J. "Black English Phonology: The Question of Reading Interference." Unpublished doctoral dissertation, University of California at Berkeley, 1970.

Meyer, B. J. F. *The Organization of Prose and Its Effects on Memory.* Amsterdam: North-Holland Publishing, 1975.

Miller, G. A. "Some Psychological Studies of Grammar." *American Psychologist* 17 (1962): 748–762.

Morrow, E. C. "The Effect of Taped Listening Lessons on the Achievement of First Grade Readers." Unpublished doctoral dissertation, Pennsylvania State University, 1972. (ED 083 559)

National Assessment of Educational Progress. *Three National Assessments of Reading: Changes in Performance, 1979–80.* (Report No. 11–R–01) Education Commission of the States, Denver, 1981.

Patterson, C. J.; Massad, C. M.; and Cosgrove, J. M. "Children's Referential Communication: Components of Plans for Effective Listening." Paper presented at the meeting of the Southwestern Society for Research in Human Development, Dallas, Texas, March 1978. (ED 158 155)

Pearson, P. D. *A Context for Instructional Research on Reading Comprehension* (Tech. Rep. No. 230). Urbana: University of Illinois, Center for the Study of Reading, February 1982.

Pearson, P. D. and Spiro, R. J. "Toward a Theory of Reading Comprehension Research." *Topics in Language Disorders* 1 (1980): 71–88.

Pearson, P. D. and Johnson, D. D. *Teaching Reading Comprehension.* New York: Holt, Rinehart and Winston, 1978.

Pratt, L. E. "Experimental Evaluation of a Program for Improvement of Listening in the Elementary School." Unpublished doctoral dissertation. State University of Iowa. 1953.

Pressley, M. "Imagery and Children's Learning: Putting the Picture in Developmental Perspective." *Review of Educational Research* 47 (1977): 585–622.

Rosenblatt, L. M. *Literature as Exploration*, 3rd ed. New York: Noble and Noble, 1976 (originally published 1939).

Rumelhart, D. E. "Notes on a Schema for Stories." In *Representation and Understanding: Studies in Cognitive Science*, edited by D. G. Bobrow and A. M. Collins. New

York: Academic Press, 1975, 211–236.

Sachs, J. S. "Recognition Memory for Syntactic and Semantic Aspects of Connected Discourse." *Perception and Psychophysics* 2 (1967): 437–442.

Samuels, S. J. "The Method of Repeated Readings." *The Reading Teacher* 32 (1979): 403–408.

Schreiber, P. A. "On the Acquisition of Reading Fluency." *Journal of Reading Behavior* 12 (1980): 177–186.

Slobin, D. T. "Grammatical Transformations and Sentence Comprehension in Childhood and Adulthood." *Journal of Verbal Learning and Verbal Behavior* 5 (1966): 219–227.

Smith, F. *Understanding Reading*. New York: Holt, Rinehart & Winston, 1971.

Smith, F. *Understanding Reading: A Psycholinguistic Analysis of Reading and Learning to Read*, 2nd ed. New York: Holt, Rinehart, and Winston, 1978.

Stein, N. L. and Glenn, G. "A Developmental Study of Children's Construction of Stories." Paper presented at the SRCD meetings, New Orleans, March 17–20. 1977.

Stein, N. and Glenn C. G. "An Analysis of Story Comprehension in Elementary School Children." In *New Directions in Discourse Processing*, edited by R. Freidle. Norwood, NJ: Ablex, 1979.

Sticht, T. G.; Beck, L. J.; Hanke, R. N.; Kleiman, G. M.; and James, J. H. *Auding and Reading: A Developmental Model*. Alexandria, VA: Human Resources Research Organization, 1974.

Straw, S. B. and Schreiner, R. "The Effects of Sentence Manipulation on Subsequent Measures of Reading and Listening Comprehension." *Reading Research Quarterly*, 1982, in press.

Thompson School District, "A Program of Primary Auding Skills: Final Evaluation Report." Loveland, Colorado, 1970. (ED 061 009)

Thorn, E. A. "The Effect of Direct Instruction in Listening on Listening and Reading Comprehension of First Grade Children." *Dissertation Abstracts*, 1968.

Trivette, S. "The Effect of Training in Listening for Specific Purposes." *Journal of Educational Research* 54 (1961); 276–277.

Weidner, M. J. "A Study of the Effects of Teacher Oral Reading of Children's Literature on the Listening and Reading of Grade Four Students." Unpublished doctoral dissertation, Boston University, 1976. (ED 140 246)

13. Integrating Reading and Writing Instruction

Fran Lehr

An impressive body of research supports the existence of a strong interrelationship among the language skills of reading, writing, speaking, and listening. Elementary school teachers are often encouraged to develop language arts programs that take advantage of those interrelationships. In particular, they are urged to explore ways of combining instruction in writing and reading as a means of improving student performance in both areas. However, many teachers are not familiar with the research and are therefore not sure of how best to incorporate the findings into their classrooms. This article provides teachers with a brief review of research concerning

From Fran Lehr, Integrating reading and writing instruction. *The Reading Teacher*, May 1981, 34, 958–966. Reprinted by permission of Fran Lehr and the International Reading Association.

the relationship between reading and writing and of the teaching strategies suggested by that research.

Reading Processes and Writing Processes

Several researchers have pointed out that writing (encoding) and reading (decoding) are related in that both involve the structuring of meaning. Elkind [ED 124 919] notes this relationship and argues that the more opportunities children have to experience the satisfaction and the trials of structuring their own writing, the better prepared they will be for interpreting the structures of others.

In a similar vein, Ribovich [ED 141 786] suggests that allowing children to manipulate through writing the structures of discourse leads them to a greater understanding of the ways in which authors structure their ideas to make it easier for readers to understand their meanings. She proposes a sequence of writing assignments beginning with exercises designed to increase children's awareness of how idea relationships are achieved in sentences. The teacher should first present children with model sentences and then have them construct their own involving such relationships as description, comparison/contrast, cause/effect, time sequence, spatial sequence, and problem solving. Once they have mastered this form, the children can move on to structuring the same ideas in paragraph form. At this stage, Ribovich points out, students begin to develop an awareness of topic sentence and supportive details, as well as use of descriptive devices and examples. Paragraph structuring, she argues, soon leads to the structuring of much longer passages and the use of transition words, headings and subheadings, and introductory and summary statements. She concludes that providing students with occasions to structure ideas through writing will help them to become

aware of what idea structuring really is thereby leading them to become more proficient readers.

Sentence Combining

Sentence combining, the act of combining several short sentences that have been derived by transformational analysis from longer ones, is best known as a technique for improving writing skills. Recent research, however, reveals that it may also be useful in developing reading comprehension.

Hughes [ED 112 421] investigated the assumption that there is a direct relationship between students' reading scores and their levels of syntactic maturity. In her study, 24 seventh grade students spent 10 to 13 weeks either in an experimental group in which they received writing exercises based on sentence combining or in a control group in which they engaged in a number of language arts activities but had no exposure to sentence combining. The results showed a close link between a student's reading level and syntactic maturity level. In addition, the reading performance of the experimental group improved significantly in the use of grammatical relations and in integration of syntactic and semantic cues.

Klein [ED 186 845] notes that the mental activity involved in sentence combining is central to both language production and language analysis. He points out that the manipulation of sentence structure and of content in sentence combining engages the participant in the internal workings of the sentence—an act essential to comprehension.

Recognizing the paucity of commercially produced sentence-combining materials available to teachers, Klein has devised guidelines to help educators produce their own materials. Among his suggestions are: (1) Start with a sensible sentence appropriate in grammatical and content complexity to the age and the ability of the intended user, then break it into its various parts; (2) design sentence combining sets in clusters so that the final product is a paragraph that, when linked with others, produces a story; (3) build exercises around various themes; (4) use the exercises sparingly so that students will not tire of them, and (5) use the exercises in a variety of instructional settings.

Writing Miscues and Reading Miscues

To better understand how children process written language both in reading and writing, Ney [ED 161 009] compared the reading and writing miscues of fourth grade students. He found a high correlation between phonological pronunciation miscues in reading and spelling miscues in writing. He also found that lexical/syntactic/semantic miscues in reading and similar miscues in writing showed distinctly different patterns: The miscues of addition and subtraction were more frequently found in reading and the miscues of omission were more frequently found in writing. From this, he deduced that the language processing skills for reading and writing are different, but that the instructional process should be similar for both. Reading and writing, he contends, should be taught as mirror images of the same process and students should be instructed in the differences between the two processes, as well as the similarities, so that their skills are enhanced. He suggests devising reading and writing strategy lessons on the basis of miscue records of readers and notes that lessons could be developed for groups of students who have similar miscue records.

Language Skills

Evanechko, Ollila, and Armstrong [EJ 115 739] used measures of reading achievement and of syntactic complexity in their investigation into the relationship between sixth grade students' reading and writing performance. They devised an experimental formula for indexing children's written language in order to identify as specifically as possible the language competencies underlying reading behavior and found a significant correlation between reading and writing performance. They discovered a higher degree of relationship between language measures and reading measures than among language measures alone—suggesting that the language indices measured different skills and that there was a strong interaction between reading and writing. Their findings indicate that reading and writing use certain skills in common and that the presence of those skills should result in better performance in both areas. Of the language behaviors indexed, fluency of language appeared to be the single most important factor in reading success, followed by competency in the use of a variety of structures leading to greater syntactic complexity. They concluded that learning activities that lead to the development and reinforcement of these two competencies would also improve reading performance and suggest the development of fluency and control of syntactic complexity in oral language as a first step.

The language experience approach (LEA) is one technique for achieving this goal. This approach integrates the teaching of listening, speaking, reading, and writing. As described by Allen [ED 034 571], LEA involves allowing students to talk about topics of interest, discuss those topics with others, listen to the language of many authors, dictate their own stories or poems to teachers or other adults, tell stories, explore writing as a recreational activity, write their own books, and relate reading to speaking and writing through hearing their own stories read aloud.

Specific LEA activities have been devised by the Wisconsin Writing Project [Smelstor, ED 179 969]. They include the writing or making of books based on students' own experiences, patterned after a model book, or written for a specific audience (a book on pet care to be placed in the waiting room of a veterinary hospital, for example). Another suggested activity is the creation of "wordless" books in which children use their imaginations to develop stories to go along with pictures arranged in a book.

By familiarizing themselves with research findings in reading and writing instruction, teachers will be able to devise more effective instructional techniques for integrating the two activities into their language arts programs. Current research reports are added regularly to the ERIC system and may be found by searching *Resources In Education* (*RIE*) and *Current Index to Journals in Education* (*CIJE*) under the headings "Reading Instruction" and "Writing Instruction."

References

Allen, Roach Van. "Language Experiences Which Promote Reading." Paper presented at the Early Childhood Lecture Series, Ypsilanti, Mich., 1969. 16 pp. [ED 034 571]

Elkind, David, "Cognitive Development and Reading." In *Theoretical Models and Processes of Reading*, 2nd edition, edited by Harry Singer and Robert B. Ruddell, pp. 331–40.

Newark, Del.: International Reading Association, 1976. [ED 124 919]

Evanechko, Peter, Lloyd Ollila, and Robert Armstrong. "An Investigation of the Relationships between Children's Performance in Written Language and Their Reading Ability." *Research in the Teaching of English*, vol. 8 (Winter 1974), pp. 315–25. [EJ 115 739]

Hughes, Theone O. "Sentence Combining: A Means of Increasing Reading Comprehension." Kalamazoo, Mich.: Western Michigan University, 1975. 73 pp. [ED 112 421]

Klein, Marvin. "The Development and Use of Sentence Combining in the Reading Program." Paper presented at the International Reading Association 25th annual convention, St. Louis, Mo., 1980. 32 pp. [ED 186 845]

Ney, James A. "Comparison of Reading Miscues and Writing Miscues." Tempe, Ariz.: Arizona State University, 1975. 32 pp. [ED 161 009]

Ribovich, Jerilyn K. "Developing Comprehension of Content Material through Strategies Other Than Questioning." Speech given at the International Reading Association 22nd annual convention, Miami Beach, Fla., 1977. 15 pp. [ED 141 786]

Smelstor, Marjorie, editor. *A Guide to the Relationship between Reading and Writing*. Madison, Wisc.: University of Wisconsin, 1979. 51 pp. [ED 179 969]

CHAPTER IV

Reading Readiness and Prereading Development

The prevailing point of view about reading readiness has shifted away from passively waiting for readiness to become evident, to active efforts to develop readiness and provide a successful early introduction to reading

Roettger opens Chapter 4 with a review of the effects of Head Start and other early intervention programs. Next, Durkin summarizes her own efforts, and those of others, to teach reading to preschool children, and cautions against drill-type reading instruction in kindergarten. MacGinitie answers the question, when should we begin to teach reading, by pointing out the many variables that influence the answer. Pikulski disparages the use of reading readiness tests and advocates an informal reading program in kindergarten, with children who do not catch on having a chance to start over again in first grade. In the final selection, McDonell and Osburn explain Clay's analysis of the language and visual concepts that beginning readers need to master.

14. Effects of Early Intervention Programs

Doris Roettger

During the past decade, we have seen increased emphasis on early childhood education in the United States. It has become axiomatic that the early years in a child's life are a critical period of growth that determines the potential for future development. According to Hunt (9), children's encounters with their environment during this period should be regulated to achieve a faster rate of intellectual development and a higher level of intellectual capacity. Bloom (3) has suggested that 50 percent of the intelligence measured at the age of seventeen was developed by the age of four and another 30 percent by the age of eight. This emphasis on the critical role of early experiences has contributed significantly to the movement toward early intervention.

Since the early 1960s, much concern has been directed toward the educational performance of minority and lower-class

From Doris Roettger, Effects of early intervention programs. In John Merritt (Ed.), *New horizons in reading.* Newark, Del.: International Reading Association, 1976. Pp. 464–471. Reprinted by permission of Doris Roettger and the International Reading Association.

children. Coleman (4) found that, as early as first grade, children from low socio-economic backgrounds scored significantly lower on most measures of school achievement than children from higher socioeconomic backgrounds. He observed that this gap widened as children moved through the grades. There is a consensus that failure is almost inevitable for the many children who come to school poorly prepared because of their impoverished environment.

Much attention has been focused on language deprivation. Deutsch (5) observed that children of low socioeconomic groups lack the knowledge of context and of syntactical regularities which lead to comprehension of language sequences. Bereiter and Engelman (1) concluded that disadvantaged children master language which is adequate for maintaining social relationships and which are satisfactory for meeting their social and material needs; however, they do not master the cognitive uses of language. What is lacking is use of language used in school to explain, to describe, to inquire, to analyze, and to compare. One of the special weaknesses in language development of lower-class children is the tendency to treat sentences as a "giant word" which cannot be taken apart and recombined. A second weakness, which may be an outgrowth of the first, is the lack of use of structure words. The prevalence of this so-called language deficiency has become one of the bases for large scale intervention programs.

In this discussion of the effects of early intervention programs, the central question is: "Can early intervention counteract the effects of deprivation?" In answering this question, other questions must be asked. "Is incidental learning or direct instruction more effective?" "Should emphasis be on cognitive learning or should attention be given to the development of the whole child?" "Should parents be involved in early intervention programs?" Early intervention programs have

become varied and sometimes confusing. It's almost like Alice's response when the caterpillar asked, "Who are you?" Said Alice, "I hardly know sir, just at present. At least I know who I was when I got up this morning, but I think I must have been changed several times since then."

In this paper I will describe various curriculum models for early intervention programs, identify the critical variations among them, and assess their effectiveness. Most preschools can be placed into one of the following categories: structured cognitive, programed or academic skills model, structured environment, and child-centered.

Structured Cognitive Programs

In the structured cognitive programs, the structure is derived from the programs' clearly stated goals for specific cognitive and language development (17). The curriculum focuses on the underlying processes of thinking and emphasizes that learning results from direct experience and action by the child. The teacher has clear guidelines of how the program is to be organized. Teacher planned situations or activities focus on improving oral language abilities, memory, concept formation, and problem solving.

One of the earliest structured cognitive programs was the Early Training Project conducted by Gray and Klaus (6, 7). They attempted to offset progressive retardation of black children living in deprived circumstances. Their intention was to make the intervention developmental rather than remedial. The criteria for judging the effectiveness of the program were performance scores on intelligence tests and reading achievement tests. The experimenters set up four groups of children: two experimental groups and two control groups. One experimental group had three summers of preschool and a second group had two summers of preschool. The summer activities were planned around two categories of variables: *attitudes* relating to achievement (achievement motivation, persistence, interest in school-type activities) and *aptitudes* relating to achievement (perceptual development and the development of concepts and language). Between the summer sessions, a project teacher visited weekly the homes of both groups. One of the purposes of the visits was to involve mother and child in activities similar to those of the summer. The control groups consisted of a local group and a group in a nearby community. Both groups took all the tests but had no intervention program.

Three years after the end of intervention, the two experimental groups remained significantly superior to the two control groups in their performance on the Stanford Binet intelligence test. At the end of first grade, the experimental children scored significantly higher than the control children on the three reading subtests of the Metropolitan Achievement Test, and at the end of second grade they were significantly superior on the word knowledge and reading subtests. While there was no significant difference between the experimental and control groups at the end of fourth grade, there was a suggestion of residual effect, since in six of seven comparisons the experimental group was superior. It is a remarkable achievement to have maintained an impact on the intellectual development through the seventh year of a study and four years after formal intervention.

In the Ypsilanti Early Education Project, three- and four-year-old children attended a Piagetian cognitively oriented preschool for two years (11, 17). Verbal stimulation and interaction, sociodramatic play, and the learning of concepts were considered more important than social behavior and other concerns of traditional nursery school programs. The families of these children received weekly home visits. Parents were encouraged to participate in the instruction of their children and to attend group meetings. A control group received no special educational services. At the beginning of the program there was no significant difference on the Stanford Binet between the experimental and control groups. When retested at the end of kindergarten, the experimental group scored significantly higher, but by the end of first grade the scores of the two groups were essentially the same. However, the experimental group scored higher than the control group on the California Achievement Test at the end of the second and third grades. In addition, elementary teachers rated the experimental group higher than the control group in academic, social, and emotional development.

Programed Academic Skills Programs

A more rigidly structured type of program is the programed or the academic skills model. The most widely used program of this type is that developed by Bereiter and Engelman (1), which is based on the premise that culturally deprived children need direct training to overcome their backwardness in skills necessary for later academic success. The area of greatest deficiency is their use of formal language. The teacher directs all activities and the children participate in highly structured, prescribed activities.

Structured Environment Programs

A third approach to intervention is a structured environment best exemplified by a Montessori curriculum. The program stresses that "children must be in touch with reality through manual activity" (15). It provides the children with self-directed and self-selected cognitive activities. Control comes from the organization of the environment rather than from the teacher as in a structured cognitive approach. The teacher is a moderator between children and materials. Kohlberg (13) found a significant increase in IQ scores in a year-long intervention program using a Montessori curriculum.

Child Centered Programs

The bulk of traditional preschool programs found on college campuses and in Headstart projects are child centered. These curricula tend to focus on the development of the whole child. The hallmark of a child centered curriculum is an open classroom where children are encouraged to express their interests and help create their own environments. The teacher capitalizes on informal experiences for learning. Considerable attention is given to social adjustment and emotional development through imitation of adult roles (17).

Evaluation studies of preschool intervention programs have primarily compared a single program with a control group which has not been involved in the program. Such studies, even when they are adequately designed, allow only the most tenuous comparisons between programs because each program is evaluated by a different experiment and conducted in a different location with a different population and with different examiners. There have been a few long ranged studies which compared different types of preschool programs using experimental procedures designed to maximize comparability of results.

Comparisons of Different Kinds of Programs

The Ypsilanti Preschool Curriculum Demonstration Project was established to study the effectiveness of three different kinds of programs (17). The programs selected were a cognitively oriented Piagetian program, a language training program following the Bereiter and Engelman Curriculum, and a unit based curriculum which emphasized social-emotional goals. After the first year, the initial findings indicated no significant differences among the three curricula on almost all measures. These measures included the Stanford Binet, classroom observations, and ratings of children by teachers and independent examiners. At the end of the second year, the results were almost the same. By the third year of the study, while there were no significant differences, the unit-based program was not matching the record it had established during the first year. This was especially true on the Stanford-Binet, which was the cognitive measure.

Karnes (12) compared the Karnes' Ameliorative program, which was a structured cognitive program, with a Bereiter-Engelman program and a traditional program with an emphasis on language development. The participants were all lower-class children. In addition, a traditional program with emphasis on psychosocial development was compared with a traditional Montessori program. The performance of the children in the Ameliorative and in the Bereiter-Engelman program was significantly better than the performance of the children in the two traditional programs and the Montessori group on the Stanford-Binet, ITPA, and Metropolitan Readiness Test. A more recent review by Bissell (2) of cognitive structured, academic skills and child-centered curricula reaches the same conclusion. Preschool programs with specific emphasis on language development and with teacher-directed strategies that provide structured activities fostering cognitive growth are more effective in producing cognitive gains for disadvantaged children than are programs lacking these characteristics.

Now let us turn our attention to Project Head Start, a major government effort to provide comprehensive intervention for preschool children. Head Start sought to bring about "greater social competence" in disadvantaged children (18). Parents and community members have been involved in planning and evaluation, and they are used as aides and volunteers. Focusing on the development of the whole child, Head Start has attempted to enhance a child's physical well being, his self-concept, his motivation, and his emotional and intellectual development.

Within federal guidelines, each Head Start site has established its own program. Many projects have adopted a traditional nursery school approach, emphasizing positive self-concept and social interaction. However, many reflect considerable preoccupation with school readiness, emphasizing that a child be able to speak in sentences, name colors, know his address, and sort shapes.

Standardized measures of performance such as IQ scores, achievement tests, and checklists of skills have been widely used by local sites for assessing the effectiveness of Head Start programs. However, evaluating the effect of the total program nationally has been difficult because of the wide variance in objectives, program delineation, and evaluation procedures.

Currently, the Educational Testing Service is conducting a longitudinal evaluation of Head Start children (16). The study is attempting to answer two questions: What are the components of early education that are associated with cognitive, personal, and social development of disadvantaged children? and What are the environmental and background variables that moderate these associations? The population was identified prior to the collection of data and is drawn nationally from four dispersed geographic regions. Information is being gathered on the family, teacher, classroom, community, and child. The emphasis is on the parent/child and teacher/child interactions, models of information processing, influence techniques, and reinforcement strategies. The ETS study will follow the same children for five years to determine the degree to which primary grade curricula are congruent with, and capitalize on, what the child has learned in Head Start. The first group of children were in Head Start in 1969–1970. The final testing should have

been completed in the spring of 1974.

The preliminary findings are that 75 percent of the children eligible for Head Start attended. It was also determined that these children performed significantly less well on a variety of cognitive tasks than those children who attended other preschools or no known preschool prior to their enrollment in Head Start. The findings also indicated that at the age of four the affective domain may not be highly differentiated. There is, however, strong evidence for differentiated personal-social characteristics. An important finding was that there was a range of variation in performance. Children from low income families exhibited a wide range of cognitive, personal-social, and perceptual functioning.

In summarizing the studies, questions must be asked in assessing early intervention programs: Does intervention contribute to success in school? How lasting are the results?

The studies discussed indicate that it is essential that goals and objectives be specifically defined for intervention programs and that day-to-day activities be centered on objectives. Evidence cited suggests that structured programs (as opposed to a traditional environmental approach) can produce significant gains through the third grade.

Within specific programs, instructional procedures must be adapted to the needs of individual children. Programs must recognize the differences between children who make progress and those who do not. Attention should be directed to specific characteristics of programs, to the children participating in them, and the interaction of the two. Hunt (10) describes this as a proper match between a child's cognitive development level and specific learning tasks.

All too often, early intervention programs have been inadequately evaluated. Although they are part of a major federal effort, many Head Start programs have been poorly evaluated at the local level. Evaluation frequently has had a low priority at local sites, and the instruments used have had low predictive validity (8). While each year's group is evaluated, few long term studies have followed children through the grades as a basis for making necessary modifications in the programs.

IQ scores have been used frequently as a criterion for assessing the effectiveness of intervention. This appears to be inadequate. Lucco (14) suggests that upward shifts in IQ performance do not necessarily reflect the cognitive development required for abstract thinking.

Other aspects of early intervention programs may be questioned. Programs seem to be designed to prepare children for success in schools as they now exist. It seems unrealistic to expect gains to be maintained unless necessary adjustments are made in the curricula of elementary schools.

In addition, children from birth through five years of age will spend a relatively small amount of time in intervention programs. Thus, these programs in themselves cannot totally offset the results of deprivation. Parents must become involved to change the home environment of the child.

The past decade has seen the emergence of early intervention programs on a wide scale. The challenge of the coming decade is the refinement of these programs on the basis of the results of evaluation.

References

1. Bereiter, Carl, and Siegfried Engelman. *Teaching Disadvantaged Children in the Preschool*. Englewood Cliffs, New Jersey: Prentice-Hall, 1966.
2. Bissell, Joan. "Effects of Preschool Programs for Disadvantaged Children," in Joe Frost (Ed.), *Revisiting Early Childhood Education*. New York: Holt, Rinehart and Winston, 1973, 223–239.
3. Bloom, B. S. *Stability and Change in Human Characteristics*. New York: Wiley, 1964.
4. Coleman, J. S. *Equality of Educational Opportunity*. Washington, D. C.: Office of Education, 1966.
5. Deutsch, Martin, et al. *The Disadvantaged Child*. New York: Basic Books, 1967.
6. Gray, S. W., and R. A. Klaus. "An Experimental Preschool Program for Culturally Deprived Children," *Child Development*, 36 (December 1965), 887–898.
7. Gray, S. W., and R. A. Klaus. "The Early Training Project: A Seventh Year Report," *Child Development*, 41 (December 1970), 909–924.
8. Hoepfner, Ralph, Carolyn Stern, and Susan Nummedal. *CSE-ECRC Preschool/Kindergarten Test Evaluations*. Los Angeles, California: UCLA Graduate School of Education, 1971.
9. Hunt, J. McV. *Intelligence and Experience*. New York: Ronald Press, 1961.
10. Hunt, J. McV. "The Psychological Basis for Using Preschool Enrichment as an Antidote for Cultural Deprivation," *Merrill-Palmer Quarterly*, 10 (July 1964), 209–248.
11. Kamii, Constance, "A Sketch of the Piaget Deprived Preschool Curriculum Developed by the Ypsilanti Early Education Program," in Joe Frost (Ed.), *Revisiting Early Childhood Education*. New York: Holt, Rinehart and Winston, 1973, 150–165.
12. Karnes, M. B., A. S. Hodgins, and J. A. Teska. "An Evaluation of Two Preschool Programs for Disadvantaged Children: A Traditional and Highly Structured Experimental Preschool," *Exceptional Children*, 34 (May 1968), 667–676.
13. Kohlberg, L. "Montessori with the Culturally Disadvantaged," in R. D. Hess and R. M. Bear (Eds.), *Current Theory, Research, and Action*. Chicago: Aldine, 1968, 105–115.
14. Lucco, Alfred A. "Cognitive Development After Age Five: A Future Factor in the Failure of Early Intervention with the Urban Child," *American Journal of Orthopsychiatry*, 42 (October 1972), 847–856.
15. Orem, R. (Ed.). *A Montessori Handbook*. New York: Capricorn Books, 1966.
16. Shipman, Virginia. "Disadvantaged Children and Their First School Experiences," in Julian Stanley (Ed.), *Compensatory*

Education for Children, Ages 2 to 8. Balti-more, Maryland: Johns Hopkins University Press, 1972, 22–66.

17. Weikart, David. "Relationship of Curriculum, Teaching, and Learning in Preschool

Education," in J. C. Stanley (Ed.), *Preschool Programs for the Disadvantaged.*

18. Zigler, Edward F. "Project Headstart: Success or Failure?" *Children Today*, 2 (November-December 1972), 2–7, 36.

15. Facts about Pre-First Grade Reading

Dolores Durkin

In 1958, it was my privilege to begin a study of children who had learned to read at home prior to entering first grade (5). At that time, reading for children younger than six was hardly being encouraged. Instead, both professional educators and society as a whole openly frowned upon this type of precociousness and predicted nothing but problems for early readers once school instruction began. Some soothsayers added to the gloom by claiming that, even if problems were avoided, the earlier learning would have no positive payoff in the future. Children who begin to read before their classmates, it was maintained, would not excel in ability in later years.

Although neither prediction was bolstered by research data, the correctness of both was taken for granted. One consequence was frequent warnings to parents *not* to teach their preschoolers to read; another was school policies that explicitly forbade reading instruction during kindergarten.

Research with Early Readers

Within such a setting, it was not surprising as I began my first study of early readers to find parents who came close to apologizing for their children's accomplish-

ments. Nor was it surprising to hear them communicate concern via questions like, "Do you think she'll be bored in first grade?" "Should I have ignored his questions about words?" "Will she be confused when they start teaching reading in first grade?"

While parent attitudes and worries were predictable, given the beliefs of the times, the details of how their children had learned to read at home were not. Prior research was nonexistent; consequently, it was anyone's guess as to how the children did, in fact, learn. Because what was uncovered in the first study was duplicated in a second (5), a brief summary of some characteristics of the home learning seems warranted.

Characteristics of Early Reading

One characteristic was that the age of four was a common time for an interest in written language to show itself. Frequently, the interest was displayed by children through questions like, "What does that sign say?" or "Where does it say that?" At other times, interest became visible through an expressed desire to learn to print. Requests and questions such as "Make me my name" and "How do you make a *b*?" were common.

From Dolores Durkin, Facts about pre-first grade reading. In Lloyd O. Ollila (Ed.), *The kindergarten child and reading*. Newark, Del.: International Reading Association, 1977. Pp. 1–12. Reprinted by permission of Dolores Durkin and the International Reading Association.

Also common was a home in which people read. Without exception, all the early readers in both studies had been read to regularly, a practice that sometimes began at a very early age. In addition, at least one parent was described, if not as an avid reader, at least as a frequent reader.

Parents of early readers also turned out to be people who enjoyed their young children; who frequently took them places; and who then spent time discussing what had been seen, answering questions, and stimulating still more. Thus, both oral and written language were common features of the lives of the early readers.

Deliberate attempts on the part of parents to teach their preschoolers to read were uncommon. Instead, the help given tended to be a response to children's questions and requests. If there were any "instructional materials," they were pencils and paper and the small chalk-boards found in almost every early reader's home. Also influential was whatever had been read to the children—trade books, encyclopedia articles, comics, and so on. Other materials that aroused curiosity about written language included: words and numbers found on everyday things such as calendars; television commercials and weather reports; newspaper headlines; menus; directions for playing games; and labels on canned goods, packages, and boxes.

Whenever instruction that was school-like in character entered into research responses from parents, it was mentioned in connection with an older sibling who had played school with a younger child. As the data eventually showed, playing school was a frequent source of help with reading and writing whenever there was a female sibling who was approximately two years older than the child who was the early reader. When the older child taught school at home, parents said her behavior seemed to be an imitation of what was happening in her own classroom. Consequently, as she changed classrooms and teachers, the school at home changed accordingly.

As all these findings point up, the two studies of early readers indicated that a "language arts approach" was an apt description of the instructional program that took place in the homes. Stimulating growth in both oral and written language abilities were various combinations of 1) interesting experiences; 2) opportunities to discuss and ask questions; 3) availability of one or more persons to respond to questions and requests related to reading, writing, and spelling; 4) availability of materials for writing; 5) positive contacts with books and reading; and 6) displays of written words and numbers that related to the children's interests (birthdays, television programs, games).

Since it appeared that the children had *enjoyed* becoming readers and writers, and since the data collected over a six-year period showed anything but negative effects for achievement in reading (5), subsequent plans were made to develop a two-year language arts program that would begin with groups of four-year-olds (7, 9). The objective of the experiment was to assemble a curriculum that would closely match the language arts "program" in the homes of early readers. The hope was for new insights about better ways for teaching beginning reading in school (8).

Meanwhile, it is appropriate to ask. "What was happening nationally insofar as the timing of school instruction in reading was concerned?"

National Developments

For a while, most schools were untouched by rather dramatic developments that became highly visible in the early 1960s. Policies governing school practices still supported not only the no reading dictum for kindergartens but also a readiness rather than a reading program for the start of first grade. In time, however, most schools began to feel and show the effects of changing expectations for young children.

Impetus for this change had its roots in the educational revolution that quickly followed the launching of the satellite Sputnik by the Russians in October 1957. Soon afterwards, an atmosphere took hold that was characterized by the demands, "Let's teach more in our schools, and let's teach it earlier!" Fostered by what must have been a national inferiority complex, rapt attention soon went to proposals from psychologists that highlighted both the learning potential of young children and the unique importance of the early years for their intellectual development.

One of the most frequently quoted psychologists, Jerome Bruner, offered his proposals in *The Process of Education*, a brief and easily read book based on a ten-day meeting convened in 1959 by the National Academy of Sciences. Included was a chapter entitled "Readiness for Learning," which Bruner introduced by stating: "We begin with the hypothesis that any subject can be taught effectively in some intellectually honest form to any child at any stage of development" (3:33). Those who took the time to read all of Bruner's book would have found little that was startling in his statement; it was simply urging schools to take another look at how they organized instruction in fields like science and mathematics. However, when the statement was quoted out of context—and it often was—it encouraged what could only be called wishful thinking about the learning potential of young children.

A publication that continued to encourage the wishing was Hunt's *Intelligence and Experience* (12), published in 1961. Unlike Bruner's book, this was a highly technical treatise in which Hunt reexamined and reinterpreted findings from a huge number of earlier studies, many dealing with animal learning. As a result of the reexamination, he proposed certain hypotheses about young children, all of which assigned special importance for intellectual development to the early years. Though offering only hypotheses to be tested, not facts to be implemented, Hunt's text was frequently referred to as providing support for "Let's teach more, and let's teach it sooner."

One other book merits attention in this discussion because it, too, exerted widespread influence on educators' notions about young children and what could be done to realize their potential. I refer to Bloom's *Stability and Change in Human Characteristics* (2), published in 1964. Like Hunt's work, Bloom's was a technical and detailed reexamination of earlier research—in this case, longitudinal studies of certain measurable characteristics that included intelligence. Concluding that the most rapid period for the development of intelligence is in the first five years of life, Bloom's book further reinforced the special importance being assigned to a child's early environment, in particular to the stimulation and learning opportunities it could and should provide.

Other National Developments

Not to be overlooked in the developments that took place in the 1960s was the new interest being shown for an age old problem: children from the lowest socioeconomic levels who start school with disadvantages that preclude adequate achievement. This concern became vocal at this period of time due to factors that were political, social, and economic in nature. Why the concern resulted in Head Start classes for young children of the poor is clearly linked to the climate of hope that had been engendered by the writings of individuals like Bruner, Hunt, and Bloom.

Although Head Start programs should have been carefully preplanned, too much pressure in the form of federal funds and political interests led to quickly organized classes that were very similar to traditional nursery schools. Some teachers did give more than the usual amount of attention to language development; others worked hard at raising the children's scores on intelligence tests. In the main, however, efforts were rare to accumulate findings about the children and the curriculum, and to coordinate Head Start programs with kindergarten and first grade classes. One result is that less knowledge about early childhood education accumulated than would have been the case had important questions been asked and better studies been done to answer them.

Unfortunately, what has to be said about Head Start is very much like what must be said now about developments specifically related to young children and reading. Let me explain.

Developments Related to Young Children and Reading

Even though the excited talk by psychologists and politicians about the unique importance of the pre-first grade years never reflected verified facts, it naturally prompted some questions about school policies that were postponing reading instruction beyond the start of the first grade. Having learned from my research that children as young as three and four can enjoy becoming readers, I was of the opinion that the questioning was all to the good. I even went so far as to envisage classrooms in which young children would be given interesting and personalized opportunities to begin reading and writing, which would avoid both frustration and boredom. Now, however, that thinking also seems wishful for, over the years, questionable practices dealing with reading have become a part of school programs for young children. Why? Do research data support practices like whole class drill on phonics for kindergarteners or, for example, a common use of workbooks and worksheets?

As it happens, research data are able to say very little about pre-first graders and reading because, first, not many stud-

ies have been carried out and, second, what has been done is anything but flawless.

Elsewhere I have reviewed in some detail both the studies and the technical reasons why the findings are open to question (9). Here, let me just quickly describe research reported in the 1960s and 1970s that focused on school instruction in reading that was initiated before the first grade. This will be done in order to demonstrate how little is known about earlier reading, including its effects upon later achievement.

Research on Earlier Starts in Reading

One of the first publicized efforts to teach reading to pre-first graders was carried out with computerized typewriters by a sociologist named O. K. Moore. Although his work with a small number of children received both immediate and dramatic attention in magazines like *Harper's* and *Time* (10, 17), Moore never published any detailed account of the research. Expectedly, subsequent use of his "$35,000 talking machine" was limited by its cost.

The earliest work with pre-first grade instruction on a schoolwide basis was done in Denver. Begun in the fall of 1960, this research can now be said to be typical of what has been reported in that no new methodology or materials were introduced. Instead, kindergarten teachers used readiness and easy reading materials from a basal series. Soon after the final report of the Denver longitudinal project (14) appeared, one reviewer lamented the excitement it would stir up because "findings were based on a weak research foundation" (15:399). Findings from the Denver project included encouraging achievement for children receiving help with reading during kindergarten, and a maintenance of their lead over nonearly readers only when "the reading program in subsequent years capitalized upon this early start" (14:59).

During the 1960s, two more studies of earlier school instruction in reading were reported in *The Reading Teacher*. One described the use of i.t.a. materials with kindergarten children and, in order to have a contrast group, with first graders too (18). When each group finished second grade and their reading scores were compared, findings indicated higher achievement for the children who used the materials one year earlier. Unfortunately, however, two kinds of data that are questionable for use in statistical tests figured in the comparison: subtest and grade-equivalent scores.

The other study reported in *The Reading Teacher* also used grade-equivalent scores to describe reading achievement (20). In addition, however, differences in intelligence test scores for the groups of children involved in the study were ignored when their reading ability was compared. In this research, the comparison was made at the end of grade three. The children involved divided among (1) some who began reading in kindergarten, (2) some who had been in the same kindergarten class but were not able to score on the reading test administered at the end of the year, and (3) some who had not lived in the community until first grade and "presumably had not been exposed to kindergarten reading experiences..." (20:596). By the end of the third grade, the highest scores were achieved by the children known to have started reading in kindergarten. Their scores from an intelligence test were also the highest, however.

In late 1970, another report of a study appeared in *Child Development* (11). This had to do with a program for children from low-income families (in this case, all blacks) that had as its aim academic success once the children were old enough for elementary school. The 1970 article, one in a series of reports about the project, discussed findings at the end of fourth grade for two experimental groups that had participated in the early school program, and

for two control groups that had not. Although prior articles had announced superior reading ability for the experimental groups, the 1970 report showed grade-equivalent scores that were closely similar to those obtained by the control subjects.

Two more reports published in the 1970s (13, 16) discussed children who could do some reading when they entered first grade; however, in neither case had the children learned as a result of school instruction.

One unpublished report (1) described the achievement of children who began to read as a result of kindergarten instruction, and also compared it with that of children who began in first grade. The data from this study prompted its author to conclude: Children who started to read in kindergarten did better in grades one to five than classmates who did not begin to read until first grade. (The early readers had higher scores on intelligence tests, but the differences were accounted for in the statistical analyses.) Because of the small number of children in the study, the researcher wisely suggested that the results "be viewed conservatively." The same suggestion applies equally well to all the other research mentioned.

Taken seriously, the phrase "View conservatively" suggests the following for professional educators who have responsibilities for kindergarten: Carefully make the decision about whether to teach reading in the kindergarten and if the decision is to teach it, thoughtfully plan the instruction so that what results is an instructional program suitable for five-year-olds.

Assuming this is a correct way to interpret the conservative view, then it is both accurate and fair to say that schools have not heeded the advice of the writer just referred to. Again, let me explain.

Kindergarten Changes

In the early 1960s, schools were pretty much as they had been for the three previous decades insofar as the timing of beginning reading was concerned. Given the "Let's teach it earlier" atmosphere, however, it was inevitable that pressure would be exerted to teach reading in the kindergarten.

One source of pressure that developed fairly quickly was parents. Bombarded by books and articles bearing titles like "Why Waste Our Five-Year-Olds?" and "You Can Teach Your Baby to Read" (4, 19), many parents questioned and complained about play-oriented programs in kindergarten. I cannot help but recall one instance of parental pressure. In this case, a highly traditional school in a small town was involved. Like so many other schools in the early 1960s, this one not only forbade reading instruction in kindergarten but also required a readiness program at the start of first grade. On a number of occasions I had discussed with the principal the possibility of introducing reading in the kindergarten in ways likely to be of interest to five-year-olds. However, each time I made the suggestion, the principal referred to the existing schedule saying, "That is the way it will be." When I pointed out that some of the first graders involved in the readiness program were able to read, he still resisted considering a change.

About a year later I happened to return to the school and, to my surprise, found the kindergarten teachers trying to teach reading. Why? Was it because the principal had sat down with the kindergarten and first grade teachers, carefully weighed with them all the relevant factors, and then made the decision to start teaching reading earlier? No, not at all.

What happened was that word got around the community that in the next town, kindergarten children were doing some reading in school. As a result, parents put the pressure on both the superintendent and the principal. One direct consequence was efforts by kindergarten

teachers to teach reading even though they had had no professional preparation for such instruction.

Some reasons why schools in other parts of the country started to teach reading earlier can be explained via the verbatim comments of kindergarten teachers. Among the explanations I have heard are the following:

"The other kindergarten teacher in this building started to teach reading so I thought I had better start, too."

"A book salesman told our principal he'd provide free phonics workbooks if they'd be used in kindergarten, so I'm using them."

"Last year my principal was curious about i/t/a readers but didn't want to risk using them in first grade. He asked me to use them here."

Perhaps these few explanations are sufficient to make one important point about the move to kindergarten reading: Decisions to teach reading in kindergarten have not always been made for reasons that would be easy to defend.

Current Instruction in Kindergarten

Whether the reasons have been questionable or sound, the fact is that most kindergartens are now attempting to teach reading. Thus, the current concern must be for the ways chosen to introduce it.

Every source of information available indicates that a program closely tied to commerically prepared materials has typically been chosen. Especially prominent among the materials are all sorts of phonics workbooks, which is why it is common to find a whole class of kindergarteners being drilled on sounds. Someone once remarked, "The saving feature of such a practice is that the children don't know what in the world is going on." While that might be so, the fact remains that some kindergarten children are experiencing instruction not likely to foster enthusiasm for reading—nor for school.

Reasons for Current Practices

Why has kindergarten instruction tended to follow commercially lined paths? There are a number of reasons, but let me name just the two that probably have been most influential.

Certainly, one reason is that very few kindergarten teachers were prepared to teach reading when it suddenly became their responsibility. Not knowing what else to do, they naturally turned to manuals and workbooks. Since most administrators associate reading with materials like basals and workbooks, they rarely encourage teachers to try something else with the younger children. Thus, there was little incentive for kindergarten teachers to try to rise above "the same old thing."

Another sad but factual reason for some current practices is that, when a workbook is visible, it is easy to convince parents that reading *is* being taught. This has meant that kindergarten teachers who had both the competence and motivation to develop imaginative, child-centered instruction also had to learn how to communicate to parents that they were teaching reading even though they were not using the usual textbooks. Only exceptional individuals would be willing to undertake both tasks; consequently, it is only in exceptional schools that reading is being taught to kindergarteners in ways that will foster the ability to read and the desire to read as well.

If more schools are to join the ranks of these exceptional ones, certain steps must be taken, and the sooner the better. As a start, it is imperative that colleges and universities, or the schools themselves, develop reading methods courses designed especially for kindergarten teachers. Such courses will not always be necessary but, for the present, they could help teachers acquire a security and a competence that all too few have. . . .

A Brief Summary

This discussion of "Facts about Pre-First Grade Reading," has shown that there really aren't very many facts because relatively little research on the topic has been done. The studies that have been carried out have flaws; thus they provide little in the way of carefully documented findings. Although none of the studies (at least none that has been reported) indicates that pre-first grade help with reading is harmful, it is suggested that future benefits will be reaped only if schools alter their instructional programs to accommodate the pre-first grade learnings. This clearly means that schools undertaking reading instruction in kindergarten must change their instruction from first grade on so that what is accomplished in the kindergarten can be used and extended in subsequent years. Introducing reading in the kindergarten, therefore, is not an isolated event but, rather, is something that ought to have repercussions throughout the entire school.

If reading instruction *is* initiated earlier than has been traditional, it also ought to be of a kind that will add enjoyment and greater self-esteem to the fifth year of a child's life. As this chapter has pointed out, the recommendation stands in great contrast to some current practices in which reading is being introduced with nothing but whole-class instruction characterized for the most part by drill and rote learning.

To effect improvement, the chapter recommended the development of reading methods courses designed especially for teachers of young children. It also pointed to this IRA publication as one step in the direction of needed help.

References

1. Beck, Isabel. "A Longitudinal Study of the Reading Achievement Effects of Formal Reading Instruction in the Kindergarten: A Summative and Formative Evaluation," unpublished doctoral dissertation, University of Pittsburgh, 1973.

2. Bloom, Benjamin S. *Stability and Change in Human Characteristics*. New York: John Wiley and Sons, 1964.

3. Bruner, Jerome S. *The Process of Education*. Cambridge, Massachusetts: Harvard University Press, 1960.

4. Doman, G., G. L. Stevens, and R. C. Orem. "You Can Teach Your Baby to Read," *Ladies Home Journal*, 80 (May 1963), 62ff.

5. Durkin, Dolores. *Children Who Read Early*. New York: Teachers College Press, Columbia University, 1966.

6. Durkin, Dolores. "When Should Children Begin to Read?" *Innovation and Change in Reading Instruction*, Chapter 2, Sixty-Seventh Yearbook of the National Society for the Study of Education, Part II. Chicago: University of Chicago Press, 1968.

7. Durkin, Dolores. "A Language Arts Program for Pre-First Grade Children: Two-Year Achievement Report," *Reading Research Quarterly*, 5 (Summer 1970), 534–565.

8. Durkin, Dolores. *Teaching Young Children to Read*. Boston: Allyn and Bacon, 1976.

9. Durkin, Dolores. "A Six Year Study of Children Who Learned to Read in School at the Age of Four," *Reading Research Quarterly*, 10 (1974–1975), 9–61.

10. Education Section. "O. K.'s Children,"*Time*, 76 (November 7, 1960), 103.

11. Gray, Susan W., and Robert Klaus. "The Early Training Project: A Seventh Year Report," *Child Development*, 41 (December 1970), 909–924.

12. Hunt, J. McVicker. *Intelligence and Experience*. New York: Ronald Press, 1961.

13. King, Ethel M., and Doris T. Friesen. "Children Who Read in Kindergarten," *Alberta Journal of Educational Research*, 18 (September 1972), 147–161.

14. McKee, Paul, Joseph E. Brzeinski, and M. Lucile Harrison. *The Effectiveness of Teaching Reading in Kindergarten*. Cooperative Research Project No. 5–0371, Denver Public Schools and Colorado State Department of Education, 1966.

15. Mood, Darlene W. "Reading in Kindergarten? A Critique of the Denver Study," *Educational Leadership*, 24 (February 1967), 399–403.

16. Morrison, Coleman, Albert J. Harris, and Irma T. Auerbach. "The Reading Performance of Disadvantaged Early and Nonearly Readers from Grades One through Three," *Journal of Educational Research*, 65 (September 1971), 23–26.

17. Pines, Maya. "How Three-Year-Olds Teach Themselves to Read—and Love It," *Harper's Magazine*, 226 (May 1963), 58–64.

18. Shapiro, Bernard J., and R. E. Willford. "i.t.a.—Kindergarten or First Grade?" *Reading Teacher*, 22 (January 1969), 307–311.

19. Simmons, Virginia C. "Why Waste Our Five-Year-Olds?" *Harper's Magazine*, 220 (April 1960), 71–73.

20. Sutton, Marjorie H. "Children Who Learned to Read in Kindergarten: A Longitudinal Study," *Reading Teacher*, 22 (April 1969), 595–602.

16. When Should We Begin to Teach Reading?

Walter H. MacGinitie

If ever there was a question that should be answered with another question, it is "When should we begin to teach reading?" The proper answer is: "What do you mean by 'begin to teach reading'?" The definitions of *beginning* to teach reading could include reading stories aloud to children, or showing them how to print their names when they ask, or casually teaching them the names of a few letters over a period of several months, or teaching them to recognize a few survival words such as "POISON," "DANGER," and "EXIT." The most common definition of what beginning to teach reading means might be something equivalent to starting to do a lesson a day from the teachers' manual of a reading series. But current practice, as defined by teachers' manuals or syllabi, is not sufficiently uniform for us to say what it means to "begin to teach reading." Among different reading programs there are considerable differences in the approach to instruction and in the rate at which it proceeds. Compare a few different teachers' manuals for the first grade and just see how different they are in both approach and pace. Furthermore, many children are being taught to read today by individualized or language experience approaches that vary enormously. Among teachers, too, there are differences in the style of presentation, the integration of reading into other tasks, and the pace at which demands on the child accumulate. It cannot be assumed that "begin to teach reading" means about the same thing to everyone.

When we should begin to teach reading also depends, of course, on the circumstances of the individual child. That is, the readiness question is involved. I have argued elsewhere (MacGinitie 1969), however, that the readiness question, too, is meaningless unless the kind of instructional program is specified. That is, we cannot answer "Is the child ready?" unless we specify "Ready for what?"

From the extensive research on reading readiness, we would expect to learn a lot about when children with different characteristics could profitably begin to learn to read. However, so much of that research has ignored the fact that children are taught in different ways, that it tells us relatively little about what abilities are important for success in any *particular* instructional program. For example, some of that research indicates that it is almost impossible for the average five-year-old child to learn to read. "Nearly every six-year-old is ready to learn *something* about reading" (MacGinitie 1969). Surely the same is true of nearly every *five*-year-old or every *four*-year-old, as long as the "something" that is to be learned is scaled to the child's background and is introduced gently enough. This possibility for appropriate scale and pace of instruction is, in my opinion, the principal argument for introducing the rudiments of reading prior to first grade.

Under our present system, we expect nearly all children to start learning to read during their first-grade year. With some of the children, the teacher will begin reading instruction right away. With others, who are deemed not as ready, the teacher may wait as much as six months or more out of the ten-month school year before begin-

From Walter H. MacGinitie, When should we begin to teach reading? *Language Arts*, November/December 1976, *53*, 878–882. Reprinted by permission of the author and the National Council of Teachers of English.

ning formal reading instruction. In the interim, these children will be given "readiness instruction."

It is interesting to observe that we are now talking about teaching reading before first grade when but a few years ago it was taboo in many schools to teach anything directly about reading as part of readiness instruction. I have never been able to understand the sort of reading readiness instruction that involves learning to discriminate a rabbit with one ear from a rabbit with two ears, but does *not* involve discriminating *a* from *b*. If early reading instruction does nothing else, perhaps it will result in more meaningful reading readiness instruction. To me, meaningful reading readiness instruction means a slow and gentle introduction to reading itself—often gamelike, often hidden in other activities.

When children are started on formal reading instruction in a given classroom, the typical procedure has been to give pretty much the same instruction to all the children, though some will have started half a year later and will proceed a little more slowly. It is easy to show that waiting half a year is *not* much of an adjustment to make for the range of abilities found in the typical first grade. In a typical first grade in the first month of school, some children will be 6¾ years old; others will not reach 6 for another two months. The children's IQs[1] are likely to range from 85 or less, to 125 or more. Under these conditions a mental age spread from less than 5 years to about 8½ years should be expected in the typical first grade classroom—a range of more than 3 years. In the face of a range of mental ability of more than three years, delaying the start of reading for some children by half a year is *not* much of a concession to individual differences. We need to provide great variation in the instruction itself.

We expect children to begin to learn to read in first grade, and those who don't are likely to be in trouble in school forev-

ermore. Evidence clearly shows that children who do not learn to read in first grade tend to be those who are the lowest achievers in most subjects clear up into secondary school (Breen 1965; Thorndike 1973–74). Part of this relationship is natural and to be expected. Some children learn faster than others. They will learn to read faster than others, and they will continue to learn a lot of other things in school faster than others.

But do we have to be so do-or-die about reading in the first grade? Yes, I'm afraid we do. At least at the present time, we do. Parents wouldn't stand for anything else; and most educators would side with them. We insist on believing that certain school tasks are divinely assigned to certain grades. We insist, by our demand that reading be learned then and there, on turning the first grade into a "child's garden of reverses" (MacGinitie 1973).

Even little children know that it's often easier for them to learn something as they grow more mature. McConkie and Nixon (1959) and Stewart (1966) conducted interesting studies of what kindergarten and first grade children think reading is and why we learn to read. They also studied the children's ideas about why some children have trouble learning to read and what happens when they do have trouble. Each child was shown a picture of a group of children and was told, "This is a group of boys and girls in the first grade. They are learning to read." Then the child was asked a series of questions, including, "Will it be hard to learn to read?" "Have you ever known anyone in the first grade who didn't learn to read?," and "Why didn't they learn how?"

"Why didn't they learn how?" Some of the answers from kindergarteners are instructive: "Maybe he was too little and couldn't do it right—maybe he was born after the other children." "He wasn't concentracing [sic] on the teacher." "I think she didn't listen or do what the teacher said." "He'll just have to get older and then learn how." "Maybe the class was too fast and he should try to start from the beginning."

"Will it be hard to learn to read?" the investigators asked. "It will if they don't know their words and if it's done fast." replied a kindergartener. These answers stress the need for reading instruction to proceed at a pace that is appropriate for the particular child. Out of the mouths of kindergarteners can come useful commentary on our curriculum.

"What will happen to a boy or a girl who cannot read?" the children were asked. "He'll be in trouble if he's lost in the desert. He'll find a mailbox, but it won't be any good. He can't write. He'll have to turn himself over to the police." A more mundane response that still recognizes the problem was, "He will learn sometime or other, and if he doesn't he will be in a thick problem."

He *will* be in a "thick problem." What can we do for first graders to help them steer clear of that thick problem? Paradoxically, one way out may be to begin teaching reading earlier than we now do.

If reading instruction is already too pressured a situation for some children in first grade, how can it help to extend reading instruction down into the earlier years? It can help simply because we can allow more time for the child to assimilate the elementary processes that are involved. The healthy thing about most early reading programs at the present time is that both teachers and students can be relatively relaxed. Whatever is learned in an early reading program is often regarded as just a start. Teacher and child can be less tense, for it is still in the first grade that we seem to believe the task *must* be accomplished. We appear to believe that first grade is early enough for frustrations and disappointments. Also, if a child does not learn to read in the early reading program, the first-grade teacher is able to start again at the beginning.

Wardhaugh (1971) has pointed out that one of the major differences between initial language learning and learning to read is that the child is required to learn to read in a relatively short time in a formal training situation. An early reading program *can* provide the opportunity for the learning of reading to be more like initial language learning. Note that I am not suggesting that early formal schooling for all children is desirable, only that a chance to learn some of the elements of reading before first grade could be helpful to many children. As a result, some children will actually learn to read rather well before first grade—an appropriate manifestation of individual differences. We should resist tenaciously, however, any steps toward making early reading achievement a standard that all children are expected to attain.

In talking about these possible advantages of early reading instruction, we should not lose sight of the initial point—that we must define what we mean by "begin to teach reading" before we can sensibly talk about the age or developmental level where it should take place. As a corollary, we need to consider some of the evidence on the mental development of children under the age of six and suit whatever reading instruction *is* given to that development. It is not yet clear what all the characteristics of a good early reading program should be. Clearly it is not appropriate simply to move down a year or two what the first grade teacher is now doing. In particular, reading for younger children should be less oriented toward teaching formal, complex rule systems than are some present first grade programs. In the first place, children seem to have difficulty analyzing language into the units that are manipulated by the rules. In the second place, the cognitive tasks that some phonics lessons represent are quite literally beyond the understanding of many six-year-olds (MacGinitie 1976).

Obviously, most children eventually learn to function according to the rules of grapheme-phoneme correspondence, for they *do* learn to read; but they do not necessarily *understand* what the rules are and what they mean.

In this sense, learning to read should be, for many children, like the initial learning of spoken language. The rules become internalized and functional, but cannot be verbalized. Being told what the rule is has *not* been the basis for learning to follow it. For example, you and I, and most six-year-olds, could say that if something is called *lun*, then two of them are *luns*. We know that if something is called a *bik*, two of them are called *biks*; and that if something else is called a *nizz*, two of them are *nizzes*. We would correctly *use* three different plural allomorphs /-z/ (in *lun-luns*), /-s/ (in *bik-biks*) and /-iz/ (in *nizz-nizzes*), but most of us, even now, do not know that there is a rule to the effect that English /-iz/ is used to indicate the plural only after affricates and alveolar and alveopalatal fricatives, that /-s/ is used only after voiceless stops and labiodental and dental voiceless fricatives and that /-z/ occurs after all other consonants and all vowels.

This example illustrates the difference between functioning according to a rule (we all do that) and understanding a rule intellectually (few of us know very much about our language in that sense). Most children learn to read by learning to function according to rules, not by gaining an intellectual understanding of the rules. After all, how many adults who are excellent readers could explain that the *s* that signifies plural is pronounced /-s/ only after voiceless stops and labiodental and dental voiceless fricatives? Yet that is the rule we all follow when we read aloud.

Many other phonological rules are involved in learning to read. Many are simpler than this, but all except the most direct are probably better learned by young children by example and practice than as rules stated as guides to pronouncing printed words. The younger the children, the harder it will be for them to use a verbalized rule as a logical proposition for analyzing written language. This fact is clear to most teachers and therefore *early* reading programs are, appropriately, not so likely to be presented as the verbalizing of formal rule systems.

I only hope that as early reading programs become institutionalized they do not become more institution-like—more formal, more uniform, more demanding, less tolerant of deviation. At the present time, early reading programs are likely to present the child with the opportunities for extensive practice and thorough acquaintance with letters and simple correspondences, with a gradual development of objectives, and with frequent, yet brief and often adventitious attention to reading that neither bores nor bewilders. Probably those features account for much of the clear success that many early reading programs have had.

Notes

1. General IQ may not be the best index of ability to learn to read, but any reasonable index you might pick as relevant to the particular reading program would show about the same range.

References

Breen, J. M. "Differential Prediction of Intermediate Grade Skills Achievement from Primary Grade Aptitude and Achievement Measures." Doctoral dissertation, University of Connecticut, 1965.

MacGinitie, W. H. "Evaluating Readiness for Learning to Read: A Critical Review and Evaluation for Research." *Reading Research Quarterly* 4 (1969): 396–410.

MacGinitie, W. H. "What Are We Testing?" In *Assessment Problems in Reading*, edited by Walter H. MacGinitie, pp. 35–43. Newark, Delaware: International Reading Association, 1973.

MacGinitie, W. H. "Difficulty with Logical Operations." *The Reading Teacher* 29 (1976): 371–375.

McConkie, G. W., and Nixon, A. J. "The Perceptions of a Selected Group of Kindergar-

ten Children Concerning Reading."
Doctoral dissertation, Teachers College,
Columbia University, 1959.

Stewart, D. Jr. "The Perception of Reading of
Kindergarten and First Grade Children."
Doctoral dissertation, Teachers College,
Columbia University, 1966.

Thorndike, R. L. "Reading as Reasoning."
Reading Research Quarterly 9 (1973–74):
135–147.

Wardhaugh, R. "Theories of Language Acquisition in Relation to Beginning Reading
Instruction." *Reading Research Quarterly* 7
(1971):168–194.

17. Readiness for Reading: A Practical Approach

John Pikulski

The field of reading has been beset consistently with controversy. There are few conclusions about how reading should be taught which are not subject to debate; there is hardly a position that can be taken which cannot be defended by the results of some study or other. Within this broad field called reading there are many specific questions that have been subjected to lively debate for at least the last fifty years. That part of reading called reading readiness has been recurringly popular and has engendered some of the liveliest debates. Hundreds of articles have been written about reading readiness, and hundreds of experiments have been conducted in an effort to better understand what it is, how it can be measured and what can be done to develop it. Yet the debate continues and widespread disagreement exists. How can a classroom teacher, usually a kindergarten or first grade teacher, deal with the concept of readiness with thirty or sixty children when the so-called experts can't agree?

The purpose of this article is to suggest that while the debates will and should go on, there are practical strategies available to classroom teachers that will allow them to come to grips with the important issues in reading readiness in a most sensible and defensible way.

The Situation As It Is

A reexamination of the concept of reading readiness is particularly timely because there is a rush in many schools to introduce a reading curriculum into kindergarten programs. There is some evidence to suggest that many kindergarten children can learn to read and that there can be a long-term, positive effect of a kindergarten reading program on later reading achievement. Experimental programs such as those by Durkin (1974–75), McKee, Brzeinski and Harrison (1966), Shapiro and Willard (1969), and Gray and Klaus (1970), offer support for the position that at least some kindergarten children can learn to read. However, while the last conclusion seems clear beyond debate, it is equally clear that not all kindergarten children can be taught to read. There, of course, is another question which should be addressed: *Should* kindergarten children be taught to read? This last question will not be discussed in this article for two rea-

From John Pikulski, Readiness for reading: A practical approach. *Language Arts*, February 1978, *55*, 192–197.
Reprinted by permission of the author and the National Council of Teachers of English.

sons: (1) No final answer can emerge. To some extent the arguments offered as answers to the question involve value judgments. Some, for example, put forth the argument that an emphasis upon reading will result in less time being devoted to social and creative activities. (2) In many circumstances teachers don't have a choice as to whether or not they will teach reading to very young children. Pressures from administrators in a school or school district or from parents are often so great that the teacher *must* teach reading.

If reading *must* be taught, how can the teacher determine which students are ready for reading instruction? The problem of coming to grips with reading readiness is usually compounded for kindergarten teachers. Many of the inservice kindergarten teachers received their training at a time when kindergarten reading was not popular; in fact, even teaching letter names or recognition of a child's own name were *forbidden* in many schools. At most, teachers were expected to develop some nebulously defined readiness skills in the course of the full kindergarten year. Determining whether or not readiness had been achieved was then the job of the first grade teachers. The organization of kindergarten classes also increases the magnitude of the problem since a teacher at that level usually sees different children in the morning and afternoon. It is not at all uncommon for a kindergarten teacher to be responsible for fifty to sixty children—all of whom must be diagnosed for readiness.

The Easy Way Out?

The citizens of the United States, at least since the turn of the century, have been quite taken with tests, and we rely on tests to measure everything from the acidity level of our garden soil to the strength of our attractiveness to members of the opposite sex. It comes as no surprise that there are tests to measure reading readiness. As a result of the pressures for kin-

dergarten reading programs, publishers now have readiness tests that are designed for administration to children at the beginning of kindergarten. For example, the 1976 edition of the very popular *Metropolitan Readiness Test* has a Level I form of the test for use at the beginning of kindergarten and a Level II form of the test for administration at the end of kindergarten or beginning of first grade. It would seem then that an easy solution to the kindergarten or first grade teacher's plight would be to give a test and find out who is and who isn't ready to read. Those ready could be taught to read while those not ready could be made ready.

The easy way out, however, doesn't really lead to a solution. The major problem is that readiness tests are far from perfect in their ability to predict who will and who will not succeed in learning to read. While scores from reading readiness tests show significant correlations with later reading achievement, these correlations are far from perfect. A sizable number of children will be misdiagnosed. One of the reasons that readiness tests are so imperfect in their predictive ability is that the methods for teaching beginning reading vary considerably from program to program and from teacher to teacher (MacGinitie 1969). For example, in the 1930s it was concluded that children generally needed a mental age of 6.5 in order to learn to read (Morphett and Washburne 1931). In the schools where the study was conducted, heavy demands were made early in the reading program so that a high degree of readiness was necessary. A lesser state of readiness might allow for success in a slower paced, less demanding program. As a matter of fact, this interaction between the state of the learner and the demands of the learning task becomes the definition of what readiness is.

Durkin (1970) proposes a very simple, sensible, and realistic definition of readiness which she borrows from the work of Ausubel (1959)—readiness is "the adequacy of existing capacity in relation to the demands of a given learning task." All too frequently we seem to have assumed that the "learning task" of learning to read was uniform, regardless of the method used for introducing reading, the skill of the teacher, the rate at which new learning is expected and a host of other factors. However, even superficial knowledge of what is done in the name of reading and reading readiness should lead to the conclusion that some teachers and some methods for teaching reading will require far more than others. A general readiness test cannot take differences in program and teacher demands into account, and therefore one very large source of measurement error cannot be eliminated if total reliance is placed in the use of test scores for predicting readiness. There are other contributors to measurement errors that cannot be discussed here. See MacGinitie (1969), Livo (1972), and Donovan (1976) for further discussion of this topic.

The other reason why the easy way out isn't really a "way out" is that the teacher is still faced with the large and important questions of what to do with or how to teach both the "ready" and "not ready" groups.

A Workable Solution

The solution to the problem of determining who is and who is not ready for reading seems quite simple and straightforward: within the first few weeks of kindergarten, and continuously thereafter, children should be exposed to regular and frequent opportunities to read. Those children who come to school already knowing how to read should be encouraged to do so. Letters, words and sentences from reading materials should be used to teach reading to those children who seem capable of profiting from reading instruction. These same materials should be used to develop additional readiness skills for those who need them. The question of ready or not

ready becomes irrelevant when children are repeatedly offered the opportunity to read. It is quite simple to tell when they are ready to begin reading because they will begin reading.

The language experience approach offers by far the most suitable methodology for implementing the above very general recommendations. That approach has been outlined in far greater detail elsewhere (Stauffer 1970; Hall 1970; Allen 1966), but a brief summary will be offered here in order to illustrate its powerful diagnostic and teaching potential when applied to the reading readiness area. In the course of the discussion which follows, particular attention will be devoted to showing how the areas of oral language development, concept maturity, knowledge of language terms, and a positive attitude toward reading can be developed. All of these areas are generally considered important aspects of reading readiness. While other factors could be added, these seem sufficient for purposes of this article.

Language Instruction for All, Reading for Some

Most teachers are somewhat familiar with a language experience approach to teaching reading; however, few teachers use this technique as a major or exclusive vehicle for teaching reading. Most teachers seem unaware of its vast potential for diagnosing the skills of a beginning reader and for individualizing beginning reading instruction. Instruction using the language experience approach can be thought of as consisting of the following segments:

Introduction and discussion of a stimulus. In order to avoid dull experience stories that are conceptually impoverished it is imperative that teachers choose carefully the topic about which children will dictate a story. A short picture book, perhaps even a wordless picture book, a science-related topic like magnets, or a social studies-related topic like life in a foreign country can be a rich source of language and concept stimulation. Through objects, pictures, slides, film strips, snapshots, and so forth, all children in a class will be able to participate in a discussion that enriches their vocabulary and makes them somewhat more familiar with some concept (e.g., what a magnetic force is). Vocabulary development and concept attainment are two very important factors that will certainly influence a child's progress in reading. All children, ready to read or not, will profit from a discussion, though there may be differences in the amount of mastery of the vocabulary and concepts introduced by students or teacher during the course of the discussion. It should be possible, however, for all students, from the slowest to the most talented, to learn something new from this phase of a language experience activity.

Children offer dictation and observe the writing of the story. All children, regardless of their state of readiness, can participate in this phase of a language experience activity. There is no need at this point to create ability grouping, no need to have test data to determine who can offer sentences or who is allowed to watch the recording of the story. Downing (1976); Meltzer & Herse (1969); Christian (1971); Kingston, Weaver & Figa (1972); Holden & MacGinitie (1972) have offered substantial evidence to suggest that children during the beginning phases of reading are likely to be quite confused about terms like "letter," "word," and "sentence," which are part of the language of learning to read. Watching the recording of a word, as a word is spoken, should help a great deal to develop the concept of what a word is. Activities which will extend and reinforce such concepts can easily be designed using language experience materials. Illustrations of such activities are offered in the next section of this article.

Perhaps an even greater readiness benefit to be derived from language experience stories is the potential for increasing a child's desire to read. The enthusiasm of children as they see their sentences recorded is impossible to ignore. The concept of reading as a meaningful, purposeful communication process is clearly being established. Many of us have suspected that far too many children do not read because they see no purpose for reading. The language experience approach either for reading or readiness instruction can certainly contribute to building motivation to want to learn to read, which may be the foremost contributor to overall readiness.

Activities to follow the dictation. In the first two phases of language experience instruction a teacher working with a wide range of student abilities needs to exert little effort to meet individual differences. All students, regardless of their state of readiness, can learn something through participation in the discussion and in observing the physical creation of the story. However, after the story has been recorded a teacher needs to have a clear picture of every child's areas of strength and weakness. The opportunities for diagnostic observation abound. Simply having several children read along with a teacher whose voice trails off, gives children who know how to read a chance to do so. Asking for volunteers to find individual words in a story can offer confirming evidence. Asking children to locate a particular letter in the story gives excellent diagnostic information about letter knowledge and visual perception skills. Calling for children to look at a word written on the board and then to find the same word in the language experience story extends the information about visual perception and adds some information about short-term memory and attention. Asking about words that rhyme or begin the same way as words in the story provides the vehicle for learning about ability to perform auditory discrimination tasks.

The list could certainly be extended. In fact, it is difficult, if not impossible, to name a readiness skill that cannot be evaluated or taught through language experience activities. It is particularly appropriate that diagnosis takes place in the context of teaching and that diagnosis is continuous. Each new story offers opportunities for observation and diagnosis. Before too many days, an observant teacher should be able to make a rather complete inventory of skills possessed and skills needed by each child, and subsequently the activities that follow the dictation can be chosen to extend and develop the skills needed by individual children—all within a meaningful, motivating language context.

While the language experience approach is more challenging to employ than the prepackaged readiness and phonics programs that are making their way into many classrooms, it holds far greater promise and eliminates the need for artificial, only partially reliable measures of reading readiness. Readiness measures retain their utility for program evaluation and for drawing conclusions about groups of children, but they do not play a critical role in diagnosing specific skill areas for individual children. However, perhaps the most encouraging aspect of a language experience approach to readiness is that if properly used, no children can "fail" in beginning reading, since no children should be asked to do something for which they are not ready. While some children are reading the language experience stories and perhaps library books as well, teachers should also be certain to have some children listening to tape recordings of these same books. Through continuous exposure to dictated stories, children who are not ready to read maintain their interest in reading and they are allowed to start reading the moment they are ready to do so. Could anything be simpler?

References

Allen, R. V. *Language Experience in Reading*. Chicago: Encyclopedia Britannica, 1966.

Ausubel, D. "Viewpoints from Related Disciplines: Human Growth and Development." *Teacher's College Record* 60 (1959):245–254.

Christina, R. V. "Learning Sight Words." In *Language Face to Face*, edited by M. Early. Syracuse, NY: Syracuse University Press, 1971.

Donovan, M. A. "The Relationship between Early Assessment and Adjusted Instructional Strategies in Reading for High Risk Learners." Paper read at International Reading Association Far West Regional Conference, 29–31 July 1976, Honolulu. (ED 136 244)

Downing, J. "The Reading Register." *Language Arts* 53 (1976): 762–766, 780.

Durkin, D. "A Six Year Study of Children Who Learned to Read in School at the Age of Four." *Reading Research Quarterly* 10 (1974–75): 9–60.

————. *Teaching Them to Read*. Boston: Allyn and Bacon, 1970.

Gray, S. W. and Klaus, R. "The Early Training Project: A Seventh-Year Report." *Child Development* 41 (1970): 909–924.

Hall, M. A. *Teaching Reading as a Language Experience*. Columbus, OH: Charles E. Merrill, 1970.

Holden, M. H. and MacGinitie, W. H. "Children's Conception of Word Boundaries in Speech and Print." *Journal of Educational Psychology* 3 (1972): 551–557.

Kingston, A. J.; Weaver, W. W.; and Figa, L. E. "Experiments in Children's Perception of Words and Word Boundaries." In *Investigations Relating to Mature Reading, 21st NRC Yearbook*, edited by F. P. Greene. Milwaukee: National Reading Conference, 1972.

Livo, N. J. *Reading Readiness: Research in Review*. Bloomington, IN: Indiana University, 1972. (ED 059 854).

MacGinitie, W. H. "Evaluating Readiness for Learning to Read: A Critical Review and Evaluation of Research." *Reading Research Quarterly* 4 (1969): 396–410.

McKee, P.; Brzeinski, J.; and Harrison, L. *The Effectiveness of Teaching Reading in Kindergarten*. Cooperative Research Project No. 5–0371. Denver, CO: Denver Public Schools and Colorado State Department of Education, 1966.

Meltzer, N. S. and Herse, R. "The Boundaries

of Written Words as Seen by First Graders." *Journal of Reading Behavior* 1 (1969):
3–14.

Morphett, M. V. and Washburne, C. "When
Should Children Begin to Read?" *Elementary School Journal* 31 (1931): 496–503.

Shapiro, B. J. and Willard, R. E. "ita—Kindergarten or First Grade?" *Reading Teacher* 22
(1969): 307–311.

Stauffer, R. G. *The Language-Experience Approach
to the Teaching of Reading.* New York: Harper and Row, Publishers, 1970.

18. New Thoughts about Reading Readiness

Gloria M. McDonell and E. Bess Osburn

Researchers, test constructors, administrators and teachers have for many years
agreed that children enter first grade in
various stages of readiness. Considerable
disagreement exists, however, concerning
this elusive concept of readiness. The most
effective way to prepare children for initial
exposure to reading is also open to question.

Since it has been essential for teachers
and administrators to discriminate between
children who are ready to read and those
who are not, many readiness tests, such
as the *Metropolitan*, the *Lee Clark*, and the
Murphy Durrell Readiness Tests have been
constructed. These tests seem to imply
that skills such as auditory discrimination,
visual discrimination, letter identification,
ability to associate letter names with an
appropriate sound, using and understanding standard English, following directions
and copying letters and letter forms are
necessary prerequisites to reading success.
Most readiness programs, through isolated drill and practice, attempt to help
children master all of these skills in
varying degrees, before they begin their
first reading book.

In 1966 Marie Clay conducted a longitudinal study involving 100 children
who had just entered schools in New Zealand. Over a period of one year, she sys-

tematically observed the behaviors of
these children as they learned to read. Her
research found that children move through
stages of readiness as they learn about two
distinct sets of concepts about print.
Unfortunately, many of these concepts are
taken for granted by literate adults, and
consequently, little attention has been
paid to helping children understand them.
The sets of concepts Clay identified have
to do with: 1) the visual concepts of print,
and 2) the language concepts about print.
While it is necessary for children to have
implicit awareness of these concepts, it is
also necessary for them to integrate the
two before they become successful readers.

The language concepts identified by
Clay which are required for success are: 1)
an understanding that print can be
turned into speech to provide a message;
2) a knowledge that pictures can be used
as a guide to that message; and 3) a realization that print must be as sensible as
spoken language.

The visual concepts are among those
which many children come to school failing to understand: (1) the directional constraints of print, that print moves from left
to right; (2) that a word is surrounded by
spaces; and (3) that the concept of word
and letter are not the same. Imagine the

From Gloria M. McDonell and E. Bess Osburn, New thoughts about reading readiness. *Language Arts*, January
1978, *55*, 26–29. Reprinted by permission of the authors and the National Council of Teachers of English.

confusion that must exist in these children's minds when teachers use terms that are so vague to them.

Finally, the New Zealand researcher found that successful readers were those who were able to integrate their knowledge of language and their understanding of the conventions of print. In her study, children demonstrated this in several ways. They used their finger to point to the words as they were reading. Dr. Clay calls this voice-print match. Another and more advanced indication of this integration was the ability of the successful reader to self-correct. Without prompting from the teacher, these readers were able to use their knowledge of the cues available to them to predict what a word might be. When this prediction seemed incorrect, either visually or because it did not make sense, they automatically reread to correct their error. These children had acquired a self-regulating ability indicating they had learned that print carries a particular message which must be reconstructed from both visual and language cues.

Perhaps the most critical finding of the Clay research is the fact that none of these concepts or readiness skills can be learned unless the child interacts with books and print. To attempt to isolate these skills for mastery apparently only slows or interferes with the rate at which they are acquired. Teachers of successful readers provide many opportunities for children to discover the relationships between print and language by giving them books to read, and then reinforcing their understanding of these relationships through writing activities.

Several Title I teachers in Fairfax County were dissatisfied with the information they received from standardized readiness tests. In order to more effectively help the children they taught, they decided to construct a readiness checklist based on Marie Clay's research (1972), and her diagnostic test (Clay 1972).

The checklist (see diagram) attempts to help teachers recognize the relationships between oral and written language that children must discover. No particular sequence is suggested by this list. In fact, the teachers found that the first item, Expects Meaning, was frequently one of the last concepts to be understood. Each of the items on the checklist was designed to allow the teacher to answer the follow-

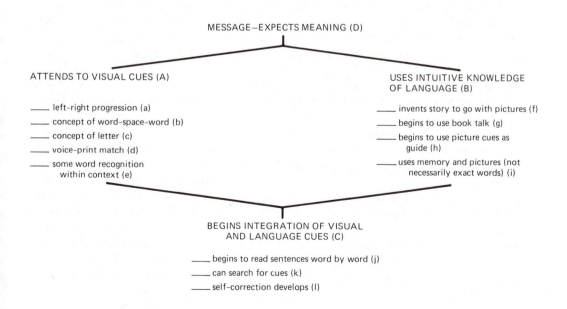

MESSAGE—EXPECTS MEANING (D)

ATTENDS TO VISUAL CUES (A)

USES INTUITIVE KNOWLEDGE OF LANGUAGE (B)

_____ left-right progression (a)
_____ concept of word-space-word (b)
_____ concept of letter (c)
_____ voice-print match (d)
_____ some word recognition within context (e)

_____ invents story to go with pictures (f)
_____ begins to use book talk (g)
_____ begins to use picture cues as guide (h)
_____ uses memory and pictures (not necessarily exact words) (i)

BEGINS INTEGRATION OF VISUAL AND LANGUAGE CUES (C)

_____ begins to read sentences word by word (j)
_____ can search for cues (k)
_____ self-correction develops (l)

ing questions about a student. The items have been labeled by letter to aid the discussion.

A. Does the child attend to the visual cues of print?
- If I am reading a story, can the child tell me where to start and where to go next? (a)
- Is the child able to point to words as I read them, thereby demonstrating knowledge of directional patterns of print? (d)
- Does the child understand the concept of words and letters? Can he/she circle a word and letter in the book? (b and c) To eliminate the good guesser, this ability should be demonstrated several times.

B. Does the child use his/her intuitive knowledge of language?
- Can the child look at a picture book and invent a story to go with the pictures? (f)
- Does the invented story, when the teacher begins to write it down, indicate the child is using a more formalized language that approximates the language used in books (book talk) rather than an informal conversational style? (g)
- Does the child recognize that the print and the pictures are related? (h)
- Can the child "read the words" of a memorized text such as a nursery rhyme, even though the spoken words are not completely accurate matches for the print? Is this recall stimulated or changed by the pictures? (i)

C. Is the child beginning to show signs of integrating the visual and language cues?
- Is he/she beginning to read single sentences word by word, pointing to each word with a finger while reading? (j)

- Can the child use all the cues available to a reader: the predictability of language, word order, a beginning sound, and an appropriateness to context while reading? (k)
- Does he/she stop and correct, without prompting, when a visual-vocal mismatch occurs? (l)

D. Does the child expect meaning from print?
- Does he/she demonstrate that a message is expected by relating a sensible story?

Although this checklist can help teachers diagnose which areas a child needs to develop, teachers found that individual items could not be successfully taught separately. Rather, a diagnosis of weakness in any area usually indicates that the child needs more exposure to print in the form of choral reading, story writing, assisted reading (Hoskisson and Krohn 1974), and so on. Certainly, just explaining the concepts is ineffective. To tell a child the meaning of "word" does not cause learning. An activity such as matching words on a word card to a chart containing a story, or matching a sentence strip and then cutting the sentence into words, involves the child in the learning process and is more likely to result in a clear understanding of the concept.

The Title I teachers of Fairfax County are indebted to Marie Clay for her significant research and for the exciting insights she has provided the whole area of the acquisition of reading. After adults master a task such as reading, it becomes difficult to know just how the task was originally learned. It has seemed appropriate to analyze the task, break it down into small parts, expect children to learn these parts in isolation, and then put them together in an efficient manner. This is an assignment which some six-year-olds find difficult to accomplish. Dr. Clay's work indicates that teachers of beginning reading need to examine their practices more closely. Such procedures as withholding books from children who have not mastered readiness skills may actually hinder their progress in acquiring these skills.

It should not be difficult for teachers to provide an environment for beginning readers that is rich in reading experiences. Perhaps this will begin to prevent or at least to minimize the numbers of youngsters who become academically unsuccessful in the first few months of exposure to formal instruction.

References

Clay, Marie M. *Reading: The Patterning of Complex Behavior*. Auckland, New Zealand: Heinemann Educational Books, 1972.

——— *The Early Detection of Reading Difficulties: A Diagnostic Survey*. Auckland, New Zealand: Heinemann Educational Books, 1972.

Hoskisson, Kenneth and Krohm, Bernadette. "Reading by Immersion: Assisted Reading." *Elementary English* 51 (September 1974): 832–836.

CHAPTER V

Beginning Reading Instruction

Teachers of all grades need to understand how beginning reading is taught. Ollila and Nurss begin Chapter 5 with an overview of the many ways in which beginning reading is taught in the United States and Canada. Aukerman describes ways in which the basal readers of the 1980s differ from those of preceding decades. Next Adams, Anderson and Durkin describe the implications for beginning reading that can be drawn from current theories concerning decoding, syntax, semantics, and the differences between spoken and written language. Frank Smith forcefully advocates a holistic, top-down approach from the beginning of reading instruction. Dykstra summarizes the results of the Cooperative Research Program in First Grade Instruction concerning the relative effectiveness of meaning-emphasis and code-emphasis programs. The chapter ends with Hall's explanation of the rationale for the language experience approach.

19. Beginning Reading in North America

Lloyd O. Ollila and Joanne R. Nurss

Instructional Methods and Materials

Beginning reading instruction in North America is skills oriented. The most commonly used material for teaching reading is the basal reader. Prior to the 1970s, basal readers consisted of readiness workbooks, preprimers, primers, and first readers for the first grade. These books were accompanied by workbooks, large pictures, and flash cards for practicing word recognition. Generally, they introduced a carefully controlled vocabulary based upon the oral vocabulary of five year olds. Many words were phonetically irregular and were taught by look-say methods with fre-

quent and systematic repetitions. Word analysis skills were introduced very slowly. Basal series have been justifiably criticized as being racist, sexist, and showing only middle class, small town, and rural families. The stories also have been criticized as uninteresting, written in unnatural language, and too dependent upon illustrations. Basal readers were often used in a lockstep fashion with the teacher's main pressure being to get every child to read "on grade level," meaning to read the appropriate grade level book. It was equally as bad to have a child "above grade level" as it was to have one "below grade level." Reading lessons as outlined

From Lloyd O. Ollila and Joanne R. Nurss. Beginning reading in North America. In Lloyd O. Ollila (Ed.), *Beginning reading instruction in different countries*. Newark, Del.: International Reading Association, 1981. Pp. 26–53. Reprinted by permission of Lloyd Ollila and Joanne R. Nurss and the International Reading Association.

in the teacher's manual consisted of introducing new words, motivating the children to read the story, guiding silent reading (page by page), posing comprehension questions following each page, reading orally "round robin" with the children taking turns reading one page around the reading circle, practicing on a relevant reading skill, and completing workbook pages and/or board work exercises to practice the new words and the reading skill. Fortunately, much of this has now changed.

Most basal readers still provide a comprehensive, sequential system for reading instruction, but the books now have stories which show a variety of races; women and girls in an equally favorable light to men and boys; a variety of socioeconomic classes; different urban settings, as well as towns and rural areas; and a variety of family patterns. Vocabulary control has been relaxed, stories are more interesting, language is more natural, and phonics instruction has been added earlier and in greater quantity. Most systems use levels instead of grades to try to overcome the lockstep labeling of children. A wide variety of additional materials such as cassettes, storybooks, filmstrips, puzzles, games, worksheets, and pictures are available to accompany most basal series.

The success of any reading program is dependent upon the teacher. In the past, many teachers misused the traditional basal series by adhering to the manual in a rigid manner. Teachers using the less structured newer materials often fail to provide an orderly sequential development of word analysis and vocabulary skills. The levels can be misused just as the grade designations were. No matter how carefully beginning reading materials are designed, the teacher is the key factor in children's learning.

Another change in current basal reading materials is the diversity in methodologies now available. In addition to analytic phonics methods, there are series using synthetic phonics methods, linguistic methods, programed methods, and a modified alphabet. Individualized reading and language experience approaches are also used in North American schools.

The analytic or meaning-emphasis approach to beginning reading stresses comprehension of the initial reading material, while the synthetic or code-emphasis approach stresses decoding of the initial material. Austin (3:506) says that ". . .few educators will disagree that reading is meaningful interpretation of written and printed symbols." The differences lie in the timing and in the emphasis on comprehension. The analytic phonics or meaning-emphasis method introduces children to some words by sight, emphasizing the meaning of the words, phrases, and sentences in the books. When the children know several words which begin with the same consonant (top, toy, to, take), they are encouraged to note the similarities of beginning letters and beginning sounds and to conclude that the sound /t/ is usually represented by the letter "t." The synthetic phonics or decoding method, on the other hand, introduces the unstressed vowel sounds and a few consonant sounds in isolation, teaching the children to discriminate the sound and to associate it with the appropriate letter. Beginning reading material consists largely of words formed by blending these sounds (for example, /a/, /m/, /t/, /r/—mat, rat, tam, ram, at, am). There have been many attempts to compare the effectiveness of these methods with a variety of conclusions. One frequently cited comparison (4) reviewed research on the code- and meaning-emphasis approaches and found that 1) the code-emphasis approaches produced better overall reading achievement by the beginning of fourth grade (nine year olds) than did the meaning-emphasis approaches and 2) code-emphasis approaches were better for children with below average and average intelligence and from low socioeconomic levels, but meaning-emphasis approaches were better for children of high intelligence and from middle and high socioeconomic levels. The debate is by no means concluded.

The linguistic approaches grew out of the work of linguists who noted that both the analytic and synthetic phonic approaches distort the phonological sounds. One type of linguistic series introduces word families in which substitutions can be made without distorting the sounds. For example, "The frog on a log with a dog." Some linguistic series use nonsense words which illustrate the decoding principle being taught but convey no meaning. The idea is to teach decoding first and to introduce comprehension later. There are many variations of the linguistic approach currently in use (2).

Programed approaches to beginning reading break down the process into small steps. Each step is presented as an item which is read (stimulus) and for which a response must be selected. The program provides immediate feedback (indicating whether the response is correct or incorrect). Reinforcement is given and additional practice may be indicated if the children make errors. Programed reading materials are usually in workbook format, but may be in a machine or computer. Students proceed at their own pace, but all children complete essentially the same material; thus the pace is individualized, but the activities are not. Programed materials are popular in behaviorally oriented classrooms.

In the late 1960s the Initial Teaching Alphabet materials (i.t.a.) from England were modified and an American i.t.a. basal series appeared. The alphabet was modified to a one-to-one phoneme-grapheme correspondence, thus reducing the task of learning to decode. The readers use a meaning-emphasis basal reader format. After children have mastered reading with i.t.a., they are given transition material to learn how to decode traditional orthography. Although i.t.a. is still used in a few systems, it has never been widely used in North America and seems to be decreasing in popularity.

Two other approaches used in North America are the individualized reading approach and the language experience approach. Individualized reading makes use of a wide variety of trade books from which children select their own reading books. The teacher listens to the children read, asks comprehension questions, and assists with appropriate skills. This method is widely used as a supplementary method in connection with a basal or language experience approach. When used alone, it places a great responsibility upon the teacher to be aware of the reading skills and their sequence, to be able to diagnose "on the spot," and to prescribe appropriate skill activities individually. Most school systems find that these demands are too severe for the average or inexperienced teacher, making this method less effective when used as the only reading approach. However, the emphasis on meaning, the interest sustained by the child's selection of the reading books, and the personal meeting with the teacher all commend this approach as one part of a reading program. The advent of a multitude of children's literature titles in inexpensive paperback format and of an interesting variety of "easy-to-read" books has made individualized reading even more popular with beginning reading teachers (6).

The language experience approach to reading is one in which children produce their own reading materials: dictating simple stories (initially a few words or a phrase) to the teacher, seeing them written down, and then reading them to the teacher. Ultimately, children write their own stories, produce books, and read them to other children. The teacher must develop a sequence of skills from each child's work and must assist the child in going from reading sentences and phrases to recognizing individual words. The language experience approach makes good use of children's oral language, integrates writing with reading, grows out of the children's own experiences, and is therefore meaningful. Language experience is used as the only approach to teaching reading in a few instances in North America. More typically, however, it is used in connection with individualized reading and a sequential skills program.

There is sufficient diversity in the United States and Canada for it to be a bit presumptuous to speak of the "typical" beginning reading program. However, in many schools children are introduced to beginning reading by learning to recognize some common words at sight (for example, their names, words related to a unit of study, words for colors or shapes, and words appearing around the room on a calendar, helper chart, etc.). Simultaneously, children learn letter sounds, letter names, and sound-letter correspondences. From that beginning, children are introduced to a basal series and taught the vocabulary and sequential skills of that series. As children develop some reading proficiency, they are encouraged to engage in an individualized reading program. Throughout the beginning reading period, children will have been encouraged to write sentences and stories to read and perhaps develop into books. The basal reader phonics program will be taught and applied in reading library books, writing stories, and playing word games.

In recent years, the systems concept has become prevalent in education and in beginning reading. A number of basal series have been developed along this line, as have many curriculum guides and special programs. In a systems approach the broad objectives are stated, the task to be accomplished is analyzed, the individual is assessed to determine which component parts (skills) have been mastered, the specific instructional objectives are stated, the instructional activities are presented, and an evaluation measure is given to determine whether the objectives have been reached. If so, the learners are taken to the next step; if not, they are "recycled" for further instruction and/or practice. The well-developed system has the goals for learning to read analyzed into the component parts in such a way that, upon completion of the system, children are proficient readers. Most schools and teachers use some modification of this systems approach (such as a diagnostic-prescriptive approach) to teaching beginning reading. The teacher has the whole process in mind and the children are made aware of the meaningful nature of the reading process; however, at any point in time, the activities might be based on one small step within the process.

The decision as to which of these methods or materials will be used for beginning reading is usually made by the local school system. The school principal may make modifications to adapt the reading program to the local community. Individual classroom teachers are given a basic curriculum to follow and a set textbook to use, however, with relatively little room for individual choice.

Both Canada and the United States have sizeable bilingual and/or non-English speaking communities (French in Quebec and Spanish in New York, Miami, and Los Angeles). In Canada, French speaking schools have been established and French speaking children are taught to read initially in French. Later many are taught to read in English, although dual French speaking and English speaking secondary schools and universities make it possible for a Canadian to obtain a monolingual education in either French or English (3). In the United States there are some Spanish speaking or bilingual (Spanish-English) schools in which children learn to read in Spanish. In most instances, however, Spanish speaking children are taught English as a second language and then given reading instruction in English. No Spanish speaking secondary schools or universities exist in the United States (except in Puerto Rico). Therefore, native Spanish speakers must learn English to complete their education.

Instructional Organization

Most North American elementary schools have single age classes taught by one teacher. The child moves to another class and another teacher each year. Classes are coeducational with mixed ability groups. Generally, classes are self-contained at the primary level with the classroom teacher teaching all subjects. The teacher's role is relatively central, especially in reading instruction. Direct instruction in reading is usually given to small groups of children. Typically, there will be three or four small groups for reading instruction in a first grade classroom. This intraclass grouping is done mainly by reading achievement level. Instruction in basic skills, practice in word recognition, and guided silent reading followed by comprehension questions will be given. Fortunately, round robin oral reading is beginning to disappear in favor of children taking turns in reading individually to the teacher or to other children. Children do oral reading for many different purposes; for example, reading directions for making something, finding a specific bit of information needed for a group project, locating a favorite passage in a story, or getting a message on a poster. While one group works with the teacher, the other groups engage in learning center activities, library reading, or written independent work. Too often, however, the same workbook pages or duplicated worksheets are provided for every child within a subgroup. A few first grade classrooms also have manipulative toys; housekeeping and block centers; and creative areas with paint, water, or sand.

In some schools, children are grouped by reading achievement levels into an interclass grouping scheme. All the children from the primary grades reading at the same level join for instruction in one teacher's room. Although this method has the advantage of reducing the range of reading levels with which one teacher must cope, there still are individual levels and learning rates present. This also means that reading must be taught in a rigid time frame which makes it difficult to coordinate instruction with the other language arts and subject areas. For these reasons, this type of organization is less common than intraclass grouping.

Open-plan arrangements, similar to those found in many British infant schools, have been developed in Canada and the United States in recent years. In some cases, buildings built in the open-plan format contain self-contained classrooms in spite of the architectural arrangements. In other cases, the physical space, staffing, and schedule have been modified to allow an informal, less structured organization. In a few cases, family grouping exists so that a class may contain children of several ages. Extensive research comparing this arrangement to more traditional organization has not yet been reported. However, a few studies have indicated that the open approach is beneficial to children's affective and creative development, but is not as successful in teaching them to read as is a more traditional organization (12).

Theoretical Background

The beginning reading methods common in the United States and Canada grow out of a theoretical understanding of reading which distinguishes between beginning reading and proficient reading. Although most American reading researchers would define reading as the process of understanding or comprehending a printed message, many see beginning reading as the process of mastering decoding skills and then applying them to "get meaning from the written message." Samuels (8) says that reading subskills (which are emphasized in beginning reading instruction) are simply a means to an end. The end, of course, is meaning. However, before the whole can be dealt with, the parts must be mastered.

The subskills important to beginning reading include visual discrimination, auditory discrimination and blending, and auditory-visual integration (all of which are essential for decoding words) and oral language development such as vocabulary, concepts, language structure, and reasoning (essential for comprehending the total written message—phrases, sentences, and paragraphs). Most American beginning reading practices are based upon this subskill analysis of the beginning reading process, teaching the two groups of subskills simultaneously.

In recent years, several American researchers (5, 9, 10) have suggested that even beginning reading is a process of extracting meaning from the written message. Goodman describes reading as a "psycholinguistic guessing game" in which the meaning of a passage is reconstructed by readers via the meaning in their minds (5). Smith (9:230) says that readers "predict their way through a passage." He also suggests that the teacher's primary instructional task is to "respond to what the child is trying to do" (10:195). Evidence that beginning readers can and perhaps do learn to read by seeing the meaningful whole instead of mastering the component parts comes from young children who are either self-taught or who learn by looking at books, writing stories, and "reading" along with competent readers (11). In discussing competence and performance in reading, Kinsbourne (7) notes that children can master all of the subskills (pass all the criterion measures) and still not be able to read, that is, not be able to integrate the subskills into the process. The North American professional literature (journals and conference papers) now is suggesting that beginning reading practices should use a meaningful, holistic approach rather than a subskills approach. School practice reflects this change in the increased use of meaningful context to teach subskills. At this time, however, most North American children are taught

to read by skills-oriented approaches and materials.

Adams, Anderson, and Durkin (1:20) suggest that beginning reading is not simply a letter and word discrimination process nor simply a psycholinguistic guessing game. Rather, they suggest that beginning reading is an interactive process in which discrimination and prediction occur simultaneously. They state that successful reading is dependent on meaning, both in the text and in the reader's mind.

It will be interesting to see the research evidence produced to support each of these theoretical models of beginning reading and the subsequent influence of that research on instructional practices and published materials in North America.

References

1. Adams, M. J., R. C. Anderson, and D. Durkin. "Beginning Reading: Theory and Practice," *Language Arts*, 55 (1978), 1925.
2. Aukerman, R. C. *Approaches to Beginning Reading*, Second Edition. New York: John Wiley, 1971.
3. Austin, M. C. "United States," in J. Downing (Ed.), *Comparative Reading: Cross-National Studies of Behavior and Process in Reading and Writing*. New York: Macmillan, 1973.
4. Chall, J. *Learning to Read: The Great Debate*. New York: McGraw-Hill, 1967.
5. Goodman, K. S. "Behind the Eye: What Happens in Reading," *Reading: Process and Program*. Urbana, Illinois: National Council of Teachers of English, 1970, 3–5.
6. Harris, L. A., and C. B. Smith. *Reading Instruction: Diagnostic Teaching in the Classroom*, Second Edition. New York: Holt, Rinehart and Winston, 1976.
7. Kinsbourne, M. "Looking and Listening Strategies and Beginning Reading," in J. T. Guthrie (Ed.), *Aspects of Reading Instruction*. Baltimore: Johns Hopkins University Press, 1976, 141–161.
8. Samuels, S. J. "Hierarchical Subskills in Reading Acquisition," in J. T. Guthrie (Ed.), *Aspects of Reading Acquisition*. Baltimore: Johns Hopkins University Press, 1976, 162–179.

9. Smith, F. *Understanding Reading*. New York: Holt, Rinehart and Winston, 1971.
10. Smith, F. *Psycholinguistics and Reading*. New York: Holt, Rinehart and Winston, 1971.
11. Taylor, J. E. "Making Sense: The Basic Skill in Reading," *Language Arts*, 54 (1977), 668–672.
12. Traub R., and others. *Openness in Schools: An Evaluation Study*. Toronto: Ontario Institute for Studies in Education, 1976.

20. Features of the Basal Series of the 1980s

Robert C. Aukerman

It is to be expected that school textbooks will reflect, in some degree at least, society's major sociological and economic concerns, which change frequently over the years. This is particularly true of social studies textbooks. Similarly, textbooks in the fields of the arts and sciences certainly must be up-to-date in order to be relevant.

One might assume that textbooks in reading would not need to react to such changes—a story being a story and a poem being a poem. And haven't we all been told that classics are classics because they set forth universal themes and deal with universal problems that transcend time and place? We might further question what difference it makes what the child reads as long as he/she is getting practice in reading. But it *does* make a difference and textbook publishers are constantly making changes and adjustments in their basal reading series to be in keeping with the spirit of the times. This is especially true in the decade of the 1980s.

A comparison of the basals of the 1980s with those of the 1950s and 1960s reveals that major changes have been made in the pupil texts of most, if not all, of the basal series. Wherever it was possible, all components, textual materials, and graphic artwork have been changed or adjusted to allow for the following.

Better Ethnic Balance

New stories have replaced others, providing realistic situations portraying ethnic and cultural mores rather than attempts (in the 1960s and 1970s) to introduce minority characters into white, middle-class neighborhood story situations.

There are more stories and poems and other selections related to the Black heritage, thus reflecting the impact of *Roots* and interest in the African tradition. The effect of the enormous migration of peoples from Puerto Rico, Cuba, Mexico, and from the islands and lands of the South Pacific and Southeast Asia also is reflected in most of the basal reader series.

Better Male/Female Balance

Equal rights for females, women's liberation, single parents, a high divorce rate, and other similar sociological changes have mandated textbook changes that portray adults as well as children in non-stereotyped roles. The latter changes show more girls in competitive sports, as just one example.

In some basal textbooks, stories have been adjusted by taking out the boy character and replacing it with a girl, but keeping the story essentially the same. For example, in one story a shepherd boy has

From Robert C. Aukerman, *The basal reader approach to reading*. NY: John Wiley and Sons, Inc., 1981. Copyright © 1981 by John Wiley and Sons, Inc. Reprinted by permission of John Wiley and Sons, Inc.

been changed to a shepherd girl. There are countless other instances where changes have been made, not necessarily to improve the quality of the reading, but apparently to appease those whose crusade for equal treatment impels them to count the number of male and female characters in the selections in the basals.

Inclusion of Handicapped

There was a time when children were protected from exposure to the handicapped! Until quite recently large segments of society looked on individuals with major injuries and/or handicaps as freaks and, frequently, people to be avoided like the plague. We may be thankful that times have changed (some, but not enough!). And basal reader textbooks in the 1980s have begun to show handicapped people in situations where they are making positive contributions to society. Moreover, a few stories are beginning to appear that depict real-life biographical vignettes of people who have overcome their handicaps to achieve greatness, stardom, and success.

Inclusion of Senior Citizens

Like the handicapped, senior citizens have also come into their own as useful contributors to society and to the quality of life for those with whom they come in contact. Respect for them and for their achievements in their mature years are new facets of the stories, articles, and biographical sketches included in the new basals of the 1980s.

Better Balance of Urban/Suburban/Rural Settings

The older basals frequently portrayed the family packing the car for a visit to "grandfather's farm." The resulting story showed grandmother and grandfather greeting the family; the exploration of the animals in the farm compound; and the departure with the old folks waving goodbye. Family

visits to the zoo, firehouse, park, and so on, were usual themes but, in the 1980s, children are more apt to be going to the mall or to a ball game, or to be doing all sorts of things without being surrounded by a smiling, happy family.

The new basals, therefore, show children skiing, skateboarding, playing hockey, eating hamburgers at McDonalds, playing on an inner-city school playground, living in a housing development environment, and or functioning in any of scores of situations that are relevant to life in the 1980s.

Deletion of Violence

This is difficult to accomplish. Indeed, it is contrary to today's environment in which most of us live. Is it something we wish to shield our children from, or is it something we do not want to portray for fear it might give them ideas to go forth and do likewise?

Many of the great classics of literature have been based on themes of murder, mayhem, war, destruction, feuding, man's inhumanity to man, torture, and death by fire and sword. The editors of the 1980 basal series have opted to leave violence to the Saturday morning cartoons, the evening TV shows, and to those who chose to read literature based on those themes outside the basic reading groups.

We will find little, if any, suggestion of violence in the selections in the new basal readers. Even wars are merely mentioned, but not portrayed. Family feuding (although all too frequent in everyday life) is a "no-no." The violence of the street gangs and motorcycle clubs, the violence of professional sports such as football and hockey, and any form of violence that even children know exists is sublimated by portrayals of the "good guys."

Better Balance of Geographic Areas

In the past, children seemed to have an aversion to reading about children in other parts of the world. Oh, yes, they did read about Heidi, and about Hans Brinker, and fairy tales with castles. Those stories appealed to the imaginative sense of awe and wonder—the magic of Disneyworld, so to speak. But the realities of children living in this world are just now being portrayed to a noticeable extent in the basal readers.

We now observe articles, poems, plays, and stories about children in places like Peru, China, the Philippines, Hawaii, Australia, the Middle East, and Africa.

A More Balanced Selection of Literary Genres

There is more emphasis on humor, mystery, adventure in the here-and-now, science fiction, advertising and persuasion, cartooning as a means of communication, and biographical vignettes of contemporary "greats" in our society.

The graphic arts that provide the setting for these selections are entirely different from the bland illustrative work that carried much of the story lines in the older series of past decades.

Vigorous Graphic Arts Components

Whereas in the past basals frequently carried the work of one illustrator throughout one entire reader (book), the new series employs scores of the best free-lance artists and photographers, which is very costly. The result is superb artwork that provides setting and mood for the reading material which it supports.

Developmental Lesson Plans

More care is shown in the new basals by supplying the classroom teachers with lesson plans that provide for developmental sequences of phonics skills, word recognition skills, comprehension skills, and so on. Most series now provide a sequence of testing to verify the acquisition of those skills in sequence. Most series also provide

scope-and-sequence charts or booklets that delineate the exact locations in the pupil texts and workbooks where the skills are introduced, reviewed, and reinforced.

Improved Literary Quality

The largely bland, nonsensical story lines that were characteristic of earlier basal series (and generated much of the criticism and many of the jokes about them) have been replaced with normal language patterns in the preprimers and primers of most series.

Even in the primers and first readers, every effort has been made to provide poetry and adapted stories from many award-winning writers of children's literature. In the higher grades, the basals of the 1980s (with the exception of two or three series) are filled with stories and poems, informational articles, biographical sketches, and science fiction selected from the works of the best contemporary children's writers. In many instances, the artwork from the original editions of their works has also been reproduced.

All of the above costs enormous amounts of money, but in a field as competitive as the basal reader field, a publisher cannot afford to settle for anything but the best in an effort to get a share of the market. As a result, children in the classroom benefit from the improved quality of the literary selections and the graphic artwork that accompanies them.

Glossary

Many of the books in the series published in the 1980s contain glossaries. They are useful additions, but only so if the pupils are taught how to use them.

The glossaries in the first-grade books generally contain the words and definitions. In the books for the more advanced grades, they usually also indicate pronunciation by means of syllabication, some type of phonics key, and accent marks. In that way, they become a bridge to dictionary usage. In fact, they can substitute for dictionaries in situations where a dictionary is not available.

Features Common to Most Basal Reader Series

Although several of the basal series are so different that they do not fit a standard pattern, it is, nonetheless, useful to have a stereotype when considering the basal series and the basal reader method. Thus, at the very beginning, we must commence with the word MOST: MOST basal series suggest this and that; MOST basal series have this component and that component; and so on.

MOST basal series have a readiness program. MOST are designed to provide practice in visual discrimination; auditory discrimination; background experiences; some exposure to alphabet letters; some learning of letter-sound relationships; some copying of shapes and letters; even some reading.

MOST provide beginning picture books with simple captions and soon some two- or three- or four-word sentences in the first preprimer. Preprimers are softbound. Usually three preprimers and the primer constitute the first half of first grade. The first reader is the second semester of first grade. It contains the first glimmer of real interesting stories, poems, and informational reading.

MOST basal series commence with the whole-word method, providing pupils with the new words in each lesson in chalkboard work just prior to reading in their pupil books.

MOST basals provide a word-identification strand that runs parallel to (but not usually a part of) the stories in the readers. The word-identification strand is based on analytic phonics, in which the children who have learned some phonics elements (letter-sound correspondences) can "figure out" what the word might be. Coupled with contextual setting, the pupil decides whether the word "makes sense."

MOST basals employ an elaborate battery of comprehension questions: Who did it? Where? When? Why? How many? How much? How do we know? Read the part that tells us . . . How would you feel? What do you think will happen next? What makes you think so?

MOST basals try to provide a balance of comprehension questions that call for facts, inferences, speculation, main ideas, supporting details, introspection, and prediction.

MOST basals provide minutely detailed lesson plans for the teachers. These include a synopsis of the story or selection; a listing of materials needed to carry on the lesson; suggestions for introducing the unit and/or lesson; a listing of new vocabulary to be placed on the chalkboard for preview; a statement of objectives for the lesson; detailed questions to be interspersed at intervals as pupils read the material.

MOST basals provide a vocabulary development strand.

MOST basals provide suggestions for the development of the associated language arts: listening, writing, composing, story-telling; drama; language-experience stories.

MOST basals provide a wide range of literary genres; realistic and imaginative fiction; biography; plays; drama; poems; informational articles; interpretive materials; fantasy; mystery; tales; and legends. In the intermediate grades there tend to be more selections from the content areas.

MOST basals provide some practice in study skills from the fourth grade onward; some provide them earlier.

MOST basals provide a strong emphasis on literary appreciation and a knowledge of literary devices in the upper-grade materials.

MOST basals employ a battery of artists and illustrators who create artwork to embellish the stories and to provide a set-ting for the stories, poems, and so on. The informational articles are frequently enriched with photographic art.

MOST basals provide pupil workbooks in which the skills are strengthened through practice.

MOST basals provide two follow-up strands—one for pupils who have not mastered the skills taught in the skills les-son and who must do some further work on those same skills, and one for those who can benefit from enrichment activities or individualized reading.

MOST basals include a number of tests: for initial assessment and placement of new pupils in the program; for pretesting before certain skills are taught; posttests to determine mastery; diagnostic tests to iden-tify weaknesses; end of unit tests for wrap-up and/or review.

MOST basal series are *very expensive* to develop; the price tag for a brand new series today might run from $10 million to more than $20 million before *one* book is sold! These costs are attributable to high office rents; salaries of editors and editorial staffs; very expensive full-color artwork; royalties for use of stories, articles, and poems; the high cost of composing, print-ing, binding, storing, advertising, and promotion of the series; and large num-bers of salespeople.

MOST basals must be revised every five years or less to make them competitive in states where basals compete for "state adoption" every fifth year. A series with a copyright date older than five years would not be considered for adoption.

MOST series undergo a constant revi-sion process.

MOST basals are greatly improved over those of 20 or even 10 years ago.

21. Beginning Reading: Theory and Practice

Marilyn Jager Adams, Richard C. Anderson, and Dolores Durkin

Anyone who knows the literature on beginning reading is forced to conclude that much still needs to be learned about what it is and how it should be taught. Those who know the literature and are also aware of what goes on in classrooms must face up to another inevitable conclu-sion; namely, the failure of classroom prac-tices to reflect what *is* known.

What *is* known with certainty is mea-ger. Even descriptions of the very nature of the reading process continue to be char-acterized by diversity rather than agree-ment. Within the framework of one conception, for example, reading is "bot-tom-up" processing. According to this interpretation, readers start with letters and, as they attend to these letters, they begin to have expectations for the words the letters will spell. As readers identify the words, they have further expectation for how these words will be strung together and what they will mean when assembled into phrases and sentences.

Constrasting with this "data driven" interpretation is one that sees reading as being "conceptually driven." Within the latter framework, reading is, to use Good-man's (1967) words, "a psycholinguistic guessing game" in the sense that readers' knowledge of language and of their world suggest certain hypotheses that are

From Marilyn Jager Adams; Richard C. Anderson; & Dolores Durkin, Beginning reading: Theory and practice. *Language Arts*, January 1978, *55*, 19–25. Reprinted by permission of the authors and the National Council of Teachers of English.

tested—that is, accepted or rejected—against what is printed. According to this interpretation, therefore, reading is "top-down" processing.

Still another interpretation, one that underlies this article, views reading as an essentially interactive process (Rumelhart 1976). From this perspective, top-down and bottom-up processing are seen to occur simultaneously, at least for a skilled reader. This makes successful reading as dependent upon the information that is in the reader's head as upon the information that is in the text. Comprehension will be obstructed, therefore, whenever a critical skill or a critical piece of knowledge is lacking. When it is, however, proficient readers find a way to compensate. They might pause and sound out a word; or, on the other hand, they might rely on top-down processes to solve the problem. In the latter case they might deduce the meaning of the troublesome word from contextual information. Both types of solutions are regularly used by skilled readers and both contribute to their success. When either top-down or bottom-up processing is followed to the extreme, however, problems arise.

The danger of relying too heavily and exclusively on top-down processing is obvious. Balance between the information that the reader brings to the text and that which the text should provide is lost. To the extent that guesses are piled upon prior guesses the individual is not really reading in any useful way.

Relying too exclusively on what is printed may also create problems. Because the human mind is a limited processor, attention directed to decoding means that attention will be taken away from other things—from what previously identified words said, for example. Limited processing capacity is an especially critical problem for new readers since many of the necessary subskills are not yet well learned and demand conscious attention.

The remaining sections of this article will consider a number of problems that beset beginning readers and will point out what they indicate for reading instruction.

Decoding

For everything to work together in a smoothly coordinated way, readers must identify words automatically. Beginners, however, are still working on that requirement. To assist them, phonics is taught. Ideally, it will be taught in a way that concentrates on patterns of letters since it is patterns, not individual letters, that suggest pronunciations. Although instructional materials now highlight patterns, some teachers continue to teach decoding skills as if decisions about a pronunciation can be made letter by letter. The persistence probably reflects the fact that the use of new materials is often affected by old procedures and habits. Such an explanation seems reasonable since materials of the past commonly assigned unmerited importance to individual letters.

Materials of the past also failed to underscore the need for flexible application of what is taught in phonics. More specifically, they failed to portray decoding as a type of problem solving that does not begin with a ready-made answer but, rather, seeks one out with the help both of a word's spelling and of the context in which that word is embedded. Teachers who keep this in mind will steer away from having children decode words presented in lists and, instead, will move toward practice that concentrates on unfamiliar words placed in sentences. Practice (of the right kind) is important because it is only rapid decoding that assists with comprehension.

Although some might take it for granted that children get sufficient and prolonged practice in decoding, classroom observations reveal something else. Once glossaries appear in books—this occurs at about the third or fourth grade level—"Look it up in the glossary" is the directive children commonly receive when they are having trouble with a new or forgotten word. While nobody would deny the value of their knowing how to use reference materials like glossaries and dictionaries, nobody could deny either that it makes little sense to spend huge amounts of time teaching phonics in the primary grades if what is taught there is put on the shelf in subsequent years.

Anyone teaching phonics also needs to keep in mind a point made earlier; namely, that the human mind is a limited processor. Because it is, the processing capacity of readers can be so taken up with sounding out a word that they may block on previously identified words. The meaning of this for teaching is clear: Have children habitually reread any sentence in which a "worked on" word occurs, once that word has been identified. Only in this way is comprehension of the sentence likely. Simultaneously, the same habit should discourage word-by-word reading, something that hardly promotes comprehension.

Syntax

Anyone interested in promoting comprehension needs to know about syntax. Syntax refers to the order of words in a phrase or sentence. Such order is significant because English is a positional language. That is, it relies heavily on word order to convey meaning. Consequently, to change order is to change meaning. Expressions like *off day* and *day off* effectively demonstrate this.

The dependence of meaning on word order indicates that even though a child's ability to decode is important for reading, it is not sufficient for success. That decoding might be sufficient is associated with a conception of writing that views it as being no more than ciphered speech. According to this view, if children can learn to translate printed words into their spoken equivalent, the problem of reading is solved. All that's needed is the application of previously acquired language skills to the deciphered text. Why such a view is an overly simple and misleading conception of reading can be explained in a variety of ways.

First of all, there is good reason to question whether beginning readers have as much competence in oral language as is often claimed. The frequent assertion that children entering school have mastered the exceedingly complex structure of our language is based on the finding that, even though young children do not produce sentences having the complexity found in adult speech, their own speech does reflect all the basic syntactic transformations. Concluding that children have mastered syntax because they can use basic grammatical structures is, however, a little like describing people as grand masters simply because they know the legal moves of the chess pieces. Not to be overlooked, either, is the evidence which indicates that children continue to make substantial gains in their ability to use and understand syntactic structures until they are at least thirteen years old (Palermo and Malfese 1972).

But, let's suppose that children do have the syntactic competence to interpret a given sentence in spoken discourse. Can it automatically be assumed that they will understand it if it were written? Our answer is "Not necessarily" for the following reasons.

Ordinarily, spoken language occurs in a rich context of external events that provides comprehension aids not found on the printed page. Or, to put this differently, the speaker is far more helpful to the listener than is the author to the reader. Furthermore, when speaking fluently, people tend to restrict pauses and breaths to syntactic boundaries. They neither speak as if every word were followed by a comma nor do they move breathlessly on in an attempt to say everything at once. Instead, they provide listeners with temporal cues that help them comprehend because they indicate meaningful units of words. Apparently the listener depends on these temporal cues for when they are distorted, comprehension suffers (Huggins 1978).

Contrasted with spoken language, written discourse is stingy in the help it offers a reader with syntax. Replacing the obviously helpful pauses of oral language is punctuation, but it is a poor substitute. Readers are pretty much on their own, then, as they attempt to group words into such necessary units as phrases and clauses. And unless they can recover the syntactic structure of a printed sentence, it doesn't matter whether they do or do not have the syntactic competence to understand its oral equivalent.

To the extent that the processes of identifying the syntactic units of a sentence are unique to reading, we might expect them to be troublesome for the beginner. It is not surprising, therefore, that studies of beginning readers' troubles have identified the failure to sample written material in phrasal units, and the tendency to indulge in many more fixations per line of the text than do mature readers (Levin and Kaplan 1970; Kolers 1975).

The failure of beginners to organize sentences into phrases creates memory problems, hence comprehension problems too. This is the case since it is the meaningfulness of a series of words that allows a listener or a reader to remember them. Recalling *ran, boy, little, to, school, the,* for example, is far more difficult than remembering the very same words presented in a meaningful order like *the little boy ran to school.*

The indisputable importance of getting an author's words organized into meaningful units if they are to be both understood and remembered raises questions about some common classroom activities. For example, word-identification practice that is routinely carried on by having children read individual, isolated words (flashcard practice) is hardly likely to foster the type of processing that the comprehension of sentences requires. Raising a

question about this type of practice, however, is not to question practice itself. To the contrary, for one of the common problems found among poor readers is the inability to identify words sufficiently quickly. Such a problem is not remedied with less practice but, rather, with different and better practice. Better practice would have children concentrate on connected words (*the girl, on the table*), not on isolated words (*the, girl, on, the, table*).

Another common classroom activity called into question by the importance of segmenting a sentence into meaningful parts is the one called "round robin" reading. This is the procedure in which one child reads aloud while others in the group are expected to follow the same material silently. Anyone who has observed the procedure soon learns that, at the beginning level, oral reading is of the halting, word-by-word kind. As such, it hardly provides an ideal model for anyone who is attempting to put an author's words together in a way that will assist with understanding them.

The great emphasis put on oral reading in the primary grades might also be encouraging still more problems related to comprehension, for it portrays reading as a performing art rather than an effort to understand what an author has written. The erroneous portrayal is undesirable because it could inhibit young readers from arriving at the understanding that reading is not saying something *to* another but is, instead, getting something *from* another.

Further Differences between Spoken and Written Language

Still more differences between spoken and written language need to be kept in mind because they also help to pinpoint the special requirements of success with reading.

One very significant difference has to do with the setting in which children acquire, use, and respond to oral language. Setting, in this case, refers to such non-language "extras" as shared experiences, gestures, facial expressions, and pointing—all of which offer considerable assistance with oral language comprehension. In the face of written language, on the other hand, readers have no extra-linguistic contexts. Instead, they must construct *mental* contexts from clues that come from the printed page and from their knowledge of the world.

For beginners, constructing the necessary contexts can be difficult. Since writers cannot do such things as point, referring expressions (words like *this, that, here,* and *there*) may be incomprehensible and so, too, may the intended referents of certain words. To illustrate this, consider a "simple" sentence like, *John said to Peter, "Come over to my house tomorrow."* If a child heard this sentence, he or she would understand that *my* referred to the speaker and that *tomorrow* referred to the day after the utterance. To read the same sentence, however, *my* has to be interpreted as meaning John's while *tomorrow* has to be interpreted as meaning the day after John spoke to Peter. For a child, these necessary changes in perspective may not be easy—at least not as easy as we commonly assume them to be.

Since fiction characteristically requires a reader both to establish and shift perspective, the traditional practice of using stories to teach beginning reading may be a faulty one. Admittedly, authors of beginning readers make generous use of pictures, which should aid children in constructing the mental contexts that comprehension requires. However, pictures can lead to other problems; namely, a reliance on pictures instead of on words, and, secondly, reduced motivation to read a story since the pictures tell it.

Semantics

Still more problems that face children when they are trying to learn to read have to do with the need to understand the meanings of words. Such a need is verified not only by the application of common sense but also by test data. Over the years, for example, a persistent research finding has pointed to the close association that exists between scores on vocabulary tests and scores on measures of reading achievement.

Research data on vocabulary itself agree with what is found when classrooms are visited; for, when they are, generous amounts of confusion about meanings are revealed (Durkin 1976). Children as advanced as fourth graders have been heard to define *border* (in the context of "South of the Border") as "Somebody who lives with you but he's not your family." In earlier grades, *bold* has been explained as meaning "not having any hair on the top of your head" while *canyon* was described as "a big gun that you use in a war."

Research data uncover vocabulary problems that are more subtle and hidden. One study, for instance, revealed unexpected complications in acquiring correct meanings for words like *give, take, buy,* and *sell* (Gentner 1975). At first, it was learned, children assign equivalent meanings to *give* and *sell*, and to *take* and *buy*. Only later are they able to deal with a second dimension of meaning for *sell* and *buy* (the transfer of money), which allows for distinctions between *give* and *sell*, and between *take* and *buy*. Other studies report well-known findings; for instance, children's tendency to overgeneralize and undergeneralize meanings. Initially, for example, a word like *brother* includes all male children but no male adults. Only with the accumulation of experiences does the true meaning come through.

Meanings for words that are in a context can create even greater problems; for, now, children must move from a wide range of possible meanings to one that fits the context. Often, knowing what does fit requires not only a knowledge of that range but also the ability to infer what is only implied in the context. At times, background knowledge is an additional prerequisite for success.

What all this says to teachers is clear: If each child's potential for reading is to be realized, attention to listening-speaking vocabularies must be viewed both as a serious and a never-ending responsibility.

Text Organization

Just as word-by-word reading thwarts comprehension, so too does sentence-by-sentence reading, since relationships also exist among sentences. Generally, classroom instruction first deals with sentence relationships through the avenue of sequence. What happened first? What happened next? And then what happened? These are frequent queries when a selection that was read is being discussed. Relationships other than sequence, however, are common in written discourse and cover such things as cause-effect relationships, explanations, elaborations, examples, exceptions, contradictions, and conclusions.

Even though comprehension depends upon success in integrating information across sentences, research on this topic with primary grade children is practically nonexistent. Nonetheless, based on the best evidence available, it appears that children have a great deal to learn about inter-sentence relationships.

Authors offer help with interrelationships through the way they organize what they write. Highly visible signs of organization, for instance, characterize most expository material. An introduction (often labeled as such) indicates what is to come, whereas a summary sketches what has been said. In between, headings and subheadings suggest what is major, what is minor, and what relates to what. Exactly how primary-grade readers use such organizational aids is unknown; for, again, research is lacking. In this case, the excessively generous use of narrative material in the early grades may be one explanation for the omission.

The structure built into written material, of course, is not the only kind that affects what is comprehended and retained. Another important kind of structure is what is built into the readers themselves in the form of experiences and information. What is used from this knowledge structure is affected by the material; but what is in the written message is also affected by what is in the reader's head. Thus, as was underscored in the initial part of this article, successful reading emerges as a highly complex, interactive process in which what the reader brings to the page is as important as what is written. That is why comprehension always is a highly personal experiences.

References

Durkin, Dolores, *Teaching Young Children to Read* (2nd Ed.). Boston: Allyn and Bacon, Inc., 1976.

Gentner, D. "Evidence for the Psychological Reality of Semantic Components: The Verbs of Possession." In *Explorations in Cognition*, edited by D. A. Norman, D. E. Rumelhart and the LNR Research Group. San Francisco: Freeman, 1975.

Goodman, K. S. "Reading: A Psycholinguistic Guessing Game." *Journal of the Reading Specialist* 4 (1967): 123–135.

Huggins, A. W. F. "Timing and Speech Intelligibility." In *Attention and Performance*, edited by J. Requin. New York: Halstead Press 1978.

Kolers, P. A. "Pattern-Analyzing Disability in Poor Readers." *Developmental Psychology* 11 (1975): 282–290.

Levin, H., and Kaplan, E. L. "Grammatical Structure and Reading." In *Basic Studies on Reading*, edited by H. Levin and J. P. Williams. New York: Basic Books, 1970.

Palermo, D. and Malfese, D. L. "Language Acquisition from Age Five Onward." *Psychological Bulletin* 78 (1972): 409–427.

Rumelhart, D. E. "Toward an Interactive Model of Reading." CHIP Report No. 56. Center for Human Information Processing, University of California, San Diego, March 1976.

22. The Teacher's Role

Frank Smith

Helping Children Learn to Read

If there is little sense in a lot of drill and exercise, what instead should be going on in the reading classroom? And the second question might be that my list of cautions about interfering with children learning to read implies that the children are already capable of some reading in the first place. What does a teacher do about a child who cannot read at all? How does a teacher get the child started? The answers to both questions are the same, since there is basically only one problem—to facilitate reading for children when they can read very little or not at all. The answers can be summed up in one basic rule and guideline for every aspect of reading instruction—*make learning to read easy*—which means making reading a meaningful, enjoyable and *frequent* experience for children.

Put in another way, the solution requires that the teacher should *read for children what they cannot read for themselves*. If a child cannot read at all, the teacher or other helpful reader must do all the reading (or provide the necessary clues) for the child. Where there are some words that the child can read, then the others must be supplied (or their identification be made unnecessary).

Reading on behalf of children helps them to achieve three important objectives in beginning to read and continuing to learn to read:

(1) *Understanding the functions of print.* It is in being read to that children find the opportunity to gain the insight that print has a purpose, that it makes a difference how print is arranged. Children cannot be *told* that written language is a part of the environment as meaningful, useful and satisfying as speech. Children must experience that insight for themselves; they must be put into situations where it can develop.

(2) *Gaining familiarity with written language.* As I have already pointed out, written language may have the same basic vocabulary and grammatical structures as spoken language but the relative frequency of various words and structures differs. Spoken and written language are put together in distinctive ways. The particular conventions of written language can make it quite unpredictable, and therefore difficult to comprehend. Constructions that are common in children's books, such as *What splendid teeth the beaver has*, or *Down the road hand in hand ran Susie and her friend* seem simple and straightforward to most of us only because of our familiarity with written language; they are not the kind of language anyone is likely to be accustomed to from everyday speech. The only way children can become familiar with written language, before they can extend their knowledge by reading for themselves, is by being read to.

(3) *Getting the chance to learn.* It is important to read to children, but even more important to read *with* them. Children get their first chance to solve many of the problems of reading when they and adults are reading the same text at the same time. It does not matter that at the beginning the children may recognize none of the words they are looking at, indeed it is in the process of being con-

Reprinted by permission of the publisher. From Frank Smith, *Reading without nonsense* (New York: Teachers College Press, © 1978 by Frank Smith. All rights reserved.), Pp. 143–49.

fronted by words that are unknown that they find the motivation and opportunity to begin to distinguish and recognize particular words, in the same way that they solve the cat and dog problem. Children reading along with an adult or other reader will look out for the words that they know and choose the additional words that they want to learn or practise.

An interesting change takes place as an adult and child read together. Initially the child's eyes wander over the pages and then follow along behind as the child strives to grasp some understanding of the relationship between the marks on the page and what is being said. But as the child develops a little proficiency in reading—especially if the passage being read is from a poem or story well-known to the child—then the child's eyes move ahead of the reader's voice. The child begins reading independently of the adult assistance. The situation is not unlike learning to ride a bicycle. For as long as the child needs adult help then the child cycles slower than the adult pushes. But as competence and confidence develop, so the child tends to pull ahead of the adult until eventually able to manage alone. No need to fear that a child who is helped at the beginning will become lazy or overly dependent on adults. The child who can take over from the adult in reading will be no more content to lag behind than the child riding the bicycle. Mastery provides its own incentive; children who can manage their own buttons and shoelaces rarely tolerate adults who insist on doing these tasks for them.

Making Sense of All Kinds of Print

In stressing the importance of reading to children I do not want to give the impression that I am talking just about *books*. In fact I think that the widespread emphasis on books in school constitutes a distorted and often obstructive approach to reading instruction. Indeed, the only books that

should be read to children or that they should be required to read for themselves are the ones that genuinely *interest* them, that contain fascinating rhymes and stories rather than the bland and unnatural prose to which many children are expected to attend, whether recounting a boring day in the life of an insipid pair of children or relating that *Sam can fan the fat cat.* The print that offers beginning readers the most insights into the meaningfulness of written language and the skill of making sense of print tends to lie outside books in the far more personal and pervasive world of their own lives. Children may learn more of the basics of reading from the brand name above a garage, the words on a sweet wrapper, or the experience of their own names on a pair of boots, than from any number of books and exercises. In natural, out-of-school surroundings, printed words exist not to be associated with *sounds* but with *sense*. Chalked on a blackboard in the classroom or printed below a picture in a book, the letters T-O-Y-S have no function, no point. But when the same marks occur in a store they convey the distinct and important meaning "This is where the toys can be bought."

The wealth of meaningful print in the environment of children can be read to them, not in any obtrusive or demanding manner but as casually and naturally as the objects in a child's environment are named. Just as children are told "There's a big dog" or "See the plane?" so adults can say "That says 'ketchup;'" and "There's the 'One-Way' sign." This simple practice will give children the opportunity to derive insights, generate ideas and test hypotheses about reading while they retain the freedom to select and control what they most want to learn whenever it makes the most sense to them. In such circumstances children learn about print and about reading in the same way that they learn about spoken language, without obvious effort or the need for formal instruction.

Reading in School

Total immersion in meaningful print is hardly a typical experience for most children in school, nor indeed can all the conditions that facilitate learning to read be easily translated into the classroom. It is in fact difficult for teachers to duplicate the richness of print that occurs naturally in the outside world, an example of the many differences between school and the world at large that children can find so confusing.

Nevertheless there are many ways in which children in school can experience printed language which has both interest and a meaning for them. Teachers can try to ensure that children often have the opportunity to read—or to hear—stories that have an intrinsic appeal, to which they will voluntarily give attention. Teachers can also make frequent use of print to forward a significant activity in some way, whether in play (keeping a store, publishing a newspaper) or in the daily routine. Printed materials and products that make sense to children in the outside world can be brought into the classroom. And there are a number of ways in which print can be emphasized in the functions of the school, for example in the identification of various classrooms and offices, washrooms and storage rooms, lockers and coathooks (all of which are often labeled too high for children's eyes). Menus constitute meaningful print, and so do posters, notices, direction signs, maps, catalogues, timetables, and telephone books, especially if they can be produced in a format children can handle, a print they can discriminate easily and a language they can understand. Not only can these and other familiar materials be used to help children learn more about reading, but they also offer the only opportunity many children may have of learning to use or make sense of the materials themselves. No one ever learned to use a telephone directory from a lecture; it is specific practice at a specific task, with sympathetic help in meaningful situations, that makes the learning of any skills possible.

At the same time that a wealth of meaningful print is provided, much of the print that is meaningless could be removed from the scene. There may be occasional justification for the use of individual letters and even isolated words as part of the decor, and lists of useful words (like the days of the week or months of the year) can at specific times have value for reference purposes. But in general the tendency should be resisted to decorate walls with sheets of print whose only function is perhaps to give adults the impression of an educational atmosphere. There is usually little need for a frenzy of labeling at the expense of windows, pictures and even soothing sections of blank wall.

Incidentally, one advantage of ensuring that children are confronted only by meaningful print, whether on the walls or in their textbooks, is that very often young children can be helped to read such print by their older or more practised schoolmates. The teacher is not necessarily or even ideally the individual who must help a child to read. The more meaningful the words to be read, the less often a child will need help and the more likely another child will be able to provide help when wanted.

Of course, providing a print-rich environment and endeavouring to avoid interference with the natural ability of children to learn does not constitute a "programme" for reading instruction. I cannot provide a consumers' report on all the different reading methodologies. Because the whole point of the analysis I have made is that no-one can rely on a programme to teach reading, in the form of a package that can be taken off a shelf or ordered from a publisher. Reading is not taught by prescription. There are hundreds of reading programmes, many of which have little relevance to reading. But even the most sensible of programmes will be little more than an aid to keeping children occupied while they are learning to read. Reading cannot be taught in the way that arithmetic is taught (not always successfully either) as a series of operations which children must learn and which can be ticked off and taken for granted as children show proficiency in each one. "Programmed instruction" scarcely scratches the surface of reading.

I am not saying that there is nothing for teachers to do, and that instructional materials have nothing to offer, but that teachers must make their own decisions about what needs to be done. The question should not be "Which method should I use?" but "How do I decide what to do now?" I have not argued that there should be no phonics, only that phonics has a widely unsuspected complexity and that children should be expected to learn about phonics only to the extent that they can make sense of the instruction. I have not said that children should not be taught the alphabet (it helps teachers and children communicate on the subject of written language) but until children have a good idea of what reading is about, learning the names of letters is largely a nonsense activity. The issue is always what a child can make sense of, and that changes with each individual teacher. Programmes should not be expected to make decisions for teachers. The question is not a simple one of whether phonics, sight-words or language experience is the best approach.

I certainly do not argue that teachers should not know about the tools of their trade, about the multitude of programmes, materials and devices that are available for their use, although a listing and evaluation of all these items would be out of place in this book. Most of the training teachers receive on the subject of reading is devoted to lectures and demonstrations about different programmes and methods. What is usually lacking is any kind of understanding of the nature of reading so that teachers can make up their own minds about when and how to use particular methods. Teachers often do not know what programmes can reasonably be expected to accomplish—how much for example a child can actually learn from phonic drills, or from sound-blending exercises—or do they know the *cost* of such programmes to the child in terms of memory overload, tunnel vision, rote learning or boredom and confusion. Teachers must be discriminating, and that requires both a familiarity with programmes and an understanding of reading. They must be able to see what makes sense.

The importance of formal programmes and of kits of materials in reading instruction is grossly overrated. Many children have learned to read without special programmes or materials at all, and many other children have probably learned despite their formal instruction. The reason there is such an emphasis on programmes today, apart from obvious commercial interests and a misplaced faith in the efficacy of technology, is a compulsion to standardize, to treat all teachers and all children in the same way. Despite talk about "individualized instruction" and "flexibility" in the classroom, the economic and political realities of education tend towards the elimination of alternatives, of differences, and of choice. Everything I have said about reading in this book is contrary to approaches that demand sequenced instruction and constant measurement, and is therefore contrary to instruction teachers may themselves receive in their own training.

23. The Effectiveness of Code- and Meaning-Emphasis Beginning Reading Programs

Robert Dykstra

In her recent book, Chall (1967) concluded that code-emphasis reading programs tend to produce better overall reading achievement, at least in the initial stages of instruction, than do meaning-emphasis programs. She defined code-emphasis programs as those which aim at the beginning to teach the pupil mastery of the alphabetic code rather than expecting from him a mature reading performance. Meaning-emphasis programs, according to Chall, are those which emphasize from the very beginning the necessity of reading for meaning, undoubtedly a more mature skill than mere code-breaking. The typical basal reading series belongs to the meaning-emphasis category. Many current programs, however, are characterized by an early concentrated emphasis on learning the alphabetic code which characterizes printed English. This is especially true of a number of recently published "linguistic" programs.

The Cooperative Research Program in First-Grade Instruction provided considerable data with which to test Chall's conclusion. Many of the projects which participated in this research venture compared the relative effectiveness of basal programs and certain innovative instructional programs, a number of which belong to Chall's code-emphasis category. The Coordinating Center at the University of Minnesota reported, in two separate volumes, the results of the combined analysis of the data which compared basal and various other programs at the end of grades one and two (Bond and Dykstra, 1967; Dykstra, 1967). The present report draws together specific data from the Cooperative Research Program pertinent to the issue of the relative effectiveness of code-emphasis programs in initial reading instruction.

Programs

Information about three relevant types of reading programs evaluated in the first-grade reading studies is presented in Table 1. Programs are categorized as conventional basal, linguistic, and phonics-first basal in accordance with Chall's classification scheme. The Programmed Reading Series was not labeled "linguistic" by Chall, but because of its claim to be linguistically based and its similarity in many respects to linguistic materials it has been placed in that category for purposes of this report.

Certain of the instructional variables which differentiate the three types of programs are presented in Table 1. More complete descriptions of these variables are found in Appendix A of Chall's book. It is apparent that conventional basal, linguistic, and phonics-first basal programs are differentiated by a number of instructional variables such as vocabulary load, type of vocabulary control, phonics load, and initial response modes. The first row of the table indicates that conventional basal programs are characterized by an early emphasis on meaning, while the various linguistic programs and the phonics-first

From Robert Dykstra, The effectiveness of code- and meaning-emphasis beginning reading programs. *The Reading Teacher*, October 1968, 22, 17–23. Reprinted by permission of Robert Dykstra and the International Reading Association.

Table 1. Classification of Reading Programs Used in the Cooperative Research Study According to Publisher, Common Label, and Certain Instructional Variables

Variables	Conventional Basal			Linguistic Approaches				Phonics — First Basal
	1*	2	3	1**	2	3	4	1***
Goals of Beginning Instruction: Reading for *Meaning* (M) or Learning the *Code* (C)	M	M	M	C	C	C	C	C
Motiv. Appeal at Beginning: *Content* (C) or *Process* (P) of Learning to Read	C	C	C	P	P	P	P	P/C
Major Criterion for Selecting Words: *Meaning Freq.* (MF) or *Spelling Regularity* (SR)	MF	MF	MF	SR	SR	SR	SR	SR
Vocabulary Load: First Year	LOW	LOW	LOW	HIGH	HIGH	HIGH	HIGH	HIGH
Phonics Instruction *Analytic* (A) or *Synthetic* (S)	A	A	A	A	A	S	S	S
Phonic Load: First Year	LOW	LOW	LOW	HIGH	HIGH	HIGH	HIGH	HIGH
Cues to Use: *Structural* (S) or *Meaning* (M)	M	M	M	S	S	S	S	S
"Set" for *Regularity* (R) or *Diversity* (D)	D	D	D	R	R	R	R	R
Structural Clues Employed: *Sounding* and *Blending* (SB), *Visual Analysis* and *Substitutions* (VAS), or *Spelling* (SP)	VAS	VAS	VAS	SP	SP	SB	SB	SB
Response Modes: *Whole Words* (WW) or *Letters First* (LET)	WW	WW	WW	LET	LET	LET	LET	LET

1* Scott, Foresman—The New Basic Readers

2   Ginn—Ginn Basic Readers
3   Allyn and Bacon—Sheldon Basic Readers
1** Barnhart—Let's Read

2   Merrill—Basic Reading Series Developed on Linguistic Principles
3   Singer—Structural Reading Series
4   McGraw-Hill—Programmed Reading
1*** J. B. Lippincott—Basic Reading

basal program belong to the code-emphasis group. It was possible, therefore, to make certain comparisons of the relative effectiveness of meaning-emphasis and code-emphasis instructional materials in beginning reading.

The experimental design utilized by the Coordinating Center enabled comparisons between basal and linguistic materials and between conventional basal programs and phonics-first basal series. The rationale underlying the analysis is presented in detail in other reports of the Cooperative Research Program (Bond and Dykstra, 1967; Dykstra, 1967). The analysis conducted by the Coordinating Center utilized data collected from various projects participating in the research program, thereby giving information about the relative effectiveness of various types of materials across a number of projects.

Achievement was measured in the Cooperative Research Study by means of a number of instruments. Oral word pronunciation was measured by the word list from the *Gates-McKillop Reading Diagnostic Test* and the Fry Phonetically-Regular Word List which was developed specifically for the research program. Accuracy of connected oral reading and rate of reading were assessed by the *Gilmore Oral Reading Test*. The *Stanford Achievement Test* was used to evaluate spelling, silent reading, word recognition, and silent paragraph comprehension.

Findings

The findings of the analysis comparing basal and linguistic programs are reported in Table 2. Relative performance of basal (meaning-emphasis) and linguistic (code-

Table 2. Reading and Spelling Achievement of Pupils in Code-Emphasis and Meaning-Emphasis Reading Programs

	Programs Compared	
Achievement variables	Conventional Basal (Meaning Emphasis) vs. Linguistic (Code Emphasis)	Conventional Basal (Meaning Emphasis) vs. Phonic/First Basal (Code Emphasis)
Oral Word Pronunciation		
Grade 1	CODE	CODE
Grade 2	CODE	———
Accuracy of Oral Reading		
Grade 1	MEANING	CODE
Grade 2	MEANING	———
Spelling		
Grade 1	MEANING	CODE
Grade 2	CODE	CODE
Silent Reading Word Recognition		
Grade 1	CODE	CODE
Grade 2	CODE	CODE
Silent Reading Comprehension		
Grade 1	MEANING	CODE
Grade 2	MEANING	CODE
Rate of Reading		
Grade 1	MEANING	CODE
Grade 2	CODE	———

emphasis) pupils on the various measures is reported for both the end of grade one and the end of grade two. At the end of first grade, 1,357 pupils were used to evaluate spelling and silent reading ability. This number dropped to 959 by the end of the second grade. Approximately 250 pupils were used at both testing points to analyze oral word pronunciation, accuracy of oral reading, and reading rate.

Linguistic pupils were better in oral word pronunciation and silent reading word recognition at the ends of both grades one and two. Pupils in the code-emphasis linguistic programs were also better spellers at the end of grade two, although the reverse was true at the end of the first grade. Therefore, it is apparent that early emphasis on learning the alphabetic code resulted in superior ability at decoding words in isolation as well as superior ability at encoding spoken words by the end of the second grade. It should be emphasized, however, that not all of the differences favoring either linguistic or basal pupils were statistically significant. The analysis was very complex because of the number of projects involved and in many cases it was impossible to come up with a simple, straightforward comprehensive test of the relative effectiveness of the two treatments. For this reason, the data presented in this article may best be used to illustrate trends. Details concerning the significance of observed differences are presented elsewhere (Bond and Dykstra, 1967; Dykstra, 1967).

Differences in accuracy of reading a connected passage orally and in understanding paragraphs read silently favored the basal pupils at both testing points. This finding lends some support to the view expressed by many reading authorities that concentrated early emphasis on learning the code to the virtual exclusion of reading for meaning may have a negative effect on comprehension. However, the differences favoring basal pupils on the second-grade comprehension test were

negligible (Dykstra, 1967, p. 105). The evidence concerning reading rate is less clear-cut. Basal pupils were faster readers at the end of grade one, but pupils whose initial instruction had been in linguistic materials were reading at a higher rate by the end of the second grade. Therefore, it does not appear that an early emphasis on learning the alphabetic code necessarily produces halting word-by-word reading, at least through the second grade.

The Cooperative Research Study also evaluated the relative effectiveness of conventional basal materials and the phonics-first reading series. Chall's analysis of this series indicated that it differs from conventional basal materials primarily in its approach to teaching and practicing new words. In other aspects of the instructional program, however, Chall found that the phonics-first basal system did not differ greatly from conventional basal readers.

The comparative effectiveness of these programs in terms of first-grade and second-grade reading and spelling achievement was evaluated. All of the performance measures at either testing point favored the code-emphasis phonics-first program. Code-emphasis pupils were superior in the word recognition and comprehension skills involved in silent reading after one year and two years of instruction. They were also better spellers at both testing points. Information regarding reading rate, oral word pronunciation, and accuracy of oral reading is available only at the end of the first grade, where all differences favored the phonics-first code-emphasis group. Furthermore, practically all of the differences reported for this particular comparison of code-emphasis and meaning-emphasis programs were statistically significant (Bond and Dykstra, 1967; Dykstra, 1967). Pupils comprising the sample for the first-grade reading measures numbered 191, while the sample used for evaluating first- and second-grade silent reading and spelling totaled 1,013 and 441 respectively.

Discussion

Data from the Cooperative Research Program in First-Grade Reading Instruction tended to support Chall's conclusion that code-emphasis programs produce better overall primary-grade reading and spelling achievement than meaning-emphasis programs. This superiority is especially marked with respect to pronouncing words orally in isolation, spelling words from dictation, and identifying words in isolation on a silent reading test. It is apparent that concentrated teaching of the alphabetic code is associated with improved initial ability to encode and decode words. This evidence reinforces the view that pupils can be helped to learn sound-symbol relationships.

It is difficult to make conclusions about the relative effectiveness of analytic and synthetic phonics programs. The relatively successful code-emphasis programs utilized both types of instruction. Evidence is also inconclusive about the relative effectiveness of unlocking a new word by sounding out the word and blending it together versus spelling the word letter-by-letter as advocated by the Bloomfield-Barnhart and Fries materials. The code-emphasis programs differed on this point, yet were relatively successful as a group in producing pupils with above-average word recognition skills. For further information on this point it would be well to look at individual studies which evaluated separately each of the types of code-emphasis programs or which compared two or more code-emphasis programs (Schneyer, 1967; Sheldon, 1967; Ruddell, 1967; Tanyzer, 1966; Hayes, 1967).

The relative effectiveness of code-emphasis and meaning-emphasis programs in influencing ability in reading comprehension is still somewhat ambiguous. Taken as a group pupils who learned to read by means of conventional basal readers were slightly superior in silent reading comprehension to pupils whose initial instruction had been in linguistic materials. However, this finding was reversed in the comparison of conventional basals with phonics-first basal materials. In this latter comparison all differences favored the code-emphasis phonics-first basal program.

It should be noted that Chall in her analysis of various types of instructional programs found the phonics-first program to differ little from conventional basals in its emphasis on comprehension, follow-up activities for a lesson, teacher guidance in reading, and similar variables. Perhaps this indicates that it is essential to direct the beginners' attention to a variety of reading tasks and to stress understanding of what is read in addition to developing the ability to decode words. Evidence seems to indicate that some direct early instruction in the more mature aspects of reading behavior may be helpful.

Conclusions regarding the influence of code-emphasis and meaning-emphasis programs on rate of reading are likewise ambiguous. At the end of the first grade pupils in linguistic programs were slower oral readers than pupils in basal programs. By the end of grade two, however, this finding was reversed. Pupils in the phonics-first code-emphasis program read at a higher rate than conventional pupils at the end of grade one, but no evaluation of rate of pupils in these programs was reported at the end of grade two. On the basis of the limited information available, there appears to be little reason for concern that first-grade and second-grade pupils in code-emphasis programs become slow, halting readers. Longitudinal data are necessary to test the long-range consequences of the two types of programs.

Similar problems exist in drawing conclusions from the data on accuracy of connected oral reading. Basal pupils read more accurately than linguistic pupils at both testing points. However, phonics-first basal pupils read more accurately than conventional basal pupils at the end of grade one. Here again the evidence can best be termed conflicting. It is likely that other variables peculiar to certain code-emphasis programs account for the lack of unanimity in the findings.

Needed Clarification

Although the study supports, in general, Chall's conclusions concerning the superiority of code-emphasis programs in beginning reading, a note of caution is in order. There is no clear evidence that the early emphasis on code per se is the *only* or even the *primary* reason for the relative effectiveness of the code-emphasis programs. The major types of programs which were compared differed in a number of respects in addition to the varying emphases on code and meaning. The possibility exists that some other characteristic the these programs (higher expectations of pupil achievement, for example) may be a more crucial element in determining pupil achievement than the emphasis on code-breaking. It is also possible that some particular combination of factors within the code-emphasis programs accounted for their effectiveness. There is some evidence for this conjecture in that the various code-emphasis programs did not appear to be equally effective. Unfortunately, studies of the nature discussed in this report compare *one complex* of instructional factors with *another complex* of instructional factors, thereby making it impossible to isolate the single characteristic (if indeed there is one) which makes one program more effective than another. Researchers interested in this question will likely have to turn to laboratory investigations.

References

Bond, G. L., and Dykstra, R. *Final Report of the Coordinating Center for First-Grade Reading Instruction.* (USOE Project X-001) Minneapolis: University of Minnesota, 1967.

Bond, G. L., and Dykstra, R. "The Cooperative Research Study in First-Grade Reading Instruction," *Reading Research Quarterly*, 2, no. 4 (1967) 9–142.

Chall, Jeanne. *Learning to Read.* New York: McGraw-Hill, 1967. P. 137.

Dykstra, R. *Final Report of the Continuation of the Coordinating Center for First-Grade Reading Instruction Programs.* (USOE Project 6–1651) Minneapolis: University of Minnesota, 1967.

Hayes, R. B., and Wuest, R. C. "I.t.a. and Three Other Approaches to Reading in the First Grade—Extended into Second Grade," *The Reading Teacher*, 20, no. 8 (1967), 694–97, 703.

Ruddell, R. "Reading Instruction in First Grade with Varying Emphasis on the Regularity of Grapheme-Phoneme Correspondences and the Relation of Language Structure to Meaning—Extended into Second Grade," *The Reading Teacher*, 20, no. 8 (1967), 730–36.

Sheldon, W. D., Nichols, Nancy, and Lashinger, D. R. "Effect of First-Grade Instruction using Basal Readers, Modified Linguistic Materials, and Linguistic Readers—Extended into Second Grade," *The Reading Teacher*, 20, no. 8 (1967), 720–25.

Schneyer, J. W. "Reading Achievement of First-Grade Children Taught by a Linguistic Approach and a Basal Readers Approach—Extended into Second Grade," *The Reading Teacher*, 20, no. 8 (1967), 704–10.

Tanyzer, H. J., and Alpert, H. "Three Different Basal Reading Systems and First-Grade Reading Achievement," *The Reading Teacher*, 19, no. 8 (1966), 636–42.

24. Linguistically Speaking, Why Language Experience?

MaryAnne Hall

The language experience approach has increasingly been employed for initial reading instruction in the last decade. In recent years, there has been growing interest in the implications of linguistic study for the teaching of reading. The term "linguistics" as related to reading instruction often signifies a beginning approach based on phoneme-grapheme correspondence through the presentation of a carefully controlled vocabulary illustrating selected spelling patterns. However, linguistics is used here with a broader application. Since reading is communication through written language, all reading, therefore, is linguistic. Knowledge about language supplied by linguists should lead to reading instruction based on accurate information about the reading process.

The relationship of reading to spoken language is basic to a linguistic definition of reading. This relationship is also basic to teaching reading through the language experience approach. Seven statements of the linguistic rationale for the language experience approach are expressed below in terms of the beginning reader.

The beginning reader must be taught to view reading as a communication process. Language experience reading is communication-centered. Attention is on communication through the medium of print just as in speaking and listening the emphasis is on communication through the medium of speech. In beginning reading, children should feel a need to communicate naturally through print just as before learning to read they had felt the need to communicate through speech. A creative and competent teacher must provide the stimuli and opportunities for children to communicate in reading and writing.

The content of personally composed stories involves concepts within the scope of children's background knowledge and interests. Communication is present as children react while discussing their ideas, as they write or watch the teacher write those ideas, and as they then read their ideas. Comprehension is present since children do understand that which they first wrote.

The beginning reader is a user of language (Goodman, 1969). The spoken language which the child possesses is his greatest asset for learning written language. The normal child from an adequate home environment has mastered the patterns of his native language by the time of school entrance. This is not to overlook the fact that his linguistic facility is by no means complete. He has much to absorb in language flexibility and elaboration; still, he has more than sufficient linguistic ability to learn to read.

In discussions of reading readiness, great attention has been given to the experience background of children, and less to their language background. When attention has been given to language factors, usually that attention has been to the extent of vocabulary and general language facility in expressing and understanding spoken language instead of how this facility operates in learning to read. The child who learned spoken language in the pre-

From MaryAnne Hall, Linguistically speaking, why language experience? *The Reading Teacher*, January 1972, 25, 328–331. Reprinted by permission of MaryAnne Hall and the International Reading Association.

school years displayed an amazing feat of linguistic performance. We should make it possible for him to learn to read with equal ease and to draw upon his existing linguistic background in doing so.

The beginning reader should understand the reading process as one of consciously relating print to oral language. As the beginning reader works with print he changes the unfamiliar graphic symbols to familiar oral language. Goodman (1968) defines reading as the processing of language information in order to reconstruct a message from print.

In the language experience approach the child finds translating print into speech greatly simplified since he is reading that which he first said. The message is easily reconstructed when the reader is also the author. In the beginning stages reading instruction must be geared to ensure success for the learner. The ease with which children can read their language should be capitalized on in language experience instruction.

Downing (1969) reports in studies of five and six year olds' views of reading that their conceptions of language are different from those of their teachers. Terminology such as "word," "sentence," "sound," and "letter" was unclear to the children in his research. He comments on the need to provide ". . . language experiences and activities which (a) *orient* children correctly to the true purposes of reading and writing, and (b) enable children's natural thinking processes to *generate understanding* of the technical concepts of language."

The beginning reader should incorporate the learning of writing with the learning of reading. Relating the written language code to the spoken code was discussed earlier as the task of the beginning reader. Learning the written code involves decoding— going from print to speech—and encoding—going from speech to print. In the language experience approach, writing is a natural corollary of reading as a child first watches the recording of thought he has dictated and as he progresses gradually to writing independently.

The integration of decoding and encoding should provide reinforcement in both processes. In studies of preschool readers, Durkin (1970) reported that interest in writing often preceded interest in reading. Dykstra (1968) reported in the National First Grade Studies that a writing component added to reading programs enhanced achievement in reading.

The beginning reader should learn to read with materials written in his language patterns. The language experience approach does use materials written with the language of the reader for whom they are intended. Reading materials should always convey meaning to a child in natural language phrasing which sounds right and familiar to him—not necessarily "right" to the ears of a Standard English speaker. For children who do not speak Standard English, the language of standard materials does not match their spoken language. While there are special materials written in nonstandard dialects, these materials are not available to all teachers of nonstandard-speaking children. Also, these materials may not fit all children in a group where they are being used. An often overlooked fact is that the limited preprimer language is also unlike the oral language of a child who does use Standard English.

The point to be remembered here is that the nonstandard speaker is a user of language. The absence of mastery of Standard English need not delay the beginning reading instruction when language experience materials are used. The teaching of oral Standard English will be another part of the total language program.

It is recommended that the teacher record the syntactical patterns of the children as spoken but using standard spelling. For example, if the child says "des" for "desk," the word will be written "desk," but if the child says, "My brother, he . . ." this pattern will be written. The language communicates, and there is sufficient language to be used for teaching beginning reading.

The beginning reader should learn to read meaningful language units. In language experience reading, children are dealing with thought units from the flow of their speech. They are not dealing with a phoneme-grapheme unit or a word unit, but with a larger piece of language. From the total running flow of speech of others in their environment they learned to talk. The child gradually learned to pick words of very high meaning, "Mommy," "Daddy," "me," and others. From one-word utterances the child progressed to two-word patterns and built his linguistic knowledge from hearing natural speech around him.

In reading from language experience, children learn to read using the meaning-bearing patterns of language. They will be exposed to reading material which is not controlled in vocabulary and which does not distort language in an effort to limit vocabulary or to emphasize phoneme-grapheme relationships. They gradually acquire a reading vocabulary by identifying words from stories which represent the natural flow of written language. Perhaps with the first experience story, children learn to read one word, perhaps two or three from the next one, and so on until their word banks represent a respectable stock of known words. These words were presented and learned, not in isolation, but in meaningful sentence and story units.

The beginning reader should learn to read orally with smooth, fluent, natural expression. The language experience approach provides oral reading situations in which children can truly "make it sound like someone talking." In the language experience approach, word-by-word emphasis in oral reading should not be permitted to occur. The teacher's model is important in illustrating fluent natural reading in the first pupil-dictated stories. In their concern that children learn vocabulary, some teachers may tend to distort the reading of experience stories with overemphasis on separate words.

Lefevre (1964) maintains that "single words, analyzed and spoken in isolation, assume the intonation contours of whole utterances. Single words thus lose the characteristic pitch and stress they normally carry in the larger constructions that comprise the flow of speech and bear meaning." He emphasizes that the sentence is the minimal unit of meaning, and that children should develop "sentence sense" in reading. In the language experience way of learning to read the beginner does learn to supply the "melodies of speech" as he reads.

The relationship of oral and written language can also be shown as punctuation signals are pointed out incidentally, with emphasis on function and meaning. For example, after a number of experience stories have been written the teacher may casually say, "This is the end of your idea—so we put a period. The next word goes with the next idea so we start this part with a capital letter."

Summary

The linguistic rationale for the language experience approach gives theoretical support to the teacher who is concerned with the implementation of this approach in teaching beginning reading. Language experience reading is truly a linguistically-based method since the relationship of oral and written language is the key to teaching children to read through the recording and reading of their spoken language. The beginning reader is a user of language who must relate graphic symbols to the oral language code he already knows. Understanding the process of language communication through language experience reading should enable the teacher to facilitate the task of learning to read for the beginner through use of relevant material which reflects *his* language. The most important consideration is how language communicates meaning—in language experience reading, *communication is the central focus*.

References

Downing, John. "How Children Think about Reading," *The Reading Teacher*, 23, December 1969, 217–230.

Durkin, Dolores. "A Language Arts Program for Pre-First-Grade Children: Two Year Achievement Report," *Reading Research Quarterly*, 5, Summer 1970, 534–565.

Dykstra, Robert. "Summary of the Second-grade Phase of the Cooperative Research Program in Primary Reading Instruction," *Reading Research Quarterly*, 4, Fall 1968, 49–70.

Goodman, Kenneth S. "Pro-Challenger Answer to 'Is the Linguistic Approach an Improvement in Reading Instruction'?" *Current Issues in Reading.* Conference Proceedings of 13th Annual Convention, Ed. Nila B. Smith, 268–276. Newark, Delaware: International Reading Association, 1969.

Goodman, Kenneth S. *The Psycholinguistic Nature of the Reading Process.* Detroit: Wayne State University Press, 1968.

Lefevre, Carl A. *Linguistics and the Teaching of Reading.* New York: McGraw-Hill, 1964.

CHAPTER VI

Measuring Reading Outcomes and Determining Needs

What are reading tests for? Harris opens the chapter by describing a dozen possible uses for reading tests, and discusses the impact of testing on morale, motivation, and achievement. Next, Betts (the originator of the informal reading inventory) provides a clear and concise explanation of this widely used procedure. Then McCracken describes how the idea of fitting the book to the child can be sold to both teachers and pupils.

Plas describes each of the kinds of scores that are available for users of standardized tests, and cautions against common misinterpretations of percentiles and grade-equivalent scores.

The Goodmans advocate the analysis of miscues in oral reading as a way to study the underlying processes of reading, and provide an example of miscue analysis. Hood, on the other hand, asserts that miscue analysis is too time-consuming to be practical for teachers and even for reading specialists, and concludes that total error scores provide a possible shortcut to the diagnostic use of miscue analysis.

25. Areas of Concern in Evaluation

Albert J. Harris

To be unable to evaluate what teachers are doing and what children are doing is to be lost in the forest with no compass. Evaluation, then, is an essential topic for the person working in the field of reading. One must not only understand some of the technicalities about how to give tests and how to score them and look up norms, but also try to discover the inner purposes of the tests—what are the tests for, and at what times evaluative procedures other than tests are needed. There are many

From Albert J. Harris, Areas of concern in evaluation. In *Significant issues in reading*. Proceedings of the Twenty-third Annual Reading Institute at Temple University, 1966. Philadelphia: Reading Clinic, Temple University, 1968. Pp. 62–72. Reprinted by permission of the author and Temple University.

areas of evaluation in reading where there are no satisfactory tests, and it becomes necessary to improvise.

Purposes of Tests

The first question is, "Why do we give tests? What purposes do they serve?" There must be more than twelve different purposes for giving tests in the area of reading but a list of just twelve should be sufficiently suggestive of the total breadth.

The first use is that of comparing the results of one group of pupils with other groups of pupils, as in a large-scale survey. The comparison may be between a class and other classes, or a school and other schools within a community, or a whole community as compared to other communities. In these kinds of comparisons, it is usually considered enough to use a test which has one overall score, or at most a very small number of parts. The concern is generally more with the question of norms than with the question of the instructional application of the results.

A second purpose is the prediction of the probable success or failure of individual pupils. Here, of course, from the end of kindergarten or beginning of first grade with readiness tests and on up through the grades, the assumption is made that what the children have done so far helps to predict what they are likely to do in the future. A report of a recent study in New York City indicates that the reading test results obtained at the end of the second grade predicted eighth-grade performance better than any intelligence measure they had utilized for the same purpose, and almost as well as any reading test given in between those grades. If this is true (and it may not be true in other communities, but it is worth checking), then it would seem to indicate that what happens in the first two grades is of crucial importance, and would point to the need for careful step-by-step checking on what beginning readers learn, before nonlearning can go too far.

A third purpose is for classification of pupils into groups for reading instruction. In some schools, reading tests are used to classify children into so-called homogeneous groups for all instruction. This is particularly prevalent in junior high schools where, very often, the results of a survey-type reading test are used to set up seventh-grade classes in numerical order from one (for brightest or best readers) to seventh or eighteenth (which are the ones reading below fourth-grade level). Of course, the term "homogeneous" cannot be used with any real accuracy. It would be preferable to call them "less heterogeneous" classes rather than "homogeneous" classes. Grouping in this way restricts the range somewhat, but anyone who has worked with so-called "homogeneous" classes has found out there are still plenty of individual differences left, no matter what is used to slice up the total population.

A fourth and somewhat related use is for the selection of pupils for special reading courses or remedial programs. Here, it seems, the reading tests that are used are usually reasonable for the purpose; but many crimes are committed in the use of tests to determine whether or not the children are capable of improving. Group I.Q. tests are often used, and a child who scores less than 90 on a group I.Q. test is often barred from the remedial program. This is in conflict with the well-established fact that, on the most widely used upper-grade and secondary school I.Q. tests, it is impossible for a poor reader to score above 90 I.Q. because he cannot read the questions. If he cannot read the questions, it is not an I.Q. test for him. It is just another reading test. Therefore, in the selection of pupils for special reading courses or remedial programs, extreme care must be exercised in what is used as a measure of reading potentiality; much more care with that than with the reading tests themselves.

A fifth use is for the measurement of specific sub-skills as a guide to group and individual instruction. Here most teachers rely on their own testing procedures, or on the use of published exercises as tests.

A sixth possible use is as a basis for the choice of instructional materials according to difficulty. Ever since Dr. Betts first published the idea of using the Informal Reading Inventory (a collection of book samples), there has been a lively argument as to the relative accuracy of standardized tests versus the book sample technique as a way of gauging the instructional materials most likely to fit the needs of individual youngsters.

A seventh use is the measurement of reading performance at intervals during an instructional program to check on the outcomes of the teaching of specific skills, or at the end of specific instructional periods as a kind of final test or check-up.

An eighth use is to compare the results of one experimental procedure with the results of other experimental procedures. In most of these research studies an appropriate battery of pre-tests is given before the teaching program is started. Then another battery of tests is given at the end of the experimental teaching period and the amounts of gain as a result of the different procedures are compared.

A ninth use is to provide diagnostic information that is useful in the analysis of both the causation and the instructional needs of children with reading problems.

A tenth use is as part of the admission requirement to certain schools or to special programs. In New York City, for example, a minimum reading test score of 7.0 is one of the entrance requirements for many of the senior high school programs. In some private schools, a reading grade of one year above the national norm is a minimum requirement for admission.

Number eleven is used as one of the requirements for pupil promotion or graduation. Many school systems still insist that in order to be allowed to enter the second grade, a first grader must score 2.0 or higher by the end of the first grade. This always seems like a echo from the dark ages, because it evidences the fact that they have no confidence in the ability of their second-grade teachers to pick up children where they are and carry them forward from there; or no interest in doing this. They are still committed to a doctrine of giving mass instruction and ignoring individual differences.

The twelfth use is to measure teacher effectiveness. This is where teachers have a very strong personal interest. "Why is the administration asking us to give the test, and what are they going to do with the scores after they get them?"

There are probably many more than these twelve kinds of uses, but these seem to be the most frequent and the most important uses of testing in the field of reading. Some of them are proper. Some of them are improper. Some of them are just misguided in the way in which they are applied. Putting the impact on teachers at the end of the list leads to the second major question—what impact does a testing program have upon the teachers and upon the children?

Impact of Tests

All classroom teachers know that when a testing program is inflicted from above it tends to engender resentment. It seems like time taken away from teaching; it involves dreary moments of just standing, watching, and waiting while the children are using up the time limit. Very often teachers resent being asked to score the tests and they show it in the way in which they do the scoring.

In a large-scale first-grade reading experiment, which was one of the 27 recipients of federal funds to take part in a cooperative, nationwide effort, all the tests were given that the central committee decided upon. The children were from twelve of the lowest achieving schools in New York City, located in Central Harlem, Bedford-Stuyvesant, and South Jamaica.

The administration of ten separate pre-tests was a disastrous experience for both teachers and children. First of all, most of the tests were much too hard for the children, and over and over again they ran into frustration as they tried to do what they were asked to do. Secondly, the teachers were inexpert in administering tests. Thirdly, anyone who has tried to give standardized tests according to standardized instructions to little five- and six-year-olds who have never been in a classroom before, and have been subjected to little or no disciplinary training at home before they arrive in September, will appreciate some of the problems of administering reading readiness tests to non-kindergarten-trained children with this kind of background. By the time the testing program was over, the morale level was down close to zero. When the teachers were told, "Well, that's over; you can now begin to teach," you could almost hear a sigh of relief coming up from all of the schools and all the teachers, and morale gradually built up. A testing program can be deleterious to the morale of children and of teachers if it is too long, and particularly, if the tests chosen are so difficult that a large number of the children experience little but frustration in taking them.

Consider some other factors. What influence does the time of year have? Standardized tests are usually given at one of two times in the year—usually in the late spring around May, but sometimes early in the year, even during the first week.

When end-of-year testing is done, the purposes are usually of three types:

(1) to provide information on which decisions concerning pupil classification for the following year will be made: decisions about promotion, about grouping, and even sometimes, decisions related to what materials to order for next year's classes; (2) to compare class with class within the school, school with school within the district, district with district within the city, and the city as a whole with other comparable cities, or if it is a small community, with similar communities elsewhere; and (3) to draw some conclusions about the effectiveness of the teacher.

As was mentioned before, this last is a tricky business. What the children learn depends partly on what they have learned in previous years. As a matter of fact, the higher up in the grades the testing is done, the more the percentage of what they do seems to be based upon what they have brought to the class at the beginning of the year, and the less it seems to depend upon what this specific teacher has been able to do during the year. If one does not take into consideration where the children were at the beginning, the judging is not of just one teacher, but of the composite effects of all the teachers the children have had.

When an attempt is made to take into account where the children were at the beginning of the year, there are many technical complications. Not only what they have learned in the past, but also what seems to be their potential for learning in the future must be considered. I.Q. as well as previous reading level has a bearing on this. In judging the effectiveness of teachers, is it sensible to judge the beginning first-grade teacher on the same scale as the teacher who has been in that grade for fifteen years, or should allowances be made for the teacher's previous background and experience?

There are all sorts of complications here. It is not at all surprising that teachers as a total group have a deep, dark suspicion of any attempt to rate their effectiveness in teaching on the basis of achievement tests given to their children. Yet in any other occupation, the practitioner's effectiveness is judged by his results; the baseball or football player is being judged by thousands of people any time he does anything. The actor, actress, musician, dancer, and so on—all are subjected to merciless evaluation every time they appear in public. Lawyers are judged by whether they win or lose cases; doctors by whether they lose a high proportion of their patients.

It is a real, professional obligation to work out some way of evaluating teacher effectiveness. If the effective teacher cannot be distinguished from the ineffective, how can the general level of performance improve? . . . This problem must be solved, in spite of its many technical complications and its intimate relationship with teacher morale.

One of the possible effects of the year-end testing program is that the teacher feels that this is a way of spying on her. As a result, some teachers are motivated to resort to defensive behavior. "It is too late for me to make any use of these results in teaching the children I have now, so this test doesn't do me any good. Therefore, I'm not really interested in whether it's accurate or inaccurate." Some teachers learn in advance which form of which test is going to be given, and teach the specific answers to specific items on the test, a very illegitimate procedure which ruins the test as a standardized test. Other teachers resort to somewhat lesser forms of sabotage such as forgetting to stop the children at the end of the time limit, or walking around the room and giving hints to children who seem puzzled. Finally, when such tests are corrected by the teacher of the children, it is surprising how few of their mistakes lower the score and how many of them raise the score. This could be a completely unconscious form of error, but nevertheless, one can understand the motivation for it.

What happens on the other hand, if instead of testing in May, the job is done in September or October? First of all, the teacher has the idea, "I didn't teach these children last year; therefore, the test can't possibly be used to evaluate what I did. They evaluate what some other teacher did with these children." She does not have the same feeling of being under scrutiny, or subjected to a form of spying. Second, she certainly ought to have the feeling, "I have almost a whole year ahead of me. If I can interpret these test results in a way that helps me improve my own planning of what to teach, what materials to use and how to use them, then the test is for my benefit more than it is for the benefit of the administration."

Now it happens that the administrator, if he is really intent upon evaluating someone, can attempt to draw some conclusions from these results about the effectiveness of last year's teacher, if he has kept the classes together as class units or if he is willing to go to the trouble of reconstructing last year's classes by collecting scores from a variety of new classes. Actually it is not often done, and when testing programs are carried out in the fall, the improvement of instruction is usually the primary and sometimes the only purpose. For this reason, fall testing programs seem definitely preferable to spring testing programs. They have far greater potential for benefiting the children and the teachers and impose far less of a threat upon anybody.

What are some of the effects of testing on learning? Pupils in general, and particularly bright pupils who are interested in getting good marks, do their best to learn what they expect to be tested on. One major difference between Phi Beta Kappa and ordinary college students is that the students who fairly consistently get A's spend a lot of time and effort trying to guess what the final examination questions are going to be. They set up lists of such possible questions and then prepare model answers for them which they then proceed to commit to memory. If they know the test is going to be an objective-type test with anywhere from one hundred to three hundred questions, they expect that a lot of these questions will be on the fine details that are contained in the footnotes in the textbook and in the charts and tables. So they pay extra attention to those. If, on the other hand, they know that the professor is addicted to using a small number of rather broad essay questions, they go over their recollection of everything he has talked about in his own lectures during the semester, trying to decide what he is most interested in and, therefore, what he is most likely to ask about. If the university keeps a file of previous exams, they will go over the exams of the past five years in that course and chart the relative probability of any one question's recurring. It is true at the college level. Very likely it is true also at the high school level and at the elementary school level.

In New York City high schools, the teachers know (at least at the junior and senior levels, or at the terminal levels in one-year courses like American History) that at the end of the course, the children are going to have to take a uniform state-wide examination. The result is that the last four to six weeks of the school year are spent reviewing the recent state-wide tests and making sure that every question that was asked in them has been thoroughly taken up and reviewed in class. This may or may not be effective in secondary school teaching. It happens to be true in practically every senior high school classroom in New York State, in every subject in which there is a state-wide test. If New York State can be used as a guinea pig, it can be predicted with confidence that as soon as the nature of the nationwide test is known, teachers will begin to teach for good performance on that test.

A second corollary is that teachers tend to neglect outcomes that are not going to be evaluated. This, it would appear, is even more serious and potentially far more deleterious. It does not mean that teachers will neglect everything that is not tested on standardized tests

given once a year. However, unless the teacher has worked out ways of evaluating the outcomes that she considers significant in her own teaching, she is going to neglect some areas that should be important, or she is never going to find out how effective her work was in promoting those particular objectives. This is especially true in those areas that are relatively more difficult to evaluate—in the development of literary appreciation, in the development of high-level and broad-ranging reading interests, in the development of critical reading skills, etc. These areas, which are the hardest to evaluate, therefore tend over and over again to be neglected by the teacher who is very much concerned about how her children are going to do on the formal testing program.

Needed Developments in Testing
Recreational reading

In the area of recreational reading there are only primitive measuring instruments, and there are many technicalities and problems in attempting to set up measuring instruments. For example, many teachers are utilizing one or another kind of individualized recreational reading program and they have all kinds of record keeping systems. Some of them are naive enough to be satisfied with the child's simply counting the number of books he has read, and they set certain arbitrary standards. Those who complete a certain number of books by such and such a date get their names on a special list or a gold star or some other mark of recognition. The inevitable result seems to be that those children who are reward-minded look for the thinnest books with the least amount of print per page and they go through them one a day. At the end of a month, they have perhaps twenty or more such books to their credit, but the total amount of actual reading might not be more than that of a child who, disregarding this reward system entirely, has plowed his way through two mature, demanding, and thick books. Simply counting the number of books read is not very effective.

The next level of operation is usually to check on the number of pages read in the book. Again it is a counting procedure. Perhaps in a remedial program where the teacher is working with small enough groups so she knows what books these are based on, and can move a child gradually to more and more mature books; this is a fully justified procedure. However, in a classroom where it is very difficult to keep track of the quality of the reading done by 20, 30, or more children, it is an incomplete way of evaluating recreational reading and needs to be supplemented by other ways of judging the quality and even the amount of reading done.

Whatever scheme is set up, there are some children who are going to find an illegitimate way to beat it. If, for example, the children's word is taken for whether they have read a book or not, without checking in some way on whether they show any signs of having read it, some children are going to be tempted to claim credit for books that they have not even opened. Other children are going to try to find out how much of the book they have to go through in order to be able to beat the teacher when she tries to check up on them. That leaves a limited number of alternatives. One is to cultivate, in the children, the belief that the teacher's evaluation is not nearly as important as what the pupil gains out of what he does. Therefore, a child who cheats the system is only fooling himself—he is not gaining from the program what will benefit him, cause him to become a better and more mature reader, or help him out in the future.

If this concept is developed, there need not be such great concern for trying to cross-check on the cheaters. However, if this attitude is not adopted by the children and the child who claims false credit is rewarded more than the child who reports honestly exactly what he did, more and more children get tempted to cheat. This is the result of an ineffective honor system at any level of school. What one rewards and what one does not reward have a tremendous effect upon the children's reaction to the reading program and specifically to recreational reading. Improper sets of rewards have worked havoc in many an otherwise well-designed recreational reading program.

Study skills

In the area of study skills, the problem is usually the lack of any attempt to evaluate what children are learning, and, as a result, a relative neglect of the teaching of *how* to study as compared to teaching what to study. More effort should be devoted in the content areas to teaching children how to tackle the material they should master. This would eliminate the need to spend so much time drilling the learned outcomes. It would be more likely to generate self-reliant and self-motivated students who will go ahead to learn not just what they expect the teacher to check up on, but well beyond it. The main point is that the way in which the evaluation program is set up has far greater effects on what pupils learn and how they learn it than most teachers have recognized in the past. Because of its tremendous impact on what students learn, the program of evaluation deserves careful and prolonged thought and planning.

26. Informal Inventories

Emmett Albert Betts

Systematic guidance in reading is, first of all, differentiated guidance. One of the first steps in systematic guidance is to estimate levels of the individual learners in the class. Until this is done, discussions of word analysis, semantic analysis, critical reading, concept development, group dynamics, and bibliotherapy deteriorate to the patter of faddists.

Basic information

To put reading instruction on a systematic basis, two questions must be answered. First, what is the highest level at which the child can read "on his own"? This is usually called the *independent* reading level. Second, what is the highest level at which the child can read under teacher supervision? This is usually called the *instructional* reading level.

Merits

An informal reading inventory has several merits. First, the teacher is given direct evidence on achievement and needs in terms of available instructional material. Second, the teacher is provided with a technique for detecting everyday needs in the classroom. Third, the child is convinced of his needs and sees how to improve his skill. The procedure is sound, understandable, and practicable.

To promote general language competence, the teacher guides her pupils in terms of their reading levels. Wholesome attitudes toward reading are fostered.

Achievement Levels

Basal level

With the exception of nonreaders, a learner usually can read material at some level of readability without *symptoms* of frustration, such as lip movement, finger pointing, word-by-word reading, tension movements, high-pitched voice, reversal errors, lack of attention to punctuation, and low comprehension. At this level he can pronounce all of the words without hesitation.

The highest readability level at which the individual can read without symptoms of frustration is the basal level. Often this is also the independent reading level. As succeeding levels of reading ability are attempted, two things happen. First, the number of symptoms increases. Second, each symptom becomes intensified.

Independent level

The independent reading level is the highest level at which the learner can read with full understanding and freedom from frustration. The reading is done without tension movements, lip movement, finger pointing, and other evidences of difficulty. Silent reading is characterized by a relatively fast rate of comprehension and absence of vocalization. Oral re-reading is characterized by rhythm, accurate interpretation of punctuation, accurate pronunciation of more than 99 percent of the words, and a conversational tone. At the independent level, the reading is fluent. The learner practices good reading habits.

Instructional level

The instructional level is the highest level at which the learner can read satisfactorily under teacher supervision in a group situation. For normal progress, this reading has the same characteristics as independent reading, with one exception. The child may require help on the recognition of words, but never more than 5 percent. If he must have help on more than one word in twenty, his comprehension bogs down. He becomes frustrated.

At a level just above the independent reading level, word recognition and/or comprehension needs may appear. If this is the only problem, the instructional level may be at this point.

Frustration level

Above the instructional level, symptoms of frustration usually increase rapidly. For example, at the next higher level, the rhythm of oral reading may tend to break and silent lip movement may be evidenced. At succeeding levels, there may be finger pointing, tension movements, a high-pitched voice, and other symptoms of frustration. This tendency to lip movement deteriorates to whispering and then to mumbling over unknown words.

Materials for Inventory

The materials used for an informal inventory are those found in a classroom equipped to meet the wide range of reading levels therein. They may be graded textbooks, graded current events materials, or other instructional materials graded in reading difficulty.

In order to guide reading development systematically, the teacher needs to have two types of information: (1) the reading achievement levels of each individual in the class, (2) the relative reading difficulty (readability) of each book used. THE AMER-ICAN ADVENTURE SERIES is graded in readability. Hence, the teacher who uses this series needs only to determine the starting level book for her group.

For an individual inventory, a series of graded materials is used. Short selections are read, beginning at a low level of readability and continuing until the individual's independent reading level is identified. Symptoms of difficulty are used as indicators of lack of achievement. . . .

Procedure for Inventory

The informal inventory is one of the most direct and effective means of appraising reading levels and needs. By using a graded series of reading materials, the teacher or clinician may observe responses in a reading situation. It is possible to estimate reading achievement levels in a well-motivated situation. In addition, specific needs may be evaluated in terms of related needs and background skills.

An informal inventory is easily administered. It is simply the observation of an individual as he reads at successively higher levels of readability. He starts at a low level, which causes no difficulty, and continues until the desired information on reading achievement is obtained.

An informal reading inventory situation may embrace an individual or a group. In a class of twenty to thirty-five pupils, there may be two or three who should be studied individually. However, the chief advantage of this no-cost inventory is that the teacher is provided with a technique for estimating reading levels and needs in *all* reading activities every day. It is as valuable in a group situation as in an individual situation.

Group inventories

Reading achievement may be assessed in two types of group situations. First, during each directed reading activity, the teacher notes both reading levels and needs. For some of the pupils, the material may be too difficult; for others, the material may be too easy. Since the teacher's obligation is to challenge all learners in a class, she uses some system of grouping.

Second, a group inventory may be administered in the same way as an individual inventory. The teacher explains to the group the purpose of the inventory and interests the pupils in finding out about themselves. She also encourages the group to note the differences in reading difficulty of the materials used for the inventory. Then each individual is given an opportunity to read in a motivated situation. This is continued with increasingly higher level materials until some members show signs of frustration.

In general, the first procedure is more satisfactory. Since modern schools use a cumulative guidance folder for each learner, the teacher usually has the benefit of the previous teacher's observations. The data is used to form tentative groups. Reassignment to groups is based on observations during directed reading activities, supplemented by an occasional individual inventory.

Individual inventories

In some instances there is a need for learning more about the reading level and needs of an individual than can be learned from a group inventory. About 10 percent of the learners in a regular classroom may profit from an individual inventory. In a corrective group, even more of the learners need to be studied in this manner. Since only five to fifteen minutes are required for each inventory, the time is well spent.

Establishing rapport

One of the chief values of an informal inventory is the understanding it gives the learner regarding his own needs. He proves to himself that he *can read* at some level. He develops self-confidence and interest.

A few minutes used for explaining the purpose and procedure of an informal inventory are well spent. How well one reads depends considerably upon the emotional climate of the situation. An understanding of what is expected is essential to rapport between the teacher and the learner.

General procedure

At each readability level, three steps are taken:

1. Oral reading at sight of a page or less.
2. Silent reading of a succeeding section of the material.
3. Oral re-reading of the material read silently.

Evaluating comprehension

Following each of the first two steps, the examiner tests the reader's comprehension. For step 3, the examiner requests the individual to read orally the parts that answer specific questions.

Different types of questions are asked in order to evaluate the reader's ability to:

1. Recall facts.
2. Associate an appropriate meaning with a term.
3. Identify a sequence of events.
4. Draw conclusions.
5. Apply information.

Estimating starting level

In order to give the learner a running start, begin with a very easy book, e.g., *Friday—The Arapaho Indian*. Usually, this starting level can be estimated from a word recognition test and general observation.

Oral reading at sight

This procedure is never used in a directed reading activity. However, it has many merits in a testing situation.

The learner is told that he is to begin reading aloud and that he will be asked questions about what he has read. He is then given a quick preview of the selection and some general questions to answer.

During the oral reading, the examiner notes hesitations, speed, rhythm, word pronunciation errors, interpretation of punctuation, and tension movements. Oral reading at sight induces difficulties. It brings to light pronunciation and comprehension needs.

Silent reading

This is standard procedure in a directed reading activity. Generally speaking, the first reading of a selection is always done silently.

After the findings on the oral reading at sight are recorded, the examiner asks the learner to continue with silent reading. One selection is read orally at sight; a succeeding selection is read silently. This silent reading is guided by sequential questions about the short selection. The learner reads silently until he finds the correct answer. He either gives the answer in his own words or re-reads orally the correct answer, depending upon what the examiner wishes to observe.

During the silent reading, the examiner notes speed, lip movement, tension movements, head movement, and other evidences of confusion or frustration. A record is kept of unknown words, comprehension scores, and other relevant information.

Oral re-reading

At and below the instructional level, the oral re-reading usually is much more fluent than oral reading at sight. At the independent reading level, the oral re-reading is done without hesitation and without symptoms of need for additional help.

There are at least two ways to approach oral re-reading. First, it may be done as a check on answers to silent reading questions. The learner merely reads answers to questions he locates by reading silently.

Second, the oral reading may be done following the completion of the silent reading activities. The learner may read orally the answers to different types of questions. Or he may re-read orally the whole selection for some specific purpose.

27. Using an Informal Reading Inventory to Affect Instruction

Robert A. McCracken

In one third grade in a traditional school, basal reading was the adopted program. It was September. Mrs. Smith was the teacher. She had taught fifteen years but she was new to teaching third grade. She asked the reading consultant for help

because the children in her reading groups were not responding well. She had inherited three reading groups from the second grade and had shifted one child.

Her top group had six children reading from a 3–2 level basal reader and doing the

From Robert A. McCracken, Using an informal reading inventory to affect instruction. In Thomas C. Barrett (Ed.), *The evaluation of children's reading achievement*. Newark, Del.: International Reading Association, 1967. Pp. 90–95. Reprinted by permission of Robert A. McCracken and the International Reading Association.

accompanying workbook exercises. The children were a joy but always finished their reading seat-work before the teacher had another activity ready. Her middle group had fourteen children reading from a 3–1 level and doing a good job. Her bottom group had eight children trying to read from a 3–1 level basal reader. They could not work independently even after instruction. They had trouble with silent reading, needed constant help when reading orally around the circle, and rarely got better than 50 percent the first time they did their workbook exercises. The teacher was using the same techniques with each group, techniques which seemed to work only with the middle group.

The reading consultant administered an informal reading inventory. The reason for Mrs. Smith's difficulties was apparent from the results. All six pupils in the top group were independent at level 3–2. All fourteen pupils in the middle group needed instruction at third reader level. All eight pupils in the bottom group were frustrated with 3–1 level material. Mrs. Smith and the second-grade teacher had recognized individual differences, knew how to conduct informal testing without

realizing it, but did not know how to record or evaluate the results.

Mrs. Smith saw the implications, but she was worried. The children would not like to be treated differently. The low group would be embarrassed by an easy book. They had read the 2–2 book last year!

The reading consultant made a chart, reproduced in Table 1. Each child took off his shoe and read his shoe size.

Each child was asked, "Why do you wear that particular shoe size?"

Pupils answered consistently, "Because it fits."

"Why don't you wear a bigger shoe? Don't you want your foot to grow faster?"

"That's crazy," a pupil said. "If my shoe didn't fit, it would hurt my foot or fall off when I run."

The reading consultant and the children talked about shoe sizes and the sequence of numerals indicating sizes. They talked about the impossibility of feet growing to be size 6 without having first been size 5 or size 4. They agreed that feet grow gradually from size 1 to 2, from 2 to 3 to 4, etc., not suddenly. They talked about book size and developed the con-

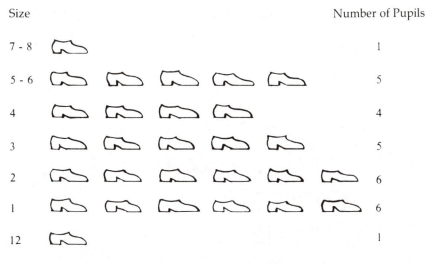

Table 1. Shoe Size of 28 Third Grade Children in September

cept that the numerals on basal readers are sizes, not grade level. They developed the concept that children learn to read book 2 after mastering book 1, book 3 after mastering book 2, etc.

The reading consultant made another chart, reproduced in Table 2. He told the children that he had measured their book sizes just as a shoe salesman might measure their foot sizes. He asked the pupils what their book sizes meant. From the top group came responses such as, "I need a harder book. Our reader is too easy. I've got a big book size." From the bottom group came responses such as, "I knew that book was too hard. I need an easy book. No wonder reading is hard."

Mrs. Smith told the children that many of them were going to shift into different books for reading instruction, that they would work in these books for one week, and that she would then ask them if their books fit. She explained that after the shoe salesman fits the shoe to your foot, he asks you to walk around a bit to see how it feels. After a week's instruction Mrs. Smith was going to ask, "How does your book fit?"

For a week the top group worked in book 4 and was assigned to choose library books for independent reading. The middle group continued reading from 3–1 level. The bottom group worked from a reader bridging 1–2 and 2–1 levels. The methods of instruction shifted slightly during this first week primarily because the children in the bottom group did not need constant attention.

At the end of the week one boy asked to change. He was the poorest reader in the middle group. He wanted to work in the bottom group. Two of the top group children said that book 4 was "Awful easy, but better than 3–2."

Some things stand out in this story:

1. *Children recognize and accept individual differences.* Teachers project adult fears when thinking that children are embarrassed by our recognizing that they are *poor* readers. The use of the word *poor* reflects this attitude. No one speaks of a *poor* shoe size. Children frequently are relieved when the teacher recognizes their difficulties. In the same way, adults are relieved when a doctor says, "You have *mal-and-sicitis*. It will take awhile but we

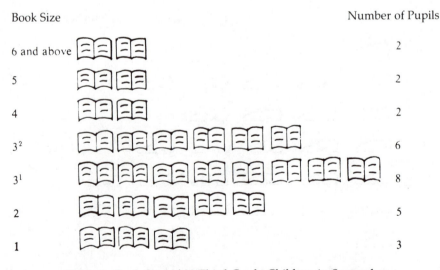

Book Size		Number of Pupils
6 and above		2
5		2
4		2
3^2		6
3^1		8
2		5
1		3

Table 2. Book Size of 28 Third Grade Children in September

can cure it." Compare reactions to this statement and to one in which the doctor says, "I don't think there is anything wrong with you. Just try a little harder to think that you're well."

2. *Children can understand the need for grouping and individual attention.* They accept book size as a concept, and they accept instruction whenever they can succeed. *Poor* readers do not object to *easy, baby* reading books if they are successful in them. *Poor* readers don't want to fail in *easy* materials. If they are going to fail, they want to fail something respectable. Failure at grade level is respectable. It is this reaction to failure in *easy* books which has led teachers to conclude that pupils reject *easy* materials.

3. *A low reading group can work independently much of the time.* The material has to be at their instructional level.

Mrs. Smith had a worry. Won't the children in group one miss the skill program? Obviously not. The children already had mastery of the skill program. Mrs. Smith had another worry. Won't the low reading group be retarded by the lack of challenge? One can infer the answer by observing the top group. The top group came to third grade with mastery of the third-grade reading program without ever having been taught from a reader harder than 2–2. Perhaps these children would have been more advanced had they had instruction at higher levels. But one cannot, on the basis of observations of top reading groups, conclude that *challenging* children makes them successful. Our most successful groups are those which have never been challenged much by reading group work. Working at an easy level with high success seems more important than challenge.

This story does not end with three groups in basal readers. The top group expanded into individualized reading without the teacher's being aware of it. Much of the reading instruction shifted to social studies and science. The success of the top group in self-selection led to the middle and bottom groups' having the same privilege. The classroom library was greatly expanded with plenty of easy picture books.

The informal testing led to a closer analysis of individual needs. Mrs. Smith assumed responsibility for continuous diagnostic observation. When a child had difficulty at instructional level, Mrs. Smith could see the difficulty because it was not shrouded with the maze of troubles which abound at frustration level. The able readers moved into projects which occasionally frustrated them, but more often just highlighted instructional needs; inefficient study skills and inefficient, ineffective note-taking stood out.

Mrs. Smith developed a sensitivity to standards of performance so that her instruction took its cue from pupils' performances, not from grade-level expectancies. The stumbling of the poor reader group no longer sounded right because that was the way the poor reading groups always sounded. The fluency of the top reading group no longer sounded right when it reflected complete independence with the material. Both Mrs. Smith and the pupils were affected by the use of the informal reading inventory, and so was the teacher of grade four the following year when the pupils did not want to be in the same book and told the teacher why. But that is another story.

28. If Not Grade Equivalent Scores— Then What?

Jeanne M. Plas

It seems that measurement specialists have finally learned what interpreters of classroom tests have known for some time now—something is not quite right with grade equivalent scores. It's a problem of miscommunication and misunderstanding resulting in misuse. Several recent articles (Echternacht, 1977; Armer, 1977) have reported some of the most common misconceptions concerning the use of grade equivalent scores. It is almost disheartening to read of problem after problem associated with a score that seems, at first glance, so straightforward and usable. It is precisely the deceptively simple nature of the expressed grade equivalent score that has been responsible for its popularity as a means of reporting pupil achievement test performance. It seems so reasonable to interpret a grade equivalent score of 3.7 as meaning only that the child performed on the test in the same way as the average third grader who takes the test in March. Yet more and more consumers are beginning to know that such a statement is an over-simplified version of what really is true. Indeed, from certain points of view such a statement can be considered false.

The test consumer might well ask why the grade equivalent score was not designed to provide more directly than it does what the user is so likely to assume given the simple nature of the grade equivalent expression. In other words, why isn't it as simple as it looks? The answer to this question lies within the purpose and function of statistics in general.

Both simple and complex statistics are designed to illustrate relationships within a set of meaningful numbers. For example, comparing any given score to the arithmetic mean (a simple statistic) will indicate how the score stands in relation to a central score, the average. The purpose of any statistic ever devised can be indicated in a way similar to this example. Statistics always stand for relationships among numbers within a group or across groups. The primary function of any statistic is to distill information regarding relationships into as simple an expression as possible. Ultimately, the highest form of the art of inventing a usable statistic involves producing a simple numerical expression that can communicate a large amount of relational information. Quite appropriately, the more complex the statistic, the more relationships it represents. Thus, an apparently simple statistical expression can represent a set of complex relationships. If it represents a number of such relationships, its interpretation demands that these relationships be incorporated into its explanation.

Each statistic used in explanation of standardized achievement test results represents a different set of relationships. Thus, there is no such thing as a "best" statistic for interpretation purposes. Each statistic merely represents relationships from a different point of view. Given the wide variety of statistics available for interpretation of standardized achievement scores, a user of tests is not bound to accept any one statistic for individual interpretation purposes. The art of test score interpretation is not dependent solely upon the statistic used. It is the

From Jeanne M. Plas, If not grade equivalent scores—then what? *Measurement in Education*, Spring 1977, *8*, 4–8. Copyright 1977, National Council on Measurement in Education, Washington, D.C.

transaction between the statistic and the user's knowledge of how the statistic "works" that makes for good test interpretation. *A test consumer should always interpret a score through use of that statistic which represents relationships that are best understood by the user.*

The remaining portion of this discussion is concerned with a simple description of important relationships[1] which underlie the most commonly used statistics within the field of norm-referenced[2] achievement testing. The majority of these statistical expressions are found in the technical and administrative manuals of commercially popular tests in use in schools today. Persons charged with interpreting achievement scores should choose the statistic that represents relationships which are most easily understood and meaningful to them.

The Raw Score

The raw score represents the total number of correct responses on a test or subtest. It tells very little about the person who took the test and nothing about performance in relation to others who have taken the test. Before the student's performance can be evaluated in terms of the performance of others, the raw score must be converted to one of the following expressions so that such relationships can be identified.

Percentile Rank

A table located within the test manual provides for quick conversion from raw score to percentile rank. The percentile rank indicates the percent of people scoring at or below an individual's raw score. Percentiles range from 1 to 99 with the mean percentile located at 50. Thus, a percentile rank of 65 shows that the individual's performance meets or exceeds that of 65% of the sample upon whom the test was normed. The relationships that need to be attended to when using this statistic grow

out of the percentile's involvement with the normal curve ($\frown$),[3] a bell-shaped curve which represents the frequency with which people distribute themselves across the range of possible scores. The normal curve illustrates that most people, approximately 68 percent, tend to score in the middle range while significantly fewer score at the lower and upper ends of the range. The normal curve-based percentile ranking system is designed to represent this situation and thus, the test interpreter must be aware of the following two relationships in addition to the basic definition of the percentile rank cited above.

The first point to be remembered is that the average range[4] on standardized achievement tests is located between the 16th and 84th percentiles. By simply subtracting 16 percent from 84 percent, the reader will discover that the 68 percent called for within the average range has been provided for through application of these two percentiles to the lower and upper limits of the average range. Thus, for example, while the 30th and 70th percentiles may appear to many to be below and above average, respectively, they are both well within the average range.

The second relationship of importance is that the distances between percentiles are not equal across the entire percentile range. A percentile of 40 is not equally distant from percentiles of 30 and 50. Thus, equal numbers of raw score points are not found from percentile to percentile. Behaviorally, this means that a child has to answer more questions correctly in order to move shorter distances within the middle range. The exact opposite is true within the above and below average ranges. In some cases, as many as five correct answers are represented between the 50th and 51st percentiles while one additional correct answer can move a child from the 90th to 95th or 1st to 5th percentile. Moving from the 50th to 55th percentile indicates less change in achievement level than does moving from the 90th to the 95th percentile.

Failure to use the above information when interpreting a percentile will always lead to erroneous conclusions. Mastery of the percentile rank concept demands that the relationships identified above be incorporated into any attempt at interpretation.

T-Score

If T-scores are suggested for use by the test publisher, a raw score to T-score conversion table is provided. Over 99 percent of all subjects will score within a T-score range of 20 through 80. The mean is located at a T-score of 50. T-scores have been designed so that the two relationships which need attention when interpreting percentiles have been accounted for statistically within the nature of this standardized scoring system. Equal distances across the T-score range can be assumed. Thus, the relationship of primary interest becomes the fact that the average group, 68 percent of the national sample, falls somewhere between T-scores of 40 and 60.

In at least one respect, T-scores provide an opportunity for clearer interpretation than do percentile ranks. The advantage is located within the initial naivete of the consumer with respect to T-scores. Since T-scores are not as popular within the common culture, there is no misinformation to be corrected as is the case with percentiles.

From another point of view, some information loss can be expected to occur through use of T-scores. For example, the fact that approximately 84 percent of those taking the test fall at or below a T-score of 60 is representative of a relationship that is not intuitively obvious. Yet such relationships need to be understood and memorized in order for the full use of the statistic to occur. The principle underlying the relationship just described is that T-scores are directly comparable to percentiles. Thus, the lower and upper limits of

the average range are equivalent for both T-scores and percentiles. Since the average T-score range is 40–60, a T-score of 40 is equivalent to a percentile rank of 16 while a T-score of 60 is equivalent to a percentile of 84. The relationship holds true across the full range of T-scores and percentiles.

Stanines

Stanines can also become readily available for interpretation through use of a raw score to Stanine conversion table located in most achievement test manuals. The word stanine is a shortened form of the term, "standard nines," which indicates that the entire normal (bell-shaped) distribution is divided into nine parts. The fifth stanine represents that group of testees which falls to the immediate left and right of the mean, and contains 20 percent of the entire sample. Although this is the middlemost group, the 5th stanine does not represent the entire average range. The average range extends from a point in the third stanine to a point in the seventh stanine. Again, approximately 68 percent of the entire sample falls within this range. The major problem when using stanines occurs when an attempt is made to interpret scores which fall in the third and seventh stanines. The lower and upper limits of the average range are imbedded within these two stanines, respectively. This means that approximately two-thirds of those who score at the seventh stanine are within the average range while approximately one-third score above the average range (and conversely for the third stanine). Thus, when only stanine information is available and the individual score falls within the third or seventh stanines, it is impossible to accurately determine performance with reference to the average range. In such cases, it is probably best to refer to such performances as borderline below average (third stanine) or borderline above average (seventh stanine).

Grade Equivalent Scores

Grade equivalent scores are the result of the conversion of raw scores into expressions which indicate achievement level in terms of academic development. Grade equivalent expressions such as 2.7 and 5.3 are to be read as second grade, seventh month and fifth grade, third month, respectively. Thus, grade equivalent scores, unlike other statistical expressions, are designed to express achievement in terms of the American public school grade level system. While statistics such as percentiles and T-scores may be rather directly applicable for use in European or Asian countries, grade equivalent scores, for the most part, are not. They are unique to the American educational system and their interpretation depends upon familiarity with that system.

The basic relationship interpretable through use of a grade equivalent score is the relationship between the individual's actual grade placement and the mean grade equivalent score obtained by the group which shares that actual grade placement. For example, in constructing grade equivalent scores it is predetermined that the mean score obtained by the sample group of second grade, seventh month testees will be identified as a grade equivalent score of 2.7. Put another way, if during the norming process the test is administered to second grade children during March (the seventh month), then the average raw score obtained by these children will convert to a 2.7 grade equivalent score. The major problem in interpreting grade equivalent scores occurs when one overlooks the fact that this mean grade equivalent score only represents the average or center score of the entire distribution. All children are not expected to score at the mean. Approximately 68 percent are expected to score around this mean. Thus, individual scores are only interpretable as they relate to a range of grade equivalent scores that represents the average group. An appreciation for the severity of the interpretation problem increases when one becomes familiar with the fact that grade equivalent average ranges or bands are very different across subtests and across grade levels.

The manual of one widely used achievement test reports that the following ranges indicate average performance (± one standard deviation) across the identified subtests at the third grade level (End of Year Testing):

Subtest	Average Grade Equivalent Range
Reading	2.3 to 5.3
Language	2.5 to 5.7
Mathematics Computation	3.0 to 4.8

The grade equivalent scores of 5.3, 5.7, and 4.8 all fall at the 84th percentile just as those identified as lower limits (2.3, 2.5, 3.0) fall at the 16th percentile. The average range varies across subtests and is more extended than might be expected. Grade placement scores of 5.0, 5.1, and 4.3 across the subtests might seem, at first glance, to indicate superior performance for a third grade child. Yet they are well within the average range. This example is not atypical. Rather, it represents the prevailing situation.

It is important to note also that, in the above example, grade equivalent scores of 5.3, 5.7, and 4.8 on reading, language and computation subtests respectively, are all representative of performances which equal or exceed that of 84 percent of the third grade children on whom the test was standardized. The performances are thus equivalent in interpretation even though represented by different grade placement scores. The easiest and best interpretation of grade equivalent scores probably is made through use of the percentile rank at which they are located.

The problem which occurs when interpreting across grade level also deserves special attention. It is located in the fact that at the lower grade levels the average range is more compressed than it is at the upper grade levels. A child who scores one grade level below the mean in the first grade in any skill area may well have scored below the average range. This is not true at the upper grade levels where such a performance (one year below grade level) may well be solidly within the average range. At the upper grade levels, a larger amount of material is covered: More years of achievement are being assessed.

Most problems associated with grade equivalent interpretation are located in a misunderstanding of the variable nature of the grade equivalent average range across subtests and across actual grade placements. Once the necessity for consulting such ranges is realized, the test consumer often will be able to locate these ranges within test manuals. This information is becoming increasingly more available as test producers become acquainted with the problems the test consumer experiences in trying to use only common sense when interpreting grade equivalent scores. As is the case with percentile ranks, common sense often is not enough when correct interpretation is the goal.

Another area of misconception specifically involves the interpretation of above average grade equivalent scores. A grade equivalent score of 7.2 on a fourth grade arithmetic subtest does *not* mean that the child is capable of performing seventh grade mathematics work. Grade equivalent scores are derived from the relationship of the student's performance to norm-referenced percentiles. They are not derived by incorporating into the test significantly above grade level work. Thus, in the example above, the fourth grade student was not asked to solve seventh grade math problems. Without giving a seventh grade test, we have no valid way of knowing how the student performs in relation to the seventh grade work.

The statistics cited above are those most commonly used in connection with standardized achievement tests. The statistic of choice always ought to be that statistic which represents relationships that are best understood by the test consumer. It is unfortunate and almost paradoxical that the two statistical expressions which have most relevance to the common culture, the percentile rank and grade equivalent score, are the two which are most easily misunderstood and misused. It is perhaps their apparent culture-relevance which is at the root of the problem. Because test consumers are familiar with the terms, they are quick to conclude that they understand the basic relationships represented by the terms. Since these relationships are intimately involved with the conception of a normal distribution, it is not always true that the relationships can be explained through use of familiar concepts and common sense. Statistical relationships must be learned and memorized if errors are to be avoided.

The person who experiences difficulty in learning and using the concepts identified above often feels incompetent due to a lack of knowledge concerning where to begin given what appears to be a massive amount of new and unfamiliar information. Such a test consumer is urged to consider a beginning that involves the concept of the average range. Each statistic associated with achievement testing is best used if the average range is located and individual scores are then related to it. Although average ranges look quite different from statistic to statistic, equivalent information is supplied. All average ranges discussed here encompass the middle 68 percent of test performances. The following table identifies the average range for those statistics referred to in this discussion:

Statistic	Average range
Percentile	16% tile—84% tile
T-score	40—60
Stanine	mid 3rd—mid 7th
Grade Equivalent Score	Highly variable across tests, subtests, and grade levels. Test Manual must be consulted.

Once the location of the average range is mastered for each statistical expression, the test interpreter is free to decide if an individual score represents average, below average, or above average performance. Further interpretation of the score depends upon mastery of the unique relationships represented by the various statistical expressions. Some of the most basic of these have been described above. Each test interpreter is free to choose a statistical expression that seems most understandable and meaningful. It is through use of such a process that consumers answer for themselves questions such as, "If not grade equivalent scores—then what?"

Notes

1. For an excellent figural description of these relationships the reader is referred to Psychological Corporation Test Service Bulletin 48 (1954) where the relationships are illustrated through visual reference to the location of standard deviations on the normal curve.
2. Interpretation of statistics associated with criterion-referenced testing is not included in this discussion. The only distribution considered is the normal distribution since it is this distribution which is most important for interpretation of standardized educational tests.

3. Percentiles are not dependent upon a normal distribution. However, percentiles used by teachers in connection with standardized tests have almost always been adapted to the normal curve. Thus, an understanding of norm-referenced percentiles is crucial for the classroom teacher.
4. Throughout this discussion, the average range is identified as the range encompassed between ± one standard deviation from the mean. However, the reader should be aware that use of the standard error of measurement dictates the conceptualization of an average range that will always be smaller than that derived from the use of the standard deviation alone. While the standard deviation provides for a range about the mean, the standard error of measurement provides a range that can be used with an individual score. It is a statistic which attempts to account for error which is attributed to the measurement process itself.

References

Armer, William. *Thoughts on Achievement Testing*: A checklist for teachers. (Unpublished manuscripts ESEA Title III, Wilson County, Tennessee, 1977).

Echternacht, Gary. Educational Testing Service. *Grade Equivalent Scores*, 1977.

Psychological Corporation Test Service Bulletin, *48. Methods of Expressing Test Scores*. New York: The Psychological Corporation, 1954.

29. Learning about Psycholinguistic Processes by Analyzing Oral Reading

Kenneth S. Goodman and Yetta M. Goodman

Over the past dozen years we have studied the reading process by analyzing the miscues (or unexpected responses) of subjects reading written texts. We prefer to use the word *miscue* because the term *error* has a negative connotation and history in education. Our analysis of oral reading miscues began with the foundational assumption that reading is a language process. Everything we have observed

From Kenneth S. Goodman and Yetta M. Goodman, Learning about psycholinguistic processes by analyzing oral reading. *Harvard Educational Review*, August 1977, 47, 317–333. Copyright © 1977 by President and Fellows of Harvard College.

among readers from beginners to those with great proficiency support the validity of this assumption. This analysis of miscues has been in turn the base for our development of a theory and model of the reading process.

In this paper we will argue that the analysis of oral reading offers unique opportunities for the study of linguistic and psycholinguistic processes and phenomena. We will support this contention by citing some concepts and principles that have grown out of our research.

We believe that reading is as much a language process as listening is. In a literate society there are four language processes: two are oral (speaking and listening), and two are written (writing and reading). Two are productive and two receptive. In the study and observation of productive language, we may analyze what subjects say or write; however, except for an occasional slip of the tongue, typographical error, or regression to rephrase, speech and writing offer no direct insight into the underlying process of what the speaker or writer intended to say. The study of receptive language—listening and reading—is even more diffi-

cult. Either we analyze postlistening or postreading performance, or we contrive controlled-language tasks to elicit reactions for analysis.

Reading aloud, on the other hand, involves the oral response of the reader, which can be compared to the written text. Oral readers are engaged in comprehending written language while they produce oral responses. Because an oral response is generated while meaning is being constructed, it not only is a form of linguistic performance but also provides a powerful means of examining process and underlying competence.

Consider how Peggy, a nine-year-old from Toronto, reads aloud. Peggy was chosen by her teacher as an example of a pupil reading substantially below grade level. The story she read was considered to be beyond her current instructional level. Peggy read the story hesitantly, although in places she read with appropriate expression. Below are the first fourteen sentences (S1–S14) from "The Man Who Kept House" (1964, pp. 282–283). In this and other excerpts from the story the printed text is on the left; on the right is the transcript of Peggy's oral reading.

Text	*Transcript*
(S1a) Once upon a time there was a woodman who thought that no one worked as hard as he did.	(S1b) *Once upon a time there was a woodman. He threw . . . who thought that no one worked as hard as he did.*
(S2a) One evening when he came home from work, he said to his wife, "What do you do all day while I am away cutting wood?"	(S2b) *One evening when he . . . when he came home from work, he said to his wife, "I want you do all day . . . what do you do all day when I am always cutting wood?"*
(S3a) "I keep house," replied the wife, "and keeping house is hard work."	(S3b) *"I keep . . . I keep house," replied the wife, "and keeping . . . and keeping . . . and keeping house is and work."*
(S4a) "Hard work!" said the husband.	(S4b) *"Hard work!" said the husband.*
(S5a) "You don't know what hard work is!	(S5b) *"You don't know what hard work is!*
(S6a) You should try cutting wood!"	(S6b) *You should try cutting wood!"*

(S7a) "I'd be glad to," said the wife.

(S8a) "Why don't you do my work some day?"

(S9a) "I'll stay home and keep house," said the woodman.

(S10a) "If you stay home to do my work, you'll have to make butter, carry water from the well, wash the clothes, clean the house, and look after the baby," said the wife.

(S11a) "I can do all that," replied the husband.

(S12a) "We'll do it tomorrow!"

(S13a) So the next morning the wife went off to the forest.

(S14a) The husband stayed home and began to do his wife's work.

(S7b) *"I'll be glad to," said the wife.*

(S8b) *"Why don't you . . . Why don't you do my work so . . . some day?"*

(S9b) *"I'll start house and keeping house," said the woodman.*

(S10b) *"If you start house . . . If you start home to do my work, well you'll have to make bread, carry . . . carry water from the well, wash the clothes, clean the house, and look after the baby," said the wife.*

(S11b) *"I can do that . . . I can do all that," replied the husband.*

(S12b) *"Well you do it tomorrow!"*

(S13b) *So the next day the wife went off to the forest.*

(S14b) *The husband stayed home and began to do his wife's job.*

Peggy's performance allows us to see a language user as a functional psycholinguist. Peggy's example is not unusual; what she does is also done by other readers. She processes graphic information: many of her miscues show a graphic relationship between the expected and observed response. She processes syntactic information: she substitutes noun for noun, verb for verb, noun phrase for noun phrase, verb phrase for verb phrase. She transforms: she omits an intensifier, changes a dependent clause to an independent clause, shifts a "wh-" question sentence to a declarative sentence. She draws on her conceptual background and struggles toward meaning, repeating, correcting, and reprocessing as necessary. She predicts grammar and meaning and monitors her own success. She builds and uses psycholinguistic strategies as she reads. In short, her miscues are far from random.

From such data one can build and test theories of syntax, semantics, cognition, comprehension, memory, language development, linguistic competence, and linguistic performance. In oral reading all the phenomena of other language processes are present or have their counterparts, but in oral reading they are accessible. The data are not controlled and clean in the experimental sense. Even young readers are not always very considerate. They do complex things for which we may be unprepared; and, not having studied the latest theories, they do not always produce confirming evidence. But they are language users in action.

Miscues and Comprehension

If we understand that the brain is the organ of human information processing, that the brain is not a prisoner of the senses but that it controls the sensory organs and selectively uses their input, then we should not be surprised that what the mouth reports in oral reading is not what the eye has seen but what the brain has generated for the mouth to report. The text is what the brain responds to; the oral output reflects the underlying competence and the psycholinguistic processes that have generated it. When expected and observed responses match, we get little insight into this process. When they do not match and a miscue results, the researcher has a window on the reading process.

Just as psycholinguists have been able to learn about the development of oral-language competence by observing the errors of young children, so we can gain insights into the development of reading competence and the control of the underlying psycholinguistic processes by studying reading miscues. We assume that both expected and unexpected oral responses to printed texts are produced through the same process. Thus, just as a three-year-old reveals the use of a rule for generating past tense by producing "throwed" for "threw" (Brown, 1973), so Peggy reveals her control of the reading process through her miscues.

We use two measures of readers' proficiency: *comprehending*, which shows the readers' concern for meaning as expressed through their miscues, and *retelling*, which shows the readers' retention of meaning. Proficient readers can usually retell a great deal of a story, and they produce miscues that do not interfere with gaining meaning. Except for S3, S8, and S9, all of Peggy's miscues produced fully acceptable sentences or were self-corrected. This suggests that Peggy's usual concern was to make sense as she read. In contrast, many nonproficient readers produce miscues that interfere with getting meaning from the story. In a real sense, then, a goal of reading instruction is not to eliminate miscues but to help readers produce the kind of miscues that characterize proficient reading.

Miscues reflect the degree to which a reader is understanding and seeking meaning. Insight can be gained into the reader's development of meaning and the reading process as a whole if miscues are examined and researchers ask: "Why did the reader make this miscue and to what extent is it like the language of the author?"

Miscue analysis requires several conditions. The written material must be new to the readers and complete with a beginning, middle, and end. The text needs to be long and difficult enough to produce a sufficient number of miscues. In addition, readers must receive no help, probe, or intrusion from the researcher. At most, if readers hesitate for more than thirty seconds, they are urged to guess, and only if hesitation continues are they told to keep reading even if it means skipping a word or phrase. Miscue analysis, in short, requires as natural a reading situation as possible.

The open-ended retellings used in miscue analysis are an index of comprehension. They also provide an opportunity for the researcher or teacher to gain insight into how concepts and language are actively used and developed in reading. Rather than asking direct questions that would give cues to the reader about what is significant in the story, we ask for unaided retelling. Information on the readers' understanding of the text emerges from the organization they use in retelling the story, from whether they use the author's language or their own, and from the conceptions or misconceptions they reveal. Here is the first segment of Peggy's retelling:

> um . . . it was about this woodman and um . . . when he . . . he thought that he um . . . he had harder work to do than his wife. So he went home and he told his wife, "What have you been doing all day." And then his wife told him. And then, um . . . and then, he thought that it was easy work. And so . . . so . . . so his wife, so his wife, so she um . . . so the wife said, "well so you have to keep," no . . . the husband says that you have to go to the woods and cut . . . and have to go out in the forest and cut wood and I'll stay home. And the next day they did that.

By comparing the story with Peggy's retelling and her miscues, researchers may interpret how much learning occurs as Peggy and the author interact. For example, although the story frequently uses "woodman" and "to cut wood," the noun used to refer to setting, "forest," is used just twice. Not only did Peggy provide evidence in her retelling that she knew that "woods" and "forest" are synonymous, but she also indicated that she knew the author's choice was "forest." The maze she worked through until she came to the author's term suggests that she was searching for the author's language. Although in much of the work on oral-language analysis mazes are not analyzed, their careful study may provide insight into oral self-correction and the speaker's intention.

There is more evidence of Peggy's awareness of the author's language. In the story the woodman is referred to as "woodman" and "husband" eight times each and as "man" four times; the wife is referred to only as "wife." Otherwise pronouns are used to refer to the husband and wife. In the retelling Peggy used "husband" and "woodman" six times and "man" only once; she called the wife only "wife." Peggy always used appropriate pronouns in referring to the husband and wife. However, when "cow" was the antecedent, she substituted "he" for "she" twice. (What does Peggy know about the sex of cattle?)

Comparing Peggy's miscues with her retelling gives us more information about her language processes. In reading, Peggy indicated twice that "said" suggested to her that a declarative statement should follow: One such miscue was presented above (see S2); the other occurred at the end of the story and is recorded below.

Text

(S66a) Never again did the woodman say to his wife, "What did you do all day?"

Transcript

(S66b) *Never again did the woodman say to his wife, "That he . . . what did you do all day?"*

In both instances she corrected the miscues. In the retelling she indicated that after "said" she could produce a question: "And then, from then on, the husband did . . . did the cutting and he never said, 'What have you been doing all day?'" Even though she had difficulty with the "wh-" question structure in her reading, she was able to develop the language knowledge necessary to produce such a structure in her retelling.

Reading and Listening: Active Receptive Processes

A producer of language can influence the success of communication by making it as complete and unambiguous as possible. The productive process must carry through from thought to underlying structures to graphic or oral production. Written production, particularly, is often revised and edited to correct significant miscues and even to modify the meaning. The receptive process, however, has a very different set of constraints. Listeners and readers must go through the reverse sequence from aural or graphic representation to underlying structure to meaning. Receptive language users are, above all, intent on comprehending—constructing meaning.

Readers and listeners are *effective* when they succeed in constructing meaning and are *efficient* when they use the minimal effort necessary. Thus, through strategies of predicting, sampling, and confirming, receptive language users can leap toward meaning with partial processing of input, partial creation of surface and deep structures, and continuous monitoring of subsequent input and meaning for confirmation and consistency. Many miscues reflect readers' abilities to liberate themselves from detailed attention to print as they leap toward meaning. Consequently, they reverse, substitute, insert, omit, rearrange, paraphrase, and transform. They do this not just with letters and single words, but with two-word sequences, phrases, clauses, and sentences. Their own experiences, values, conceptual structures, expectations, dialects, and life styles are integral to the process. The meanings they construct can never simply reconstruct the author's conceptual structures. That every written text contains a precise meaning, which readers passively receive, is a common misconception detrimental to research on comprehension.

We have argued above that reading is an active, receptive process parallel to listening. Oral-reading miscues also have direct parallels in listening. Although listening miscues are less accessible, since listeners can only report those they are aware of, still these must be quite similar to reading miscues. Anyone who has ever tried to leave an oral message knows that listening miscues are surely not uncommon. In both reading and listening, prediction is at least as important as perception. What we think we have heard or read is only partly the result of sensory data; it is more the result of our expectations.

A major difference between reading and listening is that the reader normally can regress visually and reprocess when a miscue has led to a loss of meaning or structure. The listener, on the other hand, must reprocess mentally, await clarification, or ask a speaker to explain. Furthermore, the speaker may continue speaking, unaware of the listener's problem. Readers are in control of the text they process; listeners are dependent upon the speaker.

References

Brown, Roger. *A first language*. Cambridge, Ma., Harvard University Press, 1973.

"The man who kept house." In J. McInnes, M. Gerrard, and J. Ryckman (Eds.), *Magic and make believe*. Don Mills, Ontario: Thomas Nelson, 1964.

30. Is Miscue Analysis Practical for Teachers?

Joyce Hood

"I may be old-fashioned, but I think today's experts complicate things too much. I remember when oral reading errors were errors, not miscues, and when error analysis was so easy first graders could do it. We taught a child to read the first page of a book and put up one finger for each unknown word. If all the fingers on one hand went up before the page was finished, this showed the book was too hard for that child to read."

"Maybe the method for first graders was a little oversimplified. But do you really believe a teacher who has 25 or more pupils will use modern-day miscue analysis if it takes much more time than that? Does a teacher really need to know more than the total number of errors made in proportion to the number of words that were read? As obtained in the traditional informal reading inventory (IRI), this information requires little more than first grade math skills except to count past 100 and know how to divide. In less that 30 minutes a teacher can determine a child's oral reading accuracy level and place the

From Joyce Hood, Is miscue analysis practical for teachers? *The Reading Teacher*, December 1978, 32, 260–266. Reprinted with the permission of Joyce Hood and the International Reading Association.

child in appropriate instructional materials. What else could be learned that's worth taking more time?"

With comments such as these, a veteran teacher of reading might question whether miscue analysis is really an essential diagnostic tool. It certainly takes a great deal more time than the traditional IRI. The miscue analysis procedure, as originally designed for use in descriptive research, required about 15 hours per child (K. Goodman 1973). It was recommended as much more helpful to teachers than simply counting errors (Y. Goodman 1972), but even in its adaptation to classroom use it still requires a lot of time (Y. Goodman and Burke 1972). There can be no quarrel with the assertion that valuable knowledge has been gained by means of miscue research (Allen and Watson 1976). There are some reasons, however, why miscue analysis may be of limited value for a classroom teacher or diagnostician. What information can one gain from miscue analysis, what are its limitations, and how may it be put to practical use?

Information to Be Gained

One argument in favor of miscue analysis is that its use in research has shown some oral reading errors to be good and some not so good. These findings suggest that teachers might profitably acquire a sensitivity to variations in quality of error. They should learn to respond differently to readers during instruction depending on whether they hear good errors, representing mature reading strategies, or errors signaling a need for instructional attention because they are not so good. Diagnosticians could categorize readers on the basis of observed oral reading strategies and prescribe remediation differently for children in each category. What are some of the differences in quality of errors that it might be important to note?

Not-so-good errors. Suppose a reader cannot recognize a word by sight, predict it from context, or sound it out. Reader A may try to sound it out and pronounce either a real word which doesn't fit the context or a nonsense word, or just wait for the teacher to tell what the word is. In any of these three instances, the reader has lost touch with meaning and that's not good. These undesirable errors may be referred to, respectively, as a substitution error that is not contextually appropriate, a nonsense error, and no response.

Reader B might pay more attention to the context and guess a word that makes sense, though it may or may not look much like the text word. This substitution error is better than Reader A's substitution because it shows more focus on meaning, but still it may not be very good. Suppose the error fits in with the preceding context but does not make sense when the rest of the sentence is read. It's not a good error, and, if possible, the reader should self-correct.

Reader C might take a quick peek at the following as well as preceding context before guessing an unknown word. If it fits in with the whole sentence context, Reader C's substitution is better than the errors made by Reader A and Reader B. But what if the meaning of Reader C's sentence is different from what the author had in mind? This not-so-good error suggests that too much guessing was done in relation to context and not quite enough attention was paid to the print.

It's easy to see why Readers A, B, and C have made errors. They may have paid either too little or too much attention to context, or they either knew too little about or neglected using the print. We can see several ways not-so-good errors get made, then, but where could the good errors come from?

Good errors. Reader D has accumulated lots of information about words. This reader can recognize instantly many single words in print—not only to name them, but also to recall simultaneously several of the meanings they may represent. Reader

D uses context cues to predict several meanings which may be contained in the next bit of print and uses print cues to decide which meaning may be the right one. This reader can actually focus on a word's meaning and ignore the word's name, thus identifying and integrating meanings without remembering the writer's exact words.

When reading aloud, Reader D may substitute words that mean the same as the text, such as reading *frightened* for *afraid*. Unessential words may be omitted, for example, by reading *told what he heard* instead of *told what he had heard*. Words may be inserted, such as reading *the little old lady* for *the old lady*. The writer's exact words may be read correctly but in different order, such as reading *put the tent up* for *put up the tent*. Unlike other omissions, insertions, and word order changes which do not sound sensible, these specific examples are all good errors because they represent the same meaning as the words in the text.

If some oral reading errors are good errors and some not so good, then perhaps teachers could benefit from knowing more than just how to count the errors that are made. But how reliably can good and bad errors be classified? Are there any problems in the interpretation of these qualitative error scores? Is the information to be gained useful enough to justify the extra time involved, or are there adaptations of miscue analysis more suited to practical use?

Problems in Miscue Analysis

Recently several investigators have studied the oral reading of groups of readers representing several age and ability levels. In two studies the subjects were normal to superior second grade readers (Hood 1977, Sturdivant-Odwarka 1977). In another two studies, subjects were disabled readers from fifth (Kendall 1977) and seventh grade (Leslie and Pacl 1977). In a fifth study, subjects were average to superior readers in eighth grade (Leslie and Osol, 1978). The error analysis procedure used in these studies (a simplified form of miscue analysis) had been designed for use in statistical research. Since the same procedures were followed by all researchers, some comparisons of the results of these five studies are appropriate.

The time each judge required for error analysis in these studies averaged about one hour per reader, assuming the subject read a 500-word selection and made, on the average, about 10 errors per hundred words. First, the judges counted each corrected or uncorrected error word by word. (Repetitions were not counted as errors.) The total number of errors was divided by the number of words read to determine the error rate, and the result subtracted from 100 to obtain the accuracy level. Then, each error was classified as one of eight types of errors, with two levels of graphic similarity to the text, four levels of contextual appropriateness, and two categories of correction. In each case the total number of errors classified a certain way was divided by the total number of errors made to obtain proportion scores. It is these proportion scores which provide qualitative information going beyond the quantitative information obtained in the traditional IRI.

Comparing the results of these five studies has suggested some problems with miscue analysis that limit its value as a practical tool. First, some error scores have questionable reliability. That is, the error scores one individual obtains for a child differ noticeably from those another might obtain. This is because decisions about how to classify the errors vary from one judge to another. Second, the classification of some errors as good or bad seems to differ depending on the reader's age and reading ability. Third, the relationship between passage content and the subject's experience background seems to influence the scores. Fourth, errors made by a given subject exemplify different qualities depending upon the overall reading accuracy level at which they were made.

In four of these five studies, two or more judges scored each reader's oral reading errors so that the reliabilities for each of the scores could be estimated. The scores for each error classification from each judge were averaged to obtain a single score for each error type for each child. The lowest reliabilities tended to be reported for contextual appropriateness scores, which are the most important type of scores for evaluating reading strategies. In a formal study of inter-judge reliability, the contextual appropriateness scores for a single judge were estimated to have reliabilities ranging from .52 to .77 (Hood 1975–1976). One should be very cautious in using scores with such low reliabilities for diagnosing individual differences in reading strategies.

Before beginning to evaluate oral reading errors in these studies, the judges were involved in training programs. During training, each of the judges in a study scored errors for the same group of subjects independently, and then all met to discuss their scoring decisions until agreement could be reached. Anyone who observed or participated in these discussions quickly learned that opinions of the contextual appropriateness of errors vary tremendously from one individual to another. Thus, both the subjective experience of training judges and the objective evidence in the reliability data suggest that scores obtained from one classroom teacher's scoring of a sample of errors might be quite different from the scores another teacher might obtain. A child might, then, receive a certain type of remediation based on one teacher's miscue analysis, but another type of remediation if a different teacher had determined the scores.

Factors Influencing Interpretation

Age differences in reading strategies. In describing Reader A, the first part of this article suggested that nonsense and no-response errors are not-so-good errors which indicate that a reader has lost touch with meaning. Yet the proportions of these errors and the situations in which they occurred varied in the studies cited according to the ages of subjects observed. For example, the younger subjects whose accuracy levels were low (e.g., 90% or less) made higher proportions of nonsense and no-response errors. Eighth graders made no no-response errors. But, in contrast to the younger readers, they made proportionately *more* nonsense errors if their accuracy level was high rather than low (95 compared to 90%). Eighth graders at the 95% accuracy level made proportionately more errors that did not fit the context than eighth graders at the 90% accuracy level. Also, eighth graders at the 95% accuracy level made more errors that were similar to the printed word in the text than did eighth graders at the 90% accuracy level. These findings also are the reverse of the pattern for younger readers.

Why might the scores of eighth graders differ so much from those of the second and fifth graders? In order to obtain enough errors to classify, Leslie and Osol had to select passages far above the experiential levels of their eighth grade subjects—passages these students would not normally need to read. These passages included unfamiliar words such as *proprietors*, *cavernous*, and *aqueously*. Eighth graders reading at 90% accuracy levels omitted these words, but the students reading at higher accuracy levels tried to sound them out and produced nonsense errors instead.

Under the instructions these researchers followed for error analysis, an omission could not be counted as a no-response error unless the reader said s/he did not know the word, as the younger readers often did. Certain of these eighth graders sometimes skipped over words without any hesitation; all such errors were counted as omissions. One strongly suspects that some of the omitted words were actually unfamiliar, since several other eighth graders made nonsense errors on those same words. These omissions could not be counted as no-response errors since the older readers did not admit not knowing the words. One of the problems with miscue analysis is that there is no reliable way to distinguish between words omitted inadvertently and those omitted because they are not known.

Since these results are based on passages beyond the range of these readers' experiences, they probably do not illustrate the reading strategies these eighth graders would normally use. Unless age and achievement levels are taken into consideration, miscue analysis could be more misleading than helpful in characterizing oral readers by their strategies.

Passages with estimated readabilities above readers' experiential levels. Some of the results of these five studies were related to the apparent difficulty of passage content, where the estimated readability was above the grade placement of the children who tried to read them. We have seen that some nonsense and omission errors of competent eighth grade readers seemed caused by unfamiliar content in passages they read. The effect of story content is observable in younger readers as well. Several groups of second graders read two stories different in estimated readabilities (either at or above their grade placement). One group made proportionately more nonsense and no-response errors on the above-grade-level story even though their reading accuracy level on both stories was the same (95%).

On the grade-level story, instead of these not-so-good errors, they made omissions which included the examples given in describing Reader D (e.g., *what he heard* for *what he had heard*). On the above-grade-level story, proportionately more of these younger subjects' errors were not contextually appropriate, and, in keeping with the likely loss of meaning implied by these errors, there were proportionately fewer errors which these readers could self-correct. Even at the 95% accuracy level

(instructional level according to the traditional IRI), the way a teacher might characterize a reader's strategies would differ depending upon the type of story the child had been asked to read.

Reading strategy differences at different accuracy levels. Most of the strategy differences seen in younger readers (second and fifth graders) were related to their oral reading accuracy levels. Generally speaking, when children with reading achievement at fifth grade level or lower were reading passages within range of their experiential levels, the quality of their oral reading errors varied in relation to the total number of errors made. At 95% accuracy or higher, when reading passages within range of their experiences, these young readers made proportionately more word order changes, omissions, and insertions. Proportionately more of all their errors represented the same meaning as the text, and readers more often corrected any errors that represented a meaning change. In other words, in these situations, children were reading more like Reader D.

When children were reading at accuracy levels of 90% or less, or reading passages less related to their experiences, proportionately more nonsense and no-response errors were made. Proportionately more of the errors were graphically similar to the text but were not contextually appropriate, and proportionately fewer of these not-so-good errors were corrected by the child. In this situation, then, children were reading more like Readers A, B, and C. How a diagnostician might characterize these children's reading strategies would vary a great deal depending upon the reading accuracy levels at which the samples of errors had been obtained.

If miscue analysis is to be helpful in diagnosing children's reading difficulties and in planning remediation, it must result in scores that are both reliable and characteristic of a reader's typical behavior. Yet we have seen that the scores may vary depending on the opinions of judges, on passage characteristics, and on reading accuracy levels, and their interpretation may vary depending upon the reader's age. It would seem that reliable and representative scores for a single subject could be obtained only from the reading of a variety of stories at instructional reading level with errors scored by more than a single judge. Would the improved scores be worth the extra time required to obtain them? Are there adaptations of miscue analysis more appropriate to practical use?

Practical Uses of Miscue Analysis

Developing teacher sensitivity to error quality. The results of the five studies cited in this article confirm that miscue analysis reveals differences in quality of errors and is a valuable research tool. They also suggest that obtaining reliable and representative scores for individuals may be so time-consuming as to be impractical for their use in diagnosis. Assume that a teacher would spend one hour recording and evaluating a reader's errors made on a passage of 500 words. Multiply that hour by five to represent the evaluation of five passages instead of one, and then by three to represent the scoring of this teacher and two additional judges. This increase in time would be needed to improve the reliability of scores and make them more representative of the reader's typical behavior. It seems arguable that the real value of spending this many hours in miscue analysis might be training the teacher rather than diagnosing the child.

Tallying errors from many different children would seem to provide a greater advantage to teachers than spending a lot of time on miscue analysis for only one child. By tallying a variety of errors, the teacher might develop sensitivity to the varieties of strategies different types of readers use. Comparisons of independent scoring decisions by one teacher with decisions of other teachers could help each

assess how acceptable particular reactions to children's errors might be. Such training may sensitize teachers to error quality and contribute to the appropriate use of feedback when teaching children to read. Thus all teachers could benefit from experience with miscue analysis, and the payoff would show up in the way they make decisions moment by moment while giving feedback as a learner reads aloud. But what about long-range instructional decisions? Isn't there any way miscue analysis can be put to practical use in diagnosis and remediation?

A shortcut to diagnosis and remediation. It has been shown that the quality of oral reading strategies varies depending on the accuracy level at which a child reads. Thus, the first instructional decision a teacher might make in remediating oral reading problems is to choose reading selections within a child's comfortable reading range. In the five studies cited, subjects' errors represented desirable reading strategies when they were reading at overall accuracy levels above 90%. Overall accuracy is determined by simply counting the total number of errors and dividing by the number of words in the selection. Miscue analysis research shows high estimated reliabilities (.98 to .99) for total error scores obtained by a single judge. Further, total error counts take very little time, so they could be obtained on a variety of passages and thus be fairly representative.

It seems that, practically speaking, a teacher could select appropriate instructional materials for children by means of total error scores. The teacher can assume that a more extensive miscue analysis would show a child to be using relatively more desirable oral reading strategies whenever the total number of errors made is fewer than 10 per hundred words (with errors defined according to the instructions used in the studies cited). Thus children's oral reading could show marked improvement in quality simply because of a change in the material given them to read. For a shortcut to the use of miscue analysis diagnostically, then, a teacher seems justified in using the total error score.

Perhaps the first grade method of error analysis was not so very much oversimplified after all.

References

Allen, P. David and Dorothy J. Watson, Eds. *Findings of Research in Miscue Analysis: Classroom Implications.* Urbana, Ill.: ERIC Clearinghouse on Reading and Communication Skills, National Council of Teachers of English, 1976.

Goodman, Kenneth S. *Theoretically Based Studies of Patterns of Miscues in Oral Reading Performance.* Final report. Contract No. OEG–0–9–320375–4269. Washington, D.C.: U.S. Office of Education, 1973.

Goodman, Yetta M. "Reading Diagnosis— Qualitative or Quantitive?" *The Reading Teacher,* vol. 26, no. 1 (October 1972), pp. 32–37.

Goodman Yetta M. and Carolyn L. Burke *Reading Miscue Inventory: Procedure for Diagnosis and Evaluation.* New York, N.Y.: Macmillan, 1972.

Hood, Joyce. "Qualitative Analysis of Oral Reading Errors: The Inter-Judge Reliability of Scores." *Reading Research Quarterly,* vol. 11, no. 4 (1975–1976), pp. 577–98.

Hood, Joyce. Changes in Oral Reading Strategies Associated with Elevations in Error Rate. Paper presented at American Educational Research Association meeting, New York, 1977.

Johnson, Marjorie Seddon and Roy A. Kress. *Informal Reading Inventories.* Newark, Del.: International Reading Association, 1965.

Kendall, Janet Ross. An Investigation of the Relationship between Comprehension and Word Recognition: Oral Reading Analysis of Children with Comprehension or Word Recognition Deficiencies. Paper presented at American Educational Research Association meeting, New York, 1977.

Leslie, Lauren and Pat Osol. "Changes in Oral Reading Strategies as a Function of Quantity of Miscues." *Journal of Reading Behavior,* Vol. 10, No. 4 (Winter 1978), pp. 442–445.

Leslie, Lauren and Penne Pacl. A Comparison of Oral Reading Strategies of Fourth and Seventh Grade Children of Fourth-Grade Instructional Level. Paper presented at American Educational Research Association meeting, New York, 1977.

Sturdivant-Odwarka, Anne. Oral Reading Characteristics Associated with the Language Development of Second-Grade Children. Paper presented at American Educational Research Association meeting, New York, 1977.

CHAPTER VII

Adapting Reading Instruction to Individual Differences

Although the ideal of individualized reading instruction has been advocated for half a century, practice in the schoolroom lags far behind. This chapter describes some of the newer ways to adapt reading instruction to individual needs and abilities.

McKenzie portrays ways to conduct a dialog with each pupil while working with a group and describes several every-pupil response procedures. Earle and Sanders describe ways to vary the kinds of questions asked and the length and difficulty of assignments, with special reference to subject matter classes. Whisler points out the shortcomings of round-robin oral reading, and recommends oral reading by students in pairs. Ehly and Larsen discuss the requirements for an effective use of pupils as tutors for other pupils. Hunt, one of the leading advocates of individualized reading, describes six requirements if an individualized reading program is to be successful. The chapter closes with Harris's analysis of the research on the characteristics of effective reading instruction.

31. Personalize Your Group Teaching

Gary R. McKenzie

I think individualizing instruction is a great idea. Of course I agree with the premise that each child should begin wherever he happens to be and be allowed to progress at his own rate. But what really excites me about individualization is the quality of teaching in one-to-one lessons. One-to-one teaching is almost naturally a kind of dialogue between the teacher and the student. The child is intensely involved in mental activities which produce learning, there is little misbehavior, and a great deal is learned in a short time.

Of course, in many classroom situations one-to-one teaching seems difficult to achieve. For example, when the teacher sits down with one child, the others often waste time. The exciting thing, though, is

From Gary R. McKenzie, Personalize your group teaching. *Instructor*, August/September 1975, *85*, 57–59. Reprinted by permission of the publisher.

that what happens in one-to-one lessons can serve as a model for improving group instruction. Let's take a look at techniques for preserving personalism and for establishing a dialogue with each individual when working with a group. The goals are to make each child feel that the teacher is paying attention to him as an individual, and to involve each child with every question or in every step of a process. Admittedly, this is a big order, but it is not as impossible as it may seem.

Some One-to-One Techniques

Eye contact is a way to demonstrate interest in each student. Of course a teacher cannot look into the eyes of every child at the same time, but he can discipline himself to look into the eyes of several individuals rather than looking at the chalkboard or gazing vaguely across a sea of faceless forms. He can also discipline himself to distribute his eye contact, look at *each* rather than favoring the rewarding few who always seem interested and who nod their heads in understanding. More than just "looking" is involved, of course. Much can be communicated without words. A teacher can express approval or disapproval by a quick look. He can signal encouragement, sympathy, humor.

A related technique, or rather a cluster of techniques, for communicating attention to individuals is to reply to individuals when they give responses. These techniques can range from the rather obvious practice of saying the name of the child who responds correctly, to more subtle nonverbal signs that the response was noticed. A smile, a head nod, a wink, or a pat on the shoulder as you walk past can be effective in communicating personal awareness. Even a quick glance at the student as an individual will show him you noticed his response. The teacher may comment to a child on his participation or specific responses, after the lesson is over.

This is particularly effective, even if it only happens to an individual once a day, because it shows the child the teacher is interested in him even when he may not be aware of it. Try this experiment. Pick out a couple of average or slightly below-average students and unobtrusively observe them as you teach. Notice where they look, how frequently they raise their hands . . . and also notice some positive thing they do that you can mention later on. When the lesson is over, casually and privately congratulate each individual on the positive behavior you noticed. Then watch their faces, notice their participation in the next lesson, or how they approach their seatwork. My experience is that the children will sneak more glances at the teacher, volunteer more in the future, and work harder at their lessons.

There are some questioning techniques which will increase the degree to which individuals think about the answer. For example, if the teacher asks a question and then pauses and looks around the class as if to say, "Do you know?" or "I might call on you," more children will think of a response than if the teacher calls the name first and then asks the question. Similarly, if the teacher makes it a practice to ask the question and then calls on two or three individuals in sequence before confirming a particular answer, she increases the odds of calling on a particular student, and each will realize that he is more likely to be asked to respond.

The technique of asking a child to respond in front of the group puts the individual on the spot to some extent. A thoughtful teacher can use this positively to build individual confidence by directing questions to individuals according to their ability. Eye contact, mentioned above, can pretty well tell the teacher which children are ready to respond, which aren't, and even which ones seem to be "weighing" the matter. The time to call on a slower learner is when he is likely to have the right answer.

Another very effective way to establish dialogue with individuals in group lessons is to use techniques by which each student can make a discrete overt response to every question. The intent is to get each child to process the information mentally and make a direct response, in a way that allows you to tell what he is thinking. Again this is not easy, but it is possible; and research suggests that it will be well worth the effort.

In order to get intelligible overt responses from each child in a group without slowing down the pace of a lesson to a deadly crawl, the teacher may use non-verbal forms of response from students by phrasing questions or instructions in a way that the child can answer by gesture. For example, the teacher may ask a question, pause, and then call on an individual for his answer. She could then tell the group, "If you agree with him, raise your hand; but don't raise your hand if you disagree." When this technique is used on a fairly regular basis, each child will soon learn that he has to think about the answer and listen to what his peer says, because he will have to express agreement or disagreement. Incidentally, it is crucial that the teacher look at each child to show that she notices whether or not his hand is raised; otherwise students may not bother to respond. Variations on this technique are to supply each child with two small signs, one marked "True" or "Agree," and the other marked "False" or "Disagree." Then, when the question is asked, the teacher can pause for thinking and say, "Show your card."

There are many other forms of non-verbal responses which can be used in group instruction. If a teacher asks students to read a passage silently, and then asks everyone to point to the sentence which tells some significant things, every student will read, every student will point, and the teacher can tell at a glance who understood and who didn't. This doesn't put any one individual on the spot, and it does give the teacher a chance to reinforce responses quickly by saying, "You got it, you got it, you got it—oops, you got it."

Another every-pupil-response technique is to prepare a mimeographed page of answers from which children can select in responding to oral questions. For example, an alphabet can be duplicated for each child. The teacher can hold up a picture or say a word, and ask children to point to the letter in their individual alphabets which represents the first sound they hear. Or, letter cards to hold up in response to questions can be given out. Similarly, numerals from one to twenty can be duplicated in a list, an addition or subtraction fact given, and students can be asked to point to the number that represents the answer—or, again, response cards to hold up can be made. A quick glance will, again, reinforce answers and indicate who missed what.

Older children may be asked to write numbers or single-word answers to oral questions on a sheet of paper, and the teacher can walk around, confirming correct answers with an "OK," "Good," or a tap on the shoulder. If there is a paper shortage, the erasable Magic Slates work well for this type of response; or the teacher can make individual chalkboards fairly inexpensively by painting one-foot squares of composition board with Weber Costello *Hyloplate Surface Coater*, or another such material, available at some hardware stores and most school-supply houses.

There are, of course, other techniques. If a skill is being taught, it may be appropriate to have each child state, in one way or another, what the steps in the process are before trying to do the whole task by himself. If a concept is being taught, then it is appropriate to ask students to decide whether or not a new item is or is not an example of the concept by comparing the new case with the general rule. If you want students to notice details in a passage of text or in a complex photo, ask each to point to or describe these. The focusing of attention on particular steps or details will greatly facilitate understanding and recall.

Finally, remember to use student responses to see where a student begins to make mistakes, what the source of confusion is. If, for example, you are trying to get students to discover how all insects are alike and Johnnie fails to count the legs in the first example, and Elijah says a roach has a head and a long body (rather than a head, thorax, and abdomen) you can predict what each will leave out in comparing all insects. Your next questions will clearly have to lead these students to notice what they missed. Similarly, if you are showing students how to make mobiles and Freddie says you glue the strings to the sticks before you balance the system, you can tell that Freddie is going to have trouble moving strings until they

balance. In short, your in-presentation questions can serve diagnostic purposes and tell you if everyone really understands. With feedback on what students are thinking, it is relatively easy to correct misunderstandings before they become embarrassing errors. Children will feel good about themselves and your lessons if they produce good work the first time they try a task on their own.

At the beginning of this article, I said that I think individualized instruction is great . . . and generally more effective than group instruction. But I also believe that teachers can greatly improve group lessons by attending to individuals and getting each individual to engage in a dialogue, even in group lessons. It isn't easy, but if you are having trouble with group lessons, I think you will find these suggestions helpful.

32. Individualizing Reading Assignments

Richard A. Earle and Peter L. Sanders

Any teacher who has spent more than a day or two in the public school classroom knows that students—whether they are grouped homogeneously or not—represent considerable variation in the ability to read required text material. This range of reading ability, and the variety and difficulty of subject matter text, are obstacles which can prevent effective interaction between the student and the text. Those students who are fortunate enough to have attained independence may need no special help. But what about the others? Is it "sink or swim"?

A short informal assessment of reading ability will reveal which students are less than successful in mastering their reading. Even more important are the

observations of a sensitive teacher, one who feels that if an assignment is worth giving at all, differential amounts of assistance must be provided for certain individuals and groups within the class.

Individualizing subject matter assignments is an attempt to get away from regarding a class as a monolithic "they." It means providing enough help to ensure that each student will successfully master the required reading. It does not require an individual preparation for each student in the class. Nor does it mean a different text for each individual. No one means should be singled out and used exclusively. In fact, various techniques may prove useful in different situations and in several combinations.

From Richard A. Earle and Peter L. Sanders, Individualizing reading assignments. *Journal of Reading*, April 1973, *16*, 550–555. Reprinted by permission of Richard A. Earle and the International Reading Association.

Levels of Sophistication

Not all students will find it possible to answer sophisticated questions requiring the application of meaning from subject matter reading. Some students might well profit from questions designed to identify and generalize relationships among particular facts or ideas. By the same token, poorer readers generally find it easier to locate and verify answers to specific factual questions, rather than questions requiring interpretation or application.

This suggests the first means of individualizing subject matter reading assignments. Given an important assignment, match question difficulty to the student's reading ability. Thus, each student can experience the satisfaction of mastery at some level of comprehension, while all the essential information is gleaned from the assignment. Postreading classroom discussion can be planned to ensure that the information gained by each can be shared by all.

One note of caution: It is tempting to "pigeonhole" students using this method. We have been greeted (by teachers who *thought* they were individualizing) with such statements as "These are my literal level kids, these are my interpretation level kids, and these are my application level kids." A permanent classification such as implied in this statement is not desirable. It may be detrimental to the child's learning, certainly to his continued reading growth in the subject matter classroom. Regarded as one means of adjusting the task to student abilities, however, teacher questioning at different levels can represent useful and constructive assistance.

Differential Structuring

One of the most useful techniques for differentiating subject matter reading assignments is to ask questions or give instructions which incorporate varying degrees of structure, according to the needs of different students or groups of students. "Structure" in this case means guidance built into the question itself. For example, a teacher whose "guidance" consists only of "Read Chapter 7 for tomorrow" is really saying to the students, "Some important questions about our subject matter are answered in this reading assignment, but I'm not going to tell you what questions they are. You find the answers, come in tomorrow, and in our discussion I'll let you know what the questions were. If your answers fit my questions, you will be a winner; if not, you lose."

Considerable guidance can be provided by a simple question, for example, "Read this assignment to find out such and such." While this at least provides students with some purpose for attacking the reading assignment, some students will have difficulty in locating and verifying such information, particularly in a lengthy reading assignment. For these students, a somewhat higher level of structure is in order.

Our experience suggests that reacting to alternatives is in fact easier than generating alternatives. Therefore, questions can be structured with several possible answers, the student's task being to verify one or more of the alternatives provided. Depending on the student's need for structure, alternatives can be sophisticated statements representing application, generalization, or inference, each to be supported or refuted with evidence from the reading.

On the other hand, several important details can be included in a structured question, with the student being required to verify their literal existence in the text. In some cases students who are unable to read well enough to comprehend material in paragraph and/or sentence form can be supplied with a list of single words to be verified or rejected in the light of a particular subject matter question. Combined with these techniques, even more structure can be provided by giving locational aid in the form of page and/or column number.

Some students who are overwhelmed by several pages of reading can succeed when the teacher indicates the paragraph (or even line number) where the information can be found. This approach—like most other elements of individualizing—depends on the difficulty the students are likely to have with a given assignment. It is interesting to note that some students who are labeled "nonreaders" have successfully read this subject matter assignment when questions included a little more structure. Structuring a question differentially means providing, within the question itself, enough guidance so that the student is more certain of locating, identifying, and verifying essential information contained in a reading assignment.

Collaboration by Grouping

There is an old saying that "Two heads are better than one." This particular approach to individualizing rests on the tenet that, with some reading assignments, three, four or five heads are better than one. The essential element of collaboration is teamwork—the sharing of information and skills in order to get the job done. Several forms of grouping allow the sort of team sharing that is the essence of group collaboration.

One is what we could call a "tutor" group, where one person who has a superior skill in reading can be teamed with one or more students who are not as effective. The tutor, with some direction from the teacher, might read portions of the assignment to the others, clarify directions, react to their answers, and generally provide needed assistance. In some cases, two readers of equal ability might help each other, combining information to arrive at a larger understanding than either could achieve alone. Another form of grouping is "ability" grouping, where

the class is divided into two or more groups representing different levels of reading performance.

This sort of grouping, while not recommended as permanent, is particularly useful when combined with the technique of questioning at different levels of comprehension. Still another form of grouping is "interest" grouping, where students are teamed to complete various tasks representing common interests.

Incidentally, most students, given the choice, will not select a task that appears too easy; rather, they will elect to do that which is both interesting and challenging.

Perhaps the most common form of useful collaboration in the subject matter classroom can be achieved by "random" grouping. In this form of grouping two or more students are teamed on the basis of any random means, such as their seating arrangement in the classroom. As with other forms of collaboration, the object here is to share skills and information. However, the most important element of random grouping is that it encourages an interaction among the students. In contrast to the teacher-led classroom discussion, random grouping provides each student time and opportunity to verbalize his findings, support his generalization, and question other students.

Students are sometimes uneasy or even amused by the prospect of collaborative effort. Certainly they have little opportunity for such sharing in many classrooms throughout their public school career! And the teacher may feel uneasy, perhaps equating group collaboration with cheating or improper teaching. However, two facts should be made clear regarding grouping: 1) Students *do* learn from each other by assisting or challenging their colleagues in active ways; 2) Teachers, when freed from the total absorption demanded by the lecture, are able to help, stimulate, and evaluate students in individual ways. If you regard group effort as an integral part of individualized learning, your students will catch on very quickly. Collaboration on subject matter assignments is one effective way of improving learning, especially for the less effective reader.

Selecting Appropriate Material

In the ideal classroom each student operates with material that is suited to his instructional level. We know however that this ideal is rarely the case. Some subject matter simply cannot be presented at low levels of difficulty. In other cases, money is not available to buy published materials. Or a given textbook may be required by those who design the curriculum. The net result is that most content classrooms boast a single textbook, often too difficult for the student. This situation necessitates other methods of individualizing, such as mentioned in this article. Nonetheless, when curriculum-specific materials of easier readability are available, they become another excellent means of providing each student in your class with the opportunity to master his reading assignment successfully.

Vary Assignment Length

In classrooms where coverage of the entire course takes precedence over student understanding, there is little opportunity to expect more of some students than others. However, some teachers feel that mastery of fewer understandings is more important than superficial coverage of large amounts of subject matter material. These teachers have found that yet another way to individualize reading assignments is to vary their length, that is, the number of understandings to be gained. Some students can handle lengthy assignments satisfactorily. We know, however, that others are completely overwhelmed by the prospect of ten or twelve pages of text. Hence, they avoid the pain of frustration and failure by refusing to do the assignment at all. For these students, reducing the reading assignment to manageable proportions often gives them more opportunity for success. For example, some may be directed to read only the most important sections of the material, perhaps even a single page. Others may experience success in selecting a few of the important ideas or descriptive terms. In extreme cases poor readers could be asked to do no more than verify certain key words. This particular technique is especially useful in conjunction with the differential structuring of questions.

Many students need more time to complete required reading assignments. They might be much more successful if given a few additional minutes (or hours) to complete the task. It is unfortunate that the usual public school organization—the forty-five minute period, the eighteen week semester, and the graded year—makes this sort of basic individual assistance very difficult. Nevertheless, the subject matter teacher can devise means for adjusting the time factor in reading assignments while retaining the necessary degree of guidance and control. Many sensitive teachers endorse deadlines firmly but not rigidly; they do not regard deadlines as sacrosanct. Sometimes a straightforward question, for example, "Would it be helpful if you had till tomorrow; or next Monday?" can guide the teacher in his decision. Surely it would do wonders for the student-teacher relationship by communicating the concern and flexibility that is the hallmark of the sensitive teacher. Students who finish an assignment may move on to other tasks, including the task of helping those who need additional guidance. It is important to note that additional time must often be combined with other types of assistance, as suggested in this article.

It is difficult (even dangerous) for reading specialists to suggest publicly replacing printed text with assignments that do not require reading. However, the underlying premise of this article and the major concern of most subject teachers is that mastery of the subject matter takes precedence over a student's reading development.

In point of fact, the teacher is expected to teach subject matter ideas and skills regardless of students' reading abilities. Even when the student receives separate expert reading instruction, increased reading ability is a long time coming. Therefore, when the student is severely handicapped, many important ideas can be communicated through other media, such as pictures, tapes, records, films, filmstrips, and the like. Of course, we must face the fact that complete abandonment of required reading prevents the student from improving his reading ability. He becomes forever dependent on speech alone to gather and assess information in a given subject area. It therefore seems advisable to use other media as supplement rather than as replacement.

For example, material presented orally can often be accompanied by written questions structured to provide a maximum amount of guidance. Since the questions are in written form they will require reading; hence they represent elements integral to both subject matter mastery and continued reading growth. However, to the degree that reduction or abandonment of printed material is necessary to ensure student success, the technique can be effective in overcoming the obstacles presented by reading assignments.

Summary

This article has described several techniques for individualizing reading assignments in subject matter classes. The approaches mentioned herein do not represent a comprehensive list of suggestions. Nor are they all guaranteed to be equally practical, or equally comfortable to certain teachers. Experience suggests, however, that the use of these approaches has provided many "nonreaders" with the help they needed to become successful readers—at least to some degree. That alone may be reason enough to give them a try!

33. Pupil Partners

Nancy G. Whisler

Few activities expend more classroom time, especially in primary grades, than the Round Robin Reading Circle. In this situation the teacher can commonly be seen sitting at a table within a circle of children. One student at a time reads aloud something the group most likely has already read, while the others follow along apathetically in their readers and wait their turns to perform. Under many such conditions this probably is not a worthwhile experience for students. This overused technique of hearing student after student read just so everyone in the group has a chance to read to the teacher is perhaps one of the most abused aspects of the total reading program (Zintz, 1970).

Contrary to the beliefs and persistent practices of many teachers, related research reveals that this circle-bound reading is an ineffective method of increasing reading ability. In fact, when students are required to follow along in their books, it has been shown to hinder good silent reading habits by reducing the reading rate, encouraging lip movements, foster-

From Nancy G. Whisler, Pupil partners. *Language Arts*, April 1978, *53*, 387–389. Reprinted by permission of the author and the National Council of Teachers of English.

ing silent word pronunciation, and causing inattention to content (Durrell, 1956). This frustrates both slow readers who are forced to but cannot keep up with a rapid reader, and bores the faster readers who read at a more rapid pace.

In spite of this it is unfortunate that too frequently, round robin reading is the only oral reading experience in which many pupils have the opportunity to participate. It is my belief that teachers may fall into the round robin syndrome with their students for a number of reasons: Many teachers lack knowledge about good oral reading practices which results in their inability to provide a variety of effective oral reading lessons. Pressure from students indicating the feeling that if they haven't read orally in a circle to their teacher they haven't read at all that day tends to perpetuate round robin reading. Reticence to change or give up the round robin reading circle is felt because most other teachers have oral reading circles, and teachers are not secure about and have a fear of justifying such a change to colleagues or parents. Complacency and a lack of preplanning lock many teachers into round robin reading, as this type of lesson rarely takes much teacher preparation or thought.

The preceding discussion is not intended to demean the value of oral reading as such, but rather to point out the weakness of employing the round robin reading circle as the sole reading activity in the classrooms. Purposeful oral reading tasks do have a definite place in the developmental reading programs throughout the elementary grades. In grade one, 50 percent of students' reading time is legitimately devoted to oral reading. During this year, students normally re-read orally that which they have read silently. As students progress to the second reader level this amount of oral reading decreases to about 30 percent. For students who have attained an independent reading level in a third reader or above, oral reading

becomes deemphasized and the amount of classroom time allocated to fit will surely drop to about 20 percent (Zintz, 1970).

Characteristics of Good Oral Reading Lessons

Several characteristics of good oral reading lessons are mentioned here and should be kept in mind when planning oral reading activities. (1) It is necessary that the purpose for oral reading be clearly defined and the student understands that purpose which is to entertain, to share information with others, to improve phrase reading, to gain security in oral expression, to diagnose for specific reading difficulties, to evaluate reading progress, or to check comprehension ability. The requirement that students follow along in their reader as others read has little value in attaining any of the purposes of oral reading. (2) Students need a real reason for listening to oral reading. To foster the necessary true audience situation, students should not be informed ahead of time as to the plot or story content. (3) Selection of the material is important. It should have interest and appeal for the listener. The level of difficulty must be either at the instructional or independent reading level of the reader. (4) Ideally, the oral reader is prepared and knows all the vocabulary in the selection and will encounter no difficulties during the reading. Provisions for instruction in unfamiliar vocabulary or skills should be given prior to the oral reading.

Pupil Partners: An Alternative

One possible alternative to round robin recitations is the use of pupil partners to improve oral reading and comprehension. This technique may be effectively implemented with students reading as low as the primer level. One disadvantage of the oral reading circle is that only one pupil may read at any given time. The use of pupil partners removes this "sit and wait" from learning in that more students may participate at the same time. It forces all students to take on more of the responsibility of learning themselves. Passive learners in a round robin situation frequently tune out or pretend to listen until their turn to read comes. By using the pupil partner technique both students, reader and listener, become actively involved in the reading activity.

Procedure

Pairs of students are selected to work together on the basis of similar reading level, interests, and social compatibility. Initially this activity requires a great amount of teacher direction and group support before students can effectively function without assistance. All the pairs of pupil partners are assembled in a group situation under the leadership of the teacher. One set of pupil partners is asked to help with the demonstration.

Pupil A reads the first page to Pupil B. (A whole page at a time is read in primary grades. In intermediate grades alternating readers after each paragraph is suggested.) Pupil B listens. The teacher asks Pupil A to ask Pupil B several questions about the content of what was heard. Initially pupils most likely will not be able to formulate their own questions, especially those students in grade one or two. This is when teacher guidance is necessary and so important. If neither Pupil A nor B can suggest a question, the teacher then asks if any other member of the group can ask a question relating to the reading. It will be unusual if there are any students who feel able to pose a question at this time. The teacher then suggests a question and asks Pupil A to repeat it to Pupil B. Pupil B then answers the question. A second question is then solicited and answered in the same manner.

Then Pupil B reads the next page to Pupil A, and Pupil B is directed to ask two questions on the content of that page. As assistance is needed, the teacher and the group help the demonstrating pupil partners to ask questions. Experience has shown that the first type of question that the students will be able to construct independently is the type that can be answered by "yes" or "no," such as "Did Janet sit on the step with Daddy?" Pupils A and B continue to read the remainder of the story following the same procedure alternating reading with listening and asking questions.

In a subsequent lesson the teacher and the groups of pupil partners assemble again. A different set of partners is selected to demonstrate. Gradually, students in the group will become able to pose questions such as these to each other: "Why do you think Janet was so sad?" or, "What did Daddy do to make Janet feel better?" Once this occurs the sets of pupil partners who are able to read, listen, and formulate questions are ready to read independently in pairs. They may sit together in another section of the room and read alternately on their own without teacher assistance. The teacher continues to meet with the remaining sets of pupil partners until they understand the procedure and are capable of asking questions.

Summary

Certainly most reading authorities are in agreement that definite instruction and purposeful oral reading activities should take place in the elementary reading program. Current classroom practices to foster this skill are not consistent with nor do they reflect the theories that are prevalent in the literature or the evidence that is revealed in related research studies. There continues to be an excessive emphasis on the nugatory practice of round robin reading. Pupil Partners is one oral reading activity which can be an alternative.

References

Durrell, Donald. *Improving Reading Instruction.* Harcourt, 1956.

Spache, Evelyn B. and George D. *Reading In The Elementary School.* 2nd ed. Allyn & Bacon, 1972.

Zintz, Miles V. *The Reading Process: The Teacher And The Learner.* Little, Brown, 1970.

34. Peer Tutoring in the Regular Classroom

Stewart Ehly and Stephen C. Larsen

Children have been teaching each other in the classroom for many years. In American history, older students in one-room school houses helped younger students with their lessons. In the 1960's, programs added structure on a large-scale educational basis to the peer teaching process. The term *peer tutoring* was used to identify the situation in which one child assisted and attempted to teach a school-related subject to another child. The student tutor could be older or the same age as the child being tutored (called the *tutee*). The case of two children of differing ages being involved in an instructional arrangement has been labeled more specifically as *cross-age tutoring*.

The student is an educational tool with great potential. J. L. Thomas studied the tutoring behavior of college-age tutors and fifth- and sixth-grade tutors working with second-grade students in reading.[1] The college students were senior education majors enrolled in a reading methods course. Thomas reported that the college students and the fifth and sixth-grade tutors were equally effective in producing reading gains in the second graders. The author noted certain differences in the behavior of the two groups of tutors. The college students spent a great deal of time coaxing the children into practicing reading skills. The fifth- and sixth-graders were more direct and businesslike. They accepted the fact that the second graders were having reading difficulties and that tutoring sessions were only for teaching them the materials in front of them. Few matters outside the lesson plan were discussed. The children viewed teaching and learning as expected activities that did not require explanation or apology.

The effects of peer tutoring can be very positive. The prestige gained by the "problem child" becoming a teacher is frequently incalculable. With this prestige comes the opportunity for the child to model teacher-approved, socially appropriate behavior. The child's self-esteem is boosted. He feels worthwhile. He feels needed and has the confidence that he can be successful at a learning task. This new confidence can influence the child's sense of adequacy and, subsequently, his behavior in the classroom. The "good" student has similar experiences and gains from his experiences. Tutors can also benefit by planning and working to clarify academic tasks from lower skill levels.

The child who is being tutored profits from peer tutoring experiences. The child receiving help from someone who is older or more knowledgeable will generally be more relaxed with the peer tutor. The academic and social gains from tutoring can modify the learning skills as well as

From Stewart Ehly and Stephen C. Larsen, Peer tutoring in the regular classroom. *Academic Therapy,* Winter 1975–76, *11*, 205–208. Reprinted by permission of the authors and Academic Therapy Publication, Novato, CA.

confidence, so that the child will return to the classroom with a determination to work harder.

Your Own Tutoring Program

A teacher with time and motivation can develop a peer tutoring program. Tutoring programs can begin using sectioned-off corners of classrooms, learning stations, closets, and other spaces. With administrative support, additional space and materials will permit the program to expand. Materials employed in tutoring are often developed for the situation in which they are used. Materials may be teacher-made or developed by the student tutors. Teacher-made materials insure that the tutor will cover essential learning areas with the tutee. Tutor-made materials, used effectively in several tutoring programs, have the advantage of increasing potential learning for the tutor.

Selecting and Pairing the Student

Teachers working to develop a tutoring program within their own classrooms can either ask for volunteer tutors, or they can select students with specific academic credentials. Guidelines for selecting student tutors vary. Teachers may choose students who are well-behaved but have academic weaknesses, or students who have academic and behavioral problems. Every student has something to contribute to and gain from a tutoring program, given proper training, supervision, and follow-up tutoring activities. The teacher needs to be sensitive to the limitations of the student tutors. Emotional and behavioral inconsistencies may indicate that a student with academic strengths would not be a good tutor.

When considering children to receive tutoring in a subject, the teacher can focus solely upon that student's academic weaknesses. Problems in reading and arithmetic are a common subject of tutoring; however, programs are readily developed in social studies, science, physical education, and any subject area in which students need remedial instruction. Teachers should remember that, while a student can learn by being tutored, not every student has the internal control to work over a period of time in a one-on-one relationship. They need to assess their students' abilities to cope with an individualized, remedial situation.

A teacher who has this information on her students will be able to match children in the tutoring dyad by recognizing the cognitive and affective strengths of the tutor and the needs of the tutee. The children can be reassigned to new partners if the pairing proves disruptive or nonproductive.

Training Tutors

Training procedures vary with the teacher and the requirements of the tutoring program. The teacher needs to consider her time, classroom space, and materials available to devote to training. Time required for selection and development of materials may be available so that the teacher can choose to tap resources in the school and classroom. Students may be encouraged to develop materials. Teacher guidelines and monitoring, however, help the student while planning lessons to focus on the needs of the tutee. Tutors should be well acquainted with the learning goals developed for the tutee.

The sequence in which materials are presented is an important consideration in the tutoring process. S. L. Blumenfeld has given examples in planning instructional sequences in a lesson and from session to session.[2] The emphasis is on discovering what the tutee knows, training him in a particular skill, and then reviewing periodically the acquisition and retention of skill.

The child's ability to comprehend each step in an instructional sequence controls the pace of the learning process. Tutors need to be familiar not only with the components of a tutoring sequence, but also with the materials needed at each step. A segment of any training program should be devoted to teaching the tutor to be sensitive to the tutee's adjustment and progress through the tutoring program.

Scheduling, Supervision, and Feedback

Tutoring programs vary in the length of time they extend into the school year, as well as in the length and number of sessions per week. Teachers report that, more important than the length of a tutoring program or an individual session, is the regularity and consistency of meetings by the tutoring dyad over the program's term. When a schedule has been established, stick to it. Stress with the tutors the importance of meeting on time for each session.

Students should be encouraged to seek out their teachers with questions on content and process throughout the tutoring program. In assessing whether program goals are being met, the teacher needs to monitor several processes. She must insure that tutoring sessions are occurring on schedule. She must monitor dyads to see that materials are being used appropriately, and that the tutor and tutee are working well together. Teachers vary in the amount of supervision they feel is necessary with individual children and tutoring pairs; however, the teacher can better gauge tutoring gains if she observes one in every three sessions to check on the functioning of the tutoring pair.

For the child being tutored, reinforcement may be delivered in the form of verbal praise, a star, a piece of candy, or any of a number of items. Some programs have no guidelines for giving feedback of the child's progress during tutoring. The goals and philosophy of your program will contribute to your decision on structuring the feedback process.

You will know your program is a success when big changes start occurring in the classroom. The peer teachers and students will grow academically. If changes aren't readily apparent, ask the children—they will tell you of their gains. The students are often the best judge of the benefits of a tutoring program.

Notes

1. J. L. Thomas, "Tutoring Strategies and Effectiveness: A Comparison of Elementary Age Tutors and College Age Tutors" (doctoral dissertation; Austin, Texas: University of Texas, 1970).
2. S. L. Blumenfeld, *How to Tutor* (New Rochelle, New York: Arlington House, 1973).

35. Six Steps to the Individualized Reading Program (IRP)

Lyman C. Hunt, Jr.

There are six identifiable *steps* to an Individualized Reading Program which, when successfully developed by the teacher, lead to four values basic to productive reading. These results are obtainable only through IRP and only when there is not too much stumbling on the steps along the way. Teachers must understand each step and its relative importance to the total program of individualized reading.

The six steps are:

1. Classroom environment
2. Silent or quiet reading time
3. Instructional guidance
4. Book talks and conferences
5. Skill development: USSR
6. Records and evaluation

The unique values resulting are:

1. Exploratory detective type reading
2. USSR: The ultimate reading skill
3. Self-direction in the world of print
4. L.O.B.

The purpose of this paper is to prevent stumbling on the steps, to help teachers avoid pitfalls in their efforts to build stronger classroom reading programs.

1. The Reading Atmosphere within the Classroom

The first step, and this is imperative to success, is to build an atmosphere for productive reading. Building this climate for reading takes careful nurturing; it also takes time. Each teacher's goal must be to develop productive reading on the part of each pupil. It is easy to make the mistake of leaving atmosphere to chance. This can be fatal to IRP. A climate for reading requires both endurance and endeavor on the part of the teacher. Two key factors for creating this climate are: (1) the concept of *Quiet Reading Time* and (2) skillful use of *Instructional Guidance*.

2. Quiet or Silent Reading Time

The concept underlying silent reading time is vital to developing IRP successfully. Each teacher must clearly perceive legitimate activities permissible during the Quiet Reading Period. The ideal model has each reader directing his own activities with printed material throughout the duration of the reading period. The perfect situation requires that everyone be so engaged in silent reading (or working on responses thereto) that the teacher is free to interact with pupils in a variety of ways, individually or in groups. A chart giving the framework or structure of the silent reading time helps. The chart should be very visible to each and every incipient reader. A sample chart could read:

Quiet Reading Time

1. Select a book or other printed material.
2. Read quietly (see how much you can get done).
3. Have a book talk or conference (be prepared—know what to say).
4. Record your results—write about reading—chart your progress.
5. Study vocabulary.
6. Work with a partner.

From Lyman C. Hunt, Jr., Six steps to the Individualized Reading Program (IRP). *Elementary English*, January 1971, *48*, 27–32. Reprinted by permission of the author and the National Council of Teachers of English.

The behavior of the reader is markedly different in IRP from that which he has used in the text program. Each must learn new ways of behaving. While natural for many, this new pattern is difficult for some. Some will need time and patient guidance to succeed. Success in IRP means:

1. Making wise and intelligent selections of reading material.
2. Spending large blocks of time in independent silent reading.
3. Preparing for and being ready to make his best contribution during the conference time.
4. Preparing reports, keeping records, and being ready to share his learning from books with others.

Teachers err in not giving sufficient time and effort to establishing the framework for the quiet reading period. Teachers frequently are too eager to move to conferences and book talks, leaving the silent reading to care for itself. Moving too quickly to conference activities doesn't work. Many young readers need constant and considered instruction in sustained silent reading prior to gaining the self-direction needed to make conference time worthwhile. At first these young readers need *Instructional Guidance* more than they need book talks.

3. Instructional Guidance

Serious reading covering long stretches of print is not taken seriously by some. Many boys and some girls prefer to spend silent reading time in more noisy endeavors. The gossips, those who prefer talking to reading, are common. The wanderers, those active individuals (mostly boys) who would rather rather walk around than read, need considerable attention. The wanderers usually spend excessive amounts of time searching for suitable reading material. When pressed to settle down to productive reading, 101 excuses are forth-

coming for not doing so. "Squirrels" collect books as their animal counterparts do nuts. "Squirrels" get a new book each day but are too busy gathering them to take time to read them. For them, the reading time is unproductive; little reading is completed.

Every teacher who tries IRP has gossips, wanderers and squirrels in varying degrees. Productive reading is most difficult for some. Typically about $\frac{1}{4}$ of the total group exhibit such evasive behaviors. IRP cannot succeed unless the teacher first works at moderating if not overcoming these disruptive behaviors. This is where instructional guidance is needed. And this is where many teachers fail.

The guiding principle, which should be held inviolate, is as follows: During the reading period no one may act so as to interfere with the productive reading of another. This means no interruption of one reader by another unless this interaction contributes in some way to the productivity of all concerned. Much legitimate interaction occurs among various readers. But this decree also means occasionally telling some to Sit Down, Keep Quiet and Start Reading.

The principle of non-interference of others and high productivity by each reader must be firmly established. IRP cannot succeed without it. Yet the teacher who finds this precept violated no more than a dozen times a day should not be discouraged. The teacher can err only by not attending to the problems which arise and by not working to ameliorate them. Little by little the wanderers, gossips and squirrels become readers. The basis for successful IRP has been established. Instructional guidance is crucial to creating the atmosphere of a successful Quiet Reading Time. The rule of non-interference must work.

4. Book Talks and Conferences

The Silent Reading Time, with the atmosphere of productive reading created by it, is the heart of IRP. Similarly conference time with book talks is the heart of the Silent Reading Time. Through book talks the teacher plays a key instructional role. This role must be clearly understood; otherwise efforts to build IRP will falter. In the past the role of the teacher in book talks has been poorly defined; consequently serious mistakes have been made.

First some areas of error. Teachers must not think of the first purpose of book talks as interrogating each and every reader about each and every book read. To do so is self-defeating for both teacher and reader. To the contrary, the concept that extensive reading developed within IRP is exploratory in nature (i.e. searching far and wide in print of all sorts for important ideas) must be understood by both reader and teacher. Consequently, to be successful, book talks must be based on sampling techniques. The teacher takes samples of each student's accumulated reading. Certain parts of some books are discussed; not all parts of all books. Through conversation with readers, the teacher takes samples of ideas readers have gained through a variety of situations.

To think of checking thoroughly all reading is disastrous. Thorough questioning of material read should be reserved for intensive reading which accompanies the textbook reading program; it should not be duplicated in IRP. Endeavoring to do so has been the downfall of many teachers.

Second, the conference time ought not to be used for checking oral reading errors. To think of the teacher's role as that of listening to individuals read orally is self-defeating for IRP. Again this can better be accomplished within the context of the textbook program with its oral reading groups. Teachers who try to carry the practice of oral reading checks over to the conference time of IRP find themselves overwhelmed and quickly turn back from IRP.

The essential purpose of book time is to enable each reader to reveal the signif-icance of his reading experiences. The role of the teacher is to enable the reader to convey the true meaning of what has been read. The key to book talk time lies in the questioning used by the teacher. Perceptive, penetrating questions can give insight relatively quickly into the depth of reading. Here reference is made to three articles wherein these concepts have been thoroughly developed.

1. Hunt, Lyman C. Jr. "The Key to the Conference Lies in the Questioning," *Educational Comment on Individual Reading*, H. Sandberg, ed., The University of Toledo, College of Education, Toledo, Ohio, 1966.
2. Hunt, Lyman C. Jr. "Evaluation Through Teacher-Pupil Conferences," *The Evaluation of Children's Reading Achievement*, T. Barrett, ed., Perspectives in Reading No. 8, International Reading Association, Newark, Delaware, 1967.
3. Hunt, Lyman C. Jr. "A Grouping Plan Capitalizing on the Individualized Reading Approach," *Forging Ahead In Reading*, J. Allen Figurel, ed., Part I, Proceeding of the Twelfth Annual Convention, International Reading Association, Newark, Delaware, 1968.

5. USSR: The Pinnacle of Reading Skills

Every teacher of reading should think of USSR as the pinnacle of achievement with regard to teaching skillful reading. USSR in this regard has nothing to do with our friendly Union of Soviet Socialist Republics. It is purely coincidental that the initials for this most paramount of all reading skills are identical with those of the Russian country. In this instance the initials stand for UNINTERRUPTED SUSTAINED SILENT READING.

USSR pertains to the relativity among reading skills. Basic to the concept is the consideration that silent reading is far more significant than is oral reading. Basic to the concept is the belief that contextual reading is of greater importance than are skills of recognition at the word/letter level. Basic to the concept is that the greatest reading skill to be achieved is that of sustaining silent reading over long stretches of print without interruption and without breaks. USSR cannot be achieved unless the reader has the facility to keep his mind on and flowing with the ideas.

USSR, then, is the skill which signals that the student is able to read by himself and for himself over long spans of print. Each reader must realize that his purpose in the silent reading time is to get as many of the important and significant ideas as he can through silent reading. In USSR reading is regarded as a detective-type activity. Specifically this means that the reader is not held accountable for every single idea contained in every single sentence or parts thereof. Specifically this means that the reader is oriented to search the material for ideas which are of relatively great importance, i.e., ideas of relative importance as contrasted with detail and facts of lesser importance. His task is to search out ideas that matter—ideas that make a difference.

This requires a radically different orientation to comprehension than that conveyed to the reader by the majority of current textbook programs. Both teacher and reader must understand that reading comprehension is making a series of judgments about the worthwhileness of the ideas—not remembering and repeating all that has been read.

Developing USSR in the classroom situation requires a very definite and particular set of attitudes on the parts of both the teacher and the reader. Each reader realizes that doing well means: (1) accomplishing as much silent reading as possible during the reading period; (2) keeping one's mind on the ideas; (3) responding more powerfully to high potency words and sentences; and (4) giving less attention to ideas of lesser importance.

USSR can be taught. Productive reading can be strengthened by helping each reader to realize that success means learning to sustain himself with print for longer and longer stretches of time. Any device the teacher wishes to use to help the readers attain this goal is in order. Various instructional devices help youngsters to keep track of the amount of silent reading accomplished during the reading period, i.e., through charts or through graphs or through any scheme of time-keeping which will make progress visible. Another approach is for the teacher to sit with groups in the reading circle and supervise or govern their silent reading. Here the teacher's role is simply to support and assist each youngster as he tries to get as far as he can with his printed material during his time in the reading circle. There is no oral reading around the circle; oral reading is eliminated except for having individual students verify ideas. The teacher helps with words; she assists in interpreting sentences; but more than anything else, she simply establishes the setting so that maximum amounts of silent reading can be completed by each child. The teacher helps each child to extend his own previous limits through day-to-day practice.

By using proper questions, the teacher can develop the understanding in the reader's mind that reading means getting as many big ideas out of print through sustained silent reading as he possibly can. The test for sustained silent reading consists basically of observing the youngster. Establishing situations in which sustained silent reading can be accomplished, then checking with the reader on the basic question: "Could you keep your mind on the ideas all the time you were reading?" is the essential test for USSR.

The USSR concept has significant implications for work with youngsters at the lower end of the reading scale. A gross and tragic mistake has been attempting to teach the low group readers through oral reading. The erroneous practice has been trying to get those in our low groups to sound as good while reading orally as do those in upper groups. Then, the theory goes, each will somehow become an independent reader. This approach has not worked and *cannot* work. Just attempting to reach relatively high degrees of oral reading fluency first is going at skill tasks backwards. Helping a young reader develop power of silent reading is the first priority. Teachers should make the silent reader first, and then the oral reader, not the other way around as we currently are doing. Teachers can make silent readers first if a premium is placed on doing so; fluency in oral reading will then follow naturally. More than anything else, we must realign our priorities with regard to basic reading skill areas.

6a. Record Keeping

Teachers who are developing the individualized approach to reading instruction have found it necessary to devise ways for keeping records of the children's development in reading. Some find that a card or notebook page for each child can be easily used to record notes during the pupil conferences. Others use a more formalized checklist on which the teacher periodically records observations concerning the children's performances and abilities. Such records serve as a guide for planning and a basis for reporting to parents on the child's progress.

Such record keeping is all to the good; however, some teachers get "hung up" on keeping track of things. Compulsive record keeping can be fatal for IRP. If keeping records, keeping track of books, answering questions or writing resumes on books read, takes more time than is spent by readers reading then the teacher has become lost—lost in non-essentials.

Realistically, teachers who are good record keepers will keep good records while teachers with messy desks and messy rooms will not. Similarly, youngsters who are high-powered readers and who are well-ordered will maintain good records. Conversely, low-powered readers and those with sloppy habits won't even be able to find the papers on which their records are kept. So be it. The object of the program is productive reading, not neat notepads filled with records.

As the saying goes:

> As you ramble through life, Brother,
> Whatever be your Goal,
> Keep your eye upon the Doughnut
> And not upon the Hole.

In this analogy, of course, the Doughnut is equated with productive reading, while record keeping can be the hole into which many well-intentioned teachers have fallen.

6b. And Evaluation

When the goal is that of making independent, self-sufficient and self-sustaining readers, evaluation becomes a complex matter. The evaluator must know many aspects of each child's reading. It is not enough to know whether or not each word is known. It is not enough to check on oral reading fluency. The teacher must see beyond having students answer ten questions correctly following the reading of a short passage.

The teacher must know if the young reader can perform effectively in the complex world of printed material. Does the reader find the sources important to him, and then find the truly significant ideas within them? Most important, once the proper reading material has been selected, does the reader have the staying power to follow through on long intricate passages? The ability to do this is the mark of a true reader. Any worthwhile evaluation must be predicated on this concept of reading. Fortunately each student reveals the answer to these questions through his daily performance in IRP. Evaluation becomes a self-evaluation for many. Observant teachers actually know each student's performance in reading better than in more conventional reading programs.

Four Values of IRP

The unique benefits emerging from successful development of IRP are four in number.

1. The art of extensive, exploratory reading is developed. Once the reader has learned a searching, detective approach to printed matter he has achieved a higher-level reading performance than is possible through conventional programs which concentrate on intensive types of reading.
2. USSR—the skill of sustained silent reading is acquired by some who otherwise would not have become real readers. Unless the reader can keep

going with print he has not reached the highest skill level.
3. Independence and self-direction are most difficult for some to learn, so difficult for some that self-direction is never gained. Yet it is also true that as long as one must follow teacher directions, that person is not a reader. Learning to be on-your-own in the world of print is a direct benefit of IRP for some.
4. L.O.B. is the grandest result of IRP; the result teachers who have succeeded with IRP unanimously acclaim is building LOVE OF BOOKS—a passion for reading. In IRP reading becomes a personal matter. Young readers have learned to care about books and they enjoy reading them. The personal satisfaction gained from reading is genuine. This is the ultimate difference that IRP can make.

36. The Effective Teacher of Reading, Revisited

Albert J. Harris

One of the major findings of the Cooperative First Grade Reading Studies (Bond and Dykstra 1967) was that differences among teachers are far more important in determining the reading achievement of children than differences among instructional methods and materials. Many attempts have since been made to discover why teachers who ostensibly are using the same methods can get such different results. Analytical reviews of this research have been made by Emans and Fox (1973), Medley (1977), and Rosenshine (1976, 1978). This article summarizes the research

done since a previous article, "The Effective Teacher of Reading" (Harris 1969), and develops implications for improved reading instruction.

Formal versus Informal Education

Formal educational programs are teacher centered; the teacher plans the instructional sequence and guides it step by step. Informal programs tend to be learner centered and to stress learner choices and inquiry, with the teacher functioning largely as a helper and resource person.

From Albert J. Harris, The effective teacher of reading, revisited. *The Reading Teacher*, November 1979, 33, 135–140. Reprinted by permission of Albert J. Harris and the International Reading Association.

Recent research has shown a consistent advantage of formal programs in fostering pupil achievement, in England (Bennett 1976) as well as in the United States. Reading gains tended to be greater in highly structured classrooms for children from low income families (Stallings and Kaskowitz 1974) and for middle-class suburban classes (Solomon and Kendall 1976). Permissiveness, spontaneity, and pupil choice of activities were negatively related not only to achievement but also to pupil self-esteem, inquiry, and writing ability (Solomon and Kendall 1976). Children with high IQs showed greater creativity in formal classes than in informal ones (Ward and Barcher 1975). Pupils in informal classrooms were not only lower in reading achievement but also were higher in test anxiety (Wright 1975).

Although in general the formal pattern seems more favorable to reading achievement, there is marked variability in results within formal and informal patterns, so that it is necessary to look for specific factors that influence the effectiveness of reading teachers.

Instructional Time

In a study that compared four methods of teaching reading to innercity Black first graders, there was a significant positive relationship between the time teachers spent in direct reading instruction and the average achievement of their classes (Harris and Serwer 1966). This held for all four methods, but was highest for the basal reader method. There was a nonsignificant and slightly negative relationship between reading achievement and time spent in related activities such as storytelling, use of audiovisual aids, and art correlated with reading. Cooley and Emrick (1974) also found that the time teachers spent in teaching reading had a significant effect on the reading achievement of first grade children.

Guthrie, Martuza and Seifert (1976) analyzed data from 931 instructional groups in second and sixth grades. At second grade level, classes spending large amounts of time on reading instruction made better gains than classes spending minimum time, for both high SES (socioeconomic status) children and low SES children. At sixth grade, instructional time was positively related to amount of gain in reading for low SES children, but had an inconsistent effect with high SES children. The authors reasonably conjectured that middle-class children tend to spend substantial amounts of time in reading outside of school, increasing their total reading practice and reducing the significance of differences in amount of instructional reading time in school, while low SES children are less likely to do so.

The picture is less clear in the intermediate grades, where there is a growing importance of seatwork such as silent reading and workbook exercises as one goes up the grades. In the middle grades such seatwork occupies more than half the total reading time (Calfee and Hoover 1976), and since close supervision by the teacher is usually not provided, seatwork is not counted in the research studies as part of the instructional time.

Another factor related to instructional time is the degree of pupil attention to the task, which is discussed below.

Pace of Instruction

Barr (1973–74) studied the effect of the rate at which new words were introduced in first grade classrooms. In some classrooms all children were taught at the same pace, while in others different groups proceeded at different rates. In the uniformly paced classes, the pace tended to be slow and the bright children learned fewer words than in the differentially paced classrooms. The children with slow learning rates learned about the same amount in both types of classes.

Adjustment of the pace of teaching of specific skills to the abilities of the learners is another aspect of pace that affects reading results. Tovey (1972) found that only 8% of 526 first grade children were receiving phonics teaching that was properly matched to their instructional readiness. Children who were at early first grade level in phonic proficiency were nearly all receiving phonics instruction that was too advanced for them, while children who were ready for second grade phonics nearly all were being taught what they already knew.

Difficulty of Material

In a classic study conducted in grades two through six, Cooper (1952) studied the relationship between the difficulty of a child's assigned basal reader for that child (as measured by the child's word recognition errors on a sample from that book) and the child's reading gain during the year. The easier the reader was for the child, the more progress the child made during the year. This held for both boys and girls, and for above average, average, and below average children. The best average gains were made by children who made fewer than 3 errors per 100 words. Primary children making 5% or more errors and intermediate children making 10% or more errors tended to make very small gains, so Cooper considered those percentages to represent the lower limit of the frustration level, undesirable for instruction. Percentages between those limits (3 to 5; 3 to 10) he considered of questionable suitability, and he recommended that the child's accuracy of comprehension and any signs of emotional tension should be taken into consideration. tion.

Jorgenson (1977) studied the relation of difficulty not to gain in reading but to classroom behavior. He found that the easier the material was in relation to the child's reading ability, the better her/his classroom behavior tended to be.

These studies challenge the long held belief that the ideal difficulty level for teacher guided reading instruction is an instructional level of medium difficulty— between the very easy independent reading level and the too difficult frustration level. They suggest that, when in doubt, choose the easier material.

The problem of choosing material of appropriate difficulty is complicated by the fact that the selections in a typical basal reader tend to vary in difficulty with a range of several grades (Bradley and Ames 1977). Thus a child for whom the average selection is quite easy will probably find few or no selections in that book that are frustratingly hard, while a child who needs some teacher assistance with the average selection in the book will probably find several selections that are frustrating even with teacher help.

Some teachers do not seem to realize how few unknown words it takes to make a selection difficult for a child and, with the best of intentions, keep many children struggling with material that is unsuitably hard for them.

Attention

Differences in the consistency with which children attend to the job at hand can be very large. Bloom (1976) found 15 studies in which student attention was compared with academic gain. In all but one of these studies there was a substantial positive relationship between the proportion of available time spent attending to tasks and student gain.

The fact that pupils learn when they attend to the task and do not learn what they don't attend to does not tell us how to get them to attend. To some extent individual differences in attentiveness may be constitutional and predispose some children to learning disabilities (Dykman and others 1971). But this does not explain why some whole classes attend most of the time during reading lessons and others do not. Attention may be a very desirable by-product when teaching is otherwise effective, and its opposite may be a signal that ineffective teaching is going on.

Motivation and Management

Several studies provide consistent evidence that effective teachers use praise and encouragement more than ineffective teachers do, and avoid harsh criticism, scolding, sarcasm, or other expressions of strong disapproval (Medley 1977). Orderly, teacher directed formal classrooms in which the teacher shows a good deal of warmth and uses praise generously tend to do better than teacher directed formal classrooms that are emotionally cold (Solomon and Kendall 1976). Pupil attitudes toward school tend to be more favorable in the orderly environment maintained by effective teachers.

The effective teacher seems to maintain an orderly environment with relatively little effort. This orderliness is probably a by-product of other characteristics: emphasis on academic learning, clear specification of jobs to be done, provision of appropriate materials, selection of skills based on a clear understanding of pupil needs, moving at a pace that is neither too fast nor too slow, checking work done independently as well as in groups, generous and frequent praise for effort as well as success, and provision of help when needed. When these conditions hold, children find that they can and do learn and they achieve satisfaction from learning.

Academic Engaged Time

The concept of "academic engaged time" means the time that a student spends in academically relevant activity at an appropriate, moderate level of difficulty (Rosenshine and Berliner 1977). These authors point out that teacher allocated time is not the same as student engaged time. In one class the students may be academically engaged 80% of the time, in another only 50% of the time. But the second of these classes can learn as much as the first if given proportionally more time to do it.

Rosenshine and Berliner state that direct teacher centered instruction is usually more effective than student centered instruction because it provides more academically engaged time per hour of instruction. They believe that the concept of academic engaged time incorporates most of what has been discussed above under the headings of formal versus informal instruction, instructional time, pace of instruction, difficulty of material, and attention. They point out that while informal classrooms generally have lower percentages of academically engaged time than formal classrooms, this can be compensated for by allocating more total instructional time. They also suggest that the learning and reading done outside of school by middle-class children probably add significantly to their total academically engaged time, while low SES children are less likely to benefit in this way.

Teacher Expectancies

Since the publication of *Pygmalion in the Classroom* (Rosenthal and Jacobson 1968), there have been many studies of the effects of teacher expectancies on pupil achievement and behavior. As Larsen and Ehly (1978) pointed out, expectations are neither good nor bad in themselves, and are virtually impossible to avoid. What counts is whether or not they are based on accurate perceptions of pupil behavior and whether they are flexible or rigid.

Expectations that are based on rigid stereotypes (e.g. obese children are lazy; Spanish-surname children are slow learners; girls are brighter and better behaved than boys) may distort a teacher's perceptions of individual children to the point of inducing a self-fulfilling prophecy. The teacher with such a stereotype may give a child who belongs to that group fewer instructional opportunities, less praise, and more criticism. With such treatment the child's movitation and behavior are likely to be adversely influenced, thus "confirming" the teacher's expectation. The teacher with a low opinion of the learning abilities of minority children is likely to find only the slow learning rate that he or she expected; the teacher who is convinced that such children have good learning potential encourages them to show it. With children who have reading disabilities, a teacher's conviction that the child can and will learn is a major factor in overcoming discouragement.

Attention to Pupil Needs

Rupley (1976) compared the elementary reading programs that had been identified as effective by the American Institute for Research and found that they had several types of teacher behavior in common: close monitoring of pupil progress, specifying objectives related to observable outcomes, using periodic testing in making instructional decisions, and teaching to the identified needs of the children.

Medley (1977) found that there was an important difference in the way that effective and ineffective teachers supervised independent reading activities. "When the effective teacher's pupils work independently, the teacher actively supervises them, giving careful attention to those individual children who, in the teacher's opinion, need it. The ineffective teacher who assigns pupils to seatwork leaves them pretty much to themselves; anyone who needs help must seek it."

It seems, then, that effective teachers are perceptive of individual and group needs, keep a close watch over the progress of their pupils, and provide help promptly when a difficulty becomes evident.

Conclusions

Considerable progress has been made during the past decade in discovering characteristics of effective and ineffective reading instruction, based on studies in which the amount of pupil gain in reading is the criterion.

Teaching is likely to be effective when:

- The teacher plans, assigns, and supervises the learning activities.
- Reading is scheduled for enough instructional time to accomplish mastery of the program's objectives.
- The pace of instruction is adjusted to the differences in learning rate of groups and individuals.
- Instructional material is easy enough to allow pupils to concentrate on the new words or ideas, develop fluency, and enjoy reading.
- Conditions prevail in the classroom which are conducive to good concentration and sustained attention.
- Teachers maintain order while showing warm interest in the children, and are generous with praise for their efforts.
- The proportion of lesson time spent in academically engaged activity is kept high.
- Teachers are optimistic about the learning potentialities of their pupils and do not allow their perceptions of individual differences to affect adversely the morale of some pupils.
- Teachers pay close attention to individual and group needs, are alert to signs of pupil difficulties, and provide help promptly.

There are still many issues that influence the effectiveness of reading instruction that have not been sufficiently investigated. These include the relative values of different forms of grouping and individualization, specific ways of teaching particular reading skills, relative emphasis on different kinds of questions, and possible differences in what works best with children from particular social and cultural backgrounds, to mention just a few. In another ten years we should know much more than we know now about the effective teaching of reading.

References

Barr, Rebecca C. "Instructional Pace Differences and Their Effect on Reading Acquisition." *Reading Research Quarterly*, vol. 9, no. 4 (1973–1974), pp. 526–54.

Bennett, Neville. *Teaching Style and Pupil Progress*. Cambridge, Mass.: Harvard University Press, 1976.

Bloom, Benjamin. *Human Characteristics and School Learning*. New York, N. Y.: McGraw-Hill, 1976.

Bond, Guy L. and Robert Dykstra. "The Cooperative Research Program in First-Grade Reading Instruction." *Reading Research Quarterly*, vol. 2, no. 4 (Summer 1967), pp. 5–142.

Bradley, John M. and Wilbur S. Ames. "Readability Parameters of Basal Readers." *Journal of Reading Behavior*, vol. 9 (Summer 1977), pp. 175–83.

Braun, Carl. "Pygmalion in the Reading Circle." *Academic Therapy*, vol. 12 (Summer 1977), pp. 445–54.

Calfee, Robert and Kathryn Hoover. "Reading and Mathematics Observation System: Description and Analysis of Time Expenditures." *Beginning Teacher Evaluation Study: Phase II*, vol. 3, ch. 2, Frederick J. McDonald, Ed. Princeton, N. J.: Educational Testing Service, 1976.

Cooley, W. W. and J. A. Emrick. A Model of Classroom Differences Which Explains Variation in Classroom Achievement. Paper presented at the annual meeting of the American Educational Research Association, Chicago, April, 1974.

Cooper, J. Louis. The Effect of Adjustment of Basal Reading Materials on Reading Achievement. Unpublished doctoral dissertation, Boston University, 1952.

Dykman, Roscoe, Peggy T. Ackerman, Sam D. Clements and John E. Peters. "Specific Learning Disabilities: An Attentional Deficit Syndrome." *Progress in Learning Disabilities*, vol. II, pp. 56–93, Helmer R. Myklebust, Ed. New York, N.Y.: Grune & Stratton, 1971.

Emans, Robert and Sharon E. Fox. "Teaching Behaviors in Reading Instruction." *The Reading Teacher*, vol. 27, no. 2 (November 1973), pp. 142–48.

Guthrie, John T., Victor Martuza and Mary Seifert. Impacts of Instructional Time in Reading. Presented at the conference on Theory and Practice in Beginning Reading, Learning Research and Development Center, University of Pittsburgh, June 1976.

Harris, Albert J. "The Effective Teacher of Reading." *The Reading Teacher*, vol. 23, no. 3 (December 1969), pp. 195–204, 208.

Harris, Albert J. and Blanche L. Serwer. "The CRAFT Project: Instructional Time in Reading Research." *Reading Research Quarterly*, vol. 2, no. 1 (Fall 1966), pp. 27–56.

Jorgensen, Gerald W. "Relationship of Classroom Behavior to the Accuracy of the Match between Material Difficulty and Student Ability." *Journal of Educational Psychology*, vol. 69 (February 1977), pp. 24–32.

Larsen, Stephen C. and Stewart Ehly. "Teacher-Student Interactions: A Factor in Handicapping Conditions." *Academic Therapy*, vol. 13 (January 1978), pp. 267–73.

Medley, Donald M. *Teacher Competence and Teacher Effectiveness: A Review of Process-Product Research*. Washington, D.C.: American Association of Colleges for Teacher Education, 1977.

Rosenshine, Barak V. "Classroom Instruction." *The Psychology of Teaching Methods*, 75th Yearbook of the National Society for the Study of Education, Part I, pp. 335–71. Chicago: University of Chicago Press, 1976.

Rosenshine, Barak V. "Review of *Teaching Styles and Pupil Progress* by Neville Bennett." *American Educational Research Journal*, vol. 15 (Winter 1978), pp. 163–69.

Rosenshine, Barak V. and David C. Berliner. Academic Engaged Time: Content Covered and Direct Instruction. Paper presented at the American Educational Research Association annual meeting, April 1977.

Rosenthal, Robert and Lenore Jacobson. *Pygmalion in the Classroom*. New York, N.Y.: Holt, Rinehart and Winston, 1968.

Rupley, William H. "ERIC/RCS: Effective Reading Programs." *The Reading Teacher*, vol. 29, no. 6 (March 1976), pp. 616–21.

Solomon, D. and A. J. Kendall. *Final Report: Individual Characteristics and Children's Performance in Varied Educational Settings.* Rockville, Md.: Montgomery County Public Schools, 1976.

Stallings, Jane A. and David H. Kaskowitz. "Follow Through Classroom Observation Evaluation—1972-73." Menlo Park, Cal.: Stanford Research Institute, 1974.

Tovey, Duane R. "Relationship of Matched First Grade Phonics Instruction to Overall Reading Achievement and the Desire to Read." *Some Persistent Questions on Beginning Reading*, Robert C. Aukerman, Ed., pp. 93–101. Newark, Del.: International Reading Association, 1972.

Ward, William D. and Peter R. Barcher. "Reading Achievement and Creativity as Related to Open Classroom Experience." *Journal of Educational Psychology*, vol. 67 (October 1975), pp. 683–91.

Wright, Robert J. "The Affective and Cognitive Consequences of an Open Education Elementary School." *American Educational Research Journal*, vol. 12 (Fall 1975), pp. 449–68.

CHAPTER VIII

Word Recognition and Decoding

How do children learn to figure out unknown words? This chapter includes a variety of viewpoints on this crucially important question.

Cunningham advocates a compare/contrast theory based on searching through a store of known words and comparing the new (unknown) word to those already known, rather than applying a series of rules about grapheme-phoneme correspondences. Samuels argues that accuracy in word recognition is not enough; instead, children need to learn words to the point where recognition is speedy and automatic. He recommends repeated rereading of selections as a way to develop automatic recognition.

The child who knows many phonic principles but cannot seem to blend or synthesize successive units to produce the correct word has puzzled many a teacher. Resnick and Beck point out that the usual ways of teaching blending place a strain on the child's short-term memory, and advocate a progressive blending procedure in which the child has to keep in mind only two units at a time. Jolly concentrates on the common function words that are difficult for young readers, and describes a seven-step procedure for teaching them, first in isolation, then in context, and finally in isolation again.

Goodman explains and illustrates the use of miscue analysis to develop learning strategies that stress use of meaning and context. In the final article, Lesiak narrows down phonic generalizations to thirty-two that work at least 75 percent of the time and occur with reasonable frequency; the implication is that these few are worth teaching.

37. A Compare/Contrast Theory of Mediated Word Identification

Patricia M. Cunningham

What occurs in the mind of the reader during the time lapse between encountering an unfamiliar word and successfully identifying it?

Imagine that Paula is reading along in a book. She comes to the sentence, "The man was seeking employment." The word *employment* is part of Paula's listening vocabulary, but she fails to recognize the word in print. The context is not sufficiently rich to provide her with the pronunciation of the word; Paula must me-

From Patricia M. Cunningham, A comparison/contrast theory of mediated work identification. *The Reading Teacher*, April 1979, *32*, 774–778. Reprinted by permission of Patricia M. Cunningham and the International Reading Association.

diate the identification of the unfamiliar-in-print word *employment*. That is, she must apply another tool or technique to help her identify the word.

The conventional wisdom of reading teachers would suggest that Paula goes through a process of dividing the word into syllables and then applying phonics generalizations to the letter combinations in the syllables. She would follow this route:

1. Divide into syllables between the *m* and the *p*. (Having recognized *pl* as a blend, she would not divide there.)
2. Recognize that the *y* in this case is part of a diphthong and divide before the consonant *m*.
3. Having successfully divided the word into three syllables, Paula would then apply her letter-sound generalizations to the individual syllables. The vowel *e* has a short sound. Blend short *e* and *m* to get *em*.
4. The vowel *o* has neither a short nor a long sound because of the *y*. Paula applies appropriate *oy* sound, blends to arrive at *ploy*.
5. The *e* is the only vowel in the last syllable and is not controlled by any other letter, so it too has a short *e* sound. Think short *e*, blend with other letters, *ment*.
6. Put three syllables together: *em ploy ment*. Paula has an "aha" experience. "Oh, he was looking for a job!" Paula returns to reading her book.

When asked if the previously described process is what they think they do when encountering an unfamiliar-in-print word, most adults reply that they think they apply these rules, but that it happens so fast it appears to be automatic. Many adults who can give a correct pronunciation for words they have never seen before cannot state the rules they use in arriving at a correct pronunciation.

Most think they have forgotten the rules. Upon further questioning, however, many adults will remember that they were never taught these rules. A whole generation of adults, schooled in the days before Rudolf Flesch, were taught to read by a sight-word-plus-context method. They were never taught the phonics generalizations assumed necessary for mediating the identification of an unfamiliar word. Yet, these same adults can pronounce words in isolation which they have never seen before.

There must be an alternative route to the mediation of unfamiliar words. Such an alternative route might be a compare/contrast process.

Compare/Contrast Theory

A few years ago, I synthesized a theory of mediated word identification (Cunningham 1975–76) based on the writings of Gibson (1965), Venezky (1968), Venezky and Calfee (1970) and Smith (1971). These authors show six points of agreement:

1. Mediated word identification is not a process of applying adult-taught rules, but of searching through a store and comparing the unknown to the known.
2. An unfamiliar word which cannot be recognized as a whole is segmented into the largest manageable units.
3. These units are then compared to known words, non-words, or fragments, or are tested against feature lists (i.e., mental lists of the distinguishing features of written symbols).
4. A recombining process results in a word for which the reader has an acoustic and/or semantic category.
5. Some kind of transfer is involved in the process of mediated word identification.
6. Readers form their own rules for analyzing unknown words by comparing and contrasting the unknown with the known.

The compare/contrast theory of mediated word identification would result in a different process for Paula to go through when she happened upon the unfamiliar-in-print word *employment*. Rather than applying rules, Paula would begin a search through the words in her "cognitive word store," comparing the unknown words. She would be economical in this search and would look for the largest known units. Thus if Paula knew the word *employ* and had words in her store such as *arrangement* and *installment*, she would probably segment *employment* into *employ* and *ment*, find the appropriate known words simultaneously, and then recombine to come to the "Aha—he was looking for a job!"

Let's assume, however, that Paula did not have the word *employ* in her store of known words. She would then have to break the word into smaller units. Again this segmentation would be determined by her store of known words and parts. She might break off the *em* because she knows *embarrass* and *empire*. She would mediate the identification of the syllable *em* simultaneously as she segmented.

The syllable *ploy* might not be a part of any known word. If, however, Paula had *boy* and *joy* and *toy* and *Roy* stored, she could mediate the identification of the syllable *ploy* by comparing it to the other similar known words. The same process might be used if Paula did not have in her store any words that ended in *ment* by comparing it to the known words *bent*, *went*, and *spent*.

Having arrived at pronunciations for the "largest manageable units" by searching through her store and comparing the known to the unknown, Paula must then recombine the parts and test the word against words she has heard before. She would again arrive at the correct identification.

One-Syllable Words

My original investigation into the validity of the compare/contrast theory of mediated word identification (Cunningham 1975–76) was done with a group of thirty second graders. The subjects were screened and chosen for their ability to pronounce high frequency words and their inability to pronounce similar but less frequent words. The fourteen experimental subjects received two weeks of training in comparing unknown words and non-words to known words.

The subjects were given 3 high-frequency, one-syllable words on the first day and 3 on each of the four succeeding days. These 15 words were a tangible word store, kept on individual index cards.

During the first week of treatment thereafter, the subjects were presented with 13 words and 13 non-words each day. For each presented stimulus, the subjects found the word from their tangible word store that looked most like the presented stimulus and then showed that word to the investigator. They then responded to questions which required comparing and contrasting the presented stimulus with their "look-alike" word and they pronounced both stimuli (questions such as "Where are the two words alike?" "Do they rhyme or begin alike?" "Where are the two words different?").

During the second week of treatment, the subjects were asked to try to recall the word which looked most like the stimulus and to use their tangible word store of 15 cards only when they couldn't mentally conjure up an image of their look-alike word. The purpose of this second week's activities was to help the subjects develop an internalized word store. Each day, 13 words and 13 non-words were presented.

To determine the effectiveness of the treatment in improving the second graders' ability to mediate the identifiation of words, a criterion/delayed retention word pronunciation task was designed. This task contained 10 low-frequency stimuli (one-syllable words not likely to be known by second graders), 10 non-word stimuli, and 10 two-syllable stimuli. All stimuli were novel and had been purposefully excluded from the training. This task was administered twice to all control and experimental subjects. As the criterion task, it was administered in the week following treatment. As the delayed retention task, it was administered one month following the end of treatment.

Results of a two-way analysis of variance with a repeated measure as one factor indicated that experimental group mean scores on the low-frequency stimuli and the two-syllable stimuli were significantly higher than control group mean scores at both administrations of the criterion/delayed retention word pronunciation task. There were no significant differences in the children's ability to pronounce the non-word stimuli.

Two-Syllable Words

To investigate the theory that readers might mediate the identification of unfamiliar polysyllabic words by comparing and contrasting the parts of these words to known words and word parts, I sought out a population of readers who had a store of one-syllable words but who could not pronounce two-syllable words, the syllables of which were similar to the known one-syllable words. Fourth and fifth graders enrolled in a rural school in the American Southeast were screened on two word-pronunciation tasks. The one-syllable task consisted of pronouncing 24 high-frequency words (*Bob, them, top, her,* etc.). The two-syllable task consisted of pronouncing 15 words whose syllables rhymed with the one-syllable words the children had read (e.g., *problem* for *Bob* and *them; copper* for *top* and *her*).

From the 165 students screened, sixteen were found who could pronounce 21 or more of the 24 one-syllable words and 7 or fewer of the 15 two-syllable words. The average number of two-syllable words correctly pronounced by these sixteen subjects was 4.31. (Reliability of the two-syllable word pronunciation task was .74, as estimated by the KR_{21} formula.) The subjects were also given a list of 20 two-syllable words which they were instructed to divide into syllables.

As the final task before the start of training, subjects were given an oral/aural recombining task. A native speaker had tape recorded 10 common two-syllable words, leaving a five-second interval between the syllables. Subjects individually listened to the tape and then demonstrated their ability to recombine the syllables of the word by putting the word in a sentence or giving an appropriate semantic association. Of the sixteen subjects, eight correctly recombined and gave appropriate associations for all 10 of the stimulus words. The eight remaining subjects all appropriately recombined 9 of the 10 words. Recombining the syllables of a two-syllable word was thus a *fait accompli* for this group of fourth and fifth graders, and no posttesting of their recombining ability was administered.

The sixteen subjects were divided into two groups of eight subjects each for the three-week (thirty minutes per day) treatment. The treatment was similar to that given to the subjects of the original investigation. Instead of comparing and contrasting unknown one-syllable words to known one-syllable words, these subjects compared and contrasted unknown two-syllable words to known one-syllable words. On the first day of treatment, subjects were given five index cards. On each card, they printed a one-syllable word. They were then presented with two-syllable words and asked to find the 2 one-syllable words which were similar to the parts of the two-syllable word.

The 2 one-syllable words were pronounced by a volunteer subject, and subjects noted that since the syllables of the two-syllable word rhymed with the one-syllable words, they could use the one-syllable words to decode the two-syllable word. The two-syllable word was then pronounced by a volunteer.

One-syllable words were added daily to the tangible word store. During the course of the treatment, these fourth and fifth graders matched approximately 200 two-syllable words to their store of 35 one-syllable words. They were not taught any rules for dividing words into syllables. [For a more complete description of the type of training carried out, see Cunningham (1978).]

Upon completion of the three-week training, subjects were once again given the two-syllable word pronunciation task. (These words had been purposefully excluded from the training so that they could be used as a posttest measure.) On the second administration of the 15-word two-syllable task, the mean number of words correctly pronounced was 8.01, compared with 4.31 the first time. The results of a dependent t test indicated that there was a significant difference ($p < .001$) between the two administrations of the two-syllable list.

Subjects also were once again given the list of 20 two-syllable words and instructed to divide the words into syllables. The mean number of words correctly divided prior to the training was 9.2. Following training, the mean number was 10.3. This difference was not significant ($p < .20$).

The results of this investigation must be interpreted within the limitations of the study. The most serious limitation is that subjects were not decoding words while engaged in the act of "real reading." While unfortunate, this limitation was deemed necessary in order to isolate the effect of the compare/contrast training from the variable of context. Also, the population was small and limited, and there was no control group to which results of the experimental subjects could be compared.

The "deviant" nature of the subjects, however, may lend strength to the findings. Three were classified as learning disabled, two as educably mentally retarded. Eight were enrolled in a remedial reading program. Thirteen of the sixteen children were receiving special instruction outside their classrooms and had been receiving this instruction for an average of 2.2 years.

Given the content of most remedial reading and special education programs, we can infer that all these students had been given intensive and extensive practice in the traditional "phonics." Rules for dividing words into syllables and sounding out the divided parts had no doubt been taught and retaught to this population of youngsters.

While the results of this experiment and the original experiment with one-syllable words do not prove that mediated word identification is a process of searching through a store of known words and comparing the unknown to the known rather than a process of applying a series of adult-taught rules, they do support that theory. Training in a compare/contrast strategy can result in a significant increase in the ability to decode unfamiliar words. The results also suggest that segmentation occurs as the known parts are identified and that, once the parts of a word are identified, the recombining process is automatic. The fact that the subjects did not show a significant increase in their ability to divide words into syllables adds more support to the theory that syllabication rules have more to do with dictionaries than with decoding unfamiliar words (Glass 1967, Wardaugh 1969, Canney and Schreiner 1976–77).

References

Canney, George and Robert Schreiner. "A Study of the Effectiveness of Selected Syllabication Rules and Phonogram Patterns for Word Attack." *Reading Research Quarterly*, vol. 12 (1976–1977), pp. 102–24.

Cunningham, Patricia M. "Decoding Polysyllabic Words: An Alternative Strategy." *Journal of Reading*, vol. 21, no. 7 (April 1978), pp. 608–14.

Cunningham, Patricia M. "Investigating a Synthesized Theory of Mediated Word Identification." *Reading Research Quarterly*, vol. 11 (1975–1976), pp. 127–43.

Gibson, Eleanor J. "Learning to Read." *Science*, vol. 148 (May 1965), pp. 1066–72.

Glass, Gerald. "The Strange World of Syllabication." *Elementary School Journal*, vol. 67 (1967), pp. 403–05.

Smith, Frank, *Understanding Reading*. New York, N.Y.: Holt, Rinehart and Winston, 1971.

Venezky, Richard L. Untitled remarks in *Communication by Language, the Reading Process*, James F. Kavanaugh, Ed. Washington, D.C.: United States Government Printing Office, 1968.

Venezky, Richard L. and Robert C. Calfee. "The Reading Competency Model." *Theoretical Models and Processes of Reading*, Harry Singer and Robert B. Ruddell, Eds., pp. 273–91. Newark, Del.: International Reading Association, 1970.

Wardaugh, Ronald. *Reading, a Linguistic Perspective*. New York, N.Y.: Harcourt Brace Jovanovich, 1969.

38. Automatic Decoding and Reading Comprehension

S. Jay Samuels

The role of automaticity in decoding and its effect on reading comprehension is not well understood at the present time. For years, teachers of beginning reading have been satisfied if their students were accurate in decoding words. While it is true that accuracy in decoding is necessary in reading, it is not a sufficient condition. In order to have both fluent reading and good comprehension, the student must be brought beyond accuracy to automaticity in decoding.

The need for "automatic habits" in reading is not an entirely new idea. Huey (1908, p. 104) wrote:

> Perceiving being an act, it is performed more easily with each repetition . . . to perceive an entirely new word . . . requires considerable time and close attention . . . repetition progressively frees the mind from attention to details, makes facile the total act, shortens the time and reduces the extent to which consciousness must concern itself with the process.

In Fries' (1963) book *Linguistics and Reading* we find statements about the importance of automatic habits, but the term "automaticity" is not defined, nor are there explanations of how these automatic habits are developed and measured. While there is research literature on automaticity in the psycho-motor domain, there is virtually nothing in the verbal learning-reading domain.

To appreciate the power of "automatic decoding" as a psychological process, it is necessary first to discuss the limits of human attention. A quarter of a century of research on attention has led to the conclusion that the brain acts as a single channel processor. This means that at any given moment, attention can be at only one place at a time. If two sources of information are presented simultaneously to a person, each of which demands attention for its processing, the individual finds both cannot be processed simultaneously. This dilemma has been described as the "cocktail party problem," a situation you encounter at a party where there are a number of interesting conversations going on at the same time competing for your attention. Several choices are available to a person faced with competing sources of

From S. Jay Samuels, Automatic decoding and reading comprehension. *Language Arts*, March 1976, *53*, 323–325. Reprinted by permission of the author and the National Council of Teachers of English.

information. One choice involves attending solely to one conversation and ignoring the other sources. The other choice involves attention switching. The individual may be able to follow two or more conversations by rapidly switching attention back and forth. The fact that the brain acts as a single channel communication device and can be attentive to only one information source at a time, places important limitations on the beginning reader with regard to comprehending what was decoded.

What is remarkable about automatic processes is that it enables a behavior which formerly required attention to occur without the services of attention. This is tantamount to putting a plane on automatic pilot, thus freeing the pilot to direct attention to other things. While numerous behaviors such as tieing one's shoe lace or riding a bicycle can be developed to levels which enable them to be performed without attention, it appears that the one important area of human behavior which, regardless of the amount of practice one gets, cannot be performed automatically is that of comprehending language. To comprehend either visually or auditorily presented language requires the services of attention.

At this point, a definition of "automaticity" is clear: behavior is automatic when it can be performed without attention. Under ordinary circumstances, walking is an automatic behavior. However, when the ground is icy, attention must be used to prevent falling. Another way to approach the problem of defining "automaticity," according to LaBerge (1973), is to consider two tasks which at unskilled stages could not be performed simultaneously. Two such behaviors which cannot be performed together at low levels of skill development are sight reading music while at the piano and repeating speech. After training, if both tasks can be performed simultaneously, at least one of them is automatic. Highly skilled piano players can sight read music and shadow speech. In this case, it is the piano playing which is automatic.

There are numerous examples of automatic behaviors. Ten years ago a friend who was studying to be a surgeon used a small board with pegs in order to practice surgical knot tieing. This task was sufficiently demanding that his performance was slow and he had to guide his finger movements visually. It required so much of his attention that he found it impossible to engage simultaneously in other behaviors such as watching television or conversing with others. After ten years of practice, his knot tieing became automatic.

The final example involves automobile driving, since there are interesting parallels between it and reading. At the beginning stages of driving, the student finds that the mechanics of operating the car are so demanding of attention that it is difficult, if not impossible, to comprehend conversation while driving. Once the person becomes a skilled driver, the mechanical aspects of operating the car require little conscious attention, leaving the driver free to focus attention on processing conversation at the meaning level. Only when some danger signal occurs is the driver forced to direct sustained attention back to the vehicle. When sustained attention is brought back on the mechanics of driving, it is impossible again to comprehend conversation. We find similar changes occurring in reading. At the beginning stages of learning to read, the students' attention is focused upon the decoding aspects of the task. Since processing information for meaning also requires attention, as long as the reader's attention is on decoding, what has been read cannot be comprehended.

The fluent reader, unlike the beginning reader, is able to decode automatically without the services of attention and thus is able to attend to processing meaning at the same time as decoding. Only when a new word appears is the reader's attention directed back to the task of decoding. Once the decoding problem for the new word is solved, the reader's attention can be brought back to processing meaning.

Although the beginning reader cannot easily comprehend what has been decoded because attention is not available for processing meaning, unskilled readers can access meaning by rereading a passage several times. The first few readings bring the printed material to the phonological level as if the student were "listening" to it rather than reading it. Once this point is reached, the student is able to switch attention to deriving meaning from what has been decoded. Teachers who are aware of how difficult it is for beginning readers to access meaning allow their students enough time to read a passage silently several times before testing their comprehension or asking them to read aloud. This procedure allows the student enough time and trials to switch attention to comprehending the material.

Automaticity explains a variety of reading phenomena. For example, the fluent reader claims to have read every word on the page but may not be able to recall what has been read. In this case, the student may be decoding automatically, but instead of using attention to process meaning, the student's attention is directed elsewhere on situations entirely divorced from the reading matter at hand.

Another situation explained by automaticity has to do with the student who can accurately decode a high proportion of words in a passage and still have trouble comprehending what was read, that is, "word calling." The word caller must use attention in decoding, thus preventing him or her from using that attention to process meaning.

Students who are accurate but not automatic in decoding may comprehend what they have read by means of a multiple-reading strategy. The first reading of the passage is done with attention on the decoding. With additional readings, the student may be able to direct attention to processing the meaning. The multiple-reading strategy is a slow, painstaking method. With additional practice, the student will find that he or she can reach the stage when simultaneous decoding and comprehension of the passage occurs.

Although more than a half century has passed since Huey stressed the importance of repetition and practice in the development of automatic habits, there is little more we can add today. Athletic coaches have long known that star athletes are usually the ones with the most highly developed automatic habits. Musicians have also known the value of practice as the means of a fluent performance. The time has come for teachers of reading to realize also the importance of practice beyond accuracy as a necessary condition for the development of automatic decoding. Students will learn to read fluently only by reading.

References

Fries, Charles C. *Linguistics and Reading.* Holt, 1963.

Huey, Edmund B. *The Psychology and Pedagogy of Reading.* M.I.T. Press, 1908, 1968.

LaBerge, David. "Attention and the Measurement of Perceptual Learning." [In *Memory and Cognition*, 1973, 1, 268–276.]

39. Designing Instruction in Reading: Initial Reading

Lauren B. Resnick and Isabel L. Beck

Choosing a Basic Approach

Over the years there has been substantial debate concerning appropriate strategies for initial reading instruction. Without reviewing the "great debate" (Chall 1967) over decoding as opposed to "whole-word" approaches to reading, it may be useful to point out a set of hidden assumptions that underlies the differences of opinion. Proponents of various whole-word approaches—basal reading, language experience, etc.—usually assume that good initial reading should match skilled reading performance as closely as possible. In other words, since skilled readers process units such as words and sentences, so should beginning readers—even if they can manage only a few words and sentences. Similarly, since skilled readers interpret and apply what they are reading, so should beginning readers. By contrast, a decoding emphasis in early reading assumes that the initial job is to learn the most generative form of the reading process—a form that is relatively easy to learn and that allows the learner to later approximate the performance of skilled readers. In other words, code-breaking implies teaching the basic structure of print-to-sound mapping, which is the core "subject-matter" of very initial reading.

We adopt here a code-breaking approach to initial reading. In doing so we are agreeing with the large majority of scholars—both psychologists and linguists—who argue that a fundamental task of initial reading is learning the structural relationships between written and spoken language—i.e., the grapheme-phoneme mapping that characterizes the language (Chall 1967; Diederich 1973). While virtually all scholars concerned with reading now agree that early and regular instruction in some type of code-breaking is needed, there still exist competing theories about how code-breaking itself should be taught. There are two major approaches, the "analytic" and the "synthetic." The "analytic" approach attempts to teach grapheme-phoneme correspondences to the child by having him examine displays of words that share and contrast major spelling patterns. The "synthetic" approach teaches grapheme-phoneme correspondences directly by having the child assemble words from phonemes. The main point of difference between the two approaches concerns whether or not learners should ever be asked to pronounce individual phonemes outside of the auditory context of the entire word. Proponents of the analytic approach argue that, since isolated phonemes do not occur in natural speech, the blending process of the synthetic approach unnecessarily and unnaturally burdens the child and magnifies the difficulties of his learning task.

We agree that the analytic method of teaching decoding might indeed avoid the problem of pronouncing isolated phonemes and of blending them. However, it introduces another problem that may be even more difficult for the child. Analytic decoding methods do not eliminate the need to abstract phonemes from the speech stream; in fact, they require that the child independently extract the phonemes. For at least some children, this detection of phonemes requires very extensive skills in auditory analysis and in general concept attainment strategy. By contrast, the synthetic approach provides direct help by indicating the units with which the child must deal. The child's attention is directed to the grapheme, and the phoneme is sounded; he need not discover the relationship independently. Furthermore, a natural feedback system is inherent in the process. Since phonemes do indeed normally occur in the environment of other phonemes rather than in isolation, the child can test his own verbal production (the result of blending) against what "sounds right." For example, having blended /k/ /a/ /t/ to produce *cat*, he can test to see whether he has pronounced a word that is in his aural vocabulary.

For these general reasons, we came to favor a synthetic approach to decoding instruction. However, since one of the primary pedagogic objections to this approach has been the difficulty of learning the process of blending, we sought to determine whether there was any way of simplifying or making more explicit the process of putting sounds together. For this purpose, we began with an analysis of two possible strategies of blending, one which is commonly used in initial teaching, and one which we developed while working with children who were having initial difficulty in learning.

Analysis of the Decoding Process

Two blending procedures

Figure 1 shows the general structure of the two blending routines that we examined. In each case, the routine is capable of decoding single syllable, regularly spelled words—the typical vocabulary of a beginning phonics program. At the left (Figure 1a), the procedure depicted is one in which the sound of each grapheme is given and stored; the synthesis occurs only after the final phoneme has been pronounced. We call this the "final blending" procedure, since blending is postponed until the very last step. Figure 1b, at the right, calls for successive blending. As soon as two sounds are produced, they are blended and successive phonemes are incorporated in the blend as they are pronounced.

The final blending and the successive blending routines call upon the same set of decisions and actions: finding graphemes in sequence (Component A); pronouncing identified graphemes (Component B); "storing" (remembering) pronounced sounds (Component C); deciding whether more graphemes remain to be sounded (Components D and E); blending (Component F); and, finally, in each case, matching the produced "word" against one's linguistic knowledge to determine whether the word generated is an acceptable decoding. The two routines differ only in the organization of these components, a difference in "executive" that appears to have important consequences concerning the ease of learning and of performing the decoding act.

To illustrate the differences between the two blending routines, let us use the word *cats* as an example and analyze the exact respects in which the two routines differ. The child who uses the final blending routine would proceed as follows: /k/ /a/ /t/ /s/ *cats*. The child who uses the second system would proceed thusly: /k/ /a/ /ka/ /t/ /kat/ /s/ /kats/ *cats*.

Consider the contrast between the two procedures. According to the final blending routine, each grapheme's sound is given, and the full set of phonemes in the word must be held in memory until the entire word has been "sounded out"; only then does any blending occur. But in the successive blending routine, blending

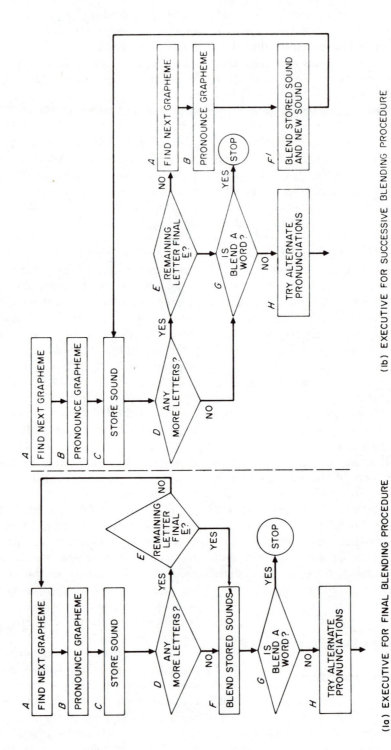

(Ia) EXECUTIVE FOR FINAL BLENDING PROCEDURE

(Ib) EXECUTIVE FOR SUCCESSIVE BLENDING PROCEDURE

Figure 1. Executive Routines for Synthetic Decoding

212

occurs sequentially at each stage at which a new phoneme is pronounced. At no time must more than two sounds be held in memory (the sound immediately produced and the one that directly precedes it); and at no time must more than two sound units be blended. Thus, the routines differ in two respects: (1) in the maximum number of sound units to be held in memory during the course of decoding, and (2) in the maximum number of units to be blended during a given attempt. The standard routine on the left requires remembering each of the separate units that the reader identifies as graphemes. The routine on the right never requires remembering more than two units.

Teaching the grapheme/phoneme correspondences

In this sequence, teachers are trained to give simple, direct statements to children and to control additional cueing or prompting in order to fade prompts deliberately and systematically.

Techniques for teaching symbol/sound correspondences are as follows:

1. the teacher models the isolated sound;
2. the children imitate the model;
3. the teacher models the sound again, this time pointing to the symbol (the letter on a printed card);
4. the children imitate the model sound, while looking at the symbol. Concurrent with the children's imitation, the teacher mouths the sound silently. In doing this, she consciously establishes a cue or prompt;
5. the children produce the sound to match the symbol, without the spoken model, but with the silent mouthing cue;
6. the teacher fades the silent mouthing cue as the children produce the sound;
7. the children produce the symbol/sound correspondence independently.

Compare the directness of the above with the indirectness and miscueing of the following procedure observed in a traditional classroom of an experienced teacher. The teacher held up a card with *m* printed on it and said, "This is an *m*. The name of the letter is *m* but the sound is /m/, as in 'mmmmountain.' I want to hear everyone say it." One child said *em*, two said /m/, another said "mmmmountain." The teacher said, "No, I want you to say the sound. Listen: /m/ as in 'mmmmountain,' 'mmmmother,' 'mmmmonkey.' Who can think of another /m/ word?" Hands went up. One child said, " 'Mmary' like my name." Teacher: "Good, Mmary. Any others?" A second child said, "We went to the mountains once. It was our vacation and we slept in a tent." With so many concepts floating about, only the most sophisticated child could extract the relevant information from the lesson. Training in the techniques of programmed teaching as described above can enable a teacher to instruct children in the basic skills with more precision.

Teaching blending

Once five symbol/sound correspondences are established they are immediately used to blend real words. A precise program for teaching the blending routine has been prepared for this purpose. You will perhaps have noted that our task analyses did not include a detailed subroutine for blending. This is because we know of no reasonably elaborated theory for how humans manage to recognize the equivalence of the single sound (e.g., /ka/) and the separate phonemes (e.g., /k/ and /a/). We know only that the equivalence is a difficult one, and that the ability to recognize it, and therefore to produce a blend, becomes greater with greater experience. In the absence of a strong hypothesis concerning the cognitive processes involved, a visual/motor analogue of the blending operation helps to organize the process for the child. We have, therefore, developed a rather ritualized procedure for blending, in which motor acts accompany the oral blending. These motor acts provide a kind of external representation of what goes on during the blending process.

For example, in the case of the word *cat*, the child who was performing the blending procedure independently would:

1. Point to the c and say /k/.
2. Point to the a and say /a/.
3. Slowly slide his finger under the ca and say /ka/ slowly.
4. Quickly slide his finger under the ca and say /ka/ quickly.
5. Point to the t and say /t/.
6. Slowly slide his finger under cat and say /kat/ slowly.
7. Circle the word with his finger and say, "The word is *cat*."

The techniques for teaching the blending procedure include a series of steps that lead the child from imitating the procedure toward performing it independently. Essentially, the teacher repeats the linking and blending of sounds three times. At each repetition, the teacher systematically fades out of the process and gives greater responsibility to the child. At the end of the sequence, the child demonstrates the procedure by himself. More specifically:

1. The teacher models the blending procedure. She models the sounds and the blends and uses finger-pointing procedures and intermittent verbal directions.
2. The children imitate the model while the teacher repeats both the verbal cues and the finger cues to assist them.
3. The teacher repeats the procedure, but this time does not model the sounds or the blends. She gives only the verbal cues and the finger cues to assist.
4. The procedure is repeated. This time, the teacher drops the verbal cues. She gives only finger cues (i.e., the prompts are faded).
5. The child performs the pointing, sounding, and blending steps independently.

A strong advantage for the teacher of this blending procedure is the precise information available for locating an error. If a child makes an error while performing the procedure, the teacher knows exactly where the error is, that is, which link in the process is incorrect. With this kind of precise information, the teacher can give him a direct prompt. For example, if the child's inability to pronounce a word was caused by a substituted or omitted phoneme, the teacher would point to the letter and ask the child to say its sound. If he hesitated, she would prompt him with a silent mouthing cue. If necessary, she would model the sound. If the error was in a blend (e.g., the *ca* in cat), she would run her finger under the *ca* and ask the child to say the blend, she would cue the blend if the child hesitated, and if necessary she would model the blend. The availability of this kind of precise information enables the teacher to adapt her behavior to the particular needs of the individual child.

References

Chall, J. 1967. *Learning to read: The great debate.* New York: McGraw-Hill.

Diederich, P. B. 1973. II. Research 1960–70 on methods and materials in reading. TM Report 22, ERIC Clearinghouse on Tests, Measurement, and Evaluation. Princeton: Educational Testing Service, January 1973.

40. Teaching Basic Function Words

Hayden B. Jolly, Jr.

Primary teachers soon discover that some of the most troublesome words for beginning and disabled readers are the three, four, and five letter words that make up the bulk of English prose. They are often referred to as "demons," a label which reflects the almost universal difficulty they cause children.

An understanding of the structural and syntactical nature of these little words makes clear why they are troublesome. First, most of the demons fit a linguistic category called "function" words, in contrast with a second broad category of words called "contentives."

Contentives (words that have "content") have a relatively definite lexical meaning—*run, red, free, slowly, woman*. Function words, or "structure words," connect the contentives and have only syntactical meaning derived from their function of relating words to each other. Contentives usually take inflectional endings and fit into one of the four major form classes: nouns, verbs, adjectives, and adverbs. Function words, on the other hand, do not take inflectional endings; they fit into the categories of prepositions, conjunctions, relative pronouns or adjectives, auxiliary and linking verbs, and articles.

As Cunningham (1980) pointed out, the fact that these words have no clear lexical meaning is one reason they cause difficulty. Beginning readers retain words with concrete meaning much more readily than function words. Contentives can usually be related to the child's experience, they can be visualized and depicted, and

they have synonyms. Consider for a moment how you would write a definition or provide a synonym for *from, which,* or *but*.

Function words are also troublesome because of the similarity of their physical features. Some of the most frequently confused forms, for example, begin with *wh* and *th: that, what, this, these, why, which*. Most children don't omit function words when reading aloud; they substitute words similar in appearance or function: *a/an, an/the, the/from, that/this, what/which*.

All children make such substitutions occasionally. When they are infrequent and do not affect meaning, the substitutions should be ignored. When function word miscues change meaning, or when oral reading fluency is adversely affected by difficulties with them, steps must be taken to sharpen their identification.

Because the function words are of such high frequency in our writing, the student who must rely on phonic analysis for their identification will be constantly involved in "sounding out" words and lose fluency and meaning. (Of the 36 words in the preceding sentence, 19 or 53% are function words, typical of their prevalence in prose.) The teacher must find ways other than phonics to develop virtually instantaneous recognition of these demons.

For the student with the most severe difficulties with function words, teaching one word at a time may be necessary. [See Cunningham's (1980) "drastic strategy."] Many pupils, however, can master the function words in groups of three or four if the teacher follows certain guidelines. I

From Hayden B. Jolly, Jr., Teaching basic function words. *The Reading Teacher*, November 1981, 35, 136–40. Reprinted by permission of Hayden B. Jolly, Jr., and the International Reading Association.

have found several guiding principles and techniques for teaching function words successful in both classroom and clinic.

Guiding Principles

Basic to the teaching strategies is a principle applicable to improving students' perception of any easily confused stimuli, visual or auditory. Karlin (1975) calls it the principle of "interference." In its simplest form, the principle suggests that the simultaneous presentation of two or more similar stimuli (in this instance words, letters, or sounds) may interfere with learning. If, for example, a student confuses *was* and *saw*, we may simply add to the confusion if we present both words together and try to point out featural differences. We should instead present *one* of the pair in contrast with dissimilar words in a single lesson and present the other in a later lesson.

Application of this principle also involves proceeding in instruction from a presentation of elements which have large featural differences toward those with finer differences. If, for example, a pupil confuses *b* and *d*, we should first present one of those letters in contrast with dissimilar letters, say *r, s, w*, and gradually move toward letters which share more features with *b/d: p, g, h*. Only after the learner is able to make quick, accurate identifications at each step should we try discrimination of *b* and *d* together.

The student who confuses the function words *this, that*, and *the* must learn to discriminate them in the same manner. If we intend to teach three or four words in one lesson, we might present *that, for, is* and *every*, words which are as different in form as possible. Only after the confused words have been taught in separate sessions, would we increase the discrimination demands by bringing them together for rapid identification.

Unfortunately, workbooks and other exercise materials commonly ask pupils to discriminate confusing items before they are prepared—to write *saw* or *was* in blank spaces within sentences, to write a short /e/ or /i/ under pictures whose names contain those sounds, or write *there, their*, or *they're* in appropriate contexts. Such exercises are only appropriate as final steps, as evaluation of previous instruction in which the elements have been taught separately. My teaching of basic function words is also guided by the belief that a pupil must discover that while the function words are meaningless out of context, they are nonetheless separate words. Many pupils do not perceive them as individual words but merely as attachments to contentives. Thus, these demons must be "overlearned" in isolation and immediately encountered in context. Frequent drill and review *are* necessary for their mastery, and simple incentive devices are helpful to stimulate independent study.

Teaching Strategy

I present three or four dissimilar words in seven steps, first in isolation, then in context, and, finally, in isolation again. A group no larger than six pupils with similar word problems is clustered in a semicircle around the teacher.

1. Three words are used in this example lesson: *this, every, was*. They are printed on small cards or paper slips for each student, the word on one side, a phrase on the other: *this* book, *every* girl, he *was* here. The students place the cards before them on the table with the isolated words in view.

2. The teacher holds up one card and directs students to look at it carefully. They are told to find and point to the card containing the word. They are told, rather forcefully, to look at the word carefully while the teacher says the word twice. Each word is identified in this manner.

3. As the teacher says each word, the students hold up the card containing the word. This step is repeated several times

until each student responds correctly and quickly.

4. The students are told that they are going to learn to spell the words. They are directed to hold up one card at a time, look at it, close their eyes and try to picture the word in their minds as the teacher says it. After visualizing each word, the students put the cards out of sight. The teacher dictates the words for spelling, circulating among the group to check their work. The students then check their spelling against their word cards and correct any errors.

5. Cards are turned over and the students run their fingers under the words as the teacher reads each phrase twice. The students are then called upon to read the phrases aloud.

6. A sheet of simple maze sentences is distributed and the students underline the correct word:

    this
Is every your book?
    was

    this
It every cold in my room.
    was

       this
We read every day.
       was

  this
I every lost in the woods.
  was

This
Every is not my book.
Was
        this
Jack fell and broke every crayon in his
        was
box.

7. In the final activity, the teacher flashes the word cards in random order several times at the pupils, who are to say each word as quickly as possible. The students may then pair off and flash the words to each other, perhaps adding a few words from previous exercises. The word-phrase cards are added to each pupil's

"Demon Kit," where they are accumulated for review.

Parent Involvement

Parents can help their children learn the function words with a gamelike activity. I send home these directions.

> Your child is having trouble with the words circled on the attached list. You can help him/her with this activity: Choose two or three words which don't look much alike. Lay a newspaper on the floor. Write one word on a slip of paper. Time your child while s/he finds and circles the word in three places on the page of newspaper. Each time s/he circles the word, s/he says it. Then, let your child time you while you search for the word in three places. Repeat with the remaining words. The one with the shortest time wins. After the game is over, call your child's attention to the circled words and encourage him/her to read any part of the context in which it appears. Another game is played by competing against time in a different way. Using an hourglass eggtimer and newspaper or magazine page, each player attempts to find and circle as many occurrences of each word as possible before time runs out. The person who finds the largest number in the time allowed is the winner.

A Motivation Aid

A simple but effective motivation aid for young children is a sheet with a large picture of a demon (mine is a typical Hallowe'en devil). Each student receives a devil with his or her problem words printed along the arms, legs, or chest. As the students master their individual words, they draw lines through them and around the chest or extremity; the line is considered a strand or rope around the demon. The demon is captured when a strand covers each word. When a word previously thought to be mastered is missed, the line is erased. My disabled readers develop an astonishing eagerness to "capture the demon."

Review and Follow-Up

One effective form of review and practice is a cloze passage requiring insertion of a number of previously studied words. Students are allowed to refer to their "Demon Kits," when stumped:

> It (was) a cold, dark night. (Every)one was in bed. Something woke me (about) midnight. I sat (up), listening. I (could) hear the wind (and) rain hitting (my/the) window. I (also) heard footsteps coming slowly up (the) stairs. "Is (this) really happening?" I (asked) myself. (Then) I heard the sound (again), louder (this/that) time. (Could/can) my demon be loose?

Following instruction on confusing word pairs, the teacher may challenge the students by presenting them together in another maze exercise:

What
⎯⎯⎯ time is it?
That

Now
⎯⎯⎯ do you get home?
How

What
⎯⎯⎯ is my book.
That

We saw a deer.
⎯⎯ was

Have you ever seen a deer?
⎯⎯⎯⎯⎯ every

This
⎯⎯⎯ books are mine.
These

Almost invariably our disabled readers with function word difficulties also have problems with oral fluency—lack of regard for punctuation, improper breathing and phrasing, and improper pitch and stress. Two techniques are useful for simultaneous development of oral fluency and function word review.

Echo reading provides the pupil with a model of proper oral reading, followed by pupil imitation of that model. Material at the pupil's instructional reading level or slightly higher is selected. The pupil is instructed to follow along with a finger under the word as the teacher reads. The pupil is told that s/he will be asked to read the sentences next, imitating the teacher.

The teacher reads one or two sentences, taking care to read with proper rate, phrasing, and stress. The pupil then "echoes," reading the same sentence(s). When the pupil fails to read properly, the teacher explains the errors and rereads the sentence; the student echoes it again.

As pupils show improvement, larger and larger segments are read before the pupil responds, leading eventually into the next strategy.

Assisted reading is little more than an extended version of echo reading. The teacher selects an appropriate story and records it on tape, taking care to use a rate that is natural but appropriate for the pupil. (Announcers on most commercially prepared read-along tapes read too rapidly for this purpose.) The teacher may slightly exaggerate pauses but uses normal pitch, stress and intonation. Pupils are directed to read along with the tape until they can read the story unassisted with the same fluency and accuracy as the model. They may have to follow the tape a number of times before reproducing it successfully. Detailed descriptions of this technique are outlined by Chomsky (1978), Carbo (1978), and Cunningham (1979).

No matter how thoroughly the demons are taught in specific exercises, students may still have occasional problems with them when reading aloud. The more students read, however, the more accurate they become in word identification generally. There is no substitute for daily recreational reading to sharpen pupils' total reading accuracy and fluency.

References

Carbo, Marie. "Teaching Reading with Talking Books." *The Reading Teacher*, vol. 32 (December 1978), pp. 267–73.

Chomsky, Carol. "When You Still Can't Read in Third Grade: After Decoding, What?" In *What Research Has to Say about Reading Instruction*, edited by S. Jay Samuels, pp. 13–29. Newark, Del.: International Reading Association, 1978.

Cunningham, Patricia M. "Imitative Reading." *The Reading Teacher*, vol. 33 (October 1979), pp. 80–83.

Cunningham, Patricia M. "Teaching *Were, With, What,* and Other Four-Letter Words." *The Reading Teacher*, vol. 34 (November 1980), pp. 160–63.

Karlin, Robert. *Teaching Elementary Reading.* New York, N.Y.: Harcourt Brace Jovanovich, 1975.

41. Using Children's Reading Miscues for New Teaching Strategies

Yetta M. Goodman

Watching and listening to children read orally can give the teacher a great deal of insight into the reading process if he views his role in the classroom as a researcher and diagnostician in addition to the more traditional teaching roles.

When Tony reads "I was a boy" instead of what was on the printed page "I saw a boy," the teacher may respond by thinking "That's wrong; I must do something to correct that behavior" or the teacher might say "That's an interesting problem, I wonder what caused that behavior? . . . what is involved in the learning process and the reading process which caused Tony to do that?"

The innovative strategies for teachers to use in teaching reading in the classroom proposed in this article will examine the major question: "How can teachers make use of children's reading miscues (errors) as a tool to help children learn to read?"

Six children learning to read have been followed since they were in their sixth month of reading instruction (Goodman, 1965). They are now at the end of their fourth year. For each of them, twenty oral reading performances have been recorded during this period. About 2,500 of the children's reading miscues (errors) have been analyzed thus far and at least that many remain to be analyzed. Certain phenomena, supported also by other research, are quite clear and have implications for teachers in the classroom.

Errors Vary

Some reading errors are better than others. The analysis of reading miscues has given a great deal of insight into the development of beginning readers. There is no question that certain types of miscues are of a higher order than others; miscues of low order give way to miscues of higher order as children become more proficient readers. Miscues must be looked at not as mistakes which are bad and should be eradicated but as overt behaviors which may unlock aspects of intellectual processing. In this case, miscues in reading give insight into the reading process. This

From Yetta M. Goodman, Using children's reading miscues for new teaching strategies. *The Reading Teacher*, February 1970, 23, 455–459. Reprinted by permission of Yetta M. Goodman and the International Reading Association.

respectability of mistakes, errors, or miscues has been supported by the vast amount of research done by Jean Piaget. "He found himself becoming increasingly fascinated, not with the psychometric and normative aspects of test data but with the processes by which the child achieved his answers . . . especially his incorrect answers" (Burke, 1969).

Examining the words children omit as they read supplies some evidence of how miscues become qualitatively better miscues as readers become more proficient. One subject omitted words he did not know and could or would not try to figure out, during early oral readings. This was evident because he often paused at these words, looked at the illustration on the page, looked at the word a little longer and then went on. In one story early in the research this subject omitted *fair*, *going*, *buy*, *stay*, *late*. In the study children were never supplied with assistance or corrections by the researcher. This technique was explained to them prior to their reading and they were encouraged to do the best they could on their own. In a story six months later, the same subject omitted two words only, *a* and *just*. The sentences resulting from the omissions were meaningful language units. The story posed problems for the child, but he had strategies for working out his problems.

When children did substitute one word for another, the substitutions showed finer discrimination of sound-symbol relationships as they became more proficient readers. Early in the study most miscues had initial or medial letters in common with the words as printed but showed little more similarity; *make* for *monkey*, *man* for *monkey*, *and* for *can* are some examples. For all subjects, based upon statistical analysis of the miscues, the children developed the ability to produce miscues which showed finer discrimination. This finer discrimination produced more miscues differing by only a single grapheme for example *man* for *men* and *lot* for *let*.

The less proficient readers tended to produce miscues which were responses to the graphic field or to a habit strength association that had been developed. A less proficient reader said *Have a Jimmy* for *What a Jump*. She had read *have* for *what* throughout two stories. *Jimmy* was called after she sounded (j, j) a few times. More proficient readers produced miscues which were more complex, involved more integration of the meaning, grammatical and sound systems of the language with the graphic input and the experience and background of the child than the miscues of the less proficient readers. A more proficient reader read *spot of fur over her nose* for *spot of fur above her nose*. The miscue made sense in the passage and was the same part of speech as the word which should have been read in the book.

Handling Errors Instructionally

Children learn to correct their own errors. In a previous study of fourth graders, Goodman concluded that "virtually every regression which the children in this study made was for the purpose of correcting previous reading" (Clay, 1967). They were less likely to correct miscues when the resulting passage sounded like language and was meaningful to them. One subject responded with *It's the Big Billy-goat Gruff* for *It's I! The Big Billy-goat Gruff*. The resulting miscue made good sense and resulted in correct sounding syntax to the ear of the child. He made no attempt at correction. The children were more likely to correct when the language prior to and including the miscue was meaningful and sounded like language to them but then conflicted with the remainder of the passage. Another subject said *Very well, he* when it should have been *Very well, be off with you*. He stopped, regressed to the beginning of the sentence again, and read the passage correctly. When the children attempted corrections of their own miscues, they were successful at least 75 percent of the time.

Words should never be introduced out of the context of language. So many things happen when words appear within the context of language. Context changes the grammatical function of words, their syntactic relation to other words, the meaning of words and often their pronunciation and intonation. The word changes depending upon whether it is in the oral language or the written language. Words should be first used with children in the most common grammatical position that the child finds them in his own language. If words appear in less common positions in reading material, teachers may compensate for this. For example, if the word *circus* is to be taught, the child will have a better chance of using more language cues to develop strategies for working it out if it appears to him first as a noun. A prereading story might be developed by the teacher.

We like to go to the circus.
There will be clowns in the circus.
The circus is coming to town.

This would avoid the difficulty that all the children in the author's study had when words were introduced in less common (to the child) grammatical positions in language. When *circus* was introduced as an adjective *circus bear, circus monkey, circus balloon* or when *river* was introduced as part of a noun phrase or as an adjective as in *Singing River* and *river man*, the children had difficulty working out the word, but when it appeared later in the story as a noun, the children often recognized the word.

Concentrate on the concept that words represent rather than on dictionary definitions. It is more important to help the children learn the underlying concept that words represent so that it will have meaning to the child within the context of the story. One subject usually had good comprehension. In one story, the word *globe* appeared eight times and the child sounded it out as /gloh + biy/ the first time he saw it. The second time it appeared, the child called

it /glo + b/ and the third time /glohb/. After that he continued to pronounce the word correctly, seemingly knowing the word. However, in the retelling of the story, comprehension was low. A globe had been on the desk in front of the child and in the illustration in the book while he was reading. The researcher pointed to the globe on the desk after the retelling of the story and asked the child, "What is this?" The child responded, "The earth." It is more important for this child to learn the scientific concept of the word globe than to teach him the sound-symbol correspondence, its graphic identity as a word or its dictionary meaning out of the context of the written language in which it was presented.

Teachers should help children make use of their miscues to provide teaching-learning strategies. Recent research in child language indicates that children have a good deal of control over their own home language when they come to school. The child's mastery of his own language is a strength which he brings to the reading task. Teachers, in an effort to improve children's reading, often work very hard on the weaknesses of beginning readers. It may be that if a child could be shown that he has strengths and if his strengths were encouraged, it might in the long run help him in improving in his areas of weakness as well.

Teachers may help children develop learning strategies by having children keep certain questions in mind as they read. Does it sound like language to you? Does it make sense to you? If not, why not? Have you read it incorrectly? Go back and reread . . . Have you read ahead? Concepts are clarified by reading more of the material. Words are often recognized when they appear a second and third time in the same story. If you still are unable to work out the problem, ask the teacher.

The teacher needs to ask himself questions before he simply gives the child the word when he is asked for help. Are the concepts unknown or partially known to the child? Is the language of the book so different from the child's language that the child needs a translation from book language to his own language rather than know just what one word is? The teacher should avoid giving the word to a child immediately or allowing other children to help when the child first encounters a problem. This will hinder the child's attempt to discover strategies to make the best use of all the language cue systems— the meaning, the sound of the longer strings of language as well as the relationship between letters and sounds. What is important in beginning reading is not the particular word but the development of strategies to use in subsequent situations. The teacher must help the child do the figuring out . . . help the child develop strategies for working out reading problems.

A caution must be kept in mind in making use of these strategies. Oral reading and silent reading are separate processes. However, oral reading provides a continuous window into the reading process and the cognitive processes taking place within children as they read.

So much happens when a child reads. If teachers are able to listen to the child's reading and try to discover why the child makes certain miscues, they will be able to diagnose children's reading problems with greater insight. With greater insight into the complexity of the reading process, the teacher can do a better job of teaching children to read.

References

Allen, P. D. "A Psycholinguistic Analysis of the Substitution Miscues of Selected Oral Readers in Grades Two, Four, and Six, and the Relationship of These Miscues to the Reading Process: A Descriptive Study." Unpublished Doctoral Dissertation. Wayne State University, 1969.

Burke, Carolyn L. "A Psycholinguistic Description of Grammatical Restructuring in the Oral Reading of a Selected Group of Middle School Children." Unpublished Doctoral Dissertation. Wayne State University, 1969.

Clay, Marie M. "The Reading Behaviour of Five-Year-Old Children: A Research Report." *New Zealand Journal of Educational Studies*, 2 (1967), 11–31.

Flavell, J. *The Developmental Psychology of Jean Piaget*. Princeton, N. J.: D. Van Nostrand Company, 1963. P. 3.

Goodman, K. "A Linguistic Study of Cues and Miscues in Reading," *Elementary English*, 42 (1965), 641–45.

Goodman, K. S., and Burke, Carolyn. *Study of Children's Behavior While Reading Orally*. (Contract No. OE-6–10–136) Washington, D. C.: United States Department of Health, Education, and Welfare, Office of Education, 1968.

Goodman, Yetta M. "A Psycholinguistic Description of Observed Oral Reading Phenomena in Selected Young Beginning Readers." Unpublished Doctoral Dissertation. Wayne State University, 1967.

Martellock, Helen. "A Psycholinguistic Description of the Oral and Written Language of a Selected Group of Middle School Children." Unpublished Doctoral Dissertation. Wayne State University, 1969.

Weber, Rosemarie. *A Linguistic Analysis of First Grade Reading Errors*. Ithaca, N.Y.: Laboratory for Research on Language Skills, Cornell University, 1967 (preliminary draft).

42. There Is a Need for Word Attack Generalizations

Judi Lesiak

Much has been written concerning the utility of word-analysis generalizations taught in basal reading series. Few have raised questions regarding the *need* of teaching at least those found to be of use in attacking unknown words. Emans (1973) has suggested that phonic generalizations with limited applicability may be better than no clue. The author's experience with elementary and junior high teachers and, more importantly, with students experiencing reading difficulties supports her contention that children *can* benefit from the teaching of those generalizations found most applicable. At present, college graduate students in a practicum in learning disabilities are working with four junior and senior high school students reading 3–4 years below grade level expectancy. The major difficulty in reading for all four students appears to be a lack of systematic word attack skills. When confronted with unknown words, particularly multi-syllable words, each student "falls-apart." Note the student who encounters the following words: *battle, saddle, button, corral*, and is unable to decode them. Knowledge of two rules of syllabication would have helped solve the problem.

Numerous studies have been conducted investigating the utility of phonic generalizations (Clymer, 1963; Burrows, 1963; Winkley, 1966; Bailey, 1967; Emans, 1967; Burmeister, 1971). Huelsman, professor in reading at The Ohio State University, interpreted results of the studies by Clymer, Burrows, Winkley, Bailey & Emans to arrive at forty rules judged worthy of further study. These forty rules were studied by Lesiak (1968) using 2925 words from the Lorge-Thorndike word list of 30,000 words. The words ranged from words common in grades one and two, to words common in the intermediate grades, to more difficult words. Two criteria were used to judge whether a rule was useful. The words selected for each rule which might apply must have totaled at least thirty, one percent of the total sample. Percentage of utility must have been at least seventy-five percent. If a rule met both criteria, it was considered useful. An attempt was made to modify any rule not useful as originally stated by re-evaluating all words. Results indicated that eighteen rules were found to be applicable as stated, ten needed modification, eight were combined to make four, and four were found to be of little or no value. The modified list of thirty-two useful word-attack generalizations is presented in Table 1.

Syllabication rules recently have come under attack for a variety of reasons (Johnson & Merryman, 1971; Seymour, 1973; Zuck, 1974). Zuck (1974) points out that syllabication rules yield a pronunciation of the written word which is different from the pronunciation of the spoken word and suggests doing away with syllabication rules. Zuck appears to see rules as useful only if they lead to precise pronunciation. However, as Bukovec (1973) states, "Phonic generalizations are designed to provide inexperienced readers with a means of translating unfamiliar printed symbols into sounds that are recognizable as words in their spoken or listening vocabularies. The primary reason for using such rules, therefore, is the achievement of word recognition . . ." (p. 271). The

From Judi Lesiak, There is a need for word attack generalizations. *Reading Improvement*, Summer 1977, *14*, 100–103. Reprinted by permission of the publisher, Project Innovations.

ability to apply the syllabication rules listed as having useful applicability in Table 1 will make the task of decoding a multi-syllable word somewhat less difficult.

Because rules are not always 100 per-cent applicable, it is wise to teach readers to be flexible. If the word doesn't sound like a known word which makes sense in context, ignore the rule. Seymour (1973)

Table 1. Useful Word-Attack Generalizations[1]

Consonant Sound Rules

Consonant Sound Rule 1:	Certain consonant letters are silent:
	a. *K* when followed by *n: knight*
	b. *W* when followed by *r: write*
	c. *gh* when preceded by a vowel: *light*
Consonant Sound Rule 2:	When two of the same consonants are side by side, only one is heard.
Consonant Sound Rule 3:	The digraph *ch* stands for three sounds:
	as in *catch* and *chair* most often
	as in *ache* less often
	as in *echelon* least often
Consonant Sound Rule 4:	When *c* is followed by *o, a,* or *u,* it has the sound of *k* as in *cat,* otherwise it has a sound of *s.*
Consonant Sound Rule 5:	When *g* is followed by *a, o* or *u,* it has a "hard" sound as in *gable,* otherwise it has the sound of *j.*
Consonant Sound Rule 6:	When a syllable ends in *ck,* the *ck* has the sound of *k* as in *lock.*

Vowel Sounds Rules

Vowel Sound Rule 1:	The *r* modifies the sound of the preceding vowel so that it is neither long nor short in a one syllable word or an accented syllable.
Vowel Sound Rule 2:	The letter *a has* the same sound (ô) when followed by *w* and *u.*
Vowel Sound Rule 3:	In the diagraphs *ai,* and *ay,* the *a* is usually long and the *y* or *i* is silent.
Vowel Sound Rule 4:	A double *e* indicates the long *e* sound.
Vowel Sound Rule 5:	The word endings *-tion, -sion,* and *-ious,* contain the schwa sound (*tion* is usually pronounced *shen* or *chen*).
Vowel Sound Rule 6:	The letters *oo* usually have the sounds *oo* as in *food* or *oo* as in *good.*
Vowel Sound Rule 7:	The two letters *ow* make the long *o* sound or the *ou* sound as in *out.*
Vowel Sound Rule 8:	The vowel in the middle (cvc) of an accented syllable (or a one-syllable word) is short unless the vowel is followed by *r,* when the short sound is modified.
Vowel Sound Rule 9:	The vowel in an accented syllable or a one-syllable word is long if it comes at the end of the syllable.
Vowel Sound Rule 10:	Whenever a syllable contains a final silent *e* preceded by a single consonant the preceding vowel is long or short. The long sound should be tried first.
Vowel Sound Rule 11:	When *y* is used as a vowel, it most often has the sound of long *e* (exceptions include long and short *i*).

Syllabication Rules

Syllabication Rule 1:	A word has as many syllables as vowel sounds, remember a final *e* is usually silent.
Syllabication Rule 2:	Whenever two consonants represent one sound (digraphs *th, ch, sh, ph, ck*) they stay together in syllabicating.
Syllabication Rule 3:	When *r* follows a vowel, it is attached to the vowel in syllabizing.
Syllabication Rule 4:	A compound word is made up of two or more smaller words. Syllable divisions occur between the words (*birth/day, mail/man*) and at other places as needed (*bas/ket/ball*).
Syllabication Rule 5:	The common word beginnings (*ad-, al-, com-, can-, de-, dis-, en-, ex-, in-, im-, per-,* and *un-*) form the first syllable of the word.

Syllabication Rule 6:	Word endings (*-cal, -ed, -ful, -ish, -ing, -ment, -ness, -tive, -sive, -ture, -tion, -sion, -ty, -ly, -fy, -ity, -less*) usually are divided from the rest of the word forming the final syllable. (Exception: the *ed* forms a new syllable only if the verb root ends in *d* or *t*).
Syllabication Rule 7:	when *le* ends a word it forms a syllable with the preceding consonant.
Syllabication Rule 8:	When two consonants or a consonant and a blend come between two vowels, the syllable division is between the consonants or the consonant and blend.

Accent Rules

Accent Rule 1:	When there is no other clue in a two-syllable word, the accent is usually on the first syllable.
Accent Rule 2:	The word endings *-al, -age, -ant, -able, -ed, -ence, -ent, -est, -er, -ful, -ish -ic -ize*(s) *-ice, -ing, -or, -ment, -ous, -ious, -ness, -tive, -sive, -ure, -ture, -tion, -sion, -ion, -ward, -y, -cy, -ry, -ly, -ary, -ery, -fy, -ity, -ate, -ance, -ship, -hood, -less, -ess,* are usually not accented. Exceptions: *-ise, -fy, -ate,* usually receive a secondary accent.
Accent Rule 3:	The word beginnings *a-, ad-, al-, be-, com-, de-, di-, dis-, en-, ex-, ir-in-, im-, ob-, per-, pro-, re-, sub-, un-, fore-, mis-,* do not receive a primary accent.
Accent Rule 4:	Two vowel letters together in the last syllable of a word (excluding suffixes) may be a clue to an accented final syllable.
Accent Rule 5:	The primary accent usually occurs on the syllable before the suffixes *-ion, -ity, -ic, -ical, -ian, -ial,* or *-ious,* and the second syllable before the suffix *-ate.*
Accent Rule 6:	In words of three or more syllables, one of the first two syllables is usually accented.
Accent Rule 7:	A beginning syllable ending with a consonant and containing a short vowel sound is likely to be accented. Prefixes are excluded.

[1] It may be advisable to introduce fewer generalizations to children. See Albert J. Harris and Edward R. Sipay, *How to Increase Reading Ability,* seventh edition, Longman, New York, 1980, pp. 390–395.

also suggests teaching children to combine rules they learned for monosyllabic words with rules learned for dividing words into syllables. Let's forget the controversy over phonetics vs. linguistics and teach students some useful basic rules to *aid* word recognition. Of course, the dictionary awaits—but certainly not for every word confronting the reader.

References

Bailey, M. The utility of phonic generalizations in grades one through six. *The Reading Teacher,* 1967, 20, 413–418.

Bukovec, J. Usefulness of phonic generalizations: a new formula. *The Reading Teacher,* December, 1973, 26, 270–274.

Burmeister, L. Final vowel-consonant-e. *The Reading Teacher,* 1971, 24, 439–442.

Burrows, A., Lourie, A. When two vowels go walking. *The Reading Teacher,* 1963, 17, 79–82.

Clymer, T. The utility of phonic generalizations in the primary grades. *The Reading Teacher,* 1963, 16, 252–258.

Emans, R. The usefulness of phonic generalizations above the primary grades. *The Reading Teacher,* 1967, 20, 419–25.

————. Linguistics and Phonics. *The Reading Teacher,* 1973, 26, 477–482.

Johnson, D., and Merryman, E. Syllabication: the erroneous VCCV generalization. *The Reading Teacher,* December, 1971, 24, 267–270.

Lesiak, J. The applicability of word attack rules. Unpublished Master's Thesis, The Ohio State University, 1968.

Seymour, D. Word division for decoding. *The Reading Teacher,* 1973, 27, 275–283.

Winkley, C. Which accent generalizations are worth teaching? *The Reading Teacher,* 1966, 20, 219–224.

Zuck, L. Some questions about the teaching of syllabication rules. *The Reading Teacher,* 1974, 27, 583–588.

CHAPTER IX

Development of Reading Vocabulary

The consistent finding that vocabulary scores are highly correlated with scores on tests of reading comprehension highlights the importance of including systematic vocabulary instruction in the reading program. Dale and O'Rourke recommend the use of procedures that go from the known to the unknown, and make maximum use of possibilities for generalizations. Pilon's enthusiasm for words is made practical through descriptions of specific ideas about how to get children excited about words and their meanings; she also lists books that can be used to arouse interest in derivations, portmanteau words, slanguage; etc. Turner explains why figurative language presents special difficulties for children and describes ten techniques for raising children's sensitivity to the meanings of figures of speech such as metaphors and similes. Criscuolo provides succinct descriptions of ten ways to build vocabulary. Miller proposes a step-by-step procedure for bridging the transition from picture dictionary to glossary, and from glossary to mature dictionary. Finally, Deighton presents the use and limitations of context in vocabulary building.

43. The Need for a Planned Vocabulary Program

Edgar Dale and Joseph O'Rourke

Vocabulary development in school must be a planned program. The research in the field indicates that this is a sound principle. Incidental teaching, alone, tends to become accidental teaching.

Beginning in the early grades, the teacher can introduce the student to vocabulary study habits that should increase transfer potential. For example, children can begin early to develop a mental filing system—a variety of ways to classify. They can learn to group words under general topics, first by a gross filing system, later through a finer system of discrimination. This approach was successfully used by the Enrichment Unit Project Staff of the Columbus, Ohio, Public Schools.

The development of vocabulary must be seen as a part of the major communication program of the school. All education is vocabulary development, hence conceptual development; we are studying words and symbols all the time. But we do need a special period at least once a week to review words and their parts, to develop principles and generalizations relating to word analysis and synthesis, and to classify and discuss words.

A systematic program of vocabulary development will be influenced by age, by sex, by income, by native ability, and by social status. A ninth-grade girl does not talk about her *dolly*. A fourth-grader does not know what a *second semester* is. A disadvantaged child may not know anything about *à la carte* or *table d'hôte*. Boys usually are unfamiliar with the colors *champagne* beige, *flamingo* pink, or *holly* green.

Geographical factors also affect vocabulary development. There are "farm" words as well as "city" words, "Southern" words as well as "Northern" words. Minority groups have special, vivid vocabularies. Any systematic program of vocabulary development must consider these factors. Since words are the names given to experiences, it is obvious that students need rich experiences to develop their vocabulary. A study trip to a farm, a museum, a planetarium, a department store, or a summer camp, attending a concert, and a ready supply of easy-to-read books all help in this respect.

Consolidation of vocabulary skills is an important part of reading. In the reading process, the student brings to and gets ideas from the printed page. He associates sound, symbol, and meaning. In reading, symbols convey meanings that are synthesized into related ideas. These symbols are words. They are perceived, understood, reacted to, and combined with previously known ideas. That is, the reading process

leads from the known to the unknown. Effective vocabulary study must proceed in the same fashion: from known to unknown words, as from *helicopter* to *lepidoptera*.

A planned vocabulary program provides the student with ample opportunity to build new concepts upon old ones. Such a program presents appropriate study materials that make effective use of the principle of transfer. Early in his education, the student must be encouraged to see relationships and make associations, be provided with the opportunity to notice that learning the word *hateful* is not like learning a completely new word if he already knows *hate*. He learns that *hate* may undergo inflectional change: that by adding suffixes to *hate* he may form such words as *hated*, *hater*, *hating*, *hateful*, *hatefully*, and *hatefulness*. With skillful guidance, the student can, at another level, make the transition from *repeat* to *repetitious*, from *imply* to *implicit*—if the word-analysis habit is fixed.

Thus greater attention to the systematic presentation of known words that take on new meanings with inflectional change can help the student learn the principle of generalization. This principle, according to Eric H. Lenneberg,[1] is one of the three major means of language acquisition.

Systematic Approach

We noted earlier that the weakness of the typical approach to vocabulary development is that it is unsystematic. Let us suppose that today a senior class in high school learns *euphoria*, *antebellum*, and *monotheism*. Tomorrow they learn *euphonious*, *ante meridiem*, and *monocular*. The third day they learn *eupeptic*, *antediluvian*, and *monomania*. This approach is unsystematic and there is likely to be little transfer. A systematic approach would be to teach *ante meridiem*, *antediluvian*, and *antebellum* as one group; *euphoria*, *euphonious*, and *eupep-*

tic as a second group; <u>mono</u>*theism,* <u>monoc</u>*ular,* and <u>mono</u>*mania* as a third. With this approach the student gets the benefit of transfer of learning.

Teaching for transfer can be begun in the early grades. For example, building on the word *telescope* (known by 87 percent of fourth-graders), the teacher can point out other words made from *scope* (from Greek *skopein,* to watch or look): *micro<u>scope</u>, peri<u>scope</u>, radar<u>scope</u>, gyro<u>scope</u>, horo<u>scope</u>, kaleido<u>scope</u>.*

The teacher can help the student form the habit of analyzing many words systematically to get clues to their meaning. For example, he might analyze *telescope* and several other *scope* words thus:

Tele means distant, far away; *scope* means see, look. When you look through a telescope you are able to see an object far away. Note also *television, telephone, telegraph,* and *telemetry,* all referring to distance.

Look at *microscope* (*micro,* small + *scope*). Germs are *small, minute,* or *microscopic.* With a microscope we see small forms of life.

A submarine has a *periscope.* Before surfacing the commander uses it to look around. The Greek prefix *peri-* means all around. What's another use for a periscope? (to look around corners). Note also *perimeter, periphery,* etc.

A *kaleidoscope* is a tube containing loose pieces of colored glass and two mirrors. If you turn the tube you see changing patterns of attractive colors. (*Kalos* is Greek for "beautiful"; *eidos* means "form.") So *kal + eido + scope* give us the word *kaleidoscope*—an instrument for seeing colored glass form beautiful designs, or, more generally, a changing pattern or scene.

Maximal Transfer Potential

A systematic program of vocabulary mastery helps the student develop a flexible mental file for storing and retrieving words. A new word isn't of much value if it is filed and lost. So a mental filing system must be active. This mental file can become a lightning-fast computer to help remember and figure out the meaning of words. The student should learn firsthand the benefits of such mental filing.

Note, for example, these words: *atypical, atheist, acentric, apathy, amoral, agonic, agnostic.* What is a useful way to file them? Actually, a dual filing system can be used. First, one learns that the prefix *a-* means not or without. Thus *atypical* means not typical. So *acentric* means not on center; *amoral* means without morals. The second file is for the root meaning, e.g., *atheist* (from *theos,* meaning God), *apathy* (not feeling), *agonic* (without an angle), *agnostic* (not knowing). Therefore, the more prefixes and roots the student has mastered, the greater his capacity for filing, remembering, and figuring out the meaning of words.

Unconsciously, the student may already have a way of filing certain words such as *apathy, sympathy, empathy,* and *pathology;* or *polygon, trigon, pentagon,* and *hexagon.* But a systematic approach to the study of vocabulary instills a conscious awareness of the associative elements in these words—the meaningful roots *path* (feel) and *gon* (angle). Knowing the element *ectomy* (cut out) helps you make associations between *tonsillectomy, appendectomy, gastrectomy,* and *neurectomy.* And knowing the root *tom* (cut) lets you see the relationship between words such as *anatomy* and *atom* (which people once thought could not be cut).

The Twilight Zone

Another fruitful way of organizing and filing words is to think of them as not known, partly known, or well known. If we visualize our vocabulary as a series of concentric circles with loose boundaries containing the words we know in varying degrees, this idea becomes clearer. We learn our new words, and thus enlarge our vocabulary, largely by sharpening the focus of those words at the edges of our knowledge, the words in the twilight zone.

The authors believe that any motivated individual can increase his working vocabulary by 10 percent. This will be, in part, a result of bringing into sharp focus these words, parts of words, and expressions which are now only partly known.

A student's score on vocabulary tests would increase sharply if credit were given for partly knowing a word, even when there was some confusion about the exact meaning. It is the daily task of the teacher to help students become more skillful in moving words from their twilight zone of confusion and partial knowledge to the broad daylight of clear understanding.

Basic Vocabulary

It is helpful to know how a child learns his first three or four thousand words. In our study of the vocabulary of inner-city children, we found that three fourths of them had a vocabulary of fifteen hundred words by January and February of their first year of school. We noted that most of these words (a) can be sensed, (b) are necessary to speak almost any sentence, (c) are in the everyday vocabulary of most people, (d) are ones which have been experienced and internalized and will never be forgotten.

How did the children learn them? First, they heard them from parents, older children, and playmates, on television and radio, on the playground and at the store. Second, they experienced them—they said things, they ate things, they touched things, they smelled things, they drank things. Their vocabulary was circumscribed only by their experiences and by the available models.

If these children had grown up in a wealthy suburb, with more opportunity to attend nursery school or kindergarten, to accompany their parents when they shopped, and to spend more time at

exhibits, zoos, parks, and children's theaters, their vocabulary would reflect their wider variety of experience.

Vocabulary and Life

When you organize and provide a vocabulary development program, you are changing the lives of students. Vocabulary growth is not at the periphery of our lives; it is central, focal. It can lead the student forward to broader experiences, which in turn generate more new experiences in logarithmic fashion.

Learning a new word carries within itself an explosive effect. We might visualize such new words as seeking further applications, nagging us to look further, study deeper. For example, when you learned the word *serendipity* (the faculty of making happy and unexpected discoveries by accident) did you then become aware of serendipities in your own life and in other people's lives? Did you become serendipity-sensitive? Perhaps you first became conscious of the word *bursitis* through having had it. Soon you discovered other people who had it and you commiserated with them on the painfulness that accompanied it.

Learning new words is a dynamic process that involves getting compound interest. New words in one's repertoire of responses are incremental, intrusive, propulsive, apparently pushing the possessor on to search for new applications. When our words change, we change.

Vocabulary Development and Conceptual Development

It is necessary to see vocabulary development as conceptual development. Even though every word is a concept, the term *concept* is both broader and deeper than *word*. If you learn the French word *l'eau* for water, you don't have a new concept but another name for a familiar concept. However, since translations are never exact there may always be some conceptual difference. For example, the word *pain* in French connotes something different from our word *bread* because the French have a different concept of bread. Further, "the bread of life" means something more than the separate meanings of the words. Concepts are developed both by generalization and by differentiation. We learn to separate "dogs" into "collies," "bulldogs," and "dachshunds." We learn to group "apples" "oranges," and "cherries" under "fruit."

Ordering Concepts

Vocabulary development means more than adding new words to your repertoire of experience. It means putting your concepts in better order or into additional orders or arrangements. To change your vocabulary is to change your life.

One big job of vocabulary development is to help students see likenesses and differences that they never saw before. They can easily learn that *believe* and *belief* are related. One is a verb and the other a noun. Indeed, one of the important gains in concept development is learning the rules for changing words from one part of speech to the other. Some are easy—*boy* to *boyish*, *zest* to *zestful*. Some are harder—*pygmy* to *pygmean*. But how do you make

an adjective out of *uncle*? *Unclean* won't do. How about *uncular*? Actually we have to make a big jump—from *uncle* to *avuncular*. Do you know what a *tress* is? Do you get a good clue by learning that it is the singular of *tresses*?

How do we designate a man from Norway? Do we call him a Norwayan even though we do call a man from America American? No simple rule applies here. Instead we used the word *Norwegian*. The point is that one's vocabulary may be inert. But it need not be. Through the use of known key prefixes, suffixes, and roots, we can daily make small and eventually large changes in our stock of words.

Although certain words are carefully fenced in—the denotative words of a science, for example—these words tend to slip away from their fenced-in denotations and acquire new meanings, or connotations. Space words become metaphorized: *pad, countdown*, and *blast-off*. Baseball expressions move into common talk and are changed in the process: *fielding questions, batting a thousand, struck out, didn't get to first base*.

Notes

1. Erick H. Lenneberg, *Biological Foundations of Language* (New York: John Wiley and Sons, Inc., 1967), p. 332.

44. Reading to Learn about the Nature of Language

A. Barbara Pilon

Our language is calorie-rich. We are a nation unafraid of borrowing. We have never penalized our citizens in any way (as have the French, for example), for using words from another nation. In our adoption of foreign terms, as was said of Shakespeare, we invade like conquerors. There is much children can learn about the nature of language through reading.

Importance of imagination. Since language itself is fluid, chameleon-like, and has an unlimited potential for change and growth, children can be helped to see that imagination (what Jan Carew (1974) has called "the third gift") is the most important element in talking about our language.

Delight and magic of words. Helping children realize the delight and the magic of words should be one of our foremost goals as language arts and reading teachers. If we can accomplish this, then many children will become "word gatherers," as was the title character in Leo Lionni's (1973) charming book *Frederick*.

Influence of words on all of us. Children also should become aware of the influence that words have upon all of us. We want our youngsters to be like Patricia Hubbell's Word Woman, who carries words with her in a jar, threading them to stars when she wants to travel (1958). We want them to be able to create, to soar and fly with language.

Teachers can explore with children, using books suggested here, to discover new vistas of the wonders and joys of language. Supplemental activities are described for teachers to use in conjunction with the books.

Linguists All: The Great Potential for Growth in Language

An easy way to show children how new words have come into our language is to make up dittos containing lists of words that have come to us from other languages. This helps children see the eclectic nature of our language. The papers can be divided into columns to show Spanish, French, Italian, German, Indian, African, and other words that we have assimilated into English. Children can be encouraged to add to the lists, including the origins of their own names. Such an exercise is bound to enhance children's self-concepts, since they will realize how many "foreign" words they know.

Children's books to demonstrate word origins

Adelson, Leone. *Dandelions Don't Bite: The Story of Words.* New York: Pantheon Books, 1972.

Ames, Winthrop, ed. *What Shall We Name the Baby?* New York: Pocket Books, 1974.

Boyer, Sophia A., and Lubell, Winifred. *Gifts from the Greeks: Alpha to Omega.* Chicago: Rand McNally, 1970.

From A. Barbara Pilon, Reading to learn about the nature of language. In J. W. Stewig & Sam L. Sebesta (Eds.), *Using literature in the elementary classroom.* Champaign, Ill.: National Council of Teachers of English, 1978. Pp. 1–12. Reprinted by permission of the author and the National Council of Teachers of English.

Epstein, Beryl, and Epstein, Sam. *What's behind the Word*? Scholastic Book Services, 1964.

Ferguson, Charles W. *The Abecedarian Book.* Boston: Little, Brown and Co., 1961.

Fletcher, Christine. *100 Keys: Names across the Land.* Nashville: Abingdon Press, 1973.

Kohn, Bernice. *What a Funny Thing to Say!* New York: Dial Press, 1974.

Lambert, Eloise. *Our Language: The Story of the Words We Use.* New York: Lothrop, Lee and Shepard, 1969.

Lambert, Eloise, and Pei, Mario. *Our Names.* New York: Lothrop, Lee and Shepard, 1960.

Mathews, Mitford M. *American Words.* Cleveland: World Pub., 1959.

McCormack, Jo Ann. *The Story of Our Language.* Columbus, Ohio: Charles E. Merrill, 1967.

Miller, Albert G. *Where Did That Word Come From*? Glendale, Calif.: Bowmar, 1974.

Stewart, George R. *Names on the Land.* Boston: Houghton Mifflin, 1958.

If we are to excite children about the "languages" they already know, then teachers must set the spark. Take familiar words—words dear to children's hearts and stomachs. Ask children if these are American words, then tell them where the words came from. Some to begin with might be:

1. *dungaree*—a Hindu word for cotton cloth called *dungri* (Epstein, 1964, p. 35).
2. *denim*—comes from France, specifically from the name of a city, *Nîmes*. The word is short for *serge de Nîmes*.
3. *jeans*—comes to us from Genoa and is short for the Italian term *jean fustian*. The sailors in Genoa wore clothes made from this kind of material. (Incidentally, jeans are also called *Levi's*, a word derived from the name of a man responsible for making Levi's so popular in this country. Words are often derived from people's names and this method of originating new terms

should be made known to children. A fine resource book to use to help children become acquainted with eponyms is Bill Severn's (1966) *People Words*.)

4. *hamburger*—from Hamburg, Germany.
5. *frankfurter*—from Frankfurt, Germany.
6. *chocolate*—from the Mexican Aztec word *chocolatl* (Epstein, 1964, p. 35).
7. *candy*—comes from an ancient language, Sanskrit, once spoken in India. The word in Sanskrit is *khanda* which simply meant piece, but was frequently employed to refer to a piece of sugar (Epstein, 1964, pp. 33–34).
8. *cafeteria*—coffee shop, from Spanish *café* (coffee).

After children have explored the books mentioned, give them lists including such words as disaster, television, and astronaut, and ask them to attempt a logical explanation of their meanings. This kind of exercise will show children one way in which language grows. In addition, it may stir a curiosity for studying the etymologies of words. This is just what we are hoping for! Other ways to show children the great elastic potential of language are the use of:

1. *Coined words.* Gelett Burgess made up his own dictionary called *Burgess Unabridged.* It contained six hundred words he thought were needed in the English language. One of the words found in current dictionaries is one Burgess created. It is *blurb* (Ferguson, 1964, p. 31). Children will enjoy making up some needed words of their own if they are given encouragement to do so. At this point no one has offered a satisfactory nonsexist word that can be used in such sentences as "Each of the children went to HIS seat," or "Every one of you is expected to do HIS share."

2. *Portmanteau words*, or blends. Lewis Carroll is famous for his use of portmanteau words in *Alice in Wonderland.* A portmanteau word (the word *portmanteau* is a French term and literally means to carry a mantle) consists of putting two words

together to make a new word. Some blends we use today, probably without thinking of the two words from which they came, are bash (bat and mash), clash (clap and crash), flare (flame and glare), glimmer (gleam and shimmer) (Farb, 1973, pp. 351–352). Other portmanteau words we all know very well include motel, brunch, and smog. Let children collect old dictionaries to find out if these words appear in them. Children enjoy making up their own portmanteau words. Provide some examples to get them started. You might try some like "submersed" in work, "innumbdated" with things to do, and a "clousy" day. One good book for children to look at which includes these patch-words is *Dandelions Don't Bite* by Leone Adelson.

3. *"Slide" words.* Slide words have come into existence either by putting two letters or a letter and a word together to make one new word. Examples of slide words are jeep and blimp. The word jeep originally was used by G.I.'s during World War II to describe a "general purpose" vehicle. Later the initials "G.P." were painted on the vehicles and the soldiers "slid" the letters together to get the word jeep. The word blimp came to us from the English who were working with "limp" airships during World War I. Their "A-limp" model did not work out, but their "B-limp" did. Eureka, blimp became a part of our vocabulary (Miller, 1974, pp. 8, 24).

4. *Slanguage.* This is a portmanteau word, used to describe the way words take on new meaning in our vocabularies, extending and enriching language. In talking with children about our language, give them examples of such words as cool, bad, mean, tough, dough, and hot. Ask the class what the standard meanings of those words are, and how they think these words took on their present meanings. Let them add to the list of slanguage words. Have them consult various modern dictionaries to see whether or not the slang meanings are included. This is one method which helps children realize that

an aspect of language is its changeability.

5. *Brand words* derived from trademarks such as zipper, nylon, Ping-Pong, Band-Aid, Xerox, and Formica. Have children note that the more deeply embedded a word becomes in our language, the more casually we treat it. We can expect, thus, that one day soon all of these words will have lost their capital letters forever. Suggest to children that they look in different dictionaries to see whether or not certain words appear in them. The words Xerox and Formica, for example, do not appear at all in the 1950 edition of *Webster's New Collegiate Dictionary*. Children may be amazed to find out that within a short time new words evolve and become important parts of our vocabulary. In addition to brand names, there are always new medical discoveries, unusual events, inventions, and social changes which necessitate creation of new words. If the children are old enough, conversations can take place about terms they know that have either come into usage recently or have new meanings attached to them. They can discuss how and why these "new" words were created. Have them look at old dictionaries to see whether or not the words transplant and pacemaker (with their medical meanings), splashdown, skyjack, and snowmobile appear. Through such an activity, children come to realize that some dictionaries in use in classrooms today most certainly do not contain words that many people will be acquainted with in the year 2001, just twenty-three years from now!

6. *Acronyms.* Discuss with pupils the origins of such words as radar (a palindromic word, which is spelled the same backward as forward), snafu, posh, scuba, and laser.

7. *People words.* Initiate curiosity about words that have come to us from people, real or imaginary. Tell them the origins of the words tantalize, Pluto (ask children why they think Walt Disney named his famous dog Pluto), and Europe (reading Greek legends such as Nathaniel Haw-

thorne's classic *Tanglewood Tales* will help give children an appreciation of the words mentioned). Other words with fascinating "people" histories which may serve as a starter list for pupils, include cereal, chauvinism, mercury, volcano, January, Mars, March, June, July, August, October, bloomer, sandwich, pasteurize, gerrymander, guillotine, cardigan, raglan, spoonerism, and boycott. Nancy Sorel's *Word People* (1970), and Severn's *People Words* (1966), help children with some of these words.

8. *Prefixes, suffixes,* and *compound words.* Many new words are incorporated into our language by the technique of adding prefixes or suffixes to root words and by putting two root words together to form new words.

The point of the foregoing itemization is to demonstrate the many strategies we employ to increase our language. Children should understand that *people* create language and that therefore *they* are capable of adding words to our English language. They can be the creators; they can be the makers of our music, not just the recipients. By working with some of these same techniques, children come to understand that one aspect of language is its ability to expand infinitely.

Changes, Changes: The Protean Nature of Words

An important facet of language is that it constantly changes sounds and meanings.

Euphemisms

Words and phrases change because people feel it necessary to "pretty up" language. A garbage man now is called a sanitary engineer, an undertaker is a mortician, a hairdresser is a beautician (Tiedt, 1975, p. 134), and the Vietnam War was referred to as an international armed conflict (Farb, 1973, p. 155). For further interesting reading about euphemisms, you may wish to look at Edwin Newman's *Strictly Speaking*

(1974). Newman feels, and he has a valid argument, that the purpose of tampering with a word or phrase is often to obfuscate and conceal its true meaning.

Etymologies

By studying the etymologies of words, children can learn that location, time, and people affect the meanings as well as the pronunciations of words. Lively discussions occur as children are told, for example, that *queen* once meant just woman (Miller, 1974, p. 39). *Girl* meant a young person (McCormack, 1967, p. 29); it did not make any difference whether the person was a boy or a girl. (Since *girl* was once a nonsexist word, perhaps its original meaning should be adopted again.) *Female*, too, was originally *femelle*, a nonsexist word which meant a small woman, but because of its obvious resemblance to the word male, it was changed to what it is today (Farb, 1973, p. 161).

Sometimes words start out with rather inoffensive meanings and change to offensive ones, or vice versa. For instance, *idiot* once meant an ignorant person, while *nice* meant ignorant or foolish. As mentioned previously, changes in meaning are occurring continually in slang. A word such as *heavy*, which could carry a negative meaning in our slanguage, now can have a positive tone.

Sometimes we hear a word, think that a mistake has been made by the person pronouncing it, and undertake to change the word to make it "right." This is what has happened to *chaise lounge*, a French term that is actually spelled *chaise longue*— a long chair. Most people, however, refer to it as a *chaise lounge*, a logical change in pronunciation and spelling since it does reflect the function of the chair (Farb, 1973, pp. 352–353). Examples of foreign words which we anglicize in pronunciation and spelling are *dandelion*—French *dent de lion* (teeth of the lion) and *real*— Spanish *royal*.

Flexibility

After reading books such as the delightful *Amelia Bedelia* series (Parish, 1963), children will be conscious that many words in English are multinyms or homophones—words that are spelled alike and sound alike but have different meanings. Words such as box, shower, bark, trunk, and run all have multiple meanings and do change their meanings depending on the context. Children enjoy extending the stories about Amelia, a silly maid but a wonderful cook who, because of her emaciated vocabulary, is always getting into trouble. Amelia invariably has a meaning for a word, but unfortunately it is always the wrong meaning. Children find her misinterpretations hilarious.

By studying the history of our language, children will know that language is made and changed by all of us. They will learn that change, not only in vocabulary but in usage and structure, is the one thing we can depend on, if a language is going to survive as a living tongue.

Punctuation Makes a Difference: The Role of Juncture in Language

Where we pause when we speak and how long we pause can make all the difference in the messages we are trying to convey. Howie Schneider, in a cartoon, "The Circus of P. T. Bimbo" (NEA, Inc., 1975), makes it clear that it is important, when advertising for an employee, to distinguish between a TIGHT rope walker and a TIGHTROPE walker. There is a difference, too, in the following two statements:

You should sit down before you eat Mother.

You should sit down before you eat, Mother.

Children enjoy making up and sharing their own sentences which prove that juncture markers are critical. However, before asking them to do this, work with them on some juncture exercises.

Children's books which include activities to demonstrate the need for punctuation

Brewton, Sara, Brewton, John E., and Blackburn, G. Meredith III. *My Tang's Tungled and Other Ridiculous Situations.* New York: T. Y. Crowell, 1973, pp. 5, 6, 8, 10.

Gardner, Martin. *Perplexing Puzzles and Tantalizing Teasers.* New York: Simon and Schuster, 1969, p. 18.

Nurnberg, Maxwell. *Punctuation Pointers.* New York: Scholastic Book Services, 1968, pp. 55–57.

———. *Fun with Words.* Englewood Cliffs, N.J.: Prentice-Hall, 1970, pp. 32–40.

Potter, Charles Francis. *More Tongue Tanglers and a Rigmarole.* Cleveland: World, 1964.

Withers, Carl. *A Treasury of Games.* New York: Grosset and Dunlap, 1964, pp. 125–126.

In these and other ways, as children read they learn about the nature of language. As we share such books and plan the suggested activities, children learn the delight of words. They come to understand the words of Emily Dickinson, who wrote:

> A word is dead
> When it is said,
> Some say.
>
> I say it just
> Begins to live
> That day.

Additional children's books for enjoyment of language development

Hanlon, Emily. *How a Horse Grew Hoarse on the Site Where He Sighted a Bare Bear: A*

Tale of Homonyms. New York: Delacorte, 1976.

Hefter, Richard. *The Strawberry Word Book.* New York: Larousse, 1974.

Hunt, Bernice Kohn. *Your Ant Is a Which: Fun with Homophones.* New York: Harcourt, Brace, Jovanovich, 1975.

Keller, Charles. *Going Bananas.* Englewood Cliffs, N.J.: Prentice-Hall, 1975.

Keller, Charles, and Baker, Richard. *The Star-Spangled Banana and Other Revolutionary Riddles.* Englewood Cliffs, N.J.: Prentice-Hall, 1975.

Tremain, Ruthuen. *Fooling Around with Words.* New York: Greenwillow Books, 1976.

References

Adelson, Leone. *Dandelions Don't Bite: The Story of Words.* New York: Pantheon Books, 1972.

Burgess, Gellet. *Burgess Unabridged.* Ann Arbor: Midway Press, n.d.

Carew, Jan. *The Third Gift.* Boston: Little, Brown and Co., 1974.

Epstein, Beryl, and Epstein, Sam. *What's Behind the Word?* New York: Scholastic Book Services, 1964.

Farb, Peter. *Word Play.* New York: Bantam Books, 1973.

Ferguson, Charles W. *The Abecedarian Book.* Boston: Little, Brown and Co., 1964.

Hubbell, Patricia. *Catch Me a Wind.* Paterson, N. J.: Atheneum, 1958.

Lionni, Leo. *Frederick.* New York: Knopf/Pantheon, 1973.

McCormack, Jo Ann. *The Story of Our Language,* Columbus, Ohio: Charles E. Merrill, 1967.

Merriam, Eve. *A Gaggle of Geese.* New York: Knopf, 1960.

———. *Small Fry.* New York: Knopf, 1965.

Miller, Albert G. *Where Did That Word Come From?* Glendale, Calif.: Bowmar, 1974.

Newman, Edwin. *Strictly Speaking.* New York: Bobbs-Merrill Co., 1974.

Ramage, Corinne. *The Joneses.* Philadelphia: J. B. Lippincott, 1975.

Parish, Peggy. *Amelia Bedelia.* New York: Harper and Row, 1963.

Severn, Bill. *People Words.* New York: Ives Washburn, 1966.

Sorel, Nancy. *Word People.* New York: American Heritage, 1970.

Tiedt, Iris M., and Tiedt, Sidney W. *Contemporary English in the Elementary School,* 2nd ed. Englewood Cliffs, N.J.: Prentice-Hall, 1975.

Warner, Bob. *The Elephant's Visit.* Boston: Little, Brown and Co., 1975.

45. Figurative Language: Deceitful Mirage or Sparkling Oasis for Reading?

Thomas N. Turner

Figurative language surrounds children. It appears in a thousand subtle forms in nearly every moment of verbal communication. Every hearing child has heard uncountable figurative expressions and understands, at least at some level, most of them. Figurative language is prominent in the dialects as well as the idioms of mainstream language. It characterizes the greater part of most slang expression. In fact, the changing slang patterns in American society can be a study in figurative expression. For example, the history of twentieth century American English can

From Thomas N. Turner, Figurative language: deceitful mirage or sparkling oasis? *Language Arts,* October 1976, *53,* 758–761; 775. Reprinted by permission of Thomas N. Turner and the National Council of Teachers of English.

be partially characterized by a series of figurative expressions used to inform people that they are attractive. Decade by decade, children have adopted expressions used by the teenagers they admired—"You're the cat's pajamas"; "You're a knockout"; "You're a real scream"; "You're real cool"; "You're far out." Children begin to imitate these slang expressions at a young age, and by the time they encounter figurative language in reading most children have a large number of slang terms in their speaking vocabularies.

That children have varied experiences with figurative language can hardly be debated. It seems, however, to be the consensus of research and opinion of reading specialists that children have difficulty in understanding figurative language in reading materials. Considering their oral experiences with figurative expression this requires some explanation. Among the factors contributing to reading difficulty, at least three logical and apparent causes seem most likely. First, understanding figurative language involves thinking which is more abstract and complex than that required for literal comprehension. Children must select meanings not normally associated with each word in the expression. Admittedly, many words have several literal meanings. The reader must often select the correct meaning of a word from a range of possibilities. However, with most words encountered in elementary reading, only a few of the possible meanings are probable. The reader can predict within a narrow selection of meanings with a high chance of success. These meanings are often closely related and the context can provide important and often obvious clues for the proper selection of a word meaning. With figurative language, readers cannot predict as easily or accurately. Meaning is hidden and unexpected. The literal meanings of the words are often contrary to the author's intended meaning. Children may be so engrossed in the labor of discovering literal meaning

that they are surprised by the figurative usage.

A second cause of children's reading difficulty with figurative language is their inexperience with the abstractions involved. There is a tendency to assume adequate experience since children encounter so many figurative expressions in oral language. However, there is no evidence that children understand the meanings of all the figurative expressions they hear and use in oral communication. Conscious, reasoned, fully developed concepts are not necessary in order to use figurative language in speaking. Children use figures of speech because they like the sound of them. They may be imitating peers, older children, adults or television. They are fascinated, as with rhyming words and nonsense syllables, with the sound and feel of the words.

A third factor to be considered is that the figures of speech encountered in reading most often are not the same ones that are encountered in oral communication. The ability to understand figuratively used language encountered in speaking and listening does not automatically imply an understanding or even an awareness of figurative expressions found in reading.

Figurative language goes beyond literal meanings. To understand it one must be able to recognize contrast, comparison, and exaggeration. Figurative language is often used intentionally to enhance the sensory images, moods and feelings which are communicated through reading, speaking or listening. Figures of speech heighten the beauty, the strength, and the appeal of the language itself. They give language a power that can be sensed almost without fathoming the meaning.

Ability to recognize and understand figurative language is crucial to successful reading. Almost all writers of literature employ many figures of speech. The problems involved in understanding figures of speech are problems germane to the entire comprehension process. Nonfiction as well as fiction, poetry as much as prose utilize such language patterns to expand meaning for the reader. There are indications of a high frequency of figurative expression in children's reading materials as early as third grade.

The common use of figurative language does not give it instructional priority. Rather, its importance lies in the ability to recognize and understand an author's ideas. To totally miss the meaning of a figure of speech may result in the reader confusing the author's message altogether. At the very least it will diminish the amount and intensity of personal meaning derived from reading.

Understanding figurative language involves readers as critical thinkers. They must read with an alertness to the possibility that the author may be attempting to communicate something other than literal meaning. Words must be considered as parts of communication. In all reading activities children must be encouraged to look for meaning. Meaning is not provided by the writer, but by the reader. This is true of literal meaning, and is even more important to comprehension of figurative language. Images and associations are supplied by the reader's imagination. When readers are trying to supply figurative meaning, they are involved in creative reading. The more imaginatively the reader interacts with the language, the richer the meaning becomes.

The objective of figurative language study is to teach children to recognize and understand it. The teacher's example alone, will not teach this skill. An initial step in teaching children to understand and use figurative language is to develop children's awareness of their own use of such language. These common oral language patterns include some of the most overused idioms and overworked phrases of English (e.g., "You eat like a horse!", "I'm really in the doghouse now!", "Cut it out!", and "You beast!").

There are many classroom approaches which will facilitate growth with figurative language. Incidental and accidental growth should not be expected of children. If untaught, figurative language will most likely remain unnoticed and misunderstood. Almost equally detrimental to growth in understanding would be an attempt to teach all types of figurative language at once. (There are at least thirteen major types of figures of speech.) A sound instructional approach appears to be one which concentrates on the simple figures and an overall awareness of figurative expression. Though it may sometimes be helpful, children need not memorize or know the names and meanings of each type of speech figure. It is more crucial that they understand what figurative language does to the meaning of what they read.

The experiences that are available through reading aloud to children provide one of the first good entry points into figurative language. Poetry is especially rich in language imagery. Teachers need to draw attention to the figures of speech. Children's levels of awareness can be raised simply through discussion of meanings. A few techniques for raising awareness and sensitivity to the meanings of speech figures in oral communication follow:

- Play a game of "nicknames." "Pet" names and nicknames are a special kind of metaphoric language. In class discussion, a number of such names can be listed on a chart or on the chalk board. Offensive names that children are hurt by might be discussed, but care needs to be taken to avoid embarrassment. Talking over the reasons these particular names are used can help children become more aware of language meaning.
- Have children collect examples of descriptions which are rich in figurative expression, and draw the object or per-

son described using literal meanings. For example, they might draw St. Nicholas from "A Visit from St. Nicholas" to fit the following description: "His droll little mouth was drawn up like a bow. The beard on his chin was as white as the snow. He had a round face and a fat little belly that shook when he laughed like a bowl full of jelly."

- Another technique involves presenting children with examples of incomplete similes. Discussion of the responses can help children realize the wide range of possible comparisons. Encourage multiple word responses.

Tall as a	_____	Happy as a	_____
Eager as a	_____	Lucky as a	_____
Sad as a	_____	Right as	_____
Pretty as	_____	Free as	_____

- Have children create similes and metaphors to describe events that change their feelings or moods. A few ideas are:

a clear sunny day
a happy optimistic person
the excitement someone feels when they receive especially good news
the feelings of a team that has just won or lost an important game
a terrible accident
a noisy confused crowd

- Discuss the figurative and literal meanings of expressive sayings and proverbs. For example:

"You're as pretty as a picture."
"Time is money."
"As ugly as sin."
"Fit as a fiddle."
"Don't beat a dead horse."
"Don't change horses in the middle of the stream."
"Where there is smoke, there is fire."
"Knock your head against a stone wall."

- Cut or have children cut titles and headlines from newspapers and magazines containing figurative language. These can be used for bulletin boards and guessing games.

- Duplicate brief poetry containing figurative language. A discussion can help children to locate and underline figures of speech and compose other ways of expressing these ideas. Children might take a short verse and rewrite it, trying to convey the same meaning literally. Or they might try to identify alternative figures to those used by the author.

- Give each child a "secret thing" to be presented through figures of speech. Though the object is never named, the class tries to guess what it is. The object can be a common household item, a toy, or something found in school. Listing things and abstract ideas can be used at a later stage.

- Have children imagine and describe something they have never seen before. Then help others to understand it by using comparison and contrast figures of speech. Possible sources for "unseen" things include:

a new invention
a new kind of vehicle
a creature from outer space
an organism that cannot be seen with a microscope
a character in a book which has no pictures
a new breed of animal that comes from crossing several breeds

- Have a "person, place, or thing of the week." Each day a "double simile" clue is given telling what the mystery is "like" and "not like." Literature may be used as the source of the mystery. For example, if the mystery were Wilbur in *Charlotte's Web*, cues to start the guessing could be:

The mystery is like a horse, but not like a chicken. (4 legged mammal)
It is like a hippopotamus, but not like a giraffe. (chubby, not tall and thin)
It is bigger than a cat, but smaller than a horse. (size clue)

It is important that children recognize the purposes of figurative language. Figurative expressions are used principally to aid in description. Through comparison, contrast, and exaggeration authors are able to expand sensory images and increase emotional identifications and associations of the reader. When everyone uses them, figures of speech may evolve into common ways of saying things. At this point they become clichés. With meanings blurred they begin to lose their power of sensory imagery. Quality reading materials supply children with figures of speech which create fresh and new sensory images. When children become involved in understanding and "seeing" these images, they are reading creatively.

46. Ten Creative Ways to Build Vocabulary Skills

Nicholas P. Criscuolo

Students read to get meaning from the printed page and to acquire knowledge. A truly competent reader is one who not only decodes words but understands the rich, full meanings behind these words whether they are used in isolation or in a contextual setting. Vocabulary development is a crucial part of the secondary program because many students at this stage have mastered basic decoding strategies and are now increasing both their receptive and expressive vocabularies at a rapid pace.

Vocabulary development eludes some students, however. This may be due to an inadequate experiential background, apathy, gaps in the reading curriculum or a host of other reasons. Two years ago, the New Haven, Connecticut public school system reinstituted the city-wide achievement testing program using the *Iowa Tests of Basic Skills Achievement Tests* (Houghton Mifflin, 1978). And for two years in a row, students at the middle school level scored consistently below big city and national norms in vocabulary. As a matter of fact, student performance in vocabulary has been the lowest in terms of all subtests on the *Iowa* both years.

Vocabulary development is too important an area to neglect. Because of the poor showing in vocabulary, the New Haven public school system instituted a series of four Basic Skills Workshops—one devoted solely to vocabulary—for all elementary and middle school teachers. Additionally, the local newspaper *The Journal-Courier*, in conjunction with the New Haven public school system, now publishes a column titled "Words of the Week" which lists selected words with their meanings for students in both English and Spanish. But this is not enough. Building vocabulary skills is an inter-disciplinary endeavor which takes place in every class. The remainder of this article will describe briefly ten creative activities for building vocabulary skills which teachers report have been successful when working with all students.

1. *What's in a Name?*—Ask each student in the class to print his or her name vertically on a piece of paper and to use words which express a feeling, emotion or describe his/her personality.
Example:

Kind	Angry
Anxious	Nervous

From Nicholas P. Criscuolo, Ten creative ways to build vocabulary skills. *Wisconsin State Reading Association Journal*, Fall 1981, *26*, 23–26. Reprinted by permission of the Wisconsin State Reading Association.

Tired   Diligent
Harried   Yearning
Youthful

This activity can be varied by having each student select another student in class and use words to describe each other.

2. *Describe It*—Ask the students to clip words (nouns) from newspapers and magazines and paste them onto a sheet of paper with ample space under each word. Have students pick a partner and exchange papers. The student's partner is asked to write three words which describe each word on the sheet under that word. Example:

frankfurter   *peddler*
dry   experienced
tasteless   sympathetic
greasy   shrewd

3. *Multiple Meanings*—Provide practice for students in discovering multiple meanings of words by putting a list of words such as *spare*, *run* and *mean* on the chalkboard. Write a sentence in which that word is used. For example:

1. Lance located the *spare* tire in the trunk.
2. The salesperson had a *mean* look on his face.
3. There was a *run* on the bank after the people read the newspaper article.

Ask the students to look up each word in the dictionary and pick out the appropriate meaning as it applies to the sentence.

Add a creative spark to this activity by encouraging the students to list as many multiple meaning words as they can think of and to write interesting sentences for each one.

4. *Swap Shop*—This activity works well with pupil teams. Direct each student to provide a certain number of colorful or descriptive words (such as eerie, delectable, flickering, towering, etc.) and to swap these words with his/her partner. Each team member must use *all* the words on the list to write an original story. Team members can share their *masterpieces* with each other or the entire class, if desired.

5. *Associated Words*—Since building vocabulary skills is an inter-disciplinary enterprise, put some subject headings on the board and ask the students to brainstorm for words usually associated with each subject. Example:

Science	*Music*	*Art*	*Math*
beaker	scherzo	collage	rectangle
microscope	concerto	hue	meter
stratosphere	triad	decal	dividend

Liven up this activity by displaying some of the objects or words mentioned or by having the students illustrate some of the words in each category.

6. *Place Names*—Using maps of the states in America, ask students to find cities and towns which use nouns, adjectives, compound words, etc. in their names.

Example:

Liverpool, Pennsylvania
Swan Lake, Mississippi
Clear Creek, Colorado
Roundup, Montana
Hot Coffee, Mississippi
Green Bay, Wisconsin

Have students label or color code these names; e.g. blue for nouns, red for adjectives, green for compound words. Students will pore over these maps to locate as many cities or towns which follow these patterns.

7. *Overworked Words*—Provide a list of overworked words such as *nice, swell, terrific*, etc. and put them in sentences with the overworked word underlined. Have students use alternate words to make the sentences more interesting and varied.

Example:
1. Martha had a *nice* expression on her face.
2. Adolph had a *neat* look about him.
3. "That's a *terrific* answer," Terry responded.

8. *Cross It Out*—Put a list of related words on the board. Add one word in each row which does not belong. Ask the students to cross out the unrelated word in each row and to write the word classification on the line after each row of words.

Example:
1. doctor   nurse   mask   accountant
   occupations
2. anxiety   tasteful   elation   anger   *emotions*
3. hotel   piano   tuna   harp   *musical instruments*

9. *Expressions*—Clip pictures from magazines and newspapers of people with a variety of expressions on their faces. Paste these pictures on tagboard with room underneath each picture. Ask the students to examine the picture and to write three words which aptly describe the expression on the person's face; e.g. *tranquil, dejected, bedraggled* and so on. As a follow-up activity, have them assume the role of this person and write a short story incorporating these words. In their stories, encourage the students to offer a plausible explanation concerning the circumstances that might have led the person depicted to feel that way.

10. *Newer Words*—The idea that our language is constantly growing needs to be reinforced with students. New words such as *mall, mart* and *metro* are recent additions to our language to describe new things and concepts. Ask students to think of additional words which have entered our language recently.

Using the dictionary and other sources of information, direct the following questions to the students:

1. Which word would have appeared in the dictionary first, *spinet* or *stereo*?   spinet
2. Which word would have appeared in the dictionary first, *sandwich* or *skyscraper*?   sandwich
3. Which word would have appeared in the dictionary first, *inlet* or *television*?   inlet

Adding words to one's vocabulary is an exciting adventure. Words and their different meanings are important for students to master if reading is to be a full and rich experience for them. The creative, classroom-tested activities for building skills described in this article will permit students to gain the maximum from their reading.

47. Stimulate Reading . . . with a Dictionary

Edith F. Miller

Making a dictionary as a class project provides a valuable addition to the reading program and can be adapted to any grade level.

As a first step, in the first grade, I prepare a set of large cards, each with a word on one side and the same word below a picture on the other side. In the lower right-hand corner of the side with the word only, I put the beginning letter of that word. This gives an added means of identifying a word—"dog" will not be

From Edith F. Miller, Stimulate reading with a dictionary. *Grade Teacher*, February 1962, 79, 51–52; 106–107. We have been unable to locate the copyright holder of this essay. Any information would be appreciated.

called "puppy," "Mother" will not be called "lady" or "woman," "ship" will not be called "boat."

The words on the cards are those with which the children are already familiar from their basic readers, from class activities, from the special weeks and holidays already passed, from writing exercise books or number study—in short, from any source the children have used.

Making the Cards

Except for the colors and a few verbs, all of the words are nouns. If the children are familiar with only the singular form or the plural form of a word, it is wise to include the other form, also, as the words are put on cards.

As soon as I start making the cards, I ask the children to help me find the needed pictures. We keep a pile of magazines on hand and the children look for the pictures, colored if possible. These are cut out and mounted. In many cases there will be duplicate pictures which are saved for later use. A good drill in reading is furnished by tacking on the bulletin board the cards which need pictures. As pictures are found, the children tack them under the cards. Later the class helps to decide which pictures shall be used on the cards.

The pack of cards may be used in a variety of ways. The teacher may show the cards, word side only, to the entire class, allowing the children to take turns reading them. The children love to see who can get the most cards. The cards may be used in the same way in a small pupil-led group. Other games may be made up by the class and played by the children in small groups. The cards also provide a good means of developing self-help when a child uses the pack or part of it by himself. Individual children may be tested on the entire pack by teacher or a pupil-partner and the words missed isolated for further drill.

Next Step

After intensive use of the pack of cards, I make a large booklet titled "Our Very Own Picture Dictionary." Each letter of the alphabet appears at the top of a page in the book with several blank pages following each lettered page. When I show the blank booklet to the children, I also show them some published picture dictionaries and picture dictionaries made by previous classes.

The children are most enthusiastic about making their own dictionaries. First their cards are sorted out according to the first letter. We play games with the sorted cards. This proves a good way for them to see, for example, that all "b" words start with the same sound, while the "a" words may have different sounds.

After this activity, we look for the pictures needed for our class picture dictionary. Many of the duplicate pictures which we did not discard are now used. The children do all the cutting and they arrange the pictures in the book in the order of the alphabetically listed words. I check this arrangement before they do any pasting. Then I print the words under the pictures.

As new words are learned, pictures are found and pasted in following the original words; thus the new words cannot be in alphabetical order. New cards are made and, if desired, these are kept in a separate pack so that drill on cards may be centered on the newly introduced words.

Personal Dictionaries

Several months after the beginning of the project, I arrange all the words alphabetically and make duplicate sheets so that each child may make his own copy of "Our Very Own Picture Dictionary." Space is left for illustrations which may be pupil-made but usually are procured from catalogues, old textbooks, gummed seals, conservation stamps, used greeting cards, informals, and magazines.

At the close of the school year, the finished picture dictionaries are taken home. Parents are always impressed with the many words that have been mastered, especially if they realize that only comparatively few words of the children's reading vocabulary can be illustrated. A copy of the dictionary is also sent to each second grade where the pupils go in the fall.

Second Grade and Up

Second-grade pupils who have not made picture dictionaries in the first grade would enjoy the project, following practically the same procedure. Whether they have had the experience in the first grade or not, any second-grade or third-grade group would enjoy adapting the idea by making "A Picture Dictionary of Science Throughout the Year," "A Picture Dictionary of the Seasons," "The Circus," or any topic they study. "A Picture Dictionary of Christmas" is always popular and the number of words added by that one theme alone is amazing.

Third-grade children may use the pack of cards or omit that part of the plan if preferred. If third-grade pupils make dictionaries toward the end of the year, they are mature enough to make up simple definitions for some of the words after studying picture dictionaries carefully. They are happy to make their dictionaries a little more like dictionaries for grownups. Of course, the teacher will have to write many of the definitions with them and for them. Pupils in the third grade and above usually prefer to draw their own pictures rather than to cut them out and paste them.

Fourth-grade pupils can write more of the definitions themselves and should also show how to pronounce each word. Since the fourth grade is the one where dictionary work is usually stressed, making a class dictionary is a natural activity for this grade and provides the needed practice in the use of the pronunciation symbols. Studying glossaries found in their own texts and in sample books helps in all

phases of dictionary writing. Thus, the transition from a picture dictionary to one with definitions and very few pictures is gradually made.

Pupils in grades above the fourth proceed in the same way. The topic chosen for the dictionary should always be one of real interest to the children. These upper-grade dictionaries will include many words other than nouns.

The dictionary made by a class may be used as a reference or as reading material by other classes, and often inspires creation of their own dictionaries by the other classes.

Transitional Step

As an intermediate step between the picture and name on a card and the "real" dictionary on a given topic, you might like to try this idea, applicable to any grade:

Choose any area where the children need some help in understanding terms—it might be art, music, science, geography, arithmetic, and so forth. Make up a list of terms which you want your children to understand. Give each child one term which can be illustrated. Have each child print his term neatly in red crayon at the top of a sheet of drawing paper. He will then draw an illustration, putting the part which illustrates the specific word in red crayon.

In arithmetic, for example, the term SUM would be lettered in red at the top of the paper and an addition example would be put on the paper in black crayon, with the answer in red. Children can see at a glance that a SUM is the answer to an addition example. However, the definition—"SUM is the answer to an addition example"—will be put on in small letters.

In geography, physical features lend themselves well to this idea; in art, it is possible to illustrate "angles," "vanishing points," "planes," and similar terms; in science, words such as "antenna," "insect," and "larva" may be clearly shown.

Every child may make as many of these sheets as desired. A border of these terms, arranged alphabetically, is a help in spelling when the children are writing on the topic. Understanding of a topic is an outgrowth of such an activity. The pupils sometimes like to make their own booklets of the words in the border, illustrating when possible. This activity could lead very naturally into making a dictionary including terms that cannot be illustrated.

Outcomes

The most important outcome of making dictionaries is that pupils will come to love words and *want* to know more and more of them and their meanings. They will become more articulate in their oral and written reports, in the expression of their thoughts and feelings. Knowledge of words increases the enjoyment of reading and greatly stimulates the desire to read.

Other outcomes include:

1. Picture dictionaries made in the primary grades provide a good foundation for the formal dictionary work of the fourth and later grades.
2. Alphabetizing is introduced sequentially beginning in the first grade and continuing until any list of words can be easily alphabetized by the children. This helps them to find words in a real dictionary easily.
3. The children experience satisfaction through the self-help their systematic study of dictionaries has made possible.
4. The number of words learned thoroughly by this one means is astounding—both words from standard lists and words from special content fields.
5. The finished dictionaries are popular with both children and their parents. The parents can see the progress the children are making in learning.
6. The practice in writing definitions is a real contribution to exact and precise English.

48. Vocabulary Development in the Classroom

Lee C. Deighton

How Context Operates

There are four general principles of context operation which can be stated with some exactness. They are stated at this point to permit their being checked against the instances of context which will be quoted later. The *first* general principle has already been stated—context reveals the meaning of unfamiliar words only infrequently. The *second* is that context generally reveals only one of the meanings of an unfamiliar word. Most words in common English usage have more than one meaning recorded in the dictionary. These dictionary entries are only an interpretation by the dictionary editors of the common denominator in a great many instances in which a particular word is used. The dictionary entries are indispensable to us as a point of departure in understanding a word. However, dictionary entries do not limit the use of words. Dictionary entries are shaped, changed, and altered by individual contexts, each of which is different. This in brief is why a single context can illuminate only one phase of a particular word. Which phase is developed will be determined by the demands of the particular context. In presenting this matter to

From Lee C. Deighton, *Vocabulary development in the classroom.* NY: Teachers College Press, Columbia University, 1959. Pp. 2–6; 15–16. Reprinted by permission of the author.

children it is worth repeating over and over again that no word has one fixed and inalterable meaning, that no one context revelation will suffice for all the later uses of the word which may be met.

The *third* principle of context operation is that context seldom clarifies the whole of any meaning. Occasionally, context will provide a synonym, but it must be remembered that synonyms are never exact equivalents. Words are not like coins of even value, to be substituted at random in the exchange of communication. Context more often provides only clues from which the reader may infer the meaning of an unfamiliar word. It is important to make clear to developing readers that the whole meaning of an unfamiliar word can never be gathered in the first encounter with it. Meaning comes from experience, and the wider the experience with a word, the richer will its meaning be for the reader.

From this follows the *fourth* general principle—that vocabulary growth through context revelation is a gradual matter. It is a matter of finding one clue here and another there, of fitting them together, of making tentative judgments and revising them as later experience requires. It is a matter of building meaning into a word over a period of years.

Limiting Factors in Context Operation

In addition to these four general principles, there are certain limitations on the effective use of contexts in classroom study. The first of these follows from what has just been said. *What a context may reveal to a particular reader will depend upon his previous experience.* It is unfortunately true that some words exist for most of us *merely* as words—as spoken sounds or printed symbols having only the vaguest of meanings for us. We have not tied these words into our personal experience. We have not objectified them. We have not applied them as labels to physical objects or to the observable qualities of physical objects or to the behavior of persons and things. We

recognize these words, and we can restate them, perhaps, in other words with more or less success, but we have not attached them to the living experience of our physical world. The degree to which we have objectified the words which compose a context will determine the success with which we use that context to uncover the meaning of an unfamiliar word.

The key words in the context may themselves be unfamiliar to the reader. Although the construction of a context may indicate to the experienced reader that an example or restatement is being given, the inexperienced reader may completely miss the restatement and assume that new material is being added. Inexperienced readers must not be expected to derive as much help from context as experienced readers get. This factor of experience is really a limitation on the effective use of contexts in classroom study.

There are two other limitations worth noting. The first of these is that the portion of context which illuminates an unfamiliar word must be reasonably close to the word if it is to act effectively. It may appear in the same sentence. It may appear in the same paragraph. It may precede or it may follow. If it follows within reasonably close space, it can be used effectively by the average reader in his average haste to cover the material in hand. If it precedes the unfamiliar word by so much as a paragraph, its effectiveness is limited. If it precedes by several pages, it has even less value except to those careful readers who take the time to re-read for understanding. In ordinary adult circumstances, there are few of us who take the time for re-reading. In classroom practice there is always time to re-read; and there could be no more salutary exercise in vocabulary development than to assist and then, as pupils experience grows, to require the pupil to dig out the preceding passages which reveal the meaning of an unfamiliar word.

There is another limiting condition in the effectiveness of context which exists irrespective of experience or reading patience. *There must be some clear-cut connection between the unfamiliar word and the context which clarifies it.* This connection may be made by repeating identical sentence structure; by repeating the construction in which the unfamiliar word occurs and by substituting a synonym; by use of pointing words or phrases such as *such as, like, for example, this, that, those,* and many others.

The importance of these constructions and these connecting words is apparent when we examine a context which lacks them. For example,

> We were flying at 22,000 feet. M. called for echelon starboard. Our Hurricanes moved into single-file, each plane to the right of the plane in front.

The unfamiliar words are *echelon starboard.* The next sentence describes an echelon starboard, but there is nothing to indicate definitely that it does. How is the reader with no previous knowledge of *starboard* or of *echelon* to know that the next sentence is not a completely new idea?

By contrast note how the parallel construction in the following example reveals what is meant specifically by *moisture.*

> The letters they carried were wrapped in oiled silk to protect them *from* moisture, either *from* water in fording streams, or perspiration of the horse.

It is not meant here that the word *moisture* is an unfamiliar word for the average reader. The example is cited simply to show the operation of context. Similar examples may be found with the same pattern involving words of real difficulty for the most widely read adult. The importance of the example is its illustration of how parallel construction ties context closely to a key word.

To restate: Context reveals the meaning of unfamiliar words only infrequently. A single context reveals only a part of a meaning of a particular word. The building of meaning from context is a gradual process. The effectiveness of context in revealing meaning is limited; it depends on the previous experience of the reader,

on the proximity of the enlightening context to the unfamiliar word, and on the clearness of the connection between the context and the word upon which it bears. . . .

Context reveals meaning most simply by outright definition. It reveals meaning by citing examples, and these contexts frequently employ signal words: *such as, such, like, especially, for example, other, this* or *these* (followed by a synonym), *the way* or *in the way that.* Occasionally, when these signal words are not employed, the linking verb is used to show the connection. A third method of explaining an unfamiliar word is the use of modifiers. A fourth method by which context reveals meaning is through restatement in which certain signal words can always be counted upon as introducing a restatement: *in other words, that is, to put it another way, what this means, which is to say,* and all the possible modifications of these. In addition restatement employs two mechanical devices as signals: the dash and the parenthesis.

The classroom study of these four methods of context revelation may reasonably be expected to yield good results for perhaps half of the context situations which will arise in classroom reading. For the other half, there are no key words and no mechanical devices. The reader must rely on inference. Sometimes these inference contexts show the connection between the unfamiliar word and the explanatory matter by employing repetition of sentence pattern, by repetition of key words, by use of familiar connecting words like *however, yet, therefore, similarly.* Frequently the connection is established only through repetition of thought or statement of its opposite.

There are many instances of inference context which contain none of these connecting devices. They may be dealt with profitably as they arise, in the hope that teacher guidance will encourage the pupil to use his own resources in reading for meaning rather than to pass by all unfamiliar words.

CHAPTER X

Improvement of Reading Comprehension

The past decade has witnessed a great upsurge of interest in reading comprehension. The articles in this chapter have been chosen to explain new concepts about comprehension and to provide bridges from the new research to classroom practice.

In the opening article, Durkin provides an overview of recent developments in comprehension theory, explains such terms as schema and story grammar, compares spoken with written language, and describes some ways to improve questioning. Strange describes the interactive model and the concept of schema, and develops seven ways to apply schema theory. Pearson concentrates on questioning and provides a clear and practical set of suggestions for changing questioning procedures to conform to schema theory.

Ruddell provides a useful taxonomy of comprehension, with eleven types of skill competencies and three comprehension levels (factual, interpretive, and applicative), Barnitz summarizes some recent research on the comprehensibility of sentences, and describes ways to combine simple sentences into compound and complex sentences to improve comprehension. Gunn and Elkins describe a program for using cloze exercises and sentence completion exercises both to enhance comprehension and improve vocabulary.

Spiegel lists and discusses ten questions that provide a useful framework for diagnosing the reasons for poor comprehension. In the final selection, Swineford employs a selection about Hitler to illustrate seven kinds of propaganda techniques and describes several ways to help students to become critical readers.

49. What Is the Value of the New Interest in Reading Comprehension?

Dolores Durkin

A quick look through current journals or convention programs is enough to reveal an unprecedented interest in reading comprehension research. More careful scrutiny would show that a large number of the writers and speakers are outside the group commonly referred to as "reading educators." While the latter have hardly been replaced as researchers, it is still true that individuals from fields like cognitive psychology, educational psychology, linguistics, and artificial intelligence are writing and speaking often enough to make their presence very apparent. How, it might be asked, have professional educators who have a special interest in reading been responding to this development?

Four Kinds of Responses

Based on what I have personally heard, four kinds of responses prevail. One is patient resignation, based on the assumption that the newcomers will soon lose their interest in reading and turn to other areas. The least patient and most vocal in this group specifically charge that many of the "outsiders" are interested in reading only because money for reading research is available and, further, that they have little or no interest in such practical but important concerns as whether or not children learn to read.

In sharp contrast, the most noticeable characteristic of a second group is gullibility. As little as one talk or one report prompts members of this group to accept and propagate a conclusion as being the final truth even when it originates from a speculative conceptualization or from research that was brief in duration, that used a small number of adult subjects, and that lacked sufficient controls. The eagerness of this group to be up-to-date sometimes means that what is propagated is so badly misinterpreted that a researcher would not recognize the finding as being his or her own.

The third response to the current wave of interest in reading comprehension is the one heard most frequently from teachers of children and teachers of teachers. It, too, is cynicism typically expressed by the contention that a re-invention of the wheel, communicated with unnecessarily technical and obscure terminology, is all that the new breed of researchers is accomplishing. Having heard for many years, for example, that what readers take to a page affects what they are able to take from it, this third group naturally thinks "So what else is new?" when certain features of schema theory are highlighted. Current discussions of story grammar evoke a similar response since part of what is said—at least at first glance—seems closely similar to content covered in undergraduate courses in children's literature.

It is possible that the cynicism characterizing this third response may be fostered by the researchers themselves because very few make an attempt either a) to show how what they are doing relates to what was done earlier by reading educators who also were researchers, or b) to pinpoint exactly how what they are doing and finding goes beyond, or is different from, what their predecessors reported. It

From Dolores Durkin, What is the value of the new interest in reading comprehension? *Language Arts*, January 1981, *58*, 23–43. Reprinted by permission of the author and the National Council of Teachers of English.

is as if reading comprehension research began in about 1970. If this interpretation is correct, greater efforts to connect the present with the past could lead not only to a better understanding of what is now going on but also to far less cynicism about the potential value of the new research.

The fourth response—the one that underlies this paper—is cautious optimism. Michael Strange, after reviewing current work with comprehension, depicts this position very effectively. He says, "It is not simply . . . old wine in new bottles but rather, finer wine in old bottles and a little new wine, too" (1980, p. 394).

With a few examples, let me show why I think Strange's description is accurate. In the process, some concerns of the new breed of reading researchers will be described and some of the terminology they use will be explained.

Schema Theory

One highly conspicuous concern is schema theory. As was suggested earlier, long before it assumed its current prominence, reading methodology courses were teaching that what readers know about a topic affects how well they will be able to comprehend what an author says about it. Since everyone's encounters with print confirm the dependence of reading on background information (now commonly referred to as *world knowledge*), even the most rebellious of students probably never objected to that part of the course. Similarly, they were not likely to raise questions when instructors urged them to provide children with varied experiences as a way of building up understandings, concepts, and vocabulary; and to review whatever experiences and concepts are relevant before children read a selection.

Currently, theorists and researchers who subscribe to schema theory are saying the same things—but much more besides as they try to uncover exactly how existing knowledge enters into, and influences, the reading comprehension process. Let me

attempt, therefore, to explain some of what they *are* saying.

Like so much of the current research with comprehension, that concerned with *schemata* (the singular form is *schema*) is interested in memory; specifically, in how knowledge is stored in the mind. Such a focus is naturally bound up with reading comprehension since both what an author says and what a reader knows must be remembered if what the author says is to be understood.

Because what goes on in the brain cannot be observed directly, how knowledge is stored and then activated for use has to be inferred. For example, how what is known is held in memory and then retrieved during reading has to be inferred from what readers do that is observable; that is, from what they do that is testable.

Based on what research subjects do (most of whom, up until now, have been adults), current theorists and researchers returned to a theory of memory that Bartlett (1932) once proposed in opposition to the belief that memory involves "separate immutable traces that represent exact copies of the original experience" (Armbruster 1976, p. 12). What was resurrected and is now being further developed is schema theory, whose basic assumption is that what is experienced (learned) is organized and stored in the brain not in a static, unchanging form but in a way that permits modification through further development.[1] Development occurs, the theorists say, when what is known (about an object, an event, a role, a process, or whatever) interacts with what is new but related.

What is already known is called a schema, which is like a concept—and then some.[2] Schemata, according to present beliefs, are arranged hierarchically. A person's schema for something like "sparrow," for instance, is thought to be one part of the more encompassing schema for "bird," which, in turn, is part of the still larger schema for "animal," and so on. Schemata may be thought of, therefore, as being networks of concepts.

For this paper, the pertinent question is, What does schema theory say about reading comprehension?

Schema theory and reading comprehension

One major tenet of schema theory is that comprehension is as dependent on what is in a reader's head as it is on what is printed. Why the theory points to this conclusion is explained as follows.

Each schema (and this is especially true for children) is incomplete. That is, certain bits of information are missing. What is missing is visualized by theorists as empty slots that are waiting, as it were, to be filled—perhaps by input from written discourse. According to schema theory, if text about sparrows includes what a reader knows as well as information that is new, it not only activates the constituents (pieces of information) of the existing sparrow schema but also (assuming the reader is able to decode the text) fills in one or more of the empty slots. This leads to a conception of comprehension that equates it with "filling the slots in the appropriate schemata in such a way as to jointly satisfy the constraints of the message and the schemata" (Anderson, Reynolds, Schallert, and Goetz 1977, p. 370). According to this view, comprehension is a process that both depends on, and develops, schemata.

Developing a schema "from scratch" is difficult, yet that is exactly what a reader must do when an attempt is made to comprehend text dealing with a topic for which he or she has no schemata. Since it *is* difficult, the reader may or may not succeed. That is, he or she may comprehend the entire text, may comprehend some of it, or may comprehend none of it. "From this follows the possibly banal, possibly profound, conclusion that reading comprehension depends eminently on what the reader already knows" (Bereiter 1978, p. 6).

Studies carried out in the framework of schema theory have begun to pinpoint even more specific implications for reading. For instance, work done by Anderson and his colleagues (e.g., Anderson, Pichert, Goetz, Schallert, Stevens, and Trollip 1976; Anderson and McGaw 1973) suggest that both the ability to make an inference and the nature of the inference itself are dependent on a reader's world knowledge. So too is the meaning of what is directly stated by an author (Anderson, Reynolds, Schallert, and Goetz 1977). That even explicit text may be interpreted in a variety of ways is said to reflect the fact that readers respond neither passively nor objectively to print but, instead, contruct its meaning themselves with the help both of the author's words and of their own schemata. This portrays reading comprehension, then, as an *interactive process* in which both text *and* world knowledge play key roles (Rumelhart 1976).

Commonly, this way of looking at reading is contrasted with two other interpretations. One portrays it as a *top-down process*; the other, a *bottom-up process*.

When reading is viewed as a top-down process, primary importance is assigned to what is in the reader's head (Smith 1971). Reading is thus seen as being concept-driven in the sense that the reader's knowledge both of the world and of language suggests certain hypotheses, which are tested—that is, confirmed, modified, or rejected—against what is printed. A top-down process is what Goodman had in mind when he referred to reading as being "a psycholinguistic guessing game" (1967).

In contrast, reading viewed as a bottom-up process is text-driven (Gough 1972; LaBerge and Samuels 1974). From this perspective, words are processed individually and sequentially, and meaning derives directly from them. Although what a reader knows is not thought to be unimportant, an author's words are assigned greater importance.

As was mentioned, it is the interactive model of reading that goes hand in hand with schema theory.

Some reactions to schema theory

Since schema theory's explanation of the way information is stored and retrieved *is* theoretical, one essential reaction is explicit acknowledgement that it is just that—a theory. And even though the growing body of supportive studies is impressive, it must also be remembered (if the theory is correct) that those conducting the research have their own schemata, which are bound to affect how they interpret data. Other researchers with other schemata might assign a different meaning to identical findings. Be that as it may, schema theory applied to reading is attractive because it supports what our own experiences as readers tell us: the more we know before we read, the more we learn when we read.

Not to be forgotten is that the very same experiences point up the need to decode whatever words authors choose to use. Keeping both sides of the reading coin in mind (world knowledge *and* text) should discourage the emergence of a bandwagon that might have classroom teachers lay aside instruction with something like decoding so that ample time is available for filling children's heads with all sorts of information. As Glass has wisely observed, "The maintenance . . . of old knowledge is no less important than the discovery of new knowledge" (1970, p. 325).

With the need for balance in the background, let's move now to possible implications of schema theory for instructional programs in reading.

Possible implications of schema theory for instruction

What I see as implications right now are not anything teachers have not heard before. For example, schema theory's attention to the dependence of comprehension on prior knowledge suggests the importance of having children recall what they know about a topic before they begin to read about it. But such a suggestion should come as no surprise to teachers, for it has been made many times in textbooks and journals. One graphic portrayal of the suggestion is Stauffer's DRTA (Directed Reading-Thinking Activity), which he proposed at least two decades ago as a way of making reading a more thoughtful and personal experience for children (Stauffer 1960). A DRTA begins with teachers' encouraging children to speculate about the content of whatever it is they will be reading, using both their own knowledge and clues found in the material—in a title, for instance, or in pictures. From this, questions emerge and, with them, purposes for reading. In discussing the pre-reading part of the outline for DRTA's, Stauffer cautions, "The reader's questions must reflect his best use of his experience and knowledge" (1969, p. 25).

The need to provide children with cognitive readiness for content subject textbooks is certainly supported by schema theory; and it, too, has been recognized by reading educators over the years. Barron (1969) and Earle (1969), for instance, influenced by Ausubel (1963) and working in association with Herber at Syracuse University, have proposed what is called a structured overview, which cannot help but bring to mind what current theorists say about semantic memory. Teachers who use the overview (a) select from a chapter the most important concepts; (b) select whatever terms are necessary for developing and understanding them; and (c) arrange the terms in a schematic diagram to show how they relate to each other. Pre-reading activities include attention to the terms, the relationships among them, and the concepts.

The point of these few illustrations is that teachers have been urged for a long time to attend to what schema theory indicates is significant for reading comprehension. This is not to claim that teachers have always followed the recommendations (Durkin 1978–79); however, since we human beings tend to pay greater heed to the advice of nonrelatives than to the counsel of family members, it is possible that teachers will now take the same recommendations more seriously as they come from the mouths and pens of cognitive psychologists and linguists.

Teachers who *are* paying attention to current theory and research are bound to have second thoughts about the way questions often function in classrooms. Typically, they are used not to facilitate comprehension but to assess it (Durkin 1978–79). With that purpose, most of a teacher's attention goes to whether or not an answer is correct. While some questions do have one right answer, schema theory reminds us that many have a number of correct answers; and it all depends not only on the text but also on the reader's schemata.

It seems almost needless to point out that schema theory also has implications for those who construct comprehension tests. While global comprehension scores have never had much meaning either for instruction or diagnosis, they clearly have even less when placed within the context of the theory. To say the least, schema theory poses a challenge to psychometricians.

Schema Theory and Story Grammar

Thus far, much that has been said about schema theory probably seems more related to expository discourse—for instance, to a chapter in a social studies textbook—than to narrative prose. If that is so, it is time to turn to what is called story grammar.

Story grammar has to do with the way stories are put together, just as sentence grammar has to do with the way sentences are constructed. As with sentences, stories are seen to have both syntactic elements (e.g., setting) and semantic content (e.g.,

information about the locale and time of the story). Whereas content varies from one story to another, the syntactic elements do not—at least not in well developed stories.

During the past decade or so, a number of psychologists have turned to stories as a possible instrument for illuminating exactly how human beings process language. What these researchers are doing with stories and subjects' recollections of them can thus be characterized as an attempt to understand understanding within the framework of schema theory.

As earlier parts of this paper pointed out, there is consensus among theorists working in that framework about the general nature of the way knowledge and understanding are acquired. That is, agreement exists that they are the product of a reciprocal interaction between a person's schemata and the information in a new event. When stories function in research as a new event, the details of their structure (as well as their content) must be known. Such a requirement prompted psychologists to try to identify the basic elements in stories; resulting from their efforts is the birth of a number of story grammars.

One of the most frequently mentioned grammars was proposed by Stein and Glenn (1979). In its most abbreviated form, their grammar identifies setting and episode as the major components of a simple story. *Setting* introduces the leading character and provides background information. *Episode* is more complex and includes an *initiating event*, a *response*, an *attempt* to satisfy a goal, a *consequence*, and a *reaction*. Figure 1, taken from the report of a study by Nezworski, Stein, and Trabasso (1979) in which the Stein-Glenn grammar was used, illustrates a single-episode structure and, further, how a story grammar functions as an analytic tool.

Bruce (1979) claims that what existing story grammars fail to capture are charac-

Figure 1. An Analysis of a Story

	The Tiger's Whisker
Setting	Once there was a woman who lived in a forest.
Initiating Event	One day she was walking up a hill and she came upon the entrance to a lonely tiger's cave.
Internal Response	She really wanted a tiger's whisker and decided to try to get one.
Attempt	She put a bowl of food in front of the opening of the cave and she sang soft music.
	The lonely tiger came out and listened to the music.
Consequence	The lady then pulled out one of his whiskers and ran down the hill very quickly.
Reaction	She knew her trick had worked and felt very happy.

ters' interactive plans and beliefs and the social setting in which they occur. He also stresses that since something like a character's intentions may have to be inferred, correct and developed schemata are essential if a story is to be correctly interpreted. Bruce effectively demonstrates this by comparing how two children retold a story they had read about a fox and a rooster. One feature of the more successful comprehender was a correct schema for fox-in-a-fable: clever and deceitful but often not sufficiently clever. "Schemata like this," Bruce observes, "allow a reader to cope with the otherwise unmanageable mass of information found in stories" (1978, p. 465).

What is especially effective about the analyses now being made of stories is the way they pinpoint how intricate a "simple" story really is. Research findings, therefore, may be headed in the direction of raising a question about the traditional use of stories as teaching material for beginners in reading who have major shortcomings not only in their ability to deal with print but also in their schemata. An analysis like that made by Bruce (1978), for instance, causes one to wonder, not why children have trouble comprehending stories but, rather, why they do as well as they do.

According to current theory, some children do well because they have a schema for "story" (that is, an internal representation of "story") that facilitates the encoding, storage, and retrieval of story information. If the elements of a given story do not conform to the schema, or if the schema itself is lacking or is poorly developed, comprehension suffers. Within this framework, then, comprehension problems may stem from flaws in an author's writing as well as from limitations in reading ability.

Unlike some of the other current work with comprehension, much of the research being done with stories uses children of various ages as subjects. This should allow it to shed light not only on the comprehension process but also on developmental differences in the ability to comprehend stories. If subjects are selected from a variety of socioeconomic backgrounds and also include bilingual children, improved understanding of how differences in world knowledge affect comprehension would be a possibility, too. One result might be guidelines for instruction and also for writing and selecting appropriate instructional material.

Comparisons of Spoken and Written Discourse

In addition to analyzing the structure and content of stories, psychologists and linguists have been examining other features of text that may influence comprehensibility. One such effort has concentrated on comparisons of spoken and written discourse (e.g., Rubin 1978; Schallert, Kleiman, and Rubin 1977). Since it is differences between the two that restrict direct contributions of oral language competency to reading, they have been of special interest. Differences that suggest what reading instruction needs to focus on will not be reviewed. As will be seen, some pertain to the medium whereas others pertain to the message.

Spoken language

As both research and experience tell us, spoken language is not always marked by elegantly constructed sentences. Consequently, listeners often have to contend with false starts, abandoned sentences, repetitions, and the like. Why all this may still be easier to understand than a writer's carefully assembled sentences is accounted for by other characteristics of spoken language.

To begin, the syntactic units of speech (e.g., a phrase) are segmented with pauses (Henderson, Goldman-Eisler, and Skarbek 1965). Apparently, listeners depend on these temporal cues, for when they are distorted, comprehension suffers (Huggins 1978). Listeners are also helped by intonation and stress (referred to as *prosodic* features of oral language), and by facial expression, gestures, eye movements, and pointing. All this is to say that speakers work hard to get their message across.

What helps them succeed is the use of words whose meanings are likely to be known to the listener. Allowing for such use is the fact that the speaker's message is often concerned with concrete, everyday objects, with shared experiences, with the immediate environment, and with a time period that is familiar to both speaker and listener. Among other things, these characteristics make it easy for the listener to know what the referents are for such potentially ambiguous words as *now, he, this,* and *here.* Identification of referents is also helped by the prosodic features of oral language. For example, saying "he" with special stress may be all that is needed to specify just who he is.

Written language

Whereas both linguistic and extra-linguistic factors facilitate communication when the medium is spoken discourse, many characteristics of written discourse complicate it. Even though written sentences are usually constructed with care, for instance, their syntax tends to be complex—certainly more complex than that of spoken sentences. In addition, their content is likely to be not only more dense but also less familiar.

While writers are hardly able to confine themselves to familiar content and simple sentences, they can and do assist readers with explanations and illustrations, and, in the area of graphic aids, with paragraph indentation and punctuation. Although marks like commas and periods should help with the segmentation that is required for communication, readers are on their own in using them. It is not surprising, therefore, that studies of beginning readers' problems identify failure to organize text into phrasal units as one deficiency (Levin and Kaplan 1970; Kolers 1975). This failure sometimes continues, for it has been identified as one of the common characteristics of poor comprehenders (Golinkoff 1975–76).

Implications of differences

Even the few differences between spoken and written language that have been mentioned have implications both for the way we think about reading and what we do to teach it.

First of all, they hardly support the contention that reading ability is no more than the ability to comprehend spoken language plus the ability to decode (Fries 1962). They thus raise a question about the related contention that the only new task for beginners in reading is to learn to translate words into their spoken equivalent.

Clearly, one additional task indicated by differences in spoken and written discourse is the need for beginners to learn about punctuation marks and their implication for deriving meaning from text. Equally clear is the need to become acquainted with, and even accustomed to, the styles of written language. What this underscores, of course, is the importance of what parents and teachers have always been urged to do: read to children. In the light of current work with comprehension, reading to children emerges not only as a means for bridging the gap between spoken and written language but also as a way to a) develop a schema for "story," b) expand vocabularies, and c) add to children's knowledge of the world.

In theory, the oral reading done by children themselves should also help bridge the gap between spoken and written language. However, the oral reading that is often heard in classrooms tends to be a halting, word-by-word rendition of a text that manages to obscure both interword relationships and syntactic units (Durkin 1975, 1978–79). Although the children's attention *is* called to features like intonation and stress, it is typically done in a way that turns the oral reading into an elocution exercise in which the overriding concern is the audience. "The erroneous portrayal is undesirable because it could inhibit young readers from arriving at the understanding that reading is not saying something *to* another but is, instead, getting something *from* another" (Adams, Anderson, and Durkin 1978, p. 23).

Readability

If readers *are* to get something from written text, its difficulty must not overtax either their knowledge of the world or their reading skills. The difficulty of text —usually referred to as its readability—is something that reading educators have studied for close to fifty years (e.g., Gray and Leary 1935; Dale and Chall 1948; Spache 1953). One result is readability formulas that use information about variables like vocabulary and sentence length to predict readability (Klare 1974–75). Words of high frequency and short sentences are, according to the formulas, signs of easy material.

Questions about readability formulas

Almost as old as the readability formulas are doubts about their ability to yield accurate information. And questions continue to be raised, spawned now by the new wave of interest in comprehension. The importance schema theory assigns to world knowledge, for instance, makes it natural to wonder about formulas that fail to consider what a reader knows about the content of a passage, and, more specifically, what he or she knows that may or may not allow for necessary inferences.

The need to make inferences enters into other questions about the common use of sentence length as a variable in readability formulas. In this case, the concern stems from recent studies (.e.g., Irwin 1980) in which it has been shown that a short sentence may be more difficult to process than a longer one because it requires a reader to make an inference about unstated information. That this is so can be seen in the following sentences:

> Add boiling water to the dry ingredients.
> After boiling the water, add it to the dry ingredients.

In a slightly different way, the sentences below also show how short sentences may require an inference, thus may be more difficult to process than longer ones.

> When John fell, he hurt his knee.
> John fell. He hurt his knee.

Adaptations of text

What happens to sentences when publishers attempt to reduce the difficulty of material in order to make it suitable for children was one concern of a study recently conducted by several linguists (Davison, Kantor, Hannah, Hermon, Lutz, and Salzillo 1980). Theirs is an important focus, since those responsible for preparing basal readers commonly use "simplified" versions of stories.

While being quick to say that "adaptors do not follow readability formulas slavishly" (p. 5), Davison et al. still concluded that "vocabulary lists (of high frequency words) and restrictions on sentence length and passage length are often given primary importance at the expense of other factors which no one would deny are related to readability" (p. 5). Additional factors identified by the researchers include the structure of sentences, the logical connections between sentences and clauses, and the coherence of topics—all of which, the researchers point out, have no objective measurement.

As current researchers continue their work with text analyses, it becomes increasingly clear that we are only beginning to understand the true nature of readability. Meanwhile, what we ask children to read may be inappropriate because it is either too easy or too difficult.

Anaphoric Devices

One possible source of difficulty that is not taken into account in current readability formulas is what linguists call *anaphoric devices*.

In the context of both spoken and written discourse, *anaphora* (the singular form is *anaphor*) can be thought of as a means for avoiding repetition and, as a result, reducing what is stated. How the two goals may be realized is illustrated below with the help of common kind of anaphor, a pronoun:

> Joel tried to open the door, but it was locked.

While the sentence above does demonstrate the two positive features of anaphora, it is not especially effective in indicating that what a speaker or writer omits must be added—that is, inferred—by the listener or reader. Some of the kinds of inferences that may be required are described in a survey of linguistic research on anaphora (Nash-Webber 1977). A little of what is described will be summarized here with the help of sentences plus comments about the mental exercises involved in comprehending them.

Examples of anaphora

That some anaphoric expressions are *ellipses*[3] is shown in the first illustrative sentence:

> Since nobody volunteered to do the dishes, grandma did ϕ.

Why readers are viewed as being active participants in the job of getting meaning from print is demonstrated by the sentence above, since comprehending it calls for adding to the end "volunteer to do the dishes." Not shown, however, is that many anaphora require a reader to make connections *between* sentences. For example:

> The room was immaculate. Even the walls ϕ had been washed.

With the above, the mental addition of "in the room" completes the message intended by the writer.

How readers may have to add to what is stated in more complex ways is demonstrated in the next three sentences. The first also shows that an adverb may function as an anaphor.

> I've shoveled the snow and scraped the ice. Park *here*.

> On the day that Marie cut her arm, her brother broke his ankle. *It* was just too much for their mother.

> Paul drives a blue Chevrolet. *That's* what I bought, but I wanted a red *one*.

In the first example, a piece of ground that is free of snow and ice must be mentally substituted for *here* if a very brief sentence is to be understood. In the next example, understanding requires that *it* be replaced by the two previously mentioned events. The third example demands even more complex substitutions. In the case of *that*, a blue Chevrolet is the referent but not the one mentioned in the first sentence. With *one*, a Chevrolet is the referent but, again, it is not the blue one in the first sentence but, rather, a different red one.

That readers must be mathematicians —at least when they encounter certain anaphora—is illustrated in two other sentences:

> Joey gave each of his three friends an apple.
> They thanked him for *them*.

> Mr. Brown met his two sons at the ballpark.
> *They* went in immediately to find seats.

The next illustrative sentence reinforces the fact that short sentences are not necessarily "simple"—at least not when an anaphor is present:

> Jeanne did not marry a banker. *He* is an accountant.

In this instance, an inference allows a reader to know that *he* refers not only to an accountant but also to the man who is married to Jeanne.

Two other sentences show the need for other kinds of mental exercises:

> Dad took the boat out to get a fish. We hope to have *it* for dinner.

> His parents live in a condominium. *They* are very suitable for retired people.

In the first example, *it* refers to a specific fish (the one dad might catch), not to the hypothetical one in the first sentence. The plural *they* in the second example helps to show that the referent is not the parent's specific condominium but is, rather, a class of objects known as "condominium."

Probably enough examples of anaphoric devices have now been given, first, to explain what they are and, second, to show some of the manipulative processes that are required for determining intended referents.

Significance of anaphora for linguists and cognitive psychologists

Anaphora are an attractive focus for study to such academicians as linguists and cognitive psychologists for the very reason that processing them may be difficult: their referents are only suggested in a text. That they are not explicitly communicated indicates that language users must themselves supply referents using both what is in the text and what is stored in their head. From this perspective, the study of anaphora can be seen as fitting in well with the current interest in learning how cognitive abilities like inferencing are acquired and, further, how they function.

Significance of anaphora for reading educators

Even the simplified account of anaphora that has been presented should be enough to suggest that they are apt to cause comprehension problems for children. More specifically, ". . . if a reader does not recognize an expression as anaphoric, or if he or she is unable to handle it as the writer intended, then there is no way that he or she can build up a correct model of the text" (Nash–Webber 1977, p. 4).

That instructional programs give anaphora the kind and amount of attention that their frequent appearance and difficulty warrant is doubtful. An examination of basal reader manuals, for instance, has shown that surprisingly little space is assigned to them (Durkin 1980). Whether this reflects too little knowledge about their pervasiveness in our language or, perhaps, insufficient appreciation of their potential difficulty, is not known.

Meanwhile, some research into children's ability to deal with anaphora in written text has been undertaken (e.g., Bormuth, Manning, Carr, and Pearson 1970; Richek 1976–77; Barnitz 1980). To illustrate what is being done and has been found, a few details about Barnitz's study will be described.

Research with anaphora

Barnitz's (1980) research concentrated on children's ability to handle the pronoun *it* in a variety of contexts that were organized under three categories. The first, labeled "Referent Type," divides into contexts in which a) the referent for *it* is a noun or noun phrase, and b) the referent is a clause or sentence. For example:

> John and his father wanted to buy *a large train set* because *it* was on sale.
>
> *Mary rides her skateboard in the busy street*, but Marvin does not believe *it*.

The second category, "Reference Orders," covers contexts in which a) *it* comes after its referent and b) *it* precedes the referent. The two sentences cited above exemplify the first subdivision; the sentence below exemplifies the second.

> Because *it* was on sale, John and his father wanted to buy *a large train set*.

"Referent Distance" is the third category. In this case, the concern is contexts in which a) *it* and its referent are in the same sentence, and b) *it* and its referent occur in separate sentences. All the illustrative sentences that have been given thus far are examples of the first subdivision, whereas the second is illustrated in the sentence below:

> John Boy and Mr. Walton went hunting for the *rattlesnake* in the woods. Mr. Walton was almost bitten by it.

It was hypothesized in the study that, for each category, the following would be easier to process:

> Type: referent is noun or noun phrase
> Order: referent precedes anaphor
> Distance: referent and anaphor are in same sentence

Findings validated the first two hypotheses but failed to confirm the third. According to Barnitz, one possible reason for the lack of confirmation is that, even though the pronoun and its referent were in the same sentence in the experimental materials (brief stories), they did not always occur in the same clause.

Some conclusions about anaphora

Some details of Barnitz's study were reported for the purpose of demonstrating to those who are not researchers that learning about children's ability to process anaphora will not be an easy or a quick process. Yet to know about it is important if instructional programs are to do a better job with an aspect of text structure that may contribute to comprehension problems.

Meanwhile, what is needed right now from linguists is information (synthesized and communicated in a way that is comprehensible to the nonlinguist) about the kinds of anaphora that occur in English.

That would provide guidance not only for researchers but also for those who teach children, who teach teachers, and who prepare instructional materials.

Questions and Comprehension

One more facet of current work with comprehension will be considered; namely, studies aimed at learning whether answering questions about a piece of prose will enhance what a reader learns. In some cases, how readers respond to questions is also used by researchers attempting a) to understand how information is processed; and b) to identify differences between good and poor comprehenders.

Before reviewing a few findings from these studies, let me first identify some of their limitations and flaws. Although negative, beginning this way seems desirable because the tendency to overgeneralize the meaning of research data has been especially widespread for this topic.

Limitations of studies

To begin, existing findings can hardly be applied to everyone since the bulk of subjects asked to respond to questions about text has been adults—often, readily accessible college students. That what is learned from the use of questions with such subjects is directly applicable to children is indeed questionable.

Placing further limitations on the general applicability of the research in this area is the common use of expository discourse. That the effect questions have on what is learned from, let's say, a chapter in a psychology textbook is identical to the effect they would have were a story being read must also be questioned.

The nature of the questions themselves—they are commonly called *adjunct questions*—is still another factor that needs to be taken into account. When researchers report on the kinds of questions they

used—and not all tell what *were* used—the questions are commonly of a type that calls for short answers taken directly and verbatim from the text. While simple recall questions do provide data that are easy to analyze, using only one kind of question places further limitations on the general value of findings.

What also cannot be overlooked in these studies is that subjects usually answer questions right after they have read a passage. While what is recalled immediately is important to know, what readers continue to remember is important, too. Yet, the research done thus far never deals with the kind of delayed recall that is both meaningful and desirable in the real world. (After all, if something is worth remembering, it is important to know what to do to help children remember it for more than a day or a week.) Nor has the research been of a duration that allows a researcher to learn whether the effects of questions change with continued use. As Faw and Waller point out, "Long-term studies are not popular in most areas of psychology, and prose learning is no exception" (1976, p. 713).

Keeping all these limitations in mind, let's turn now to what has been reported about the effects of questions.

Questions: a means for understanding information processing

That readers learn more—that is, recall more—when questions are posed about the content of text than when no questions are used is one consistent finding. Presumably, questions have a positive effect because they prompt a reader to pay closer attention to the content. Such an effect is the reason questions are sometimes discussed in the context of mathemagenic activities. *Mathemagenic* is a term coined by Rothkopf "to refer to attending phenomena" because they "give birth to learning" (Rothkopf 1970, p. 325).

Other researchers (McGaw and Grotelueschen 1972) have reported data suggesting that questions inserted into a passage promote what they call "backward review" and "forward shaping." Still others (Rickards and Hatcher 1977–78) have hypothesized that certain kinds of questions help readers assimilate new material in relation to what is already known. Such a function parallels what Ausubel proposed as being the value of advance organizers (Ausubel 1963).

With the help of computers, several more studies have identified what might be called focusing behavior as a variable that relates both to adjunct questions and to what a reader learns by trying to answer them (Alessi, Anderson, and Goetz 1977; McConkie, Rayner, and Wilson 1973; and Reynolds 1979). Together, findings from these studies suggest that a question increases inspection time and the cognitive effort that a reader gives to what is considered relevant for his or her purpose; in this case, answering the question.

Questions: a means for augmenting what is learned

Researchers concerned with questions as a possible means for improving prose learning have placed them both before and after relevant passages. A frequently quoted study by Rothkopf (1966), whose findings are somewhat typical when subjects are adults, has been summarized by Anderson and Biddle:

> College students read a twenty-page . . . selection . . . on marine biology. Two questions were asked either before or after each two- or three-page passage. The questions were of the completion type requiring a one or two word answer. People who received adjunct questions did substantially better than controls on repeated criterion test items[4] regardless of the posi-

tion of the questions . . . People who answered adjunct questions after, but not before, the relevant passage also showed a small but significant advantage on new test items (1975, p. 91).

Researchers who have conducted studies similar to the one just summarized have especially underscored the effects of question placement on learning. Even though differences in what is learned (based on answers to simple recall questions) are sometimes very small, the following observations have still received widespread attention:

1. Questions posed before a passage is read increase what is learned about content that relates to the questions.
2. Questions placed after the relevant passage increase what is learned about content that relates to them and, in addition, increase what is learned about different content.

The usual explanation for differences in the effects of pre- and post-questions is that the latter do not circumscribe a reader's attention in the way that the former do.

Questions: implications of the research for instructional programs

Even though a large number of topics that have won the attention of current researchers are omitted from consideration in this paper, questions and their effect on learning from text *is* considered because findings on this topic have generated misinterpretations which, if taken seriously by reading educators, are likely to have anything but positive effects on instructional programs. "Don't ask children questions before they read because that will curtail what they'll learn" is a prime example of what I believe to be an unfounded, premature interpretation of the data. Unfortunately, it also is a common one in spite of the limitations of the research.

Not taken into account by such an interpretation are more recent studies in which (a) children are subjects, and (b) more than simple recall questions are asked. In reviewing the more recent work, Wilson reached the conclusion that findings are highly contradictory. "One notes," she writes, "that the majority of studies with public school pupils have found no significant results for question placement" (1980, p. 100).

Since the bulk of the research done thus far does suggest that questions (regardless of their placement) foster increased learning, posing them to children appears to be one device for promoting comprehension. However, since the same research indicates that questions have this positive effect because they encourage readers to give more time and concentrated attention to what is related to answering them, anyone who asks questions should feel obligated to choose only those that deal with important content. As Frase has observed, questions "may lead a reader to stray from, as well as move toward, desirable learning outcomes" (1977, p. 43).

To those of us who teach, then, the research seems to be saying, ". . . if we wish to produce better comprehenders, we must begin by becoming better questioners" (Hansen 1977, p. 65). Some time ago, findings from an extensive, year-long study by reading educators (Wolfe, King, and Huck 1968) made the same point: the level of children's responses closely mirrored the level of the questions posed by teachers.

In Conclusion: Some Personal Reactions

The review of research that was done to write this paper prompted a number of reactions, some of which have already been mentioned. One unstated but overriding reaction is a clearer, more explicit recognition of the amount of inferencing that is required by the nature of what is central to so much of the research: the human mind. A related reaction, therefore, is restlessness since it is so easy for inferences to be wrong.

Stating such reactions here is not done for the purpose of casting doubt on the value of what is being attempted by cognitive psychologists, linguists, and others. Rather, it reflects the conviction that the researchers *and* the consumers of their reports need to be very careful—more careful than some have been—about making distinctions between hypotheses, conjectures, and inferences on the one hand and, on the other, well-established facts.

Related to this is the tendency of current researchers to refer in their reports to certain studies in a way that implies they prove whatever point is being made. However to read the original reports of the studies runs the risk of learning that they may be sufficiently flawed or limited in scope as to prevent them from proving anything.

All this was reminiscent of graduate school years because professors of reading were also quick to cite studies to back up their recommendations. If the topic was reading readiness, for instance, it could be taken for granted that the research reported by Morphett and Washburne (1931) would be referred to as offering proof that a mental age of about 6.5 years is a requirement for success with beginning reading. Not easy to forget is the shock that was experienced when the report itself was read and the limitations of the research were seen. A little of the same feeling developed while reviewing some of the current work with comprehension. To keep us all from ending up in the undersirable position of thinking that we know more than we really do, it would be helpful if writers of research reports used the citation and the interpretation of another writer only when they themselves have read the report and agree with the interpretation. Otherwise, studies may exert influence even when their quality is poor.

Additional observations about the current research brought to mind the analysis of studies of beginning reading carried out by Chall (1967). Although looking at an entirely different body of research, she found what I found: too many isolated studies; too little replication; practically no long-term studies; and too much unquestioning allegiance to one position. Because of the similarity, the words of Santayana kept coming to mind as reports were examined: "Those who cannot remember the past are condemned to repeat its mistakes."

With such a prediction in the background, it was only natural to wonder why there wasn't more evidence in the examined reports of attempts to uncover what others in a different area of specialization—for instance, reading education—might have done previously on the same or a related topic. Although it is only natural for someone like a cognitive psychologist to want to communicate with his or her own colleagues, current work with reading does need to be placed in a setting that recognizes what was done and learned in the past. Otherwise, the special contribution of the new research may not be evident.

The desire to communicate with one's own colleagues has another drawback—at least for those who are interested in moving from research data to possible implications for instruction. It fosters studies that tell us more than we need to know for our purposes. Take the case of anaphora as an example. What linguists know about them has important implications for instructional programs; however, linguists speaking to other linguists are more apt to pursue analyses that are even more technical and minute than to work on syntheses of what is already known. Yet it is the syntheses that could be helpful to reading educators.

What this suggests is the need for more cooperation and communication between academicians and reading educators. I propose that the latter could help not only by participating in research (starting at the planning stage) but also by offering reminders about education, classrooms, and children. Since so much of the current work with comprehension concentrates on increasing learning from prose, let me use that topic to illustrate some reminders.

Education

Education is primarily concerned with *long term* effects; therefore, researchers need to examine the effect over time of whatever type of intervention they choose to study.

Related to this is the fact that *transfer* is at the core of effective education. While it is helpful to know what increases learning from prose, it is necessary to know, too, what children do with a piece of text when they are on their own, both when they have something like questions available and when they do not. This means that researchers who study the effect of adjunct questions or structured overviews should not think that their work is done when positive effects are found. Instead, they should next try to learn whether there is any carry over to independent reading. If none is found, the next question is, What can be done to promote transfer?

Classrooms

With all that has to be done in classrooms, teachers can hardly use everything being recommended for increasing learning from prose. They need answers, therefore, to questions like: Which of the various treatments increase learning the most? Is there a differential effect depending on kind of learning and kind of text?

What needs to be investigated, too, is whether an intervention used by a researcher with subjects will have the same effect when it is used by a teacher with students. This clearly calls for studies that are done in classroom settings.

Children

Anyone who knows about children in classrooms is keenly aware of the great differences among them. Before any research findings can be generalized, therefore, systematic replication of studies using subjects who vary in age, intelligence, reading ability, and socioeconomic background is essential. Persistent efforts to try to learn why differences in findings occur when different subjects are used are also necessary if an understanding of all the data being collected is ever to be achieved.

Notes

1. Trace theory and the conception of brain function as being static were natural for the 1930s since, at the time, the telephone switchboard was used as a model for understanding the mind. With the computer as the current mechanical model, it is equally natural now to find widespread acceptance of schema theory.
2. *Frame* is sometimes used as a synonym for *schema* (Minsky 1975).
3. An ellipsis is an omission of one or more words from a sentence.
4. This refers to the same questions asked after the entire passage was read.

References

Adams, M. J.; Anderson, R. C.; and Durkin, D. "Beginning Reading: Theory and Practice." *Language Arts* 55 (1978): 19–25.

Alessi, S. M.; Anderson, T. H.; and Goetz, E. T. "An Investigation of Lookbacks During Studying." *Discourse Processes* 2 (1979): 197–212.

Anderson, R. C. and Biddle, W. B. "On Asking People Questions about What They Read." In *Psychology of Learning and Motivation* (Vol. 9), edited by G. Bower. New York: Academic Press, 1975.

Anderson, R. C. and McGaw, B. "On the Representation of Meanings of General Terms." *Journal of Experimental Psychology* 101 (1973): 301–306.

Anderson, R. C.; Pichert, J. W.; Goetz, E. T.; Schallert, D. L.; Stevens, K. V.; and Trollip, S. R. "Instantiation of General Terms." *Journal of Verbal Learning and Verbal Behavior* 15 (1976): 667–679.

Anderson, R. C.; Reynolds, R. E.; Schallert, D. L.; and Goetz, E. T. "Frameworks for Comprehending Discourse." *American Educational Research Journal* 14 (1977): 367–381.

Armbruster, B. B. *Learning Principles from Prose: A Cognitive Approach Based on Schema Theory* (Tech. Rep. No. 11). Urbana: University of Illinois, Center for the Study of Reading, July 1976.

Ausubel, D. P. *The Psychology of Meaningful Verbal Learning*. New York: Grune & Stratton, 1963.

Barnitz, J. G. "Syntactic Effects on the Reading Comprehension of Pronoun-Referent Structures by Children in Grades Two, Four and Six." *Reading Research Quarterly* 15 (1980): 268–289.

Barron, R. F. "The Use of Vocabulary as an Advance Organizer." In *Research in Reading in the Content Areas: First Year Report*, edited by H. L. Herber and P. L. Sanders. Syracuse, NY: Syracuse University Reading and Language Arts Center, 1969, 29–39.

Bartlett, F. C. *Remembering*, Cambridge, England: Cambridge University Press, 1932.

Bormuth, J. R.; Manning, J.; Carr, J.; and Pearson, P. D. "Children's Comprehension of Between and Within Sentence Syntactic Structure." *Journal of Educational Psychology* 61 (1970): 349–357.

Bereiter, C. "Discourse, Type, Schema, and Strategy—A View from the Standpoint of Instructional Design." Paper presented at AERA National Convention in Toronto, Canada, 1978.

Bruce, B. *Analysis of Interacting Plans as a Guide to the Understanding of Story Structure* (Tech. Rep. No. 130). Urbana: University of Illinois, Center for the Study of Reading, June 1979.

———. "What Makes a Good Story?" *Language Arts* 55 (1978): 460–466.

Chall, J. S. *Learning to Read: The Great Debate.* New York: McGraw-Hill, 1967.

Dale, E. and Chall, J. S. "A Formula for Predicting Readability." *Educational Research Bulletin* 27 (1948): 11–20.

Davison, A.; Kantor, R. N.; Hannah, J.; Hermon, G.; Lutz, R.; and Salzillo, R. *Limitations of Readability Formulas in Guiding Adaptations of Texts* (Tech. Rep. No. 162). Urbana: University of Illinois, Center for the Study of Reading, March 1980.

Durkin, D. "The Little Things Make a Difference." *Reading Teacher* 28 (1975): 473–477.

———. "Reading Comprehension Instruction in Five Basal Reader Series." Unpublished paper, University of Illinois, 1980.

———. "What Classroom Observations Reveal about Reading Comprehension Instruction." *Reading Research Quarterly* 14 (1978–1979): 481–533.

Earle, R. A. "Use of the Structured Overview in Mathematics Classes." In *Research in Reading in the Content Areas: First Year Report*, edited by H. L. Herber and P. L. Sanders. Syracuse, NY: Syracuse University Reading and Language Arts Centers, 1969.

Faw, H. W. and Waller, T. S. "Mathemagenic Behaviors and Efficiency in Learning from Prose Materials: Review, Critique, and Recommendations." *Review of Educational Research* 46 (1976): 691–720.

Frase, L. T. "Purpose in Reading." In *Cognition, Curriculum, and Comprehension*, edited by J. T. Guthrie. Newark, DE: International Reading Association, 1977.

Fries, C. C. *Linguistics and Reading.* New York: Holt, Rinehart, & Winston, 1962.

Glass, G. V. Editorial. *Review of Educational Research* 40 (1970): 323–325.

Golinkoff, R. M. "A Comparison of Reading Comprehension Processes in Good and Poor Comprehenders." *Reading Research Quarterly* 11 (1975–1976): 623–659.

Goodman, K. S. "Reading: A Psycholinguistic Guessing Game." *Journal of the Reading Specialist* 4 (1967): 123–135.

Gough, P. G. "One Second of Reading." In *Language by Ear and by Eye*, edited by J. F. Kavanagh and I. G. Mattingly. Cambridge, MA: M.I.T. Press, 1972.

Gray, W. S. and Leary, B. E. *What Makes a Book Readable?* Chicago: The University of Chicago Press, 1935.

Guthrie, J. T. "The 1970s Comprehension Research." *Reading Teacher* 33 (1980): 880–882.

Hansen, C. "Comments on Purpose in Reading." In *Cognition, Curriculum and Comprehension*, edited by J. T. Guthrie. Newark, DE: International Reading Association, 1977.

Henderson, A.; Goldman-Eisler, F.; and Skarbek, A. "Sequential Temporal Patterns in Spontaneous Speech." *Language and Speech* 8 (1965): 236–242.

Huggins, A. W. F. "Speech Timing and Intelligibility." In *Attention and Performance*, edited by J. Requin. Hillsdale, NJ: Lawrence Erlbaum Associates, Publisher, 1978.

Irwin, Judith W. "The Effects of Explicitness and Clause Order on the Comprehension of Reversible Causal Relationships." *Reading Research Quarterly* 15 (1980): 477–488.

Klare, G. R. "Assessing Readability." *Reading Research Quarterly* 10 (1974–1975): 62–102.

Kolers, P. A. "Pattern-Analyzing Disability in Poor Readers." *Developmental Psychology* 11 (1975): 282–290.

LaBerge, D. and Samuels, S. J. "Toward a Theory of Automatic Information Processing in Reading." *Cognitive Psychology* 6 (1974): 293–323.

Levin, H. and Kaplan, E. L. "Grammatical Structure and Reading." In *Basic Studies on Reading*, edited by H. Levin and J. P. Williams. New York: Basic Books, 1970.

McConkie, G. W.; Rayner, K.; and Wilson, S. "Experimental Manipulation of Reading Strategies." *Journal of Educational Psychology* 65 (1973): 1–8.

McGaw, B. and Grotelueschen, A. "Direction of the Effects of Questions in Prose Material." *Journal of Educational Psychology* 63 (1972): 580–588.

Minsky, M. "A Framework for Representing Knowledge." In *The Psychology of Computer Vision*, edited by P. H. Winston. New York: McGraw-Hill, 1975.

Morphett, M. V. and Washburne, C. "When Should Children Begin to Read?" *Elementary School Journal* 31 (1931): 496–503.

Nash-Webber, B. L. *Anaphora: A Cross Disciplin-*

ary Survey (Tech. Rep. No. 31). Urbana: University of Illinois, Center for the Study of Reading, April 1977.

Nezworski, T.; Stein, N. L.; and Trabasso, T. *Story Structure Versus Control Effects on Children's Recall and Evaluative Inferences* (Tech. Rep. No. 129). Urbana: University of Illinois, Center for the Study of Reading, June 1979.

Reynolds, R. E. "The Effect of Attention on the Learning and Recall of Important Text Elements." Unpublished doctoral dissertation, University of Illinois, 1979.

Richek, M. A. "Reading Comprehension of Anaphoric Forms in Varying Linguistic Contexts." *Reading Research Quarterly* 12 (1977): 145–165.

Rickards, J. P. and Hatcher, C. W. "Interspersed Meaningful Learning Questions as Semantic Cues for Poor Comprehenders." *Reading Research Quarterly* 13 (1977–1978): 538–553.

Rothkopf, E. Z. "The Concept of Mathemagenic Activities." *Review of Educational Research* 40 (1970): 325–336.

———. "Learning from Written Instructive Materials: An Exploration of the Control of Inspection Behavior by Test-like Events." *American Educational Research Journal* 3 (1966): 241–249.

———. "Some Theoretical and Experimental Approaches for Problems in Written Instruction." In *Learning and the Educational Process*, edited by J. D. Krumboltz. Chicago: Rand McNally, 1965.

Rubin, A. D. *A Theoretical Taxonomy of the Differences between Oral and Written Language* (Tech. Rep. No. 35). Urbana: University of Illinois, Center for the Study of Reading, April 1978.

Rumelhart, D. E. *Toward an Interactive Model of Reading* (CHIP Rep. No. 56). San Diego: University of California, Center for Human Information Processing, March 1976.

Schallert, D. L.; Kleiman, G. M.; and Rubin, A. D. *Analyses of Differences Between Written and Oral Language* (Tech. Rep. No. 29). Urbana: University of Illinois, Center for the Study of Reading, April 1977.

Schank, R. and Abelson, R. *Scripts, Plans, Goals, and Understanding*. Hillsdale, NJ: Erlbaum, 1977.

Smith, F. *Understanding Reading*. New York: Holt, Rinehart, & Winston, 1971.

Spache, G. "A New Readability Formula for Primary-grade Reading Materials." *Elementary School Journal* 53 (1953): 410–413.

Stauffer, R. G. "Productive Reading-Thinking at the First Grade Level." *Reading Teacher* 13 (1960): 183–187.

———. *Teaching Reading as a Thinking Process*. New York: Harper & Row, 1969.

Stein, N. L. and Glenn, C. G. "An Analysis of Story Comprehension in Elementary School Children." In *New Directions in Discourse Processing* (Vol. 2), edited by R. R. Freedle. Hillsdale, NJ: Erlbaum, 1979.

Strange, M. "Instructional Implications of a Conceptual Theory of Reading Comprehension." *Reading Teacher* 33 (1980): 391–397.

Wilson, M. M. "The Effects of Question Types in Varying Placements on the Reading Comprehension of Upper Elementary Students." *Reading Psychology* 1 (1980): 93–102.

Wolfe, W.; King, M. L.; and Huck, C. S. "Teaching Critical Reading to Elementary School Children." *Reading Research Quarterly* 3 (1968): 435–498.

50. Instructional Implications of a Conceptual Theory of Reading Comprehension

Michael Strange

This article represents a synthesis of ideas gathered from many sources. I am no longer sure as to the origin of all of them, but I have tried to give due credit when I can. The basic premise is that we are in need of order when it comes to teaching children to comprehend what they read. My particular orientation suggests that we need a theory of reading comprehension from which to teach.

There is in teaching an attempt to minimize the theoretical and maximize the practical. I am convinced that this is counterproductive, and that one of the problems in education is that we have too few useful theories. As Pearson and Johnson (1978) state: "Nothing is more practical than a good theory."

Prior to becoming convinced of the usefulness of a theory it is necessary to understand that a theory is not a fact or a law but an attempt to explain something that takes into account what we think we know. A theory is dynamic, it will change as we learn more, and one attempt will give way to later attempts that explain better. Even though a theory may not completely explain, it is still useful, since it provides a structure with which to observe and evaluate what occurs. A theory also allows us to make predictions that something should happen in a particular way.

In teaching, a theory becomes useful when it allows us to interpret what children do as well as make judgments concerning appropriate instruction that children may need. In addition, a theory becomes useful when it allows us to plan meaningful instructional episodes and provide appropriate practice activities.

Comprehension Instruction

In a recent paper (Durkin 1978), the state of instruction in reading comprehension is characterized as no instruction. Durkin spent considerable time observing reading instruction in elementary classrooms to determine what is actually done in the name of teaching comprehension. What she found is that less than 1% of the time is spent in actual instruction. Much greater amounts of time are spent in such activities as assessing comprehension, giving assignments, and helping with assignments.

When I speak of much greater amounts of time, I am not speaking of mere statistically significant differences but massive differences. For example, the ratio of time spent on assessment and time spent on instruction was greater than 25 to 1.

Some might argue justifiably that assessing comprehension (the asking of questions relevant to what has been read) is a necessary phase of instruction. If this is granted and these two categories combined, they still account for less than 20% of the time. And what of the questions we are asking? Guszak (1967) found that the vast majority of teacher questions call for the recall of details. In almost any taxonomy of thinking, these types of questions

From Michael Strange, Instructional implications of a conceptual theory of reading comprehension. *The Reading Teacher*, January 1980, *33*, 391–397. Reprinted by permission of Michael Strange and the International Reading Association.

typically call for low level thinking. They are essentially memory tasks.

If we are to judge by what we see being done to improve reading comprehension, we must conclude that we know very little about the process. We seem tied to a skill hierarchy notion that promotes comfort in the seeming precision of the skills and the objectives that come with them. We treat the skills as discrete behaviors with little or no attempt to help children generalize these skills to new situations. We also seem willing to accept that children, who are capable of sitting down in front of a television set and understanding the complex plot and relationships in *Wonder Woman*, are unable to read and understand the simple plot and relationships in the narrative of a romp involving two children and their dog.

This Particular Theory

There is a continuing debate among reading experts about whether the reading process is primarily top down or bottom up. Those who adhere to a top down position believe that the reader brings more information to the page than the page brings to the reader. In other words, when someone is reading s/he has a good deal of prior knowledge about the world and this prior knowledge is used to make good guesses about the nature (relationships, episodes, characters, etc.) of the text. The reader proceeds to confirm or modify the hypotheses as well as to appreciate the nuances that a particular author might bring to the text.

Those experts who adhere to a bottom up position believe that the page brings more information to the reader than the reader brings to the page. The reader begins reading with little information about the text and the print is sequentially processed until the message is completely understood. The reader continues to gather more information from the page.

These positions are also referred to as concept driven (top down) and text driven (bottom up).

Rystrom (1977) provides a number of logically derived reasons why neither position can provide a total description. If reading were exclusively top down, it would be highly unlikely that any two people would read the same text and arrive at the same general conclusion. It is also unlikely that we would learn anything new from texts if we relied solely on our prior knowledge. For similar reasons Rystrom concludes that reading can not be exclusively bottom up. If it were, there would be no disagreement about the meaning of a text. In addition, there would be no possibility of personal interpretations based on differences such as preconception, age, experience, occupation, etc.

He proposes an alternative conceptualization labeled matrixing that has come to be known as an interactive model after the work of Rumelhart (1976). In an interactive model, the reading process is described neither as exclusively top down nor bottom up, but rather involves both the reader and text working in concert to reveal a meaning.

The process is begun when the reader begins attending to the print. As soon as possible, the reader begins using prior knowledge to begin making decisions about the print. At one level, these decisions are primarily intraword decisions which we might call decoding, and at another level, these are interword decisions which are the beginnings of comprehension.

The interword decisions affect the intraword decisions by predicting which words are likely and which letters might be expected. The intraword decisions affect the interword decisions by helping to confirm or reject certain hypotheses about the meaning as well as providing information for new interword hypotheses. Both work together to gather information for hypotheses about the overall meaning. Other sources of information that may have nothing to do with the print are also being used to give the passage some unique meaning for the particular reader.

Rystrom (1977) provides the following example to illustrate the process. The reader sees the sentence "The Indian rode off into the sunset." The reader thinks: (1) I once drove into a sunset. (2) I was driving toward California. (3) California is west. (4) I was driving west. (5) The Indian must be riding west.

Statement 5 is clearly an inference that we would accept as evidence that the reader understood the sentence. Statements 2, 3, and 4 have no representation in the text, but are certainly useful in getting the meaning. In addition, questions like the following are also answerable. (1) What time of day was it? (2) What was the mood? The answer to question 1 is inferred in much the same way as statement 5, and question 2 is answerable depending on the reader's prior experiences with Indians, solitary horsemen, riding off and sunsets.

When we begin to think about comprehension as an interactive process, it becomes necessary to understand an additional concept. Recently, there has been a good deal of interesting work done in the area of reading comprehension under the label of schema theory (Rumelhart 1976; Anderson, Spiro and Anderson 1977; Adams and Collins 1977). Schema theory seeks to explain how new information acquired while reading is meshed with old information already in our heads. It is helpful to think of a schema (singular of schemata) as a concept, although a schema is meant to be more inclusive than a concept.

As a person reads, certain elements in the text trigger a certain schema in our head. When we read the sentence about the Indian, all our previous knowledge about Indians becomes useful in understanding this text. We have knowledge about the dress of Indians, culture of Indians, white men and Indians, Indian social structure, etc., that is cued for use by the word Indian in the text. We don't know how much of this previous knowledge is necessary for understanding this text until we read further. As we read the word *rode* we cue our knowledge about transportation. People ride on trains, planes, horses, etc. We also have experience about Indians and transportation and so predict that this Indian was riding on a horse. It is certainly possible that this Indian was riding on something else, but given our prior knowledge, the most probable interpretation is riding on a horse. Similar things happen for sunset and the interaction of Indians, transportation, and sunset.

Schemata are not static however, and can be changed in a number of ways. Say that we add to our sentence "on a motorcycle." Motorcycles are part of our transportation schema, but not of the Indian and transportation schemata called up by this sentence. There is nothing in our Indian schema, however, that actually prohibits riding on motorcycles, so we change our schema for this sentence, deleting horse and accepting motorcycle. Riding motorcycles is also added to our Indian schema, making this happenstance a slightly more probable interpretation the next time we read about Indians and transportation.

Schemata are not limited to objects. We also have schemata for episodes (purchasing something), roles (father), events (parades), etc. The basic principle involved regarding comprehension and schema theory revolves around the idea that we comprehend print in terms of existing knowledge and that this knowledge is changed at the point of contact between what we know and what is new. It also suggests that the most important skill is inferencing and that recall is important only as it assists a reader in making an inference. This is an important point when we consider the findings of Durkin (1978) and Guszak (1967) mentioned earlier.

Applications of the Theory

One of the uses of a theory is to allow us to examine what we know and observe in an effort to understand phenomena more completely. It also allows users of the theory to make predictions. The following applications of an interactive model and schema theory do not require major changes in what we do. It is not, however, simply a case of old wine in new bottles, but rather, finer wines in old bottles and a little new wine, too.

Use number 1: The importance of prereading instruction

We are currently urged to spend time prior to reading to motivate and to provide purposes for reading for children. If you accept the schema point of view, prereading instruction should also focus on alerting children to the relevant schemata for the story, assuring that the schemata are sophisticated enough to understand the story, and finally, helping children make predictions about how the schemata will interact in the story they are about to read.

Use number 2: vocabulary instruction

Schema theory suggests that vocabulary instruction should be given greater emphasis than it currently is. If words are labels for schemata, then the more words a child has, the more precise s/he can become in selecting appropriate schemata. If a child thinks that all equines are labeled horses s/he might have some difficulty with *Morgan, Clydesdale, Zebra, Appaloosa*. In addition, a compound word like *Zebrawood* would be beyond comprehension.

The theory also predicts that it is more effective and efficient to learn a new word

through synonyms and antonyms than going immediately to a dictionary.

Use number 3: analysis of question and answer relationships

Questioning taxonomies suggest that certain questions elicit certain types of thinking. In reading, we typically break questions down into literal and inferential ones. Pearson (1978) provides a refinement of these categories by proposing a taxonomy for analyzing question/answer relationships.

A question and answer are *textually explicit* when both are derived from the text and the relationship between them is explicitly cued by the text. Consider the following example of a textually explicit question/answer relationship provided by Pearson (1978):

> Up at Basset Lake, a man was ice fishing using minnows for bait. Two pet crows helped him fish. They pulled on the lines with their beaks. And they put their feet on the line to keep it from slipping into the hole. Because the crows were smart, they got a meal. So did the clever fisherman.
>
> Q: Why did the crows get a free meal?
> A: Because the crows were smart.

A question/answer relationship is considered *textually implicit* if both question and answer are derived from the text, but there is no expressed grammatical cue tying the question to the answer. If the student provided an answer like the following, the question/answer relationship would be textually implicit.

> A: Because the crows helped him fish.

There is yet a third question/answer relationship that Pearson calls scriptally implicit that I will call *schema implicit* for the sake of consistency. A question and answer share a schema implicit relationship whenever a plausible nontextual response is given to a question derived from the text. Consider the following response to our question about the crows.

A: Because they proved their worth to mankind.

Textually explicit question/answer relationships require literal recall. Textually implicit question/answer relationships require text-to-text inferences. Schema implicit question/answer relationships require text-to-schema inference. Pearson likens these to reading the lines, reading between the lines, and reading beyond the lines.

Use number 4: importance of recall and details

Both Durkin (1978) and Guszak (1967) remark that teachers spend large amounts of time on recall and noting details. However, memory tasks and noting details are helpful only to the extent that they focus on information useful in changing or integrating existing schemata. In most cases this requires some type of inference. It would be appropriate to say that any inference question is by definition more important than any recall or detail question, and that more time should be spent on helping children make inferences then we now spend.

Use number 5: comparing stories

If we have schemata for phenomena that we have experienced, it seems logical that we have schemata for stories. There is evidence that children do have such schemata (Baker and Stein 1978) and research involving story grammars holds promise for determining their requirements.

The basic premise is that for simple stories there is a generalizable structure (grammar) that is useful in comprehending the stories. Some story grammars are

extremely elaborate and complex and others are less so.

One of the less complicated versions is that proposed by Stein and Glenn (1978). Their grammar holds that a story is composed of the setting and one or a series of episodes. The setting introduces the main character and provides a context for the story. Each episode contains a goal for the episode, motivation for attaining the goal, attempt(s) to reach the goal, the consequence of the attempt(s), and a reaction to the consequence.

Significantly, story grammars appear to be culture specific, and readers' comprehension is higher when they are dealing with stories patterned on a schema from their own culture (Kintsch and Greene 1978).

What the research on story grammars and the interactive model suggests is that a story should not be dealt with as a discrete experience. Learners should be helped to compare characters, events, goals, etc., in one story to those in another.

Use number 6: modeling/simulating

The interactive model of reading can be characterized as a dialogue between our schema and the text. This dialogue is typically carried out silently, but it need not be. After a section of a story has been read, teachers could model this dialogue using two simple strategies, recall/compare (you know what that reminds me of?) and predict/justify (I think that such and such will happen because . . .). Observing this simulation of the comprehension process, children can see mature comprehension as a continuous process, not as a reaction to questions.

Use number 7: understanding miscomprehension

Perhaps the most useful application of a schema and interactive view of reading comprehension is the analysis of miscomprehension. [I choose this term for the same reason Goodman (1965) chose the term "miscue" for inexact oral responses to print. Looking at a child's response as only right or wrong is overly restrictive and ignores what the child may be doing appropriately.]

What are some possible explanations for the responses that we observe when discussing a story with children?

1. No existing schema: A very real possibility, especially with young children, is that they lack certain critical schemata with which to understand a story. This is also a possibility when a story assumes a particular cultural background and the readers' cultural background is different.

2. Naive schema: In some cases readers may have the beginnings of appropriate schemata, but they are not sufficiently developed to allow for the events in a story. Imagine, for example, a child whose schema for restaurant only includes fast food restaurants reading about the misadventures of a waiter at a four-star French restaurant.

3. No new information: Some children will have well developed schemata, and a particular story may provide nothing that is not already accounted for by the child's schema. This is often the case when reading about very common experiences. The details that make up the experience are lost since they are predictable and well understood.

4. Poor story: In some children's stories the appropriate schemata are not sufficiently cued to assist the child in integrating them in order to achieve full understanding. In basal readers, where the authors work within the constraints of a controlled vocabulary and limited word analysis skills, it is not always possible to develop the necessary schemata fully.

5. Many schemata appropriate: Many stories allow the reader to bring different schemata to bear on the episodes involved. This results in different interpretations for the same events. In certain cases, each of these interpretations is appropriate if we understand the prior experiences of the reader. Different interpretations of the Bible are good examples of this possibility.

6. Schema intrusion: Pearson (1978) calls this scriptal intrusion, but again, for the sake of consistency, I will call it schema intrusion. This occurs when the response to a question comes from the child's head and no plausible line of reasoning connects it to the story. The response is merely wrong.

7. Textual intrusion: Pearson suggests that this is another type of response that can be considered wrong. In this case, a child seems to overrespond to one or more words in the text. The child's response is based on the text, but no plausible line of reasoning connects the question and the response.

The usefulness of this theory lies in helping teachers to examine what children do and to plan instruction which will help the children acquire appropriate schemata for comprehending the reading materials they encounter.

References

Adams, Marilyn and Allen Collins. *A Schema-Theoretic View of Reading*. Center for the Study of Reading, Technical Report No. 32, University of Illinois at Urbana-Champaign, 1977.

Anderson, Richard, Rand Spiro, and Mark Anderson. *Schemata as Scaffolding for the Representation of Information in Connected Discourse*. Center for the Study of Reading, Technical Report No. 24, University of Illinois at Urbana-Champaign, 1977.

Baker, Linda and Nancy Stein. *The Development of Prose Comprehension Skills*. Center for the Study of Reading, Technical Report No. 102, University of Illinois at Urbana-Champaign, 1978.

Durkin, Dolores. *What Classroom Observations Reveal about Reading Instruction*. Center for the Study of Reading, Technical Report No. 106, University of Illinois at Urbana-Champaign, 1978.

Goodman, Kenneth. "A Linguistic Study of Cues and Miscues in Reading." *Elementary English*, vol. 42, no. 6 (October 1965), pp. 639–43.

Guszak, Frank. "Teacher Questioning and Reading." *The Reading Teacher*, vol. 21, no. 3 (December 1967), pp. 227–34.

Kintsch, Walter and Edith Greene. "The Role of Culture-Specific Schemata in the Comprehension and Recall of Stories." *Discourse Processes*, vol. 1, no. 1 (March 1978), pp. 1–13.

Pearson, P. David. The Text and Task in Reading Comprehension. Paper presented at the International Reading Association Convention, Houston, Texas, May 1978.

Pearson, P. David and Dale Johnson. *Teaching Reading Comprehension*. New York, N.Y.: Holt, Rinehart and Winston, 1978.

Rumelhart, David. *Schemata: The Building Blocks of Cognition*. Center for Human Information Processing. Technical Report No. 79, University of California, San Diego, 1978.

Rumelhart, David. *Toward an interactive Model of Reading*. Center for Human Information Processing. Technical Report No. 56, University of California, San Diego, 1976.

Rystrom, Richard. "Reflections of Meaning." *Journal of Reading Behavior*, vol. 9, no. 2 (Summer 1977), pp. 193–200.

Stein, Nancy and C. G. Glenn. "An Analysis of Story Comprehension in Elementary School Children." *Discourse Processing: Multidisciplinary Perspectives*, R. Freedle (Ed.), Hillsdale, N.J.: Ablex, Inc., 1978.

51. Asking Questions about Stories

P. David Pearson

Questions have a long tradition in teaching reading. Beginning with the Directed Reading Lesson Plan suggested by William S. Gray in the Twenties, their presence in the daily lives of students and teachers has been well documented in both student textbooks and teachers' manuals.

Outside the context of a reading lesson, there is something a bit peculiar about a teacher asking students questions about stories that the students know the teacher *has already read*: In most everyday situations, people ask other people questions about stories they *have not yet read*. However, the question-answer session accompanying reading lessons (and lessons for reading content area textbooks) has become such an integral part of life in classrooms that it has assumed a sense of reality and "naturalness" within that context. It is likely that this naturalness is reinforced when students and teachers encounter similar sorts of questions on teacher-made and standardized tests. Students and teachers alike seem to accept it as a fact of life.

Given the importance of questions in classroom life, teachers have an obligation to their students to ask useful questions— questions that increase the likelihood that students will:

1. focus their attention on important aspects of the text
2. relate information in a text to the most appropriate set of background experiences
3. create a coherent framework for understanding and remembering the text, or

4. allow students to practice cognitive skills that they will ultimately be able to use on their own

Teachers must avoid questions that misdirect students. Such questions can focus students' attention on trivial aspects of the text, direct them to an inappropriate set of background experiences, lead them to a fragmented view of a text, or leave them dependent upon a teacher for skill application. In other words, misleading questions nurture precisely the opposite behaviors from questions of high quality.

The purpose of this paper is to present a set of guidelines that teachers can use to make sure that they are asking useful questions rather than misleading or trivial questions as they guide their students to an understanding of stories and informational articles they read. While many of these guidelines apply to all texts, some apply especially to stories. And indeed the focus in this paper is on using these techniques with stories rather than informational texts.

Questions should focus student attention on appropriate background experiences. It is commonplace these days to regard reading comprehension as a process of relating the new (new ideas in a text) to the known (background experiences that readers carry around in their heads). In fact much recent research has suggested that background knowledge is a major, if not *the* major, determinant of text comprehension. Hence the kind of discussion that precedes a story or an article can be critical in helping students understand and remember key elements of that text.

From P. David Pearson, *Asking questions about stories*. Ginn Occasional Papers, No. 15. Columbus, Ohio: Ginn and Co., 1982. Reprinted with permission of the author and Ginn and Co.

There is a particular line of pre-reading questions that has proved quite successful, when used with stories, in promoting both comprehension of the literal meanings stated by a text as well as comprehension of ideas only implied by a text (Hansen & Pearson, 1980). This questioning strategy involves eliciting statements from students about what they would do in a particular circumstance (the circumstance is chosen to correspond closely to one that the story's main character or protagonist will encounter). Then the teacher tells the students that the character is faced with a similar situation and asks them to predict what he or she will do (older students write down their predictions). Finally, after reading the story, the students discuss the protagonist's actions along with their predictions and their assessment of what they themselves would have done.

The remarkable result of this technique is that students not only exhibit better comprehension of the key ideas discussed and predicted; they also exhibit better comprehension of other, sometimes unrelated, text elements and implied ideas. The technique seems to elicit *deeper* processing of the text as a whole. We believe that this deeper processing occurs because of the increased motivation that comes from having a more personal "stake" in reading. Students seem to want to compare their hypothesized behavior with the protagonist's actions.

The technique is not difficult to implement. It involves these steps:

1. Read the selection.
2. Select 3 or 4 key points: the moral of the story, a key goal of the protagonist, compelling motivation, or crucial action.
3. Establish a set of "What if . . ." questions, for example,
   a. Have you ever found yourself in a situation where you didn't know what your parents would want you to do?

What did you do? What happened?
   b. What would you do if you found yourself alone in the middle of a forest fire and did not know your way out of the woods?
4. Establish a set of comparable predictions for the protagonist(s)
   a. William, the hero of our story, doesn't tell his parents the whole truth. What do you think will happen to him?
   b. Henrietta, the main character in our story, finds herself alone in the middle of a forest fire. What do you think she will do to protect herself or get out of the fire?
5. Have the students read the text or text segment.
6. Have students compare their own hypothesized behaviors, their predictions, and the actual actions of the character(s).
7. Check out their comprehension of other key elements of the story.

We have tried out a similar technique with expository writing. But it differs in that students are asked what they expect to find in the article rather than what they think the characters will do. For example, before reading a selection about pollution, a teacher might ask,

What do you know about pollution? What kinds are there? How does the air or the water get polluted? What can we do to reduce or eliminate pollution?

With a sort of collective group "map" about the topic outlined on the chalkboard, the teacher can then ask students to predict what aspects of their map will be addressed in the article. After reading the article, the students' map of their predictions and the content of the article can be compared, using both specific and general comprehension questions.

Whether a selection is expository or narrative, the essential tasks of the teacher are (1) to select key ideas from the selection for the hypothesis and prediction activities and (2) develop questions that tap into the relevant areas of students' background knowledge.

We have demonstrated the power of these techniques in several studies. It works for both exposition and narrative and it is particularly effective at increasing levels of inferential comprehension. The latter finding should not be surprising since inferential comprehension, by definition, requires readers to establish connections between text ideas and ideas that can only come from readers' stores of background knowledge.

Questions should focus student attention on important aspects of the text. Imagine yourself as a subject in the following experiment. You are faced with a 27-page segment from Rachel Carson's *The Silent Spring*. After each page you have to answer a question dealing with a key date in the text or, alternatively, a key name. Page after page this procedure is repeated. All the time you are reading the text (which comes up paragraph by paragraph on a computer screen), the experimenter is measuring the amount of reading time you devote to each text segment (sentence and/or paragraph). A curious thing happens. Without any cue from the experimenter, you unconsciously start spending more time reading text segments containing key dates (or alternatively key names). In other words, you learn what is expected of you (the pattern of questions sinks in) and you allocate your attention accordingly!

Now think about the implication that such a repeated pattern of questions has for students. Students who are constantly bombarded by a barrage of low level detail questions (What color blouse was Susan wearing? Which wagon was Tom riding in? Who played the trombone?) soon learn that, in future encounters with text, they should attend to low level details. The

danger, of course, is that such details may not be important to the central thread of a story or the theme of an expository text. Little wonder, then, that students so exposed have trouble summarizing the selection or drawing inferences to prior knowledge; they have *learned* to avoid such strategies.

This is not to say that detail questions have no place in a reading program; to the contrary, details are crucial to building a coherent representation of the text. The point, which is elaborated in the next section, is that details are important to the degree that they fill in important slots in the overall structure of a story or an exposition. The color of Susan's blouse is important if it is a clue to "whodunit" in a mystery; the particular wagon Tom rode in is important if we know that the red, but not blue, one had a bad wheel; the identity of the trombone player is crucial if we know that the victim was hit over the head by a musical instrument. In other contexts, however, each of these facts might be trivial.

Questions should create a coherent framework for understanding and remembering the text. The solution to the problem of "trivial detail" questions could take two forms: Don't ask any detail questions, or ask only for important details. Both forms of the solution have merit. And thanks to the work of Isabel Beck and her colleagues at the University of Pittsburgh, we have a single strategy for accomplishing both (Beck, McKeown, McCaslin, & Burkes, 1979).

Beck and her associates suggest that teacher questions for narratives should be developed from a "story map" created for each narrative students encounter.

A story map is an idea taken from recent work by psychologists aimed at characterizing the general structure of children's narratives; in other words, a story map defines what most stories have in *common*. A story map consists of the following key elements of a story: the setting (including place, time and major characters), the problem (most stories represent characters' attempts to solve problems), the protagonist's goal (usually to alleviate the problem), the set of attempts to achieve the goal (usually the major events in the story), and the resolution (usually achieving the goal and alleviating the problem). Another way to think of a story map is that it would look like a first-rate summary of the setting and a plot of a narrative.

Beck and her associates examined the guided reading and follow-up discussion questions found in several popular basals. They concluded that for many stories, the *sets* of questions appear to have no guiding rationale. The questions are in error in two ways. Quite often they are too localized, too page or even too sentence specific. Hence, the questions bear no relationship to one another; they do not form a *line* of questions. Often, also, while questions may be directed toward prior experience of the students, they may not tap into those experiences that will aid student's understanding of the story in question. In short, Beck et al. found that the questions for guiding and discussing selections were likely to lead to a less than coherent and integrated understanding of the selection.

In their stead Beck et al. recommend that teachers and basal reading publishers should use story maps to guide their generation of questions for narratives.

The task is not as difficult as it may seem. Just begin with a setting question,

(1) Where and when did the story occur?

Then ask, Is that information important to the story's understanding? If so, leave the question in (or create alternative questions for it). If not, omit it. Then ask a protagonist question.

(2) Who is the hero or heroine (or heroes or heroines)?

Then ask a problem question, which might take a variety of forms,

(3) What is Susan's problem?
(4) What did Susan need?
(5) Why is Susan in trouble?

Usually, the problem question will encompass the goal question (because the goal is usually to alleviate the problem). If not, form a separate question, such as,

(6) What does Susan need to do?

Next, generate a set of questions that will get students from the problem/goal to its ultimate resolution. This set of questions will tie together the major "events" of the story. Do not be misled into believing that these questions tap mere "sequence." Granted they occur in sequence, but a "causal chain" better characterizes the relations among events. Events lead, often inevitably, toward one another; they do not simply precede and follow one another. This point is important because it has critical implications for the kinds of questions that are asked to elicit this part of the story map.

"Why" . . . questions, "What happened because" . . . questions, and "What did X have to do before he could do Y" . . . questions are as likely, if not more likely, to comprise this component of the story map questions as are "What happened next . . ., What happened before" . . ., and "What happened after" . . . questions. One other point: Not all the answers to these questions will be found in the text. This is true because often authors omit important character motives (a part of the causal chain) on the grounds that readers will be able to infer them easily. However, answers will always come *either* from the text *or* the readers' prior knowledge about topics and stories of the type represented by the text. Hence a set of event eliciting questions might include,

(7) What was the first thing Susan tried to do to get rid of her tooth?

Fish Story
Robert Tallon

"I've got to get out of here!" Little Fish said. "I'm tired of swimming in the same water. I want a bigger pond."

Big Cat, walking by, heard him. "May I be of help?" Big Cat asked.

"I want to see the world," Little Fish said.

"The world is beautiful up here, really beautiful," Big Cat said. "The flowers and the trees are beautiful. So is the ocean just over the hill."

"Ocean! Old Fish told me about the ocean," Little Fish said. "Can you take me there?"

"Sure," said Big Cat. "First, I'll have to go home and get a bag to carry you in."

"Please hurry back," Little Fish said.

Big Cat came back with a big bag. He put it into the water. Little Fish swam inside.

"Thank you," Little Fish said.

"I'm glad to help a friend," Big Cat said. He licked his lips.

Big Cat ran through the woods.

"How beautiful! Is that a flower?" Little Fish asked.

"It's a flower," Big Cat growled.

"Could we stop?" Little Fish asked.

"No," Big Cat yelled.

"Where is the ocean?" Little Fish asked.

"Just over the hill," Big Cat said. "Now, quiet! You're asking too many questions."

"I'm sorry," Little Fish said. "It's so new to me."

Big Cat ran over the hill and into a house. Little Fish looked around at the pots and pans on the walls. "Is this the ocean?" he asked.

"No. It's my kitchen," Big Cat said. "I'm going to cook you!"

Little Fish shook. "Why me?" he asked.

Big Cat sang to himself as he got a pan ready. "Didn't Old Fish ever tell you about Cats and Fishes?" he asked.

"Are you a Cat?" Little Fish asked.

"Yes, Big Cat's the name. And I'm going to eat you."

"But I'm all bones," Little Fish cried.

"Quiet! I'm trying to read this cookbook," Big Cat said. "I'm starved!"

"Big Cat, wait, please!" Little Fish yelled. "Just look at me. I'm all bones. I'd be just a snack for you. But I know a Big Fish. He's so big, he'd fill this kitchen."

Big Cat looked at Little Fish. "Just where is this big fish?" he asked.

"Back at the pond. He's big enough to last you a month," Little Fish said. "If you take me back, I'll get him for you."

"How?" Big Cat asked.

"Have you got some ketchup?" Little Fish asked.

"What if I do?" Big Cat answered.

"He just loves ketchup. Just take me back," Little Fish said. "Bring a string and some ketchup. Leave the rest to me."

Big Cat took up the bag with Little Fish. He took another bag with the ketchup and raced back to the pond. He put Little Fish into the pond. Then he let down the string with the ketchup.

Little Fish swam out of the bag. "How wonderful to be back in my beautiful pond," he thought. He swam around and around.

Big Cat jiggled the string. "Hurry up, Little Fish. Get your friend. I'm starved!" he said.

Little Fish grabbed the string and swam down with it. "OK, Big Cat," Little Fish called. "Pull it up!"

Big Cat pulled on the string. He pulled and pulled—and landed his catch. It was an old bike!

"You tricked me!" Big Cat yelled. He jumped up and down.

Little Fish laughed as he swam to the center of the pond. "It was just a Fish Story," he sang out. "It was just a Fish Story for a Big Cat!"

Reprinted from The Ginn Reading Program, Level 8, Unit 2, by permission of Ginn and Company

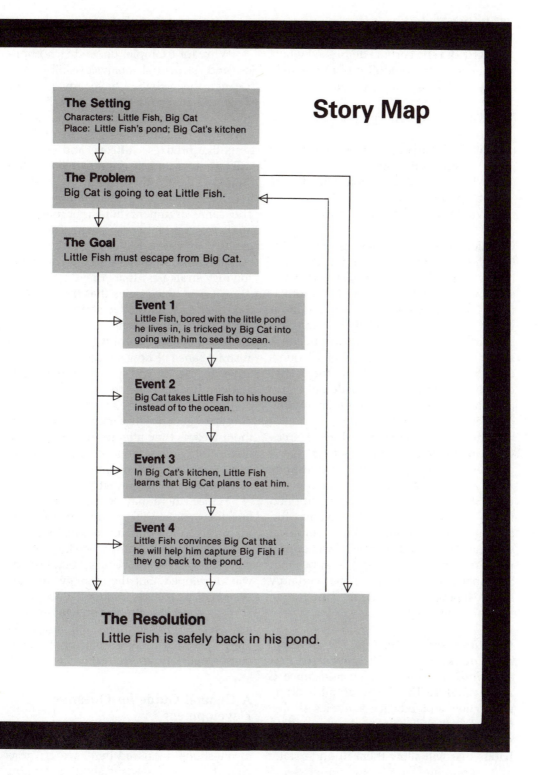

The Setting
Characters: Little Fish, Big Cat
Place: Little Fish's pond; Big Cat's kitchen

Story Map

The Problem
Big Cat is going to eat Little Fish.

The Goal
Little Fish must escape from Big Cat.

Event 1
Little Fish, bored with the little pond he lives in, is tricked by Big Cat into going with him to see the ocean.

Event 2
Big Cat takes Little Fish to his house instead of to the ocean.

Event 3
In Big Cat's kitchen, Little Fish learns that Big Cat plans to eat him.

Event 4
Little Fish convinces Big Cat that he will help him capture Big Fish if they go back to the pond.

The Resolution
Little Fish is safely back in his pond.

(8) What did she do when that wouldn't work?

(9) Why did she become depressed when her mother wouldn't pull the tooth?

(10) Why did her friend Gwen feel sorry for Susan?

(11) Why did Gwen suggest they play soccer?

(12) What happened when Susan got involved in the game?

(13) What happened when she forgot about her tooth?

(14) What lesson did Susan learn?

Questions (13) and (14) also get at resolution and story moral. Thus the cycle ends. Notice that questions (7)–(12) vary from sequence orientation to result to motivation. Nonetheless all of them are integrated via the story map. By the way, the story map technique does not and cannot specify in advance the number of questions appropriate for a given story. That decision can and must be made only after a teacher has decided what the main flow of ideas is for a story.

The claim implicit in Beck et al.'s critique of existing questions sets is that a coherent and integrated *line* of questions will lead toward better story understanding. Students will be better equipped to see relationships among events and among types of events. While empirical verification of this claim must await appropriate research, the notion is appealing. Systematic *lines* of questions certainly seem superior to random barrages of unrelated questions.

Questions should lead to the development of skills that will transfer to new situations in which teacher assistance is not available. The hope of all reading instruction and practice activities is that those efforts will help to develop within students the independent skills and habits that will allow them to understand and appreciate stories and other selections when they encounter them "on their own." In fact, there is not much

point to instruction that does not lead to independence.

Why, for example, do we teach phonics and structural analysis skills? Not because the activities have any intrinsic merit; rather, because we believe that students who are equipped with rules and a sense of predictability about structural patterns like prefixes, suffixes, and syllables will be able to decode unknown words "on their own." In other words, we believe that these skills have broad *transfer* value. The same argument holds, or ought to hold, for comprehension instruction and practice activities. We ought to be developing within students a set of problem-solving strategies that they can apply (transfer) to new stories that they read by themselves. What better strategy can we develop among students, in order to help them understand narrative text, than an abstract sense of how stories are made. In other words, if we systematically guide students to integrate the major elements of the stories they read, they ought to develop a generic story map that will serve them well as they attempt to sort out and tie together new settings, characters, problems, goals, motivations, events, and resolutions in new stories that they encounter.

Hence, there may be a side benefit to question generation guided by a story map: Not only will this teacher strategy serve to enhance comprehension of the story for which the specific set of questions was developed, but the strategy, applied systematically and frequently to many stories, should lead to the development of an internal abstract sense of story, *The Story Map*, that becomes part of students' comprehension repertoire.

A General Guide for Question Development

Given the four general goals about the role of questions discussed here, we can now come to some consensus about generating questions for stories that students read. That consensus represents an attempt to balance these goals where they conflict and to integrate them where they mesh with one another.

1. Begin a lesson with questions that focus student attention on appropriate background experiences.

This guideline seems so intuitively obvious that its inclusion might be questioned. Yet it is so central to the comprehension process that it should never be overlooked or omitted. If students' background knowledge is fairly well-developed for the content, it is simple to tap into it. Questions like (15) or (16) will do quite nicely.

(15) What do you know about farms?
(16) Have you ever been on a farm? Tell us about it.

If, however, background knowledge is not well-developed, teachers must ask themselves something like, "Well, if students don't know about jaguars, what *do* they know about that I can use as an anchor point or analogy?" Then questions like (17) would come into the picture.

(17) Today we are going to read a story about a family of jaguars in South America. Now, a jaguar is a little bit like a house cat, a little bit like a wolf, and a little bit like a sports car. Let's figure out how a jaguar is like these things.

2. If possible, allow students to use background knowledge to predict what might happen in the story.

Such questions usually focus on a problem one of the protagonists has and how he or she solves it.

(18) If you were lost in the forest and needed food, how would you get it?
(19) The jaguar family in the story is

running out of food. How do you think they will find it?

3. Set up a purpose that lasts as long as possible throughout the story.

Quite often the prediction strategy in 2 above takes care of the purpose setting automatically; students read to verify, disconfirm or modify their prediction, and that takes care of a purpose for reading. If that is not the case, then fairly general purpose setting questions, like (21) or (22) but not (20) are in order.

(20) When you read this story, find out what the jaguar family's problem was.
(21) When you read this story, find out what the jaguar family's problem was and how they tried to solve it.
(22) What did the jaguar family try to do to solve their problem?

Note that the purpose imposed by question (20) ends as soon as the problem is located but that questions (21) and (22) last throughout the story.

4. During the guided reading (usually during the reading in the primary grades and immediately following the reading in the intermediate grades), ask questions that tie together the important elements in the story map.

Remember that a story map is not so much a sequence of events as it is a *causal chain* of events. The questions (7)–(14) illustrate a typical set of story map questions.

5. Immediately following reading, return to the purpose setting question(s).

There is no reason to give a purpose setting question if you do not follow it up. In fact if you do not follow it up, students will learn not to take seriously the purpose setting questions you give. The follow-up question does not have to take precisely the same form as the pre-reading questions, but it must get at the same information. For example (21) might be paraphrased as (23).

> (23) Let's list in order the three things the jaguar family did to find food.

6. In discussing the story, follow this sequence for question generation: (1) Retell the story map at a fairly high level of generality. (2) Take students "beyond the information given" by asking them to compare this selection to their own experience or to another selection, or by asking them to speculate about how these characters might react in a new situation. (3) Return to the selection to appreciate the author's craft.

Recapitulation can be either mundane or creative. Whatever you do here, do not simply repeat the earlier story map questions. Either save them for this part of the discussion (a valuable idea especially in the intermediate grades), or review the story in some novel way: dramatize it, make a time line of events, or make a causal flow chart of events as in (24).

> (24) See flow chart below.

We have had good success getting students as young as eight to depict a story in flow chart form. They can either write out or picture the events. We have even taught them to use circles to visualize goals and motives, some of which might not be explicitly stated in the story. Having students occasionally complete such a flow chart may even help them to build a *general* framework for understanding stories.

Taking students "beyond the information given" is a necessary and relatively simple step. Questions like (25)–(28) are illustrative of a wide range of possible questions.

> (25) Did you think the jaguar family acted wisely? Why or why not?
> (26) What would you have done in their situation?
> (27) How would the pioneer family in the last story have solved the problem?
> (28) What would the jaguar family have done if invaders had taken over their hunting territory?

Similarly, appreciating the author's craft is both a necessary and simple step. Returning to the text to appreciate good dialogue, colorful language, vivid action, clever use of words, idioms or metaphors are representative of a range of activities that should occur here.

> (29) What is your favorite part of the story? Read it aloud; we'll listen. . . . What made you like that part?
> (30) On page 31 what words make you feel frightened?
> (31) How does the author tell you that the youngest jaguar feels proud?
> (32) On page 37, the author lets you know that jaguars are fast but he doesn't say "fast." How does he tell you they are fast?

Concluding Statement

John Downing, in his new book, *Reading as Reasoning*, makes a plea for educators to help children make sense of their world of reading by appealing to a principle he calls "cognitive clarity." He believes that teachers have the responsibility to struc-

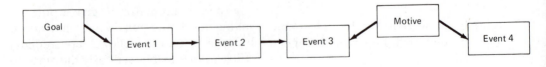

ture students' learning environments so that they see patterns of regularity and predictability. The students build sets of expectations about what reading is all about, and they use these expectations to guide their independent reading.

The same principle of cognitive clarity, helping students make sense of that part of the day we call reading time, is the motive force behind the suggestions I have offered in this paper. It is my hope that both teachers and textbook authors will keep that principle in mind as they develop questions to ask students about the stories they read. For if they do, they will help students: see the relationship between what they read and what they already know; read with definite purposes in mind; understand the central thread of stories they read; apply these notions when they read independently; and, appreciate the language, humor, suspense, and action that characterizes good literature.

References

Beck, I., McKeown, M. G., McCaslin, E. S., & Burkes, A. M. *Instructional dimensions that may affect reading comprehension: Examples of two commercial reading programs* (Tech. Rep.). Pittsburgh: University of Pittsburgh, Language Research and Development Center, 1979.

Downing, J. *Reading as reasoning.* New York: Academic Press, 1980.

Hansen, J., & Pearson, P. D. *The effects of inference training and practice on young children's comprehension* (Tech. Rep. No. 166). Urbana: University of Illinois, Center for the Study of Reading, April 1980.

52. Improving Classroom Comprehension

Robert B. Ruddell

The development of reading and listening comprehension abilities is a major objective of any classroom reading program. The development is critical to the success of each child—critical because these comprehension skills directly affect the ability of the child to *derive, interpret,* and *apply* meaning in an effective way.

The comprehension skills affect success throughout the primary, intermediate, junior high, and high school years. Grasping meaning from printed and oral language, and interpreting and applying it, will be equally important as the student moves into the college setting or into a trade and assumes independent responsibility for his or her future direction.

The comprehension of written or spoken language directly involves language and thought: *language* in the sense that the child's linguistic structure and his or her store of meanings provide the currency for representing ideas; *thought* as the child cognitively uses and manipulates ideas, guided by the reading or listening purpose. The end result is interpretation and meaning.

Because of the necessary involvement of language in comprehension, the successful comprehension program must take into account the child's language background. Also, directly related to this, the child's range of experience, concerns, anxieties, hopes, and perception of self must

From Robert B. Ruddell, *Improving reading comprehension.* The Allyn and Bacon Reading Newsletter, No. 1. Undated. Reprinted by permission of Allyn and Bacon.

be taken into account, for all influence the meaning derived from written and oral language. In the words of the French novelist Proust, "Every reader reads himself."

What is comprehension? The available research seems to indicate that it involves a cluster of related mental or thinking abilities rather than a single mental process (1, 2, 3, 4, 5, 6). High-priority abilities identified include vocabulary knowledge, understanding of word meanings, ability to draw inferences, and "seeing the intent or purpose of an author, judging the mood or tone of a selection, and perceiving the literary devices by means of which the author accomplishes his purposes"(4).

It is obvious that these comprehension abilities include much interpretation and application of what we read and hear.

However, teachers' questions in the classroom tend to be largely literal and factual. Approximately 70 per cent of teacher question time is devoted to literal, detail-type questions, and only 30 per cent to questions of an interpretive or applicative nature (2, 5). This emphasis on factual questions may actually detract from understanding of what is read, rather than help it. Frank Guszak of the University of Texas believes that such questions "lead the student away from basic understandings of story plots, events, and sequences" (2). As teachers, we need to be aware of the possibility that extensive use of factual questions may cause students to miss the overall meaning of the text.

Comprehension is often seen only from the standpoint of specific skill com-

Table 1. Pathfinder Comprehension Taxonomy

Skill Competencies	Comprehension Levels		
	Factual	Interpretive	Applicative
Details			
Identifying	•	•	
Comparing	•	•	•
Classifying		•	•
Sequence	•	•	•
Cause and Effect	•	•	•
Main Idea	•	•	•
Predicting Outcomes		•	•
Valuing			
Personal judgment	•	•	•
Character trait identification	•	•	•
Author's motive identification		•	•
Problem Solving			•

petencies such as identification of details, understanding the sequence of events, recognizing cause and effect, selecting the main idea, and predicting outcomes. Such a view leads to the belief that the development of these competencies will automatically account for higher thinking processes. This is not the case. Comprehension operates at different *levels* as well as in terms of different *skills*. Table 1 shows three such levels, factual, interpretive, and applicative, and integrates these with specific skill competencies.

Notice, in the table, the addition of two critically important skill competencies to those already identified. These two are valuing and problem solving. The first of these accounts for personal judgment, character trait identification, and author's motive. The second incorporates the more involved problem solving process.

The uniqueness of this view of comprehension is that the various skill competencies can be dealt with across the three comprehension or thinking levels— in most instances. At the *factual* level, the student is asked to identify and recall specific facts and ideas presented in the selection. The *interpretive* level requires that the reader go beyond the stated particulars of a selection, manipulating the information in it to arrive at an inference not stated in the text. Finally, at the *applicative* level, the reader or listener applies or transfers understandings to new situations, situations that go beyond the context of the story. Applicative questions will frequently involve a personal response level as the reader or listener relates to his or her own reservoir of experiences.

A brief illustration of each of the three levels may help to clarify understanding of them. Chapter Eleven of E. B. White's classic, *Charlotte's Web*, opens with a beautiful description of the farm on a foggy morning and Lurvy's trip to the barnyard where he discovers to his astonishment a neatly woven message in block letters which reads "SOME PIG!" (7). After a student has read this, we might ask: "What

was written in the web?" This question requires the student to operate on the *factual level* using the skill competency *identifying details*. The question: "Why did Lurvy, the hired hand, feel weak?" requires the reader or listener to utilize and manipulate information presented to go beyond what is explicitly stated in the story. It engages the reader or listener at the *interpretive level*, using the specific skill competency of *cause and effect*. And finally, "How would you have reacted if you had been the very first person to see Charlotte's web that morning?" fosters a higher-level thinking process at the *applicative level* and the skill competency of *predicting outcomes* or *valuing—personal judgment*, depending on the intent of the question.

One point of caution is in order as you adapt this framework to your classroom comprehension needs. You will need to examine the reading matter carefully to determine whether or not a particular question is answered directly in the text. If so, regardless of your intent, the question is at the factual level and cancels your efforts to ask an interpretive or applicative level question. For example, the question: "Why was Lurvy in the barnyard that morning?" on first encounter might be viewed as an *interpretive level* question using the *cause and effect* skill competency. Upon close examination of the text, however, we find the sentence: "Even Lurvy, who wasn't interested in beauty, noticed a web when he came with the pig's breakfast" (7, p. 77). In fact, the question requires a literal-type response at the basic *factual level* using a *cause and effect* skill competency—*not* an *interpretive level* response.

In framing questions, you will find that the children's responses are a very valuable guide. Your sensitivity to these responses can be gauged through listening to a ten minute recording of one of your guided reading discussions. Such a recording will enable you to examine which thinking level processes you are fostering in your classroom and which skill competencies you emphasize; it can also give you information about the appropriateness of your questions relative to the students' responses. A careful examination of the interaction between you and the students will allow you to plan for a balance of skill competencies and comprehension levels so that all facets of comprehension are developed.

Even without a recorder, you can make yourself more aware of the kinds of questions you use in your guided reading discussions and design them to achieve a balance of competencies and levels. Such a balance can be extended to content-area instruction as well. Comprehension levels and skill competencies are as applicable to discussions of social science, science, and mathematics as to free-reading literature experiences.

The time, energy, and effort that you spend in developing your comprehension program will be more than repaid in the increased comprehension abilities of your students. Their ability to interpret information and to better understand their world have a direct relationship to their concerns, anxieties, hopes, and perception of self. All of these can be profoundly influenced by the meaning your students derive from their encounters with written and spoken language.

References

1. Benjamin S. Bloom et al., eds., *Taxonomy of Educational Objectives: Handbook I: Cognitive Domain* (New York: David McKay, 1956).
2. Frank J. Guszak, "Teacher Questioning and Reading," *Reading Teacher*, 21 (1967), pp. 227–234.
3. John Guthrie, *Cognition, Curriculum, and Comprehension* (Newark: International Reading Association, 1977).
4. Roger T. Lennon, "What Can Be Measured?" in Russell Stauffer, ed., *The Role of Tests in Reading*, Proceedings of Annual Education Conference, 9 (Newark: University of Delaware Press, 1960), pp. 67–80.
5. Robert B. Ruddell, *Reading-Language Instruction: Innovative Practices* (Englewood Cliffs: Prentice-Hall, Inc., 1974), pp. 361–408.
6. Norris M. Sanders, *Classroom Questions* (New York: Harper and Row, 1966).
7. E. B. White, *Charlotte's Web* (New York: Harper and Row, 1952), p. 77.

53. Developing Sentence Comprehension in Reading

John G. Barnitz

There can be little doubt that during the 1970s reading education has undergone many advances in the area of comprehension. Prior to the seventies there was a strong emphasis on word decoding skills (Gray 1960). That focus was challenged through the psycholinguistic movement (Goodman 1970, 1973; Smith 1973) with an increasing interest in the role of children's knowledge or "schema" in comprehension (Anderson 1977). Current thinking on reading focuses on the interaction of many factors: the child's conceptual development (e.g., world knowledge), cognitive

From John G. Barnitz, Developing sentence comprehension in reading. *Language Arts*, November/December 1979, 56, 902–908; 958. Reprinted by permission of the author and the National Council of Teachers of English.

development (e.g., memory, perception), language development (e.g., syntax, word structure), educational factors (methods, materials, teachers), and other aspects of the child's background (socioeconomic status, cultural experiences).

One growing line of research during the sixties and seventies is the study of the effect of syntax on children's ability to comprehend written language. Two questions can be asked: What syntactic structures are difficult for children to comprehend? How does the reading/language arts teacher help promote the comprehension of difficult syntactic structures? In the pages which follow a few of the many syntactic studies on children's reading comprehension will be reviewed, and various practical teaching methods for promoting sentence comprehension in context will be outlined.

Before proceeding, it is first necessary to understand the relationship of language to reading. There is more to helping children to be "on their own in reading" than teaching word attack strategies or hierarchies of skills (Gray 1960). A fluent reader is a thinking language user. In the reading-communication process, a reader samples information from the text by means of the various subsystems of language. Three of the cue systems of the reading-language process were specified by Goodman (1973). With the *graphophonic* system readers may use their knowledge of the relationships of the spelling system to oral language. Yet, this subsystem is only a small part of the reading process. With the *syntactic* system readers have intuitions about the sentence structure of language as a means of predicting meaning of a sentence. With the *semantic* system readers use their knowledge of the world and previous content to construct a meaningful representation of the ideas in the passage.[1] With the close relationship of language to reading kept in mind, the role of syntax in reading comprehension will now be discussed.

Selected Research Studies

That there is a close relationship between the maturity of sentence structure of children's oral language and their reading achievement has been well documented in the 1960s (Strickland 1962; Ruddell 1965). It was later demonstrated that children's acquisition of oral syntax is both systematic and continuous throughout the school years and that children develop language at different rates (C. Chomsky 1969; Loban 1976). To illustrate the role of sentence structure on children's reading comprehension in the middle grades, two studies on pronoun-referent structures will be briefly discussed (Richek 1977; Barnitz 1978, 1979).

Consider the relative difficulty of the following paraphrase alternation for third graders (Richek 1977):

> John saw Mary and *John* said hello to Mary.
> John saw Mary and *he* said hello to her.
> John saw Mary and ϕ said hello to her.

Each of the sentences differs in the structure of the second clause, where the second occurrence of *John* is either repeated, pronominalized or deleted through basic transformations of English (N. Chomsky 1957, 1965). Target sentences like these were embedded in short passages followed by a test question based on the target structure. In Richek's study third graders were able to comprehend the repeated noun form of the alternation more easily than the pronominalized noun form, which in turn was easier than the structure with the deleted noun.

In yet another study involving pronoun-referent structures, Barnitz (1978, 1979) demonstrated the effect of various sentences containing the pronoun *it* upon the reading performance of children in grades two, four and six. Like the previous study, target structures were embedded in short passages. For each grade, some of the findings were: (1) Pronoun-referent structures where the referent is a noun or noun phrase were more easily recalled after reading than structures where the referent was a clause of sentence. The following sentences are examples:

> John and his father wanted to buy *a large train set*, because *it* was on sale. (noun phrase referent)
> Mary rides her skate board in the busy street, but Marvin does not believe *it*. (sentential referent)

Similarly, (2) structures in which the pronoun follows its referent were generally easier to recall after reading than the structures in which the pronoun precedes its referent. While the above examples contain *forward* reference with the antecedent preceding the pronoun, the following examples are parallel versions with *backward* reference:

> Because *it* was on sale, John and his father wanted to buy *a large train set*.
> Marvin did not believe *it*, but *Mary rides her skate board in the busy street*.

In the overall study, it was claimed that children are generally able to comprehend pronouns by the time they reach the upper grades. These studies illustrate that the role of syntactic structure is important in the comprehension of a monosyllable word.

While syntax is demonstrated to be a variable in reading comprehension, it is not yet clear to what extent the content of the sentences affects their comprehensibility. A study by Bormuth, Manning, Carr and Pearson (1970) investigated the relative difficulty for fourth graders of as many as fifty-five target structures. However, one of their taxonomies was challenged by Lesgold (1974) who demonstrated that there is much variability in the difficulty of sentence structure. Likewise, Pearson (1974) found that more complex structures or longer sentences involving cause-effect

relations often were easier for children to read, especially if the cause-effect relation between two sentences was marked by *because*, as in the following pair:

> Because the chain broke, the machine stopped.

> The chain broke. The machine stopped.

Thus short simple sentences are not necessarily easier to read than more syntactically complex sentences. Furthermore, as Bransford and McCarrell (1974) reported, the sentence:

> The notes were sour because the seam split.

is almost incomprehensible, unless the reader relates the sentence to prior knowledge in context (*bagpipe*). Thus, the reader's knowledge of the world plays an important role in sentence comprehension.

In short, although syntax is demonstrated to have an effect on reading, not always will a potentially difficult syntactic structure be problematic, especially if the content of the passage matches the knowledge background of the child. Certainly, not all children will need help with all aspects of sentence structure comprehension because of background knowledge and different rates of language development. Thus, the teacher must understand, through ongoing informal diagnosis, the knowledge and language background of the child (see Marcus 1977). Once the teacher decides a child needs help with certain aspects of text structure, the following techniques for teaching syntactic aspects of reading may be helpful.

Teaching Sentence Comprehension in Context

Helping children find meaning through difficult sentence structure is an important task for the classroom teacher. Yet this assertion does not imply that formal grammar instruction by itself will help children read. Rather than labeling parts of speech or diagramming sentences, the child must learn how to derive meaning from syntax. Many of the techniques for teaching syntactic aspects of reading can be classified into the following categories: paraphrase techniques, cloze techniques, manipulation of text, sentence building and combining, and questioning. However, these categories are not mutually exclusive.

Paraphrase Techniques: Asking children to restate what they have read has been a common element in the teaching of reading. However, techniques for paraphrasing can be refined to help young readers recognize and understand that different structures could have similar meanings. Pearson and Johnson (1978, pp. 87–88) incorporate paraphrasing in a variety of ways. One way is through "sentence matching," where the child chooses the sentence with similar meaning, as in their example with active and passive sentences:

Susan hit the ball.

a. The ball was hit by Susan.
b. Susan was hit by the ball.
c. Susan was hit ball by.

A variation of this method is to present a child with a list of three sentences, two of which are paraphrases, and to ask the child to identify the one that does not match. A third way is to ask the child to produce an alternate way of communicating the same idea. The value of paraphrase techniques is that children may be led to use their intuitions about how sentences are related in language as a means of comprehension.

Cloze Techniques: The cloze procedure (Taylor 1953, Bormuth 1968), a readability technique whereby every nth word is deleted for the reader to supply the missing word, may be adapted for use as a technique for teaching sentence-level comprehension. For teaching reading to speakers of English as a second language, Norris

(1970, p. 26) suggests using a cloze-like activity for supplying structure words from the reading material, as in the example:

> All cultures seem to be _____ a continuous state _____ change.

Similarly, Pearson and Johnson (1978) suggest the use of a fill-in-the-blank problem as one of the techniques for teaching, for example, clues to causal relations (p. 115) or sequence (p. 121):

> The machine stopped _____ the chain broke.
> _____ so _____ because _____ unless
> John started the car _____ he shifted it into drive.
> _____ after _____ before _____ earlier.

To give practice in logical completions, Norris (1970, p. 27) suggests this activity:

> You can trust Henry to take good care of your money, for he is very _____ (honest, angry, evil, distant)

Cloze-like techniques may give children opportunities to use their knowledge of the world and syntactic structure to predict meaningful relationships in a passage.

Manipulating the Text: Unlike the paraphrase techniques where the *student* recognizes or produces a paraphrase, another technique is the manipulation by the teacher of a difficult passage. Three different types of text structure manipulation can be identified: (1) manipulate the format of the passage to mark phrase boundaries; (2) rewrite parts of a story to include structures which are contained in the child's oral language; and (3) for non-standard English speaking children, include forms which are part of the reader's dialect.

Text structure manipulation of the first kind was a technique used in a research experiment by Mason and Kendall (1978) to see if reorganizing a passage will aid children's comprehension, especially for children who may have difficulty in readily identifying meaningful phrase units. It was found that good readers generally have the ability to identify meaningful units of structure, but poor comprehenders show difficulty with complex structures found in texts beyond third grade. Two of the ways that clauses can be marked are: the parsing of the text or writing the complex sentences in simpler sentences, preserving meaning in both cases. Sample formats from the study are:

Standard: Dick will be in grade five and though he enjoys math he likes art class best.

Parsed: Dick will be in grade five
and though he enjoys math
he likes art class best.

Short Sentence: Dick will be in grade five. He enjoys math. He enjoys art.

Some of the findings of the study were that middle grade children required more time to read the parsed or short sentence version, but displayed lower error rates in recall after reading a marked version, than in the standard version. Furthermore, the manipulation of the text helped the scores of the low ability readers. This technique may prove useful in helping low ability readers.

A second type of text manipulation is the rephrasing of difficult structures by the teacher. Thus, without changing the propositional content, the teacher could rewrite the structure, as in the following example:

What was hit by the torpedo was the enemy destroyer

The torpedo hit the enemy destroyer.

This may aid children in understanding difficult prose, if the teacher feels that the student cannot comprehend certain structures.

Finally, a third type of text manipulation, proposed in the late sixties and early seventies as a means of facilitating the beginning reading of minority children, is the dialect reader. The goal of a dialect reading program was to incorporate aspects of language that are used in the vernacular dialect of the child. Thus, a line of text could be "My mama pretty" in an "everyday talk" version and "My mama is pretty" in a "school talk" version (Leaverton 1973). Although in the Leaverton project black English speaking children were able to learn to read in the "everyday talk" version, the issues of dialect interference and dialect readers in reading education remains controversial (Laffey and Shuy 1973, Goodman and Buck 1973, and Cullinan 1974).

Building and Combining Sentences: Sentence manipulation activities may take different forms: sentence transforming or paraphrasing (discussed earlier), sentence building, and sentence combining.

Sentence building activities were suggested by Ruddell (1974, p. 166), where children are led to expand on simple sentences as in the following example:

Rico bats.
Rico bats (the) (ball).
Jackson bats (the) (ball).
Rico and Jackson (bat the ball)
(They) bat the ball.

This activity is related to other sentence manipulation techniques. Combs (1977) suggests using a sentence combining activity similar to the one developed by O'Hare (1973) for teaching writing. Thus, students may combine simple kernel propositions by conjoining or embedding:

The hunter chased the anteater.
The anteater raided the ant hill.
The hunter lives in a cabin.
The hunter, who lives in a cabin, chased the anteater which raided the ant hill.

Children may also be helped to do the reverse of the above activity by decomposing difficult multi-embedded sentences to determine the basic ideas conveyed. These activities may help children use their knowledge of how simple structures are compacted into more sophisticated structures.

Activities based on sentence manipulation have been developed over the past two decades, especially after theoretical advances were made in the study of grammar in the late fifties and early sixties (see Chomsky 1957, 1965). Transformational generative grammar was established as a theory to characterize the knowledge of a native speaker-hearer of language. Part of this knowledge involves the potential to produce and understand an infinite set of sentences by means of phrase structure and transformational rules. While Chomsky did not intend the formal aspects of his theory to be taught in the classroom (e.g., tree diagrams, syntactic formulae), the teacher can capitalize on some of the insights about language to help children become aware of how their language works, how sentences can be manipulated in relation to meaning, and how their intuitions about language relate to comprehending written language. Sentence manipulation techniques may prove to be a promising activity in the reading-language comprehension classroom as long as the activities are related meaningfully to the story and as long as the focus is not on grammatical formulae.

Questioning: Using a variety of question types has classically been a part of teaching reading comprehension (see Bormuth 1970). In teaching sentence level comprehension of causal relations, for instance, Pearson and Johnson (1978, p. 114) suggest probing children's understanding after reading a selection by using questions containing different surface clues to a cause-effect response, as in the following examples:

Why did John have to go downtown?
Under what condition will Susan's mother give her a piece of cake?
What will happen if Susan cleans her room?

Questions can easily be adapted to any syntactic structure (Bormuth et al. 1970). Thus, asking the child to recall the antecedent of a pronoun would guide the child's reading of pronoun-referent relationships.

Conclusion

For every technique for teaching comprehension, the teacher must relate instruction to the immediate needs encountered in the particular story the child is experiencing. Isolated exercises become useless if the skill is not related to the entire reading experience. It is important to stress sentence structure as a clue to meaning rather than isolated components of language. The teacher must also allow children the opportunity to use their native intuitions about language and their knowledge of the world to predict the meaning of the passage. Thus, helping children through "inductive strategies" to discover meaning should be the focus of language-reading teaching (Marcus 1977, Ruddell 1974). An inductive approach should be used "to create awareness of the ways sentence development can contribute to description, so that youngsters can expand and combine sentences more effectively in order to sharpen meaning" (Ruddell 1974, p. 166). Furthermore, as Eskey (1970, p. 319) points out: "Reading is a skill, that is something students *do*, some kind of inductive method seems to be called for within which the student can work his own way up from simple structures that he knows to the complex constructions that are largely new to him." Wilson (1973) suggests reviewing the known pattern, presenting the new pattern, and guiding the students to generalize how the sentences convey meaning. A more general rationale for inductive teaching in the language arts is summarized by Marcus (1977, pp. 297–298). The students can improve their intrinsic motivation, their retrieval of information, their retention of concepts and skills, their overall interest and involvement. Inductive strategies are adaptable for small groups and for individual children. For a child to learn strategies for discovering meaning from text is a very important basic skill in reading.

This article has outlined many ways in which teachers may help children discover the meaning of sentences. However, there is certainly more to comprehending written language than the meaning of individual sentences. For an understanding of the structure of larger discourse, text cohesion or intersentential relationships, the teacher may consult Halliday and Hasan (1976). For an understanding of teaching comprehension of longer discourse, the teacher will benefit from reading Pearson and Johnson (1978). The teaching of comprehension of written discourse by incorporating children's language and children's knowledge of content is an exciting horizon for the 1980s.

Notes

1. A significant amount of research is being conducted in this area at the Center for the Study of Reading at the University of Illinois at Urbana-Champaign. A series of technical and practical reports on a wide variety of topics is available from the Center for the Study of Reading, 174 Children's Research Center, University of Illinois, Champaign, Illinois 61820.

References

Anderson, Richard C. "Schema-Directed Processes in Language Comprehension." Technical Report No. 50. Urbana, IL: Center for the Study of Reading, University of Illinois, July 1977.

Barnitz, John G. "Children's Development of Syntactic Aspects of Reading Comprehension: Pronoun-Referent Structures." Unpublished Doctoral Dissertation, University of Illinois at Urbana-Champaign, 1978.

Barnitz, John G. "Reading Comprehension of Pronoun-Referent Structures by Children in Grades Two, Four and Six." Technical Report No. 117. Urbana, IL: Center for the Study of Reading, University of Illinois, March 1979.

Bormuth, John R. "The Cloze Readability Procedure." *Elementary English* 65 (1968): 429–36.

Bormuth, John R. *On the Theory of Achievement Test Items*. Chicago: University of Chicago Press, 1970.

Bormuth, John R.; Manning, John; Carr, Julian; and Pearson, P. David. "Children's Comprehension of Between and Within Sentence Syntactic Structure." *Journal of Educational Psychology* 61 (1970): 349–357.

Bransford, John D. and McCarrell, Nancy S. "A Sketch of a Cognitive Approach to Comprehension: Some Thoughts About What It Means to Comprehend." In *Cognition and Symbolic Processes*, edited by W. G. Weimer and D. S. Palermo. Potomac, MD: Erlbaum Press, 1974.

Chomsky, Carol. *The Acquisition of Syntax in Children From Five to Ten*. Cambridge, MA: M.I.T. Press, 1969.

Chomsky, Noam. *Syntactic Structures*. The Hague: Mouton & Co., 1957.

Chomsky, Noam. *Aspects of the Theory of Syntax*. Cambridge, MA: M.I.T. Press, 1965.

Combs, Warren E. "Sentence Combining Practice Aids Reading Comprehension." *Journal of Reading* 21 (1977): 18–24.

Cullinan, Bernice (ed.). *Black Dialects and Reading*. Urbana, IL: National Council of Teachers of English, 1974.

Eskey, David. "A New Technique for the Teaching of Reading to Advanced Students." *TESOL Quarterly* 4 (1970): 315–322.

Goodman, Kenneth S. "Reading: A Psycholinguistic Guessing Game." In *Theoretical Models and Processes of Reading*, edited by H. Singer and R. B. Ruddell. Newark, DE: International Reading Association, 1970.

Goodman, Kenneth S. "Analysis of Oral Reading Miscues: Applied Psycholinguistics." In *Psycholinguistics and Reading*, edited by F. Smith. New York: Holt, Rinehart & Winston, 1973.

Goodman, Kenneth S. and Buck, Catherine. "Dialect Barriers to Reading Comprehension Revisited." *Reading Teacher* 27 (1973) 6–12.

Gray, William S. *On Their Own in Reading*. Glenview, IL: Scott, Foresman & Co., 1960.

Halliday, M. A. K. and Hasan, R. *Cohesion in*

English. London: Longman, 1976.

Laffey, James L. and Shuy, Roger (eds.). *Language Differences: Do They Make a Difference?* Newark, DE: International Reading Association, 1973.

Leaverton, Lloyd. "Dialect Readers: Rationale, Use and Value." In *Language Differences: Do They Make a Difference?*, edited by J. Laffey and R. Shuy. Newark, DE: International Reading Association, 1973.

Lesgold, Alan M. "Variability in Children's Comprehension of Syntactic Structures." *Journal of Educational Psychology* 66 (1974): 333–338.

Loban, Walter. *Language Development: Kindergarten Through Grade Twelve*. Urbana, IL: National Council of Teachers of English, 1976.

Marcus, Marie. *Diagnostic Teaching of the Language Arts*. London: John Wiley & Sons, Inc., 1977.

Mason, Jana M. and Kendall, Janet R. "Facilitating Reading Comprehension Through Text Structure Manipulation." Technical Report No. 92. Urbana, IL: Center for the Study of Reading, University of Illinois, June 1978.

Norris, William E. "Teaching Second Language Reading at the Advanced Level: Goals, Techniques and Procedures." *TESOL Quarterly* 1 (1970): 17–35.

O'Hare, Frank. *Sentence Combining: Improving Student Writing Without Formal Grammar Instruction*. Urbana, IL: National Council of Teachers of English, 1973.

Pearson, P. David. "The Effects of Grammatical Complexity on Children's Comprehension, Recall, and Conception of Certain Grammatical Relations." *Reading Research Quarterly* 10 (1975): 155–192.

Pearson, P. David and Johnson, Dale D. *Teaching Reading Comprehension*. New York: Holt, Rinehart and Winston, 1978.

Richek, Margaret A. *Reading Comprehension of Selected Paraphrase Alterations: Pronominal Forms*. Unpublished Doctoral Dissertation, University of Chicago, 1974.

Richek, Margaret A. "Reading Comprehension of Anaphoric Forms in Varying Linguistic Contexts." *Reading Research Quarterly* 12 (1977): 145–165.

Ruddell, Robert B. "The Effects of Oral and Written Patterns of Language Structure on Reading Comprehension." *The Reading Teacher* 18 (1965): 270–275.

Ruddell, Robert B. *Reading-Language Instruction: Innovative Practices*. Englewood Cliffs, NJ: Prentice Hall, 1974.

Smith, Frank. (Ed.). *Psycholinguistics and Reading*. New York: Holt, Rinehart and Winston, 1973.

Strickland, Ruth G. "The Language of Elementary School Children: Its Relationship to the Language of Reading Textbooks and the Quality of Reading of Selected Children." Indiana University, Bloomington. *Bulletin of the School of Education* 38 (1962): 1–131.

Taylor, Wilson, L. "Cloze Procedure: A New Tool for Measuring Readability." *Journalism Quarterly* 30 (1953): 415–433.

Wilson, Lois Irene. "Reading in the ESOL Classroom." *TESOL Quarterly* 7 (1973): 259–288.

54. Clozing the Reading Gap

V. Patricia Gunn and John Elkins

Cloze procedure was developed more than twenty-five years ago, and since then hundreds of examples of its use have been reported. Many teachers have found cloze useful in gauging the readability of text. Typically cloze involves the deletion of a portion of the words in a passage and readers are asked to insert a sensible word in each blank space.

One distinctive feature of Australian reading practice during the past decade has been the use of cloze procedure for the

From V. Patricia Gunn and John Elkins, Clozing the reading gap. *Australian Journal of Reading*, August 1979, *56*, 144–51. Reprinted by permission of the authors and the publisher.

items in comprehension tests. Tests by McLeod (1967), McLeod and Anderson (1972), and Elkins and Andrews (1974) have been widely used. Observation of children's attempts at such tests suggested that much diagnostic information could be obtained. A belief that diagnosis is most valid in a teaching rather than a testing situation and that cloze procedures could prove effective in teaching as well as in testing led to the research described in this article.

Cloze Procedure and Reading Comprehension

As a teaching technique, cloze programs are frequently suggested for improving reading comprehension although few report have considered which aspects of the cloze program are effective in stimulating performance. There is often the implication that benefits mainly stem from changes in the reader's role from passive receiver or word by word caller, to active participant who must respond to the message (Jongsma 1971). This conception of the reader's role further implies that comprehension depends not only on the content of the message but also on the characteristics of the reader who is taking an active synthesising role (Neisser 1967).

The characteristics of the reader which most influence this role include motivation, past experiences, and the development of language and cognitive structures. If a child's reading comprehension skills are to be improved, it would seem that these are the important characteristics to be considered and further developed.

Extending Readers

Relating these characteristics to the design of a cloze program suggests first that the material be of interest to the reader. It should also attempt to extend the range of concepts already within the child's experience and, while it should be related to the reader's present development of language and cognition, it should also offer the opportunity to go "beyond the information given" (Bruner 1973). The cloze task seems to require the reader to construct hypotheses and to alter these in the face of conflicting evidence.

It should be noticed, however, that not all appropriate responses to a cloze exercise involve active learning. For instance, *the dog wagged his* _____, requires only a low level of conscious processing for solution. If active learning is to be encouraged as a pre-requisite for the development of comprehension skills, this type of over-learned response is not as relevant as one which requires a deeper level of processing and the application of problem solving skills: *Their island is so* _____ *you can walk around it in a few* _____ (Elkins and Andrews 1974).

Conscious Awareness

The next stage of conscious awareness appears to be involved in thinking aloud and in verbalising about one's own processing strategies. It is interesting that many writers have recommended this as a follow-up to the completion of cloze exercises (Jongsma 1971).

In order to talk about their choice of words, children must not only be aware of the appropriate reasons for choosing a response but they must also be able to explain their reasons to others and, if necessary, defend their choice. Ryan's [in press as of this writing] review of meta-linguistic development would suggest that conscious awareness would be beyond the capabilities of younger children, even though they may have used appropriate strategies and arrived at an acceptable solution. It does seem, however, that this may be less apparent for exercises in which the missing element is a label, name or concrete description rather than a relationship.

Using Context Clues

In order to foster the connection between the child's present skill and its later application, cloze exercises should also be followed by the teacher directing attention to ways of using the same strategies in future reading. By drawing attention to the specific factors which led to an acceptable response and demonstrating with more examples, the teacher may heighten the child's perception of context as a source of semantic and syntactic cues both for word attack and word meaning.

It is customary for reading teachers to adopt a systematic approach to the teaching of phonic skills and structural analysis. One of the aims of a cloze program is to help children develop a systematic use of context clues.

A Cloze Program at Year 3*

The writers devised a series of exercises to be given regularly by teachers at the Year 3 level. Each exercise took approximately half an hour to complete and four exercises were scheduled for each week.

Word Attack

The initial tasks required only the overlearned type of response. Nursery rhymes, definitions and familiar expressions provided sentences in which a missing word is highly predictable from the remaining context. This allowed teachers to demonstrate to children that they have already developed a skill in using prediction which will be useful to them as a reading strategy.

In later exercises, predictability was enhanced by using stories written by children of a similar age. By using these stories it was believed that there would be less chance of a mismatch between the conceptual and language structures of the children and those of the written passages.

*"Year 3" refers to level in school, not age—Eds.

A language experience approach (Balyeat and Norman 1975) would be most suitable for individual use from both a predictability and motivational point of view but the present scheme seems to be an appropriate compromise for classroom use, irrespective of the reading approach adopted by the teacher.

The passages included narrative, fantasy, and exposition with cloze blanks for every fifth word or every fifth content word or in some cases, the deletion of a certain form class. In addition, shorter exercises required the completion of a sentence or paragraph so that instead of filling in a missing word, the child had to provide complete phrases or sentences which were compatible with the text provided. It was intended that the children would be stimulated to process words and phrases immediately for meaning and to start making predictions about missing information. Examples included:

1. Into the blazing building ....
2. In the train ....
3. If it gets in ....

Although this kind of exercise serves a useful purpose, a sentence completion task does not expose children to the extra cues which are available in connected discourse. For this reason, they are not suitable as sole methods of building prediction skills. A cloze passage has the advantage in that it can be used to demonstrate that semantic and syntactic cues are not necessarily bound by sentence limits. This is an important feature and the need to direct children's attention to these cues seemed particularly necessary since an earlier study comparing the oral reading errors of third graders with their cloze errors had suggested that children tended to process words around the cloze blanks only at the phrase level. They made significantly more errors acceptable at phrase rather than sentence level in their cloze responses but not in their oral errors, perhaps because a cloze blank is perceptually conspicuous for young children and so influences their processing strategies. To counteract this tendency, the practice of reading the mutilated text before starting the exercise was followed throughout (Bortnick and Lopardo 1973) and some exercises were expressly designed to give practice in using cues well removed from the required response blank. This is illustrated by the first word missing in the following story.

> One day, Peter saw a _____ in the window of the hobby shop. Peter _____ a very determined boy and would _____ anything to get what he _____. He really wanted his boat.

Vocabulary Development

As well as giving children practice in the use of context clues to fill in missing words or phrases, other exercises were designed to help children learn that the same kind of clues can also be used to provide the meaning of an unknown word. One such passage introduced the word *luminous* in the final paragraph.

> So Becky coated paper _____ a special luminous paint. If she put the painted paper _____ a lamp, it would trap the light. The paper glowed for hours and Becky was _____ to write in the dark.

A sentence completion test including the item:

> Luminous means ....

was given before and after the class completed the cloze exercise. This indicated that 19 out of 60 children were able to give the correct meaning after but not before reading the cloze story, and one child responded with what is almost an unsolicited testimonial:

> *At thirst I thout it ment dark now I know it means light.*

Other vocabulary exercises included passages in which only certain descriptive words were deleted, for example, those describing a sound or movement. These gave children an opportunity to compare stereotyped descriptions with possible alternatives. Class suggestions for sounds, _____ of birds, and _____ of children, included *tweet, whistle, song, chirp, cheep, chatter* and *squawk* for the first word omitted but the second word was chosen from the noisy end of the scale: *yell, scream, shout, cry, call, chatter* (only one of seventy children suggested *laughter!*).

This type of exercise is also suitable for use with older readers and, if an extract from a story or poem is used, the author's choice of words can later be compared and contrasted with the class versions.

Diagnosis

Also included in the program was a variety of exercises designed to draw attention to the role of function words and to check children's understanding of the relationships expressed. These included transition words signalling cause and effect (*because, so*), contrast (*but*), time order (*before, after, then, next, when, while, as soon as*) and condition (*if . . . then*). In most cases these were first used in a cloze story but in conventional cloze tasks with no given sample of words from which to choose a response, many children responded with *and* to signify any form of continuing relationship. The different relationships were then later examined further in exercises of varying task demands:

> One day, when John and Peter were _____ home, they saw a little _____. The kitten was very dirty and _____ to be hungry. The boys took her _____ and gave her some _____.
> Next day, John and Peter went back to the ....
> and ....
> After a _____, a boy came up and said "..........................."

John and Peter were _____ that the kitten was _____ back to her home but they were a little _____ to see her go.

1. The children went swimming so
....
2. The children went swimming but
....

Choose your answer from one of these words: *so, if, because.*
1. He is tired _____ he did not sleep well last night.
2. Ann liked reading _____ she wanted a book for her birthday.

The exercises indicated that some children of this age do not fully understand these relationships. The distinction between *so* and *because* was not known and many children confused the meanings of sentences in which *before, after, as soon as* were used in such a way that the written order did not correspond to the event order. This latter confusion has been well documented in research into children's oral language development (Clark 1971) and it may be anticipated that the difficulties would become even more pronounced in a task which involves production within a reading and writing framework.

Other difficulties which have been reported by researchers into children's language development were also identified. These included reversible sentences, tag questions, pronoun referents and the ask-tell distinction investigated by Chomsky (1969). Of these, the most prevalent confusion lay in the question-answer concept which has implications also for punctuation, since the confusion was often reflected in errors in the use of inverted commas and question marks.

The girl asked the boy what to feed the cat. The girl said, ...

The children's answer to this was often *cat food* or *why don't you feed him cat food?* or *Kit-Kat.* We had noted a similar phenomenon in the first passage of the *GAP Reading*

Comprehension Form R (McLeod 1967), where the following sentence occurs:

"Will _____ be a jet pilot when you grow _____?" mother asked Tom.

Nine per cent of a fifth grade sample wrote *I* for the first response which may indicate both egocentrism and a continuing difficulty with this form of construction.

The use of cloze techniques augmented by sentence completion exercises proved to be a convenient classroom method of diagnosing linguistic confusions. In keeping with present beliefs that children extract their own rules from their language environment, it seems that the next step will be for teachers to devise models in a form which children can readily interpret. For instance, question-answer situations in the classroom and time-order examples may be cued by pragmatic considerations.

I put on my shoes *after* I put on my socks.
Before I get dressed in the mornings, I get out of bed.

Results of the Cloze Program

In addition to its diagnostic value, the cloze program was effective in raising children's reading comprehension skills (measured by standardised tests) after both an initial and a subsequent period of eight weeks. It may be inferred that the task demands of the exercises, the language interaction which followed, and teacher-directed attention to specific applications, all contributed to growth in the conceptual and linguistic skills which influence comprehension. The relative contribution of these three factors is not known and indeed varies from individual to individual.

Further Ideas on Using Cloze

It should also be noted that each of these factors (the type of cloze exercises, the nature of the language interaction, and the transfer of strategies to other reading) may exist at different levels. Tasks may vary from those requiring a low level of conscious processing to those demanding a high level of reasoning ability. The language interaction may change from an abbreviated almost telegraphic supply of labels to a sophisticated analysis of linguistic processing. Teacher-directed attention may at first focus on highly predictable context but may later be expanded to the use of transition clues and inference from more abstract textual materials.

Each of the factors may be varied according to the characteristics of the individual learner and, at different ages, children may benefit from programs attempting to match these factors to present needs and development. We believe that teachers could use cloze at any stage of reading proficiency providing that appropriate levels of these three factors are selected. Gardner (1975), for instance, showed that high school students have considerable difficulty with logical connectives: it seems likely that cloze could be useful in drawing the attention of adolescent readers to the function of connectives in expository material.

References

Balyeat, R. and Norman, D. LEA-cloze comprehension test. *The Reading Teacher*. 28, 555–560, 1975.

Bortnick, R. and Lopardo, G. An instructional application of the cloze procedure. *Journal of Reading*. 16, 296–300.

Bruner, J. S. *Beyond the Information Given*. New York: W. W. Norton, 1973.

Chomsky, C. *The Acquisition of Syntax in Children from 5 to 10*. Cambridge, Mass.: MIT Press, 1969.

Clark, E. V. On the acquisition of the meaning of before and after. *Journal of Verbal Learning and Verbal Behavior*. 10, 266–275, 1971.

Elkins, J. and Andrews, R. J. *St. Lucia Reading Comprehension Test*. Brisbane: Teaching and Testing Resources, 1974.

Gardner, P. L. Logical connectives in science: a preliminary report. *Research in Science Education*. 5, 161–175, 1975.

Jongsma, E. *The Cloze Procedure as a Teaching Technique*. Newark, Delaware: International Reading Association, 1971.

McLeod, J. *Gap Reading Comprehension Test*. Melbourne: Heinemann, 1967.

McLeod, J. and Anderson, J. *Gapadol Reading Comprehension Test*. Melbourne: Heinemann, 1972.

Neisser, J. *Cognitive Psychology*. New York: Meredith, 1967.

Ryan, E. B. *Metalinguistic Development and Reading* (in press).

55. Ten Ways to Sort Out Reading Comprehension Problems

Dixie Lee Spiegel

Consider two kinds of children to be found in nearly every classroom. Child One has been carefully instructed in reading comprehension skills. He's been taught how to identify details, find the main idea, determine sequence, draw conclusions. Yet his responses to questions about a story offer no evidence that he understands what he's just read.

Child Two's reading instruction has been holistic, focused on the reading experience itself rather than on prepara-

Reprinted by special permission of *Learning*, the Magazine for Creative Teaching, March 1979. © 1979 by Pitman Learning, Inc.

tory skills training. She has just read the same story as Child One and is trying to take part in a carefully guided discussion. But she too demonstrates no understanding of what she's read.

Do these children really have a problem with comprehension? Is it possible that the problem lies, not with the child but rather with the reading selection, the teacher's attitude or the teacher's questions?

Comprehension is usually defined as the student's ability to reason from reading, to use the information given or implied in a story to extract the author's meaning.

Many so-called comprehension problems are not really failures to comprehend the author's message. When a child fails to respond correctly to a comprehension task, the teacher should consider ten problems that masquerade as comprehension difficulties before sending the child back for more direct practice in comprehension skills. The following ten questions will help teachers sort out reading comprehension problems.

1. Was the Reader Able to Decode Most of the Words in the Selection?

The question may seem almost too obvious. Yet it can be overlooked in haste, or impatience, or mistaken confidence that the children learned certain preliminary lessons some time ago. It is clear, nevertheless, that the child who must spend a great deal of energy identifying words will have little attention left for identifying ideas.

If a student does not seem to understand a passage, the teacher should investigate the student's ability to decode the passage. This need not happen every time a child gives a wrong answer, of course. However, if a child seems generally confused about a whole selection, the teacher should ask the child to pick out a particularly difficult passage and to read it aloud.

If the problem appears to involve decoding, the teacher should take steps to ensure that the student's next assignment will involve material at an appropriate level of decoding difficulty.

2. Did the Reader Understand the Specialized Vocabulary of the Selection?

Decoding can't happen when the code is too complex. For example, the following reading task for adults is analogous to selections that many children face:

> *Glucocorticoids exert an antiinsulin action in peripheral tissues and make diabetes worse. In the diabetic, they raise plasma lipid levels and increase ketone body formation, but in normal individuals the increase in insulin secretion provoked by the rise in blood glucose obscures these actions.*

Although most young readers are not confronted by *glucocorticoids* and *ketone bodies*, they do regularly meet technical words that are new to them. These may be highly specialized words, such as *steppe* or *longitude*, in social studies. They may be words that are familiar in form but that have an unfamiliar meaning within the context of the passage at hand, such as *cabinet* in social studies or *product* in mathematics. Inability to understand even one or two important words can lead to failure to understand an entire passage.

The message to teachers should be clear: Give careful attention to technical vocabulary. Introduction of specialized words prior to their appearance in a reading assignment will help students quickly recognize those words in print. It will also alert readers to important points in the selection before they start reading.

3. Did the Reader Follow Directions?

The inability to follow directions is indeed a comprehension problem, and it is especially common when children are completing workbook assignments. The teacher should not confuse such a problem, however, with failure to understand the selection on which the workbook assignment is based.

For example, a student may understand completely the story about Aunt Hetty and the missing petunias but may not follow the direction to "circle the sentences that do not describe Aunt Hetty."

Teachers can help prevent such problems by ensuring that students understand the directions before beginning the task. This can be done in at least two ways. First, the directions can be given and then rephrased, either by the teacher or by a student. Often students will not understand directions given in one form but may understand them if they are expressed in a slightly different manner.

The second way to ensure that the directions are understood is to have all the children do a sample question together. This procedure not only clarifies the directions but also provides a written guide for students to follow.

4. Did the Reader's Experiential Background Interfere with Comprehension?

Another adult reading task, parallel in difficulty to the tasks many children may encounter, is this passage from *Murder Must Advertise* by Dorothy Sayers:

> *The innings opened briskly. Mr. Barrow, who was rather a showy bat, though temperamental, took the bowling at the factory end of the pitch and cheered the spirits of his side by producing a couple of twos in the first over. Mr. Garrett, canny and cautious, stonewalled perseveringly through five balls of the following over and then cut the leather through the slips for a useful three.*

Any reader not familiar with the game of cricket will have trouble conjuring up a visual image while reading the passage. A child reading about little Sally getting lost in a huge department store may have similar trouble if the child has never been in any store bigger than the local market.

If the reader's background is markedly different from the author's—or the teacher's—a "wrong" interpretation of a passage is possible. This interpretation may be perfectly legitimate in terms of the reader's personal experience.

The teacher should determine the relevance of students' experiential backgrounds before reading begins. This can often be done through informal discussion. If students don't seem to have the background necessary for successful comprehension, the teacher can either introduce the students to the necessary concepts or alter the assignment.

5. Was the Reader Interested in the Selection?

Teachers may find it difficult to discriminate between those students who can't comprehend and those who simply can't get interested. Asking children whether or not they are interested often doesn't work. Most children aim to please, and they often won't admit it if they're bored.

Teachers can minimize motivational problems by helping children set specific purposes for reading. When students have questions they are seeking to answer, their comprehension is likely to be enhanced. Teachers should also try to introduce reading assignments in such a way that students' curiosity is piqued or their enthusiasm aroused—unlikely results when students are simply told to "read pages 12 through 26 and answer the questions on page 27."

If the teacher can't think of a good, interesting reason for reading the selection, maybe it *shouldn't* be read!

6. Was the Reader Able to Express the Answer Correctly?

Many children have severe problems with written composition, spelling or penmanship. They are unable to write their ideas coherently and legibly. Teachers must be careful to distinguish between such composition problems and comprehension problems. One way to do this is to ask students to give answers orally when their written reponses cannot be deciphered. A student might also dictate the answers to an aide, another student or a tape recorder.

Some children have great difficulty expressing their ideas orally. They know what they want to say but cannot find words to express themselves. The teacher may find distinguishing between problems of oral expression and genuine problems of comprehension quite troublesome. It is wise, in this case, to enlist the aid of a language therapist.

7. Did the Reader Forget What He or She Read?

Reading is of little use if the child immediately forgets what has been read. However, it is important to differentiate between a memory problem and a comprehension problem because the remedial work will be very different. When a student responds to questions with "I forget," the teacher should allow the student to search back in the text for the answers. If the student still cannot identify the correct answers, the problem is probably more severe than just poor memory.

Students who have been taught the skill of note-taking and who take notes as they read can improve their comprehension. Writing down notes not only helps the student's memory but also presses the reader to interact with the text, to make decisions about the importance and organization of what is being read. If the child *still* forgets what was read, the notes can serve as a quick reference.

8. Did the Reader Understand the Question?

Whenever a student answers a question with an evident non sequitur (Question:

"Why do you think Aunt Hetty planted petunias in the first place?" Answer: "She planted them in her window boxes"), the teacher should consider the possibility that the question is at fault. The misunderstanding might be caused by the form in which the question is asked, not by the student's lack of knowledge.

The teacher can find out if the question has been heard by asking the child to repeat the question. If the student can do this accurately but apparently does not understand the query, the teacher should rephrase the question or have another student explain what was asked.

9. Could Both the Teacher's and the Child's Answers Be Right? Or Could the Child's Answer Be Right and the Teacher's Wrong?

When teachers ask questions with specific answers in mind, they sometimes don't accept other legitimate answers from students. The expected answer may be based on the teacher's interpretation of the author's message or on the answer suggested in the teacher's manual. Teachers must be open to the possibility of several correct answers.

Experienced teachers also know that their own interpretations or the answers given in teacher's manuals may on occasion be dead wrong. No teacher should stick blindly to such an answer. Teachers as well as students should be critical readers. A teacher should not accept every answer a child offers, of course. But the teacher should examine every answer on its merits, not with a preconceived notion of one right answer.

10. Are the Questions Asked of the Reader Warranted by the Text?

Written language has limitations. Even the best texts and stories may include passages that are obscure, ambiguous, awkwardly constructed or superficial. Unfortunately, question writers—perhaps seeking a tenth item to round out an exercise section—may focus on such faulty passages. Before making an assignment, teachers should read scheduled material and attempt to answer questions in the same manner that the child will have to. Close reading by the teacher may disclose such writing faults as a key pronoun with an uncertain antecedent or an important fact given so little emphasis that a reader's eyes races over it. Both kinds of flaws can make comprehension difficult for the reader.

These ten questions should help the teacher to distinguish true comprehension problems from other kinds of problems that are sometimes more profound but often much simpler to solve. Asking these questions can, in the long run, save valuable instructional time for both teacher and learner.

56. The Perils of Reading

Edwin J. Swineford

Teachers who teach students how to read may damage the students to the extent that they guarantee the students' early obsolescence as thinking and functioning members of society. In teaching students to read there is a real danger that the teacher has contributed to the students' future self-destruction by building in certain attitudes and skills which fail to vaccinate them against the ravages of the ubiquitous propagandists who spread deadly germs in the battle for the minds of men.

Let's try an experiment: Assume you are a history student studying World War II. Read the following short excerpt from a 165-page book on Adolf Hitler:

The Führer on His Travels

by the S. S. Brigade Chief,
Julius Schreck
(deceased) Date: 1936

Never before has a leading statesman come to know his country and his people as thoroughly as Adolf Hitler. Whether by automobile, airplane, or by train, his travels always resulted in a more thorough getting acquainted with his people. During the beginnings of his National Socialistic Movement he recognized with foresight the importance of the fastest means of transport, especially the automobile, and he made use of this means in spite of modest development at that time. Even today the Führer prefers the automobile because he regards it as important to remain in touch with his fellow countrymen and old fellow warriors. During the great political struggle for power it has turned out that the Führer through the motorization of his entourage was far ahead of his political adversaries. We have taken many a trip during those years of struggle during which the going was rough and we could only fight our way through by presence of mind and by sheer force. No alarming news would keep the Führer from penetrating the headquarters and camps of the Red and Black enemies. Often straight through wild heaps of Bolshevistic organizations and past demonstration parades of the other parties; sometimes our car was completely surrounded by thousands of misguided fellow citizens.

From Edwin J. Swineford, The perils of reading. *Language Arts*, September 1975, *52*, 816–819; 851. Reprinted by permission of the author and the National Council of Teachers of English.

But again and again we have witnessed how a raised fist suddenly was lowered under the penetrating look of the Führer. How many of these misguided German workers looked in those days for the first time into the eyes of that man who was supposed to be their opponent, only to become in one stroke fanatic members of his movement. When his work and affairs of state permit, the Führer, even today, sits not only in his office, but he drives out into the land and walks amid the people. Then he sits again in his Mercedes car and bobs up here and there, one day in the rural region, another day in Baden, in Ruhrgebiet, in Saxony, in East Prussia, along the sea coast: in short, there is no province into which the Führer does not travel. At the wheel of the car, behind the windshield, I then hear suddenly astonished and enthusiastic exclamations. "Hitler," or "the Führer is there," and often the people do not notice who has just passed through their town. Only after the column of cars has passed, the three heavy cars become noticeable and then it all becomes clear to them who has just passed. Usually the children are the first to recognize the Führer. In the same moment there begins a race for the car. There is usually a short way to a large gathering of people, to the choking of many roads, and finally we must stop many times so that the Führer can shake the hands of the enthusiastic people and accept the flowers or occasionally sign a few cards. Long trips the Führer undertakes only in an open car, which he does not even close during an official affair when it starts to rain. To the advice of those around him he has only one answer, "as long as the storm-troopers and the formation have to stand in the rain, we can also get wet." Thousands were witnesses when he bare-headed, and clothed only in his brown shirt, reviewed the parade of storm-troopers during the annexation, or the return of the Saar to Germany.

Already in his first car his place was right next to the driver. Today, after three years as Reich Chancellor he has not deviated from it. He also determines the routing of the trip, for the Führer likes to use side roads and to enjoy Germany's landscape outside the large traffic arteries.

In the old days when the Führer was not yet as well known as today it was much simpler. In those days many a time we could stay overnight unrecognized in a small country inn or have a meal there. Today this has changed. Like a storm the news of the arrival of the Führer travels through the villages and cities through which our road takes us. Many spread the news in their joy, calling the next village, and then the inhabitants of that place who never have seen their Führer wait for us in order to greet him at the arrival of the car.

When we come through a village, everyone is there, young and old, clubs and schools, mothers with children on their arms, quickly the main street is changed into an ocean of flags, the girls of the Hitler youth try to bring the car to a stop, but time presses on. The Führer has to meet his appointment at a predetermined hour for hundreds of thousands in the scheduled speech are waiting for him. Then with a big jump, a large muscular man leaps on the car; he is the blacksmith of the village. Now the Führer has to decrease his speed and immediately the car is surrounded by the inhabitants of the village. Everybody would like to press the hand of the Führer. Women with children in their arms cannot get close, they hold the little ones, Germany's future, over the heads of the enthusiastic crowd as if to say, "you belong to him."[1]

Many students would be able to read this material in three or four minutes and would be able to show their comprehension of it by answering such questions as: Who wrote it? How did Hitler travel? As isolated reading the content would probably seem interesting, but unimportant. What is important are the defensive reading skills and attitudes the reader brings to the material. With my subtle urging you were trapped into an extremely clever and diabolical piece of Nazi propaganda, starting as many people did, down a road that ultimately led to the oven doors of the crematorium.

Material of this type places a tremendous burden on the young reader. What skills does the reader have to get at it? What attitudes toward printed material does the reader have? The student reader is particularly vulnerable, for reading teachers utilize many of the techniques of the propagandist and psychotherapist in teaching reading.

Some of the perils of reading are revealed in examining how the propagandist puts content together, uses special devices to persuade, and operates from a set of propaganda principles that are psychologically destructive. Let us analyze the content, techniques, and basic principles of this piece of propaganda:

Content

1. It seems obvious that the article was put together by the staff of the Propaganda Ministry and was not written by Julius Schreck. Schreck was one of Hitler's chauffers (1922–1936), valued as a body guard and street brawler. He was well known by the crowds who watched Hitler's auto caravan.

2. As an Austrian, Hitler was late in getting to know "his country." He did not appear in Germany until 1924.

3. When compared to the activity of his political opponent, Paul Von Hindenburg, Hitler did in fact travel extensively across Germany in political campaigns where he went through the countryside, sometimes making as many as ten speeches a day. His personal trips were more to be by himself than to keep in touch with people.

4. Before 1936 military style political attacks were made on opponents who were verbally and physically abused by the Brown Shirts. For this reason Hitler wore a steel-lined military cap and bulletproof vest and traveled in an armoured Mercedes, manned by picked street brawlers who were the nucleus of the elite S.S. troops. His route changes and affinity for back roads stemmed from his constant fear of assassination.

5. Party members in each village were alerted ahead of the arrival of the motorcade. With party banners flying and filled with uniformed huskies, the heavy Mercedes was an exciting sight even for those who did not support Hitler. Later, S.S. troops patrolled the crowds, slapping the faces of those who did not "shape up."

6. Hitler's love of children, and the masses, was a fiction invented by Joseph Goebbels whose family of five children were all poisoned later in Hitler's Berlin bunker.[2]

Propaganda Techniques

1. Card stacking: Only that information is presented which favors the predetermined themes which were woven throughout the 133 pages of the book. The discussion on content reveals some of the information left out in the card stacking.

2. Plain Folks: Visible and verifiable evidence that Hitler was just "one of the guys," an ordinary individual just like everyone else, runs through the entire book.

3. Name-calling: Labels and loaded words are used in seeming innocence in this first chapter and repeated consistently in all thirteen chapters. Examples include: great political struggle, red and black ene-

mies, many bolshevistic organizations, raised fist, rise to power, return of Saar, old days, old warriors.

4. Bandwagon: You are led to believe by the narrative and photographs of rallies that everyone is doing it, come on in and join the group. Leni Riefenstahl's film of the 1936 Nuremberg Rally supplemented the book and is said to be the most effective propaganda film ever made. Examples: never before; already; misguided fellow citizens; hundreds of thousands were witnesses; like a storm; everyone is there; oceans of flags; you belong to him.

5. Testimonial: This technique involves getting individuals you know or respect to support you. The propaganda exhibit was claimed to have been written by Schreck, the chauffeur with the Hitler-type mustache who was recognized by thousands. Testimonials include: old warriors, children, soldiers, blacksmiths and thousands of farmers and hard-working city people, all of whom are seen in the photographs. Other testimonials were by people they trusted.

6. Glittering Generalities: Broad, non-specific phrases that sound good, but have little substance are used to trap you—S.S. Brigade Chief; never before; getting acquainted; great political struggle; old fellow warriors; rise to power; his work; common man; old days; everyone is there.

7. Transfer: The use of a symbol to represent something it was not intended to represent is the last of the seven techniques used. One such example was the imputation of daring, bravery, and strength to Hitler because he used the airplane and powerful Mercedes car. The child-like faith and honesty of children who mob Hitler's car with flowers is used to suggest similar child-like qualities in Hitler. A crass political trip is written up as a dangerous military campaign aimed at the heart of a ruthless enemy.

Since the propaganda used in this article was produced by Goebbels' Propaganda Ministry it seems appropriate to note some contemporary principles of propaganda quoted from Hitler's *Mein Kampf* and from writings of Goebbels himself. You will quickly see how they were used:

1. From verifiable facts and half-truths comes the over-riding big lie. The people more easily fall victim to a big lie rather than a little one since they themselves lie in little things and would be afraid of lies that are too big.

2. Several simple messages must be presented as part of a campaign and repeated like a drum beat. Propaganda must be limited to a very few points and used like slogans.

3. There is no reason for half-hearted messages; superlatives are needed and the deified individuals must be one of the folks, but possessed with a magnetic reserve.

4. The propagandist must know his people, the terrain, and be pitched for the present, touching nerves, frustrations, loves, and guilt feelings.

5. The masses love a commander, not a petitioner. The masses would sooner salute than vote. There must be a crusade to enlist the undecided who have an unconscious desire for propaganda or simple solutions to problems blown out of proportion by the propagandist.

6. Don't regard the common people as more stupid than they are; their feelings decide more than reason so aim at their emotions and a limited degree to their intellect.

What are the implications of this exercise for teachers of reading? In particular, what can teachers who teach reading do to help since it appears that in the teaching of reading there are also inherent many perils which threaten the student with propaganda fall-out. The following suggestions, while not new to many reading teachers, may have a new urgency and emphasis:

1. In teaching reading emphasize that reading is only one of the several ways of communicating or acquiring knowledge. In our "reading" dominated schools we tend to close off or denigrate other avenues for building meaning, developing in the students an almost blind faith in the printed word and the source from which it comes.

2. Examine your own belief in the importance of reading and books in the total life of youth. You may be infected with "book lust" and enjoy a blind faith that learning to read will solve all the problems faced by young people. It is interesting that psychologists studying the mass murderers in the extermination camps of the Third Reich have discovered common factors that characterize the group. Reading retardation was not one of them. Hitler was an omnivorous reader, particularly in his early Vienna days. As a self-taught historian he shows the horrors of unskilled labor. What the teacher sets out for the student to read, and the prereading screening the student has gone through, may be more important than the food the student eats. All books are, to a certain extent, biased, consisting of various portions of truth, half-truths, and lies. Someone said that all polemics (including this article) are a lie, a form of exaggeration wherein facts are marshalled as persuasive arguments to snare the reader.

3. Be aware of the hazards inherent in some methods used for teaching reading. These hazards seem to exist in the gray area where the techniques of the psychotherapist and the propagandist overlap with the techniques of the reading teacher. There is a danger of "over-kill" and unforeseen psychological "fall-out" with the blind use of techniques that may produce profound psychological effects. The pupil may become a reading person, but may also be an easily conditioned victim for the first propagandist that comes along. It is known that the student often remembers the feelings experienced while reading, rather than the content read. Teaching a pupil to read involves opening the door to that person's very essence.

4. Help the students develop defensive reading attitudes and skills. Before leaping into the printed material the student should habitually stop, look and listen. He/she needs to know that one can't read all the books that are available.[3] A British writer has stated that teachers are "paper secreting organisms." They need to know themselves and what is being brought to the material. Very early one should develop the practice of monitoring what is read and talking back to what has been read.

5. The reader needs answers to such questions as: Who is making this available to me? Why? Who is saying it? Why is this person qualified to write on it? Who is the publisher and when was it published? What is the target audience? What are the implications of the title and what topics are covered according to the index? table of contents? What have others said about it? On what facts is it based? What references are used? Are pictures and illustrations accurate and authentic? What are the hypotheses employed? What techniques of the persuader are used? What action is expected of me? Is it logical? At what point are half-truths or lies introduced? Is it moving through unverified stereotypes and cliches? Are the words "empty shells" and word-symbols overloaded with "freightage"?

Society is laced with networks of biased communication designed to serve the interests of others. The student's susceptibility to this assault, as well as ability to penetrate it, is related to early experiences in learning how to read. Providing the student with "crap-detection" devices, or lecturing on how the hidden persuaders fake content is not enough. The teacher of reading should examine the process employed in teaching reading, looking critically at techniques used by the propagandist. By emphasizing defensive reading techniques the period of reading may be minimized and the teacher can make certain that he/she doesn't rob the student of a part of self and produce a student with strings attached, ready to be pulled.

Notes

1. Because of space limitations, cuts have been made from the original German copy.
2. Over 100 sources, including films and photographs were used as a basis for this analysis of the content.
3. H. H. Bancroft's treatment of the West up to 1900 filled 39 volumes, or approximately 35,000 pages.

CHAPTER XI

Reading for Content

As children progress in school, emphasis shifts from learning to read, to reading to learn. This chapter contains articles concerning study-type reading that have broad applicability in a variety of content areas. Herber and Nelson point out that when teachers use questions to direct students' reading, there is an implicit assumption that the students already have the reading skills needed; an assumption that often is wrong. They advocate the use of simulation to guide students along a series of steps toward independent study. Tutolo describes interlocking and noninterlocking study guides and argues persuasively for the use of such guides.

Brown, Campione, and Day describe experiments in which children are taught strategies such as cumulative rehearsal and self-testing when memorizing, and how to summarize information. Readance and Moore recommend use of the "encoding specificity principle"—presenting similar cues during both prereading and postreading activities. Rickards reports on some recent research on the value of making written notes. In the final selection, graphic literacy, a topic not often discussed by reading specialists, is described by Fry, who presents a taxonomy classifying the different kinds of graphs in use, and emphasizes the importance of developing the ability both to comprehend and to draw graphs.

57. Questioning Is Not the Answer

Harold L. Herber and Joan B. Nelson

The interrogatives "who, what, where, when, why, and how" are standard tools for the inquiring reader. A reader who can apply these interrogatives independently has the necessary skills for selecting pertinent information, for developing concepts by perceiving relationships within and across that information, and for syn-thesizing those concepts with others drawn from previous experience.

These interrogatives are also basic to *questioning*, a teacher's most frequently used instructional tool. Most teachers regularly use questions to guide students' reading of text materials, believing this to be an effective way to help students

From Harold L. Herber and Joan B. Nelson, Questioning is not the answer, *Journal of Reading*, April 1975, *18*, 512–517. Reprinted by permission of Harold L. Herber, Joan B. Nelson and the International Reading Association.

acquire the information and ideas in the text. Some teachers are also aware that reading skills are implicit in the application of questions to text materials. These teachers have two objectives in their use of questions: (1) to teach the content in the text, (2) to teach the reading skills necessary for answering the questions being asked.

The validity of these two objectives seems obvious. However, a careful reflection on what these objectives assume, particularly the second one, raises serious questions about that validity. When one directs students' reading with questions, there is an implicit assumption that students already have the reading skills necessary for a successful response to those questions. If the students do indeed possess those skills, then such questioning is perfectly valid. But if students in fact do not already have those skills, then directing their reading with questions that assume they do is misdirected teaching.

Is it valid to use a teaching procedure which, on the one hand, is designed to teach a skill but, on the other hand, assumes prior possession of that skill in order to perform the required task? This is what happens when a teacher attempts to teach interpretation, for example, by asking interpretive questions of students who need help in learning how to interpret. If students can answer the interpretive questions, do they not already possess the interpretive skills? If they do not possess the skills, does asking questions that require the use of the skills really teach them the skills?

It seems very probable that for instruction in how to read with good comprehension, questioning is not the answer.

Consider what is assumed for students by the science teacher in the following lesson on pollution. The reading selection in the science text focuses on carbon monoxide as a major air pollutant. The authors have organized their information and ideas using the cause-effect pattern of organization. Some of the cause-effect relationships are explicit; others are implicit. To acquire the information and to perceive the concepts imbedded in the material, students need to be able to read for cause-effect, an important part of the comprehension process.

Prior to giving the reading assignment, the teacher and students engaged in appropriate activities to prepare for the reading. Assume, then, the teacher knew that his students needed help in learning *how* to read for cause-effect. His instructional purposes were (1) to develop students' skill in reading for cause and effect and (2) to guide their learning of the content of the reading selection. To aid in accomplishing those purposes, he gave them the following questions:

1. What percentage of all air pollution is caused by carbon monoxide?
2. Why is carbon monoxide a major pollutant?
3. How does CO poisoning affect a person's body?
4. Where does much of our CO poisoning come from, other than automobile engines?
5. What is the most obvious way to reduce air pollution?
6. How do society's priorities relate to air pollution?
7. What have you observed concerning pollution that suggests people would rather not face reality?

Some of these questions are at the literal level. Others are at the interpretive, requiring students to perceive cause-effect relationships across information from several places in the text. Still others are at the applied level of comprehension, requiring students to synthesize ideas from the reading selection with ideas from other sources or experiences.

Are these good questions? Surely they are. Are they appropriate questions? No, they are not, *if* the intended objectives are to be believed. The questions may be appropriate for students who already know how to read for cause-effect relationships, but they are premature for those who lack the experience and skill. For students who have not learned how to manipulate information and ideas in this fashion, questions that in reality assume possession of that skill do little to develop it. Using questioning to direct students' search for information or ideas assumes at least some competency and independence in the process essential for the search.

Questions Are Valuable

None of this is to suggest that questioning is poor teaching procedure in the absolute sense. Speeches have been given, conferences organized, papers, articles, and books written on questioning as an instructional device. Anyone conversant with education cannot doubt the appropriateness of questioning.

The art and science of questioning is fundamental to good teaching. Well-formed questions can stimulate both critical and creative response from students as they interact with one another or the text material. Questions can be adjusted to the needs of students and their ability to respond, ranging from simple to profound, concrete to abstract. Good questions can reinforce the reading skills that students already have by providing practice on the application of those skills. Many teachers use study guide questions for that purpose. Good questions, accompanied by reinforcing feedback on the nature and quality of the responses, can raise the students' levels of sophistication in their use of the reading skills implicit in those questions. Many teachers provide students with study guide questions to serve as the basis for small group discussions to accomplish that purpose.

But what happens when students do not possess the skills to practice or reinforce? What does one do when questions do not seem appropriate or do the job? It is very likely that there needs to be a procedure that is preliminary to the application of good questioning strategies. This could well be the application of good *simulation strategies.*

Consider a different approach to the same lesson on carbon monoxide. The teacher guides students through the same appropriate activity to prepare them for reading the text. The purposes for reading are the same. But the manner in which the teacher guides the students is different. The following materials are given to the students and the teacher goes over the directions orally to make certain they understand how to perform the task.

Carbon Monoxide

Part I. Directions: Here are twelve sets of words or phrases and numbers. The words or phrases in each set are separated by a line. You are to decide if the first word or phrase in a set stands for a possible cause of what the second word or phrase stands for. The numbers at the end of each set tell you the page, paragraph, and lines where you can find the information to help you decide. Work together to make your decisions. Be ready to show the information in the text that supports your decisions.

1. Carbon monoxide/more than 51 percent air pollution (113,1, 1–3)
2. Automobile engines/80 percent carbon monoxide emissions (113,1, 6–7)
3. Incomplete combustion/significant percent of CO emissions (113,1, 4–7)
4. Carbon monoxide/danger, illness, death (113,2, 1–3)
5. One gallon gasoline/three pounds CO (113,2, 6)
6. Mild CO poisoning/highway accidents (114,1, 1–2)
7. Faulty exhaust systems/poisoned people (114,1, 9–11)
8. CO poisoning/oxygen starvation (114,2, 1–2)

9. Hemoglobin and CO/strong chemical bond (114,2)

10. Heavy smoking/permanent combination of hemoglobin and CO (115,0, 4–6)

11. Inhaling CO/trouble with hearing (115,1, 9–11)

12. Reduction in traffic/obvious remedy (115,1, 1)

After part one is completed by students and discussed, they do part two. Again, the teacher goes over the directions to insure understanding of the task.

Part II. Directions: Read each of the following statements. Check those you believe to be reasonable. Think about the work you did in Part I of this guide as well as other ideas you have about pollution.

1. People will risk their lives to have what they want.

2. What a person wants is not always what he needs.

3. Good replaces bad more easily than bad replaces good.

4. What you can't see won't hurt you.

5. A surplus can cause a shortage.

Now, what is the difference between the two lessons and the procedures they represent? The obvious difference is that one is based on a set of questions while the other is based on a set of words and phrases and a set of statements. But within that obvious difference is an important distinction and the potential for *simulation*.

You will note that the materials for the second procedure really present possible answers to the questions posed in the first procedure. But the *teacher* asked those questions *of himself* rather than of his students. As a skilled reader of science material, he was able to discern the cause-effect relationships and to express them by a series of related words or phrases as well as by a set of sentences. He then took these, his own answers to his own questions, and presented them to his students

as a series of alternatives for them to consider. Their task was to take those "answers" and determine if the information in the text or ideas from their store of knowledge and experience either supported or denied their validity or reasonableness. Students discussed the alternatives among themselves in small groups and later with the teacher. In those discussions the question that was constantly raised in reference to decisions about the validity of alternatives was "What's your evidence?" Students responded to that question by identifying information from the text or ideas from their experience to justify their decisions. Thus, they went through a simulation of the process the teacher went through when he created those alternatives in the first place.

As a skilled reader, the teacher could perceive relationships within the information and could state those relationships. On the other hand, when students are not skilled readers, they may experience great difficulty doing what the teacher can do well. But when asked to find support for statements that do express possible relationships across information in the text, they can locate that information. In finding support for the statements, the students deal with the text in almost the same way the teacher did in creating the statements. They develop a feeling for the skill the teacher had to apply when creating the statements.

Simulation can be defined as an artificial representation of a real experience; a contrived series of activities which, when taken together, approximate the experience or the process that ultimately is to be applied independently. As it pertains to the process of comprehension in reading, simulation would be to contrive a set of activities which approximate what one does when one comprehends independently. In our example, the activity approximates reading for cause and effect, providing a representation of that experience. Repeated over time, experiences of this type give students a feeling for processes which are part of reading comprehension.

Independent Questioning

With that feeling as the base and the reference point, and with the confidence that comes from success, students then can respond more readily to questions that require the application of the skill in order to produce their own answers. The teacher can explain that the process is almost the same; they still look for relationships and they still think about what ideas those relationships represent; but now they develop their own expressions of those relationships. With the previous simulated experience providing a pattern to follow, they are in a much better position to produce such answers than if they had not had that experience.

The principle operating here is that it is easier to recognize information and ideas than it is to produce them. Using that principle as applied to the difference between responses to statements and responses to questions, one can establish an instructional sequence that moves students along a continuum of independence.

1. The teacher prepares statements for students' reactions. References are added to indicate where students might look in the text to determine if there is information to support the statements (page, column, paragraph, if necessary).

2. The teacher prepares statements for students' reactions. No references are given.

3. The teacher prepares questions for students to answer. References are added to indicate where students might look in the text to find information which, when combined, might answer the question.

4. The teacher prepares questions for students to answer. No references are given.

5. Students survey the material, raise their own questions and answer them.

6. Students produce statements of meanings, concepts, and ideas as they read.

Within each of these steps in the sequence one can accommodate a range of ability and achievement by the sophistication of the statement or question. Steps 1 through 4 are teacher-directed; steps 5 and 6 are student-directed.

Earlier it was stated that using questions to guide students' reading in order to develop reading skills is really based on the assumption that students already have the skill; otherwise they would not be able to answer the question. To be sure, the simulation as represented in steps 1 and 2 in the above sequence also makes some assumptions, but not nearly so many. Students identify, they do not produce, the valid responses. The assumption is that when they encounter the information in the text they will see the connection between that information and the statements. If they do not, it may be because the statement is too abstract. So you make it more concrete, adjusting statements just as you would adjust questions.

The next time you guide students' reading, ask yourself the questions you would normally ask them—questions that deal both with the content of the selection and the comprehension process essential to understanding that content. Then give the students your answers as a series of alternative statements to respond to. Depending on your students' achievement levels, you may want to provide references for them as suggested above. Make certain the statements aren't too sophisticated for them. However, do not be afraid to have the students think beyond the literal level of comprehension. Then be ready for responses and for justifications you may not have thought of yourself. These will come if, after students have responded to the statements and are discussing them with you, you keep asking the all-important question, "What's your evidence?"

And *where* does all of this happen? Right in the regular content area classroom, of course. And *who* does it? The regular classroom teacher. *How?* As indicated above. *When?* As often as it seems profitable; as consistently as time and logic will allow. *Why?* Because students need the help; they need to be shown how to do what their teachers require them to do. *What?* We said, "Because . . ."

58. The Study Guide— Types, Purpose and Value

Daniel J. Tutolo

Students' poor comprehension of expository texts is a problem that concerns most content teachers. A contributing factor is the extensive concept load found in most content area texts. The reader simply does not know what ideas are important and what topics deserve concentrated study.

The teacher can improve student learning by designing study guides which lead the learner to the important concepts explained in the textbook. This article will define the study guide and provide an example of both the interlocking and non-interlocking types. The purpose of study guides will be clarified, and this author's opinion will be offered concerning the value of guides.

A study guide is a teaching aid written by the teacher to be used by the student to assist the student in developing reading skills for the purpose of enhancing comprehension of textual material. A guide is usually a typewritten copy keyed to the textbook that can be placed beside the text while the student is reading. The student refers to the guide, then the text, or vice versa. Or, the student may refer back and forth to guide and text while reading the associated text.

The guide represents a plan or strategy to be followed by the learner to enhance comprehension. The guide, as written by the teacher, identifies a reading task or objective and offers a plan or strategy for the reader. The assumption is that comprehension will be enhanced when directions which stipulate goals are in close proximity to the textual material containing the relevant information.

The guide is a simulator of the experience and understanding which the teacher wants the student to have. It assumes that many students have difficulty reading expository text and must be guided carefully so as to experience success at their level of competence.

Guides can be designed to lead students through levels of comprehension from literal to interpretive to applicative. Or, they can be designed to focus on internal patterns of paragraphs like comparison/contrast, cause/effect and main idea/detail. Or, they can be designed to lead students through specific skill development like conclusions, arguments, relationships and generalizations.

Types of Study Guides

Interlocking study guide. In the case of the interlocking study guide, statements

From David J. Tutolo, The study guide—types, purpose and value. *Journal of Reading*, March 1977, *20*, 505–507. Reprinted by permission of Daniel J. Tutolo and the International Reading Association.

proceed from the literal level of meaning (Herber's model, 1970) to the interpretive level of meaning to the applicative level of meaning. The three levels of thinking required of the reader do not intermix. All literal questions are grouped together, all interpretive questions are grouped together, and so on. The sequence of thinking in the interlocking guide always moves from literal to interpretive to applicative.

By keying the statements in some way, the guide can serve as a valuable help in individualizing instruction. Suppose that all literal statements are marked with one star (*). Immature readers can be asked to respond to these statements, while average and brighter students can be expected to respond to two-star and three-star statements. Thus the class is divided into three ability groups all following the same guide yet responding to different parts of the guide.

Research is not yet clear whether concentrating on one kind of thinking is a better approach to learning. Certainly, however, this approach can insulate some students against failure. An immature reader who is guided to respond to literal statements and questions is far more likely to be successful, particularly if this student has a history of quitting or giving up when confronted with complex reading tasks.

Noninterlocking study guide. In the case of the noninterlocking study guide, no such hierarchical thinking is encouraged. The teacher is free to include in the guide any direction that will help the reader to process the information (Cunningham and Shablak, 1975). The thinking necessary for understanding might vary from literal to application and back to literal again as the reader moves through the connected discourse.

The purpose of the study guide is to prepare a plan for reading the text. One way to eliminate the need for study guides is to write expository texts that are easier for students to read. The problem is, as we know, at what level we write these texts when reading levels of students in a typical class are likely to vary considerably. The usual formula used to measure this variance, as suggested by curriculum experts, is two thirds of the median chronological age of the students. With fifteen year olds, this means a spread of reading achievement of ten years.

Interlocking Levels Guide

Read "Tragedy" on page—of your textbook. After you have completed the reading, respond to this study guide. Try to answer correctly without returning to the text material. However, if you are not sure of an answer feel free to reread the assignment and then mark your study guide. Notice that the guide has questions and statements separated into three categories. Section one—the one starred items—calls for your recall of facts as stated in the text. Section two—the two starred items—calls for a different kind of thinking called interpretation. Here you must decide what the author meant by what was said. Section three calls for a third kind of thinking called application. In this section you will be expected to use the facts and interpretations to solve a problem.

Remember, read the account carefully and try to respond without going back to the text. This guide will attempt to measure your recall of information. If, after you have carefully read the guide, there are answers you are not sure about, feel free to return to the text to reread.

Now: Read "Tragedy."

Tragedy

The townspeople regarded "Death Hill" as appropriately named. Over the years sixteen lives had been lost as a result of automobile accidents on the dangerous turns. Despite flasher lights warning of the peril, visitors to the area often miscalculated the turns, with the result of bent fenders and bruised egos. The fatality rate in the teens indicated the problem was far greater than property and ego damage alone.

It wasn't until the town lost two of its own on the second and most dangerous turn that talk began in earnest of building a bypass around "Death Hill." State engineers had been contacted and a preliminary study was now in progress. In projects of this type the state paid ninety percent and the local townspeople ten percent. Most local people considered the project cheap at any price for they had known Becky and Jerry all of their lives. Each time they met the family survivors here or there around town, it served as a silent reminder of the loss that could have been avoided.

Factual questions: Remember, a fact can be verified by going directly to the text for the answer.

Code: * literal   ** interpretation
       *** application

* According to townspeople "Death Hill" was
  A.   a poor nickname
  B.   appropriately named
  C.   a passing fancy
  D.   the greatest local problem

* The preliminary study was intended to determine the cost of
  A.   a tunnel through the hill
  B.   widening the highway
  C.   a bypass
  D.   extensive safety measures

Interpretation: Remember, you are to try to determine what the author meant by what was said.

** What is meant by "the town lost two of its own"? Write a one paragraph explanation: _____

** Select the answer that most nearly represents what the author meant when he said "most local people considered the project cheap at any price."
  A.   Cost is no object where safety is involved.
  B.   This was one death too many.
  C.   The ninety percent—ten percent ratio was appealing.
  D.   Local conscience was now involved.

Application: Considering the facts and ideas as expressed, can you solve these problems?

*** Assume you are the editor of the local newspaper. Six months has passed since City Council received the preliminary report and no action has yet been taken. Write an editorial encouraging positive action on the part of Council to approve a bypass road.
*** The City Council has approved the bypass and now must raise $100,000 as its portion of expenses to construct the bypass. Suggest ways the community can raise this amount.

Noninterlocking Levels Guide

Code: * literal
         ** interpretation
         *** application

* Read paragraph one of "A New Way of Life for Americans." When energy was abundant and cheap we could produce goods more _____.
*** Read paragraph two carefully. List several reasons why this adjustment would be difficult for Americans.
** In paragraph three what is meant by "increasing the quality of life"?
*** Reread paragraph three with this question in mind. Is it better to produce many different kinds of breakfast cereals to appeal to every taste or to limit production only to cereals that are tasty and high in nutritional value? Respond to the question in writing. Tell why you feel as you do.

A New Way of Life for Americans

The energy shortage can be expected to influence the cost of goods and services for years to come. When energy was abundant and cheap we could produce goods more economically and thus sell them at a lower per unit cost. Now that energy is expensive and goods produced higher priced we must make more careful choices about the things we buy.

Perhaps we will have to give up the idea of an extensive wardrobe, two cars for every family, two or more weeks vacation every year, and other signs of our affluent society. One very visible sign of affluence which may be on the decided decline is the department store loaded with consumer goods to appeal to every taste. This adjustment will be difficult for a nation used to consuming so much.

But, when we look at the future it may better to produce and sell products which increase the quality of life rather than simply appeal to insatiable wants. Appealing to our insatiable wants never made us very happy anyway. Perhaps if we direct our efforts as a nation toward producing and consuming goods that enhance the quality of life, we can look forward to a society which takes a more realistic view of wants and the satisfaction of these wants. With the energy shortage upon us this new way of thinking is worth a try.

It perhaps makes more sense to adopt a book which most students in the class can read and then prepare study guides to enhance comprehension of the students. This is easier said than done. Certainly high school teachers are not going to spend countless hours generating study guides to assist all students. It often is easier to set the book aside and assume the responsibility for lecturing and providing the information in other ways.

Teachers, however, might be convinced to generate study guides on those parts of the textbook which contain essential ideas, concepts, and generalizations. Let us suppose that a teacher selects some key concepts that are taught in November of the school year. The teacher carefully prepares the study guide to aid in comprehension of these concepts. The teacher wants mastery of these concepts because instruction throughout the rest of the year will build on these basic ideas. An hour spent generating a guide is an investment that pays dividends many times throughout the year.

If we keep in mind that a study guide once generated can be used over again the next year, we truly have a good investment in teacher time and not an intrusion on important teacher time.

At any rate the use of the study guide makes textbook teaching easier. One can reason that the textbook is not that important and all would agree. Yet, 80 to 90 percent of teachers use a text adopted by their school district. Textbooks are likely to be around for a long time. The problem is not the textbook, in my view, but rather the inflexible use of the textbook. Study guides increase this textbook flexibility and make it possible for more students to be successful in their reading.

References

Cunningham, Dick and Scott L. Shablak. "Selective Reading Guide-O-Rama: The Content Teacher's Best Friend." *Journal of Reading* vol. 19, no. 5 (February 1975), pp. 380–82.

Herber, Harold L. Teaching Reading in Content Areas. Englewood Cliffs, N.J.: Prentice-Hall, Inc., 1970.

59. Learning to Learn: On Training Students to Learn from Texts

Ann L. Brown, Joseph C. Campione and Jeanne D. Day

The general theme of this paper is how we can devise instructional routines to help students learn to learn. The dominant questions which have motivated training studies in developmental psychology are: can we improve upon students' spontaneous performance, and can we enhance their ability to perform future tasks of the same kind? Training studies aimed at improving students' academic performance can succeed by adding substantially to the students' knowledge; or they can succeed by instructing students in ways to enhance their own knowledge (i.e., in promoting learning to learn activities). It is this latter outcome that we now think is most desirable. A historical review of training studies in developmental research will provide a framework within which to place our recent research. Consideration will be given to the shift in emphasis from a concentration on instruction aimed at improving student performance per se to the current emphasis on instruction aimed at improving students' self-control and self-awareness of their own learning processes.

Historically, training studies in developmental research have aimed at inculcating deliberate strategies for promoting recall of information. But rote recall, although valuable, is not the only desirable outcome of learning activities. Often we want to enhance students' ability to understand the significance of the material they are learning rather than to improve their ability to recall it. Activities that promote recall need not necessarily be optimal for promoting other learning outcomes. Because of the dominance of deliberate memory strategies in training research, we will begin with a brief consideration of this literature and then proceed to discuss training aimed at bringing students to understand the significance of learning strategies, particularly in relation to school tasks such as studying texts.

Strategies of Rote Recall

The most commonly studied strategies of rote recall are rehearsal, categorization and elaboration, and a great deal of research has been conducted to examine the developmental progression in the acquisition of these strategies. Rehearsal, repetition of items to ensure their memorability, is an activity that can be carried out on material that has no inherent meaning, such as a phone number. It can be, and often is, a brute force approach that does not demand any understanding of the significance of the material being processed. The learner is required merely to repeat segments of material until they can be rote recalled. Categorization as a strategy to enhance recall demands that any categorical organization inherent in the material be familiar to the learner and be used to design a plan for learning. Elaboration is a strategy whereby the learner imposes meaning or organization on material to render it more comprehensible.

The degree to which active transformation of the material is required, and the degree to which it is necessary to introduce, refine or combine elements of different strategies, determines the age of initial use and developmental trajectories. In general, however, the emergence of such strategies tends to be dependent on the degree and recency of formal schooling. In schooled populations, they emerge in a recognizable form between five and seven years of age and continue to be tuned and refined throughout the school years. Also common to the developmental course of these strategies is an intermediate stage called a production deficiency, where the child does not produce the strategy spontaneously but can be prompted or instructed to do so quite readily. Training studies in developmental research were initially aimed at examining the intermediate stage of production deficiencies for a variety of theoretical reasons. In some cases, however, the aim was to help younger or slower children produce strategies that they would rarely come to produce spontaneously (Brown, 1974; Brown & Campione, 1978), and it is these "instructional" studies that we will consider next.

Training Rote Recall Strategies

To simplify a very extensive literature, there are three types of training which have been attempted. The first group, and by far the most heavily populated, is the *blind training* study. By this we mean that students are not active conspirators in the training process. They are induced to use a strategy without a concurrent understanding of the significance of that activity. For example, children can be taught to use a cumulative rehearsal strategy by initially copying an adult, but they are not told *explicitly* why they must act this way or that the activity helps performance or that it is an activity appropriate to a certain class of memory situations, not just this particular task and setting. In the task of free recall of categorizable materials, children can be tricked into using the categorical structure by clever, incidental, orienting instructions (Murphy & Brown, 1975), or the material can be blocked into categories (Gerjuoy & Spitz, 1966), or recall can be cued by category name (Green, 1974); but the children are not told why, or even if, this helps recall. In elaboration tasks, children can be induced to provide an elaborated encoding of a pair of unrelated items but they are not informed that this activity can be an effective learning strategy (Turnure, Buium, & Thurlow, 1976). All of these tricks lead to enhanced recall because the children are producing an appropriate activity. They fail, however, to result in maintenance of generalization of the strategy; that is, the children neither use the activity subsequently on their own volition, nor transfer the activity to similar learning situations. This is scarcely surprising as the significance of the activity was never made clear.

An intermediate level of instruction, *informed training*, is where children are both induced to use a strategy and also given some information concerning the significance of that activity. For example, children may be taught to rehearse and receive feedback concerning their improved performance (Kennedy & Miller, 1976), or they might be taught to rehearse on more than one rehearsal task; that is, they are trained in multiple contexts so that they can see the utility of the strategy (Belmont, Butterfield, & Borkowski, 1978). In the categorization task, students may be given practice in putting items into category, *and* informed that this will help them remember, *and* cued by category on retrieval failure (Burger, Blackman, Holmes, & Zetlin, 1978; Ringel & Springer, 1980). These training packages result in both improved performance on the training task and maintenance of the activity by the child when faced with subsequent similar problems. There is some evidence of generalization, but so far the evidence has been very near; that is, the generalization task is very similar to the training task (Brown & Campione, 1978, in press).

The third level of instruction, *self-control training*, is the level where children are not only instructed in the use of a strategy, but are also explicitly instructed in how to employ, monitor, check, and evaluate that strategy. The number of studies that have employed this combination are few, but preliminary results do indicate that the strategy-plus-control training packages are the most successful at inducing not only enhanced performance but also transfer of training to appropriate settings (Brown & Campione, in press). We will illustrate this type of training with one study from our laboratory (Brown, Campione, & Barclay, 1979).

Recall-readiness training study

We were interested in teaching mildly retarded, grade school children the simple skill of checking to see if they knew material sufficiently well to be tested. This is an essential prerequisite for effective studying and one that young children have difficulty understanding (Flavell, Friedrichs, & Hoyt, 1970). Therefore, we devised a simple task where we could make the self-checking demands of such studying activities quite explicit. The hope was that with the essential elements made clear in a simple situation, we could look for transfer to more complex, school-like learning tasks.

The simple training task consisted of presenting the students with a list of pictures, too long for them to recall without using some deliberate memory strategy. They were told to study the list for as long as they liked until they were sure they could remember all the picture names. Even given unlimited study time, performance was initially poor, with students terminating study rapidly, long before they could recall the items.

During the training portion of the study, children were taught strategies which could be used to facilitate their learning of the lists, along with the overseeing or monitoring of those strategies. The latter aspect of training was accomplished by employing strategies that included a self-testing component and by telling the children to monitor their state of learning. For example, two effective strategies are cumulative rehearsal and anticipation. Anticipation involves active attempts to recall an item before looking at it, and rehearsal involves repetition of a small subset of the list. These activities both act as an aid to memory and provide information about its current status (i.e., if the learner cannot anticipate the next picture in a list, this provides the requisite knowledge that the list, in its entirety, is not yet known).

There were two groups of trainees: The older children were approximately 11 years old with mental ages of 8 years; the younger children were 9 years old with mental ages of 6 years. The older children taught the strategies involving a self-testing component improved their performance significantly (from 58 percent correct to almost perfect accuracy), whereas those in a control condition did not. These effects were extremely durable, lasting over a series of posttests, the last test occurring one year after the training had ended. The younger children did not benefit much from training. They improved their performance significantly only on the first posttest, which was prompted (i.e., the experimenter told the children to continue using the strategy they had been taught). In the absence of such prompts, they did not differ significantly from their original level of performance. Even though the younger and older children did not differ in their level of original learning, they did differ in how readily they responded to training.

Given the successful result of training for the older students, we examined whether they had learned any general features about self-testing and monitoring on the simple laboratory task which they could transfer to a more school-like situation, learning the gist of prose passages. The students were asked to read and recall several short stories commensurate with their reading ability. They were permitted unlimited study time and were asked to indicate that they were ready to risk a test only when they felt confident that they could recall the essential information. Students who had received training on the list-learning tasks outperformed untrained students on four measures of efficiency: (1) the total amount recalled, (2) the ratio of important material to trivia included in their recall, (3) time spent studying, and (4) overt indices of strategy use (such as lip movement, looking away, and self-testing, etc.) Training on a very simple self-checking task did transfer to the school-like task of studying texts. We believe that an effective technique for inducing the rudiments of mature studying behavior is to (a) simplify the task so that the basic rules can be demonstrated, (b) train an appropriate learning strategy, *and* (c) train the self-monitoring of that strategy.

From our early work with training simple learning strategies, we came to two general conclusions (Brown & Campione, 1978, in press): Children should be fully informed participants in any training enterprise (i.e., they should be helped to understand why they should be strategic and when it is necessary to be so), and they should be trained in the self-management of the strategies they must deploy. The degree of explicit training needed on any one task will depend on the starting competence of the children and their general speed of learning. For slower children, or those with little prior knowledge, it might be necessary to make each step explicit. This is usually the case with mentally retarded students (Campione & Brown, 1977). Brighter, better informed students tend to show faster learning and some spontaneous transfer, and, therefore, it is often not necessary to make explicit all the steps of learning and the need for transfer, and so forth. The degree to which it is necessary to make each step explicit is a measure of the child's zone of potential development or region of sensitivity to instruction. (See Brown & French, 1979, for a discussion of this Vygotskian concept.)

Coming to Understand the Significance of One's Activities

Recall of information is often demanded in schools, both verbatim recall as in vocabulary tests and gist recall as when the student is required to reconstruct the essential meaning of a text. Developing strategies that aid recall of information is, therefore, a worthwhile activity. Recall of information, however, is not the only desirable outcome of learning, and strategies that promote recall of information are not always the most appropriate for enhancing other learning outcomes. For example, Nitsch (1977) found that different kinds of practice were needed to ensure that learners could remember the definition of concepts, as opposed to ensuring that they could readily understand new instances of the concepts. A similar finding was reported by Mayer and Greeno (1972) concerning the appropriate training for students learning the binomial distribution. Repeated practice in using the formula or rule led to very accurate performance on subsequent problems of exactly the same form as training, whereas training aimed at explaining the significance of the components of the formula led to somewhat less accurate rule use but far better performance on alternate statements of the problem class.

In order to design appropriate training, we need to analyze the question: training for what? Similarly, in order to become really effective learners, children must analyze the learning situation for themselves.

Effective learning involves four main considerations: (1) the activities engaged in by the learner, (2) certain characteristics of the learner including his/her capacity and state of prior knowledge, (3) the nature of the materials to be learned, and (4) the critical task. In order for the psychologist or educator to devise a training program, it is necessary to consider all four aspects of the learning situation. For example, consider learning from texts. Any strategy (learning activity) one might adopt should be influenced by the inherent structure of the text (its syntactic, semantic and structural complexity, its adherence to good form, etc.), the extent to which the text's informational content is compatible with existing knowledge (characteristics of the learner), and the test to which the learning must be put (critical task, i.e., gist recall, resolving ambiguities, acquiring basic concepts, understanding instructions, etc.). As psychologists, interested in understanding and promoting learning, we must appreciate the complex interactions implicit in this characterization of the learning situation, and we argue that this is exactly what the student must do. In order to become expert learners, students must develop some of the same insights as the psychologist into the demands of the learning situation. They must learn about their own cognitive characteristics, their available learning strategies, the demands of various learning tasks and the inherent structure of the material. They must tailor their activities finely to the competing demands of all these forces in order to become flexible and effective learners. In other words, they must *learn how to learn* (Bransford, Stein, Shelton & Owings, 1980; Brown, 1980). As instructors our task should be to devise training routines that will help the student to develop the understanding of the learning situation. In principle, training can be aimed at all four points. In fact, the majority of studies have aimed at training strategies or rules for prose processing. We will again illustrate strategy training approaches with a series of studies from our laboratory concerned with helping students to improve their summarization skills.

Training Strategies for Summarization

The ability to provide an adequate summary is a useful tool for understanding and studying texts. For example, an essential element of effective studying is the ability to estimate one's readiness to be tested, and we dealt earlier with simple procedures for ensuring at least a primitive form of such self-testing (Brown, Campione & Barclay, 1979). A commonly reported sophisticated method of testing one's level of comprehension and retention and, therefore, one's preparedness for a test, is to attempt to summarize the material one has been reading. This is quite a difficult task for immature learners. After considering many examples of children's failures and experts' successes when summarizing texts, we identified six basic rules essential to summarization (Brown & Day, Note 1). These operations are very similar to the macrorules described by Kintsch and van Dijk (1978) as basic operations involved in comprehending and remembering prose.

Two of the six rules involved the *deletion* of unnecessary material; one should obviously delete material that is trivial. Grade school chilren are quite adept at this if the content of the material is familiar (Brown & Day, Note 1). One should also delete material that is important but redundant. Two of the rules of summarization involve the *substitution of a superordinate* term or event for a list of items or actions. For example if a text contains a list such as "cats, dogs, goldfish, gerbils and parrots," one can sustitute the term pets. Similarly, one can substitute a superordinate action for a list of subcomponents of that action, for example, "John went to London," for "John left the house," "John went to the train station," "John bought a ticket," and so forth. These rules are roughly comparable to Kintsch and van Dijk's generalization rules. The two remaining rules have to do with providing a summary of the main constituent unit of text, the paragraph. The first rule is *select a topic sentence*, if any, for this is the author's summary of the paragraph. The second rule is, if there is no topic sentence, *invent* your own. These operations are roughly equivalent to Kintsch and van Dijk's integration and construction rules.

These operations are used freely by experts (rhetoric teachers) when summarizing texts (Brown & Day, Note 1). Do less sophisticated readers realize that these basic rules can be applied? To examine the developmental progression associated with the use of the basic rules we looked at the summaries produced by students from grades 5, 7, and 10 and various college-aged groups. The youngest children were able to use the two deletion rules with above 90 percent accuracy, showing that they understood the basic idea behind a summary. For the more complex rules, however, developmental differences were apparent. Students became increasingly adept at using the superordination and select topic sentence rules, with college students performing extremely well. The most difficult rule, invention, was rarely used by fifth graders, used on only a third of appropriate occasions by 10th graders, and on only half of the occasions when it was appropriate by four-year college students. Experts, college rhetoric teachers, used the invention rule in almost every permissible case. But junior college students performed like seventh graders, having great difficulty with the invention rule and using only the deletion rules effectively.

We explained this developmental progression in terms of the degree of cognitive intervention needed to apply each rule. The easier deletion rules require that information in the text be omitted and the intermediate topic sentence rule requires that the main sentence contained in a paragraph be identified. The more difficult invention rule requires that learners supply a synopsis in their own words. It is the processes of invention that are the essence of good summarization, that are used with facility by experts, and that are most difficult for novice learners.

Helping Students Learn to Learn from Text

The two sets of studies used as illustrations, the recall-readiness (Brown, Campione, & Barclay, 1979) and summarization (Day, 1980; Brown & Day, Note 1) training studies, were selected because they are excellent examples of what we can do readily and what we have more difficulty in accomplishing. For example, with detailed task analyses, experts' advice and intensive training, we were able to help remedial college students improve their ability to summarize texts. But the texts were very easy for them, that is, they were texts of fifth-grade readability level and were focused on familiar contents. Therefore, instructions to delete trivia met with compliance. If the texts had concentrated on less familiar content or had been more structurally complex, it is not clear that the instruction to delete trivia would be so easy to follow. One must have some background concerning the content knowledge to enable one to recognize trivia readily.

There are two general classes of problems that can impede effective studying: inefficient application of rules and strategies, and impoverished background knowledge. The child may lack the necessary strategies to engage in appropriate learning activities and we have ample evidence in the literature of children's lack of strategic knowledge. Alternatively, children may lack the requisite knowledge of the world to understand certain texts that presuppose adequate background experience. In principle, instruction can be aimed at overcoming one or both these problems.

Consider instruction in rules and strategies. If adequate performance depends on the application of a set of rules and these rules can be specified exactly, then it should be possible to design instructional routines that introduce the uninitiated to these possibilities. For example, providing children with concrete procedures to help them continue studying and self-testing until ready for a test improves study performance in young children (Brown, Campione, & Barclay, 1979). Instructing students in efficient self-question techniques is also an effective training procedure (Andre & Anderson, 1978–1979). Sensitizing young readers to the logical structure of text and the inherent meaning in certain passages again helps the less able reader (Bransford, Stein, Shelton, & Owings, 1980). The more detailed understanding the instructor has of effective rules for reading and studying, the more readily can those rules be trained. Our work with summarization rules is a case in point. Merely instructing students to make their summaries as brief as possible and to omit unnecessary information was not an explicit enough guide for junior college students. Exact specification of the rules that could be used to achieve this aim, however, was an extremely effective instructional routine. Quite simply, the more we are able to specify the rules used by experts, the more we will be able to successfully instruct the novice.

The second major impediment to effective learning is a deficient knowledge base. If the text deals with topics that the reader is not familiar with, it will be difficult for the reader to understand the significance of the material, to select main points and disregard trivia. One answer to this problem is to select texts that deal with familiar material. But, whereas the teacher may actively attempt to provide the requisite background knowledge for a particular text, she/he cannot always do this. To overcome the impediments to effective reading caused by a lack of knowledge, one must set about increasing the learners' general store of information. While this is no doubt desirable, even necessary, it certainly takes time. The only prescription for training which follows a diagnosis of deficient knowledge is one of general enrichment, which few schools have the resources to provide.

Learners must themselves consider the four points and their interaction—perhaps as described in the following: (1) *Learning activities:* The learner should consider the available strategies, both general and specific. Specific strategies could be the rules for summarization just described, while general strategies could be variants of such general comprehension and study-monitoring activities as generating hypotheses about the text, predicting outcomes, noting and remediating confusions, and so forth (Baker & Brown, in press; Brown, in press b). (2) *Characteristics of the learner:* The learner should also consider his/her general characteristics such as a limited immediate memory capacity for meaningless materials and a reservoir of appropriate prior knowledge. Thus, the learner should not overburden his/her memory by attempting to retain large segments of texts, too many pending questions, too many unresolved ambiguities, and so forth (Baker & Brown, in press). The learner should attempt to tie the information content into any prior knowledge possessed, to activate appropriate schemata (Anderson, 1977; Brown, Smiley, Day, Townsend, & Lawton, 1977), to seek relationships or analogies to prior knowledge (Brown, in press a; Simon & Hayes, 1976; Gick & Holyoak, Note 2) to see the information in the light of knowledge he/she already has. (3) *Nature of the materials:* The learner should also examine the text itself for the logical structure of the material, its form as well as its content. Although meaning does not reside in the text alone, authors are sometimes helpful in cueing meaning. They flag important statements by such devices as headings, subsections, topic sentences, summaries, redundancies and just plain "and now for something really important" statements. Students can be

made aware of the significance of these cues and induced to actively seek help from such sources. (4) *Critical task:* The learner should consider the aim of the learning activity, the purpose of his/her endeavors; he/she should also be aware that different desired outcomes require different learning activities and thus learn to tailor efforts accordingly.

What we are advocating here is an avoidance of blind training techniques and a serious attempt at informed, self-control training, that is, to provide novice learners with the information necessary for them to design effective plans of their own. The essential aim of training is to make the trainee more aware of the active nature of learning and the importance of employing problem-solving, trouble-shooting routines to enhance understanding. If learners can be made aware of (1) basic strategies for reading and remembering, (2) simple rules of text construction, (3) differing demands of a variety of tests to which their information may be put, and (4) the importance of activating any background knowledge which they may have, they cannot help but become more effective learners. Such self-awareness is a prerequisite for self-regulation, the ability to orchestrate, monitor, and check one's own cognitive activities.

Notes

1. Brown, A. L., & Day, J. D. *The development of rules for summarizing texts*. Unpublished manuscript, University of Illinois, 1980.
2. Gick, M., & Holyoak, K. *Analogical reasoning in adults*. Unpublished manuscript, University of Michigan, 1979.

References

Anderson, R. C. The notion of schemata and the education enterprise. In R. C. Anderson, R. J. Spiro, & W. E. Montague (Eds.), *Schooling and the acquisition of knowledge*. Hillsdale, N.J.: Lawrence Erlbaum, 1977.

Andre, M. D. A., & Anderson, T. H. The development and evaluation of a self-questing study technique. *Reading Research Quarterly*, 1978–1979, *14*, 605–623.

Baker, L., & Brown, A. L. Metacognitive skills of reading. In D. Pearson (Ed.), *Handbook of reading research*. New York: Longman, in press.

Belmont, J. M., Butterfield, E. C., & Borkowski, J. G. Training retarded people to generalize memorization methods across memory tasks. In M. H. Gruneberg, P. E. Morris, & R. N. Sykes (Eds.), *Practical aspects of memory*. London: Academic Press, 1978.

Bransford, J. D., Stein, B. S. Shelton, T. S., & Owings, R. A. Cognition and adaptation: The importance of learning to learn. In J. Harvey (Ed.), *Cognition, social behavior and the environment*. Hillsdale, N.J.: Lawrence Erlbaum, 1980.

Brown, A. L. The role of strategic behavior in retardate memory. In N. R. Ellis (Ed.), *International review of research in mental retardation* (Vol. 7). New York: Academic Press, 1974.

Brown, A. L. Learning and development: The problems of compatibility, access and induction. *Human Development*, in press. (a)

Brown, A. L. Metacognitive development and reading. In R. J. Spiro, B. C. Bruce, & W. F. Brewer (Eds.), *Theoretical issues in reading comprehension*. Hillsdale, N.J.: Lawrence Erlbaum, 1980.

Brown, A. L. & Campione, J. C. Permissible inferences from the outcome of training studies in cognitive development research. *Quarterly Newsletter of the Institute for Comparative Human Development*, 1978, *2*, 46–53.

Brown, A. L., & Campione, J. C. Inducing flexible thinking: A problem of access. In M. Friedman, J. P. Das, & N. O'Connor (Eds.), *Intelligence and learning*. New York: Plenum Press, in press.

Brown, A. L., Campione, J. C., & Barclay, C. R. Training self-checking routines for estimating test readiness: Generalization from list learning to prose recall. *Child Development*, 1979, *50*, 501–512.

Brown, A. L., & French, L. A. The zone of potential development: Implication for intelligence testing in the year 2000. *Intelligence*. 1979, *3*, 255–277.

Brown, A. L., Smiley, S. S., Day, J., Townsend, M., & Lawton, S. C. Intrusion of a thematic idea in children's recall of prose. *Child Development*, 1977, *48*, 1,454–1,466.

Burger, A. L., Blackman, L. S., Holmes, M., & Zetlin, A. Use of active sorting and retrieval strategies as a facilitator of recall, clustering, and sorting by EMR and non-retarded children. *American Journal of Mental Deficiency*, 1978, *83*, 253–261.

Campione, J. C., & Brown, A. L. Memory and metamemory development in educable retarded children. In R. V. Kail, Jr. & J. W. Hagen (Eds.), *Perspectives on the development of memory and cognition*. Hillsdale, N.J.: Lawrence Erlbaum, 1977.

Day, J. D. *Training summarization skills: A comparison of teaching methods*. Unpublished doctoral dissertation, University of Illinois, 1980.

Flavell, J. H., Friedrichs, A. G., & Hoyt, J. D. Developmental changes in memorization processes. *Cognitive Psychology*, 1970, *1*, 324–340.

Gerjuoy, I. R., & Spitz, H. Associative clustering in free recall: Intellectual and developmental variables. *American Journal of Mental Deficiency*, 1966, *70*, 918–927.

Green, J. M. Category cues in free recall: Retarded adults of two vocabulary age levels. *Amercan Journal of Mental Deficiency*, 1974, *78*, 419–425.

Kennedy, B. A., & Miller, D. J. Persistent use of verbal rehearsal as a function of information about its value. *Child Development*, 1976, *47*, 566–569.

Kintsch, W., & van Dijk, T. A. Toward a model of text comprehension and production. *Psychological Review*, 1978, *85* (5), 363–394.

Mayer, R. E., & Greeno, J. G. Structures differences between learning outcomes produced by different instructional methods. *Journal of Educational Psychology*, 1972, *63*, 165–173.

Murphy, M. D., & Brown, A. L. Incidental learning in preschool children as a function of level of cognitive analysis. *Journal of Experimental Child Psychology*, 1975, *19*, 509–523.

Nitsch, K. E. *Structuring decontextualized forms of knowledge*. Unpublished doctoral dissertation, Vanderbilt University, 1977.

Ringel, B. A., & Springer, C. J. On knowing how well one is remembering: The persistence of strategy use during transfer. *Journal of Experimental Child Psychology*, 1980, *29*, (2), 322–333.

Simon, H. A., & Hayes, J. R. The understanding process: Problem isomorphs. *Cognitive Psychology*, 1976, *8*, 165–190.

Turnure, J. D. Buium, M., & Thurlow, M. L. The effectiveness of interogatives for promoting verbal elaboration productivity in young children. *Child Development*, 1976, *47*, 851–855.

Vygotsky, L. S. *Mind in society: The development of higher psychological processes.* M. Cole, V. John-Steiner, S. Scribner, & E. Souberman (Eds.). Cambridge, Mass.: Harvard University Press, 1978.

60. Strategies for Enhancing Readiness and Recall in Content Areas: The Encoding Specificity Principle

John E. Readence and David Moore

Much emphasis in recent years has been placed on pre-reading strategies that enhance comprehension of text material. Research begun by Rothkopf on mathemagenic behaviors (1965, 1972) and Ausubel on advance organizers (1968) points to the necessity of providing pre-reading experiences to enhance cognitive readiness, comprehension, and subsequent learning efficiency. Rothkopf (1970) defines mathemagenic behaviors as those activities that help students achieve certain instructional objectives specified previously. He found that study aids such as adjunct questions "shape" what students learn from text material. Thus, students' reading behaviors can be adapted to fit specific tasks. Ausubel (1968, 1978), on the other hand, bases his research on the concept of meaningful verbal learning. His operationally defined advance organizers are intended to serve as an aid to learning and retention of concepts. According to Ausubel, learning is maximized as advance organizers help students associate new information to prior knowledge.

The importance of pre-reading strategies has been emphasized more recently in a line of research investigating mental schema and its effect on processing connected discourse (Anderson, Spiro, & Montague, 1977). Schema has been defined as one's pre-existing knowledge, or "a kind of mental framework based on cultural experience into which new facts are fitted" (Clark & Clark, 1977, p. 168). Rumelhart and Ortony (1977) have proposed a "top-down" model of reading that includes schema as crucial to the reading process. Top-down processing requires an activation of schema to form conceptual expectations within which new learnig takes place. With the reconstruction of prior knowledge from one's mental framework, learners are able to associate new to known information and also make assumptions about concepts which are not explicitly stated in the incoming information. Failure to adequately utilize existing schema is said to deter or inhibit learning. Additionally, Herber and his associates at Syracuse University have created a line of

From John E. Readance and David Moore, Strategies for enhancing readiness and recall in content areas: The encoding specificity principle. *Reading Psychology*, Fall 1979, *1*, 47–54. Reprinted by permission of the publisher.

applied research that does much to validate cognitive readiness activities at the secondary level (1969, 1973, 1977). All this diverse input has focused attention on activating pre-existing knowledge and creating expectancies before students undertake the difficult task of learning from content textbooks (Readence & Moore, 1978). Readers who fail to associate new to known information may be unable to process the heavy conceptual load in subject-matter textbooks, and it may result in lack of comprehension.

While there can be little quarrel that pre-reading strategies are important, it must be remembered that the pre-reading stage is but only one part of the total instructional lesson. Perhaps just as important is the post-reading phase. It is in this stage that concepts are refined, extended, and reinforced. Unfortunately, post-reading activities and their theoretical rationale are not currently as extensively researched as their counterpart, the pre-reading activities. This is curious, as post-reading strategies seem to greatly enhance future retrieval possibilities for newly learned concepts (Estes & Vaughan, 1978). Therefore, it seems appropriate for educators to pursue instructional strategies that first establish cognitive readiness for learning and then later bring about retrieval of that learning.

Some interesting research has suggested the possibility for such instructional strategies. Wood (1972) found that retrieval processes in learning are facilitated when similar cues are presented during both the pre-reading and post-reading stages. Tulving and Thomson (1973) have described this phenomenon in their writing on memory processes as the encoding specificity principle. The encoding specificity principle functions, first, as one learns new information under certain conditions, and, second, as those same conditions stimulate retrieval of the information. In other words, pre-reading stimuli first provided

in a learning situation for purposes of cognitive readiness may also be used in a later, retrieval situation to reconstruct the learning.

Instructional applications of the encoding specificity principle offer some promising methods to help students cope with content area text information. If a stimulus is provided readers for pre-reading, readiness purposes, that identical stimulus may be presented in a post-reading situation as a cue to more effectively enable students to retrieve the material read. What follows, then, is a discussion of instructional strategies for content reading which have been adapted to capitalize upon the encoding specificity principle.

Structured Overview

The structured overview (Barron, 1969; Earle, 1969) was designed as a means to provide cognitive readiness by pre-teaching the technical vocabulary of a content lesson. It is derived from the work of Ausubel (1968) on advance organizers and provides students with a framework of the relationships among content vocabulary.

Briefly, the teacher performs a task analysis of a reading passage and selects the concepts to be stressed. The teacher next selects terms from the passage that are necessary for understanding those concepts. These terms are arranged in a schematic diagram to convey their relationships and thereby illustrate the key concepts. Any words previously learned by students may be added to provide clarity in the overview. Finally, the teacher evaluates the overview to make sure it can be easily interpreted and that it conveys the major concepts to students.

For illustrative purposes, the key concepts, key vocabulary, and accompanying structured overview of an introductory lesson in U.S. Government are presented here.

Key concepts

1. The U.S. Government consists of three main branches.
2. A system of checks and balances maintains a balance of powers between the branches.

Key vocabulary

U.S. Government   executive
judiciary   judicial review
veto   legislative
override   checks and balances

Structured Overview

When presenting an overview, teachers should thoroughly explain the meaning of each new term, its relation to other terms, and the overall scheme. Teachers should pose questions to the students and encourage discussion as the overview is presented. Simultaneous exploration of the overview by the teacher and students is also an aid to better understanding.

To adapt the structured overview so as to capitalize upon the encoding specificity principle, the teacher again presents the overview during the post-reading phase. As a pre-reading strategy, the overview serves to activate students' prior knowledge and preview the upcoming information; in the post-reading phase, the overview serves as a stimulus that enables students to retrieve and reconstruct relationships among concepts found in the text. Either verbal or written responses may be employed to insure thoughtful consideration by students.

Outline

Outlines can be an excellent instructional tool for students; likewise, they can be an abysmal waste of time. The outline should not be so detailed that it becomes cumbersome, but rather, it should contain only the important ideas to be stressed in a sequentially ordered, main idea-supporting detail paradigm. Structured thusly, the outline serves as a practical and useful tool for instruction.

Teacher-prepared outlines can be employed as easily as structured overviews to utilize the encoding specificity principle. Initially presenting an outline of upcoming text will serve to activate students' prior knowledge and develop expectancies; the later presentation of the outline will serve as a stimulus to retrieve concepts acquired during the actual reading. Just as with the structured overview, teachers are encouraged to involve students through questions and discussion whenever possible. An outline based on the same passage as the structured overview presented earlier is offered below. It is shown here to illustrate the similarities and differences between the two instructional formats.

U.S. Government

1. The U.S. Government consists of three branches
   a. Legislative
   b. Executive
   c. Judiciary
2. Checks and balances maintain the balance of power
   a. Appeals
   b. Veto
   c. Judicial Review

Anticipation Guides

The anticipation guide (Herber, 1978) is a variation of a study guide and is designed to generate higher-order thinking about a topic prior to reading. Unlike a traditional study guide, students react to statements before they read in order to become attuned to the major ideas of a selection. Statements used in the anticipation guide are developed by the teacher to point out those major ideas and themes. Some statements constructed for the guide should be supported by the text while others should be opposed by it. They should all deal with concepts familiar to students. Below is an example of an anticipation guide that deals with a quotation by Martin Luther used in an English class.

Even if I knew certainly
the world would end tomorrow,
I would plant an apple tree today.

You	Author	Statement
_____	_____	1. Since you only go around once in life, you should grab for all the gusto you can get.
_____	_____	2. Death waits for no man.
_____	_____	3. Don't put off until tomorrow what you can do today.
_____	_____	4. It is better to be optimistic than pessimistic about the future.

The statements should be recorded on paper and presented for students' reaction. They check statements with which they agree and then prepare themselves to defend their reactions through class or small group discussion. This phase of the anticipation guide is the pre-reading phase wherein cognitive and affective readiness is developed. After reading the passage, students are instructed to reread the guide and then respond again to the statements. This time, however, the task is not only to determine their own reactions to the statements but to determine what the author's reactions might be. A thorough discussion of the statements from both viewpoints follows the second presentation of the anticipation guide. This discussion is designed to refine, extend, and reinforce the ideas presented throughout the lesson. This second presentation of the same statements serves as the cue for retrieval of higher-order concepts, thereby completing the paradigm of the encoding specificity principle.

Directed Reading-Thinking Activity

The Directed Reading-Thinking Activity (DRTA) (Stauffer, 1975) is intended to develop students' abilities to set purposes for reading, comprehend factual information, and read critically. This is accomplished by helping students utilize their experiential background in efforts to predict the author's message. Hansell (1976) has discussed the DRTA in relation to improving content area reading.

The DRTA is essentially a process of previewing, predicting, reading, and verifying. Students are directed first to examine special aspects of text such as the title, subtitles and any pictorial aids. These stimuli for prediction are largely the same as those attended to during the Survey phase of SQ3R as elaborated by Aukerman (1972) among others. From their initial inspection, students are encouraged to make predictions about the content of the selection. Discussion and evaluation of the predictions is encouraged. Students' inspection and subsequent predictions about the text, then, form the cues for encoding specificity.

Once predictions have been made, students are directed to read the selection for verification. Following the reading, students compare their predictions with the information found in the selection and evaluate the match. At this point students must produce evidence from the text to support their predictions. Once this is done, succeeding portions of text are previewed and predictions are refined, extended or new ones are generated.

Thus, the DRTA incorporates the dual-processing aspects of the encoding specificity principle. Students are directed to make predictions based upon portions of text and their experiential backgrounds in the pre-reading phases of the strategy. The post-reading phase, then, consists of retrieving information from the selection highlighted by the identical cued stimuli, the students' own predictions.

Adjunct Questions

Adjunct questions are placed either before or after portions of text and have a "shaping" effect on the study procedure utilized while learning from text (Rothkopf, 1972). Adjunct questions focus students' attention on specified learning objectives. A great deal of research has been conducted regarding specific effects of adjunct questions, and one study, in particular, helps describe the relationship between adjunct questions and the encoding specificity principle. Bruning (1968) hypothesized from his research on review techniques that the identical set of pre- and post-questions simultaneously enhance students' review of learning and confirm whether relevant prior knowledge was mobilized for learning activities.

Bearing in mind the interaction of dual processing in the principle of encoding specificity, the Bruning study indicates a potential for the use of identical pre- and post-questions in reading text material. Pre-questions induce readers to attend to specific information in text; post-questions act to retrieve that information. Especially when the information to be processed is conceptually based, adjunct questions incorporating the encoding specificity principle may be advantageous.

Reviews by Faw and Walter (1976) and Frase (1970) among others, have cautioned that the type of question asked of students will influence their learning from text. In particular, literal or factual level questions enhance the learning of specific facts but tend to inhibit overall, incidental learning. Conceptually based, nonliteral questions, on the other hand, facilitate both relevant and incidental learning; i.e., such questions contribute to the acquisition of ideas as well as facts. Teachers should bear this in mind when constructing adjunct questions to enhance comprehension of their specified objectives. The use of a taxonomy of comprehension questions as recommended by Sanders (1972) or Hunkins (1972) is suggested for those individuals seeking further clarification in question construction.

In summary, the authors have discussed a principle of learning along with several instructional strategies which encompass both cognitive readiness for and enhanced retrieval of textual information. The strategies are by no means the only alternatives available to teachers as they employ the encoding specificity principle; however, they are offered as examples for perusal and as specific strategies for teachers seeking an efficient means to aid students in learning from text.

References

Aukerman, R. C. *Reading in the secondary school classroom*. New York: McGraw-Hill, 1972.

Ausubel, D. P. *Educational psychology—a cognitive view*. New York: Holt, Rinehart and Winston, 1968.

Ausubel, D. P. In defense of advance organizers: A reply to the critics. *Review of Educational Research*, 1978, 48, 251–257.

Barron, R. F. The use of vocabulary as an advance organizer. In H. L. Herber & P. L. Sanders (Eds.), *Research in reading in the content areas: First year report*. Syracuse, New York: Syracuse University Reading and Language Arts Center, 1969, 29–39.

Bruning, R. H. Effects of review and test-like events within the learning of prose material. *Journal of Educational Psychology*, 1968, 59, 16–19.

Clark, Herbert & Clark, E. *Language and psychology* NY: Harcourt Brace Jovanovich, 1977.

Earle, R. A. Use of the structured overview in mathematics classes. In H. L. Herber & P. L. Sanders (Eds.), *Research in reading in the content areas: First year report*. Syracuse, New York: Syracuse University Reading and Language Arts Center, 1969, 49–58.

Estes, T. H., & Vaughan, J. L., Jr. *Reading and learning in the content classroom*. Boston: Allyn & Bacon, 1978.

Faw, H. W., & Waller, T. G. Mathemagenic behaviours and efficiency in learning from prose materials: Review, critique and recommendations. *Review of Educational Research*, 1976, 46, 691–720.

Frase, L. T. Boundary conditions for mathemagenic behaviors. *Review of Educational Research*, 1970, 40, 337–347.

Glynn, S. M., & DiVesta, F. J. Outline and hierarchical organization as aids for study and retrieval. *Journal of Educational Psychology*, 1977, 69, 89–95.

Hansell, T. S. Increasing understanding in content reading. *Journal of Reading*, 1976, 19, 307–310.

Herber, H. L. *Teaching reading in content areas* (2nd ed.). Englewood Cliffs. NJ: Prentice-Hall, 1978.

Herber, H. L., & Barron, R. F. (Eds.). *Research in reading in the content areas: First year report*. Syracuse, NY: Syracuse University Reading and Language Arts Center, 1973.

Herber, H. L., & Sanders, P. L. (Eds.). *Research in reading in the content areas: First year report*. Syracuse, NY: Syracuse University Reading and Language Arts Center, 1969.

Herber, H. L., & Vacca, R. T. (Eds.). *Research in reading in the content areas: Third year report*. Syracuse, NY: Syracuse University Reading and Language Arts Center, 1977.

Hunkins, F. P. *Questioning strategies and techniques*. Boston: Allyn & Bacon, 1972.

Readence, J. E., & Moore, D. *Teaching strategies that enhance 'top down' comprehension in the content areas*. Paper presented at the Annual Meeting of the College Reading Association, Washington, D.C., October, 1978.

Rothkopf, E. Z. The concept of mathemagenic activities. *Review of Educational Research*, 1970, 40, 325–336.

Rothkopf, E. Z. Some theoretical and experimental approaches to problems in written instruction. In J. D. Krumboltz (Ed.), *Learning and the educational process*. Chicago: McNally, 1965, 193–221.

Rothkopf, E. Z. Structural text features and control of processes. In R. O. Freedle & J. B. Carroll (Eds.), *Language comprehension and the acquisition of knowledge*. Washington, D.C.: Winston & Sons, 1972, 315–335.

Rumelhart, David E. & Ortony, Andrew. The representation of knowledge in memory. In. R. C. Anderson, R. J. Spiro, & W. E. Montague (Eds.), *Schooling and the acquisition of knowledge*. Hillsdale, N.J.: Erlbaum, 1977.

Sanders, N. M. *Classroom questions: What kinds?* NY: Harper & Row, 1966.

Stauffer, R. C. *Teaching reading as a thinking process*. NY: Harper & Row, 1975.

Tulving, E., & Pearlstone, Z. Availability versus accessibility of information in memory of words. *Journal of Verbal Learning and Verbal Behavior*, 1966, 5, 381–391.

Tulving, E., & Thomson, D. M. Encoding specificity and retrieval processes in episodic memory. *Psychological Review*, 1973, 80, 353–373.

Wood, G. Organizational processes and free recall. In E. Tulving & W. Donaldson (Eds.). *Organization of Memory*. N.Y.: Academic Press, 1972, 49–91.

61. Notetaking: Theory and Research

John P. Rickards

Notetaking is one of the most encouraged and common activities of students. Hartley and Davies (1978) reported that roughly 90 percent of the American and British students (N = 123) sampled for their study indicated that notetaking was an "important activity," and over half of the American students indicated that they have been "encouraged and/or given instructions in the taking of notes." Yet,

This article is reproduced with special permission from the copyright holder, National Society for Performance and Instruction, 1126 Sixteenth Street, N.W., Suite 315, Washington, D.C. 20036. This article is from *Improving Human Performance Quarterly*, Fall 1979, Vol. VIII, No. 3. (*Improving Human Performance Quarterly* was discontinued in 1979.)

an intuitive analysis suggests that it could help or hinder performance.

On the one hand, notetaking forces the student to actively process material by organizing it, "sifting through" material for the essential ideas, and even attempting to associate it with prior knowledge. On the other hand, however, notetaking may interfere with the learning of new information, especially information on which no notes are taken. The notetakers may be so preoccupied with writing down notes that they may miss some points, especially from material presented in lecture form.

The Encoding and External Storage Hypotheses

The encoding hypothesis suggests that the act of taking notes results in some sort of transformation of passage material. The precise nature of this transformation has not yet been fully specified, but it likely involves some processing beyond rote learning, such as "sifting out relevant material" (Di Vesta & Gray, 1973, p. 13) or "distinguishing the parts and determining the structure of the material" (Hartley & Davies, 1978, p. 27). In a similar vein, Peper and Mayer (1978) argue that notetaking forces the learners to organize new information and assimilate it to their cognitive structure. The major empirical implication of the encoding hypothesis is that the mere act of taking notes without any opportunity to review such notes will enhance performance.

The external storage hypothesis, on the other hand, suggests that notes are taken as a means of storing information in some fashion for later use as review. Hence, the external storage idea implies that notetaking per se is not facilitative of recall. Only if learners are given the opportunity to review their notes prior to recall is notetaking effective.

In the experiments conducted by Di Vesta and Gray (1972, 1973), they showed

that a group which took notes (NOTE TAKE condition) was invariably superior in passage recall to a group which did not take notes (NO NOTE condition), thereby providing support for the encoding hypothesis. In their review of the literature, Hartley and Davies (1978) found sixteen investigations providing support for the encoding hypothesis and eighteen studies providing no support for it, including two investigations in which a no notetaking condition was significantly superior to a notetaking one. Without a detailed analysis of each investigation included in the tally, it is difficult to assess the value of Hartley and Davies' (1978) summary statement regarding the encoding hypothesis. Such an analysis is forthcoming in a report by Ladas.[1]

In a general sense, Peper and Mayer's (1978) results may shed some light on the above findings. While notetakers and nonnotetakers may not vary from each other in *total* recall, Peper and Mayer (1978) found that notetakers recalled more general, conceptual information than nonnotetakers. Also, all investigators previous to Peper and Mayer had only employed recognition or verbatim recall tests which may not have been sensitive to differences produced by notetaking. For example, Peper and Mayer (1978) found that notetakers generally performed better on "far-transfer" items and worse on "near-transfer" items than nonnotetakers. Near transfer items required learners to apply the formula given in a previous lesson to problems similar to those in the lesson, while far transfer items demanded learners to go beyond the specific lesson information by answering, for example, a "What if?" type question. While Peper and Mayer's (1978) results are only marginally significant in some cases, the data are quite important in suggesting some possible subtle effects of notetaking on the encoding of information.

Fisher and Harris (1973) reported results which suggested that notes serve both an encoding function and an external storage function, at least on a test of immediate recall. In their experiment, the NOTE HAVE condition exceeded the NOTE TAKING condition which, in turn, was superior to a NO NOTES condition. On the delayed test, however, only the NOTE HAVE condition was superior to the NO NOTES group.

Carter and Van Matre (1975) argued that the Fisher and Harris study did not represent a "strong test" of the external storage hypothesis, since it involved conditions in which the review of notes period occurred immediately after the passage rather than just before testing on a long term retention test. They further argued that this latter-mentioned experimental arrangement more closely approximates the typical use of notes by students. Using this arrangement for their NOTE HAVE conditon, Carter and Van Matre's results demonstrated that the NOTE HAVE group recalled more than the NOTE TAKE group or the NO NOTES group, including a NO NOTES group which mentally reviewed the passage prior to the criterion test. The NOTE TAKE group equalled the NO NOTE groups on the performance measure. From these findings, they reasoned that in order to benefit from notetaking, students must have them for review just before the test. That is, Carter and Van Matre's results supported the external storage hypothesis but not the encoding hypothesis.

In general, there is considerable support for the external storage idea, despite the fact that in many instances only a "weak test" (review immediately after reading rather than just before a delayed retention test) has been provided. Again, aware of the problems associated with study counts, Hartley and Davies (1978) found eight investigations in which recall was increased by reviewing versus not reviewing notes. Only three studies reported no significant differences in this regard.

In all of the foregoing experiments, no separation was made between recall of material from the notes and recall of material not from the notes (nonnote recall). Separate analyses of this sort are important because the external storage idea suggests two possible functions for notes: a *rehearsal* function, whereby enhanced recall is only due to recall of material from the notes just reviewed. In this case, a NOTE HAVE condition would be superior to a NO NOTES condition in recall of notes, but not in nonnote recall; alternatively, a *reconstruction* function suggests that the recall of notes allows learners to reconstruct parts of the passage on which no notes were previously taken. Consequently, a NOTE HAVE condition would exceed a NO NOTES condition in both notes recall and nonnotes recall.

Separation of total free recall into notes recall and nonnote recall by Rickards and Friedman (1978) demonstrated that the only advantage of note having over note-taking was in the recall of material contained in the notes themselves. It could be, however, that nonnote recall was subject to a floor effect. A maximum of only 3 items was recalled in this measure. This was likely due to the length of the retention interval (one week), the difficulty of the material (brain anatomy), and the type of test given (free recall, hence no cues).

In another performance measure used by Rickards and Friedman (1978) which did employ cues (the completion test), the results were somewhat different. On this measure, both the NOTE HAVE group and the NOTE TAKE group exceeded the NO NOTES/MENTAL REVIEW group in overall recall, thereby suggesting that some advantage was accrued by simply taking notes. These results supported the encoding view of notetaking (Di Vesta & Gray, 1972). More importantly, however, they were pertinent to the external storage view as well.

Rickards and Friedman (1978) used Johnson's (1970) method for calibrating text sentences in terms of their "structural importance." This method was developed via a normative assessment procedure which involved asking readers to rate each text sentence as to its importance to the overall meaning or semantic content of the passage being presented. Sentences rated as high in structural importance were the more abstract, general statements (in many instances, topic sentences), whereas sentences rated as low in structural importance were often statements representing specific examples and illustrations. Since the NOTE HAVE group was superior to the NOTE TAKE group in recall of high structural importance completion test items contained in the notes and low structural importance items *not* contained in the notes, these results support the reconstruction hypothesis. More specifically, it appears that recall of high level material from the notes enabled learners to recall lower level passage material that had *not* been previously recorded in their notes.

Test Mode Expectancy and Notetaking

Another issue of importance in notetaking research is test mode expectancy. Researchers (Hakstian, 1971; Weener, 1971) have found no difference in both total test performance and number of notes taken between learners expecting a multiple choice test and those anticipating an essay examination. But, in each of the above studies, the only dependent measure of notes employed was the total amount of notes taken. While quantity of notes taken may not vary as a function of test mode expectancy, the quality of such notes may.

Consistent with the work of previous investigators Rickards and Friedman (1978) found no effect for test mode expectancy on the number of notes taken or on total test performance. Those expecting an essay test, however, chose for notetaking sentences of greater importance to the overall meaning of the passage

than those expecting a multiple choice test. Furthermore, the essay group recalled more high structural importance items than the multiple choice group, and vice versa for low structural importance items. Assuming that essay test expectancy created a greater focus on high level, idea-oriented passage material, perhaps dependent measures testing applications or inferences would have yielded yet other differences in performance between these two groups.

Individual Differences in Notetaking

A final variable of vital importance in notetaking research is individual differences. Firstly, there is some evidence to suggest that learners perform better when allowed to use their preferred as opposed to their nonpreferred learning strategy (Annis & Davis, 1978; Fisher & Harris, 1974). Since, however, the nonpreferred strategy condition involved forced constraint to use a strategy one would not normally use, it could easily have depressed performance.

Weener (1974) found that some students naturally take a detailed set of notes, while others chose to take a much less detailed set. On both an immediate and a delayed retention test, detailed notetakers recalled less information than those who took fewer notes. Perhaps, students who took fewer notes concentrated more of their attention on the main ideas or general concepts in the material, thereby allowing them to reconstruct some passage details at the time of recall. Weener did not have any measure of the relative importance of the notes taken nor did he separate NOTES RECALL from NON-NOTES RECALL, so further experimentation is needed to test this hypothesis. Also needed is some measure of intellectual ability, since intelligence may have been a confounding variable in the Weener (1974) experiment.

Peters (1972) used "learning efficiency" as an individual difference variable which was determined by examining the difference in recall between a list of definitions recorded at a fast rate (190 words/minute) versus a list recorded at a normal rate (136 words/minute). In a subsequent lecture, notetaking debilitated the performance of the low efficiency listeners. For high efficiency listeners notetaking did not interfere with recall and in some cases was advantageous to recall. Interestingly, when the lecture was presented at a fast rate (200 words/minute), notetaking generally reduced performance in the Peters (1972) investigation. This finding seems to support the notion that in the process of taking notes one may not be able to adequately attend to the ongoing "flow" of information, at least when the flow is rapid. In a related experiment, Aiken, Thomas, and Shennum (1975) found superior performance when notes were taken between segments of a lecture rather than during it.

Using memory ability as an individual difference variable, Berliner (1971, 1972) demonstrated that notetaking was an effective learning strategy only at high levels of memory ability. Learners low in memory ability recalled more when simply asked to pay close attention to the lectures. However, Berliner only employed a recognition test requiring literal comprehension as a dependent measure. Peper and Mayer (1978) showed that low ability notekers performed worse on "near transfer" items but better on "far transfer" items than nonnotetakers. Hence notetaking may actually benefit low ability learners, but not on tests demanding verbatim recall.

And finally, using junior high and high school students as subjects, Brown and Smiley (1977) experimentally distinguished students who take notes of their own volition ("spontaneous notetakers") from those who require explicit directions to take notes before doing so ("induced notetakers"). In their experiment spontaneous notetakers took notes on material of greater importance to the overall meaning of the passage than did induced notetakers. Also, relative to the induced notetakers or the no strategy subjects, the spontaneous notetakers displayed increased recall of the important units of the texts. Brown and Smiley (1977) conclude that "students need knowledge concerning texts, knowledge concerning strategies, and knowledge concerning the interface of these factors before they can study strategically (p. 24)."

Summary and Conclusions

Notetaking is frequently encouraged and widely used as a learning strategy. Early research from 1925 until about 1970 was primarily correlational in nature, whereas recent notetaking research is more experimental and process-oriented.

A review of the literature suggests that notetaking can be a helpful learning strategy. There is some evidence that it aids performance even when the notes are not reviewed before the test. This may especially be the case with test items that require students to transfer the knowledge gained in a lecture to related hypothetical situations.

It appears also that notetaking can be even more effective when notes are reviewed prior to a test. Such review may not only enhance recall of material contained in the notes, but also recall of material on which no notes were taken.

It seems that the type of test one expects (essay or multiple choice) does not affect total recall or the total number of notes taken. However, the type of test expected does seem to influence the kind of notes taken. Expecting an essay exam may lead to students taking notes on the main ideas of a lecture/passage, while the anticipation of a multiple choice test may lead to students taking notes on details.

In the absence of any induced test mode expectancy, students seem to take notes on material containing the main ideas of a passage/lecture and recall more general information than nonnotetakers.

Notetakers may organize the material better as well.

Students may differ in the number of notes they take. Students who take too many notes may perform less well than those who take fewer notes and perhaps concentrate on the main ideas of a passage/lecture.

Some students may be less able than others to take notes and listen to a lecture at the same time. The more efficient listeners may benefit from notetaking, while the less efficient listeners may find notetaking debilitative to their performance. Depending upon the nature and the complexity of the material, notetaking may be more effective when taken at "breaks" in a lecture rather than during the lecture itself.

While notetaking may not benefit low ability learners on test items requiring simple recognition or verbatim recall, it may benefit them on items demanding some sort of high level transfer.

And finally, students who spontaneously take notes appear to benefit the most from notetaking. Relative to spontaneous notetakers, induced notetakers appear to take notes on material of lesser importance to the overall meaning of a passage/lecture and the material they recall is of lesser importance as well.

One possibly fruitful line of inquiry for notetaking research would involve further qualitative analyses of the notes of the best spontaneous notetakers. Particular things to look for in this regard might include the degree of organization and the amount paraphrased as opposed to verbatim material in the notes. Especially important here would be an analysis of the nature of any paraphrasing by these expert notetakers. Brown and Smiley (1977) were the first to express an interest in analyses of this sort, although, to date, nothing has appeared in the literature which goes beyond an examination of the rated importance of the notes. Further qualitative analyses may ultimately enable us to improve the comprehension and recall of slow learners by teaching them effective notetaking strategies.

Notes

1. Ladas, H. S. A macroanalytic approach to summarizing research applied to studies on the value of taking notes. (Working title), in progress.

References

Aiken, E. G.; Thomas, G. S.; & Shennum, W. A. Memory for lecture: Effect of notes, lecture rate, and information density. *Journal of Educational Psychology*, 1975, *67*, 439–444.

Annis, L., & Davis, J. K. Study techniques and cognitive style: Their effect on recall and recognition. *Journal of Educational Research*, 1978, *71*, 175–178.

Berliner, D. C. Aptitude-treatment interactions in two studies of learning from lecture instruction. Paper presented to the American Educational Research Association, New York, February, 1971.

Berliner, D. C. The generalizibility of aptitude-treatment interactions across subject matter. Paper presented to the American Educational Research Association, Chicago, April, 1972.

Brown, A. L., & Smiley, S. S. The development of strategies for studying prose passages. (Tech. Report No. 66.) Urbana, IL: Center for the Study of Reading, University of Illinois, October, 1977.

Carter, J. F., & Van Matre, N. H. Note taking versus note having. *Journal of Educational Psychology*, 1975, *67*, 900–904.

Crawford C. C. The correlation between college lecture notes and quiz papers. *Journal of Educational Research*, 1925, *12*, 282–291. (a).

Crawford, C. C. Some experimental studies of the results of college note-taking. *Journal of Educational Research*, 1925, *12*, 379–386 (b).

Di Vesta, F. J., & Gray, S. G. Listening and note-taking. *Journal of Educational Psychology*, 1972, *63*, 8–14.

Di Vesta, F. J. & Gray, S. G. Listening and note-taking: II. Immediate and delayed recall as functions of variations in thematic continuity, note-taking, and length of listening-review intervals. *Journal of Educational Psychology*, 1973, *64*, 278–287.

Fisher, J. L., & Harris, M. B. Effect of note-taking and review on recall. *Journal of Educational Psychology*, 1973, *65*, 321–325.

Fisher, J. L., & Harris, M. B. Effect of note-taking preference and type of notes taken on memory. *Psychological Reports*, 1974, *35*, 387–391.

Hakstian, A. R. The effects of type of examination anticipated on test preparation and performance. *Journal of Educational Research*, 1971, *64*, 319–324.

Hartley, J., & Davies, I. Note-taking: A critical review. *Programmed Learning and Educational Technology*, 1978, *15*, 207–224.

Howe, M. J. A. Repeated presentation and recall of meaningful prose. *Journal of Educational Psychology*, 1970, *61*, 214–219.

Johnson, R. E. Recall of prose as a function of the structural importance of the linguistic units. *Journal of Verbal Learning and Verbal Behavior*, 1970, *9*, 12–20.

Peper, R. J. & Mayer, R. E. Note taking as a generative activity. *Journal of Educational Psychology*, 1978, *70*, 514–522.

Peters, D. L. Effects of note-taking and rate of presentation on short term objective test performance. *Journal of Educational Psychology*, 1972, *63*, 276–280.

Rickards, J. P., & Denner, P. R. Inserted questions as aids to reading text. *Instructional Science*, 1978, *7*, 313–346.

Rickards, J. P., & Friedman, F. The encoding versus the external storage hypothesis in note taking. *Contemporary Educational Psychology*, 1978, *3*, 136–143.

Weener, P. D. The effects of recall mode and recall interval expectancies on note-taking and recall. In F. J. Di Vesta; N. M. Sanders; C. B. Schultz; & P. D. Weener, Instructional strategies: Multivariable studies of psychological processes related to instruction. ARPA Semi-Annual Report (Order No. 1269), 1971, 59–73.

Weener, P. Note-taking and student verbalisation as instrumental learning activities. *Instructional Science*, 1974, *3*, 51–74.

62. Graphical Literacy

Edward Fry

Graphical literacy is the ability to read and write (or draw) graphs.

Isolated elements of graphical literacy already exist in most school curriculums, but as a concept it is not well developed or well taught. Some aspects of map or graph reading are taught in social studies curriculums. In a few reading courses, these simple graphical reading skills are subsumed as part of "study skills." Bits and pieces of graph drawing appear in vocational or mechanical drawing classes, mathematics classes, or in the art department. However, what I am proposing here is literacy in graphs that begins to approach word literacy.

Cognitive Psychology Background

The use of graphs to communicate information has been around since or before written verbal language. Pictures, maps, and other types of graphs have been used throughout the ages. However, educators have recently become more interested in nonverbal communication as part of the cognitive movement in psychology.

From Edward Fry, Graphical literacy. *Journal of Reading*, February 1981, 24, 383–389. Reprinted by permission of Edward Fry and the International Reading Association.

Researchers have pointed out some interesting things; for example:

> In nearly all right-handers, and in about 70 percent of the left-handers, the left hemisphere (of the brain) employs an analytic, sequential strategy appropriate for verbal proposition information. The right hemisphere characteristically uses a global or holistic, synthetic or appositional strategy, such as one might use in looking at a painting, where parts acquire meaning through their relation to the whole (Whittrock, 1978).

Another cognitive psychology approach has been through the study of imagery. Paivio (1974) has found that pictures and instructions to generate images facilitate memory. Levin (1976) has found that both children and adults remember pictures of objects better than names of objects. Graphs are an interesting way of presenting schemata or as Confucius is reputed to have said, "A picture is worth a thousand words."

Reading Teacher's Role

I am proposing that reading teachers are well equipped to take active educational leadership in graphical literacy because they already have many skills that are readily transferable. For example, it is quite possible to teach map comprehension by asking such typical reading comprehension questions as:

What is the main idea of this map? (To show the location of a housing tract)
What details support this main idea? (Tract location in the center of the map, only roads leading to the tract clearly marked)
What is the author's purpose in drawing this map? (To sell houses)
How are the details interrelated? (Does road location have anything to do with rivers or mountains?)

What new vocabulary is used? What new symbols? (Arroyo, off ramp) (300m, R-1 zone)

I need not go on, but perhaps already you can see that many, if not most, typical "reading comprehension" types of questions can be asked of a map. A map is only one kind of graph; many types of reading comprehension questions can also be asked of a bar graph, a time line, or other kinds of graphs.

Singer and Donlan (1980) suggest that graphs could be taught using the Directed Reading Activity (DRA), which is similar to some types of reading lessons where the teacher conducts a prereading discussion including new vocabulary and background. The student reads the graph, then does activities related to the graph including answering comprehension questions or possibly drawing similar graphs.

Reading teachers, or teachers interested in reading, are further qualified to take a leadership role in graphical literacy because they are already part of the literacy education area and part of the communications field. Their knowledge of everything from individual differences to tests and measurements can be applied, and they are used to working with material from many subject matter areas.

But before going further into graphical literacy, let us give a more complete definition of graphs with a taxonomy and some examples. Most of what I am calling graphs fall into the five areas outlined in A Taxonomy of Graphs shown in Figure 2: Lineal, Quantitative, Spatial, Pictorial, or Hypothetical. See Figure 1 and Figure 2 for details.

Graph Uses

Graphs are used because they quickly communicate a concept often better than words. Even though many of them contain some words or numbers, the basic transmittal of information is nonverbal.

Figure 1. Illustration of the Taxonomy of Graphs

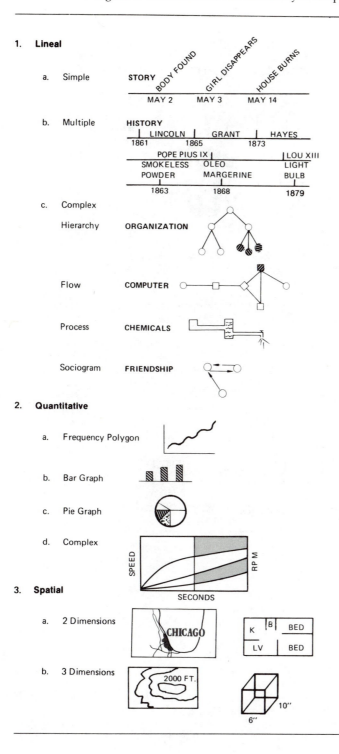

1. **Lineal**

   a. Simple

   b. Multiple

   c. Complex

      Hierarchy

      Flow

      Process

      Sociogram

2. **Quantitative**

   a. Frequency Polygon

   b. Bar Graph

   c. Pie Graph

   d. Complex

3. **Spatial**

   a. 2 Dimensions

   b. 3 Dimensions

(continued)

Figure 1. (continued)

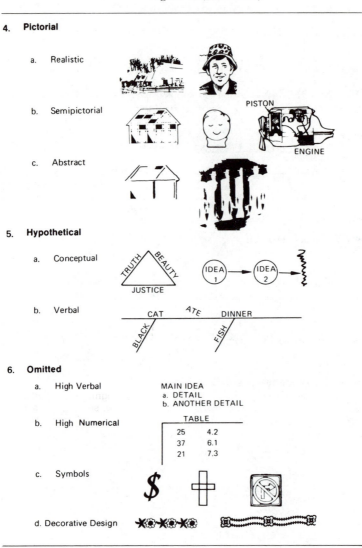

4. **Pictorial**

   a. Realistic

   b. Semipictorial

   c. Abstract

5. **Hypothetical**

   a. Conceptual

   b. Verbal

6. **Omitted**

   a. High Verbal

   b. High Numerical

   c. Symbols

   d. Decorative Design

Figure 2. A Taxonomy of Graphs

1. *Lineal graphs* - Sequential data
   a. *Simple lineal* - For example, a time line or simple nonbranching flow chart can be used in history, literature (a story line), or directions.
   b. *Multiple lineal* - Parallel lines. For example, a set of three time lines that show terms of office of presidents, with a parallel line showing inventions, and a third parallel line that shows the reigns of English kings or queens.
   c. *Complex lineal* - Complex lines that have branching, feedback loops, and diverse data. For example, a computer programmer's flow chart; a process chart; or a hierarchy chart for a business or governmental organization, a geneaology chart, or a sports tournament elimination chart.

2. *Quantitative graphs* - Numerical data
   a. *Frequency polygon* - Gives continuous data, can best show trends. For example, a normal distribution curve, growth curves, stock market fluctuations.
   b. *Bar graph* - Gives discrete data points, can best show the difference between two amounts. For example, it can contrast the size of enrollment for three different years.
   c. *Pie graph* - Best shows percent by various areas.
   d. *Complex numerical graphs* - Engineering graphs, multiple data graphs, higher mathematics graphs. For example, graphs drawn in logarithmic units, multiple line or multiple variables.

3. *Spatial graphs* - Area and location
   a. *Two-dimensional* - Represent something flat. For example, road maps, floor plans, football plays.
   b. *Three-dimensional* - Represent height or depth plus length and width. For example, a map with contour lines showing mountains or valleys, mechanical drawings, or building elevations that accurately show dimensions.
Basically, spatial graphs show the location of a point or the location and size of a line (one dimension), area (two dimensions), or volume (three dimensions). By use of special indicators or multiple graphs, different time periods can be shown.

4. *Pictorial graphs* - Visual concepts
   a. *Realistic* - More or less what the eye would see without significant distortion or elimination of detail. Can have an angle or point of view, selection of subject matter, selection of composition, background, and content. For example, photographs or realistic drawings, single or multiple color.
   b. *Semipictorial* - A recognizable image but with noticeable distortions in form, color, content, or omissions of detail. For example, most Picasso paintings, schematic drawings showing cutaway or exploded engine, cartoons, or outline drawings.
   c. *Abstract pictorial* - Highly abstracted drawing which, however remote, has some basis in visual reality. For example, a single line across a space might represent the horizon; a vertical line, a person; a series of squares, a row of automobiles. Abstract drawings or graphs nearly always require some context, verbal explanation, or prior experience with the type of abstraction.

5. *Hypothetical graphs* - Interrelationship of ideas
   These graphs have little or no basis in visual reality.
   a. *Conceptual graph* - An attempt to communicate abstract ideas by using lines, circles, and other forms, with or without words or symbols. For example, a philosopher who labels the sides of a triange "truth, beauty, justice"; a theoretical model of the reading process with boxes labeled "short-term memory and long-term memory."
   b. *Verbal graph* - The use of graphical arrangements of words or symbols to add meaning to the words. For example, a sentence diagram, semantic mapping.

6. *Intentional omissions from the Taxonomy of Graphs*
   a. *High verbal omission* - On the borderline between having some graph qualities and being purely verbal would be a typical outline with main idea and supporting

(continued)

Figure 2. (continued)

---

details, or posters and advertisements composed with different sizes and styles of type that show emphasis or are aesthetically pleasing.

   b. *High numerical omission* - Arrangements composed mostly of numbers, such as statistical tables, are omitted.

   c. *Symbols* are omitted because, for all practical purposes, they are the equivalent of a word. Typical examples are rebuses or glyphs (like the outline of a man on a restroom door, a cross on a church building, and road sign arrows).

   d. *Decorative design* - Designs whose main purpose is decoration, not conveying concepts, are omitted.

Combinations - Nearly any kind of graph can be combined. An example of a combination would be a mechanical drawing, which is a type of spatial graph (3b), but which could approach the reality of a picture (Section 4, Pictorial). Another example would be a bar graph, which is quantitative (2b), but which can use drawings or photographs of images; for example, car production is seen as many little cars piled on top of each other.

Graphs pack a high density of information into a small area. A very large statistical table can often be compressed into two or three simple lines on a frequency polygon graph. And even more than that, a curved line is an infinite number of points (if you remember your geometry), and theoretically every point can be read or interpreted, whereas a table necessarily has a fixed number of points. For many people, looking at a curved line shows a trend better than looking at a page of numbers.

The ability to read graphs is becoming increasingly important because they are being more widely used in newspapers, magazines, textbooks, and television presentations. Computers are learning to draw graphs in order to simplify massive amounts of statistics or complex mathematical data. Offset printing, now so widely used, makes the reproduction of graphs easier than former printing processes. Students in today's schools can look forward to an increasing use of graphical presentations on computer terminals, in print and in classrooms.

Drawing Graphs

Reading and comprehending graphs is only half of graphical literacy. The other half is the ability to draw them. Students need to draw them so that they can better communicate ideas, so they can use them in studying, and so they can better understand them.

Drawing a graph can be a creative communicating experience similar to writing a paragraph or a story. There are many ways to express the same idea graphically, just as a writer can express a written idea in a variety of ways. Someday we may see a course in creative graphing just as we now have creative writing. In the meantime a unit of a reading, communications, or writing class might well be devoted to graphing.

Graphing, or expressing ideas graphically, is already a well established part of some study skills courses. It should be developed. Outlining, summarizing, notetaking, and underlining are all fine study techniques; but they are all essentially verbal. Graphing can add another very important dimension to study techniques. Once the students start to think about applying graphing whenever possible, they will be amazed at how often it can be applied.

Teachers can help to develop graphing ability by making assignments just as they now do for writing. For example, take a section of a history book, science article, or short story and ask the students to make as many graphs as they can to illustrate ideas in the material.

Another interesting lesson for teaching graphing is to take a newspaper article, budget statement, or some other piece of writing with numerical data and ask the student to attempt to make a graph. You will often find that the article does not contain enough information to draw a complete graph. The students will learn that a graph contains far more information than most typical prose paragraphs about data. Or stated another way, the graph more succinctly conveys the information.

Valuing Graphs

We teach reading and writing because we value reading and writing. We teach mathematics because we value mathematics. We will only teach graphical literacy because we value it. If we do value graphical literacy, here are some things we can do.

- Allow some time for graphical literacy in the curriculum.
- Ask reading comprehension type of questions about graphs.
- Select texts that have a good use of graphs.
- Talk to students about the importance of graphs.
- Grade graphs in student papers.
- Work on extending the types of graphs a student uses.
- Have a graphing contest and prizes.
- Invite art and drafting teachers to reading and English classes to talk about graph use and development.
- Use graphs yourself on the chalkboard or the overhead projector in explaining ideas.

Conclusion

Graphical literacy—the ability to both comprehend and draw graphs—is an important communication tool that needs more emphasis in the school curriculum.

Reading teachers, by virtue of their experience teaching reading comprehension, their practice in using materials from many fields, and their knowledge of educational principles, are qualified to teach graphical literacy and aid other teachers in developing units in this subject.

Furthermore, reading teachers often teach some graphing techniques in study skills segments of their courses, and these need to be further developed.

Helping students to develop graphical literacy can be akin to creative writing as a creative experience. Students should be encouraged to use graphing in all types of written communication and in study.

Finally, if graphing is to be included in the curriculum of reading, English, and most other subjects to a greater extent, it needs to be more highly valued. Some techniques for showing greater value for graphical literacy include graphing assignments and greater recognition on the part of teachers of the communication value of graphs.

References

Fry, Edward. *Graphical Comprehension*. Providence, R. I.: Jamestown Publishers, 1981.

Levin, Joel R. "What Have We Learned about Maximizing What Children Learn?" In *Cognitive Learning in Children: Theories and Strategies*, edited by J. R. Levin and V. L. Allen. New York. N.Y.: Academic Press, 1976.

Paivio, A. "Language and Knowledge of the World," *Educational Researcher*, vol. 3 (1974), pp. 5–12.

Singer, Harry, and Dan Donlan. *Learning from Text*. Boston, Mass.: Little, Brown, 1980.

Whittrock, Merl C. "The Cognitive Movement in Instruction," *Educational Psychologist*, vol. 13 (1978), pp. 15–29.

CHAPTER XII

Recreational Reading

In our concern with developing comprehension and study skills, we sometimes forget that one of the major objectives of a well-balanced reading program is development of the habit of reading for pleasure. Finding out what children would like to read is not always easy, and Dulin provides useful descriptions of instruments for measuring reading interest and attitudes. Next, Wagner summarizes what is known about the impact of TV on reading and school work in general.

Huus describes six approaches to the use of literature in school, and advocates combining them into a total literature program. Gentile and McMillan propose greater emphasis on humor, describe developmental changes in appreciation of humor, and suggest humorous books enjoyed at different ages. Criscuolo provides a wealth of ideas about how to motivate reluctant readers. And in the last reading, Hickman argues that our understanding of children's responses to literature is best studied through ethnographic research conducted in the classroom.

63. Assessing Reading Interests of Elementary and Middle School Students

Ken L. Dulin

The measurement and evaluation of various aspects of students' affective orientation toward reading and reading materials have long been topics of concern to teachers. This presentation focuses on three new measurement tools: 1) an *attitude* inventory designed for assessing elementary and middle school students' general feelings toward reading; 2) an *interest* inventory designed to tap these students' preferences within and among various reading topics, reading genre, and print forms; and c) a *motivational* survey designed to plumb the relative motivational appeals various teacher procedures and classroom practices hold for these students. Materials included are copies of the three instruments, scoring and interpretation procedures for each, and initial validation statistics for all three.

From Ken L. Dulin, Assessing reading interests of elementary and middle school students. In D. L. Monson & D. K. McClenathan (Eds.), *Developing active readers: Ideas for parents, teachers, and librarians.* Newark, Del.: International Reading Association, 1979. Pp. 2–15. Reprinted by permission of Ken L. Dulin and the International Reading Association.

The Wisconsin Reading Attitude Inventory, Form II

This questionnaire (really a *battery*) has four distinct parts, each of which can be used separately or in combination with any or all of the other parts.

Part I is the Dulin-Chester Scale, the second version of a project Bob Chester (now of the University of British Columbia) and I began about two years ago. Since that time, this scale has been administered to several thousand children, has proven to be quite reliable, and has been published in *Tests and Measurements in Child Development: Handbook II*, Orval G. Johnson, Editor, Jossey-Bass Publishers; and in *Teaching Children to Read*, Richard J. Smith and Dale D. Johnson, Addison-Wesley Publishing.

The Dulin-Chester Scale is scored fairly simply. All the *odd numbered items* (1, 3, 5, 7, and so on) are scored 1, 2, 3, 4, or 5 from the left hand box to the right hand box; and all the *even numbered items* (2, 4, 6, 8, and so on) are scored 5, 4, 3, 2, or 1 from left to right. When summed, then, the total scores possible from this section can run from a low of 20 to a high of 200, with the 45 to 65 range of scores seen, as a result of our past testing, as "average."

Part II of the total inventory is the Estes Scale, developed by Tom Estes of the University of Virginia and first published in the *Journal of Reading*, November 1971. It's scored by awarding individual points of 5, 4, 3, 2, and 1 to As, Bs, Cs, Ds, and Es for all of the *positive* items (2, 5, 7, 10, 14, 15, 18, and 19) and awarding 1, 2, 3, 4, and 5 to As, Bs, Cs, Ds, and Es for all of the *negative* items (1, 3, 4, 6, 8, 9, 11, 12, 13, 16, 17, and 20). Here, too, the summed scores can run from a low of 20 to a high of 100, with the 65 to 90 range seen as average. The Estes Scale, updated and revised, is available with scoring keys and manual, from the Virginia Research Association, Box 5501, Charlottesville, Virginia 22902.

Part III was simply a little experiment Bob and I were interested in, since it used a ratio kind of measurement (i.e., the dividing up of the parts of a constant sum to show relative attitudes), and so we include it. Surprisingly, it turned out to be a quite good measurement device. When we added together the number of points the subjects gave to the first two categories, "Reading Books" and "Reading Magazines and Newspapers," we found that sum correlated highly with all of our other measures.

Part IV consists simply of some self-rating scales. We used them (plus many other things) as criterion measures during our field testing.

FORM II
THE WISCONSIN READING ATTITUDE INVENTORY
Ken Dulin and Bob Chester
The University of Wisconsin at Madison

NAME _____ DATE _____

SCHOOL _____ TEACHER _____

GRADE IN SCHOOL _____ SEX _____

(circle one)

DIRECTIONS

The test you're about to take is called an "attitude inventory." Instead of measuring what you KNOW, it is designed to measure how you FEEL about something. This particular attitude inventory deals with books and reading.

I. The first part of the inventory consists of a series of choices to be made between different leisure-time activities, some dealing with reading and others not. You're to indicate your choices by marking a series of scales, and it works like this.

At each of the two ends of each scale there'll be an activity, something you could do in your spare time if you wanted to. If you'd *much* rather do one of the activities than the other, mark the box *nearest to* that activity, like this:

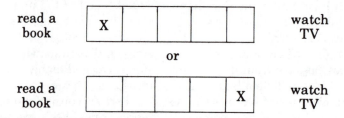

or

Or, if you'd *sort of* rather do one or the other, mark the box *second* from that activity, like this

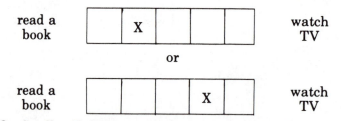

or

Or finally, if the two activities are *absolutely equal* in your mind, mark the middle box, like this

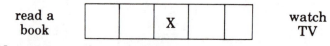

Now go on to the real choices.

WHICH WOULD YOU RATHER DO?

THIS...	OR	THIS...

1. listen to the radio □□□□□ read a book
2. read a book □□□□□ clean up around the house
3. play a musical instrument □□□□□ read a book
4. read a book □□□□□ shine your shoes
5. write a letter □□□□□ read a book
6. read a book □□□□□ watch television
7. play with a pet □□□□□ read a book
8. read a book □□□□□ take a nap
9. do some work around the house □□□□□ read a book
10. read a book □□□□□ read a magazine
11. draw or paint a picture □□□□□ read a book
12. read a book □□□□□ fix something to eat
13. call a friend on the phone □□□□□ read a book
14. read a book □□□□□ play a solitary game
15. read a newspaper □□□□□ read a book
16. read a book □□□□□ look at pictures
17. do a cross-word puzzle □□□□□ read a book
18. read a book □□□□□ work on a craft or hobby project
19. work on a school assignment □□□□□ read a book
20. read a book □□□□□ listen to records

II. Now, to take the next part of the inventory, you're to *grade* twenty statements in terms of how you feel about them. If you STRONGLY AGREE with a statement, give it an A; if you TEND TO AGREE with it, give it a B; if you feel FAIRLY NEUTRAL about it, give it a C; if you TEND TO DISAGREE with it, give it a D; and if you STRONGLY DISAGREE with it, give it an E. Be sure to read each statement carefully before you circle a grade for it, and be sure to grade *every* statement.

1. Reading is for learning but not for enjoyment.   A   B   C   D   E

2. Money spent on books is well-spent.   A   B   C   D   E

3. There is nothing to be gained from reading books.   A   B   C   D   E

4. Books are a bore.   A   B   C   D   E

5. Reading is a good way to spend spare time.   A   B   C   D   E

6. Sharing books in class is a waste of time.   A   B   C   D   E

7. Reading turns me on.   A   B   C   D   E

8. Reading is only for grade grubbers.   A   B   C   D   E

9. Books aren't usually good enough to finish.   A   B   C   D   E

10. Reading is rewarding to me.   A   B   C   D   E

11. Reading becomes boring after about an hour.   A   B   C   D   E

12. Most books are too long and dull.   A   B   C   D   E

13. Free reading doesn't teach anything.   A   B   C   D   E

14. There should be more time for free reading during the school day.   A   B   C   D   E

15. There are many books which I hope to read.   A   B   C   D   E

16. Books should not be read except for class requirements.   A   B   C   D   E

17. Reading is something I can do without.   A   B   C   D   E

18. A certain amount of summer vacation should be set aside for reading.   A   B   C   D   E

19. Books make good presents.   A   B   C   D   E

20. Reading is dull.   A   B   C   D   E

III. This third part of the inventory calls for a bit of math ability. Your job this time is to *divide up 100 points* among the following ten things in terms of *how desirable* you feel they are as leisure activities. Remember, the total should come out to 100.

Activities	Points
Reading books	
Reading magazines and newspapers	
Watching television	
Playing musical instruments	
Doing craft and hobby work	
Listening to the radio	
Writing letters	
Listening to records	
Painting or drawing pictures	
Sleeping or napping	
Total	100

IV. And finally, to tell us a few things about *yourself*, please respond to the following three scales by circling the answer to each which *best describes you.*

1. Compared to other people your own age, about *how well* do you think that you read?

1	2	3	4	5
a good deal better than most	somewhat better than most	about as well as most	somewhat less well than most	a good deal less well than most

2. Compared to other people your own age, about how much do you feel you *like* to read?

1	2	3	4	5
a good deal more than most	somewhat more than most	about as much as most	somewhat less than most	a good deal less than most

3. And finally, compared to other people your own age, about how *much* reading do you feel you do?

1	2	3	4	5
a good deal more than most	somewhat more than most	about the amount as most	somewhat less than most	a good deal less than most

Thanks for your participation. Now please turn this in to your teacher.

The Dulin-Chester Reading Interests Questionnaire

This instrument combines two things: The survey of reading interests by topics, genre, and print forms; and the motivational survey regarding teacher procedures and classroom practices.

The project was developed for the reading people of the Oconomowoc, Wisconsin, Public Schools. It has also been used in many other places, and has been slightly adapted for other applications. It has turned out to be highly reliable and quite useful.

The scoring is quite straightforward, simply the conversion of the A-B-C-D-E grades to numbers (5, 4, 3, 2, and 1) in parts I through IV and the retaining of the raw scores in parts V through VII. When we conceptualized the parts as we were developing them, we looked upon Part I as dealing with Reward Systems, Part II as dealing with Teacher Motivational Devices, Part III as dealing with Follow Up Activities after a lesson, and Part IV as Enrichment Activities after a lesson. Part V is Topics about which to Read, Part VI is Reading Genre, and Part VII is Reading Print Forms.

As far as "norms" are concerned, this concept doesn't really mean much related to an interest inventory; more important is the fact that the instrument appears to be quite reliable (gives consistent information).

READING INTERESTS QUESTIONNAIRE
Ken Dulin and Bob Chester
The University of Wisconsin at Madison

Name _____ Date _____

School _____ Grade _____ Teacher _____

Some of us like to read a lot and others don't, but almost all of us read at least sometimes for one reason or another. That's what this questionnaire is about: *why* people read.

I. Sometimes for example, people read because their teachers or parents *reward* them for reading.

Here are ten possible rewards a person could get for reading, some of them pretty good rewards and some others not so good. To show how *you* feel about each of them, *grade* each reward, A or B or C or D or E. Here's what each grade means:

A = I feel this would be a *very good* reward for reading.

B = I feel this would be a *fairly good* reward for reading.

C = I feel this would be only an *average* reward for reading.

D = I feel this would be a *fairly poor* reward for reading.

E = I feel this would be a *very poor* reward for reading.

For each reward, circle the grade you're giving it.

1. getting a grade for how much reading you do   A   B   C   D   E

2. getting extra credit for how much reading you do   A   B   C   D   E

3. getting your name on a bulletin board for how much reading you do   A   B   C   D   E

4. getting stars on a chart for how much reading you do   A   B   C   D   E

5. getting money for how much reading you do   A   B   C   D   E

6. getting prizes for how much reading you do   A   B   C   D   E

7. getting free time in school as a reward for extra reading you've done   A   B   C   D   E

8. getting a certificate to take home for extra reading you've done   A   B   C   D   E

9. getting to go to other classes to tell about books you've read   A   B   C   D   E

10. getting excused from other class work as a reward for extra reading you've done   A   B   C   D   E

II. Sometimes things *teachers* do encourage us to read. Please grade the following ten things to show how much you think they'd encourage *you* to read. Here's what the grades mean this time.

A = I feel this would *certainly* encourage me to read.

B = I feel this would *probably* encourage me to read more.

C = I feel this *might* encourage me to read more.

D = I'm pretty *sure* this *wouldn't* encourage me to read.

E = I'm *quite sure* this *wouldn't* encourage me to read more.

Again, circle the grade you're giving the activity.

1. having the teacher read a book to the class at a chapter a day   A   B   C   D   E

2. having the teacher read to the class the first few pages of books that you can then check out if you want to   A   B   C   D   E

3. having the teacher act out parts of a story or book before you start to read it   A   B   C   D   E

4. having the teacher take your class to the school library now and then   A   B   C   D   E

5. having the teacher tell you about the lives of authors of books you can read   A   B   C   D   E

6. having the teacher tell about the places where stories in books take place   A   B   C   D   E

7. having the teacher tell about books he or she has read   A   B   C   D   E

8. having the teacher explain some of the hard words in a book or story before you read it   A   B   C   D   E

9. having the teacher give you some oral questions about a story in a book before you start reading it   A   B   C   D   E

10. having the teacher give you some written questions to answer *while* you're reading a story or book   A   B   C   D   E

III. Now, here are some things you might do *after* reading a book or story in class. Grade them by these grades.

A = I'd *like* to do this.

B = I'd *sort of* like to do this.

C = I'm *not sure* if I'd like to do this.

D = I *don't think* I'd like to do this.

E = I'm *sure* I wouldn't like to do this.

1. take a written test on how well you understood a story you've read   A   B   C   D   E

2. take a written test on how much you can *remember* about a story you've read   A   B   C   D   E

3. take an oral test on a story or book you've read   A   B   C   D   E

4. use some of the new words in a story or book you've read for word-study   A   B   C   D   E

5. write a book report about a book you've read   A   B   C   D   E

6. give an *oral* report on a book you've read   A   B   C   D   E

7. write your own ending to a story or book you've read   A   B   C   D   E

8. do a crossword puzzle with some of the new words in a story or book you've read   A   B   C   D   E

9. match some of the new words in a story or book you've read with their definitions   A   B   C   D   E

10. take a spelling test on some of the new words in a book or story you've read   A   B   C   D   E

IV. And finally, here are some *extra* things you could do after reading a story or book. Grade them with *these* grades.

A = I'd *really like* to do this.

B = I'd *sort of* like to do this.

C = I *might or might not* like to do this.

D = I'm *fairly sure* I wouldn't like to do this.

E = I'm *quite sure* I wouldn't like to do this.

1. make a play out of a story or book you've read

    A   B   C   D   E

2. make a picture to go with a story or book you've read

    A   B   C   D   E

3. have a discussion in class about a story or book you've read

    A   B   C   D   E

4. write a story of your own about people you've met in a story or book

    A   B   C   D   E

5. go to a movie or play made from a story or book you've read

    A   B   C   D   E

6. meet the author of a story or book you've read

    A   B   C   D   E

7. listen to a record of an author reading his or her own story

    A   B   C   D   E

8. look at pictures of the people you've read about in stories or books

    A   B   C   D   E

9. look at pictures of the places you've read about in stories or books

    A   B   C   D   E

10. have the school librarian visit class and tell about books you can read

    A   B   C   D   E

V. That's all the grading for you to do. This time you're to *number* certain kinds of reading to show how you feel. Give your favorite thing to read about number 1, your next favorite number 2, and so on, down to number 10. Here are your choices. Be sure to give *every type of reading* some number.

TYPE OF READING	NUMBER
about sports and athletics	
about hobbies and crafts	
about travel and faraway places	
about animals and pets	
about adventure and romance	
about careers and occupations	
about religion and religious people	
about science and inventions	
about science fiction and tales of the supernatural	
about detective stories and mysteries	

VI. These next two parts of the questionnaire will call for a bit of Arithmetic ability. This time you're to *divide up 100 points* (think of dividing a dollar into cents) among five kinds of reading to show how much you like each of them. Each kind can get anywhere from 0 points to the whole 100, but remember that *the overall total must equal 100.* Here they are.

KINDS OF READING	POINTS
full length books about imaginary people	
nonfiction stories and books about real-life people	
short stories about imaginary people and events	
plays	
poetry	
TOTAL	100

VII. And finally, for the last part of the questionnaire, *divide up 100* points to show how much you like different *types* of reading material. Any one type can get from 0 to 100 points, but you should try to give at least *some* points to each.

TYPES OF READING MATERIAL	POINTS
magazines	
newspapers	
comic books	
hardbound books	
paperback books	
TOTAL	100

That completes the whole questionnaire. Thanks for finishing it all. Later on your teacher may share with you how most of your class felt about all these things. Now please turn in your questionnaire to your teacher.

Using These Instruments

The best uses of the reading attitude measures would probably be as measurements before and after some sort of experimental treatment (say, a USSR program) or simply as overall measures of fall to spring changes in your students. Also, you might want to use the basic scores yielded by the various scales as guides to grouping practices, to individual counseling, or to other curricular decisions.

As for the Reading Interests and Teaching Practices instrument, we found at Oconomowoc that many interesting relationships were uncovered when we compared the interests and opinions of high, average, and low ability groups of students and high, average, and low attitude groups of students.

This instrument has been published in the same handbook mentioned above for the Dulin-Chester Scale and served as the basis for several research papers presented at the Great Lakes Regional IRA Conference in Milwaukee.

64. The Effects of TV on Reading

Lilya Wagner

Television has often been dubbed the "electronic pied piper." This nickname appears to be appropriate when one considers that children spend one-sixth of their time between birth and age 18 watching television (Berger, 1976). Children spend more time in front of the TV than in any other activity except sleeping (Huston-Stein and Wright, 1979).

According to Gilbert (1978), the Ninth Annual Gallup Poll of the Public's Attitudes toward the Public Schools found that the average American child, 12 years old or younger, spends two hours per day (including school days) viewing television, 30 minutes reading (not schoolwork), and 45 minutes doing homework. By the time a teenager graduates from high school, 15,000 hours will have been spent before the TV screen (Waters, 1977).

Television is, without doubt, a way of learning. Feinberg (1977, p. 78) maintains that "mass media have singularly shaped and molded this generation of students, and television, more than any other medium, has created passive, disinterested learners who have abdicated responsibility for their own education." It is her belief that students in a classroom, conditioned to "station breaks," cannot sit quietly, but must fidget, rustle papers, and move about restlessly. Also, because students are accustomed to "turn off" anything they do not wish to hear, they can turn off instruction as effectively as a commercial. In addition, teaching is often seen as a noise that invites attention, and students choose to ignore it, much as they ignore anything on TV that does not grab their attention. In short, few classrooms can cope with the competition of TV as a setting for learning.

Because schools function on the premise that the bulk of learning takes place through reading, what we learn there is based on our ability to read. However, reading teachers and all teachers concerned with their students' reading abilities are now dealing with young people whose linguistic frame of reference is television.

Much has been written about television and violence, television and models for children, and the general impact of the truncated episode, the phenomenon of quick problem solving. Yet how TV has affected reading is seldom considered specifically. If, in the minds of educators, reading has not lost its stature as the primary means of acquiring knowledge, then questions such as the following should be considered. What affect does TV have on academic achievement, which is inextricably tied to reading? How is reading interest affected by TV? Is there a difference in the effect of TV on good learners versus poor learners? Does TV hamper creativity; that is to say, does it rob the students of the ability to conjure up mental images, something that reading is said to promote? Does TV destroy the art of critical reading?

In reviewing the research literature which attempts to answer these questions, only that which directly related to students in middle or high school was considered. In some cases, if the research covered a wide age range, yet was applicable to the teen years of schooling, it was included. Television was defined as commercial TV, not educational TV or isolated programs

From Lilya Wagner, The effects of TV on reading. *Journal of Reading*, December 1980, 34, 201–206. Reprinted by permission of Lilya Wagner and the International Reading Association.

designed to promote various learning possibilities.

Television and Intelligence

When Starkey and Swinford (1974) studied 226 fifth and sixth graders, they found that viewing time was negatively related to intellectual level, and the relationship appeared to grow stronger in the high school years. The average viewing time per week was 28 hours for girls and 30 for boys, but the brighter child was more discriminating in viewing habits and time, and better readers watched less TV than poor readers.

Schramm, Lyle, and Parker, in a benchmark study completed in 1961, had already reported that the poorest students in school were the heaviest users of television. Brighter children were heavy viewers until age 11, and then they turned more to reading. However, if children of high mental ability continued to be avid watchers in their teen years, they tended to do less well on knowledge tests and in school than those who spent less time viewing TV.

In 1978 Busch looked at possible changes that might have taken place since the Schramm, Lyle, and Parker research. She found that low ability students received the greatest portion of their information from TV, whereas high ability students read newspapers, magazines, and books for further information. In addition, slower students, as they progressed through the grades, noticed their own poor reading ability and increasingly began to rely on TV for information. Busch also discovered that students of low reading ability are not very discriminating in their viewing. She quotes one student as saying that television is used like "chewing gum for the eyeballs."

Busch concluded that her study supported the Schramm, Lyle, and Parker study in most respects. It is her contention that students can learn from TV, but that the saturation point is reached by age 12,

after which students' total knowledge declines as TV viewing increases. In addition, the intelligence of a student determines to some extent how much effect TV, and reading, will have on his or her learning.

In 1966 Witty published the results of surveys conducted over 15 years to that date. He found a significant negative correlation between amount of TV viewing and students' IQ. For fifth grade pupils in the lower fourth of their class on IQ, the hours watched averaged 28, while those in the upper fourth on IQ viewed for only 20.5 hours. The gap narrowed only slightly for sixth grade pupils; those in the lower fourth viewed for 27.5 hours, while those in the upper quartile averaged 21 hours weekly.

As indicated in these studies, intelligence does appear to be related to the amount of time a student views TV. This, in turn, affects students' reading habits. High ability students tend to be devotees of television until they reach their teen years; after that, the majority increasingly turn to reading material. If low ability students are not encouraged to improve in reading ability and reach the point where reading becomes an easily managed means of adding to knowledge, they will continue to seek out TV as a way of learning. The inability to read, frequently brought on by a lack of practice, leads to increasing dependence on TV for information, resulting in a further neglect or avoidance of reading.

TV and Academic Achievement

Witty's (1966) early review of studies suggested that TV viewing was negatively related to reading achievement. Fifth grade pupils who scored in the lower fourth in their classes on the California Reading Test averaged 27 hours of viewing weekly, as compared to 21.5 hours by the pupils in the upper quartile. Sixth graders in the lowest quartile watched 26 hours per week, while those in the upper fourth averaged only 21 hours.

However, Himmelweit, Oppenheim, and Vince (1960) maintained that television had not created viewers who were markedly better or worse at any school subject, and both Starkey and Swinford (1974) and Fisher and Bruss (1976) also found only a slight relationship between reading ability and the amount of time spent watching TV.

Childers and Ross (1973) agreed, saying that "there seems to be little evidence that different amounts of televiewing, independently or together with student intellectual factors, have any correlation with students' grades in elementary school" (pp. 318–19). Furthermore, Childers and Ross state that parents and teachers should not blame televiewing for low scholastic achievement. They say that "the mean number (3.31) of hours watched daily has changed very little in the last 20 years. The practice of punishing a child by curtailing his viewing of television would seem to have little substance" (p. 319).

Do students themselves have an opinion of how TV viewing may affect their scholastic standing? In a study designed to collect information about the television habits and opinions of seventh and eighth grade pupils, Ridder (1963) found no significant relationship between academic achievement and the total number of hours spent viewing.

The above indicates that scholastic achievement, which to a great extent depends upon a student's ability to read, is not adversely affected by the amount of time the individual spends watching television. However, recent research is decidedly limited and this would prevent any definite conclusions.

TV and Interest in Reading

On occasion, TV stimulates viewers to read books. According to Witty (1966), 25% of elementary school pupils stated that TV presentations had led to their reading certain books. Indeed, TV tie-ins appear to be preferred in the books read by both boys and girls (Hamilton, reported by Barth and Swiss, 1976). However, the interest in reading stimulated by TV remains narrow, due to the small number of literature-oriented programs.

Can TV raise the maturity of children's tastes? Himmelweit, Oppenheim, and Vince (1960) stated that viewing stimulated children's interests, especially in nonfiction. However, Schramm, Lyle, and Parker (1961) were uncertain about TV's effect on children's tastes. They stated (p. 154) that

> so far as television builds a child's tastes at all, we have to assume that it operates to reinforce whatever tastes a child can satisfy from it. Now if it were sufficiently varied that a child could satisfy almost any level of taste and could experiment with widely different selections, this would not be worrisome. But the truth is that television is not greatly varied, and is mostly on the level that will appeal to a very broad audience. In that situation, will television in time shape children's tastes to its own offering?

It is unfortunate that the question posed by Schramm and his associates cannot be adequately answered almost two decades later because of the scarcity of research relative to television and interest in reading. Certainly the volume of written material on the market would indicate that interest in reading has not vanished, but whether TV has stimulated or hindered this interest, or has had no effect whatsoever, is not clear at this point.

Reading and Creativity

TV is frequently accused of creating a passive generation, unable to use imaginations fully and simply waiting to be entertained, rather than creating entertainment for themselves. If this is true, then an effect on reading should be apparent, because reading allows opportunity for creating pictures in the mind. "In reading," Winn (1977, p. 54) wrote, "the mind transforms abstract symbols into sounds and the sounds into words; it 'hears' the words, as it were, and invests them with meaning learned in the spoken language."

Winn further stated that in reading we create our own images, and these reflect our own experiences and individual needs. Yet in viewing TV, we must accept what we receive. No transformation takes place. "It may be," she added, "that television-bred children's reduced opportunities to indulge in 'inner picture-making' account for the curious inability of so many children today to adjust to nonvisual experience." She described TV as a one-way transaction, requiring the taking in of sensory material in one particular way.

A study cited in *Newsweek* (Waters, 1967) gives an example. A University of Southern California research team exposed 250 mentally gifted elementary pupils to three weeks of intensive television viewing. "Tests conducted before and after the experiment found a marked drop in all forms of creative abilities except verbal skill. Some teachers are encountering children who cannot understand a simple story without visual illustrations" (p. 65).

Fisher and Bruss (1976) also tested for a relationship between TV and perceptual passivity, or rigidity, the degree to which one tends to adhere to a mental set. Their results suggested that viewing TV promotes perceptual passivity; that is, if a child is watching more than 37 hours per week, she/he may be developing a rigid view of her/his environment. They further suggest that TV relates negatively to reading comprehension, but positively to vocabulary.

Since schools tend to promote and reward creativity, the passive character of television cannot be ignored. A child need exert little effort in concentration and understanding, and it is possible that creativity is stifled.

Television and Critical Reading

In reading, the reader can determine the pace according to personal needs. If the material is interesting, or not profound, it can be read quickly. But if critical reading is required, the reader may slow down. However, on TV the images move quickly. There is no flexibility in pace. This may lead to more shallow comprehension of the material. If so, a viewer may lose the ability to be critical of the information received.

Feinberg (1977, p. 79) says, "Perhaps the most disturbing aspect of television's impact lies in its creation of a generation of viewers incapable of making critical judgments about the media or their world or themselves." In this way, learning may become synonymous with exposure, and without critical tools available, they may indeed become the same in actuality.

There is an apparent void of research in this important area. If discriminating reading is a vital part of a student's learning skills, then it is imperative that researchers address the task of discovering how television affects this factor.

Summary and Conclusions

As can be seen, research on television and its effects on reading has dealt with vital concerns. Also apparent is the scarcity of such research. If educators continue to design school programs based on reading, writing, speaking and listening, then it is crucial that we discover what specific effects television has on reading skills and ability.

According to the research that is available, intelligence affects a child's viewing and reading habits. Students of lower intelligence watch more TV, while those of higher ability turn to reading with increasing frequency as they mature. However, if they continue their extensive TV viewing, their ability to achieve declines.

Which is the cause and which is the effect? No clear-cut answer is possible. A students' academic standing in an educational system based largely on reading does not appear to be greatly influenced by TV. Creativity does seem to be hampered because of television's one-way transaction. Students' interest in reading is increased if there is a tie-in to a TV program. Otherwise, the conclusions are not definite.

Teachers and administrators must recognize TV's existence and power and understand its impact on young people. This may mean development of new curricula, designed to teach students who have been deeply influenced by TV and find the school's orientation toward reading somewhat confusing. Rutstein (1972, p. 137) states:

> Teachers should learn to appreciate how TV shapes their students' views of themselves, of their friends, of school and of the world. But most importantly, teachers should discover how TV conditions students for formal education. Nurtured on TV since infancy, today's child is a picture and image oriented student who sits in a classroom being taught by a word oriented teacher.

Feeley (1975) wrote a pertinent article on the effect of TV programs which are designed to teach reading. Her conclusion is relevant. "This overall preference for viewing . . . was one of the most revealing findings of this study, indicating clearly that this is a *watching* generation" (p. 800). Few would contend her point. The question is: What are the implications for reading?

References

Barth, Rodney J., and Thom Swiss. "The Impact of Television on Reading." *The Reading Teacher*, vol. 30 (November 1976), pp. 236–39.

Berger, Arthur Asa. *The TV-Guided American*. New York, N.Y.: Walker and Co., 1976.

Busch, Jackie S. "Television's Effects on Reading: A Case Study." *Phi Delta Kappan*, vol. 59 (June 1978), pp. 668–71.

Childers, Perry R., and James Ross. "The Relationships between Viewing TV and Student Achievement." *The Journal of Educational Research*, vol. 66 (March 1973), pp. 317–19.

Feeley, Joan T. "Television and Reading in the Seventies." *Language Arts*, vol. 52 (September 1975), pp. 797–801.

Feinberg, Susan. "The Classroom's No Longer Prime Time." *Today's Education*, vol. 66 (September/October 1977), pp. 78–79.

Fisher, Richard, and William Bruss. "The Viewing of TV, Perceptual Passivity, and Reading." *Colorado Journal of Educational Research*, vol. 15 (Spring 1976), pp. 33–37.

Gilbert, Steven S. "Television, Families, and Schools." *Independent School*, vol. 37 (February 1978), pp. 29–35.

Himmelweit, Hilde T., A. N. Oppenheim, and Pamela Vince. *Television and the Child*. London, England: Oxford University Press, 1960.

Huston-Stein, Aletha, and John C. Wright. "Children and Television: Effects of the Medium, Its Content and Its Form." *Journal of Research and Development in Education*, vol. 13 (Fall 1979), pp. 20–31.

Ridder, Joyce M. "Pupil Opinions and the Relationship of Television Viewing to Academic Achievement." *The Journal of Educational Research*, vol. 57 (December 1963), pp. 204–06.

Rutstein, Nat. "Kids and TV: Challenge to Teachers." *The Reading Teacher*, vol. 26 (November 1972), pp. 134–37.

Schramm, Wilbur, Jack Lyle, and Edwin B. Parker. *Television in the Lives of Our Children*. Stanford, Calif.: Stanford University Press, 1961.

Starkey, J. D., and H. L. Swinford. *Reading? Does Television Viewing Time Affect It?* ED 090 966. Arlington. Va.: ERIC Document Reproduction Service, 1974.

Waters, Harry F. "What TV Does to Kids." *Newsweek*, vol. 89 (February 1977), pp. 63–70.

Winn, Marie. "The Hazards of the Plug-In Drug." *Parents' Magazine*, vol. 52 (June 1977), pp. 38, 54–56, 60.

Witty, Paul. "Studies of Mass Media." *Science Education*, vol. 50 (March 1966), p. 122.

65. Approaches to the Use of Literature in the Reading Program

Helen Huus

This paper appraises some of the approaches currently labeled "literature teaching," and then it describes a total program. The literature program is here defined as a planned program of teaching that uses books of recognized quality to achieve the following objectives: enjoyment (including imagination stretching); acquaintance with the literary heritage; an understanding of what constitutes literature; application of literature in personal living; and the ability to evaluate, appreciate, and develop personal tastes. By *literature* is meant the writing kept alive through time by its beauty of style or thought—writing that is artistic in form and which appeals to the emotions. Literature worthy of the designation has layers of depth that allow the selection to be reread countless times, and each rereading uncovers meanings hitherto unrecognized or forgotten. Gerber maintains that literature is "written for people to read; it is designed to evoke feeling and belief and not just understanding and not just a sense of form" (2). *Literature for children* means classical or contemporary writing of such quality that children can understand what is read or heard.

Program Approaches

The literature program is distinct from the teaching of reading, yet is tightly interwoven with it. Students must learn how to read before they can read independently; although, ideally, the literature program need not wait until this phenomenon occurs. Learning begins as soon as the child is born. Mothers sing lullabies, recite verses, and play patty-cake before infants can make both hands meet, and story reading continues in preschool years when parents or baby sitters take the time.

The planned literature program, however, begins with school and usually is approached in six different ways in various combinations: (1) free reading by children, (2) reading aloud to children, (3) guided and supplementary reading, (4) topical units, (5) creative sharing, and (6) a combined program that includes literature teaching.

Free Reading

A literature program of free reading is variously organized but it usually provides a certain amount of time each week for students to read books of their own choosing. Pupils are usually not free *not* to read, but they are free to read what they wish and supposedly what they can—even comic books, series like Nancy Drew or The Hardy Boys, and maybe *Mad Magazine!*

Last year one elementary school gained quite a reputation as "A Reading School." Each afternoon after lunch, "Please Do Not Disturb" signs were hung on every door to inform anyone who came that a reading period was in progress. During this half hour, everyone in the building read: the students, the teachers, the principal and his secretary, and the janitor!

Free reading does have a place in the literature program. It allows pupils to read what they wish, to not finish every book

From Helen Huus, Approaches to the use of literature in the reading progam. In Bonnie S. Schulwitz (Ed.), *Teachers, tangibles, techniques: Comprehension of context in reading.* Newark, Del.: International Reading Association, 1975. Pp. 140–149. Reprinted by permission of Helen Huus and the International Reading Association.

they start, to select material considered by interested adults to be too difficult or too easy for them, and to pursue one topic relentlessly.

However, free reading has disadvantages, even when it is only part of a total literature program. The approach assumes that pupils have a wide range of choices available on many topics of varying levels of difficulty so that they can find what they want to read and be able to read it. This is not always the case. In addition, some pupils may stay too long on one level and fail to progress to books of greater depth; some may read superficially and be satisfied with only cursorily following a story plot or with merely looking at pictures; and others may have difficulty in choosing books from those available and thus may waste their time. The free reading done at home has similar advantages and disadvantages, provided the reader has a suitable place to read.

If free reading is only one prong of a total program, it can contribute by capturing and extending the readers' interests and by easing pupils into a more structured approach.

Reading Aloud

In some schools, the only literature offered for oral reading is that presented during the ten- or fifteen-minute period set aside for the teacher or a student to read aloud to the class. The material may consist of short stories, poetry, or a chapter-a-day from a longer book.

When the reader is well prepared and when the book is chosen with the total class in mind, such oral reading is often interesting and enjoyable. Furthermore, since pupils are not doing the reading for themselves, they have no responsibility other than listening; they can hear books with a vocabulary and language structure beyond their current competencies, and being unhampered by problems of reading, they can focus on actions and ideas; they can hear the beauty of the language

as it sounds; and they can listen to stories that they ordinarily might miss. Some pupils would shun poetry completely, and few boys today are likely to pick out *Alice in Wonderland* for their free reading, although one sixth grade boy did admit to reading *Little Women* because he had heard it was a good book.

On the other hand, when someone reads aloud, pupils may be relatively passive and thus profit less from the experience than they would have if they had read the book themselves. Books selected for reading aloud can take into account the interests of a majority of the students or the known interests of a given age group, but such books may fail to capture the interest of other individuals. Regardless of age, those who have not learned to read are dependent upon those who can read. For some pupils, a pressure to learn to read can be generated because they want so much to read for themselves a story they enjoyed hearing; other pupils may be completely satisfied to continue their dependency and simply listen. In any case, listening to fine stories and poems read well orally is another important prong of the program for literature and is one way children become acquainted with their literary heritage.

Storytelling can be placed in the same category as reading aloud, for it has most of the same advantages and disadvantages. The fact that a storyteller usually has no book between himself and the listener is often cited as the crucial contribution. However, a storyteller who feels the responsibility of fidelity to the author's composition may still wish to have the book as a prompter, if needed.

Storytelling falls short as literature when the teller takes great liberties with the vocabulary and syntax of an author's writing and gives pupils, at best, a poor substitute that happens to be the teller's personal version of the story. It is also a disadvantage when the storyteller fails to submerge his own personality in favor of the work.

A library story hour is subject to the same pitfalls, for even though pupils hear a story read or told, the literary experience depends upon the quality of the selection, the authenticity of the rendition, and the attention to elements constituting literature. Unless the latter is present, pupils have a pleasant and comfortable time hearing old favorites and getting acquainted with new stories, but they may not be progressing in their literature learning.

Guided and Supplementary Reading

Guided reading and supplementary reading refute some of the criticisms leveled at free reading. In the guided program, students are given help in selecting the books they wish to read, with consideration given to a variety of types and topics and to levels of quality and difficulty. Guidance is apparent when librarians color-code books for difficulty or place books on shelves by topic and grade level. Just making a book available in the library, classroom, or at home is another subtle way of channeling the pupils' choices.

More pointed guidance is given in school subjects when additional readings are recommended on the topic studied. Alert teachers note possibilities before the topic is initiated and procure the recommended books so that they are available at the outset. Library books enhance the regularly assigned lessons by expanding and explaining ideas which a textbook, of necessity, merely generalizes. Biographies can bring to life persons who are mentioned only briefly in a line of text. Whole eras, countries, or concepts can be illustrated through narration, drama, poetry, fiction, and pictures.

However, not all supplementary reading can be classed as literature for some informational books are trite, stilted, made-to-order books devised to reach a ready market. In contrast to such books are the beautifully written factual accounts like the animal stories of Mary and Conrad Buff or Jean George; the biographies of James Daugherty or Jean Lee Latham; the historical fiction of Elizabeth Janet Gray or Rosemary Sutcliff; or the almost-true accounts of Laura Ingalls Wilder, Kate Seredy, and Carol Ryrie Brink. While fewer literary books on useful topics serve as supplementary reading materials in subject areas, the distinction between quality writing and reportorial recitation must be recognized.

Relating literature to other school subjects serves to reinforce both and helps pupils realize the range of style possible when dealing with varied topics such as elephants, snow, frontier life, or ancient Peru. Literature may fire a student's imagination for far away places or unresearched areas and may have a lasting influence on his vocational choice or avocational pursuits. The background pupils acquire through well-written informational books stands them in good stead later, and the experience with factual books of quality helps acquaint students with literary elements—irrespective of topic—which may provide motivation for further, more advanced reading about peoples, places, and things. Supplementary reading, then, has a place as another prong in the total literature program.

Topical Units

The approach to literature that utilizes units on a topic or subject, a type of work, or the style of writing also is related to supplementary reading.

Topics like "People of Other Lands," "The Oregon Trail," "The City," "Animals that Live in the Sea," "Plants that Move," "Machines," and "The First Thanksgiving" are familiar to teachers. In some classrooms, literature is organized around calendar topics—"September," "Fall," "Halloween," "Book Week," "Veterans' Day," "Thanksgiving," and so on through the year.

A topic like "Spring" can lead in several directions. One might focus on "Growing Things," starting out with plants and animals and promoting books such as *Maple Tree* by Millicent Selsam, *Lookout for the Forest* by Glenn Blough, and *Green is for Growing* by Winifred and Cecil Lubell. "Animals and How They Grow" could be introduced through Holling Clancy Holling's *Pagoo* which tells of the life of a hermit crab, and Herbert Zim's books that follow life cycles in *Monkeys, Elephants, Rabbits,* and *The Great Whales*. Reptiles could be introduced through Robert McClung's dramatic *Buzztail*, the story of a rattlesnake, as well as John Hoke's *First Book of Snakes* and Barbara Brenner's *A Snake Lover's Diary*. Books about birds, insects, and human beings could be added as the topic expands and as pupils are led to see similarities among all the growing things which struggle for survival.

Other topics comparing and contrasting older classics like *Little Women* and *Tom Sawyer* with modern counterparts like *Up a Road Slowly, Island of the Blue Dolphins, It's Like This, Cat,* and *Henry Reed, Inc.* provide the basis for a literature unit where relationships between parents and children, siblings, peers, or sexes can be discussed.

Young children might compare contemporary editions of Mother Goose illustrated by Tasha Tudor, Brian Wildsmith, Philip Reed, Marguerite de Angeli, and Harold Jones with classical editions illustrated by Kate Greenaway, Randolph Caldecott, Walter Crane, L. Leslie Brooke, and Blanche Fisher Wright. Pupils can note the inclusiveness of the collection, versions used, color, action, period depicted, and placement of illustrations in relation to the verses.

Types of literary works might be featured, such as biography, folk and fairy tales (which could be coupled with other topics such as France, Japan, or Brazil), tall tales, poetry, plays (though these are few for the elementary school), myths, hero tales, and picture books.

"American Tall Tales" might be chosen as pupils read and compare the exploits of John Henry, Paul Bunyan, Pecos Bill, Joe Magarac, Febold Feboldson,

Mike Fink, Tony Beaver, Stormalong the Sailor, and other half-true heroes such as Davy Crockett, Johnny Appleseed, and perhaps Daniel Boone and Buffalo Bill. Anne Malcolmson's *Yankee Doodle's Cousins* still gives a fine overview of these characters and can easily be followed by books about each individual.

Style is another common denominator for a topical unit, and books containing various types of humor—exaggeration or funny characters—could be compared. Various figures of speech, realistic conversations, lifelike portrayals of characters, or variations in levels of language are other dimensions of style to be discussed.

For illustration, suppose a unit or lesson focuses on the simile as a figure of speech. The teacher first might explain that unknown objects and ideas can be made real and understandable when compared to something the reader already knows. Borten's *Do You See What I See?* (1) contains similes on nearly every page. In this book the author discusses lines, shapes, and colors. Note how her similes in these descriptions relate both to content and to feeling:

> Lines can bend in a curved way, too. A curved line is like a swan, full of beauty and grace. It can rise and curl slowly, as lazy as smoke. It can twirl like a dancer, or flow and swirl like water in a stream full of speckled fish.
>
> A circle is a "shape"—a merry, cherry shape. It can roll like a ball, or float like a bubble, or turn like a ferris wheel. It can be calm as the moon, as gentle as a curled-up kitten, or as fat and jolly as Santa Claus.
>
> Different colors make us feel different ways, just as lines and shapes do. Red is hot like a crackling fire, and blue is cold like a mountain stream.
>
> Yellow is warm like the sun's rays, and green is as cool as a crisp leaf of lettuce.

Poetry, too, contains pictures. Tippet's poem, "The Park" (4), describes the lights that shine "as bright and still/ As dande- lions/ On a hill." Kuskin's snake "moved like a ribbon/Silent as snow," (3) and Lewis' trumpet "honks and it whistles/ it roars like lion/ With a wheezing huffing hum" (3). Children understand the idea and later can make their own comparisons and eventually learn the term.

According to the National Assessment of Educational Progress reports on litera- ture, more than half of the 9- and 13-year- olds expressed personal involvement with the literary works and made a value judg- ment or evaluation of them. At most, about a third of these age groups were able to analyze, describe, and interpret the works. Although more than half of these pupils evaluated the material, apparently they were unable to support their evalua- tions through analysis and interpretation. These pupils may not know how to ana- lyze and interpret literary works. The types of analyses and interpretations expected may be beyond the mental capac- ities of certain age groups; some pupils may lack the experiential background nec- essary for interpretation; and some may lack the vocabulary to express ideas they recognize but cannot verbalize.

If the National Assessment test appraises the objectives accepted for liter- ature teaching, then the implication for schools is clear: Pupils need help in sup- porting their value judgments of the worth and in finding the meanings of the mate- rials they read.

Topical units or lessons have the advantage of focusing on a common thread, allowing pupils to see how various authors approach similar ideas or prob- lems. Pupils can make comparisons and contrasts and begin to discern levels of quality among works of comparable con- tent, genre, or style. Eventually, the ear- marks of quality are identified, and students improve in their ability to evalu- ate. Since a class or a group of students usually works together on a topical unit, opportunities for discussion, interchange, and sharing of ideas are possible, and a

teacher can structure the lessons to pro- vide continuity and coverage. Also, stu- dents are introduced to topics and ideas that they might not consciously seek out independently, thus providing them with a fuller, richer literary experience than if left completely to their own devices.

Disadvantages of a topical-unit ap- proach include the problem of finding topics that appeal equally to all members of the group and of obtaining adequate material of quality on a variety of different reading levels for these topics. Additional difficulties can occur in organizing and synchronizing the various activities, espe- cially if more than one topic is selected and several groups are working simultane- ously. Since individual choices would be restricted within the range of topics treated, students might also be less likely to carry over their reading into out-of- school life. Topical teaching could become routine and humdrum, though this is more a fault of poor use of the plan than of the plan itself. For many programs, units form the crux of literature teaching per se and are the central core around which other aspects cluster.

Creative Sharing

In some classrooms, including those at university level, the study of literature for children is approached as a vehicle for cre- ative sharing through oral reading and storytelling; through writing compositions, original stories, critiques, and analyses; or through art activities like modeling, paint- ing, cutting, and pasting. In this approach, discussions, choral readings, reports and reviews, dramatizations, puppet shows, pantomimes, charades and other games, murals, dioramas, overhead projection, slides, filmstrips, tapes, and records abound during the literature period.

The chief advantages of using such activities as an approach to literature are the obvious interest generated in the chil- dren and their chance to share the prod- ucts with other groups and classes, parents, and casual visitors. Such tangible evidence relating to books can also serve as a means of evaluating pupils' understanding of their reading, at least on a superficial level, for literal interpretation is usually necessary to complete most of the projects developed.

There is danger, however, that creative activity may replace the literature itself, and the time allocated for reading may be usurped for production. Similarly, evaluation may become restricted to creative output and may be diverted from aspects of language and feeling to skill with paint and paper. While creative arts and literature complement each other very well, the art period can capitalize upon ideas gained from literature, and each activity may be given its place in the weekly schedule.

A Total Program

The learning of literature—its content, style, interpretation, emotional overtones, quality, and humanness—requires a total program that incorporates the aforementioned approaches into a flexible, overall plan. Such a plan makes provision for free reading, listening to stories and poetry read aloud, utilizing library books to supplement the content subjects, reading at home, focusing on a topical unit, learning about elements that constitute literature, and creatively sharing enjoyable books and poems. But the total program should also provide pupils with opportunities to achieve objectives at progressively higher levels as they read literature of increasing complexity and depth.

A structured program need not necessarily be formal or restricted. A teacher who recognizes and accepts the objectives of literature teaching, who knows the materials and can help pupils reach the objectives, can plan lessons that, to a casual observer, may seem to be very freewheeling in their execution. Once the lesson or series of lessons has been thought through, the teacher is free to

teach a lesson as planned or to depart from it as the situation demands. What is constant is the conscious movement forward toward achieving the goals and a knowledge of what to do to create this forward movement. The real test, perhaps, will not come until the pupil leaves school and enters the working world where other pressures prevail for his time, energy, and attention.

Conclusion

This discussion on approaches to literature in the elementary school has focused on the ways in which literature teaching is included in the ongoing activities of the school program. The content, activities, and evaluation of such a program have not been treated; obviously, attention must be given to the selection of concepts and content, then to the materials and activities that are utilized to obtain the objectives, and, finally, to the evaluation program that uncovers the achievement of the pupils and the strengths and weakness of the program.

Yet, until proven wrong, teachers must assume that teaching literature does have lasting positive effects. The challenge is to help each student enjoy good books, improve his taste, and become acutely aware of the way literature enhances his living, enriches his experience, and sharpens his insights into the very humanity of man. A total program of literature has a chance to succeed in meeting the challenge.

References

1. Borten, Helen. *Do You See What I See?* New York: Abelard-Schuman, 1959.
2. "English Teachers Commend Free Response Exercises in Literature Assessment," *Newsletter* of the National Assessment of Educational Progress, 6 (February 1973), 4.
3. Kuskin, Karla. *In the Middle of the Trees.* New York: Harper & Row, 1958.
4. Tippett, James, "The Park," from *I Live in the City.* New York: Harper & Row, 1927, 1955.

66. Humor and the Reading Program

Lance M. Gentile and Merna M. McMillan

A brief glance at the history of the United States reveals a nation born of revolution and violence. Unfortunately, not only do these elements continue to defile life in this country, but today a person must cope with the innumerable problems of a highly technological and "pressure packed" environment. Therefore, in addition to acquiring specific skills to earn a living, it is vital that people develop a sense of humor to sustain them in times of stress. Durrell (1956, p. 320) stated:

Humor is a highly important characteristic of the American tradition and an extremely useful part of social intercourse. It provides balance, encourages cooperation, reduces emotional pressure, relieves dullness and opens conversation.

The current "back to basics" movement and mounting concern about the reading difficulties of so many young people portend an overly serious direction in education. While school, and the reading program in particular, provide ideal opportunities to deal with humorous or witty material, quite often this aspect is overlooked or viewed as being "out of place" in the standard curriculum. Many individuals contend that school is a place where people prepare to make a living rather than a life.

Laughter and mirth are more visible among young people away from the classroom. Hallways, gymnasiums, playgrounds, restrooms, and cafeterias are the "acceptable" places to show emotion, but a return to the pupil's desk from any of these areas is generally a signal to "straighten up."

In his book, *The Atrocity of Education*, Arthur Pearl (1972) deplored the lack of humor and affect in most of what students are asked to read. In particular he criticized readings describing work functions for their gross distortions. Pearl said (pp. 69–71):

The reader is unable to share the humor—or the heartache—that is part of all work activities. There is an absence of detail. No children's book writer of today is doing for the truckdriver or any other occupation what Mark Twain did in the nineteenth century for the riverboat pilot.

Pearl cited a section from Twain's *Life on the Mississippi* detailing the manner in which a pilot directed landsmen in moving a gangplank. This passage is so vivid, it could be reenacted as a play, or students might model its style, language, or characterization through role-playing activities. Mark Twain's writing comes alive; it has substance, whereas so much of what is written for today's students is contrived. Small wonder most youngsters are not excited or "turned on" by their reading experiences and greatly prefer watching endless hours of violent television.

In earlier years TV accentuated humor and comedy through shows like Sid Caesar and Imogene Coca's "Your Show of Shows," "The Colgate Comedy Hour," Jackie Gleason's "Cavalcade of Stars," Art Linkletter's "People Are Funny," and so on. Comedians such as Danny Thomas, Red Buttons, Jack Benny, George Gobel, and George Burns and Gracie Allen dominated prime time viewing.

From Lance M. Gentile and Merna M. McMillan, Humor and the reading program. *Journal of Reading,* January 1978, *21,* 343–349. Reprinted by permission of Lance Gentile, Merna McMillan and the International Reading Association.

Today these programs and people have been replaced by "cops and robbers" series whose themes are violence, perversion, and emotional trauma. This damaging influence may well contribute to an absence of humor and lightheartedness among young people.

Corcoran (1976, p. 22) described a week-long experience at the International Platform Association's Convention in Washington, D.C., where he observed a teenagers' speech contest:

It has been a solemn performance all around. When William Howard Taft III comes forward to present the winner's trophy, he appears stunned. He turns to the contestants and says: 'I've never heard such seriousness from those so young. I just hope they cheer up as life goes forward.' He asks the teens, who are now fidgeting nervously, 'I wonder if there are any light stories each of you could tell?' Silence and uncomprehending glances. 'Is there *one* light story among you?' More silence. 'I've proved my point,' Taft sighs.

It is essential that reading programs provide ample opportunities for students to experience life's whimsical, preposterous, zany, and nonsensical characters and events. For purposes of inner harmony and peace, no single human phenomenon is as healthy, spontaneous, honest, and soothing as laughter.

Notwithstanding the salubrious side effects of funny material, reading at this level often demands critical thinking and great insight. The development of the latter constitutes one of the most crucial comprehension skills. It affords individuals a much purer and more amusing view of themselves and their surroundings. Out of the overflow of good humor and comedy comes a healthy sense of proportion or sanity. People who have balanced their personal qualities and fondest values readily perceive their incongruities and absurdities. Allport (1961, p. 292) noted:

Perhaps the most striking correlate of insight is the sense of humor. In one unpublished study where subjects rated one another on a large number of traits, the correlation between ratings on insight and humor turned out to be .88. Such a high coefficient means either that personalities with marked insight are also high in humor, or else that the raters were not able to distinguish between the two qualities. In either case the result is important.

A sense of humor develops among people in rather distinct stages. Its growth is dependent on age and experience. Gesell, Ilg, and Ames (1956, pp. 343–46) summarized this development from 10 years of age and above. An awareness of this successive progression will help the reading teacher provide materials and design humorously appealing experiences for each age group. For each phase we provide a partial bibliography as a starter.

Age 10: Humor is of the literal or obvious type and quite often not funny to adults. Some of it is slapstick, but much of it is a reaction to anything unexpected.

Trade Materials

Alexander, Lloyd. *The Marvelous Misadventures of Sebastian.* New York, N.Y.: Dutton, 1970.

Brewton, Sara and John Brewton. *Laughable Limericks.* New York, N.Y.: Crowell, 1965.

Fast, Howard. *Tony and the Wonderful Door.* New York, N.Y.: Knopf, 1968.

Hoke, Helen. *Jokes, Jokes, Jokes.* New York, N.Y.: Grolier, 1963.

Masin, Herman. *For Laughing Out Loud.* Englewood Cliffs, N.J.: Scholastic Book Services, 1974.

Wilson, Dagmar. *Jokes, Riddles, and Funny Stories.* New York, N.Y.: Grosset & Dunlap, 1959.

Comics and Cartoons

Aragones, Sergio. *Mad as the Devil.* New York, N.Y.: Warner Books, 1975; *Mad about Mad.* New York, N.Y.: New American Library, 1970.

Archie Comics Ed. *Everything's Archie.* New York, N.Y.: Bantam Books, 1972.

Debartolo, Dick. *Mad Look at Old Movies.* New York, N.Y.: Warner Books, 1973.

Ketcham, Hank. *Dennis the Menace: Short Swinger,* 1976; *Dennis the Menace: Who Me?,* 1976. New York, N.Y.: Fawcett World Library.

Mad Libs, no. 1, 1958; no. 5, 1968; no. 6, 1970; no. 7, 1974. Los Angeles, Calif.: Price/Stern/Sloan.

Schulz, Charles. *Peanuts,* 1952; *Peanuts Classics,* 1970. New York, N.Y.: Holt, Rinehart & Winston.

Walker, Mort. *Beetle Bailey #9: Shape Up or Ship Out.* New York, N.Y.: Grosset & Dunlap, 1974.

Age 11: Humor is "corny" and often smutty, with much laughing at misbehavior and minor accidents. The child can understand a little adult humor, but his/her own humor is of a different type and still based at a literal, concrete level.

Trade Materials

Clark, David. *Jokes, Puns, and Riddles.* New York, N.Y.: Doubleday, 1968.

Cole, William. *Humorous Poetry for Children.* Cleveland, Ohio: Collins-World, 1955.

Fox, Sonny. *Jokes and How to Tell Them.* New York, N.Y.: Putnam, 1965.

Haskins, James. *Jokes from Black Folks.* New York, N.Y.: Doubleday, 1973.

Malone, Mary. *Here's Howie.* New York, N.Y.: Dodd, 1962.

Preston, Edna. *Barrel of Chuckles,* 1972; *Barrel of Fun,* 1973; *Barrel of Laughs,* 1974. Englewood Cliffs, N.J.: Scholastic Book Services.

Comics and Cartoons

Debartolo, D. and J. Torres. *Mad Look at TV.* New York, N.Y.: Warner Books, 1974.

Ketcham, Hank. *Dennis the Menace: Just for Fun.* New York, N.Y.: Fawcett World Library, 1976.

Mad Magazine Ed. *Mad at You.* New York, N.Y.: Warner Books, 1975.

Martin, Don. *Mad Adventures of Captain Klutz.* New York, N.Y.: New American Library, 1974.

Schulz, Charles. *Peanuts Revisited,* 1970. New York, N.Y.: Holt, Rinehart & Winston. *Snoopy and His Sopwith Camel,* 1974; *Snoopy and the Red Baron,* 1976. New York, N.Y.: Fawcett World Library.

The World's Worst Knock-Knock Jokes, 1974; *. . . Doctor Jokes,* 1974; *. . . Riddles,* 1974; *. . . Jokes,* 1974; *. . . Moron Jokes,* 1974; *. . . Monster Jokes,* 1974; *. . . Psychiatrist Jokes,* 1974; *. . . Golf Jokes,* 1974. Los Angeles, Calif.: Price/Stern/Sloan.

Age 12: This stage is marked by many practical jokes of an obvious kind, teasing and some exchange of banter with adults.

Trade Materials

Adler, Bill. *Hip Kids' Letters from Camp.* New York, N.Y.: New American Library, 1973.

Byfield, Barbara. *Book of Weird.* New York, N.Y.: Doubleday, 1973.

Cahn, Victor. *Disrespectful Dictionary.* Los Angeles, Calif: Price/Stern/Sloan, 1974.

Gerles, Bill. *Jokes, Riddles and Other Funny Things.* New York, N.Y.: Western Publications, 1975.

Insult Dictionary: How to Snarl Back in Five Languages. Los Angeles, Calif.: Price/Stern/Sloan, 1970.

Lewis, George. *Dictionary of Bloopers and Boners.* Englewood Cliffs, N.J.: Scholastic Book Services, 1974.

Roylance, William. *Complete Book of Insults, Boasts and Riddles.* Englewood Cliffs, N.J.: Prentice-Hall, 1970.

Comics and Cartoons

Jacobs, F. and B. Richard. *Mad about Sports.* New York, N.Y.: Warner Books, 1972.

Jaffee, Al. *Mad Book of Magic and Other Dirty Tricks.* New York, N.Y.: New American Library, 1970.

Lear, Ed. *Ed Lear's Nonsense Coloring Book.* New York, N.Y.: Dover, 1971.

Mad Magazine Ed. *Mad Strikes Back.* New York, N.Y.: Ballantine, 1975.

Prohias, Antonio. *Fourth Mad Declassified Papers on Spy vs. Spy.* New York, N.Y.: Warner Books, 1974.

Schulz, Charles. *Snoopy,* 1958; *Peanuts Every Sunday,* 1961. New York, N.Y.: Holt, Rinehart & Winston.

Age 13: Humor is rather less obvious and more reserved than at earlier or later stages; the beginnings of sarcasm mark this stage of development.

Trade Materials

Anobile, Richard. *Drat: W. C. Fields*. New York, N.Y.: New American Library, 1973.

Blair, Dike. *Books and Bedlam*. Middlebury, Vt.: Vermont Books, 1962.

Garagiola, Joe. *Baseball Is a Funny Game*. New York, N.Y.: Bantam, 1974.

Heller, Jack. *Jokesmith's Jubilee*. New York, N.Y.: Scholastic Book Services, 1971.

Kearne, Bill. *Just in Pun*. New York, N.Y.: Scholastic Book Services, 1969.

Lauber, Pat. *Jokes and More Jokes*. New York, N.Y.: Scholastic Book Services, 1967.

Lewis, Martin. *The Quotations of W. C. Fields*. New York, N.Y.: Drake, 1976.

Masin, Herman. *Baseball Laughs*. Englewood Cliffs, N.J.: Scholastic Book Services, 1969.

Comics and Cartoons

Brandel, Max. *Mad Book of Word Power*. New York, N.Y.: Warner Books, 1976.

Friedman, Les. *Eggbert: The Fun Born*, 1976; *Belly Laughs*, 1975; *Funny Side Up*, 1975. New York, N.Y.: Pocket Books.

Ketcham, Hank. *Dennis the Menace: Dennis Power*, 1975; *Dennis the Menace: Where the Action Is*, 1975. New York, N.Y.: Fawcett World Library.

Lariar, Lawrence. *The Teen-Scene*. New York, N.Y.: Dodd, 1966.

Mad Magazine Ed. *Fighting Mad*, 1974; *Boiling Mad*, 1973. New York, N.Y.: Warner Books.

Walker, Mort. *Beetle Bailey #1: Beetle Bailey*, 1968; *Beetle Bailey #4*, 1970; *Beetle Bailey #7*, 1973; *Beetle Bailey #11*, 1975. New York, N.Y.: Grosset & Dunlap.

Age 14: Humor is used against parents or others in authority; smutty jokes among members of one's own sex and dislike of parents' jokes are characteristic of this age group.

Trade Materials

Armour, Richard. *It All Started with Columbus*, 1976; *. . . With Eve*, 1963; *. . . with Europa*, 1955; *. . . with Hippocrates*, 1966; *. . . with Freshman English*, 1973; *. . . with Marx*, 1958; *. . . with Stones and Clubs*, 1967; *Golf Is a Four-Letter Word*, 1964. New York, N.Y.: McGraw-Hill.

Behrens, Frank. *Dante's Infernal Guide to Your School*. New York, N.Y.: Simon & Schuster, 1971.

Critchfield, J. and J. Hopkins. *You Were Born on a Rotten Day*. Los Angeles, Calif.: Price/Stern/Sloan, 1975.

Everhart, Jim. *The Illustrated Texas Dictionary of the English Language*, vols. 1, 2, 3, 4. Lincoln, Neb.: Cliff's Notes, 1973.

Everhart, Jim. *CB Language*. Lincoln, Neb.: Centennial Press, 1976.

Ferrell, T. *Sneaky Feats*, 1975; *More Sneaky Feats*, 1976. Mission, Kan.: Sheed & Ward.

Fidell, Jeanette. *Jokes, Jokes, Jokes*. New York, N.Y.: Scholastic Book Services, 1976.

Comics and Cartoons

Schulz, Charles. *Peanuts Double*, vol. 1 and 2, 1976; *Peanuts for Everybody: Selected Cartoons*, 1975. New York, N.Y.: Fawcett World Library. *Peanuts Jubilee: My Life and Art with Charlie Brown*, 1976. New York, N.Y.: Ballantine Books.

Age 15: Evident at this stage are the beginnings of the ability to laugh at oneself and to see something funny when teased or "kidded." Also emerging at this time is the understanding of irony as a form of humor.

Trade Materials

Buchwald, Art. *I Never Danced at the White House*. New York, N.Y.: Fawcett World Library, 1976.

Elliott, B. and R. Goulding. *Write If You Get Work: The Best of Bob and Ray*. New York, N.Y.: Random House, 1975.

Harron, D. *K.O.R.N. Allmynack*. Buffalo, N.Y.: Gage Publications, 1976.

McGeachy, D. P. *Gospel According to Andy Capp*. Atlanta, Ga.: John Knox Press, 1973.

Stokes, Jack. *Mind Your A's and Q's: Useless Questions to Dumb Answers*. Garden City, N.Y.: Doubleday, 1977.

Wilde, Larry. *The Official Democrat/Republican*

Joke Book. New York, N.Y.: Pinnacle Books, 1976.

Wood, Rob. *The Book of Blunders.* Kansas City, Mo.: Hallmark Cards, Inc., 1974.

Comics and Cartoons

Hart, Johnny. *B.C.: Big Wheel,* 1976; *B.C.: Dip in Road,* 1976; *B.C.: Great Zot I'm Beautiful,* 1976; *B.C.: It's a Funny World,* 1976. New York, N.Y.: Fawcett World Library.

Kelley, Walt. *Pogo's Body Politic,* 1976; *Pogo Revisited,* 1974. New York, N.Y.: Simon & Schuster.

Parker, Brant and Johnny Hart. *Wizard of Id: "Long Live the King,"* 1975; *Wizard of Id: No. 8,* 1976. New York, N.Y.: Fawcett World Library.

Schulz, Charles. *Peanuts for Everybody.* New York, N.Y.: Fawcett World Library, 1975.

Age 16 and above: Ability to understand more subtle forms of humor, such as satire, for example, participation in adult jokes, and the beginnings of spontaneous humor on an adult level mark this stage of development.

Trade Materials

Adler, Bill. *How to Be Funny in Your Own Lifetime.* Chicago, Ill.: Playboy Press, 1973.

Busch, Wilhelm. *Bushel of Merry Thoughts,* W. H. Rogers, trans. New York, N.Y.: Dover Publications, 1971.

Hughes, Langston. *Book of Negro Humor.* New York, N.Y.: Dodd, 1965.

Johnson, Charles. *Black Humor.* Chicago, Ill.: Johnson Publications, 1970.

McKenzie, E. C. *Eighteen Hundred Quippable Quotes.* Grand Rapids, Iowa: Baker Books, 1973.

Nash, Ogden. *I Couldn't Help Laughing.* Philadelphia, Pa.: Lippincott, 1957.

Reit, Seymour, Ed. *America Laughs: A Treasury of Great Humor.* New York, N.Y.: Crowell-Collier Press, 1966.

Rosenberg, Marvin, Ed. *The Best Cartoons from Punch.* New York, N.Y.: Simon & Schuster, 1952.

Schirmer, Mathilda. *The Bedside Book of Humor.* Chicago, Ill.: People's Book Club, 1948.

Scoggin, Margaret. *More Chucklebait.* New York, N.Y.: Knopf, 1949.

Untermeyer, Louis. *Treasury of Great Humor.* New York, N.Y.: McGraw-Hill, 1972.

Magazines (samples sent on request)

Dublin Opinion: The National Humorous Journal of Ireland, Gordon Clark, Ed. First published in 1922. Dublin Opinion Ltd., 193 Pearse St., Dublin, L, Ireland.

Funny Funny World, Martin A. Ragaway, Ed. First published in 1971. 407 Commercial Center St., Beverly Hills, Calif. 90201.

Harvard Lampoon, James H. Siegelman, Ed. First published in 1876. 44 Bow St., Cambridge, Mass. 02138.

Journal of Irreproducible Results, Alexander Kohn, Ed. First published in 1955. Society for Basic Irreproducible Research, Box 234, Chicago Heights, Ill. 60411.

Mad, William Gaines and Albert B. Feldstein, Eds. First published in 1953. E.C. Publications Inc., 485 Madison Avenue, New York, N.Y. 10022.

National Lampoon, Douglas C. Kenney, Ed. First published in 1970. Twentieth Century Publications, 635 Madison Avenue, New York, N.Y. 10022.

Private Eye, Richard Ingrams, Ed. First published in 1961. Pressdam Ltd., 34 Greek St., London W1, England.

Worm Runner's Digest and Journal of Biological Psychology, James V. McConnel, Ed. First published in 1959. Box 644, Ann Arbor, Mich. 48107.

References

Allport, G. W. *Pattern and Growth in Personality.* New York, N.Y.: Holt, Rinehart & Winston, 1961.

Corcoran, John H. Jr. "At Last a (Slim) Chance to Make the Big-Time." *The National Observer* (October 23, 1976), p. 22.

Durrell, Donald D. *Improving Reading Instruction.* New York, N.Y.: Harcourt Brace Jovanovich, 1956.

Gesell, A., F. L. Ilg and L. B. Ames. *Youth: The Years from Ten to Sixteen.* New York, N.Y.: Harper & Row, 1956.

Pearl, Arthur. *The Atrocity of Education.* New York, N.Y.: E. P. Dutton, 1972.

67. Dr. Criscuolo's 30 Miracle Motivators for Reluctant Readers

Nicholas P. Criscuolo

1. Character Clues. Have students develop a list of statements (clues) about a book character and see how many have to be given before a group can guess who the character is. A continuing activity can develop from questions in envelope pockets on the bulletin board. One envelope labeled "Who am I?" might present questions about characters, such as "I'm a monkey who took a trip around the world. Who am I?" Another, labeled "Where did it happen?" might include questions about events in different books.

2. Reference Preference. Have pupils make a collection of quotations from favorite books which describe ideas or feelings about evildoers; people, places, or things; foolishness and folly; sadness; happiness.

3. Birthday Gift. As part of the birthday celebration for a pupil, let him pick his favorite story from those you have read to the class; then read it aloud at an appropriate time.

4. Book Kite. Draw a kite with a long string. Display books recently read. Ask students to draw small pictures of major events from one of the books. Those pictures will comprise the bows to the kite's tail. A large picture of a class favorite, drawn by a group of youngsters, can comprise the body.

5. Panel Discussions. Panel discussions of books read by pupils are interesting. No two members of the panel have to have read the same book. Pupils can discuss problems faced by the major characters in stories. They can compare stories and react to the solutions. Some guiding questions: (1) What major problem did the main character face? (2) How was it solved? (3) How would you have handled it? (4) How does your solution differ from those of other members of the panel? The class or panel may also discuss favorite characters, how they are alike or different.

6. Story Sections. Cut into sections a story from a children's magazine or book that is no longer usable. Distribute the sections. Have each student carefully prepare his section so it can be read to the class. Since most pupils have not read the story in its entirety, they will be interested in how it unfolds in each pupil's section.

7. Class Journalists. A class newspaper is an excellent project for sparking interest in reading. Be sure each pupil makes a contribution. You'll need editors, artists, staff writers, and so on. Plan a section on "New Books We Have Read," another on "Riddles and Jokes."

8. Rebus Reading. A great deal of fun! In certain spots of a sentence or paragraph, pictures are substituted for words. Ask children to create a rebus story to match a book they're reading. Suggested resources for rebus writers can include an alphabetized list of service words—*on, at, all,* and so on. Some students might enjoy stockpiling a rebus reservoir. Pictures of objects, people, and obvious actions can

From Nicholas P. Criscuolo, Dr. Criscuolo's 30 miracle motivators for reluctant readers. *Instructor,* November 1977, 87, 48–50. Reprinted by permission of the publisher.

be clipped, collected, and put into envelopes for future rebus-writing sessions.

9. How Do They Compare? Secure different editions of the same children's books—*Alice in Wonderland, Mother Goose, The Wizard of Oz.* Ask pupils to compare different styles and types of illustrations—fantasy versus realism, color versus black and white, line drawings versus paintings or collage. Ask which style they prefer for a particular book and why.

10. Clipping Service. Magazines and newspapers are an excellent source of pictures and articles on leaders and events important in world affairs. Set up a clipping file as a stimulus for further reading about them.

11. Poetry Club. Children with a poem they really like are eligible to join the Poetry Club. They must write it in a personal notebook, illustrate it, and save it for the club. When the day for Poetry Club arrives, all with poems to share read them to the class, showing illustrations.

12. Read-a-Long. Special design a read-a-book special train. The first child to finish five books becomes engineer. The next becomes brakeman. The rest become passengers. Snapshots can be pasted onto the train as soon as children finish reading five books. Before the year is up, chances are every child will be riding the Read-a-Long Special!

13. Reading Tree. Secure a tree branch and mount it in an old coffee can containing sand. Tie several paperback books on the twigs of the branch. This will capture the interest of kids, who can pick a book from the tree.

14. Who's Who. Have each child write his name and address on a page in a large loose-leaf notebook, and list hobbies, personal information, and the types of books he or she enjoys. Children then use the notebook for reference in sending to classmates holiday greetings, get-well letters, or books they think the recipients would enjoy.

15. Ready Resources. Every community has resource people who may share their talents and experiences. Travel, for example. Invite persons who have visited foreign countries to show slides and artifacts and to discuss experiences so that as children read stories set in these countries, reading will come alive. Or if kids are into mysteries invite a detective to class.

16. Crossword Puzzles. Have students use vocabulary words from a book or story to make crossword puzzles on graph paper. They should write a question sheet for it and hand in an answer sheet. Check and distribute the puzzles to other students to work out in their free time.

17. Look It Up! Prepare questions which need to be researched in the school library. A prize might be awarded to the youngster who completes the assignment first. Starter questions might be: Who holds the world's record for catching the largest shark? Is Los Angeles north or south of San Francisco? What was the score of the 1962 Cotton Bowl Football Game?

18. You've Got My Vote! After completing a unit of stories in basic reading texts or a book, hold an election of favorite characters. Have children write and deliver short "speeches" pointing out the qualities of storybook friends. Then, by voting, pare the number of nominations down to two. Pick a campaign manager, prepare slogans, design pins. Finally, have children vote for their favorite book or story character.

19. Pen Pals. Everybody loves to read letters. Begin a pen-pal program that will assure weekly letter exchanges. If students wish, have them share letters received. They'll eagerly await the mailbag!

20. Classified Ads. Have children make up classified ads and read them to each other. For instance: *Found: One blue shoe at corner of Fox and Evergreen Streets. Must prove ownership by trying on shoe. Call Mrs. Carter at 329–9764.*

21. Popular TV Shows. Two popular TV shows, one on the rerun circuit, are "I've Got a Secret" and "This Is Your Life." They can be used to motivate children to read. For the "I've Got a Secret" game, a youngster pretends he is either the character or author of a book. Other students try to figure what event from the book is his secret. For "This Is Your Life," one student becomes the surprised guest—a character from a book—and other students appear to recall events that happened to them in the book.

22. Fun Box. Start a Fun Box in your room. Select jokes, puns, limericks, and cartoons from magazines and newspapers . . . and make up your own. Write or type each on slips of paper and put in the Fun Box.

23. Something Special. Each month have the librarian list new library materials. Make two copies. Scan the list for items of interest to your kids. When a new book or other material suits one, write his name next to the title on the list. Give one copy to the librarian so the item will be reserved, and use the other for yourself. Then tell the child you've reserved something special for him at the library and he can go there to pick it up.

24. Important Notice Board. Put up an Important Notice Board in your room, containing notices of assemblies, field trips, and other important events. Keep the information concise: *where, when, who, what.* It can also be used by the children to

notify classmates that at a specified time they will be reading a limerick, rhyme, poem, or giving a brief report on a "fantastic" book.

25. Unusual Place Names. Some towns in the United States have unusual and interesting names. Ask pupils if they have ever visited any—Birds Landing, California; Kit Carson, Colorado; Fly, Ohio; Panther Burn, Mississippi; and the like. Motivate students to read about these places by writing to their chambers of commerce for literature.

26. Cartoon Capers. Encourage students to create cartoons for the bulletin board. All that's needed is white construction paper and felt pens. Students can glean ideas from song titles, TV programs, newspaper and magazine ads, and so on. Try these: "Don't Fence Me In," "Try It, You'll Like It!" "Fly Me to the Moon!" "Everybody Wants a Piece of the Action," "Pie in the Sky."

27. Shadow Panels. To add dramatic effect for pupils telling a story or narrating a play, have them make "shadow panels." From colored construction paper, cut silhouettes of characters and scenes. Mount on sheets of white tissue paper. As pupils tell stories, they exhibit shadow panels for each scene, holding them against light so silhouettes stand out.

28. Book of Rhymes. Ask the class to make up and illustrate a book of rhymes. For openers, perhaps, did you ever see a dish fish? Did you ever see a ring swing? Did you ever see a clip flip? Did you ever see a book look? Place the book in the Reading Corner for extra reading.

29. Armchair Travelers. If children have read a travel book, let them present an illustrated lecture using postcards, photographs, slides, and pictures clipped from magazines. As a backdrop, a large poster of a particular country can be used to add flavor to the presentation.

30. Collage Posters. Add a creative spark to reading by making collage posters. Ask each student to select a recently read book and make a list of main ideas, characters, and other important story elements. Bring in old magazines from which the children can cut letters, words, phrases, pictures, or parts of pictures that illustrate or spell out items on their lists. Remind them to include cutouts of titles and authors. Next, ask each student to select a brightly colored piece of construction paper and arrange and paste the cutouts on it.

These activities are designed to turn reluctant readers into eager, enthusiastic ones. Skills and drills are important, but thrills whet reading appetites.

68. Children's Response to Literature: What Happens in the Classroom

Janet Hickman

Most methods of studying response to literature begin with imposed questions. *Which book would you choose? What do you like about it? What do you think about it? Can you retell the story? Can you explain?* Such direct approaches (*e.g.* Applebee 1976; Benton 1979; Terry 1974) have yielded valuable information on children's preferences and on their understanding of and expectations about literature. But are there still other perspectives on children's response to books that might be worth having? In order to deal with this concern, it is necessary to look at response in a way that does not set deliberate limits on the evidence. In other areas of language, researchers (Graves 1973; Griffin 1977) have broadened their data base and our understanding by focusing on a process within a natural context. Consider, then, a child and a book in a real classroom setting.

Ben's teacher is showing her kindergarten-first grade group the new selection of books she has brought from the public library to add temporarily to their reading center. When she holds up *Pezzetino* by Leo Lionni, six-year-old Ben scoots closer from his place within the circle of children on the carpet.

"Oh, that's my favorite book!" says Ben. He reaches out for it, hugs it to his chest, and kisses the cover. Around the group, nods and smiles show that others recognize this title and seem to understand Ben's feelings about it.

Later in the day, when part of the first graders' work is to spend ten minutes sharing a book with a kindergartener, it is *Pezzetino* that Ben chooses. Following this sharing, the teacher invites some of the children to talk with her in a small group about their books.

Ben says, "I like *Pezzetino* because of all the colors 'n stuff, and the way it repeats. He keeps saying it. And there's marbleizing—see here? And this very last page . . ." Here Ben turns to the end of the book and holds up a picture for the group to see. "He cut paper. How many think

From Janet Hickman, Children's responses to literature: What happens in the classroom. *Language Arts*, May 1980, 57, 524–529. Reprinted by permission of the author and the National Council of Teachers of English.

he's a good cutter?" Ben conducts a vote, counting the raised hands that show a majority of the group believes Leo Lionni to be "a good cutter."

Some of the things we can infer from this account would also be evident in other kinds of response studies. *Pezzetino* is a book that Ben is particularly interested in; he knows it well enough to tell it to another child, using the pictures as a guide; perhaps surprisingly, he is able to make comments that show attention to form and to the author-illustrator as creator. Yet a descriptive, holistic approach permits other insights as well. For one thing, it emphasizes certain qualitative aspects of response. Kissing a book cover is certainly a more eloquent testimony to preference than any mark on a checklist. And of course Ben's actual selection of the book in a free choice situation is a better indicator of the strength of its attraction than any statement of intent to choose could be.

More important, however, this approach calls attention to the fact that specific responses to books always occur within a context. In a less supportive environment, Ben might have said nothing—or something quite different—about *Pezzetino*. At any rate it is worth noting that on the day in question, his most elaborated comments did not come with first sight of the book, even though it was already familiar; they came at the end of a sequence of experiences which provided a variety of opportunities for him to think about and talk about the story.

Studying Response in Context

Ben's encounter with *Pezzetino* is excerpted from a study (Hickman 1979) that looked at children's response to literature as expressed in a school setting. The method was primarily ethnographic, with a full time participant observer making notes and gathering supplementary data in taped interviews and photographs over a period of four months. Some ninety chil-

dren in three multi-age classrooms spanning kindergarten through grade five were involved. Although the children roughly represented a middle range in socioeconomic and achievement levels, the site was not chosen because it represented typical or average classrooms, but because literature was much in evidence there, as an important part of an integrated language arts curriculum. Since teachers identified their classroom structure as informal and since the architectural plan of the school was open space, it was feasible for an observer to move freely from one classroom area to another in order to keep a running account of events that reflected the children's contacts with literature.

In this environment, books were readily available and frequently shared. They were seen as valuable experiences in themselves as well as material for reading and models for writing. Since the children had considerable freedom in choosing their tasks and their working companions, and were almost always welcome to make quiet conversation, it was possible to note the form and content of spontaneous expressions of response as well as their participation in teacher-planned activities.

Analyzing Unsolicited Expressions of Response

One of the advantages of ethnographic research in classrooms is that it covers a range of events and situations that are excluded from more tightly structured studies. In this case, the informal talk among children and with interested adults, the book-choosing times, and the work periods all provided new perspectives on response in terms of where and when and how it is expressed. For example, here is a bit of an October afternoon's activity in the second-third grade group:

Jenny is seated at a desk beside the book rack, looking at Silverstein's *Where the Sidewalk Ends*, one finger marking the poem entitled "Sick."

When the observer asks, casually, if this book has any spooky poems in it, Jenny says, "The teacher read us one. Wait, I'll find it." She looks for, and finds, "The Deserted House" and reads it aloud, stumbling but persistent. By the time she finishes that one and begins to read "Sick," Lori is looking over her shoulder. When Lori begins to join in, Jenny tries to shush her. But Amanda has come up on the other side, laughing at the poem and also joining in on occasional phrases.

Next, Jenny wants to read "Melinda Mae," and Amanda concurs, explaining to the observer that "it took this girl a *whole month* to eat a whale!" She turns the page to show the illustration of the mostly-eaten whale. Then Jenny reads the poem, and repeats the ending for effect: "Eighty-nine years!" Amanda does not comment on the difference between "a whole month" and eighty-nine years.

As the work period has progressed, other children around the room have turned to books. Keith has claimed Fleischman's *McBroom's Ghost*, which the teacher has been reading aloud, and is reading it for himself. Doug is stretched out on the floor with *Glory, Glory How Peculiar*, a book of song parodies, singing to himself, "D-A-V-E-N-P-O-R-T spells Davenport." Jeannie and Sandy are trying to get a look at it too, but Doug is keeping the book to himself.

Teresa and Amy and Shari have gone to the listening center at the edge of the classroom, where there are two filmstrip viewers. Today they are looking at one of the stories in the *Clifford the Big Red Dog* filmstrip series. At least one of the girls is acquainted with Clifford, and there is a lot of pointing, with smothered giggles, as the pictures tell the story.

One of the striking things about this account, which is typical of the data gathered in the study, is the way sociability and book experiences are intertwined. On their own, children did not sit together to discuss a book in any sustained way, with the sort of formulated critical statements that adults might use. It is evident that they did talk to one another about books, however, offering brief comments about content, about liking the material, and about their familiarity with it. Much of the time these comments functioned as invitations to share the selection; Jenny's directive "Wait, I'll find it" was a promise to produce the material itself as an appropriate substitute for talking about it.

Other behaviors also indicated a generalized impulse to share. Children frequently read together or to one another, or pointed out discoveries they had made about the pictures or the text. The opportunity to show a book to a friend, to giggle over it, offer a private opinion, even argue a little, seemed to keep children interested and in contact with books they might otherwise have dismissed. In addition, this spontaneous sharing was sometimes a prelude to, as well as motivation for, the formulation of more discerning statements.

Incidental insights—the answers to questions one would not think to ask—are also a product of the systematic observation of children's spontaneous behavior.

Two first graders are working on a mural based on *Tikki Tikki Tembo* by Mosel. The observer says, "Carl, tell me about your picture."

"Well," says Carl, "here's the old man with the ladder and here's where they live and here's the well, and wait a minute . . ."

He goes to the bookcase and comes back a few minutes later, empty-handed.

"What were you looking for, Carl?"

"That book, *Tikki Tikki Tembo*."

"Can't you tell me about it without the book?"

"Nope."

Over and over again, children demonstrated greater willingness to express a response if they could have the book in hand, except in cases where the story was thoroughly familiar. One interpretation would be to infer an unwritten rule, *Talk about a book you can touch*, which apparently operated here with considerable force. This raises a question about the comparative validity of studies that do and do not include actual contact with books, and presents a strong argument for the importance of children's direct access to books in the classroom.

Another advantage of looking at children's unsolicited response is in gaining indirect information on their knowledge about literature. Telling clues about children's acquaintance with stories and their mastery of literary conventions appear unhidden in their free compositions. By studying both their stories on paper and stories in drama (in the play corner, or presented as skits for other class members), one can learn something of their knowledge of beginning and ending markers, manipulation of the narrator's point of view, and the handling of set structures like those in folk tales. Kindergarten and first grade students, for instance, made "a play" which ended with the entire cast of monsters piled in a heap on the carpet, presumably having reaped a just reward at the hands of the hero, who had left the scene. At this point a small voice announced from the middle of the pile, "And we lived happily ever after." The intent to convey an appropriate sense of ending is clear.

Contrast this with an informal production created and staged by a group of fourth and fifth grade girls who wanted to present an ecology theme in a folk tale format.

The title is "Queens and Trees Don't Mix." The queen calls in the woodcutter, telling him that there is a paper shortage and that the trees must be cut. When the woodcutter sets to work, two squirrels appear and complain that he is destroying their home. The woodcutter declares that squirrels can't talk, but he nevertheless reports the incident to the queen, who doesn't believe him. This sequence is repeated, but the third time, the queen hides behind a bush and hears the squirrels for herself. She invites them to live with her in the palace. The woodcutter continues his work, and everyone is happy. All the characters dance in a circle midstage, singing a parody of a rhyme from *Where the Sidewalk Ends*: "Ickle me, tickle me, pickle me, poo/We want to live in the palace with you."

These girls demonstrated not only their knowledge of the conventions of folk and fairy tales, such as talking animals and patterns of three, but also their ability to manipulate those conventions for their own purposes. Their way of marking the end is of particular interest. Like the younger children, they recognized the need for a formal closing; unlike the younger children, they were able to provide one that was unique to their production as well as specifically appropriate to its content.

Nature vs. Nurture

Such comparisons call attention to the question of development: what differences necessarily exist between the responses of younger and older children? One of the benefits of gathering evidence within classroom settings is the opportunity to see how expressions of response to literature fit into larger developmental patterns. Predictably, in this study the youngest group used their bodies more in expressing response, bouncing with excitement, for instance, or physically demonstrating meanings when words eluded them in the course of a discussion. Younger children tended to focus on pieces or parts of stories, while older ones were more able to deal with a story as a whole.

In oral responses there were some pronounced differences in form. A first grader seems to have caught the meaning of *The Little Red Hen* in saying that the lesson to be learned from the story was "When someone already baked the cake and you haven't helped, they're probably just gonna say no." A fifth grader, answering the same sort of question about *Tico and the Golden Wings*, said, "Everybody's different, and you shouldn't be jealous." Both children understood their respective stories, although the younger child's expression was particularized in terms of the story from which it came, while the older child's statement was generalized, or disembedded from the text. Given what we know about language and cognitive development, this movement toward abstraction is also a predictable change.

What is most notable about the theme statements, however, is that they would probably never have occurred at all without an adult to begin the discussion and set the stage. The teacher influence was a far-reaching one. Thus while it was evident that children were bound by certain developmental constraints, it was equally evident that even the youngest children frequently expressed response in ways that had been directly or indirectly taught.

Experienced observers would be likely to agree that the opening example of Ben sharing *Pezzetino* with a small group indicates prior adult guidance in looking at and talking about picture books. In fact, much of what Ben said was a direct reflection of his classroom experience. One of the teacher's consistent efforts was to provide books that were related in some way, by theme (scary things) or genre (folk tales) or author. Leo Lionni's work had been brought into sharp focus for Ben, and the illustrator's basic techniques had been pointed out, with various books displayed together for comparison. In daily read-aloud sessions that covered a wide range of books, the teacher frequently remarked about repetitive passages or asked children to identify refrains. In this context, it is easier to understand Ben's "I like . . . the way it repeats. He keeps saying it." Ben's poll of the group on the subject of Lionni's technical skill was also a learned strategy; his teacher often asked for a show of hands on matters of opinion. In view of the background, is it fair to say that Ben's reaction to *Pezzetino* was simply imitative? Probably not. To this observer he appeared to be genuinely involved in both the story and in the task of talking about it. The comparison and focus strategies had been developed through exposure to many books and were used selectively and for the most part appropriately here.

The Nurturing Environment

If there is anything that becomes particularly clear in an ethnographic classroom study, it is the importance of what the teacher does. In this case, such research provides a needed link between our understanding of children's response to literature and our understanding of how literature might best be approached in the classroom. At the very least, it permits description of learning environments in which lively and interesting expressions of response have occurred.

Teachers who are working to create such an environment—one that facilitates and nurtures children's interaction with literature—may find it helpful to consider the basic outlines of what happened, regularly, in Ben's classroom:

1. Many books were provided, not just in the nearby library resources center, but in the classroom area itself. These books were of sufficient quality to bear rereading and reflection, and many of them had been chosen around a focus so as to invite comparison.

2. Books were made immediately accessible to children, with plenty of time for making choices and for reading.

3. Literature was read aloud to the children every day. New selections were introduced with comments that often

pointed out the connections between one book and another.

4. Books were discussed with the whole group, with small groups, and with individuals. Free comment was encouraged, but a focus for talk was provided as well. Literary conventions were made explicit and critical terminology was furnished when children had the idea but needed the words.

5. Opportunities were provided for children to work with literature through various other activities—art, writing, drama, and the like—with allowance for the necessary time, space, and material. Children were encouraged to share or display this work and to talk about the story which prompted it.

6. Long-term, cumulative experiences with literature were planned for, giving children the chance to return to familiar books in a variety of ways.

Although no formal guide for the study of literature was used in this classroom, Ben and the others had wide opportunities to experience and respond to it.

In sum, our understanding of children's response to literature will be enriched by studying what happens in the classroom. Research methods based on ethnography are time-consuming and demanding, but they carry important advantages, allowing for qualitative judgment, for making some distinctions between spontaneous and learned responses, and for description of the contexts in which certain kinds of responses are expressed. This broader perspective, so close to the teacher's natural angle of vision, can furnish practical insights for those who want to facilitate and encourage the expression of response to literature in their own classrooms.

References

Applebee, Arthur N. "Children's Construal of Stories and Related Genres as Measured with Repertory Grid Techniques." *Research in the Teaching of English* 10 (Winter 1976): 226–238.

Benton, Michael. "Children's Response to Stories." *Children's Literature in Education* 10 (Summer 1979): 68–85.

Graves, Donald. "Children's Writing: Research Directions and Hypotheses Based Upon an Examination of the Writing Processes of Seven Year Old Children." Unpublished doctoral dissertation, State University of New York at Buffalo, 1973.

Griffin, Peg. "How and When Does Reading Occur in the Classroom?" *Theory into Practice* 16 (December 1977): 376–383.

Hickman, Janet Gephart. "Response to Literature in a School Environment, Grades K-5." Unpublished doctoral dissertation, The Ohio State University, 1979.

Terry, Ann. *Children's Poetry Preferences: A National Survey of Upper Elementary Grades.* Urbana, IL: National Council of Teachers of English, 1974.

Children's Books

Bridwell, Norman. *Clifford the Big Red Dog.* New York: Scholastic Book Services, 1969.

Galdone, Paul. *The Little Red Hen.* New York: Seabury Press, 1973.

Fleischman, Sid. *McBroom's Ghost.* Illustrated by Robert Frankenberg. New York: Grosset and Dunlap, 1971.

Keller, Charles. *Glory, Glory, How Peculiar.* Illustrated by Lady McCrady. Englewood Cliffs, NJ: Prentice-Hall, 1976.

Lionni, Leo. *Pezzetino.* New York: Pantheon, 1975.

———. *Tico and the Golden Wings.* New York: Pantheon, 1964.

Mosel, Arleno. *Tikki Tikki Tembo.* Illustrated by Blair Lent. New York: Holt, Rinehart and Winston, 1968.

Silverstein, Shel. *Where the Sidewalk Ends.* New York: Harper and Row, 1974.

CHAPTER XIII

Some Special Issues Concerning Reading Instruction

This chapter contains articles on a variety of topics that have not been addressed fully in the preceding twelve chapters, but which deal with issues that are important in reading instruction.

The first three articles describe alternatives to traditional teaching procedures. Anderson describes four oral reading methods that can be used in developmental or remedial teaching. Efta advocates Reading in Silence (uninterrupted silent reading of self-selected materials). Spiegel describes and compares six alternatives to the typical basal reader lesson plan.

The next two papers discuss the development of reading rate and flexibility. Brown emphasizes the importance of teacher expectations in the development of reading rate and presents results which indicate that rates considerably higher than the usual results are attainable. Schachter describes the use of content area texts, newspapers, magazines, and phone books to develop flexibility in rate and teach skimming and scanning.

The remaining articles each cover a different topic. Anderson and Coates explain the use of cloze to determine the reading difficulty of texts. Noonan emphasizes the importance of including parents in the reading program. Finally, O'Donnell describes computer assisted instruction and computer managed instruction, and presents an optimistic picture of the role of microcomputers in the schools of the future.

69. The Missing Ingredient: Fluent Oral Reading

Betty Anderson

The rising popularity of reading-skill management systems and criterion-referenced testing seems to be leading to fragmentation of developmental reading instruction. The mastery of isolated reading skills, which such programs emphasize, may not lead to fluent reading ability with comprehension. Traditional remedial reading approaches (Monroe 1932; Gillingham and Stillman 1970) also stress mastery of spe-

Reprinted from Betty Anderson, The missing ingredient: Fluent oral reading. *Elementary School Journal*, January 1981, (81), 173–177, by permission of the University of Chicago Press. Copyright 1981 by the University of Chicago Press.

cific skills; consequently, students who fail in classroom reading programs based on specific skills are not likely to respond favorably to similar remedial programs. There may be a need for such skill-oriented programs to include "reading practice" to build fluency. Oral reading techniques offer possibilities that could provide this missing ingredient.

Four oral reading methods which have been used as developmental or remedial programs or supplementts will be described below. All have reported successful applications or experimental research and offer promise for classroom and clinical use. The methods are neurological impress, echo reading, assisted reading, and repeated readings.

The Neurological Impress Method (NIM) was developed by Heckelman (1966). It is a simultaneous oral reading method with the teacher and student sitting side by side sharing a book. The student is a little in front of the teacher so the teacher's voice is directed into the student's ear. At first the teacher, reading at a moderate pace, will lead. Sentences and paragraphs are reread as needed until fluency is achieved. When the student gains ability and confidence, he should lead, with the teacher reading softly and a little behind the student. During all the reading the teacher points to the words with her finger in a smooth movement across the page. The student may take over the finger movements when able, perhaps with the teacher at first guiding his finger along. The usual NIM treatment procedure involves daily 15-minute sessions for a total of 8–12 hours. No word analysis instruction, vocabulary, or comprehension discussion is included.

Heckelman (1966) tried out the process in a pilot project involving twenty-four students in Grades 6–10. In this uncontrolled project the mean gain was 2.2 years, with the instruction period no more than 7.5 hours. A follow-up controlled study with significant gains for the impress group was also cited by Heckel-

man (1966) in his original description of the technique. Other researchers who have reported success with this method include Langford, Slade, and Barnett (1974) and Hollingsworth (1978).

The impress method does not require skilled training on the part of the teacher and thus can be readily used by teacher aides, interns, volunteers, or peer tutors. Stinner (1979) trained sixth graders to read with fourth-grade learning-disability students using NIM. There was no difference in the gains between students reading with the sixth graders and another group reading with the researcher. Heckelman (1966) also suggests that NIM may be used in small-group settings with techniques which utilize a microphone, earphones, and visually projected material. He indicates that the use of individual headsets is essential so the teacher's voice (from the microphone) is received directly in the student's ear.

Materials to be used with impress reading can be varied and should interest the student. At first, material at a level a little below the student's current performance is recommended. Easy material is quickly replaced by books, stories, newspapers, and so forth at increasingly higher levels.

The impress method is an attractive remedial approach. It has been documented as a successful method, requires little or no instruction, and can be used by assistants. In addition a student usually will respond positively within 4 hours of instruction with NIM. So if it is not the appropriate method for a student, this will become apparent in a short time and another remedial approach can be tried.

Echo Reading is another oral reading method with fluency as the goal. In this approach the teacher reads first, and the student echoes what the teacher has just read. Thus the teacher serves as a model for phrasing and expression as well as word identification. The material can be read by phrases or sentences, whatever is necessary for successful echoing. Schneeberg (1977) used this method to introduce books to students in a study that involved follow-up practice with tapes. After echo reading with the teacher, the students listened and reread the story at a listening center. Finger pointing is utilized in echo reading as in the neurological impress method. The teacher or the student uses his finger under the line of print as a moving guide to the material as it is read.

Chomsky (1976) has had personal success with a different approach to echo reading. She recommends using a short, interesting book near the student's instructional level. The story is taped and the student listens, reads, and rereads until he can read the entire story fluently. There is no direct oral reading with the teacher with this technique. The student listens to the whole book daily and then listens and reads sections orally with the tape or records sections alone after listening. When the student can read the book independently, he reads it to the teacher, and then many opportunities to share it— with parents, peers, or younger children— are provided.

Other instruction is included to insure that pupils go beyond mere memorization of the book. This involves comprehension, sight vocabulary, phonics, and structural analysis activities using flash cards, games, and writing. Only words from the stories are used, and frequent reinforcement with the story context is emphasized.

Chomsky developed the method with five remedial readers from a third-grade class. They worked with the taped books and activities for 4 months and achieved overall reading gains ranging from 1 to 9 months. More impressive than the pre- and posttest scores were the changes in attitude toward reading and the improvement in self-concept regarding their ability to read. The students felt that they could and would read following the echo reading activities.

Another practitioner who has worked with taped books is Carbo (1978). In an uncontrolled study she reported an average gain of 6 months over a 3-month period with eight learning-disabled pupils. A word study skills program was introduced as a supplement to the tape reading after the pupils gained a basic vocabulary and self-confidence in reading.

Assisted Reading is a three-stage, oral instructional approach for beginning readers (Hoskisson 1977). Stage I starts at about age 4 or 5 with the teacher or parent reading aloud and the child repeating it as in echo reading. This procedure is followed as they read through the book by phrases or sentences. The material is read and reread as much as the child's interest allows. The teacher runs her finger along the line of print while either she reads or the child rereads. In stage 2 the teacher reads aloud and leaves out words she thinks the child can supply. Once again the child's interest provides the signal when to start stage-two reading. The child will start to read some of the words or lines along with the teacher or may ask to read it alone. Role switching characterizes stage three, with the child reading most of the material and the teacher supplying any needed words to maintain fluency.

Limited experimental evidence has been reported regarding the success of assisted reading (Hoskisson, Sherman, and Smith 1974). Groff (1979) has questioned the validity of this method as a beginning instructional approach but considers assisted reading activities acceptable as supplements to beginning reading programs.

Hoskisson (1975*a*) also suggests that assisted reading be used as a supplement to other reading programs. For example, it could be included as teacher-directed instruction with reading groups, as follow-up reading practice with teacher aides, or with parents working with remedial readers. In another classroom adaptation (Hoskisson 1975*b*), sixth graders served as tutors for high-risk first-grade pupils. The student tutors read to and with the beginning readers. Mean reading achievement scores in April were 1.6 for the first graders in this uncontrolled study.

As a supplement to developmental or remedial programs, assisted reading does seem to offer promise. Parents, aides, volunteers, interns, or pupil tutors are all potential assistants for this method. Research evidence is needed to determine the effectiveness of assisted reading whether as a beginning reading method or as an integral part of skills oriented programs.

Repeated Readings is another oral reading technique to build fluency. It is suggested by Samuels (1979) as a supplement in developmental reading programs, and he particularly encourages its use with special education students. It is a simple procedure to implement in the classroom, and aides or volunteers can handle much of the operation.

To start a student on repeated readings, the child selects an easy, interesting story to read. The teacher marks off a short passage from the story (only fifty to 200 words), and the student prepares this material by reading and rereading. When the student is ready, the passage is read orally to the teacher, who records the speed and word-recognition errors on a graph. More practice reading follows, with another oral reading to the teacher recorded on the graph. This procedure continues until the rate of eighty-five words per minute is reached. Then another short passage is marked off for practice, oral reading, and recording on the graph.

Students can use tapes for the reading practice if needed. Samuels reports that the student is able to read without the tapes after some practice. The graph serves as a motivator, showing progress and success.

Samuels's data indicate that repeated readings result in steady progress in rate and decrease in word-recognition errors. In addition, the first reading of each successive passage starts at a higher rate and lower number of errors. The repeated-reading practice increases the reader's fluency.

Gonzales and Elijah (1975) report similar results with rereading activities. They investigated the difference in word-recognition errors for students reading at third-grade level for first and second oral reading of passages over 175 words. Five of the six categories of errors reported at instructional level decreased on second reading, and all six error categories decreased at frustration level. Significant decreases occurred in two error categories out of five at the instructional level and three of the five categories at frustration level. These researchers suggest that the practice of rereading during a developmental reading lesson is a useful procedure.

In summary, these four oral reading teaching strategies all stress practice to increase fluency, but each is slightly different. Neurological impress involves the teacher and student reading material simultaneously, while echo reading has the student reading after a teacher model (whether in person or on tapes). Assisted reading progresses from echo reading to a joint oral cloze procedure with first the student and later the teacher filling in the needed words. In repeated readings the student practices alone and presents the completed material to the teacher, repeating the process until a criterion of rate is reached. All four approaches place a heavy emphasis on fluency, and any skill work that is included is of less importance.

An advantage to these approaches is compatibility for instruction by paraprofessionals. Since they are primarily practice techniques, other readers can implement them, freeing the teacher for instructional tasks. Another advantage is in their adaptability. While each approach is presented as a particular method with specific procedures to be followed, all have been adapted in various ways without diminishing their usefulness. Thus the practitioner should feel confident about including adaptations to fit any particular group or situation.

The increasing emphasis on isolated skill mastery in reading programs presents a need for reading practice. These oral reading techniques offer a variety of ways to include it, whether in developmental or remedial programs. They may be the missing ingredient to many reading programs.

References

Carbo, Marie. "Teaching Reading with Talking Books." *Reading Teacher* 32 (December 1978): 267–73.

Chomsky, Carol. "After Decoding: What?" *Language Arts* 53 (March 1976): 288–96, 314.

Gillingham, Anna, and Stillman, Bessie W. *Remedial Training for Children with Specific Disability in Reading, Spelling, and Penmanship*. 8th ed. Cambridge, Mass.: Educators Publishing Service, Inc., 1970.

Gonzales, Phillip C., and Elijah, David V., Jr. "Rereading: Effect on Error Patterns and Performance Levels on the IRI." *Reading Teacher* 28 (April 1975): 647–52.

Groff, Patrick. "Critique of Teaching Reading as a Whole-Task Venture." *Reading Teacher* 32 (March 1979): 647–52.

Heckelman, R. G. "Using the Neurological-Impress Remedial-Reading Technique." *Academic Therapy Quarterly* 1 (Summer 1966): 235–39.

Hollingsworth, Paul M. "An Experimental Approach to the Impress Method of Teaching Reading." *Reading Teacher* 31 (March 1978): 624–26.

Hoskisson, Kenneth. "The Many Facets of Assisted Reading." *Elementary English* 52 (March 1975): 312–15.(*a*)

Hoskisson, Kenneth. "Successive Approximation and Beginning Reading." *Elementary School Journal* 75 (April 1975): 443–51.(*b*)

Hoskisson, Kenneth, "Reading Readiness: Three Viewpoints." *Elementary School Journal* 78 (September 1977): 45–52.

Hoskisson, Kenneth; Sherman, Thomas M.; and Smith, Linda L. "Assisted Reading and Parent Involvement." *Reading Teacher* 27 (April 1974): 710–14.

Langford, Kenneth; Slade, Kenneth; and Barnett, Allyson. "An Examination of Impress Techniques in Remedial Reading." *Academic Therapy* 9 (Spring 1974): 309–19.

Monroe, Marion. *Children Who Cannot Read*. Chicago: University of Chicago Press, 1932.

Samuels, S. Jay. "The Method of Repeated Readings," *Reading Teacher* 32 (January 1979): 403–8.

Schneeberg, Helen. "Listening While Reading: A Four Year Study." *Reading Teacher* 30 (March 1977): 629–35.

Stinner, Mary Catherine. "The Use of Neurological Impress Method in Accelerating Reading Levels in Selected Disabled Children." Master's project, University of Central Florida, 1979.

70. Reading in Silence: A Chance to Read

Martha Efta

"RIS will now begin!" announces the student leader, having previously checked to see if I am comfortably seated with book in hand. Within moments 16 books open and silence prevails in room 106, a normally active, bustling group of educable mentally retarded children ranging in age from 7 to 10 years. Only the ticking of the timer and the rustling of pages can be heard. Everyone is "reading."

Finding the Right Name

Reading in Silence (RIS) is my class adapted name for the practice of silent reading without interruption for a predetermined period of time. RIS is representative of USSR, an acronym for uninterrupted sustained silent reading as introduced by Lyman C. Hunt, Jr., of the University of Vermont in the early 1960's. Other names include Robert McCracken's Sustained Silent Reading (McCracken, 1971) and Marvin Oliver's High Intensity Practice (Oliver, 1970).

For several months, the children repeatedly asked for clarification of the USSR acronym. Simpler, more understandable terminology to describe this daily practice seemed necessary. The children responded by offering alternate names which were then posted and voted upon. RIS received a unanimous vote.

Giving Students a Chance to Practice Reading

Teachers of slow learners know that reinforcement is an integral part of learning any skill. RIS provides an opportunity to personally integrate skills. It is *not* a total reading program. It *is*, simply, an activity providing the children with the opportunity to practice their reading skills privately. Too often we instruct and assume that the children will practice. But how often do we consistently provide the opportunity for practice? RIS is an attempt to do so.

Setting up the Rules

RIS encompasses the practice of the total reading act including the integration of the reader's sight word vocabulary, decoding skills, comprehension, background experiences, and degree of enjoyment. It can easily be incorporated into any program. The general rules as concisely outlined by McCracken (1971) are as follows:

1. Each student must read silently.
2. The teacher reads adult fare materials, thus setting an example.
3. Each student selects a single book, magazine, or newspaper. No book

changing during the period is permitted. A wide range of materials must be available.
4. A timer is used.
5. There are absolutely no reports or records of any kind required.
6. The teacher should begin with a whole class or large group of heterogeneous students.

Ganz and Theofield (1974) also offered helpful suggestions in beginning a sustained reading program.

I first heard about these ideas in a graduate course. The professor seemed enthusiastic about the idea and assured us we would feel the same once we tried it. As I listened to the description of this assignment, I became apprehensive. "It'll never work in my class! My hyperactive children and nonreaders will never last 3 minutes! When can I fit it into the schedule?" After giving serious thought to the rules outlined above, I decided to amend them slightly with my children. Explanation of the practice was discussed, and this more simplified procedure was introduced and posted.

1. Choose any books you wish (with a limit of three).
2. Stay in your seats. (Later the option to sit anywhere was incorporated.)
3. Read silently.
4. Teacher reads; guests read.

We "sustained" for 3 minutes the first day with no infractions. A minute was added every other day until a period of 13 minutes was reached. This seems to be the limit for a silent reading session with this group of primary children.

Even though there are certain guidelines for RIS, we also allow for flexibility. Presently, RIS begins after the noon recess break. This seems to be a good time for the children and me to reorient ourselves to the classroom atmosphere. We all assemble our reading material and show our readiness by placing the signal flag (a square labeled RIS stapled to a straw) on our desks. The student leader for the week checks all signals, puts the sign out on the door ("Silent reading in progress. If you come in, bring a book!"), and signals for all to "find your places." The timer is set. "RIS will now begin!" I vary the time interval from 10 to 13 minutes depending on the daily classroom climate, which fluctuates from a settling calm to an energetic whirlwind.

Dealing with Infractions

Occasional infractions do occur including the whispering to a neighbor or reading aloud. Instead of ending the RIS period at the moment of interruption as suggested by Frank Greene (1971) and others, the student leader quietly and calmly walks to the reader and removes the book. If the reader has previously selected another book, he may continue reading with the second book. If he has not selected another book, he must quietly sit and wait for the buzzer. In this way, the continuation of RIS for the allotted time allows the students who do follow the rules to continue to read with little interruption. When the timer buzzes, the leader announces "RIS is now over."

To provide added incentive, RIS is tied into our behavior modification system. The student leader is responsible for awarding a point to all readers who have followed the established rules. In order to earn *his* point, the student leader must organize and carry out the RIS procedures and address himself to any major infractions.

Seeing Exciting Changes in Students

From the onset of RIS, the students have demonstrated some exciting and favorable behavior changes such as independent decision making, self discipline, sharing, student leadership, student interaction, and broadened reading interests. The

enthusiastic rush to select their day's reading materials following noon recess is indicative of the children's interest and eagerness for RIS. The children seem to delight in the adultlike responsibility of selecting their own reading matter.

Materials provided in the classroom include newspapers, magazines, encyclopedias, picture books, controlled beginning vocabulary readers, and library books. Students have offered books such as comic books, sports program booklets, and discarded textbooks from an older brother or sister.

It is interesting to watch the sharing of the different types of materials among the children. Book chatter and bartering occur, and developing salesmanship abilities are evident in comments such as "You've *got* to read this one; it's so funny" and "Oh, there are two copies of this book. Do you want one?"

Independent decision making plays an important role in the personal development of all children, especially slow learners. The self selection of reading materials for RIS affords them such an opportunity.

When children are given time to practice reading in school, they are also in control of their reading pace and style. One may opt to flip through a selection prior to reading it, read the conclusion first, or read only the intriguing parts. Using their own personal combination of reading strategies, they attempt to find meaning and enjoyment from print without adult or peer intervention. RIS is for enjoyment and not for answering teacher questions or work-sheet problems. Many become absorbed in their reading matter appearing disappointed when the timer buzzes. "Oh, I read *this* far?" is a delightful comment to hear.

Sharing an interesting picture or story situation with the total class has become a daily spinoff activity from RIS. "This Dr. Seuss book has the funniest person in it who does the craziest things" and "Here's a picture in this encyclopedia of Jaws, the great whale. He's out looking for food!" are spontaneous "book reports" of an enjoyable nature.

As a result of RIS, "attention span increases, self-discipline improves, self-selection of reading materials becomes more sophisticated, acceptance and enjoyment of reading improves, and reading skills are refined and extended" (Oliver, 1970, p. 69). My students, many of whom are hyperactive and some of whom are nonreaders, appear to enjoy the quietness of RIS and the opportunity to read. "Reading" for children who daily put forth *so* much effort into learning a single sound or a new sight word is indicative of a beginning reader's positive experience with RIS. "I really like RIS because it's so quiet and peaceful" and "Nobody is walking around, so I don't get mixed up" suggest that RIS is positively affecting the entire learning atmosphere.

Sharing and Modeling

Sharing and modeling are integral components of RIS. Not only the sharing of materials has occurred but also the sharing of reading spots. Children are found under the television stand, behind the piano, and squeezed together on a carpet. As I delve more deeply into my current novel, sharing an occasional picture or a situation from my book seems to be appreciated. My reading behavior is being mirrored. Children have made and are using their own special bookmarks.

One day a nonreader, who consistently flipped pages as he hurried through book after book, was so engrossed in watching a friend read that he sat immobile, staring for the entire RIS period. Modeling the reading behavior of his friend, he began, in subsequent RIS periods, to scan, through use of his finger, each sentence word by word.

In addition, many student leaders have demonstrated exceptional leadership capabilities as they organize the daily RIS

proceedings, thus serving as role models for subsequent student leaders. When weekly jobs are awarded, this leadership role is the most coveted position.

Measuring the Effects

Is this daily activity effective? Are the children learning? One study (Evans & Towner, 1975) compared reading achievement over 10 weeks using sustained silent reading versus selected commercial practice materials commonly used as supplement to a basal instructional program. Findings on the Metropolitan Achievement Test indicated that "SSR as a form of practice was neither more nor less effective than a multi-material form of practice" (p. 156).

Future researchers should consider the effects of SSR on the reading interests, skills, and behavior changes of children. It will be important for all investigators to follow a uniform set of guidelines, such as those outlined by McCracken (1971). The length of the study should be appropriate, so as to allow for the integration of reading skills. If we, as educators, believe in individual differences in learning styles and instructional methodology, we need to use statistical measures that will determine the compatibility between RIS and changes in individual children.

RIS is as much a part of our day as handwriting, arithmetic, and lunch, and the children question if they think it has been forgotten. "Oh we've *got* to have RIS today; I want to finish my book" and "I told my friend I'd sit by him today" are heard in their pleas for RIS. The children and I really look forward to the opportunity to read silently and without interruption. Although it is difficult to measure, I am observing exciting changes in reading interests, self discipline, decision making, sharing, student interaction, and student leadership. Sustained silent reading can be a dynamic, enriching, positive experience for you and your students.

References

Evans, H. M., & Towner, C. Sustained silent reading: Does it increase skills? *The Reading Teacher*, 1975, *29*, 155–156.

Ganz, P., & Theofield, M. B. Suggestions for starting SSR. *Journal of Reading*, 1974, *17*, 614–616.

Greene, F. P. *High intensity practice*. Course handout from Syracuse University Clinic, 1971.

McCracken, R. A. Initiating sustained silent reading. *Journal of Reading*, 1971, *14*, 521–524, 582 and 583.

Oliver, M. E. High intensity practice: The right to enjoy reading. *Education*, 1970, *91*, 69–71.

71. Six Alternatives to the Directed Reading Activity

Dixie Lee Spiegel

For many years the Directed Reading Activity (Betts, 1946) has been the primary format for basal reader lessons. The DRA is based on sound psychological and educational principles and its step-by-step format is easy to follow. And yet since its inception educators have been searching for alternatives, not because the DRA is not valuable, but because too much of even a good thing is too much. Teachers may become bored doing the same thing day after day. More seriously, students may approach their basal reading lesson with a sense that its most important aspect is going through steps of the rite and that it has nothing to do with life beyond the reading group. Most seriously, teachers may stop *thinking* about what they are doing and just follow the prescribed steps with little attempt to adjust to their students' actual needs.

Alternatives to the DRA do exist. Six such alternatives—ReQuest, the Directed Reading-Thinking Activity, the Expectation Outline, the Pre-reading Guided Reading Procedure, Word Wonder, and Semantic Webbing—are presented here as techniques that use many of the basic principles of the DRA while adjusting to the needs of specific materials and groups of students.

The DRA

The DRA taps many of the important aspects of reading instruction. Step 1, Preparation, introduces new vocabulary and helps students identify both the printed form and the relevant meanings. In Step 1, background information helps children understand concepts in the story. Specific purposes for reading, set by the teacher, give readers a focus for their efforts at comprehending the story. Motivation is provided so that the student will *want* to read the selections.

Step 2 of the DRA is Guided Silent Reading. The teacher directs children to read portions of the story in order to find the answers to specified questions. After each portion is read silently, the teacher assesses student understanding by questioning.

In Step 3, Oral Reading for Specific Purposes, children read certain sentences aloud. The "specific purposes" often

From Dixie Lee Spiegel, Six alternatives to the Directed Reading Activity. *The Reading Teacher*, May 1981, *34*, 914–920. Reprinted by permission of Dixie Lee Spiegel and the International Reading Association.

include those of sharing the location of an answer or of developing oral reading skills, such as reading with expression.

For Step 4, Skill Development, the basal reader manual identifies certain skills within decoding, comprehension, oral reading, or perhaps study skills that a particular story may help develop. Teachers are given questions to ask, examples to cite, and activities to use to help students improve in these skills.

The last step in the DRA is Enrichment. Too often teachers spend so much time on the first four steps that the Enrichment step is never used. The students may be so busy completing activities prescribed by the manual that they have little time to extend their understanding of the concepts, to investigate other resources, or just to sit back and enjoy some new ideas.

These steps of the DRA are one way to guide student reading. However, not every story needs to be approached in this manner and not every student needs to be led through these steps. Even if the story and the child *do* need these steps, it's tedious to approach the basal reader in the same manner day after day.

The following alternatives retain the essential steps of the DRA and yet avoid the tedium of doing the same thing each day. Teachers can choose a strategy to suit their mood, the characteristics of the story, and the needs of the students. The activities can be used on the spur of the moment, as they require very little teacher preparation and draw most of the energy and ideas from the children themselves.

Six Alternatives

Six alternatives to the DRA are presented in a grid in Table 1. To use the grid, a teacher determines which aspects of the DRA are necessary for the story and important for the students. Then the teacher chooses an activity from the grid that meets these requirements, by itself or in combination with another activity. This activity replaces the DRA from the teacher's manual for that one lesson.

For example, with a basal story on a familiar topic for which students have a good background and vocabulary, the teacher might choose the DRTA. At another time, a group of students may be impatient with Guided Silent Reading, but not yet be able to set their own purposes for reading. ReQuest solves that dilemma. Semantic Webbing and Word Wonder can

Table 1. Alternatives to the Directed Reading Activity

	ReQuest	DRTA	Expectation Outlines	Prereading GRP	Word Wonder	Semantic Webbing
Preparation						
vocabulary	X		X	X	X	
background	X		X	X	X	X
purpose and motivation	X	X	X	X		X
Guided silent reading		X	X	X		X
Oral reading for specific purposes		X	X	X	X	X
Skill development	X	X	X	X	X	X
Enrichment						

Note: All of these activities allow more time for enrichment. Most of them increase motivation so that students will spontaneously seek enrichment activities.

be combined to give special attention to vocabulary needs and problem-solving techniques. An examination of each of these activities will show how they can best be used.

ReQuest

Manzo's ReQuest procedure (1969) is especially appropriate for students who need guidance in thinking above the literal level. In ReQuest, both students and teacher read just the title and first sentence of a story and look at the picture on the page. Then the students ask the teacher anything they wish about that sentence.

The teacher answers all questions, hypothesizing where necessary and modeling the way to think about possible answers. The teacher praises students for asking questions above the literal level and answers literal questions without comment. After the students have asked all the questions they can think of, the teacher poses additional questions above the literal level.

For the second sentence, the teacher may question first and the students second. They alternate going first until the students are seething with impatience to read the story.

With ReQuest a teacher-class dialogue such as the following might take place:

(There is a picture of a woman walking down a road with an empty basket on her arm. The first line of the story is: "Mrs. Green is going to visit her friend, Mr. Gardner."

Sam: Why does she have a basket?

Teacher: That's a good question, Sam. She probably has a basket because she's going to bring something back in it. Maybe she's going to the store after she visits Mr. Gardner. Or maybe he has a garden and has promised her some vegetables.

Maria: Why isn't she driving her car to Mr. Gardner's house?

Teacher: What a good question! That question has lots of possible answers. It could be that she doesn't have a car, or

maybe she's trying to lose weight, or maybe Mrs. Green is energy conscious and is saving gas, or maybe her car is in the garage for repairs.

Candy: Where is Mrs. Green going?

Teacher: To visit her friend, Mr. Gardner. (Note that this question is not reinforced because it is at the literal level and that the child is not scolded or embarrassed for asking a literal level question.)

ReQuest gives an opportunity for vocabulary questions to come up in a meaningful context and only as the students identify their need. It gives the teacher an opportunity to assess the students' background for the story (through asking questions) and to enhance it where necessary. Purpose and motivation arise from the questions that are asked, since these questions emerge from the students' concerns and experiences.

In ReQuest, the Guided Silent Reading of the DRA is bypassed because the children are motivated and curious to find out the answers to their questions. ReQuest also has no oral reading step but does insure excellent opportunities for oral language interaction. Skill development centers around developing higher level questioning and thinking skills through teacher reinforcement and modeling. ReQuest also provides the teacher opportunity to assess student needs in these areas.

Directed Reading-Thinking Activity (DRTA)

The Directed Reading-Thinking Activity (Stauffer, 1969) is a good alternative when vocabulary and background pose no problems. In it, each student hypothesizes about the story. After defending the reasonableness of their hypotheses, the students read the story to find out if their guesses were right. Proof of each answer is given by reading appropriate sentences aloud.

Let us return to Mrs. Green and her visit to Mr. Gardner. In the DRTA the reader surveys the entire story in order to settle on a specific hypothesis. From just the first picture, however, the following hypotheses might be generated:

> I wonder where Mrs. Green is going. (Since the child has not yet read any of the text, this is a perfectly acceptable question.)
>
> I guess she's going to buy food since she has a basket with her.
>
> I wonder why Mrs. Green is walking and not in her car.

The DRTA emphasizes the DRA Preparation step of setting purposes and instilling motivation, but the purposes and motivation come from the children, not the teacher. For Guided Silent Reading the students are guided by their own active searches for answers to their questions and to their peers' questions. For an exceptionally long story, the steps of hypothesize, read, and prove may be used more than once, but for most basal stories the silent reading will be in one "gulp."

The DRTA's oral reading is purposeful: Students repeat their hypotheses and then read the portions of the story that offer proof for or against their hypotheses. For skill development, the children are growing in their ability to ask appropriate questions, to set their own purposes, and to find proof for their answers. Some critical and inferential reading skills may also be developed as students offer different kinds of proof.

Expectation Outline

An Expectation Outline is best used for a factual story and therefore would be appropriate for social studies and science texts as well as for factual stories in basal readers. For an Expectation Outline, students are asked to tell what they expect to learn in a story about spiders, for example. As the students suggest questions (such as What do they eat? Will they kill you? How do they have babies?) the teacher groups related questions on the chalkboard without comment.

When all questions have been asked and categorized, the teacher directs the class's attention to one group of questions at a time and asks the children to make up a heading or title for those questions. "Where do spiders live?" "Why do spiders make webs?" "Why are webs so sticky?" and "Why do spiders make different kinds of webs?" could be labeled "Webs." Next the children read the story to find the answers to those questions, reading aloud the proof. Unanswered questions could be posted on a bulletin board to stimulate reading in other resources.

With an Expectation Outline, many vocabulary words are brought to the students' attention as questions are written on the board. The teacher can comment on these terms while writing them, thus insuring that the terms are understood as well as recognized in print. As the children offer questions, the teacher can assess their readiness to deal with the concepts. If no one realizes that spiders build webs, the teacher can stop and fill in the necessary background.

Purpose and motivation are again provided by the students, and silent and oral reading are much like in the DRTA. Skills in prereading anticipation, categorizing, and identifying answers to specific questions are developed.

Prereading Guided Reading Procedure

The prereading Guided Reading Procedure (Spiegel, 1980) is an adaptation of Manzo's GRP (1975). When used as a prereading activity, the GRP focuses on reminding students of what they already know about a topic. As with the Expectation Outline, the prereading GRP is especially useful with factual material. Students are asked to tell everything they know about the topic and the teacher records all responses on the chalkboard or on chart paper, numbering each piece of information. No editing is done by the teacher, nor is anything categorized at this point.

When the students are unable to give any more information about the topic, they search the recorded information for inconsistencies or for information they feel is incorrect. The numbers of inconsistent information are circled and connected. For example, No. 6, "Spiders kill people," would be joined to No. 28, "Spider bites hurt but you don't die." Questionable information is marked with a question mark.

Next the children suggest four or five categories under which the information could be grouped and assign each piece of information to one of those categories. Last of all, the students read to find out if the information they have listed is accurate.

The prereading GRP serves many of the same functions as the traditional DRA, but adds the advantages of diagnosis and increased student involvement and confidence. The Preparation step of the DRA is completed in several ways. The teacher can determine what vocabulary and conceptual background the students have and what needs to be developed before reading the story. The students set their own purposes for reading by identifying inconsistent, incorrect, and missing information. They are motivated to read both by their own purposes and by the confidence that arises from finding out that they already know a lot about this topic.

As with the Expectation Outline, silent and oral reading are purposeful and are guided by the student rather than the teacher. Students receive meaningful practice in developing the important skills of prereading anticipation, critical reading, categorizing, and setting purposes.

Word Wonder

Word Wonder (originally devised by Paula Hodges, a graduate student at the University of North Carolina at Chapel Hill) is most helpful when the teacher suspects the students need help with vocabulary items and concepts for a certain story. In its simplest form, the students tell what words they expect to find in a story about a trip to the zoo or making doughnuts and then read to find out if they were right. In its more complex form, the teacher lists words and the children decide whether each word is likely to appear in the story, giving a rationale for each decision. The teacher should purposely include words apt to be chosen incorrectly so that postreading discussion can center around children's misconceptions.

For example, if the children are to read a story involving modern Navajo children, the teacher might propose the words: *adobe, reservation, Arizona, fierce, North Carolina, teepee, buffalo, dry, poor, savage, sheep, schools.*

If the children do not select *adobe* or *reservation*, they may not understand the meanings or visual forms of those words, and the teacher would then preteach them. On the other hand, if the children choose *teepee, fierce,* and *savage*, the teacher might be wise to reserve comment. When the students find that those words or ideas are *not* in the story, discussion can focus on misconceptions. Postreading discussion should also include investigation of whether "wrong" guesses were "bad" guesses or if the author just didn't choose to use those words.

Word Wonder fulfills the vocabulary step of the DRA, but in a diagnostic manner. Vocabulary words are pretaught only when necessary. Similarly, background is assessed as the children offer or react to the words and is filled in as necessary. Purpose and motivation may arise from the vocabulary discussion, but additional comprehension-oriented purposes may need to be set. If silent reading needs to be guided more purposefully, combining Word Wonder with the DRTA or Semantic Webbing is appropriate. Oral reading takes place when the students show where they found the vocabulary of interest. Skill development takes place primarily in the areas of vocabulary development and in pre-reading anticipation.

Semantic Webbing

Semantic Webbing (Freedman and Reynolds, 1980) focuses on comprehension, as do the DRTA, ReQuest, prereading GRP, and Expectation Outline. In Semantic Webbing, the teacher identifies an aspect of the story that the students should think about especially clearly. This aspect is written on the board inside a circle, posed as a core question, such as "Why would Mrs. White go to see the policeman instead of calling him on the phone?" Student hypotheses ("She doesn't have a phone" "She is afraid to stay in her house" "She has a crush on the policeman" "She wants help immediately") are recorded as web strands branching from the circle.

Justifications for each hypothesis are given and recorded in yet another set of branches radiating from the hypotheses, called strand supports. For "She doesn't have a phone," justifications might include poverty, dislike of mechanical devices, or malfunctioning equipment. As a last preparation step, strand ties are drawn between strands related to each other in ways the teacher or students wish to emphasize. For example, a strand tie called fear might be drawn between "She is afraid to stay in her house" and "She wants help immediately."

Then the students read the relevant section of the story to find the answers to the core question and to find out which, if any, of their supporting reasons were right. The procedure can be used for just one central issue in the story or can be repeated as new issues need to be clarified.

Semantic Webbing provides little in the way of vocabulary or background development and is therefore most appropriate for stories about familiar topics or themes. Semantic Webbing does, however, build specific purposes for reading and develops motivation. Silent reading is guided by these purposes and oral reading evolves naturally out of them. Development in the skills of prediction, purpose setting, and critical reading takes place.

These six alternatives to the DRA are offered as alternatives that allow variety within the basal reader lesson while still attending to the needs met by the DRA. They also allow the teacher to match children's needs and story characteristics. Several of the six alternatives have a diagnostic aspect so that all children don't automatically receive instruction prescribed by the authors of a basal manual. Almost no advance preparation is required and there is virtually nothing to grade. Last of all, these procedures may free up teacher and student time and energy for that most-neglected portion of the DRA— enrichment.

References

Betts, Emmett. *Foundations of Reading Instruction*. New York, N.Y.: American Book Company, 1946.

Freedman, Glenn, and Elizabeth G. Reynolds. "Enriching Basal Reader Lessons with Semantic Webbing." *The Reading Teacher*, vol. 33 (March 1980), pp. 677–84.

Manzo, Anthony V. "Guided Reading Procedure." *Journal of Reading*, vol. 18 (January 1975), pp. 287–91.

Manzo, Anthony V. "The ReQuest Procedure." *Journal of Reading*, vol. 13 (November 1969), pp. 123–26.

Spiegel, Dixie Lee. "Adaptations of Manzo's Guided Reading Procedure." *Reading Horizons*, vol. 20 (Spring 1980), pp. 188–92.

Stauffer, Russell G. *Directing Reading Maturity as a Cognitive Process*. New York, N.Y.: Harper and Row, 1969.

72. Techniques for Increasing Reading Rate

James I. Brown

For teachers of reading, today's tremendous proliferation of printed material is a dramatic reminder of the need for increased reading rates. The veritable avalanche of print necessitates a closer examination of any and all techniques for meeting that need. My special concern in this paper is with teaching techniques especially useful with students at the senior high, college, and adult levels. Within this context, a strong pragmatic orientation seems indispensable.

Formulating an Objective

The first step in arriving at techniques for the improvement of rate is to formulate, carefully and thoughtfully, a specific objective. As a sample, consider the Efficient Reading course at the University of Minnesota.

> *Objective: To help each student develop the maximum rate possible, without significant loss of comprehension.*

This statement of objective is intentionally open-ended so as to encourage maximum progress and provide desirable latitude for individual differences. After all, while a typical college class initially averages around 250 words-per-minute, with 60 percent comprehension, the range may be from 160 to 420 words-per-minute, with comprehension of from 20 to 90 percent.

Checking Available Aids

Once a reading rate objective has been phrased to your complete satisfaction, the next step is to examine all available resources of help in reaching that objective. Resources include films for use with regular motion picture projectors and films for use with special projectors. The latter include various kinds of *accelerators*, with shades, wires or lights to hasten the eyes down a printed page; and they include *tachistoscopes* for sharpening perceptual skills and increasing span. And not to be overlooked are *vocabulary-building aids* in film, TV, slide, card, or textbook form. The substrata-factor research by Holmes and Singer (1) indicates that vocabulary deserves predominant emphasis, since it contributes 51 percent to reading speed—far more than any other first-order factor.

Aids versus Techniques

With today's profusion of aids for increasing rate, how important are techniques? The first adult classes in reading taught at Minnesota in 1949 suggest an answer. At that time, we were using two aids, a tachistoscope and the Harvard Films, with accompanying readings. That very first class initially averaged 213 words-per-minute, with 79 percent comprehension. By the end of the course students had progressed to 519 words-per-minute, but they showed a disappointing drop to 55 percent comprehension.

For the very next class, the teacher of the first group used the same aids, materials, and tests. One change was made. Some new techniques were added. Initially, the second class averaged 283 words-per-minute, with 70 percent comprehension. Final results were 721 words-per-minute, with 66 percent comprehension.

From James I. Brown, Techniques for increasing reading rate. In John E. Merritt (Ed.), *New horizons in reading.* Newark, Del.: International Reading Association, 1976. Pp. 158–164. Reprinted by permission of James Brown and the International Reading Association.

In short, the first class read 2.4 times faster with a loss of 24 percent in comprehension. The following class read 2.5 times faster with only a 4 percent loss. Such evidence suggests that, while teaching aids are indeed important, the techniques we use with those aids are even more important.

Identifying Attitudes

Once a teacher sets an objective, surveys the available aids, and recognizes the vital importance of techniques, he should determine exactly what techniques are best. The teacher's success in determining techniques depends on knowing the students and himself well. To be effective, all techniques must be solidly grounded on an awareness of which student and teacher attitudes are helpful. Here, student feedback is crucial.

One student's performance will serve as an example. Initially, the student read at 170 words-per-minute, with 30 percent comprehension. In over a week he moved up only to 190 words-per-minute. When the instructor suggested he try a faster speed, the student shook his head. "I don't get much even when I read slowly and carefully. I wouldn't get anything if I went any faster." That remark revealed a personal roadblock. Until that block was removed, no teaching aid could be effective.

Only when attitudes, such as the one described, are identified and catalogued can one begin to develop specific techniques to circumvent deleterious effects. Building a checklist of such roadblocks, to be used at the beginning of the course to identify problems, provides invaluable help in selecting or devising appropriate techniques. Repeated at the end, the checklist serves equally well to evaluate success in meeting student needs.

At the University of Minnesota, we use a checklist of some thirteen possible reasons for rate difficulty. Students check the one which seems most apropos. During a recent quarter, "Fear of missing something" was checked most frequently by 53 percent initially and by only 22 percent at the end of the quarter. "Lack of confidence" was checked by 38 percent initially and by less than 1 percent at the end.

Student attitudes help or hinder in achieving objectives but so do teacher attitudes toward students and their capabilities.

Research by Rosenthal (2), first with mice and then with grade-school children, has led to the concept of "self-fulfilling prophecy." According to that research, teachers communicate very subtly their own attitudes and expectations toward individuals in their class, leading them to perform better or worse than they might have performed otherwise.

Consider the implications of that research for teachers of reading. For example, if a teacher is absolutely convinced that 800 words-per-minute is the top limit as a reading rate, class results would tend to reflect that limiting attitude. Or, consider a teacher who is skeptical about the effectiveness of a certain teaching aid. That skepticism will tend to permeate his efforts and be communicated to his students, vitiating the effectiveness of that aid.

Evidence bearing on this theory accidentally surfaced in our own program. A relatively new teacher taught a section of reading for the class hour devoted solely to the developing of scanning speed and accuracy. Fourteen scanning practice problems were planned, interspersed with suggested tips for increased efficiency. Normally, by the end of the hour, students are scanning at an average top rate of about 15,500 words-per-minute, with excellent accuracy. The new teacher was not told what to expect and was quite pleased with his results—an average of 2,161 words-per-minute on identical problems. Without realizing it, he had apparently conveyed to his students his belief that 2,000 words-per-minute was about all that could be expected.

If they are to bring maximum results, any techniques for increasing reading rate must be solidly based on insights drawn from careful evaluation of student and teacher attitudes. In one sense, this step may be more important than the actual techniques themselves. Once a proper foundation is laid, everything done during each class hour for the entire course will tend to fall into place. Separate technique minutiae will combine to make larger constellations.

Motivational Techniques

At this point, suppose we examine some sample or model constellations to suggest the many possibilities.

Active self-discoveries. Active self-discovery involves translating information normally conveyed by lecture into a heuristic or self-discovery form to generate heightened interest and more active student involvement. The difference between being told something and discovering it for ourselves is cardinal. Keats catches so well the excitement of discovery in his sonnet, "On First Looking into Chapman's Homer," a portion of those realms of gold making up the reading teacher's domain. Furthermore, so much of what goes on in a reading class can easily be translated or restructured into this general technique format.

For example, suppose you want to explain how, as a person now increases his rate, he soon reaches a top limit. Faster reading would result in skimming or skipping. With data from preceding classes, students can determine that the demarcation line would be, on the average, 336 words-per-minute.

Translate that information into an active self-discovery technique, however, and enjoy the quickened interest and enthusiasm. You raise the question. Your students discover the answer. Just give them these directions. "Read the directed selection at your absolute top reading rate. Don't skip. Don't skim. Read every single word, but read at your present top rate. The resulting figure will mark your exact upper reading limit, beyond which you must begin to skim or scan."

This one example should suggest how to restructure much of what is done in class into active self-discovery form.

Visual expeditors. The second general type of motivational technique might be labeled visual expeditors. These expeditors involve translating information into visual form, sometimes in combination with the heuristic. To time students as they read articles in class, teachers sometimes write on the blackboard or use a slide or transparency with reading time in minutes and seconds indicated.

It takes only a slight restructuring to translate that practice into a true visual expeditor. Instead of reading time in minutes and seconds, convert that information into a direct word-per-minute reading figure. When a student looks up after completing an article he immediately knows his word-per-minute rate. Take this a step further. If the figures go up only to 800 words-per-minute, students will be encouraged to consider that rate an upper limit. If the figures go up to 1,200 words-per-minute, a different expectancy is communicated. Such visual expeditors play an important role and students often raise their heads to check the figures.

1,000 Club. Perhaps the most useful visual expeditor for our adult classes has been the 1,000 Club card, a small card which fits nicely into a billfold. The club is described to the class a little past the halfway mark in the course, when interest may tend to lag. The club is unique in that it has no meetings, no dues, no officers, and no responsibilities—just honor. Any student who achieves at a certain level receives a signed card which reads as follows:

THE 1,000 CLUB
OFFICIAL MEMBERSHIP CARD

This is to certify that

_____

has achieved a reading speed of 1,000 words a minute or faster, with a comprehension of 80 percent or better, in the University of Minnesota's course in "Efficient Reading," Rhetoric 1147.

Date: _____

Attested: _____
                    (Instructor)

Instructional Techniques

Next, let us turn from motivational techniques to an examination of sample instructional techniques.

Pacing. Perhaps the most common, and certainly one of the most useful, techniques for increasing rate is pacing. Pacing is predicated on the theory that we can do things under pressure that would be impossible otherwise. Pacing is the underlying principle at work in all reading films and accelerators. Furthermore, by using a stop watch and spoken commands, any teacher may pace any individual or entire class through any selection at a desired rate. Since pacing is so well known, no further amplification is needed here.

Determining the best practice rate. This instructional assignment, the active self-discovery type, involves the reading of seven selections. Students graph their results, noting interrelationships between rate and comprehension. Students are told to read the first selection very slowly and then to read each of the remaining six from 75 to 125 words-per-minute faster than the preceding one, despite any adverse affect on comprehension. The resulting graph should reveal, among other things, students' present optimum practice rates. A secondary value is in removing the common attitudinal barrier summed up in the phrase, "the faster you read, the less you comprehend."

The best comprehension for about 70 percent of the students is not achieved at their slowest rate. The graph makes that point nicely, freeing them from undesira-

ble stereotypes and attitudes which limit progress. The assignment also generates added reliance on the self-discovery technique.

It is relatively easy to get each student to circle his best comprehension score or scores and make the point that optimum results come from practicing beyond the rate at which he comprehended best. Practicing what you do well stops progress, just as additional hunt-and-peck typing keeps you from mastery of the touch system.

Using specialized reading-type skills. Still another technique involves the teaching of such specialized skills as surveying or overviewing, skimming, and scanning. These are important skills in their own right and deserve to be taught. Our concern here is to teach them in such a way that they make a major contribution to increasing reading rate.

Sequence is of particular importance. For example, when introducing skimming as a reading-type activity, have the class skim an article immediately *after* doing a timed reading. This insures meaningful comparisons. After providing complete directions as to how skimming is done, you raise the question, "Exactly how do reading and skimming rates differ and what about resulting differences in comprehension?" It is helpful to use a timing slide with suitably high rate figures to reinforce the expected rate advantage. Later, additional skimming practice is scheduled to fit immediately *before* a timed reading. Students will soon notice the accelerating effect of that juxtaposition and take advantage of it in better organizing their out-of-class reading.

Surveying and scanning can be treated in the same way and used as rate accelerators, as well as skills in their own right.

Individual progress sheet. One last technique involves a specially designed, single-page record sheet with space for entering records of every reading activity. The sheet is organized so as to present a de-

Table 1. Results

Version 1				Version 2				Version 3			
Initial		Final		Initial		Final		Initial		Final	
rate	comp	rate	comp	rate	comp	rate	comp	rate	comp	rate	comp
252 —	63%	1548 —	62%	314 —	72%	889 —	74%	293 —	64%	903 —	66%
	6.1 times faster				2.8 times faster				3.0 times faster		

veloping picture of progress, as well as to pinpoint difficulties. Each student picks up his sheet when he comes in, makes entries during class, and leaves it afterwards. The teacher has an accurate check of class progress as well as of individual problems needing attention.

Results

In conclusion, a capsule look at results from three quite different structurings of efficient reading (Rhetoric 1147) provides added perspective for evaluating the kinds of techniques discussed. (See Table 1.)

1. Regular version: 3 credits. Meets for 30 45-minute periods (22½ hours of class time). This version involves direct student-teacher interaction, as described.
2. *Independent study cassette version*: 3 credits. No classroom time. Lectures, timing and pacing tapes, texts, and study guide provide instruction. Sixty-two students have enrolled since its recent inception. This version involves no face-to-face contact—only mail contact with the lessons.
3. *Independent study TV version*: 3 credits. Twelve 30-minute TV lessons—six hours of viewing. This version has had over 22,000 paid enrollments from open or closed circuit broadcasting. It provides a visual instructor but no live face-to-face relationship—only mail contact for the lessons.

For the visual TV medium, it was possible to multiply the use of visual expeditors, achieving unexpectedly good results considering the limited six-hour viewing time—results which point up the efficacy of such expeditors.

Finally, let me quote Hallock Hoffman—flier, sculptor, and photographer. He once divided mankind into the "quick and the dead." In his view the quick "are people who can hear questions" and the dead "are people who know answers." The quick are the pioneers, feeling the spell of unknown frontiers—the tug of discovery. The dead are settled stolidly into the comfort of a tidy, well-explained, questionless world.

Hopefully, you should consider this paper as not an answer but a question, leading you on to those further self-discoveries which make teaching the genuinely satisfying experience it is.

References

1. Holmes, Jack A., and Harry Singer. "The Substrata Factor Theory: Substrata Factor Differences Underlying Reading Ability in Known Groups at the High School Level," Final Report Covering Contracts 538, SAE 8176 and 538A, SAE 8660. U.S. Office of Education, Department of Health, Education, and Welfare, 1961.
2. Rosenthal, Robert, and Leonore Jacobson. *Pygmalion in the Classroom*. New York: Holt, Rinehart and Winston, 1968.

73. Developing Flexible Reading Habits

Sumner W. Schachter

Many students with reading problems seem to be unwilling or unable to vary their reading rates (Gibson and Levin 1975, Karlin 1975, Spache 1976, Golinkoff 1975–1976, Spache and Spache 1977). Obviously, all readers can vary their rates to some extent (when we look up a telephone number, we don't read the whole phone book), but many poor readers tend to read "the whole thing."

Often students approach reading as a task involving attention to and decoding of every word on the page (Karlin 1975, Spache 1976, Golinkoff 1975–1976). These students benefit especially from activities that help them develop more flexible reading rates.

Skimming and scanning both refer to rapid reading during which the reader does not direct attention to all of the information on the page. Scanning is fast reading to obtain answers to specific questions (Karlin 1975, Spache and Spache 1977), while skimming is rapid reading to find out what something is about or a general idea (Karlin 1975, Spache and Spache 1977). In classrooms, the two terms are often used synonymously to refer to rapid reading for some specific purpose.

Flexible reading habits should be taught systematically from kindergarten through high school. Basal readers, content area texts, newspapers, magazines, nd phone books are the basis for appropriate activities.

Young children can be asked to skim and scan pictures, wordless picture books, and posters. They can scan the newspaper to find a specific letter of the alphabet, a word, or a picture.

Activities for flexible reading can be done informally or formally in almost any reading situation. Given a reading book, text, newspaper, menu, or novel, a reader can be taught to skim or scan for a variety of purposes. The teacher directs the students to "Find the place where . . .," "Find the sentence in which . . .," "Underline ten nouns," "Locate the names of the people who . . .," "List the places mentioned on page . . ."

Using a Phone Book

Both the white and yellow pages of the local phone directory can be used to help students develop flexible reading habits. Questions should be given to the students in advance. The teacher may control the difficulty of the task by limiting the amount of printed material that the reader must scan. For example, the directions may state a specific task: "Write the name of the third person on page 48." "Turn to page 50 of the yellow pages. What is the phone number of Anderson's Lumber Store?" As pupils develop greater flexibility and efficiency, assignments may be made longer and the orienting questions less specific.

White pages
Where can you find fire and police phone numbers?

On what page can you find the phone number of Okanela Lodge?

How many families in Basalt have last names beginning with "Z"?

What town does Patrick Harmon live in? What's his phone number?

From Sumner W. Schachter, Developing flexible reading habits. *Journal of Reading*, November 1978, *29*, 149–152. Reprinted by permission of Sumner Schachter and the International Reading Association.

What is the phone number for the Silt City Hall?

What page is your phone number on?

Yellow pages

Where can you get airline tickets in Glenwood Springs?

On what page can you find out about buying motorcycles?

Find the phone number of a tattoo parlor.

Can you go to a hardware store in New Castle?

For variety, these activities may be timed, done in cooperating or competing groups, as whole class activities, or in learning stations. Students can make up their own questions for peers to answer.

The timing and recording of reading activities may focus students' attention upon their reading rates. The reading performance of students is likely to improve if they become aware of their reading rates, how these rates fluctuate, what factors affect reading rates, and how their rates improve.

Using the Local Newspaper

The local newspaper is a useful resource for a variety of skimming and scanning activities. The classified ads are used for activities similar to those done with a phone book.

What color dog was lost?

Where can I call to buy a horse trailer?

How much does a condominium cost?

How much does a 10 × 45 foot mobile home cost?

News articles may be used for finding specific information or reading for the general idea.

Who protested at the Carbondale board meeting?

What were the citizens protesting?

When was the meeting?

When was the master plan for zoning developed?

Who presented the petition?

Tell students to scan the article as quickly as possible to find the answers to the questions.

The students could also be instructed to skim the entire article (and to record reading time) and then write a short summary or paraphrase of the article. After skimming the article, the students could be asked to answer several questions. If they cannot, they should be directed to reread the relevant portions of the article.

Using the Table of Contents

Students can be directed to find specific information from the table of contents of a basal reader or textbook. This activity not only helps the reader develop and practice flexible reading habits, but also helps students learn about the kinds of information available in the book. Similar kinds of activities may be constructed using indices or glossaries.

How many stories are in this book?

On what page would you find a story about a typewriter?

Who wrote "Winning Magic"?

Which story titles tell us the name of a main character?

Turn to the story "I'm Not Dumb Anymore" and find out where the story takes place.

Find out the names of the people in the story "A Surprise for Anna."

Using Content Area Textbooks

Students should work with directed activities in content area studies to develop additional flexibility in reading as well as knowledge and study skills in that particular subject. We can assist students by telling them in advance what questions we want answered. Then they can read the chapter looking for the specific information, without having to read every word.

What is the chapter about?

Look at the paragraph headings and then write a short paragraph telling what the chapter tells us.

List the qualifications necessary to be President.

Read under "The President's Assistants" to find out which president had to decide whether or not to use the atomic bomb.

Read under "The President's Cabinet" to find out how many departments there are.

Now read (skim) the whole chapter and try to answer these questions.

Who actually elects the president?

Is the power of the president limited in any way?

What are some of the president's duties?

Who determines what the Vice President does?

Students should be led to realize that the printed page holds a variety of information. At times, only some of that information is relevant to a particular task. By developing activities in which students successfully extract information by skimming and scanning, we can help them develop flexible reading habits and the confidence to use those habits in appropriate settings.

These activities do not imply that a reader never reads "the whole thing." We do read whole paragraphs, chapters, and books. Many of us have read a favorite novel from cover to cover several times. We have memorized lines of poetry and plays. We have read and reread while studying for exams. However, we chose to do these things. We had the flexible reading habits that enabled us to vary our reading performance and choose how best to use our time. We must help students develop habits that enable them to decide how best to use their time as well.

References

Frase, Lawrence T. "Purpose in Reading." *Cognition, Curriculum, and Comprehension*, John T. Guthrie, Ed., pp. 42–64. Newark, Del.: International Reading Association, 1977.

Gibson, Eleanor J. and Harry Levin. *The Psychology of Reading*. Cambridge, Mass.: The M.I.T. Press, 1975.

Golinkoff, Roberta M. "A Comparison of Reading Comprehension Processes in Good and Poor Comprehenders." *Reading Research Quarterly*, vol. XI, no. 4 (1975–1976), pp. 623–59.

Karlin, Robert. *Teaching Elementary Reading: Principles and Strategies*. New York, N.Y.: Harcourt Brace Jovanovich, 1975.

Spache, George D. *Diagnosing and Correcting Reading Disabilities*. Boston, Mass.: Allyn and Bacon, Inc., 1976.

Spache, George D. and Evelyn B. Spache. *Reading in the Elementary School*. Boston, Mass.: Allyn and Bacon, Inc., 1977.

74. The Teacher's Dilemma: How to Gauge the Suitability of Reading Materials

Jonathan Anderson and Jim Coates

When teachers meet a new class of students at the beginning of a course of studies, they often have little reliable evidence of the reading abilities of their students. Teachers may also be unsure of the difficulty of some of the reading materials available for students undertaking the course (Coates 1977). This can lead to frustrating and disillusioning experiences for both teachers and students. Part-way through the course teachers may discover that certain students cannot understand an important section of the work because the materials are too difficult for them to read. Three questions of fundamental importance may be posed by teachers in this situation.

1. What means are available to find out whether my students can read this book with understanding?
2. Why are John, Peter and Mary unable to read this book?
3. How can John, Peter and Mary be helped to overcome their reading problems?

This article attempts to provide an answer to the first question.

Matching Readers and Reading Materials

Whether reading materials are suitable for students depends to a large extent on whether the reading level required to understand the materials corresponds with the reading level of a large majority (at least 80 per cent) of the students in the class. Among the ways of gauging this correspondence between reading ability and reading difficulty might be mentioned:

- using professional judgement, that is subjective evaluation (can be hazardous);
- testing the suitability of the materials by making a representative selection (sample) of the materials and setting questions requiring students either to write short answers or answer orally;
- developing an objective test from selected passages and requiring students to answer multiple-choice questions based on the passages (this is more difficult than it seems and besides there is no way of knowing whether the language of the questions or the language of the passages is the major stumbling block);
- measuring the reading difficulty of the materials with a formula and using another test to determine the reading level of the class;
- administering cloze tests to ascertain whether most students can read and understand the material.

Of these various methods cloze procedure has certain advantages in that:

- it provides a reasonably objective measure;
- it can be constructed quickly and is relatively easy to mark;
- it involves only one test administration and can be considered as a learning exercise; and

From Jonathan Anderson and Jim Coates, The teacher's dilemma: How to gauge the suitability of reading materials. *Australian Journal of Reading*, August 1979, 2, 135–142. Reprinted by permission of the authors and the publisher.

- it is a global measure, gauging whether students can read and understand the structure of the sentences as well as main words (one reason it is used extensively with English second language students).

The Cloze Procedure

Cloze procedure was developed as a measure of the readability of written material which takes the reader into account. In this respect cloze procedure differs radically from the element counting readability formulae. Perhaps the major limitation of the readability formula is that factors within the reader such as his motivation, his familiarity with the topic, his facility with language are not considered.

Cloze procedure is a simple yet subtle technique. It is a technique which can be applied by any teacher who wishes to gauge the reading difficulty of a particular passage or book for a particular group of pupils. All that the technique requires is for words to be mechanically deleted from a passage, say, and given to a group of subjects with instructions to restore the missing words. A subject is given a score of one for each word he correctly replaces. If, for example, one reader replaces many words correctly, then the passage is for him more readable than for another reader who correctly replaces only a few words. As an example of a cloze test made over a passage, every fifth word has been deleted from the following sentences and replaced by a standard-length blank:

> Once upon a time _____ was a little girl _____ sang. She sang with _____ birds as they chirped _____ the hedges. She sang _____ the wind as it _____ in the trees. She _____ as she skipped along _____ road to school.

There are a number of questions that immediately spring to mind about cloze procedure. Which words are deleted? How many words are deleted? Does a word have to be replaced exactly to score

or will a synonym do? And perhaps the most important question of all: Does the method measure reading difficulty? Before trying to answer these questions, we should examine the logic or rationale of cloze procedure.

Rationale of Cloze Procedure

Consider a sentence like *The birds _____ in the trees*. English grammar requires some verb to fill the blank (e.g., *sang, chirp, built*) though the tense of the verb is not indicated. Meaning also determines to some extent what the missing word should be, for some words are more likely than others. For example, *chirped* or *sing*, even in the very limited context, is more probable than *ate* or *climb*. Fries (1963) identified three layers of language meanings—the layer of meanings carried by the lexical items, the layer of meanings carried by the grammatical structures, the layer of social-cultural meaning. Cloze procedure taps these three layers of meanings for, as McLeod (1965) stated, to successfully replace a word ". . . requires a familiarity with the grammatical structure of English, an understanding of lexical meaning and, if the passages selected are concerned with a variety of experiences familiar in a given culture, they reflect to some extent *social-cultural* meaning." Thus, for example, the sentence *For breakfast we had bacon and _____* is more likely to be completed in Australia by *eggs* than, by say, *porridge* or *yams*.

The theory behind cloze procedure goes something like the following. A source or encoder produces a message. In the present discussion the source would be the writer and the message, a passage of printed English. The language patterns of the message are mutilated by some mechanical procedure. That is, words are deleted and to denote these, blanks are inserted. The message reaches a receiver or decoder, namely, the reader. To decode the message cloze procedure requires the reader to make the most likely replacement in the light of his language system and the cues that are available.

Cloze procedure is a measure of the correspondence of language habits of source and receiver when the code of the message (that is, the language) is common to both. Taylor (1953) in introducing cloze procedure, stated:

> . . . [it] appears to be a measure of the aggregate influences of *all factors* which interact to affect the degree of correspondence between the language patterns of transmitter and receiver (p. 432).

There is a substantial body of research evidence (Rankin 1959; Bormuth 1962, 1963; Anderson 1967, 1976) indicating that cloze procedure is a reliable and valid technique for measuring the suitability of reading materials for a particular group of students.

Cloze Procedure in the Classroom

Some general guidelines for preparing cloze tests by the classroom teacher may be laid down:

1. Select passages of about 200–300 words in length.
2. Delete words regularly throughout each passage (say, every sixth or seventh) and replace with blanks of a constant length. This gives tests containing 40–50 items.
3. Administer cloze tests to pupils.
4. Score the tests by giving one point for each word correctly replaced. Misspellings, phonetic spellings, or responses where the intention is clear are not counted wrong since cloze tests are measures of comprehension, not of spelling.
5. Calculate each pupil's cloze score (the total number of exact replacements) and the cloze score for each passage (the total number of exact replacements made by all pupils).

The two scores obtained in Step 5 allow the teacher to order his/her pupils in terms of comprehension ability and to order passages in terms of reading difficulty. It is also possible to infer from cloze scores the probable ease that a student or group is likely to encounter with similar reading material. The interpretation of cloze scores is discussed below, but first some more detail about actually constructing and scoring cloze tests over sample passages from textbooks or other learning materials.

The questions most frequently asked about cloze procedure concern frequency of word deletions, type of word deletions, number of deletions, and cutting across all of these, scoring procedures.

Frequency of Word Deletions

The two most commonly employed deletion systems in cloze studies are random and regular word-deletion. A regular deletion is preferable though both systems have the advantage in that they are mechanical and completely objective and require no training in test construction for their use. A variety of word deletion frequencies has been reported, from every twelfth to every fifth word omitted. In one sense the deletion of every fifth word is the most efficient of these, providing as it does more blanks for passages of given length, though experience favors a less frequent rate, like every sixth or seventh, especially with younger readers.

Type of Word Deletions

In the construction of cloze tests all words may be potential deletions or deletion may be restricted to words of a certain grammatical class or to *key* words. Taylor (1957) contrasted three types of word deletions: *any* words, *hard* words (adverbs, verbs and nouns) and *easy* words (verb auxiliaries, conjunctions, pronouns and articles). He found that generally the *any-word* deletions correlated highest with pre-reading knowledge, immediate recall and aptitude and the *easy-word* deletions, lowest. Deletion of *hard words* was the best measure of prior knowledge of technically worded content. Taylor concluded that for testing reading comprehension and aptitude the *any-word* form is superior to the *easy form* and generally superior to the *hard form*. For contrasting readability levels, however, Taylor concluded that only the *any-word* form seems justifiable:

> To restrict deletions to particular kinds of words is to ignore the fact that those kinds may not occur equally often in different materials. The difference in frequency of occurrence may itself be a readability factor; if so, its effect should be included in—not excluded from—the results (Taylor 1957, p. 25).

Number of Deletions

The number of items in a cloze test involves such considerations as testing time, fatigue, and test reliability. Taylor (1956) suggested that "a series of about 50 blanks is roughly sufficient to allow the chances of mechanically selecting easy or hard words to cancel out and yield a stable score of the difficulty of a passage, or the performance of an individual." Bormouth (1964) considered the question of test length in relation to complex problems of sampling involved and also concluded that 50 unselected items (blanks) was usually sufficient to ensure stable estimates.

Scoring Procedures

Several procedures have been reported for scoring cloze items. The most common is where credit is given only if a subject replaces a blank with the exact word that was deleted. Allowing credit for synonyms, or for words that make sense, or even for words of the same grammatical class, are other scoring methods advocated by some.

Experimental evidence of the relationship of these different scoring procedures is in close agreement (Anderson 1976). Which to use then depends very much on the teacher's purpose. Since there is little difference between the different scoring methods, the more objective exact replacement scoring method is preferred if the purpose is to scale passages in terms of difficulty or rank students according to reading ability. If on the other hand, the purpose is to develop students' powers of vocabulary, the exact replacement scoring method is least preferred.

Should teachers regard, as rather inflexible, scoring correct only responses that match the words deleted, then certainly synonyms and other likely responses may be accepted too. The net effect, over passages of sufficient length, is usually to raise everyone's score by a more-or-less constant amount. As indicated, this may be important when the procedure is used as part of a teaching exercise; it is usually not important when assessing the suitability of a particular text for student use.

Interpreting Cloze Scores

An important question is the interpretation of a score on a cloze test. What score indicates comprehension? Some answers are provided from research if exact replacement scoring is used. The findings from several studies, summarised by Anderson (1976), suggest scores between 40 and 60 per cent indicate that the reading material is suitable for use at the *instructional level*, that is with some help from a teacher; scores above 60 per cent indicate material suitable at the *independent level*, or for reading on one's own; scores below 40 per cent indicate material likely to be too difficult—hence *frustration level*.

The 40/60 per cent cut-off points are fairly approximate but are usually sufficient for the purposes here. They allow teachers to assess fairly readily the suitability of reading materials for particular groups of students. If accepted as such, the teacher has a useful classroom tool to assist in matching reader and book without recourse to complicated readability formulae or the need to administer standardised reading tests. Furthermore, cloze tests constructed over learning materials do not conflict with but rather are a part of the teaching-learning process.

It is important to inject a note of warning. The results of a single cloze test of students' reading ability need to be treated with some caution as individual students can perform poorly due to a variety of factors such as, for example, lack of basic reading skills, non-native speaker background, or too difficult concepts. Teachers need to consider cloze test results along with other information they have on students' performance. It may be that a particular passage was more difficult than the teacher expected.

A careful analysis of students' cloze results may produce clues as to the reasons for their poor performance. The type and pattern of students' errors may be significant—it can for instance, point to basic structural English second language problems or to lack of word knowledge.

In a Nutshell

Cloze procedure is a relatively simple tool for examining the reading difficulty of books and it may be applied in the classroom. The theoretical justification for cloze procedure is based on modern communication theory and linguistic analysis of language. The procedure allows both an assessment of the reading comprehension of pupils and the ordering of reading materials in terms of difficulty.

References

Anderson, J. *A Scale to Measure the Reading Difficulty of Children's Books*. St. Lucia: University of Queensland Press, 1967.

Anderson, J. *Psycholinguistic Experiments in Foreign Language Testing*. St. Lucia: University of Queensland Press. 1976.

Bormuth, J. R. Cloze tests as measures of readability and comprehension ability. Unpublished doctoral dissertation, Indiana University, 1962.

Bormuth, J. R. Cloze as a measure of readability. *Proceedings of the International Reading Association*. 8, 131–134, 1963.

Bormuth, J. R. Experimental applications of cloze tests. *Proceedings of the International Reading Association*. 9, 303–306, 1964.

Coates, J. R. Cloze procedure: A method of determining the suitability of reading materials. *ACT History Teachers' Journal* (CHATTA) 3, 18–21, 1977.

Fries, C. C. *Linguistics and Reading*. New York: Holt, Rinehart and Winston, 1963.

McLeod, J. *Gap reading comprehension test manual*. Melbourne: Heinemann, 1965.

Rankin, E. F., Jr. The cloze procedure—its validity and utility. *Eighth Yearbook of the National Reading Conference*. 8, 131–144, 1959.

Taylor, W. L. Cloze procedure: a new tool for measuring readability. *Journalism Quarterly*. 30, 415–433, 1953.

Taylor, W. L. Recent developments in the use of 'cloze procedure'. *Journalism Quarterly*. 33, 42–48, 1956.

Taylor, W. L. 'Cloze' readability scores as indices of individual differences in comprehension and aptitude. *Journal of Applied Psychology*. 41, 19–26, 1957.

75. Parents as Partners in Reading Development

Norma Noonan

As teachers we accept responsibility for teaching children to read or facilitating the process for those who need little teaching. In doing so we should not underestimate the importance of the home or the part played by close cooperation between home and school in helping children along the road to literacy, and in developing positive attitudes and life-long habits of reading.

Some factors we might consider are:

- In the pre-school years the home is the educational agency that has equipped children with the competencies they bring to school.
- The home has the greatest single influence on children's learning, particularly on that of young children.
- During the school year children spend approximately six hours at home or in activities directed by the home for every one hour spent at school.
- Home environment helps to determine children's attitude to learning. Attitude contributes largely to success or failure.
- Positive attitudes are created more by consistent good example than by precept. It is wise for school and home to co-operate in setting this example.
- Children's sense of security in their home environment contributes to the emotional stability that enables them to learn more readily. The school can be a help to the home in developing and maintaining a supportive environment.

What can the school do to foster the school/home partnership in reading development?

- Ensure that parents know the school's policy on reading and inform them of changes in policy or implementation of it.
- Assure parents of their welcome to the school, of the value placed upon their involvement in school activities and be prepared to discuss what the school is trying to do in its reading programs.
- Understand the hopes and aspirations parents have for their children and realise that in entrusting them to schools they are trusting us with their most precious *possessions*.
- Inform parents honestly and tactfully about their children's progress—helping them, where necessary, to have realistic expectations for their children.
- Where additional help is necessary, share with parents knowledge of how to help their children so that home and school work together using appropriate methods and materials.
- If parents are involved at school in reading programs, give clear guidance on what they are to do and methods to use. Be available to assist with any problem that arises.

What assistance or advice can the school give to parents about their role in reading development?

Reading ability grows out of language ability. Starting from the early years parents can do much to develop children's facility in the use of language. When children begin to read, parents can encourage them, supplement school programs with leisure reading at home, help to give purpose for and foster a love of reading.

Suggestions the school might offer parents:

From Norma Noonan, Parents as partners in reading development. *Australian Journal of Reading*, August 1978, 1, 61–64. Reprinted by permission of the author and the publisher.

- Talk to children from a very early age. For example, talking to babies when bathing, dressing, settling, or playing enables them to become aware of intonations and rhythms of speech long before they can speak. Babies of a few weeks old are aware of oral communication and are stimulated by it. As they grow, they begin to associate speech sounds with objects and oft-repeated phrases with their accompanying actions. Talk *to* children long before they learn to answer.

- When children begin to respond with sounds and actions, later with words, phrases and sentences, talk *with* them. Repeat their own words, show pleasure in their verbal achievements, thus reinforcing their importance. Add new words and phrases as occasions arise.

- Continue to provide interesting and stimulating experiences at the children's level of development and talk with them about the experiences. Experience alone does not develop language or underlying concepts. Children need experiences, help in interpreting the experiences and opportunity to develop ideas and language about the experiences.

- Listen actively to children's contributions to the conversation. Pay attention to children's statements and questions and display interest by your own answers or comments. The richer the language interchange between adults and children, the easier it is for them to learn the vocabulary, to develop concepts and gain control of language patterns.

- Continue to hold conversations with children throughout their school years, thus showing interest in them as people and in their ideas, while at the same time exposing them to an increasingly wide vocabulary and extending their range of ideas.

- Select books to read to children, paying careful attention to interest level, language level, content, format and attention span. Read regularly and with

enjoyment to children. A toddler can enjoy picture books with an interested adult. The shared experience of a bedtime story is still enjoyed by children.

- Buy books at children's interest and achievement level—with children's help or as *surprises*—so that they can begin their own library. Read the books yourself so you'll know what your children are reading and so you can enjoy the excellence of some children's books.

- Read, yourself, in front of children, setting a good example. Talk about your reading in front of children. This is motivation for children. Children of parents who don't read seldom become avid readers.

- Read interesting excerpts from newspapers to children or, if they are able to read them for themselves, discuss or ask opinions about an article. For example "Did you read the article in today's paper about 'Sandmining at X'? What do you think about it?" or "That's a part you might like to read because it's about the place we went to last Sunday. You might like to read it and take it to school to tell the class any other interesting things you know about it."

- Show an interest in what children are reading at school and what is borrowed from the library. Go with them to the library, borrowing for yourself and other adults. Make library visits a part of family life.

- Encourage children to read wherever reading occurs in their daily lives. On car trips, shopping, at places of relaxation or entertainment, encourage reading and understanding of environmental material. As children are old enough, show them how and let them practise filling in forms, using guides, maps and directories. Ability to survive and function effectively in society requires ability to read and understand these types of material.

- Become involved with the school. Attend parent or grade days/nights when possible. Get to know the school's policy on reading, the teacher's assessment of the child's capabilities and how the child copes with reading tasks. If possible, become involved in a parent group that assists with reading. If your child is having difficulty, work with the school in helping to overcome it to the best of the child's ability.

- Accept your child for what he or she is, whatever the ability level, and have a positive attitude towards achievement at that ability level. Never allow a child to feel that limited ability is a sign of lesser worth as a person.
- Praise where praise is due—conscientious effort, neatness, industry—for there are many occasions one can give genuine praise.
- Encourage children to read a little of their own written work for you regularly. Children's writing can be interesting and enjoyable. Help your child write, illustrate and publish a book for friends or relatives. If you can print well, type or illustrate, you might volunteer for that job.
- Set aside a time and place for the child to study and give help where needed. Try to make study a part of the normal household routine rather than a chore or a punishment.
- Do not allow tension or criticism to become part of helping your children. If they do not understand the work or cannot do it, clear instruction, given cheerfully and patiently, is needed. The feeling that they are not living up to parent's expectations contributes to some children's unhappiness and results in disinterest or failure.
- Encourage children—and carry it out yourself—to use reference books and materials to increase knowledge. For instance, the family might be planning a picnic at a storage dam. Collect leaflets supplied about it, read and discuss; using reference material go to the different locations about the dam and point them out or have children locate and point them out; look up reference material at home or from the library to find out more about dams. This stimulates children's interest and provides the necessary example of adult learning. A scrap book of the experience could be compiled, using photographs, leaflets, adults' and children's comments. It could be kept as a family record or presented to the school library.
- If children need help with reading, find out from school or teacher how best to do it. Reading with them or listening to them read helps.
- Buy word games and play them with your children. The school may have ideas that can be adapted or reference books to lend you. Simple commercial games, such as Picture, Pairing and Sound Lottos, Dominoes Sequence Cards, Crosswords, Bingo cards for specific skills, Rummy games, Scrabble, Spelling Phun, can be bought and played with children. Using their sight vocabulary words or phonic elements, Bingo boards can be made.
- In brief—enjoy an active interest in your children, their reading and other school activities; work with, rather than for or against them, in reading activities; and set a good example so they can see the relevance, excitement and importance of literacy in their lives.

76. Computer Literacy, Part II: Classroom Applications

Holly O'Donnell

The mention of computers in the classroom can invoke a myriad of images. Some might remember Hal from "2001: A Space Odyssey." Others might envision a monolithic structure with blinking lights. To others, the computer might be a typewriter with a visual display.

In fact, the first general-purpose electronic digital computer . . . became operational in 1945 and filled a very large room. With the introduction of microcomputers in the 1970s, however, computer size diminished to the extent that some became portable. Today computers are small and affordable—as evidenced by their growing use in the classroom.

John Hinton [ED 196 409] notes that "although [computers'] first use in school has frequently been to do extensive computations, they are capable of much more. They can draw pictures and make music. They can drill in rote memorization, tutor in all subjects, or simulate in areas too costly or too dangerous to experience in real life. And they can store, sort, and retrieve large amounts of data with ease, speed, and accuracy."

With this array of capabilities, one might suspect the teacher would no longer be needed. In addressing this question, the Florida State Department of Education [ED 190 120] responded: "It does seem apparent that, as computerized methods and materials become more effective and useful, proper planning could allow teachers' roles to shift gradually from delivering information to those of managing the instructional process. Teachers could have more time for guiding individual progress, while computerized resources perform time-consuming drill and record-keeping activities."

Schools can choose between two types of computer systems. With the *time-sharing system* several users harness the power of a larger system. An example is the PLATO system developed by the Control Data Corporation. An alternative is a *standalone microcomputer system* that is entirely self-contained with both an input/output terminal and a small processor in the same physical location [Florida State Department of Education, ED 190 120].

For instructional purposes, many schools use a combination of the two: a time-sharing standalone microcomputer that can act as a temporary terminal to a time-sharing system, until the user receives a desired program, then breaks the communication link with the main computer and runs the program as a self-contained unit [Florida State Department of Education, ED 190 120].

Regardless of system, the computer's instructional possibilities are many. This article will distinguish between computer assisted instruction (CAI) and computer managed instruction (CMI), and relate some of their applications to reading.

Computer Assisted Instruction

Don Grimes [ED 161 433] defines CAI as a process in which the learner interacts directly with lessons that are displayed on a cathode ray tube or are printed out by a terminal. According to James vonFeldt [ED 160 044], CAI is most often used for drill and practice, tutorials, dialogue, and simulations and games. Generally, CAI is pro-

From Holly O'Donnell, Computer literacy, part II: Classroom applications, *The Reading Teacher*, February 1982, 35, 614–617. Reprinted by permission of Holly O'Donnell and the International Reading Association.

grammed instruction; the student receives a stimulus and responds at his/her own rate.

The responses are made with a keyset resembling a typewriter. George Mason and Jay Blanchard [ED 173 771] write, "The students type in the letters A, B, C, D, or E to indicate their choices for multiple choice questions or they type in Yes, No, True, False, or missing terms in incomplete statements . . . Even younger children can respond to the touch-sensitive panel which may be attached to PLATO terminals."

According to research cited by Don Grimes [ED 161 433], drill and practice programs in elementary reading and mathematics showed good results.

In a pilot project using CAI at Bath Elementary School (Ohio), students gained an average of 2.4 months in reading proficiency during the months they used the computer. Most of these users became faster, more careful readers, possibly because the computer prints as though a person were typing the materials, thus the video terminal trained several slow readers to read faster. All 100 sixth grade students used the computer daily either for remediation or enrichment. After the teacher selected the appropriate program, the student worked on the terminal for 20 minutes each day until the program was completed. The terminals were also available for the students and their parents after school hours four nights a week. According to the sixth grade teacher, "The terminals' best asset was the immediate feedback that prevented the students from practicing a mistaken method of operation . . ." [ED 195 245].

CAI in beginning reading was developed over 12 years at Stanford University [Fletcher ED 155 634]. It included exercises on letter identification, sight-word vocabulary, spelling patterns, phonics, word comprehension, and sentence comprehension. The developers observed that (1) curriculum development became less theory driven and more pragmatic, especially in decoding instruction; (2) the use of games, stories, and other motivational materials decreased; (3) literal and interpretive comprehension instruction can be presented at the fourth-grade through sixth-grade reading curriculum; (4) it was simpler to schedule CAI in a central location for all members of a classroom at one time than to present CAI to one student at a time; (5) beginning reading achievement was about the same for boys and girls under CAI.

If used properly, computer assisted instruction seems to have a positive influence upon student achievement. Other positive attributes, according to James vonFeldt [ED 160 044], include its ability to interest students of all ages, the feedback of the information provided by the computer that can be applied not only to the learning process but also to the teaching process, and the fact that CAI lessons can be modified easily for other applications.

Computer Managed Instruction

Moursand (1980) defines computer managed instruction (CMI) as the use of the computer as a record keeper, diagnostic tester, test scorer, and prescriber of what to study next. The report on instructional computing developed by the Florida State Department of Education [ED 190 120] describes a typical CMI system as "one in which students take tests on machine readable sheets, and the sheets are scored through a machine. The results are then processed and summarized by a computing system. The summary may include a diagnosis of problems and prescriptions for further study."

A CMI system for reading developed by the Belvedere-Parkway Elementary School in Calgary contains 329 behavioral objectives ranging from kindergarten to eighth grade levels, with testing performed online [Brebner et al., ED 198 793].

When the student's name is entered, the system accesses the appropriate record on the student file and prints out the number of the test booklet that the student should complete. The student then reads the multiple choice questions from the booklet and types the answers on the keyboard. The program scores these replies and stores the results for further analysis. Testing continues for 20 minutes, until a choice is made not to proceed further, or until the approximate working level of the student is reached (the last correct response beyond which the student gives five successive incorrect answers). The student summary report may then be obtained. It lists the objectives mastered, those needing review, and those that are wrong. The summaries provide useful teacher-student conference material. A class summary groups the students by objective into three sets—students who know the objectives listed, students who need to review the objectives, and students who need to learn the objectives. The class summary also lists a variety of prescriptions for each of the student sets. After five years of experience, the school found that CMI led to individualization, which in turn led to better reading achievement and improved attitudes toward learning.

Both CAI and CMI can enhance teaching and learning. The report by the Florida State Department of Education [ED 190 120] identifies several special-needs populations who without instructional computing may never receive the attention they deserve: students requiring remediation in basic skills, students with learning disabilities, students in low population courses, accelerated learners, and transfer students. Applications of CMI and CAI offer logical solutions to problems these

and other student populations bring to school.

As computers become more readily affordable and as more instructional programs are developed and refined, schools will have the opportunity to experiment with CAI and CMI thereby increasing our understanding of the computer's potential as well as its limits.

References

Bath Elementary School. *Results of Computer Assisted Instruction at Bath Elementary School*. Cleveland, Ohio: Martha Holden Jennings Foundation, 1979. 26 pp. [ED 195 245].

Brebner, Ann, and others. *Teaching Elementary Reading by CMI and CAI*. 1980. 23 pp. [ED 198 793]

Fletcher, J. D. *Computer-Assisted Instruction in Beginning Reading: The Stanford Projects*. Pittsburgh, Pa.: Pittsburgh University, Learning Research and Development Center, 1976. 65 pp. [ED 155 634]

Florida State Department of Education. *More Hands for Teachers. Report of the Commissioner's Advisory Committee on Instructional Computing*. Tallahassee, Fla.: Florida State Department of Education, 1980. 39 pp. [ED 190 120]

Grimes, Don Marston. *Computers for Learning: The Uses of Computer-Assisted Instruction (CAI) in California Public Schools*. Sacramento, Calif.: California State Department of Education, 1977. 15 pp. [ED 161 433]

Hinton, John R. *Individualized Learning Using Microcomputer CAI*. Aptos, Calif.: Cabrillo College, 1980. 26 pp. [ED 196 409]

Mason, George E., and Jay S. Blanchard. *Computer Applications in Reading*. Newark, Del.: International Reading Association, 1979. 115 pp. [ED 173 771]

vonFeldt, James R. *An Introduction to Computer Applications in Support of Education*. Rochester, N.Y.: National Technical Institute for the Deaf, 1977. 12 pp. [ED 160 044]

CHAPTER XIV

Teaching Reading to Children with Special Needs

This final chapter provides an introduction to the special needs in reading of three groups of children; those with reading disabilities, those whose progress in reading is poor because of linguistic and/or cultural differences, and those with a very special intellectual potential.

Harris explains the diagnosis of reading disabilities as the process of finding answers to the questions: who, what, where, how, and why? Frostig describes some special corrective teaching methods that can be used in the regular classroom. Harris then surveys recent developments in remedial reading, including medical and psychological as well as educational treatments.

Masland calls attention to the ways in which language and cultural differences can interfere with word recognition and comprehension, using samples of oral reading of black and Hispanic children to show the importance of distinguishing between true reading errors and dialect renditions. Lamb analyzes alternative ways of dealing with nonstandard dialects in the classroom. Gonzales explains how one can assess a child's level of English competence and the structural level of the reading material, as a basis for lesson planning for children to whom English is a second language. In the final selection, Trezise calls attention to three ways in which intellectually gifted children can be helped to become critical and creative readers.

77. The Diagnosis of Reading Disabilities

Albert J. Harris

Sometimes names that we use to label certain things or objects or events are very impressive, but when we look more carefully into the meaning we find that the label does not really tell us any more than a much simpler term would convey. Medical specialists, for example, have devised quite a number of special terms to describe difficulties in learning to read. For example, the term *alexia* simply means inability to read. This can be subdivided into *acquired alexia* (loss of ability to read as a

From Albert J. Harris, The diagnosis of reading disabilities. In *Corrective and remedial reading: A report of the sixteenth annual conference and course on reading*. Pittsburgh: School of Education, University of Pittsburgh, 1960, Pp. 31–37. Reprinted by permission of the author and Harry Sartain.

result of damage to the brain), *congenital alexia* (the person has never been able to read), or *developmental alexia* (the person has not developed any reading ability). Another favorite medical term is *dyslexia*, which simply means *that there is something wrong with the person's reading*. The term *strephosymbolia* simply means twisted symbols, or in other words, the individual has a reversal tendency.

The term *diagnosis* also seems formidable to some teachers. It is derived from Greek roots which mean "to know through" or "to know thoroughly." Taking this word out of the medical setting and applying it educationally, it refers to what is really a straightforward process. When we are diagnosing a difficulty, what we want to do is to find out what is wrong, what caused it, and what can be done for it. That is what diagnosis means as applied to reading disability.

Continuing the effort to explain diagnosis in plain and simple English, we may regard the diagnostic process as one that consists of asking five kinds of questions. These questions are summarized by the well-known little words: who, what, where, how, and why.

The first of these, *who*, means: who are the children who need special help? All children whose reading seems to be significantly below grade level need some special attention. Within this large group, usually consisting of one-quarter to one-third of all the children, we have to make some differentiations. We need to distinguish, first of all, between those whose reading problem is just one aspect of generally slow mental development and those who have the potentiality of making considerable improvement. The generally slow child, who is usually reading close to his mental ability level and sometimes manages to read somewhat above it, does not need a remedial program, but rather a total curriculum which is adapted to his limited learning abilities. He needs to be recognized and appreciated for doing the best that he can, and relieved of the pressure of trying desperately and vainly to come up to the normal group. The other children, who are below both the standards for age and grade and their general level of intellectual functioning, are children with reading disabilities, ranging from slight to severe.

Children who have slight to moderate reading disabilities are generally able to be helped considerably by the classroom teacher, working with them either in groups and helping them in the areas of their greatest difficulty, or providing them with some highly individualized help in the general classroom setting. The remainder, the severely disabled readers, need a much more careful diagnostic study and need to be given remedial help individually or in quite small groups, and usually outside of the classroom setting.

The task of estimating the mental ability of a retarded reader is not an easy one to solve. In the primary grades, the group intelligence tests in common use do not require any reading, and therefore are less likely to underestimate seriously the intelligence of a poor reader than the tests used above the third grade. The majority of the group intelligence tests now in use in schools at the fourth-grade level and above present most of their questions in printed form, so that the child who cannot read the question is automatically low. For this reason, group intelligence test results must be interpreted with caution when trying to establish the mental ability of a poor reader. Individual testing by a trained psychologist is generally much more accurate in indicating what the child is able to do.

Assuming that one has a dependable measure of the child's mental age or level of mental development, it is simple to determine his average level of reading performance, express it in terms of an age score, and compare it with his mental age. If the mental age is significantly higher, there is a disability, and the greater the discrepancy, the more serious the disability.

The second question, *what*, asks: at what level can the child read? In answering this question, we find that teachers and school administrators tend to place too much reliance on the scores obtained from standardized reading tests. While average and good readers tend to get most of their scores on such tests by actually reading and answering the questions, the scores of poor readers are often based largely on guess-work and so they frequently overestimate the level at which the child can really read. Standardized reading tests are very good instruments for comparing groups and for measuring rate of progress of groups. They are somewhat less satisfactory as measures of the status or progress of an individual child.

Increasing emphasis has been given in the past few years to the actual tryout of a child in a book to see if the book fits him. Usually we try to distinguish between the instructional level, at which the child can read fairly well when given instructional assistance of the usual sort, and the independent level, at which he can read for pleasure and without any assistance. Determining these levels for the disabled reader is extremely important, since we find over and over again that one of the reasons that certain children do not improve is that the materials with which they are being taught are just too hard for them.

With disabled readers, it is unsafe to rely on silent reading alone. It is necessary to listen to the child's unrehearsed oral reading in material of varying levels of difficulty, and to test his sight vocabulary and word analysis skills.

The next question, *where*, is an inquiry into the specific reading skill or skills that are central to the child's difficulties with reading. For example, let us assume that a sixth-grade child scores at fourth-grade level in a standardized silent reading test. Presumably his reading comprehension is quite inferior. But if we test his word rec-

ognition skills, we find that they are even more limited, since he has a small sight vocabulary and cannot read many words of greater than second-grade difficulty. Under these conditions, it seems evident that the word recognition problem is more central than the comprehension problem, or, in other words, he cannot understand the material primarily because there are too many words that he cannot recognize. The special help that he would need would have to concentrate more on word recognition skills than on comprehension. Similarly, many children who are very slow readers are slow readers because they have to hesitate and pause to puzzle out words, and again the central difficulty would not be the rate problem but rather a word recognition problem.

The next question, *how*, signifies: how does the child proceed in reading? What is he trying to do? What goes on in his mind? Here we can ask a number of questions, all of which are highly significant.

First, how does he attack words? Does he read only the words that he knows and wait to be told the others, or does he make some effort to figure them out? If so, does he try to sound words letter by letter, or by phonograms, or does he try spelling the word, or some other technique? In order to be able to answer these questions it is helpful to try the child on words presented individually rather than in continuous material, because some children have become such expert guessers that many of their shortcomings in word recognition pass unnoticed when they are allowed to guess from context. Furthermore, it is very helpful, when the child does not recognize the word immediately, to ask him to do his thinking out loud so that you can find out what he is trying to do and why it works or doesn't work. This is perhaps the most helpful single technique in reading diagnosis that I know. Sometimes more can be learned by listening to a child as he tries to figure out two or three words than can be gained from hours of other kinds of testing in terms of providing insight and understanding about the child's difficulties.

A second question is, how does the child approach the reading material? With what intentions, expectations, or mental set? Is he reading to try to find out something, or is he just trying to say the words? In oral reading is he reading to himself out loud, or is he trying to read with expression so as to communicate to others?

A third area of inquiry is, how does the child feel about reading? Many children who have difficulties in reading approach printed material with fear and trepidation. They may anticipate that they will make many mistakes and that somebody will laugh at them. They assume it is going to be difficult and frustrating. If this is true about a child, then obviously helping him to change these feelings to more constructive ones would have to become a major objective in trying to help him. Answers to this kind of question are sometimes not easy to obtain, but once the child trusts you he will very frequently be able to tell you frankly just how he does feel about reading.

A fourth area of inquiry is, how does the child respond to instructional help? Does he seem indifferent, resistive, passively accepting, or gratefully enthusiastic? If he is already enthusiastic, perhaps one can concentrate on *what* to teach him; but if he displays very little responsiveness, perhaps major attention will have to be given to motivation for a considerable length of time, and skills development may have to be kept at a minor level of importance. It is desirable to inquire not only into his response to instruction in general, but whether he responds differently to different kinds of activities or different kinds of material. Sometimes finding a book that appeals greatly to a child's special interest may provide a magic key to getting him started. Sometimes a child who is a slow learner with one method of instruction may respond ever so much faster to a different method.

Experimental tryout of a variety of materials and a variety of teaching approaches may play a very important and practical part in the total diagnostic program.

The final question, *why*, is an attempt to get to the heart of causation. The causation of reading difficulties is very complex and frequently there are more causal handicaps for a particular child than we need in order to account for the difficulties that he is experiencing. Sometimes even in an intensive study by a group of specialists in a clinic it is difficult to do more than conjecture as to what the causes really were when the difficulty started several years ago. Nevertheless, the effort to find out what causal handicaps have interfered with the child's learning is very worthwhile, and even if we do not find full and complete answers, we often discover contributing factors or handicaps about which something can be done.

It would be a mistake to assume that it is always necessary to understand the causes in order to help the condition. From a practical standpoint, it is useful to make a diagnostic distinction only when there is a difference in treatment involved. For example, if there are half a dozen kinds of organisms that can cause a sore throat and they can all be treated with the same antibiotic, a sensible physician does not bother to make laboratory tests to decide which particular organism is the cause this time. Instead, he prescribes the antibiotic and the sore throat gets cured. On the other hand, if there is an abdominal pain and he does not know whether it is a digestive disturbance or an inflamed appendix, it is very important for him to make a diagnostic differentiation because the treatment of these conditions has to be so different.

In reading diagnosis, the first differentiation that has to be made is between those children whose problems are specific to reading and those who are generally slow. In this way we narrow our range of special inquiry to those children who can really profit from special attention. We look through the accumulated school records for any information that they can throw on how long he has had trouble in reading, what previous teachers have recorded about him, recorded intelligence and achievement test results, attendance, physical factors, conduct and personality rating, and so on. A talk with his mother is desirable. This search may or may not cast light upon the causation. We should then proceed to a straightforward analysis of his reading problems, leading to the formulation of a teaching plan. If the parents are cooperative and interested, it may be helpful to suggest that the possibility of a significant visual or other physical defect be checked by comprehensive private examinations.

At this point it is proper to proceed with a remedial program, even though several areas of causation have not been explored at all deeply. If the child responds well to remedial help, it is an academic question whether or not we ever get answers to those questions. If after a reasonable period of tryout the child is making very disappointing progress, it is wise to try to get additional diagnosis in those areas that have not previously been covered. For example, it may be desirable to find out, through referral to a psychologist, psychiatrist, or mental hygiene clinic, whether the child's emotional problems are such that he cannot at present profit from remedial instruction. Proceeding one step at a time, in this way, we are able to avoid wasting our precious resources of psychological and psychiatric examinations, which are usually limited in availability, and use them for those cases that really need them, rather than giving every child a thorough diagnostic study.

In summary, diagnosis is nothing more than the application of a straightforward, common sense, problem-solving approach to the study of children who have difficulties in reading. We try to find out what is wrong, what caused the difficulty, and what can be done for it. We do it by intelligent use of our common question words—who, what, where, how, and why? We first single out those children who require special attention to their reading, and then we try to find out the level at which they can profitably be taught, specific reading skills that need to be tackled first, the incorrect procedures that the child is using so that we can correct them, and, finally, we try within the limitations of the study procedures available to us to find the causes of the child's poor reading and what handicaps may still be preventing him from effective learning.

78. Corrective Reading in the Classroom

Marianne Frostig

Three major approaches to the teaching of reading may be distinguished, principally on the basis of the materials commonly used. With the so-called basic approach the teacher uses the familiar basic readers, and the children are usually grouped according to reading achievement. During the reading lesson the children are told about the material they will read, and new words are introduced before they read. The individualized reading approach permits each child to make his own selection from a great variety of books, magazines, and pamphlets. The teacher gives assist-

From Marianne Frostig, Corrective reading in the classroom. *The Reading Teacher*, April 1965, *18*, 573–580. Reprinted by permission of Marianne Frostig and the International Reading Association.

ance as needed. Each of these approaches has advantages and disadvantages for a total communication program. The language experience approach meets many of the disadvantages of the other two since in this approach the reading material is mainly composed by the children themselves. They tell their experiences in class and the teacher writes them down for later reading.

All of these approaches to the teaching of reading are valuable and each supplements the others. They are the three major lines of approach, and none can be neglected. Nevertheless, in teaching reading to children who have learning difficulties, whether the cause is emotional disturbance, brain damage or a developmental language disorder, it is necessary to modify and augment these approaches. This paper is devoted to an account of a variety of ancillary methods which should be used to supplement these approaches when teaching children with learning difficulties. But I should like to state most emphatically that these additional techniques can be used very effectively in the regular classroom as well as with exceptional children. They can speed up the process of learning to read for all children and help eliminate nagging difficulties that might impede even a relatively proficient learner.

Labeling

During World War I, Kurt Goldstein developed methods to rehabilitate soldiers who had suffered brain damage because of gunshot or shrapnel wounds. He found that some of those who had lost their reading ability were unable to regain the skill when taught by the regular methods because the symbolic functions of their brains had been impaired. Reading involves a double symbolic process, for not only are the spoken words symbols, representing real things or events (the word *chair* stands for a real chair, *house* for

a real house, *running* for a certain type of locomotion), but the printed words are symbols also, standing for the combination of sounds that make up the words.

To help soldiers whose ability to master symbols had been impaired by cerebral dysfunction, Goldstein introduced a method of matching words to pictures. Kindergarten teachers now often use a similar method by putting labels on objects or pictures in the room. When a child first sees the configuration of the word *chair*, it is meaningless to him, but when he sees it paired with either a real or pictured chair he can understand what it means. The child at this stage is only labeling, however; he cannot be said to be reading until he is able to recognize and understand the word alone, unsupported by the object or picture.

In teaching children with reading difficulties by this method, we usually start with just two words. The two words, cut out from an old workbook, and their matching pictures are put in an envelope fastened to the back of a page, ready to be matched with either the word or pictures pasted on the front of the page. When the child can match the words and pictures well, the identical two words are used again on the next page, but with a new word added, and this system is maintained. All three words are used on the third page, plus a fourth word. The matching can be repeated indefinitely, since the material to be matched is always available. The child should switch frequently between matching words with pictures and matching pictures with words. The words should be joined in as many ways as possible to form simple phrases or sentences. The words *run* and *Billy* can be written "Run, Billy" or "Billy, run," or "Billy, Billy run!" for instance.

This method is, of course, limited by the fact that only words for concrete objects or depictable actions can be matched with pictures. Conjunctions and other parts of speech which exist for the purpose of organizing language cannot be illustrated. Such words as *the, to*, and *and* have to be added gradually to the illustrated words so as to make phrases and sentences. These words have to be learned by repetition, but only in the context of phrases or sentences in which their function is clear.

The labeling method has been found of particular value in teaching children suffering from specific dyslexia or more pervasive defects, such as mental retardation, who fail to learn by any other method. The process requires careful use and preparation by the teacher, but usually need not be maintained for an extended period. When the child has learned to match from nine to twelve words, he will very likely indicate that he has developed the ability to visualize words and will no longer need the help of pictures.

The Highly Controlled Vocabulary

All books designed for children just learning to read employ a vocabulary which is controlled to some degree, with new words being introduced slowly and with frequent repetition. But in teaching children who have learning difficulties, this process needs to be intensified. In preparing such children for reading a preprimer, for instance, it is advisable for the teacher to first compile original books for them, using the same vocabulary that is used in the preprimer. The teacher thus has control over the pace at which vocabulary is accumulated and can eventually provide each child with encouraging success when he tackles the printed book.

The teacher should write in the right upper corner of each page of each child's book the words that the child has learned in the order of their original presentation. In the middle of the page the same words are presented in story form. As soon as the child knows a few words, this presentation is made in as lengthy units as possible—phrases, sentences, and finally

paragraphs—rather than in the individual words or two-word phrases which necessarily characterize learning by the matching method. Emphasizing larger word units avoids chopped and relatively meaningless learning, which lessens interest and fails to instill a feeling for the structure of language.

One or two new words should be introduced daily, and repeated daily for a sufficient period of time to insure overlearning. The list of words in the upper corner constitutes a record of the sequence. If a word is missed, the teacher can go back to the page on which this word was first introduced and review the succeeding pages. When necessary, a page is prepared without new vocabulary for the purpose of review. It is helpful to give the children familiarity with reading different kinds of print by composing the reading matter in the book from words cut from old textbooks, newspapers, and magazines, as well as from words written by hand in both articulated and cursive writing. Illustrations can be gathered similarly from a variety of sources or can be made by the children themselves.

Proper names which occur at this stage in most preprimers are best omitted, because they are not common vocabulary and because it is best to teach the children to think in a less specific way at first than by reading stories about a single family. The appropriate proper names can be introduced when the rest of the vocabulary has been learned and the child is about to read the book itself. When the child has learned to read one book in this way, he should learn to read others in a different series at a similar level before progressing to the vocabulary and stories of the next level.

Other commercially available books may be used in addition to primers and preprimers in such a way as to insure sufficient repetition of each word. For instance, the series called Easy Readers, published by Wonder Books, New York, has a highly controlled vocabulary and a great deal of repetition, but as with all commercial books, some words are repeated as many as thirty times and other words only a few times. Before giving these books to the children, therefore, all words which are likely to cause difficulty should be written on flash cards and learned beforehand. Words which are missed by the child in reading the book should also be written on flash cards or listed on a chart and taken home by the child for review.

The Easy Readers may also be used to develop other reading skills. A list of printed questions concerning the text can be prepared, glued to cardboard, and inserted in a pocket on the last page of the book. These questions help the child in developing certain areas of reading comprehension or reading skills, such as finding a certain bit of information on a particular page, finding the main idea of the story, finding a word which rhymes with a given word, and so on.

Teaching reading by the use of a highly controlled vocabulary can be adapted to work with both the usual basic readers and individualized reading programs. Insuring adequate mastery of the vocabulary beforehand greatly enhances the probability that the child will enjoy what he reads and will acquire increased motivation.

The Child's Own Book

A third auxiliary method consists of constructing a book based on each child's own experiences and using it according to the principles of the language experience approach, in which reading, writing, and oral language are integrated. The fact that the child's own experiences constitute the subject matter does much to assure his interest and cooperation.

The child is presented with a booklet made from newsprint stapled between sheets of construction paper, and he is told that the teacher is going to help him to make his own book. The teacher will necessarily have to steer the child closely to make sure that the vocabulary is appropriate to the child's level and is augmented sufficiently slowly. On the first page is pasted a photograph of the child, or a picture of any boy or girl, and the name of the child is written beneath it. Then one or two more words may be added so that a simple sentence can be written: for example, "I am Billy," or "See Billy." In writing the next page, the child can be asked what he saw recently that interested him, and the sentence constructed accordingly. It might read, "Billy, Billy, see the car," or "I see a dog." The incident to which this new word, *car* or *dog*, refers is discussed, and the simple sentence may have all the qualities of a real adventure for the child.

I recall how successful this method was with Jim, a little boy from Alaska who had been sent to us because he had not been able to learn to read. He was at first very homesick for Alaska. His teacher talked with him about what he liked best there, and he told how he went out in a boat to fish with his father. For the first page of Jim's book, the teacher put a picture of a father standing by a boat, and the words were, "Jim, see the boat." Jim and his teacher talked about the construction of the boat, how it would be launched, and so on. For the second page, the teacher wrote under a picture of a father beckoning his son: "Jim, ride in the boat. See the boat, Jim. Jim, ride in the boat. See, Jim, see! See the boat." Jim told how the first time he went out in the boat he was so excited that he could not sit still and his father told him not to jump in the boat. So his third page read: "Jim, ride in the boat. See Jim ride. See Jim jump. Jim, Jim, jump not in the boat. Jump not in the boat, Jim." In the upper right corner of the first page the words used were written: *See, Jim, the, boat*. On the second page, the words used were written in the same order in the right hand corner: *see, Jim, the, boat, ride, in*. The words on the third page were: *see, Jim, the, boat, ride, in, jump, not*.

In this way the story was developed, and the entire preprimer vocabulary introduced with sufficient repetition. For the adult the story may seem somewhat inane, but for the child it represented a series of most pleasurable experiences.

Besides learning to read the words, the child should be taught to write them as soon as possible, and he should be encouraged to read his book to other children and discuss with them the contents of his book and theirs.

The Child's Own Book method need not be restricted to young children. It was found to be equally effective for teaching a group of nonreading adolescent girls between thirteen and seventeen years of age in a camp for juvenile delinquents near Los Angeles. These youngsters had not even mastered the preprimer vocabulary, and an attempt to teach them from a printed book would have evoked only a scornful refusal to work. The idea of making books of their own, however, caught their interest. Surprisingly, they did not choose as their subjects the lives of film stars or stories of crime or romance, as might be expected, but cooking, travel, and flowers.[1] When they had learned a basic vocabulary in the manner described above, they were told that they were now equipped to read a preprimer. They were at first reluctant to try, until it was suggested that they should imagine they were mothers wanting to read a story to their children, or older sisters reading to the younger members of the family. This imaginative touch stimulated them to read aloud in turn from a preprimer, and they were delighted with their accomplishment.

Phonics

The purpose of teaching phonics is to help the child to recognize the association between the phoneme and the grapheme—between the auditory stimulus, the sound, and the printed word or symbol. It is often possible to teach reading without the aid of phonics by using the whole-word method, but in our experience, the latter method is difficult, if not impossible, for children with certain disabilities in visual perception, nor does it give a child a tool with which to attack new words. It seems, therefore, that the whole-word method should be augmented by instruction based on phonics.

Teaching a child to associate the sounds of the language with the written symbols is especially difficult in English, because of the great disparity between many of the spelling and phonetic rules. Even the greatest admirers and promoters of the phonic methods, such as the author of *Why Johnny Can't Read*, cannot claim that more than 80 percent of the words in the English language are phonetically written, and many maintain that the proportion is less. It is even difficult to teach rules of exception, since there are exceptions to the exceptions. For instance, when the letter *i* appears in short syllables, it is pronounced as in the word *bit*, *except* when it appears before the letters *nd*, when it is pronounced with a long sound (as in *kind*), *except* in the word *wind*, referring to air in motion.

For this reason, we place greater emphasis upon a functional approach to phonics than upon a systematic teaching of phonetic rules, but it must be acknowledged that opinion on this question is divided. Sabaroff (5), for instance, found that an experimental group of low achievers made progress with systematic instruction in the rules of phonics.

Color Cues

Our usual method is to associate phonemes with graphemes from the beginning, writing each distinct sound in a word in different color. The first words to be introduced are, of course, phonetically "pure," and it is best to introduce words containing short vowels first, then words with long vowels, and finally more complex sounds, such as diphthongs and digraphs. Where letter groups are pronounced uniformly, as, for example, the combination *ur* in the words *hurt, curtain, turn,* the letters in the group are written in the same color, to help the child learn the pronunciation of that particular combination. Sometimes it is necessary to teach a child to read only the initial letter in a word, at first, then the last letter, and finally the middle letter or letters. In these cases, the appropriate letter only is colored. Colors can also be used to teach syllabification, each syllable of a word being written in one color. Silent letters, such as the *e* in *those,* can be indicated by an appropriately insubstantial stippled effect so that the letter does not stand out from the background. We have not generally found it necessary to use the same color for one sound consistently, except in a few instances in which a child shows a particular difficulty which he can be helped to overcome by receiving a consistent cue, but we have found it useful to use consistently one color for *all* of the long vowels, and one other color for all of the short vowels.[2]

Kinesthetic Methods

The sense modality basic to the reading process is of course vision. Accurate space and form perception are essential. But when a child has disturbances in visual perception, the visual modality can be supported by the auditory even at the beginning of reading (as with the phonic instruction described above) and also by the kinesthetic modality. As kinesthetic activities are largely a matter of tracing, they not only provide training in reading but serve also to further writing and spelling skills.

Kinesthetic methods have other advantages as well. They form a bridge between the experience of an act extended in time, which occurs when we hear, and the experience of an act extended in space,

which occurs when we see. Whenever we say a word or read it aloud, we experience an act which is extended in time. The *v* at the beginning of the word *visual,* for instance, is heard before the *l* at the end of the word. But when we read silently, we usually take the word in at a glance, and all of the letters seem to be perceived at the same time. The word is no longer perceived as extended in time, but as extended in space. It may be that it is just this translation from a spatial dimension to a temporal one, and vice versa, which makes it difficult for a child to associate words which he hears with the printed word. The kinesthetic method helps overcome the problem by forming a bridge between the auditory stimulus and the visual one. When we write or trace a word, it takes *time* to write it; we perceive that a time span elapses while we are writing. We also experience a spatial dimension as we see the word "grow" from left to right on the page. When a word is presented kinesthetically, therefore, it has both a temporal and a spatial dimension, which makes it easier for the child to connect the two experiences of seeing and hearing.

There are many modifications of the kinesthetic method. Pulliam (3) has suggested that children write in grooves, experiencing in this way the movement of the word and learning its kinesthetic pattern. For children with severe motor defects, it is helpful to write in clay or on some similarly resistant surface. Many clinics advocate the Fernald method (2) of first tracing words with the fingers and then writing them.

Blind Writing

The blind writing kinesthetic method deserves a detailed account because of its effectiveness with children whose visual perception is inadequate, as is often the case with children who have minimal brain damage.

Recent research (1, 4) has shown that even in small children the visual experience is stronger than the haptic one. ("Haptic" means the dual experience of touch and kinesthesia, which are combined, for instance, in taking an object in one's hand and feeling it totally while moving a finger over it to experience its shape.) When the children were first shown something which they experienced visually, and then felt the same object without looking at it, their final description of the object was in visual terms rather than in terms of touch. Because of this natural predominance of the visual modality, a child with a severely distorted visual perceptual sense is very seriously handicapped. It is necessary in these cases to train the child's less effective, but at least unimpaired, kinesthetic abilities so that he can perceive accurately by movement, as blind children can do. The kinesthetic modality can then be used to guide the visual one.

To teach the child to write and read by the blind writing method, the teacher first writes the letter or word on the chalkboard at a height which can easily be reached by the child. Then the teacher guides the child's hand while he traces the word with closed eyes. The elimination of visual stimuli enables him to concentrate entirely upon the kinesthetic experience. While the teacher guides the child's hand, she pronounces the word slowly, trying to use as much time for saying the word as the child takes in tracing it. With repetition, the teacher will feel the child's hand begin to follow the lines of the word independently. She can then remove her hand while he continues to trace, without opening his eyes and without her assistance. The next step is to have him make the connection between the kinesthetic and the visual modality by looking at the word as he traces it, and then as he writes it. The child is finally asked to find the word on a page in his book, to read the sentences in which it appears, and then to write it again. The use of cursive writing is a great advantage because of the uninterrupted flow of the kinesthetic pattern the child perceives, even though he has to make the association between the written and printed forms of the word.

Causes of reading difficulties. Difficulties in reading occur not only because of a specific difficulty with the reading process itself. They may be due to disabilities in comprehension or to a lag in any other area of development, such as in perception, motor skills (especially eye movements), language, and social and emotional development. The possible difficulties in any one of these areas are legion. But the corrective methods described above can be used with all children in the regular classroom during corrective reading.

Notes

1. A catalog is often a most helpful source for illustrations. In this instance a Sears Roebuck catalog and a National Park brochure were used.
2. We have not discussed the use of the Augmented Roman Alphabet in teaching reading because we have had no experience with it. It would seem to be a very worthwhile method, however.

References

1. Birch, Herbert G., and Lefford, A. "Intersensory Development in Children," *Society for Research in Child Development Monographs*, vol. 28 (1963).
2. Fernald, Grace M. *Remedial Techniques in Basic School Subjects.* New York: McGraw-Hill, 1943. P. 349.
3. Pulliam, Roy A. "Invented Word Cards as a Sensori-Motor Aid in Vocabulary Development," *Peabody Journal of Education*, 23 (July, 1945), 38–42.
4. Rock, I., and Victor, J. "Vision and Touch: An Experimentally Created Conflict Between the Two Senses," *Science*, 43 (February, 1964), 3606.
5. Sabaroff, Rose. "A Comparative Investigation of Two Methods of Teaching Phonics in a Modern Reading Program: A Pilot Study," *Journal of Experimental Education*, 31 (March, 1963), 249–56.

79. What Is New in Remedial Reading?

Albert J. Harris

This article is a third survey of developments in remedial reading in the U.S. The first, in 1966, surveyed the 50 year period from 1916 to 1965. The second, in 1976, reviewed the decade ending with 1975. The present article takes another look, with particular attention to new developments in treatment.

First, some comments on developments in the field of learning disabilities and their implications for reading specialists. As of September, 1978, new federal regulations setting guidelines for the identification and education of the learning disabled went into effect in the U.S. According to those regulations, diagnostic evaluation requires a multidisciplinary team that must include the child's teacher and one person qualified to give individual diagnostic examinations; that person may be a psychologist, a speech therapist, or a remedial reading teacher. The study must include classroom observation and an individual intelligence test.

The team must file a written report giving the reasons why it does or does not classify the child as learning disabled. The main criterion to be used is evidence of a severe discrepancy between the child's achievement and his/her potential.

The intent is to limit the category of learning disabled to the severely disabled, made up of not more than 2 or 3% of the school population. For each child classified as learning disabled, a detailed individual educational plan has to be prepared, stating shortterm and longterm objectives and specifying who is responsible for what.

Since 1970 there have been many reports of school districts in which the development of learning disability programs was accompanied by cuts in remedial reading services. In some states, the learning disability label was applied indiscriminately to children with a wide variety of problems. The new procedure should lessen those abuses.

Best available estimates place the national incidence of reading disability in shcool children at about 15%. Since only 2 to 3% are classifiable under the new law as learning disabled, most disabled readers remain the responsibility of classroom teachers and reading specialists. However, if reading specialists are to remain available to these children despite budget cuts, the reading specialists must devote time and energy to public relations. This can be a very important activity for local reading councils. If reading specialists do not convince parents and administrators that their services are valuable and necessary, who will?

It is to be hoped that the fields of reading and learning disabilities will grow closer in the future. Each group can learn from the other, to the benefit of the children. Reading specialists should have some background in the psychology and education of exceptional children, in psychological testing, and in behavior modification. Learning disability teachers need much more training than many of them have received in the techniques of remedial teaching. Both groups need to understand each other's professional jargon and role responsibilities. These issues have been discussed in greater detail in recent articles by Harris (1980a, b) and Artley (1980).

From Albert J. Harris, What is new in remedial reading? *The Reading Teacher*, January 1981, 34, 573–580. Reprinted by permission of Albert J. Harris and the International Reading Association.

Medical Therapies

The study of reading and learning disabilities has become a multidisciplinary effort, and several kinds of medical specialists have become involved. In addition to psychiatrists, neurologists, pediatricians, and ophthalmologists, who have been involved for many years, nutritionists and allergists have entered the field. Many of the newer medical ideas about the causation and medical treatment of learning problems are highly controversial.

One new medical theory links reading disability to poor functioning of the mechanisms that control balance and movement—in other words, the cerebellum (a large brain center behind and below the cerebral cortex), and the semicircular canals of the inner ear. De Quiros and Schrager (1978) stated that when automatic reflex control of balance is inadequate, conscious control of balance interferes with concentration in learning situations. Frank and Levinson (1976–77) also reported a high incidence of vestibular disturbance in reading disabilities, which they called "dysmetric dyslexia," and stated that Dramamine and other medications for motion sickness were helpful in such cases. Ayres (1978) developed a sequence of physical exercises to improve the automatic functioning of the vestibular system.

Medical attention has been focused on diet as a cause of hyperactive behavior and learning disorders. The Kaiser-Permanente diet advocated by Feingold (1976) eliminates foods and drinks that contain additives, dye or natural salicylates, thus excluding not only desserts, candy, and soft drinks, but also most breads and cereals, many meats, and many fruits and vegetables. Other physicians have criticized the research on which this treatment is based as inadequate and insufficient (Spring and Sandoval, 1976; Sieben, 1977).

Caffeine in coffee, tea, and cola drinks has been blamed for making children overstimulated (Powers, 1975); but other evidence indicates that caffeine may have a quieting effect on hyperactive children (Firestone, Poitras-Wright and Douglas, 1978). The use of massive doses of certain vitamins, called megavitamin therapy, is a hotly contested medical issue (Cott, 1977; Sieben, 1977). The presence of too much or too little of certain minerals in human tissues may or may not be linked to learning disabilities (Sieben, 1977). Even fluorescent lighting in the classroom is claimed to have a deleterious effect on the behavior of children (Painter, 1976–77). Still another medical controversy involves the idea that learning disability may result from an allergic reaction of the brain, that can be treated with cortisone and similar drugs (Wunderlich, 1973).

These medical controversies are not for the reading specialist to decide. Parents must take the responsibility for choosing their physicians and for following, or not following, their advice.

Psychological Therapies

Individual psychotherapy, group psychotherapy, and family therapy have been with us for many years. Reading specialists recognize that many disabled readers have serious personality problems that require the diagnostic consideration of a psychiatrist or psychologist, and may require some form of psychotherapy. The reading specialist's task is to make appropriate referrals of such cases.

The practice of behavior modification based on Skinnerian principles of learning is not new, but the form of it called *cognitive behavior modification* is quite recent. The general idea is that children's behavior is strongly influenced by what they say to themselves in inner speech, and that one can change behavior by helping them to change this inner dialogue. This involves the use of models for the learner to imitate, and the use of reinforcement or rewards when the desired changes occur. Thus the child who has been saying to herself/himself "It is too hard so I might as well not try" may be helped to verbalize "It is hard, but I can do it if I really try" (Meichenbaum, 1977).

This approach suggests that we have been paying too much attention to the counting of errors and not enough to what goes on in the child's mind when s/he is reading. Without becoming behavior therapists, reading specialists can become more sensitive to a child's thoughts and feelings that influence how s/he behaves in a reading situation.

Suggestopedia is the term used by Lozanov (1975) to describe his system of instruction in which the use of positive suggestion is emphasized. His followers have established a Society for Suggestive-Accelerative Learning and Teaching that has headquarters in Ames, Iowa, and publishes a journal. The system assumes that most individuals have the potential for greatly improved learning and that a combination of positive suggestion and relaxation can release individuals to perform very rapid learning.

A report by Pritchard and Taylor (1978) described the application of suggestopedia in teaching poor readers. Periods of active instruction alternated with passive activities such as lying down, breathing in time to a metronome, listening to suggestions emphasizing the students' worthiness, and encouragement to visualize words on an imaginary "magic drawing board."

An application of suggestopedia in second grade reading instruction involved seven steps: physical relaxation, mind calming, recall of earlier pleasant learning experiences, active presentation, concert review, practice, and test. In the active presentation the children were told to visualize reading as a house in which each apartment represented a vowel, and to visualize the words containing that vowel as items of furniture within the apartment (Somsky, 1980). This is similar to the techniques used by memory experts.

Suggestopedia is a new development in the application of psychological techniques to education, and one worth watching.

Educational Therapies

A number of modifications of the Fernald kinesthetic method of teaching severely disabled readers have been described. One of them is "blind writing," in which the child traces the word with eyes closed and only after s/he is able to trace it correctly does s/he open the eyes and start to associate the visual form with its auditory and kinesthetic representations. Three-dimensional letters may be used, or the child's hand may be guided through the tracing. This procedure is said to work with neurologically immature or damaged children who need a reduction in the total amount of sensory stimulation they must handle (Blau and Blau, 1968).

Zorotovich (1979) conjectured that one boy who seemed unable to learn words by the Fernald VAKT procedure might have a functional gap preventing cooperative action of the two cerebral hemispheres, with symptoms comparable to those of the cases reported by Sperry, Gazzaniga and Bogen (1969) in which the two hemispheres were surgically separated. The child seemed unable to learn the word shape by tracing with the dominant hand. Fernald tried having him trace with the nondominant hand, which was easy for him, but his coordination with that hand was insufficient for writing the word. Simultaneous tracing with the nondominant hand, writing with the dominant hand, and saying the word was found to work. This is a report of only one case, but there may be many others like him. Zorotovich wrote that she thought her procedure had promoted the integration of the two hemispheres.

A procedure described by van den Honert (1977) is based on the notion that poor progress may be due to interference by the nondominant hemisphere with the reading process controlled by the dominant hemisphere. She used stereophonic earphones with recorded reading instruction going through the right ear to the left (dominant) hemisphere, while the right hemisphere was kept busy with recorded music fed to the left ear. She also attempted to eliminate conflict between the right and left visual centers by blocking out the vision of the right eye (p. 23). She found a dramatic increase in rate of learning for seventh graders, but not for ninth graders. She also said that both the auditory and the visual blocking were required for good results.

The so-called "neurological impress" method (Heckelman, 1966) involves having the teacher and pupil read a selection together almost simultaneously. At first the teacher's voice is slightly in the lead, providing cues for the child; gradually the child takes over. Word recognition is said to develop painlessly through the repeated prompting provided by the teacher. This kind of procedure has been recommended by Carol Chomsky (1978) for use with children who have become resistive to decoding drills. It is probably more useful as a supplementary procedure than as a complete remedial method. Hollingsworth (1978) has recently reported favorable results with the impress method, using recorded selections listened to through earphones.

Samuels (1979) has advocated the method of repeated readings as a way to improve fluency and make word recognition increasingly automatic. The child reads a selection of 50 to 200 words orally, and rate and number of errors are charted on a graph. He rereads the material to himself while the teacher is checking other children, and then reads the same selection to the teacher, who enters the new time and errors on the graph. This is continued until a rate of 85 words per minute is achieved; then the child moves on to another selection. With successive selections, most children start with more speed and fewer errors. A read-along procedure can be combined with the repeated readings.

Meares (1978), a remedial teacher in New Zealand, reported that some of her least successful remedial readers seemed to have a special kind of difficulty in perception of print. When she asked them what the page looked like, they seemed to be seeing a figure-ground reversal; instead of seeing black letters against a white background, the white seemed to be the foreground against a black background, looking like white rivers or dams. She said that such children seemed to be aided by reduced contrast between print and background, minimal space between words and lines, and small size print; thus they seemed to be helped by the opposite of what makes for better legibility for most readers.

The innovations described above are small-scale explorations that have not yet been followed up by controlled research. It is important for remedial teachers to know about them and be prepared to try them with pupils who seem unable to learn from conventional remedial procedures.

There are certain basic principles of successful remedial reading instruction that have not changed in the past 50 years. They include the following:

1. The vital importance of beginning at a low enough level, and with small enough steps, to insure initial success.
2. The development of a pleasant rapport between teacher and each pupil.
3. The need for flexibility in choosing both method and materials, paying attention to the child's feelings as well as aptitudes.
4. Particularly early in the remedial program, taking very small steps with ample review and repetition.
5. Using materials that combine high interest appeal with low difficulty.
6. Using progress charts to record progress toward important objectives.
7. Keeping lines of communication open with the child's classroom teacher and parents.

8. Celebrating the child's successes and arranging for praise and support from other significant adults and children.

9. Keeping in mind the need for application in connected reading of skills that may need some development in isolation.

10. Maintaining the child in the remedial program until s/he has acquired sufficient skill to carry on in the regular homeroom reading program, and has started the habit of reading on his/her own.

These 10 principles are basic, and are independent of the particular procedures for teaching decoding and comprehension that are used. They are common to programs that look superficially to be quite different, yet may be alike in basic characteristics. The reading specialist who combines flexibility and resourcefulness with unlimited patience will achieve successful results with most disabled readers.

References

Artley, A. Sterl. "Learning Disabilities Versus Reading Disabilities: A Vexing Problem." In *Inchworm, Inchworm: Persistent Problems in Reading Education*, edited by Constance M. McCullough, pp. 119–24. Newark, Del.: International Reading Association, 1980.

Ayres, A. Jean. "Learning Disabilities and the Vestibular System." *Journal of Learning Disabilities*, vol. 10 (January 1978), pp. 30–41.

Blau, Harold, and Harriet Blau. "A Theory of Learning to Read." *The Reading Teacher*, vol. 22 (November 1968), pp. 126–29, 144.

Chomsky, Carol. "When You Still Can't Read in Third Grade: After Decoding, What?" In *What Research Has to Say about Reading Instruction*, edited by S. Jay Samuels, pp. 13–30. Newark, Del.: International Reading Association, 1978.

Cott, Allan. "A Reply." *Academic Therapy*, vol. 13 (November 1977), pp. 161–71.

de Quiros, Julio B., and Orlando L. Schrager. *Neuropsychological Fundamentals in Learning Disabilities*. San Rafael, Calif.: Academic Therapy Publications, 1978.

Feingold, Benjamin F. "Hyperkinesis and Learning Disabilities Linked to the Ingestion of Artificial Food Colors and Flavors." *Journal of Learning Disablities*, vol. 9 (November 1976), pp. 551–59.

Firestone, Philip, Helene Poitras-Wright, and Virginia Douglas. "The Effects of Caffeine on Hyperactive Children." *Journal of Learning Disabilities*, vol. 10 (March 1978), pp. 133–41.

Frank, Jan, and Harold N. Levinson. "Seasickness Mechanisms and Medications in Dysmetric Dyslexia and Dyspraxia." *Academic Therapy*, vol. 12 (Winter 1976–1977), pp. 133–53.

Harris, Albert J. "Current Issues in the Diagnosis and Treatment of Reading Disabilities." In *Inchworm, Inchworm: Persistent Problems in Reading Education*, edited by Constance M. McCullough, pp. 111–18. Newark, Del.: International Reading Association, 1980a.

Harris, Albert J. "Five Decades of Remedial Reading." In *Forging Ahead in Reading*, edited by J. Allen Figurel, pp. 25–33. Newark, Del.: International Reading Association, 1968.

Harris, Albert J. "An Overview of Reading Disabilities and Learning Disabilities in the U.S." *The Reading Teacher*, vol. 33 (January 1980b), pp. 420–25.

Harris, Albert J. "Ten Years of Progress in Remedial Reading." *The Reading Teacher*, vol. 31 (October 1977), pp. 29–35.

Heckelman, R. G. "Using the Neurological Impress Remedial Technique." *Academic Therapy Quarterly*, vol. 1 (1966), pp. 235–39.

Hollingsworth, Paul M. "An Experimental Approach to the Impress Method of Teaching Reading." *The Reading Teacher*, vol. 31 (March 1978), pp. 624–26.

Lozanov, Georgi. "The Suggestological Theory of Communicating and Instructing." *Suggestology and Suggestopedia*, vol. 1, no. 1 (1975), pp. 1–14.

Meares, Olive. "Some Children Talk about Print." Mimeographed. Auckland, New Zealand: North Shore Reading Clinic, 1978.

Meichenbaum, Donald. *Cognitive-Behavior Modification: An Integrative Approach*. New York, N.Y.: Plenum Press, 1977.

Painter, Marilyn. "Fluorescent Lights and Hyperactivity in Children." *Academic Ther-*

apy, vol. 12, no. 2 (Winter 1976–1977), pp. 181–84.

Powers, Hugh W. S., Jr. "Caffeine, Behavior, and the LD Child." *Academic Therapy*, vol. 11 (Fall 1975), pp. 5–19.

Pritchard, Allan, and Jean Taylor. "Suggestopedia for the Disadvantaged Reader." *Academic Therapy*, vol. 14 (September 1978), pp. 81–90.

Samuels, S. Jay. "The Method of Repeated Readings." *The Reading Teacher*, vol. 32 (January 1979), pp. 403–08.

Sieben, Robert L. "Controversial Medical Treatments of Learning Disabilities." *Academic Therapy*, vol. 13, no. 2 (November 1977), pp. 133–48.

Somsky, JoLene. "Teaching with Love." *Society for Suggestive-Accelerative Learning and Teaching*, vol. 5, no. 1 (1980), p. 2.

Sperry, R. W., M. S. Gazzaniga, and J. H. Bogen. "Interhemispheric Relationships: The Neocortical Commisures: Syndromes of Hemisphere Disconnection." *Handbook of Clinical Neurology*, vol. 4. New York, N.Y.: John Wiley, 1969.

Spring, Carl, and Jonathan Sandoval. "Food Additives and Hyperkinesis: A Critical Evaluation of the Evidence." *Journal of Learning Disabilities*, vol. 9 (November 1976), pp. 560–69.

van den Honert, Dorothy. "A Neuropsychological Technique for Training Dyslexics." *Journal of Learning Disabilities*, vol. 10 (January 1977), pp. 21–27.

Wunderlich, Ray C. *Allergy, Brains, and Children Coping.* St Petersburg, Fla.: Johnny Reads, 1973.

Zorotovich, Betty. "Hand Centers That Cause and Cure Alexia." *Academic Therapy*, vol. 14, no. 4 (March, 1979), pp. 469–77.

80. The Reading Program and Its Potential Obstacles for Minority Children

Susan W. Masland

Teaching reading effectively in a multiethnic classroom is, in most ways, like teaching reading effectively in any other kind of classroom: the teacher is concerned with developing a well-rounded program in which children not only learn skills for effective reading, but also develop positive attitudes toward reading. If the teacher lacks the special knowledge required to meet the needs of learners in a multiethnic classroom, they may encounter obstacles in three components of the reading program: the teaching of word attack skills, the teaching of comprehension skills, and the use of instructional materials. These obstacles are examined here in the hope that classroom teachers, reading specialists, and administrators can learn to recognize the impediments and avoid creating them.

Word Attack Skills

Whatever children's racial or ethnic background, they need strategies for figuring out words they encounter while reading. Teachers typically check their students' progress by listening to them read. Teachers listening to a child whose dialect differs considerably from their own often find it difficult to determine whether a misread word, or miscue, is a reading error or a rendering of that word in the child's dialect. This problem is evident in transcripts of two third-graders who read the same passage. John is a black dialect speaker,

Reprinted from Susan W. Masland, The reading program and its potential obstacles for minority children. *Elementary School Journal*, March 1979, *79*, 250–254, by permission of the University of Chicago Press. Copyright 1979 by the University of Chicago Press.

and Carmen comes from a Spanish-speaking home. In the transcripts, each time the student departed from the text, the student's rendering was entered directly above the original word. The transcripts are presented in Figure 1 and Figure 2. The words in boxes are considered reading errors; the words not enclosed in boxes are considered dialect renderings of the text.

At first glance, it looks as if the two children are inaccurate, sloppy readers. Both children said words that do not appear on the page. The classroom teacher who is unaware of the influence of dialect on the reading process might conclude that the children are poor readers because of their home language. The teacher might decide to drill John and Carmen on all the words they "missed."

Closer inspection of the transcription reveals that John pronounced *goes, store, with,* and *first* according to the sound system of black dialect. "Ask her can he stay home" is black dialect for the original text and completely retains the meaning of the sentence.

In Carmen's oral reading, some words are different from the text, because of the influence of her home language, which is Spanish. Her pronounciation of *think, with,* and *if* is typical of the pronunciation of Spanish-speaking children who are learning English. These changes have not affected her comprehension of the words. The miscues in boxes, however, indicate words that depart from the text and are not the result of imposing the Spanish sound system or grammar.

The teacher's response to the children's reading errors, the miscues in the boxes, would depend on the extent to which they affect meaning. If their miscues significantly altered the meaning, the teacher would need to help John and Carmen make more effective use of their word attack strategies in order to get closer to the author's message.

If changes in the text are due to dialect, the teacher would do well not to demand standard English pronunciation from the young readers. It is difficult for teachers to know whether dialect differences in pro-

John's Oral Reading

      go   sto   wiv

"I think he goes to the store with his

[friend]   can he

mother. Ask her if he can stay home

 [today]   [he] [con]

this time. Then we can get the club-

 [starried] firs [maybe]

house started first thing Monday."

Figure 1. Transcript of Reading by a Third-Grader Who Speaks a Black Dialect

Carmen's Oral Reading

theenk [go]   duh   wid heez

"I think he goes to the store with his

[friend]   eef

mother. Ask her if he can stay home

[today]   [he] con ged duh

this time. Then we can get the club-

houz [stored] theeng [maybe]

house started first thing Monday."

Figure 2. Transcript of Reading by a Third-Grader Who Is Bilingual

nunciation and grammar interfere with learning to read standard English. There is little research evidence that reading comprehension is affected by the child's dialect (1).

If teachers believe that interference from dialect is significant, they are likely to be persistent about correcting children's speech. Constant correction under the guise of teaching reading, however, has profound negative side effects. Children who speak nonstandard English during oral reading run the risk of being considered poor readers when the criterion for evaluation is "correct" pronunciation rather than the child's understanding of the written message. A disproportionate number of black dialect speakers and bilingual children may find themselves in the lowest reading groups, subject to the psychological impact of this kind of labeling, solely because at times their pronunciation and grammar differ from the teacher's.

Children whose speech is constantly corrected will probably refrain from active participation in oral and written activities of the reading program, for in these activities their home language is very noticeable. The children may develop the notion that the reading process is a hostile one, and they may be turned away from the enjoyment of reading merely because their language differs from standard English.

Teachers who understand the system of the dialects their children speak will dismiss all-too-prevalent misconceptions of these speech characteristics as random errors, sloppy diction, or ignorant speech. These teachers can make a number of appropriate responses to dialect, responses that benefit black children as well as white children in any classroom:

1. During reading activities, the teacher accepts and values the oral and the written language of children who are bilingual or speak black dialect; the teacher does not constantly correct "errors."

2. The teacher does not try to teach standard English pronunciation during a child's oral reading of a text. The main objective becomes full comprehension rather than accurate rendering of standard English sounds.

3. The teacher helps all the children gain an important understanding about the English language: different dialects offer different ways of expressing the same idea. Helping children to appreciate the differences is a realistic goal for teachers in multiethnic classrooms in which many varieties of English are spoken.

Comprehension

Children's comprehension is related to many variables. Two of them are particularly important in a multiethnic classroom. First is the experience that the reader brings to the page. In a sense, a reader will get from the page only what he or she brings to that page in prior understanding of the content and the language of the text, in attitudes toward reading, and in expectations of what should happen as the eye meets the print. Weaknesses in any one of these three areas will hamper the reader's effective interaction with the author's ideas.

In multiethnic classrooms teachers need to work hard to determine the nature of the gap between reader and author. Teachers cannot rely on the comfortable notion that their students have had similar experiences and thus are similar in their readiness to read a particular selection. Teachers need to consider several questions. What language structures used by the author may be unfamiliar to some of the readers whose primary dialect or language is not standard English? What background of experience does the author assume the readers bring to the page: do the readers have the necessary background? What concepts and words may be used in a way that is unfamiliar to some of the children? Teachers need to build readiness for reading a particular selection by carefully assessing their materials in order to identify potential barriers caused by the author's language structures, ideas, and vocabulary. Likewise, teachers need to assess the children's level of experience with the author's language structures, ideas, and vocabulary.

The second variable that affects children's comprehension is their understanding of what they are to do when they read. This understanding evolves largely from the quality of the comprehension questions teachers ask. The quality of the questions, in turn, is seriously affected by expectations teachers have. Some teachers lower their expectations for minority students because of their language differences.

Minority children may have difficulty speaking English or may speak a dialect that differs from standard English. Teachers perceive what they consider to be the children's weakness in decoding and general language proficiency and too often assume that the cognitive skills must also be weak. Consequently, teachers focus on word attack skills and devote less time to comprehension instruction, which usually is limited to questions that require recall or literal comprehension. After all, teachers reason, if children cannot speak the language very well, all we should expect from them is attention to the facts and the details of the stories they read. The damaging result is that instruction to develop comprehension proceeds on the simplest level only.

Teachers need to be sure that all children view reading as a meaningful encounter with print, not a meaningless process of calling out "correctly" pronounced words or culling endless facts from the material. Minority children at any level of proficiency in standard English need to be helped to think critically and creatively about what they read.

Reading Materials

A third major component of a well-rounded reading program is freedom for children to select from a wide variety of materials they can read for pleasure. Besides being appropriate for the children's reading levels, the materials need to fit the children's reading interests. One widely held assumption is that children want to read about people who are like them in racial or ethnic background. Children are also curious about people who are very different.

With these reading interests in mind, we should ask ourselves two major questions to determine how well we are accommodating the needs of children in a multiethnic classroom. Do materials portray blacks and other minority groups? Are blacks and other minority groups portrayed in positive, realistic settings that avoid stereotypes? Answers to these questions are essential if we are concerned with helping all children gain a healthier view of themselves and others in American society.

In our examination of instructional materials as well as library books, we can analyze the story content, the illustrations, and the author's tone. A systematic way for teachers to begin their analysis is offered in the book *Starting Out Right: Choosing Books about Black People for Young Children* (2). The authors propose several categories that describe how blacks and other minority characters are often depicted in children's books. Two categories the authors use are the Oasis Syndrome and the Ostrich-in-the-Sand Syndrome. In the Oasis Syndrome many characters are pictured, but only one is black. In the Ostrich-in-the-Sand Syndrome the author avoids dealing with prejudice or discrimination, merely hinting at it and thus oversimplifying the issues.

How can teachers use what they learn from an analysis of their materials? Should books be removed from the shelves if they portray blacks and other minority groups as stereotypes? If teachers can find no books in their classroom or school libraries that meet criteria for nonracist books, the problem extends beyond the classroom and is an appalling statement about the school itself. A retreat to the all-white world of literature is not the answer. Instead, teachers should make sure that the school budget for materials is used to purchase acceptable books about blacks and other minorities for classroom and school libraries. Teachers should insist that a wide selection of these books is readily accessible to all the students. The books reviewed by Latimer and associates (2) provide a starting place.

At times teachers may want to use a racist book in an open discussion about stereotyping. In a carefully planned sequence of discussions, children could be taught to identify stereotyping and its harmful effects. Books that would not meet the criteria for acceptance developed by Latimer and associates (2) could thus become a vehicle for learning about racism. Teachers' effectiveness in these discussions depends on their awareness of stereotyping and the rigor with which they evaluate their materials to learn where minority groups are portrayed in a manner that demeans them.

Teaching reading in a multiethnic classroom is like teaching reading in any other classroom except for some additional requirements of the teacher. Acknowledging and fulfilling these requirements could make all the difference in children's attitudes toward reading as well as their accomplishments in and through reading.

References

1. Susan W. Masland. "Black Dialect, Linguists, and Elementary School Teachers: Avoiding the Blind Men's Elephant." Paper presented at the Seventh Annual Linguistics Symposium, The University of Wisconsin, Milwaukee, March 18, 1978.
2. Bettye I. Latimer (editor). *Starting Out Right: Choosing Books about Black People for Young Children*. Bulletin No. 2314. Madison, Wisconsin: Wisconsin Department of Public Instruction, 1972.

81. Dialects and Reading

Pose Lamb

Although other processes may also be involved in the reading act, there is, currently, general agreement that reading is at least a *language* process and a cognitive process. The successful reader is engaged in what Sticht and others (20: 11) term "languaging,"[1] combining conceptual and linguistic activity. The close relationship between cognitive and all facets of language is brought into clear focus in considering dialect and its influence on reading achievement. Cazden (2) defines dialect as "a variety of spoken language that initially represented divergent geographic origins but may now represent social groups within a community." Dialect speakers, typically, can be understood by other speakers of the language used and, while the dividing lines are not at all clear, this criterion is the most frequently applied in differentiating between a dialect and a language. West (25) contends: "One of the most common, and valid, characteristics of the language is mutual intelligibility. . . . Within a single language community, particularly if it is large, there will probably be subgroups who speak the common language, but with differences in

From Pose Lamb, Dialects and reading. In R. E. Shafer (Ed.), *Applied linguistics and reading*. Newark, Del.: International Reading Association, 1979. Pp. 40–50. Reprinted by permission of Pose Lamb and the International Reading Association.

pronunciation, vocabulary, or other linguistic components. But as long as the different subgroups still understand each other, the language variations are called dialects.'' If one accepts as valid the almost stereotypic language strands—phonology, morphology, syntax, semantics, and vocabulary—*all* reflect the influence of dialect and that variant of dialect, ideolect, which signifies the unique and highly creative nature of each person's language.

It has already been noted that dialects reflect various geographic regions and various levels of society as well. One might wish that the adoption of the speech and writing patterns of one's family and other close associates didn't have such tremendous implications for personal, academic, and vocational or professional success, but such is not the case. Some dialects are much more prestigious than others, and those who don't speak a prestigious dialect operate at a disadvantage—minor or major, depending upon a variety of other factors, but a disadvantage, nonetheless.

To accept as reality the existence of prestigious and nonprestigious dialects is not to suggest that dialects exist in some rank order of acceptability. Cazden (2) makes this point very well.

> Is there in fact a single variety of English used by educated speakers throughout the United States? The answer to this question depends upon which aspect of language is being considered. In pronunciation there is no single standard. Regional variations in ''accent'' exist and are widely accepted without social stigmatism . . . In syntax, by contrast, a single standard does seem to exist.

The entire issue of variability in code-switching is extremely complex and of great interest to educators. Nonstandard dialect speakers comprehend standard dialects at the receptive level, aurally at least; and, when the situation demands it, many, if not most, can produce it as well. It should also be noted that those classified as standard dialect speakers occasionally make homophones of *pin* and *pen*, omit the *h* sound at the beginning of *who* and *when*, and have been known to minimize or even omit part of *-ed* and *-ing* endings. It appears that Noam Chomsky's goal of the ideal language user has yet to be reached. The problems created will be referred to later when dialect readers are discussed as potential aids in solving the dilemma related to black pupils' reading achievement.

While it is true that there is some controversy regarding the precise nature of standard dialect, and it is clear that there is tremendous variability in both standard and nonstandard dialects, most would agree that the language the majority of middle and upper class youngsters use when they begin school does *not* provide a barrier to achievement in reading. This condition is not equally true for low socioeconomic-status (SES) children, and there is justifiable concern for their poor achievement. Some writers, researchers, and/or educators have suggested that a major cause for this poor achievement is the poor match between the nonstandard dialect the low SES children speak and the standard language of the text and trade books they read. For this reason, the primary focus of these remarks will be on low SES children and the relationship between their productive and receptive language competencies. Because so much attention has been directed toward low SES black children, they are the focus of most of the recent data reported and opinions summarized. It should be stated that many blacks, for a variety of reasons, speak standard English, and cannot easily be distinguished from white speakers of standard English. A number of solutions have been proposed, based upon different premises; and, to date, none has the unqualified support provided by a mass of empirical data.

First to be discussed is the *eradication* theory, which is based upon the premise that black language is deficient and reflects the limited cognitive development of most blacks. Bernstein's concepts of restricted (low SES) and elaborated (middle and upper SES) codes are central to this solution. Low SES children must learn to use standard English exclusively, not only to succeed academically but because their cognitive functioning will be strengthened. The first flaw in this theory is that it is completely impractical. Nonstandard dialects will never be eradicated, nor probably should they be. To say that children who speak nonstandard English will be more successful academically, if they learn to operate comfortably with middle class language, is different from saying they must completely abandon a language which has served their communication needs very well and is the language used by those individuals who are significant to them.

Adoption of this eradication approach would probably have little impact on most reading programs because authors, publishers, and teachers currently operate on the assumption that low SES children can at least understand divergent dialects and that the dialect presented in the readers and/or trade books is an appropriate language for instruction. The extent to which nonstandard dialect interferes with reading achievement has *not* been determined, and until we have conclusive evidence that the interference is major and seriously detrimental, it is not likely that basic reading materials will change. As they are, such materials are probably not viewed negatively by the eradicationists, particularly since the language model presented *is* standard English, with little consideration for the variations in pronunciation, word endings, and syntax typical of some varieties of nonstandard English.

The second proposal for dealing with nonstandard dialects could be called bidialectal or biloquial. It represents a compromise, a middle position, between the eradicationists and the small groups who contend that complete acceptance of non-standard dialect is the humane, the democratic, the equalitarian solution to the problem. Advocates of the bidialectal position suggest that, by providing an alternative dialect, one permits the child access to the middle class world—and perhaps greater opportunity for academic and professional success—without depriving him of the code, which makes it possible for him to continue to operate effectively with those who are closest and most significant to him.

Fasold and Shuy (22) note:

> Most linguists will agree that a speaker of any language will make linguistic adjustments to specific social situations. These adjustments in phonology, grammar, and lexicon will range anywhere from the obvious adjustments between adults and small children to the more complicated sociolinguistic switching between school, home, and playground talk. Those who advocate the adoption of biloquialism feel that the teacher's job is *not* to eradicate playground English, or any other kind. Instead, teachers should help children to make the switch comfortably from one setting to another.

Acceptance of a biloquial or bidialectal solution to the problems of the young child who brings a variety of nonstandard English to his first encounters with print raises several issues. The first issue has just been suggested. If variation between textbook language and the child's language is viewed as a barrier to successful beginning reading, is one justified in recommending delay in introducing, or even emphasizing, standard English? Specifically, should exposure to -*ed* endings, the *is* copula, pronunciation of *r*'s and *l*'s accompany the first reading lessons in which these prominent nonstandard dialect features occur? The answer depends upon how serious the mismatch is.

Knapp's findings (*11*) are of some significance in considering this issue of interference. She studied the relationship of sex, age, ethnic group, and socioeconomic status to the development of an awareness of the social significance of language dialects. Eighty children, grades one and five, were given four tasks. They were asked to indicate the differences in paired sets of sentences, one in black English (BE) and the other in standard English (SE). Next, they were asked to identify whether BE and SE sentences were said "the right way" or "the wrong way" from a teacher's point of view. Finally, they were asked to identify speakers of black English and standard English by race and then by social class. Knapp reports: "The resulting data revealed that awareness of the social and racial significance of dialect does increase from first to fifth grade. On the other hand, awareness of standard forms as being what a teacher would say . . . was already well established by first grade." This study suggests, at least, that bidialectalism is achieved without much direct instruction, and at a fairly early age. Desire to please the teacher is strong among most first graders and appears to be a stronger factor in sucessfully stressing the need for code switching than telling young children they will get better grades or find better jobs if they are comfortable with standard English in appropriate situations. Knapp further concludes: "The Labov hypothesis that early adolescence is the stage during which the child becomes aware of the social significance of dialect characteristics is applicable to the current group of subjects, but there may be resistance among black children to identify with their own dialect."

Torrey (*23*) studied the language patterns of twenty-seven Harlem, New York, second graders. She reports:

These children were interviewed and tested to find their competence in spontaneous speech, oral and written

comprehension, oral reading, and explicit grammatical knowledge in standard English morphemes often missing in Black English. The data show large individual differences in the ability to use standard forms and low but significant correlations between speech and reading performance.

Gumperz and Hernandez-Chavez (*6*) contend:

There is little if any experimental evidence . . . that the pronunciations characteristic of urban black English actually interfere with the reading process . . . on the contrary, a recent study, using testing procedures specifically adjusted to black children, shows that children who fail to distinguish orally between such word pairs as "jar" and "jaw," "toe" and "tore" "six" and "sick" are nevertheless able to distinguish between them in written forms.

It cannot be stressed too strongly that the results of these studies, and others, suggest great variability in the black English items used and, probably of more significance to reading teachers, great variability in the ability to switch codes and to operate with standard English in both the productive and receptive facets of language.

Simons (*17*) has prepared an extraordinarily thorough review of the research relating to dialect interference with reading achievement. He concludes:

It is not possible to draw any firm conclusions about the existence of phonological interference on the basis of available evidence. However, the evidence there is tends to be negative. There is also insufficient data about grammatical interference, but what there is also tends to be negative.

However, the generally negative but inconclusive evidence reviewed here, even discounting the methodological and conceptual problems with the research, suggests that the original strong hypothesis of reading interference may have to be revised and qualified to take into account other factors. It appears likely that if black dialect interferes with the acquisition of reading skill, it does not interfere for all black dialect speakers in all educational situations.

The lack of definitive evidence regarding the phonological, morphological, and syntactic items in black dialect which cause the *most* interference with successful reading achievement, and the body of evidence suggesting that there is great variability in the nature of the dialects characterized as "black," call into question one of the most frequently proposed solutions to the dialect-reading problem: the use of dialect readers. These are books in which the same selection is written two ways—in standard English and nonstandard English—and the two versions appear side by side. Typically, only one area of divergence—the absence of the copula, perhaps—is worked on at a time, and the two dialects gradually become one. That is, by the end of a series, "school talk" and "everyday talk" are indistinguishable. Strickland opposes the use of dialect readers (21).

> While agreeing with the premise that divergence between the language of the learner and the language of the school impedes the acquisition of reading skills, I must disagree with the use of nonstandard dialect materials as a solution to the problem. These are my reasons:
> 1. Such a program must assume that there is one universal nonstandard dialect which all disadvantaged black children speak. In effect, it may impose upon some children another dialect with which to contend besides standard English which they will inevitably meet.
> 2. Most black parents object to the use of such books as initial instructional materials for reading. Whether or not their objections are based upon misinformation is unimportant when one considers the potential erosion of school-community relations and the resultant disruption of the learning process which would follow.

It might be added that teachers' frequently negative attitudes toward black English, especially when black English is given the status of being printed in a book, can be a barrier to learning as serious as that presented by the nonstandard language itself. Strickland continues:

> 3. The use of initial reading materials which are based on the individual child's own language might be a better alternative. Personal experience stories using the child's dictation as the content and the teacher as scribe can serve as an important tool for introducing reading.

She concludes with a plea for better teacher training—a clear and urgent need.

The language experience approach, to which Strickland refers, has been suggested as a means of helping a child see a match between his speech and written language. Cramer (3) writes:

> The language experience approach is predicated on the notion that reading can be most meaningfully taught when the teaching materials accurately reflect the child's own experience as described by his language. The language of instruction, then, must be that which proceeds from the wealth of linguistic, conceptual, and perceptual experience of the child. A child is more likely to learn to read when the activities associated with the approach have functional relationships with his language, experiences, needs, and desires.

The possibility of a negative teacher attitude can also be a serious deterrent to pupil achievement if this approach is used. Efforts to combine instruction in reading with lessons on standard grammar are not likely to be productive. Furthermore, major adjustments in the syntax the child dictates could result in a linguistic mismatch and a diminished self-concept on the part of the pupil. "He workin" or "She be home" must be genuinely accepted by the teacher and written as dictated, in the syntactic sense, at least. (There appears to be general agreement that phonological elements of nonstandard dialects would be difficult to transcribe and would make the transfer to standard English at least as difficult as the transition from i.t.a. to t.o. The syntax, however, should be recorded *as dictated*.)

So much has been written in praise of the language experience approach, particularly for "culturally different" pupils, that it is beginning to assume the dimensions of a panacea. In addition to the teacher attitude problem referred to previously, two items from the writers' personal experience with the approach may help to put language experience in perspective. The approach is no more a panacea than is any other. First, in a study comparing the achievement test scores of innercity pupils, five classes using language experience and five using a modified basal reader approach, results showed no statistically significant difference between the two groups. Further, it was noted on several occasions the pupils could not recall with a high degree of accuracy the precise language they had dictated only the day before. On a positive note, it should be stated that all five of the language experience teachers requested permission to use the approach the following year, although the project had ended.

In concluding the discussion of the varying proposals made by those favoring biloquialism or a bidialectal approach, the following comment by Smitherman (*19*) is especially appropriate: "Black English is an important topic of concern in educational circles since its speakers comprise the largest group of minority students (and, of course, black idiom speakers outside of school are the largest group of minority dialect speakers). For, make no mistake about it, bidialectalism concerns itself with the situation of ethnic and class minority students. Don't ever think for one minute that anybody is talkin [sic] about makin [sic] white and/or middle class kids bidialectal." According to Smitherman, the thrust is entirely toward making the "outsiders" talk like "insiders."

The position taken by Smitherman, and others, is that black English is a perfectly valid language, which should be accepted as it is. In fact, it might be as justifiable to ask standard English speakers to become comfortable using black English, or any other nonstandard variety of English as to do the reverse—certainly a provocative suggestion! Whether one is willing to go this far, it is clear that one's attitude toward black English or any other nonstandard dialect will significantly influence the way one teaches pupils who use it. It very well may be that this represents the most fruitful area of future research. Changing teachers' attitudes toward nonstandard dialects, in a more positive and accepting direction, may prove to have more positive effects on the reading achievement of pupils who speak these dialects than changing materials, or methods, or insisting on changing the children's language in a total or basic sense.

Despite the evident concern and the wealth of data which have been accumulated, it is clear that one still must seek solutions for helping speakers of nonstandard dialects achieve success in reading. It is possible that one large part of the solution to this major educational problem is not through reading methods or materials but through the teachers who work with these pupils. As teachers acquire more positive attitudes toward the worthiness of pupils and parents and learn to respect their dialects as useful and valid, although different, then the reading problem may become far less serious. The hypothesis is well worth testing!

Notes

1. Languaging: Representations of conceptualizations by properly ordered sequences of signs, or the inverse process of understanding the conceptualizations underlying the sequences of signs produced by others.

References

1. *Black Dialects and Reading*. Bernice E. Cullinan (Ed.). Urbana, Illinois: National Council of Teachers of English, 1974.
2. Cazden, Courtney B. *Child Language and Education*. New York: Holt, Rinehart and Winston, 1972, 200.
3. Cramer, Ronald. "Dialectology: A Case for Language Experience," *Reading Teacher*, 25 (October 1971), 33–39.
4. "From 'The Standard of Pronunciation' in Funk and Wagnalls New 'Standard' Dictionary of the English Language," in James Sledd and Wilma R. Ebbitt (Eds.), *Dictionaries and That Dictionary*. Chicago: Scott, Foresman, 1962, 39–41.
5. Gantt, Walter N., Robert M. Wilson, and C. Mitchell Dayton. "An Initial Investigation of the Relationship between Syntactical Divergency and the Listening Comprehension of Black Children," *Reading Research Quarterly*, 10 (1974–1975), 193–211.
6. Gumperz, John J., and Eduardo Hernandez-Chavez. "Bilingualism, Bidialectalism, and Classroom Interaction," in Courtney Cazden, Vera John, and Dell Hymes (Eds.), *Function of Language in the Classroom*. New York: Teachers College Press, 1972, 105.
7. Hall, Edward T. "Listening Behavior: Some Cultural Differences," in Johanna S. DeStefano and Sharon E. Fox (Eds.), *Language and the Language Arts*. Boston: Little Brown, 1974, 130–134.
8. Hockman, Carol. "Black Dialect Reading Tests in the Urban Elementary School," *Reading Teacher*, 26 (March 1973), 581–583.
9. Hutchinson, Jane O'Shields. "Reading Tests and Nonstandard Language," *Reading Teacher*, 25 (February 1972), 430–437.
10. Johnson, Kenneth R. "Teacher's Attitude toward the Nonstandard Negro Dialect: Let's Change It," in Johanna DeStefano and Sharon E. Fox (Eds.), *Language and the Language Arts*. Boston: Little Brown, 1974, 148–159.
11. Knapp, Margaret O. "Awareness of Black Dialect by First and Fifth Graders as Related to Race, Socioeconomic Status and Sex," EdD thesis, Rutgers University, 1974, abstract, 100.
12. Labov, William, "From 'The Logic of Nonstandard English'," in Johanna DeStefano and Sharon E. Fox (Eds.), *Language and the Language Arts*. Boston: Little Brown, 1974, 134–148.
13. MacGinitie, Walter. "Research Suggestions from the Literature Search," *Reading Research Quarterly*, 11 (1975–1976), 7–35.
14. Pederson, Lee A. "Social Dialects and the Disadvantaged," *Language Programs for the Disadvantaged*. Report of the NCTE Task Force on Teaching English to the Disadvantaged. Urbana, Illinois: National Council of Teachers of English, 1965, 236–249.
15. Rystrom, Richard. "Language Patterns and the Primary Child," *Reading Teacher*, 26 (November 1972), 149–152.
16. Sawyer, Janet. "Dialects, Education, and the Contributions of Linguists," *Language Programs for the Disadvantaged*. Report of the NCTE Task Force on Teaching English to the Disadvantaged. Urbana, Illinois: National Council of Teachers of English, 1965, 216–220.
17. Simons, Herbert D. "Black Dialect and Reading Interference: A Review and Analysis of the Research Evidence," unpublished paper, mimeographed, 1974.
18. Smith, Nila Banton. "Cultural Dialects: Current Problems and Solutions," *Reading Teacher*, 29 (November 1975), 137–141.
19. Smitherman, Geneva. "Grammar and Goodness," *English Journal*, 62 (May 1973), 774–778.
20. Sticht, Thomas G., et al. *Auding and Reading*. Alexandria, Virginia: Human Resources Research Organization, 1974.
21. Strickland, Dorothy S., and William A. Stewart. "The Use of Dialect Readers: A

Dialogue," in B. E. Cullinan (Ed.), *Black Dialects and Reading*. Urbana, Illinois: National Council of Teachers of English, 1974, 147.

22. *Teaching Standard English in the Innercity*. Ralph Fasold and Roger Shuy (Eds.). Washington, D.C.: Center for Applied Linguistics, preface, xii.

23. Torrey, Jane W. "The Language of Black Children in the Early Grades," *Studies in Developing Competence in Standard English I.* Research report, National Institute of Child Health and Human Development, 1972, abstract.

24. Wanat, Stanley. "Language Acquisition: Basic Issues," *Reading Teacher*, 25 (November 1971), 142–147.

25. West, Fred. *The Way of Language: An Introduction*. New York: Harcourt Brace Jovanovich, 1975.

82. Beginning English Reading for ESL Students

Phillip C. Gonzales

Of the 7.6 million youngsters in U.S. schools who are nonnative English speakers (Waggonner, 1978), only about a half-million are in bilingual or English as a Second Language programs (Gonzalez, 1979). An additional one million limited speakers or nonspeakers of English will probably enroll in formal schooling annually during each of the next few years. Meeting this challenge must be one of the major educational concerns of the 1980s.

Nowhere is this concern greater than in the area of initial reading instruction. While the value of initiating reading instruction in the child's strongest language is well documented (Modiano, 1968; Gamez, 1979; Grieve and Taylor, 1952), determining when to begin or transfer to English reading instruction remains an important educational question, with inadequate guidelines provided by most reading methods textbooks. Most reading specialists agree that the language of print should not exceed the child's oral language proficiency, yet we have had no usable method of determining this level.

Furthermore, although there is agreement that language improvement should be an important component of reading instruction at all levels, particularly for English as a Second Language (ESL) students, specific recommendations regarding linguistic comprehension and development are often not provided.

This article describes procedures currently used by teachers of Spanish/English bilinguals in the Pacific Northwest. Field research on these procedures was conducted by Cardona and Williams (1980) and the procedure is used by migrant education teachers in 52 Washington school districts. Specifically, the following questions will be addressed: (1) How can teachers easily and accurately determine the stage of English language proficiency of children who are not native speakers of English? (2) How can teachers assess the linguistic demands of first grade basal reader textbooks used for initial reading instruction in English? (3) How can teachers ensure proper linguistic preparation for comprehending the reading selection?

From Phillip C. Gonzales, Beginning English reading for ESL students. *The Reading Teacher*, November 1981, 35, 154–162. Reprinted by permission of Phillip Gonzales and the International Reading Association.

Second Language Acquisition

English language skills of nonnative speakers develop in a definite, sequential fashion resembling that of native speakers (Dulay and Burt, 1974; Krashen et al., 1976; McLaughlin, 1977; Chun, 1980). The English skills are acquired in developmental stages during which predictable linguistic behaviors are manifested. These behaviors, although variant from those expected from adult users of English, reflect the child's understanding of the recurrent structures and patterns of language at that given time (Guskin, 1976).

The stages of linguistic development (Cardona, 1980) are shown graphically in Figure 1, the Oral Language Index. The lefthand column lists, in order of acquisition, the syntactic forms first appearing and expected at each of the eight stages. The righthand column gives the order in which the learner acquires semantic structures. In both cases, reference is to productive language ability rather than to receptive ability (speaking rather than listening).

When a child is first introduced to an English speaking environment, the language comprehended and used will be

Figure 1. Cardona Oral Language Index: Stages in acquisition of English*

Acquisition of syntax	*Acquisition of Semantic Structures*
Stage 1	
1. Yes/no answers	1. Sentences with 1 part:
2. Positive statements	agent or object or locative
3. Subject pronouns: *he, she*, **etc.**	(attribute + noun = 1 part)
4. Present/present habitual verb tense	2. Sentences with 2 parts:
5. Possessive pronouns: *my, your*, **etc.**	agent + action
	or + object
	or + locative
	action + object
	or + locative
	+ locative
Stage 2	
1. Simple plurals of nouns	1. Substitution of pronouns for nouns
2. Affirmative sentences	2. Fragmentary grammar
3. Subject and object pronouns (all)	3. Beginning regularization of sentence order
4. Possessives: *'s*	4. Sentence with 3+ parts:
5. Negation	agent + *to* action/infinitive/ + object, or
6. Possessive pronouns: *mine*, **etc.**	action + agent + object or locative, or
	agent + object + action or locative
Stage 3	
1. Present progressive tense	1. Regularized sentence order
2. Conjunctions: *and, but, or, because, so, as,* etc.	2. Conjoining with *and*, using deletions
	3. Addition of modifiers:
	agent + (modifier) action + object or
	locative
Stage 4	
1. Questions: *who? what? which? where*	1. Sentence with 4 parts:
2. Irregular plurals of nouns	agent + action + 2 other parts, selected
3. Simple future tense: *going to . . .*	from:
4. Prepositions	additional agent, agent modifier, action
	modifier,
	1–2 objects, object modifier, locative

Figure 1. (continued)

Initial Reading Readiness	1. Sentence with 5+ parts:
	agent + action + 3 other parts:
	   additional agent, agent modifier,
	   additional action, action modifier, 1–2
	   objects, object modifier locative
	   object modifier locative

Stage 5
1. Future tense: *will*
2. Questions: *when? how?*
3. Conjunctions: *wither, nor, neither, that, since,* etc.

Stage 6
1. Regular past tense verbs
2. Questions: *why?*
3. Contractions: *isn't,* etc.
4. Modal verbs: *can, must,* etc., and *do*

1. Permutations in word order
2. Substitution of phrases and clauses for sentence parts

Stage 7
1. Verb tense: Irregular past
2. Past tense questions
3. Auxilliary verbs: *has, is*
4. Passive voice

Stage 8
1. Verbs: conditional
2. Summary of verb forms
3. Verb tense: the imperfect
4. Conjunctions: *though, if, therefore,* etc.
5. Verb mood: subjunctive

---

* Adapted from Cardona, 1980

---

limited. It is not uncommon for a second language learner to exhibit a "silent period" at first (Krashen, 1978; Brown, 1979). As comfort increases, the child begins to experiment with language. This experimentation follows a consistent path suggestive of a universal process among language learners (Corder, 1967; Ervin-Tripp, 1974; Dulay and Burt, 1972, Chun, 1980).

At Stage 1, one and two-word utterances resembling holophrastic and simple telegraphic speech are heard. Through these utterances—usually consisting of nouns, verbs, or a combination of the two—the speaker is able to speak of people, situations, or activities immediately present, is able to utter "yes" and "no" to many situations, and learns to use "verbal formulas" that enable him or her to social-ize with peers and use activities as language learning opportunities (Wong-Filmore, 1976). Employing these verbal formulas, children appear to understand what is going on in a given situation. Common utterances might include "my turn," or "me next," both indicating a willingness to be included in an activity.

Lexically, over-generalizations and over-extensions of meanings are common. Often, too specific a reference is given to a word (e.g., *dog* meaning either a specific dog or referring to all animals with four legs and a tail). Egocentric speech, where children may practice English pronunciation and simple sentence structures before using them with their peers, may also be heard (Brown, 1979).

At Stages 2 and 3, students begin to use more regularized language in sentence-like utterances. They are able to communicate concrete and immediate information to peers in a variety of contexts. Communication by whatever means appears to be the concern. Frequently, mixing of English and native language occurs at this stage (Wong-Filmore, 1976).

At each subsequent stage, additional sentence parts are incorporated into basic sentence structures. These parts can be modifiers, additional agents, actions, or objects (Menyuk, 1969). The addition of this extra part provides the best indication of increase in the complexity of language acquired (Dale, 1976).

Now, language use becomes somewhat complex, with prepositional phrases (Stage 4) and conjunctions (Stage 5). By the end of Stage 5, abstractions of language are observed in metalinguistic manipulations. Students have a language they can use in making judgments regarding correctness of form and in discussing what language is and how it functions. Such language is related to initial reading readiness (Downing, 1979; Mattingly, 1979) and is manifested by children who can and often do request feedback regarding the "correctness" of their language (Wong-Filmore, 1976).

Lexical knowledge and use become more refined as the child has opportunities to practice language in a variety of situations. Several hundred words may be understood at this point.

At Stages 6, 7, and 8, students begin to substitute phrases and clauses for major parts of sentences. Moreover, they begin to experiment with changes in order of parts of sentences (permutation), thereby demonstrating their new flexibility in language use. Conceptually, at this stage, the learner is capable of using language in situations in which problem solving, hypothesis testing, or abstract thought is involved. The grammar learned during these stages of acquisition (conditionals, subjunctive, passive voice, etc.) allows for this manipulation of thought.

Assessing the Child's Language

The preceding description of language developmental stages can be used in assessing the language proficiency of ESL learners. The child's language can be assessed by using samples taken from informal, spontaneous, unthreatening situations in which the teacher/tester and student are discussing a topic, activity, or experience (Tarone, 1979; Rosansky, 1976; Cazden, 1972). Formal, elicited talk—where form and not communicative value is the focus of attention—tends to limit language production (Gonzales, 1980). The child's language sample can be tape-recorded for later transcription and analysis.

Analysis involves two steps. First, examine the language sample for characteristic grammatical forms (i.e., evidence of use of subjunctive case, auxiliaries, types of verbs, conjunctions, prepositions, etc.) and their location on the Oral Language Index (Figure 1). For example, "I was hit by a car" contains an example of the passive voice—Stage 7.

Second, examine the type of grammatical structure. The parts of the utterance are identified and counted. The major sentence parts include: (1) agent (subject), (2) action (verb), (3) object (either indirect or direct), (4) locative (denoting place), (5) phrases (particularly prepositional phrases), (6) modifiers (either adjectival or adverbial), (7) clauses (especially if substituted for basic parts of a sentence). Finally, regularization of the sentence is checked. At this point, examine the sentence to see if the language sample follows the usual English order: agent, action, object, or locative. For example, consider "(You) take it and put it in my mouth." Analysis is as follows: (agent)-action-object-action-object-locative. This is a six-part sentence indicative of Stage 5.

Figure 2 is a language sample and its analysis. It is not a complete transcription of the sample, but it contains utterances

Figure 2. Sample from a child's speech

Severo is a 10 year old who repeated the second grade due to difficulties experienced with beginning reading instruction.

Teacher: What do you see in this picture?
Student: 1. The police girl are ticket for a car.
          2. And the firemen giving the lady a flower.
          3. The girl is in a car.
          4. A little boy is down there.
          5. A lady is looking for a dish.
          6. He is eating pop.
          7. He is opening the window.
          8. She's calling somebody.
          9. And this man is picking box for a truck.

Analysis:		Stage of Acquisition
Type of Language		
A. Verbs—exclusively present tense, present progressive		3
B. Prepositions: Sentences 1, 3, 5, 9		4
C. Structures: Regularized order		
	Sentences 7, 9: agent-action-object	3
	Sentence 2: agent-action-object-object	4
	No sentences include more than four parts	

---

representative of those exhibited by the student. The teacher talk is omitted.

It is apparent from the sample that Severo is employing syntactic and structural forms indicative of Stage 4. No evidence of Stage 5 or above was found in the sample. Additionally, no evidence of substitutions or permutation (involving a change in word order) was found. Furthermore, Severo did not use sentences that contained an additional agent, modifiers, or additional action. Thus he might have difficulties if placed in reading materials that required production and understanding of the future and past tense of verbs, response to "why" questions, or sentences with five or more parts.

Although one sampling of a child's language may not provide a complete indication of competence, it does provide direct evidence of the types of language forms and structures that the child is able to use in conversations and therefore presumably comprehends. Lacking, of course, is an indication of the specific vocabulary and conceptual background of the child.

Determining a child's command and use of various syntactic forms and structures is necessary if the teacher does not want to run the risk of attempting to teach reading with printed language containing syntax far in advance of the child's understanding and productive abilities. This is especially important at the beginning stages of learning to read.

The assessment of the child's language skills suggested in this article is unidimensional. However, it offers a means of determining the level of a child's syntactic development that is so often ignored in initial reading instruction.

Assessing a Text's Linguistic Demands

Assessment of the linguistic demands of a first grade reading book is conducted in a fashion similar to that employed with the oral language sample. The story sample in Figure 3 is taken from a series designed for

Figure 3. Sample from a basal reader, first grade level*

Hot Corn Muffins

Text: 1. Jen Hen is digging and digging.
2. Jen Hen is planting corn.
3. Jen Hen digs and digs, and digs and plants.
4. Chuck Chipmunk and Chub Cub are running up the hill.
5. Chuck Chipmunk is running with a big sack on his back, and Chub Cub is running with a fishnet in his hands.
6. It is hot, and Chuck and Chub are hot.
7. They stop at Jen Hen's cabin and sit on a rock to rest.
8. "I am going up the hill."
9. "I am going fishing with this net."
10. And I am hot!

Analysis:

Type of Language	Stage of Acquisition
A. Verb: Present tense, present progressive (mostly)	3
Simple future (sentences 8 and 9)	4
B. Prepositional phrases: Sentences 5, 7, 8, 9	4–5
C. Structures: Regularized order	
Sentences 1, 3, 7: agent-action-action	5
Sentence 3: five parts	5
Sentence 7: seven parts	6+

* Robinett, Ralph F., Paul W. Bell, and Pauline Rojas. "Hot Corn Muffins." *Miami Linguistic Readers*, Level 6, pp. 4–6. Lexington, Mass.: D.C. Heath and Co., 1970. Reproduced by permission of the publisher.

the linguistically different student. The sample is only part of one story, yet it contains language representative of the remainder of the selection.

While the grammar is relatively low in complexity (Stages 3 and 4), many of the semantic structures are from Stage 5 or 6. Therefore, the structures would pose more difficulty for readers than would the grammatical forms. Severo, for example, would conceivably have difficulty understanding some of the structures at Stage 5 and above but would comprehend the grammatical elements of this story sample.

Examining the linguistic demands of a textbook used for reading instruction and comparing it with the language competence a student exhibits will certainly provide the teacher with useful information regarding how and perhaps when to teach English reading to the ESL learner. If too much disparity exists between the capabilities of the child and the language found in the text, reading instruction would necessitate deliberate teaching of those language structures and grammatical forms. If the child exhibits language of the type found in the text, then the reading lesson could be focused on understanding the story's content and on learning the decoding skills of reading.

Preparing the Child for the Reading Lesson

Any good instructional introduction to a new reading story includes the following components: conceptual background of experience related to the story content and review of new and difficult vocabulary in the story. What is often omitted in this introduction is a linguistic preparation of the child for the new and difficult grammatical forms and structures. The following suggestions help with this concern.

Using the Oral Language Index, the

teacher can readily determine those structures that may prove difficult for any second language English speaker. These structures and grammatical forms can then be deliberately taught, ensuring that the language of the text does not interfere with comprehension of the story.

As the child's language may be somewhat limited, abstract discussions of language would be totally inappropriate and ineffective (for example, telling the student just beginning to read: "A sentence with two 'actions' describes two habitual activities occurring simultaneously"). More concrete means of communication should be employed.

The most direct and perhaps the best instruction is concrete, involves a hands-on activity or experience, and employs comprehensible language appropriate to the situation (see Figure 4). For example, the sentence "Jen Hen digs and plants" can be role-played, with the student acting out the continuous actions described. Of course, the relationship between the child's movements and the language should be pointed out to the child.

Visuals (iconic images) depicting what is not understood by the student should also help. For example, the sentence "Chuck Chipmunk is running with a big sack on his back" contains two prepositional phrases. A student not yet able to produce sentences with two prepositional phrases may have difficulty understanding such a structure. Here, discussions of the visuals (such as in picture reading) with the teacher using simple, comprehensible language would aid the student. (This particular story contains many useful pictures of what is going on in the story. Most basal readers contain good visuals.)

Simplification of the language found in the text would also help the learner comprehend the structures. Using the Oral Language Index as a guide, the teacher can reduce the complexity of the structure to one within the reach of the second language learner. For example, a sentence

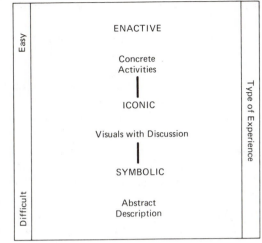

Figure 4. The terms *enactive, iconomic,* and *symbolic* are taken from Bruner (1964).

such as "Jen Hen digs and plants, and digs and plants" can be rewritten into four very simple "agent-action" sentences such as "Jen Hen digs" and "Jen Hen plants." Compound sentences can also be simplified. For example: "Chuck Chipmunk is running with a big sack on his back, and Chub Cub is running with a fishnet in his hands" can be written into six simpler sentences. "Chuck Chipmunk is running. Chuck Chipmunk has a big sack. The sack is on his back. Chub Cub is running. Chub Cub has a fishnet. The fishnet is in his hands."

Benefits for the Teacher

Using the processes suggested in this article may initially require time for the teacher to learn to use the Index and to assess the proficiency of children's language and the linguistic demands of the text. However, the advantages of the procedures, which help provide appropriate and comprehensible reading education, far exceed the disadvantages. Six outcomes from using the procedure have been reported by teachers and students who have received training. (1) Teachers become familiar with the hierarchy of levels of linguistic development and the process of language development. (2) Teachers learn to identify difficult grammatical structures and forms in reading selections. (3) Teachers learn to listen to the quality of their students' language production with the intent of scheduling instruction to accommodate a linguistic skill level and to prepare students for the difficult language forms and structures encountered in print. (4) Teachers learn about the relationship of language use and reading. (5) Teachers learn to apply the Index automatically as they teach. (6) Teachers can readily determine the linguistic readiness of English as a Second Language learners for initial English reading.

Teachers want to do a good job in helping nonnative English speakers learn to read. For this, they should be able to assess the language abilities of these children; they must be able to determine the linguistic demands of the stories used; and they must provide sufficient preparation for the nonnative and perhaps limited-English speaking child to adequately comprehend the language of the stories. Otherwise, nonnative English speakers may essentially be acquiring the skills of "decoding" written language which they do not understand.

The approach suggested in this article is particularly important in determining when and how to introduce the nonnative English speaker to initial reading instruction. These students are in the danger of being assigned English language reading materials before they have the linguistic base to handle the written language. A linguistic approach should help prevent some of the difficulties we have experienced in attempting to teach limited-English speakers before they are ready for such instruction.

References

Brown, Daphne M. *Mother Tongue to English*. Cambridge, England: Cambridge University Press, 1979.

Bruner, Jerome. "The Course of Cognitive Growth." *American Psychologist*, vol. 19 (1964), pp. 1–15.

Cardona, Carlos. "Oral Language Index." Unpublished manuscript, University of Washington, Seattle, Washington, 1980.

Cardona, Carlos, and Carl Williams. "The Effectiveness of the Use of the 'Oral Language Index' in Assessing the Entry Level for the Introduction of English Reading to Bilingual Children." Unpublished research, Washington State Migrant Education Service Center, Sunnyside, Washington, 1980.

Cazden, Courtney B. *Child Language and Education*. New York, N.Y.: Holt, Rinehart and Winston, 1972.

Chun, Judith. "A Survey of Research in Second Language Acquisition." *The Modern Language Journal*, vol. 64 (Autumn 1980), pp. 287–96.

Corder, S. Pit. "The Significance of Learners' Errors." *International Review of Applied Linguistics*, vol. 5 (November 1967), pp. 162–69.

Dale, Philip S. *Language Development—Structure and Function*. New York, N.Y.: Holt, Rinehart and Winston, 1976.

Downing, John. "Psycholinguistic Basis of Cognitive Clarity." Paper presented at the University of Victoria International Reading Association Research Seminar on Linguistic Awareness and Learning to Read, Victoria, British Columbia, June 26–30, 1979.

Dulay, Heidi, and Marina Burt. "Goofing: An Indicator of Children's Second Language Learning Strategies." *Language Learning*, vol. 22 (December 1972), pp. 235–51.

Dulay, Heidi, and Marina Burt. "Natural Sequences in Child Second Language Acquisition." *Language Learning*, vol. 24 (June 1974), pp. 37–54.

Ervin-Tripp, Suzan. "Is Second Language Learning Like the First?" *TESOL Quarterly*, vol. 8 (June 1974), pp. 137–44.

Gamez, Gloria. "Reading in a Second Language: Native Language Approach vs. Directed Method." *The Reading Teacher*, vol. 32 (March 1979), pp. 665–70.

Gonzales, Phillip C. "What's Wrong with Basal Approach to Language Development?" *The Reading Teacher*, vol. 33 (March 1980), pp. 668–73.

Gonzalez, Josue. "The Future of Bilingual Program Evaluations." Keynote address delivered at the 1979 N.A.B.E. International Bilingual, Bicultural Education Conference, Seattle, Washington, May 7, 1979.

Grieve, D. W., and A. Taylor. "Media of Instruction." *Gold Coast Education*, vol. 1 (1952), pp. 36–52.

Guskin, Judith T. "What the Child Brings and What the School Expects: First and Second-Language Learning and Teaching in Bilingual-Bicultural Education." In *The Bilingual Child—Research and Analysis of Existing Educational Themes*, edited by Antonio Simoes. New York, N.Y.: Academic Press, 1976.

Krashen, Stephen. "The Mother Model for Second-Language Acquisition," In *Second-Language Acquisition and Foreign Language Teaching*, edited by Rosario C. Gingras. Arlington, Va.: Center for Applied Linguistics, 1978.

Krashen, Stephen D., Victoria Sferiazza, Lornal Feldman, and Ann K. Fathman. "Adult Performance on the SLOPE Test: More Evidence for a Natural Sequence in Adult Second Language Acquisition." *Language Learning*, vol. 26 (June 1976), pp. 145–52.

Mattingly, Ignatius G. "Reading, Linguistic Process, and Linguistic Awareness." Paper presented at the University of Victoria International Reading Association Research Seminar on Linguistic Awareness and Learning to Read, Victoria, British Columbia, June 26–30, 1979.

McLaughlin, Barry. "Second-Language Learning in Children." *Psychological Bulletin*, vol. 84 (May 1977), pp. 438–59.

Menyuk, Paula. *Sentences Children Use*. Cambridge, Mass.: The M.I.T. Press, 1969.

Modiano, Nancy. "National or Mother Language in Beginning Reading: A Comparative Study." *Research in the Teaching of English*, vol. 2 (Spring 1968), pp. 32–43.

Rosansky, Ellen. "Methods and Morphemes in Second Language Acquisition Research." *Language Learning*, vol. 26 (December 1976), pp. 409–25.

Tarone, Elaine. "Interlanguage as Chameleon." *Language Learning*, vol. 29 (June 1979), pp. 181–91.

Waggonner, Dorothy. "Non-English Language Background Persons: Three U.S. Surveys." *TESOL Quarterly*, vol. 12 (September 1978), pp. 247–63.

Wong-Filmore, Lily. "The Second Time Around." Unpublished dissertation, Stanford University, Stanford, California, 1976.

83. Teaching Reading to the Gifted

Robert L. Trezise

In the past five or six years, there has been a phenomenal resurgence of interest in gifted and talented students—on the national, state and local levels. After a period of little or no interest in special programming for these youngsters, educators everywhere are now beginning to ask, "What can we do for gifted students?" This mushrooming of interest in gifted students should be of particular interest to teachers of reading.

Perhaps it may seem paradoxical, however, to even consider the question of reading in relation to the gifted. After all, intellectually gifted students almost by definition are very good readers and usually learn to read with amazing facility— sometimes as if by some magical, osmotic means. Indeed, it is well known that gifted children often teach themselves to read before beginning school, as was the case with close to half of the gifted youngsters in Terman's monumental study, "Genetic Studies of Genius" (1925).

What's more, gifted children not only read very well, but they tend also to be highly motivated to read. In fact, books and printed matter in general are often their passion. Affinity for reading, in short, is practically the *sine qua non* of intellectual giftedness.

Then why an article on teaching the gifted to read?

It is my feeling that just as the superlatively accomplished Olympic-bound swimmer is in the greatest need of brilliant coaching, so does the excellent reader need special and intensive reading instruction, for in spite of the prevailing myth that the gifted can take care of themselves,

this is no more true of the intellectually gifted than the athletically gifted. Talent requires careful nurture, as any Olympic coach or mentor of the gifted knows.

However, though the gifted do need reading instruction, this instruction usually should not be of the kind that focuses on basic decoding skills. If a child comes to school knowing how to read or learns to read at a rapid rate in the early grades, he or she should not be required to plod along through the drills and exercises dealing with the enabling skills. Yet, sad to say, this is exactly what happens to many bright children in the early elementary grades—they know how to read, but they are required to learn again, this time by the prescribed method. As a result, maddened by the pedestrian pace, and bored with consonant blends and diphthongs, the child who already can read or is able to learn to read by cognitive leaps and bounds and intuitive flashes frequently becomes frustrated early in a school career and becomes an embittered, cynical student.

What can be said, then, about what a reading program for the gifted should be?

The research on gifted students over the years has stressed that these students are not only advanced in their learning skills, but that they learn in ways that are somewhat different from the average youngster. Most distinctive among the higher cognitive processes often possessed by these youngsters is the ability to conceptualize, especially to unify or synthesize experiences and facts into original solutions. Such conceptualizing involves language or symbolic behavior, ability to

From Robert L. Trezise, Teaching reading to the gifted. *Language Arts*, November/December 1977, 54, 920–924. Reprinted by permission of the author and the National Council of Teachers of English.

organize, broad experience, and creative flexibility. These youngsters tend to gravitate to the abstract, seek complexity, learn through complex associations, and respond to questions from a moral and ethical standpoint.

Reading programs for gifted children, then, should include objectives appropriate to the needs and learning styles of this particular group of youngsters. Relating these learning qualities to a reading program for gifted students means that these students are likely to want to deal not simply with what happens in their books, but with the significance of the events and how those events are related to things they have read in other books and to their own life experiences. Perhaps they will want to consider the social, moral, and ethical significance of the themes of their stories and how various authors deal with similar themes and situations. The role of the reading teacher should be to encourage the students in this direction; that is, to delve more and more deeply into what they have read, even though they may appear to be making a simple story more complex than perhaps the author intended it to be. But that is the way gifted readers like to, and should, respond to what they read.

There are undoubtedly many appropriate reading objectives for the gifted student, but I would stress the following three: Gifted students should receive reading instruction designed to encourage them to read: 1) more widely, 2) more critically, and 3) more creatively.

To read more widely: We live in a veritable Golden Age of children's literature. Attractive, well-written books are available to children on virtually all topics and themes—written by some of our best authors, illustrated by some of our most outstanding artists. Themes of universal concern are dealt with in elementary-level books. Titles like *The Dead Bird* (Brown 1958) (death), *William's Doll* (Zolotow 1972) (sexual identity), *Ramona the Brave* (Cleary 1975) (non-conformity), *Mom, the Wolf Man, and Me* (Klein 1972) (value systems in conflict), *Blubber* (Blume 1974) (cruelty among children) are examples of excellent books with significant themes that gifted students should be led to and which they have the abilities to deal with. Unfortunately, teachers of reading often don't know the best of children's literature themselves and, therefore, aren't able to bring their gifted students to these marvelous books, and thereby widen their reading horizons. Most reading teachers know their Scott Foresman, Houghton Mifflin, or Ginn reading series backwards and forwards but they are less likely to know the books of Judy Blume, M. E. Kerr, Norma Klein, Virginia Hamilton, or Judith Viorst.

Good readers are always author-conscious, and a reading program for the gifted should increase the children's awareness of who is writing, what is being written, what the themes are, what the styles. Gifted children are usually good readers, and they usually love to read. But it is the teacher's role to further broaden their reading horizons by bringing them to the infinite variety of books that are now available.

All children, of course, should be exposed to outstanding children's literature. But considering the gifted child's ability to respond at a depth beyond the average reader's, and an eagerness to take part in discussions about books that deal with universal themes, the use of the best of children's books is especially appropriate for this group of youngsters. Robert Frost once said that the whole purpose for going to school is to get the impression fixed for life that there is a book side to everything. In an age of mass communication, Frost's view may begin to sound a bit anachronistic. But for the gifted student, who has the potential to be "book-centered," this purpose should be still relevant. It is the job of reading teachers, through the use of the best of children's books, to keep this purpose in mind as they work out a reading program for gifted students.

To read more critically: Contrary to the all too common view that reading is "saying the words," reading is essentially a thinking process—a process of transforming visual symbols into meaning. With gifted students who so readily master basic decoding skills, this view of reading should be stressed. Yet too often, if children talk about what they have read at all, it is only to recall specific facts, recitation style. Critical reading for the gifted must go beyond lower cognitive levels: these children should be encouraged to summarize and paraphrase what they've read, to apply what they've learned from one situation to another, to analyze what they've read, to gather their insights together into new thoughts, and to make judgments about the values embedded in what they've read. In other words, to do the kinds of things with what they read that are so appropriate to their learning styles.

Like comprehension skills in general, critical reading skills can and should be consciously and systematically taught. Gifted students should be allowed and encouraged to dissect what they read from both the standpoint of content and style and to speculate on the validity and basic truths of books. Gifted students can enjoy discussing with others of similar ability what they consider to be the author's purpose or theme, the appropriateness of the treatment of a topic, the believability of the plot and characters, or how various books deal with a similar theme in different ways. Being "critical" may have acquired an undeservedly negative connotation; it should be considered a quality to be desired and developed. A reading program for gifted youngsters should indeed include developing critical reading (thinking) skills as a basic objective.

To read more creatively: While reading more critically is mainly a matter of convergent thinking—albeit convergent thinking at the higher cognitive levels—creative reading is more divergent in nature. In teaching to divergent, creative reading objectives, the teacher leads students *out* from what they have read. Opposite to the truncating "But we're off the subject" (a convergent comment), teaching strategies that encourage creative responses to what has been read use books as a means of creating new thoughts and ideas. Creative readers vault beyond the books they read—a behavior to be encouraged by teachers. The Hilda Taba discussion strategies (Trezise 1972) are a particularly good means of doing this, since they ask students to make inferences about how characters feel, why they felt that way—and then ask children if anything like that ever happened to them? How they felt? Why? What did they do? For example, if the children have read *Hey, Dummy* (Platt 1971), the creative response to the book would not be a discussion of the story itself, although this is where the discussion would start, but of similar experiences the children have had, how they felt, what they did. Before the discussion is through, gifted children—even the very young ones—will undoubtedly deal with the universal theme of man's inhumanity to man.

Creative readers bring themselves to the reading process—their own ideas, feelings, attitudes, and values; and the teacher of the gifted consciously attempts to get this to happen. For the creative reader, books are more than storehouses of thought—they are grist for their own thinking. *Creative Reading for Gifted Learners: A Design for Excellence* (Labuda 1974) is a useful resource in creative reading.

All of the objectives discussed above depend upon group discussion. I feel there is no substitute for putting groups of gifted students together, including on a multi-grade basis, to discuss what they have read. Older and younger gifted children often share similar interests, and discussions can center around particular themes, even though the specific books dealing with those themes may differ. In any case, in conducting discussions, teachers, aides, or volunteers should be well-versed in the art of asking open questions, for the quality of a student discussion is, after all, heavily determined by the level of the discussion leader's questions. Ideally, a discussion leader should be continually aware of the cognitive level of the questions being asked; and especially in discussions with gifted children, the leader should consciously seek to move the level of the discussion from lower to higher cognitive and affective levels. A useful resource for gifted readers is offered through the *Junior Great Books* program.[1] In this program, discussion leaders are trained to ask good questions about what the students have read—questions that are designed to heighten the students' critical reading abilities.

Today many school districts and individual buildings are redesigning comprehensive reading plans so that the reading program will represent a consolidated and integrated effort. If we are to deal with the massive reading problems, such a coordinated effort is indeed appropriate.

In formulating our plans, while stressing the importance of assisting the disabled reader, we must not, as is almost always done, overlook the gifted student. We owe these talented students an education that is appropriate to their ability level. Thus, every reading plan, every reading management system, every build-ing reading program should include specific reading objectives for gifted readers—objectives that are appropriate to their abilities, interests, and learning styles.

Notes

1. Information concerning the Junior Great Books Reading and Discussion Program for Students from Second Grade through Senior High School may be obtained by writing to: The Great Books Foundation, 307 N. Michigan Avenue, Chicago, IL 60601.

References

Blume, Judy, *Blubber*. Scarsdale, N.Y.: Bradbury Press, 1974.

Brown, Margaret W. *The Dead Bird*. New York: W. R. Scott, 1958.

Cleary, Beverly. *Ramona the Brave*. New York: Morrow, 1975.

Klein, Norma. *Mom, the Wolf Man and Me*. Boston: G. K. Hall, 1972.

Labuda, Michael. *Creative Reading for Gifted Learners: A Design for Excellence*. Newark, Delaware: International Reading Association, 1974.

Platt, Kin. *Hey, Dummy*. Chilton, Pa.: Radnor Press, 1971.

Terman, Lewis M., *et al. Genetic Studies of Genius; Mental and Physical Traits of a Thousand Gifted Children*. Stanford University Press, 1925. Vol. I, pp. 271–272.

Trezise, Robert L. "The Hilda Taba Teaching Strategies in English and Reading Classes." *English Journal* 61 (April 1972): 557–580, 593.

Zolotow, Charlotte. *William's Doll*. New York: Harper and Row, 1972.

Index

academic engaged time, 198
accenting generalizations, 225
acronyms, 233
adaptations of texts, 257
adapted reading program, 417
adjunct questions, 261, 330
adult reading, 24–29
  Also see literacy
advance organizers, 261, 326
affixes, 234
alexia, 416–417
allergies and reading disability, 428
alphabetic method, 2
alphabetic-phonetic reading systems, 4, 5
alphabetic principle, 14
analytic instructional approaches,
  see meaning-emphasis approaches
analytic phonics, 117, 140, 210
anaphoric devices, 257–260
  Also see pronoun referents
answers, ability to express, 300–301
anticipation guides, 328–329
applicative level of comprehension, 285, 309
assessing,
  reading ability, 25, 26
  functional literacy, 27
  reading readiness, 107–112
  reading interests, 344–357
  reading needs, 416–420
  language development, 446–447
  linguistic demands of a text, 447–448
assignment length, varying, 183
assisted reading, 218, 385–386
attention, 197–198
attention to pupil needs, 199
automaticity, 207–209

background knowledge,
  see prior knowledge

back to basics movement, 24
bandwagon (propaganda technique), 305
basal level, 153
basal readers, 4, 6, 7, 9, 17, 116–117, 122–126,
  133, 136, 259
beginning reading, 116–145
  comparison of approaches, 14–17, 136–141
  when to begin, 103–107
  choosing an approach, 210–211
  Also see code-emphasis approaches,
    mean-emphasis approaches, First Grade
    Studies
behavior modification, 428
bidialectalism, 438–441
bilingualism, 119
black English, *see* dialects
blending procedures, 211–214
blind writing, 425–426
bottom-up models/processing, 126, 127, 251,
  268
brand words, 233

card stacking (Propoganda technique), 304
categorization, 318
causation, 419
cause and effect, 291, 309
child centered programs, 92
children's literature, *see* literature
child's own book technique, 423–424
  Also see language experience approach
classroom management, 198
clauses, 290
cloze,
  as a measure of readability, 406–409
  as a teaching device, 289, 293–298
code-emphasis approach programs, 14, 117,
  136–141, 210
codes, restricted and elaborated, 63, 438
cognitive behavior modification, 428

cognitive clarity, 282–283
cognitive psychology, 80, 337
cognitive readiness, 327
cognitive skills, 32
coined words, 232
collaboration by grouping, 182–183
color cues, 424–425
compare/contrast theory of word
    identification, 203–207
comprehension, 283, 286
  taxonomy, 284–286
  Also see listening comprehension, reading
    comprehension
computer assisted instruction (CAI), 413–414
computer literacy, 413–415
computer managed instruction (CMI), 414–415
computerized (talking) typewriter, 13, 98
concept development, 229–230
concepts,
  about print, 112–115, 132, 133
  development of, 229–230
  ordering, 230
conceptual expectations, 326
conceptually-driven models, *see* top-down
    models
conferences, individual, 191–192
connectives, 298
connotations, 230
conscious awareness, 294
conservation (Piaget), 71
consonants, 224
content subjects, 180–184, 308–343
contentives, 215
context, 221, 245–247
context clues, 245–247, 295
controlled vocabulary technique, 422–423
convergent thinking, 454
corrective reading, 420–426
CRAFT Project, 41, 148, 196
creative reading, 454
creative sharing, 367–368
creativity and television, 360–361
critical reading, 454
  and TV, 361
critical task, 324
cross-age tutoring, 187

data-driven models, *see* bottom-up models
decoding, 17, 127–128, 202–207, 207–209,
    215–219, 223–225, 299
decomposing sentences, 290
denotive words, 230
details, noting and recalling, 271, 276

diacritical markings, 5
diagnosis, 416–420
  of reading readiness concepts, 112–115
  use of cloze, 296–297
  of reading comprehension problems,
    298–302
dialect readers, 290, 440
dialects, 63–64, 143, 432–434, 436–443
dictionary, 242–245
differential structuring of questions, 181–182
direct instruction, 16
directed reading activity (DRA), 391–392
  alternatives to, 392–396
Directed Reading-Thinking Activity (DRTA),
    252, 329–330, 393–394
disabled reader, 417, 427
discrimination, visual, 32
DISTAR, 16, 91
divergent thinking, 454
DRA, *see* directed reading activity
DRTA, *see* Directed Reading-Thinking Activity
Dulin-Chester Reading Interests
    Questionnaire, 351–357
dyslexia, 417, 422

early reading, *see* pre-first grade reading
echo reading, 218, 384–385
eclectic approach, 42
educational therapies, 429–430
elaborated codes, 63, 438
elaboration, 318
encoding hypothesis, 332–334
encoding specificity principle, 326
English as a second language, 119, 443–451
eradication theory, 437–438
ESL students, 443–451
ethnography, 378, 381
etymologies, 234
    Also see word origins
euphemisms, 234
evaluation, 146–152
every-pupil response technique, 179
Expectation Outline, 394
experiental background, *see* prior knowledge
expository material, 131
extra-linguistic factors, 130, 255
external storage hypothesis, 332–334

factual comprehension, *see* literal
    comprehension
Feingold diet, 428
Fernald method, *see* Kinesthetic method
figurative language, 236–240

figure-ground reversal, 430
final blending, 211–213
First Grade Studies, 10, 14, 15, 136–141, 195
flexible reading habits, 402–404
flow chart, 282
fluency, 144, 383–387
focusing behavior, 261
following directions, 299–300
Follow-Through, 15
formal educational programs, 195–196
free reading, 363–364
frustration level, 154
function words, 215–219
functional literacy, 27,
   Also see literacy, illiteracy

generalizations, decoding, 223–225
gifted chilren, 452–455
glittering generalities (propoganda technique),
   305
grade-equivalent scores, 160, 163–164
grammatical function, *see* syntax, syntactic
   cues
grapheme-phoneme relationships, *see* symbol-
   sound associations
graphical literacy, 337–343
graphophonemic cues, 287
graphs, 337–343
group instruction, ways to personalize,
   177–180
grouping,
   for instruction, 120
   collaboration by, 182–183
guided reading, 281
   in recreational reading, 365

habits, reading, *see* reading habits
haptic experience, 426
Head Start, 92–94, 97, 98
hemispheric dominance, 429
hemispheric processing, 429
history of reading instruction and research,
   1–12
holistic approaches to reading instruction,
   34–36, 37–38, 121,
homogeneous groups, 147
humor in the reading program, 369–374
hyperactivity, 428

idioms, 238
illiteracy, 11
imagery, 77–81
independent level, 153

independent questioning, 312–313
independent reading, *see* recreational reading
individual differences,
   adapting instruction to, 177–201
   in note taking, 334–335
individualizing reading assignments, 180–184
   190–195
individualizing reading assigments, 180–184
inductive teaching strategies, 291–292
inferencing, 251, 256, 271
   Also see cognitive skills
informal reading inventories, 148, 153–156,
   156–159
information processing, 167, 260
initial teaching alphabet (i.t.a.), 9, 118
instructional level, 154, 197
instructional materials, history of, 1–12
instructional organization, 120
instructional time, 196
intelligence tests, 147
interactive model/processes, 121, 127, 131, 251,
   268–272, 286
interest and reading comprehension, 300
interests, reading, *see* reading interests
interlocking study guide, 313–315
interpretive level of comprehension, 285, 309
intervention programs, 89–95
interword decisions, 268–269
intonation patterns, 75, 80, 144
   ·· *Also see* pitch, stress
intraword decisions, 268–269
intrusions
   scriptal, 272
   textual, 272
i.t.a., *see* intial teaching alphabet

juncture, 75, 235
Junior Great Books program, 455

Kindergarten, reading instruction in, 99–101,
   107–108
Kinesthetic methods, 425, 426, 429

labeling technique, 421–422
language, 283
   and reading, 31, 38–39, 59–87, 105, 128, 142
   development of, 59–65, 444–446
   variations in, 63–64
   reading to learn about nature of, 231–236
   spoken, 287
   comparison of written and spoken, 128–130,
      131, 142, 143, 254–256
   assessing development of, 446–447

language arts, interrelatedness of, 85
language concepts, and reading readiness, 112
language deprivation, 90
language-experience approach (LEA), 15, 87,
     109–111, 118–119, 142–145, 295, 440–441
learner characteristics, 324
learning activities, 324
learning disability, 427
learning strategies, *see* learning to learn
learning to learn, 317–325
left-to-right principle, 32
letter names, 32
letter-sound correspondence, *see* symbol-
     sound associations
limited processing capacity, 127, 128, 307
linguistic demands, assessing texts, 447–448
linguistic, rationale for LEA, 142–145
linguistic readers/approaches, 9, 13, 118,
     136–141
listening comprehension, 74–85, 283
     and reading comprehension, 169–170
literacy, 21, 22, 26
     functional, 27
     graphical, 337–343
     Also see illiteracy
literal comprehension, 284, 285
literature,
     programs, 363–368
     children's responses to, 377–382
look-say method, *see* whole-word method

manuals, 259
materials,
     selecting appropriate, 183, 197, 405–409,
          435–436
     difficulty of, 26–27, 197
     examining nature of, 324
mathemagenic activities/behaviors, 260, 326
meaning-emphasis reading
     approaches/programs, 14, 33, 117,
          136–141, 210
measurement of reading achievement and
     needs, 146–176
mediated word identification, 203–207
medical therapies, 428
megavitamin therapy, 428
mental abilities, estimating, 417
metaphors, 230, 238
microcomputers, 413
minority children, 89–95, 229, 432–436,
     436–443, 443–451
     Also see dialects, bidialectalism, non-English
          speakers

miscomprehension, understanding, 271–272
miscue analysis, 165–170
     critique of, 170–176
miscues, 433
     reading, 45–50, 87, 165
     writing, 87
     using for teaching strategies, 219–222
     Also see miscue analysis
modeling/simulating, 271, 390
models of reading (process), 45–53, 120–121,
     126–127, 251
     Also see bottom-up, interactive, top-down
          models/ processing
monitoring word recognition, 221–222
morphological development, 60
motivation, 198, 374–377
multiethnicity in texts, 122

NAEP, 22, 27
name-calling (propoganda technique), 304
narratives, 276
neurological impress method, 384, 430
non-English speakers, 443–451
noninterlocking study guide, 314, 316
nonstandard speakers, 143
     Also see dialects
norm-referenced tests, 160, 161
notetaking, 301, 323–328, 331–337

one-to-one teaching, 177–180
open-plan schools, 120
Oral Language Index, 444–446
oral reading, 4, 20, 129, 144, 185, 383–387
     Also see round robin reading
outlines, 328

pacing, 196–197
paraphrase technique, 289
parents,
     helping children learn function words,
          217
     as partners in reading development,
          410–412
peer tutoring, 187–189
people words, 233–234
percentile rank, 161–162
perceptual learning, 40
phonics, 58, 135, 424
     intrinsic, 8
     value of, 14, 15, 17–18, 56–58, 70
     lessons, 105
     analytic, 210–211
     synthetic, 210–211

Also see blending procedures, decoding, symbol sound associations

phonic generalizations, 203, 223–225

phonological development, 59–60

phonology, 75

phrasal units, 129, 254, 255, 290

Piagetian theory, 70, 71, 91

picture cues, 130

pitch, 75, 80

plain folks (propoganda technique), 304

portmanteau words, 232–233

post-reading strategies, 327

prediction, 281

pre-first grade reading, 95–102, 104–105

preoperational stage, (Piaget), 70

prereading development, 89–115

prereading Guided Reading Procedure, 394–395

prereading instruction, 270

pre-reading questions, 275–276

pre-reading strategies, 326, 327

print,
   understanding functions of, 132
   making sense of, 133–134

print-rich environment, 133, 134

prior knowledge, 142, 250, 268, 274–276, 281 283, 288, 300, 301, 323, 448–449
   Also see schema theory

problem solving, 285

professional books on reading, 4, 6, 7, 8

programmed academic skills programs, 91

programmed reading approaches, 9, 118, 136

Project Literacy, 14

pronounalization, *see* anaphoric devices, pronoun referents

pronoun referents, 287–288
   Also see anaphoric devices

propaganda, 302–307

prosodic features, 79–80, 255
   Also see pitch, stress

psycholinguistic guessing game, 45–52, 121, 126

psycholinguistic processing, 165–170

psycholinguists, critique of contribution of, 53–58

psychological therapies, 428–429

punctuation, 80, 144, 235, 255, 257

pupil partners, 184–187

purpose-setting questions, 281

questioning techniques, 178–180, 308–312

questions, 253, 267, 291, 301
   differential structuring of, 181–182

and comprehension, 260–283

asked by teachers, 268–284

taxonomy of, 270, 384–286

asking about stories, 274–283

guide for developing, 280–282

understanding of, 301

value of, 310–312

rate of reading, *see* reading rate

raw score, 161

readability,
   of materials, 26–27
   formulas, 256–257
   cloze, 406–409

reading,
   components of, 31–34
   and writing instruction, 85–88

reading achievement/ability,
   status of in U.S.A., 20–25, 25–29
   possible reasons for decline in, 23 –24

reading acquisition, compared with language acquisition, 38–39, 65–74, 105

reading along with children, 133

reading assignments, individualizing, 180–184

reading attitudes inventory, 345–350

reading comprehension, 18, 131, 167–169, 248–307
   and listening comprehension, 78–80
   and automatic decoding, 207–209
   diagnosing problems, 298–302
   and schema theory, 250–251
   and questions, 260–262
   sentence, 286–293
   and cloze procedure, 294
   and minority children, 434–435

reading disabilities, 427

reading habits, 27–28

Reading in Silence (RIS), *see* sustained silent reading

reading instruction,
   history of, 1–12, 12–19
   contrasting views about, 30–58
   when it should begin, 103–107
   beginning reading, 116–145
   adapting to individual differences, 177–201

reading interests, 435
   assessing, 344–357
   and TV, 360

reading process(es),
   nature of, 303–34
   and writing processes, 86

reading programs, characteristics of successful, 41–42

reading rate, 140, 397–401
    flexibility, 402–404
reading readiness, 8, 9, 89–115, 142, 262
    tests, 108–109, 112
    checklist, 113–114
reading terminology, *see* terminology of
        reading instruction
reading tests, 6
    readiness, 108, 149
    purposes of, 147–148
    impact of, 148–151
    recreational reading, 151–152
    study skills, 152
    Also see informal reading inventories
reading to students, 132–133, 364–365
reading vocabulary, 144, 226–247
    need for a planned program, 226–230
    developing, 240–247, 270, 296
    and reading comprehension, 299
    problems, 130
reasoning ability, *see* cognitive skills,
    inferencing
recall, 301, 318–322, 326–331
recall-readiness, 319–321, 326–331
record keeping, 194
recreational reading, 151–152, 344–382, 435
rehearsal, 318
reluctant readers, motivating, 374–377
remedial reading, 427–432
repeated readings technique, 386, 430
rephrasing, 290
ReQuest, 393
restricted codes, 63, 438
retellings, 168
round robin oral reading, 129, 184–185

scanning, 402
schema, 272, 326
schema implicit questions/answers, 270
schema intrusions, 272
schemata, 81, 250, 251, 268
schema theory, 81, 250–254, 269–270
scientific alphabet, 5
scriptal intrusion, 272
scriptally implicit question/answers, 270
second language acquisition, 444–446
segmentation,
    auditory, 32, 68, 105
    visual, 68
self-corrections, 220
semantic cues, 287
semantics, 130–131

Semantic Webbing, 396
sentence-by-sentence reading, 131
sentence building, 290
sentence combining, 77, 86–87, 290
sentence decomposing, 290
sentence comprehension, 286, 293
silent reading, 6, 190–191
    Also see sustained silent reading
similies, 239
simulation strategies, 310–312
skilled reading, 208
skills approaches, 14, 16, 116
skimming, 402
slang expressions, 237
slanguage, 233
"slide" words, 233
slow learners, 417
spelling method of teaching reading, 3
Standard English, 63, 143
stanines, 162
story grammar, 81, 253–254, 255, 271
story map, 276–280, 281
storytelling, 364
structure words, *see* function words
studying, 323
stress, 75, 80
structured cognitive programs, 90–91
structured environment programs, 91–92
structured overview, 252, 327–328
study games, 313–317
study skills, 152
    Also see learning to learn
subskill approaches to reading instruction, 34
    35, 36, 38, 39–43, 120–121
    Also see skills approaches
successive blending, 211–213
suggestopedia, 429
summarizing, 322–325
supplementary reading, 365
sustained silent reading (RIS), (SSR) (USSR),
    192–194, 387–391
syllabication, 203
    generalizations, 223, 224–225
symbol-sound associations, 32
    teaching, 213
    Also see decoding, phonics
syntactic complexity, 87
syntactic cues, 287
syntactic development, 60–63
syntactic units, 256
syntax, 75, 128–129
synthetic phonics, 117, 140, 210–211

synthetic reading approaches, *see* code-
    emphasis approach programs
system approach, 119

taped books, 385
talking (computerized) typewriter, 13, 98
task analysis, 14
teacher attitudes, 440–441
teacher-centered programs, 195–196
teacher effectiveness, 195–201
    evaluating, 149–150
teacher expectancies, 198–199
teacher's role, 132–135
television, effects on reading, 24, 358–362
terminology of reading instruction, 68–69,
    110, 143
testimonial (propoganda technique), 305
test interpretation, 160–165
test-mode expectancy, and notetaking, 334
test scores, types of, 160–165
text organization, 131
text structure, 76
text structure manipulation, 289–290
textual intrusion, 272
textually explicit questions/answers, 271
textually implicit questions/answers, 271
theories of reading, *see* models of reading
top-down models/processing, 126, 127, 251,
    268, 326
topical units, 365–367
tracing techniques, *see* kinesthetic techniques
transfer (propoganda technique), 305
transfer of skills, 280

transformational grammar, 291
T-score, 162
tutors, 182, 187–189
TV, *see* television

USSR, *see* sustained silent reading

vestibular disturbances, 428
visual discrimination, 32
voice-print match, 113
vowels, 224

whole-word method, 3, 4, 5, 13
Wisconsin Reading Attitude Inventory,
    345–350
word attack, *see* decoding
word-analysis, *see* decoding
word-by-word reading, 131, 144, 256
word-calling, 209
word identification, *see* word recognition,
    decoding
word meaning, 26, 221
    Also see reading vocabulary
word origins, 231–234
world knowledge, *see* prior knowledge
word recognition, 32, 129, 202–207, 221–222,
    432–434
    Also see decoding
Word Wonder, 395–396
writing, integrating with reading instruction,
    85–88, 143
    Also see language experience approach
writing miscues, 87